INTO THE DEPTHS OF HISTORY

RESEARCH ON MARX'S
HISTORICAL MATERIALISM

INTO THE DEPTHS OF HISTORY

RESEARCH ON MARX'S HISTORICAL MATERIALISM

by Chen Xianda

Translated by Li Ruiping

CANUT INTERNATIONAL PUBLISHERS

Istanbul ▪ Berlin ▪ London ▪ Santiago

Published in 2010 by China Renmin University Press

Original Chinese Copyright © 2010, Third Chinese Edition
ISBN: 978-7-300-07041-8

This book is published in cooperation with the Humanities and Social
Sciences Foundation China (中华社会科学基金).

Canut International Publishers
Published by Canut International Publishers
Canut Int. Turkey, Balipaşa Cad. 155a, Tel : +90-212-5124356, Istanbul, Turkey
Canut Int. Germany, Heerstr. 49, D-47053, Duisburg, Germany
Canut Int. UK, 12a Guernsay Road, London E11 4BJ, England
Web: http://www.leftreader.com
E-Mail: canut@leftreader.com

English Print edition: *Into the Depths of History. Research on Marx's
Historical Materialism*, February 2014

ISBN: 978-605-4923-06-9

English Digital Edition:

ISBN: 978-605-4923-05-2

Printed in England
Lightning Source UK Ltd.
Chapter House
Pitfield
Kiln Farm
Milton Keynes
MK11 3LW
United Kingdom

CONTENTS

PUBLISHER'S FOREWORD

Globally, recent years have seen a revival of interest in the nature and utility of Marx's historical materialism theory. Debate amongst historians and philosophers on Marx's assertions on the role of man as the subject of history also the relations between his practice view and historical materialism has been a hot topic. No wonder this is the case in Chinese academia, which is one of the leading spots of vigorous Marxist philosophy studies, today. The book we present here, which firmly adheres and innovatively interprets Marx's materialist concept of history, addresses the main discussions in the interpretation of it. The author Chen Xianda is among the leading researchers of history and theories of Marxism in China, who greatly influenced several important debates in the Chinese academia in the last three decades, including those on Marxist humanism, the role of superstructure, ontology and practical materialism. In the generous appendix part of the book with six articles we have included his important contributions to these debates, which also include his ideas on the present problems of Marxist philosophy in China and the world.

It is a well known fact that opponents of Marxism still frequently attack for its supposed neglect of subject and society's political, ideological superstructure, which Marx and Engels themselves have referred as early as *The German Ideology*, pointing to the reciprocal action of base and superstructure and their dialectical interaction. However, Marxism and main components of its system as an open book keeps being innovated and gives new answers to these refutations from a new height reflecting our time. As Xianda underlines: "Social science can fully become as accurate as natural science. To do this, the first thing is to determine its nature accurately, that is, to have a scientific understanding of the macroscopic laws of history. Different from living organisms, the social organism has its unique laws. The various systems in society have their special structures and functions, but they are interrelated and constitute an indivisible whole. It is impossible to understand society without grasping the laws of social development and without analyzing the nature and complex causality in social phenomena. However, human understanding of society cannot rest on the qualitative analysis, and quantitative analysis should be conducted wherever it is possible. With the emergence of world-wide technological revolutions, the spread of the system theories, control/simulation theory, information theory and even mathematical methods being applied into social sciences provides conditions for the accurate grasp of the quantitative determination of social phenomena. The mutual permeation between natural science and social science is a progressive tendency, and Marxism philosophy researchers should face the world and the contemporary era, and summarize the new achievements in those technological revolutions. The achievements in natural science enrich and affirm instead of reducing the scientific character of the materialist conception of history. No methods offered by natural science can replace the materialist conception of history, and history has proved that the methods of positivism and empiricism were unsuitable."

This meticulous work includes and discusses in detail, closely related by the historical circumstances, every step in which Marx formed and developed the materialist conception of history in his writings including his *Anthropology Notes* and his discussions on prehistoric societies. The author gives special attention on the thoughts Marx and Engels had similarities and even agreement with their contemporaries especially Feuerbach and followers of Hegel. Naturally each philosopher has his own specific formation which applies for Marx, his differences with his contemporaries carefully discussed by the author gradually and at the certain point of time rapidly led him to establish the materialist concept of history. As Chen Xianda emphasized: "All social life is essentially practical." This conclusion of Marx is highly condensed and contains some important principles of historical materialism. The view of practice is the kernel running all through Theses on Feuerbach. Marx introduced practice into the theory of knowledge and more importantly into the conception of history. The combination of the view of practice and the conception of history is a striking feature of *Theses*. Proceeding from the idea of labour as the essence of man to labour as the essence of social life, the door of the materialist conception of history was finally opened in examining human society, to examine it in human practical activity. For this reason, Engels called Theses "the first document in which is deposited the brilliant germ of the new world outlook", and as "the genesis of historical materialism.

The book also discusses the ideas and preferences which led Marx to study French, European Revolutions and political economy which were critical for his progress.

I hope this comprehensive book will further promote the dialogue efforts among the Marxism researchers throughout the globe and enable new generations grasp the essence of Marx's materialist concept of history. Thanks are owed to a number of members of editors of China Renmin University Press who have encouraged and supported us when several difficulties arose when translating and editing the text. In particular I would like to thank our translator, Li Ruiping who did a hard job.

Cem Kizilcec
February, 2014
London

FOREWORD

Man is said to rarely live to 70,

And, yet I am nearly 80 and still feel energetic.

Provided that I can teach, walk and type on the keyboard,

I will continue to work hard and devote myself to academic research.

Chen Xianda
December, 2006
Written at Shouzhuo Study, Yi Yuan

PREFACE

Mankind explores the mysteries of the world while transforming it, whether in the natural sphere or in the social sphere. The numerous discoveries in the intellectual history radiate with wisdom like glistening stars in a summer night, of which the brightest one is historical materialism established by Marx. It discovers the general laws of the development of human society and uncovers the long-standing curtain on the social organism. No wonder that Engels highlighted the epoch-making historical contribution of Marx's materialist conception of history, and praised it as the first great discovery of his life in the famous funeral oration on March 17, 1883, at the grave of this departed friend who had gone through thick and thin together with him.

Marxism is a unified whole of mainly: Philosophy, economics and the theory of scientific socialism. However, the materialist conception of history in Marxist philosophy is indeed a concentrated and vivid expression of Marx's originality and outstanding contribution. Some principles of dialectics and epistemology can find their original form with his forerunners. The thoughts of naïve materialism and dialectics had appeared in ancient Greece, and Hegel was the first one in history to elaborate the general laws of dialectics in the form of idealism, and the French materialists of the 18th century and Feuerbach established the materialist principle of ontology and epistemology. However, in the social sphere, it is a different story.

Although mankind has also been exploring this sphere for a long time and there have been sprouts of certain materialistic views, they were idealistic as a whole. Unlike in the sphere of nature and epistemology, new theories cannot be formulated through inversion, rejection, elimination and supplement in the social and historical sphere; all the outstanding cultural heritage of mankind must be summarized and history and the reality should be restudied to reveal the laws of history itself which have never been discovered. It is really a more arduous task to advance from the surface into the depth of history wrapped in layers of various and complex ideologies, complex motivations and accident.

Social science can fully become as accurate as natural science. To do this, the first thing is to determine its nature accurately, that is, to have a scientific understanding of the macroscopic laws of history. Different from living organisms, the social organism has its unique laws. The various systems in society have their special structures and functions, but they are interrelated and constitute an indivisible whole. It is impossible to understand society without grasping the laws of social development and without analyzing the nature and complex causality of social phenomena. However, human understanding of society cannot rest on the qualitative analysis, and quantitative analysis should be conducted wherever it is possible. With the emergence of world-wide technological revolutions, the spread of the system theories, control/simulation theory, information theory and even mathematical methods applied into social sciences provides conditions for the accurate grasp of the quantitative determination of social phenomena. The mutual permeation between natural science and social science is a progressive tendency, and philosophy researchers should face the world and the contemporary era, and summarize the new achievements in those technological revolutions. The achievements in natural science enrich and confirm instead of reducing the scientific character of the materialist conception of history. No methods available in natural science can replace the materialist conception of history, and history has proved that the methods of positivism and empiricism were unsuitable. Franz Mehring said, "Historical materialism is not a closed system which takes the final truth as its destination."[1]. This is undoubtedly an excellent view. The materialist conception of history is not problem-solving; it cannot provide ready-made answers to the complex and changing history, but it does provide scientific theories and methods to help people find correct answers. However progressive the means and tools to understand history are, the first discovery of the materialist conception of history, which expels idealism from the sphere of history, is always a milestone in the course of human knowledge. Like Prometheus, Marx illuminated the social and historical sphere which had been groping in darkness for a long time with the light of the materialist conception of history.

Even though Marx and Engels are two persons, they are like one person. They have their own characteristics and styles, and yet they are the co-founders of the same ideological theoretical system. Before collaborating once again with Marx in Brussels in the spring of 1845, Engels had reached the same conclusion with that of Marx through his own exploration. This book focuses on Marx, but we will never forget Engels' historical contribution to the establishment and defence of the materialist conception of history.

Chen Xianda
December, 2010

---

1   Mehring: In Defence of Marxism, p. 25, Beijing: People's Press, 1982.

INTRODUCTION

HUMAN'S EXPLORATION ON THE LAWS OF HISTORY

Rousseau sighed, "The most useful and least perfect of all human studies is that of 'man'".[1] This is true. Man is concerned first and foremost about himself, but it is precisely himself whom he has not understood for a long historical period. The relatively small scale of production and the biases of the exploiting class limit people's historical horizon. Although people can go deep into nature, they stay on the surface of history in social life. However, neither history itself nor people's understanding of history will stop. People keep exploring in the social sphere just as they do in the natural world. The materialist conception of history established by Marx is the rare brilliant fruit of human exploration of history.

---

1 Rousseau: Discourse on the Origin and Foundation of Inequality among Mankind, p. 62, Beijing: The Commercial Press, 1962.

I

It is with nature that man begins his course of materialist philosophy. Natural materialism is very close to and yet far from historical materialism, which can be fairly described by a Chinese idiom of "a short distance away, and yet poles apart."

They are very close to each other, because they share the same materialistic principle. The argument of historical materialism that social being determines social consciousness is consistent with the principle of general materialism that being determines consciousness. It seems that general materialism can step into the door of historical materialism after extension, expansion and deduction.

Yet they are actually far from each other. The materialistic understanding of nature started in ancient Greece, where philosophers regarded the ἀρχή, material arche, as the origin of the universe, and expressed their view on the material unity of the world in the simplest form. However, the road leading natural materialism to historical materialism has been rough and rugged, strewn with thorns, which has been explored by mankind for more than two thousand years. How onerous and distant the road is!

Why is that? One of the main reasons is that society is not a simple extension of nature. It has its own special forms of expression and laws, and thus must be studied specifically. Logically, Lenin made an absolutely right judgment about the consistency between historical materialism and natural materialism in terms of its theoretical principle, which states that "materialism in general recognizes objectively real being (matter) as independent from the consciousness, sensation and experience, etc. of humanity. Historical materialism recognizes social being as independent from the social consciousness of humanity. In both cases, consciousness is only the reflection of being, at best an approximately true (adequate, perfectly exact) reflection of it."[2] However, this relationship between them could be perceived only after the establishment of historical materialism, so Lenin's judgment is a summary of an established fact. Before that, this relationship was hidden. There has been no lack of intelligent materialist philosophers for more than two thousand years, but none could logically derive historical materialism from the principles of materialism.

---

2   Lenin Selected Works, 2nd edition, Volume 2, p. 332, Beijing, People's Press, 1972.

In the natural world, what people see is matter and movement; while in the social sphere, what they see is human will and their acts. Society is the product of human activity which is conducted by people who have consciousness, passion and different purposes. However, not all their purposes can produce expected results, which appear as a series of accidental events, and specific historical events have unrepeatable uniqueness. This subjectivity, uniqueness and randomness presented by social life serve as a "drop-leaf" between nature and society. Even for those relatively firm materialists, when they turn their eyes from nature to society, and as soon as they enter the social and historical sphere, almost all of them plunged into the abyss of idealism by this drop-leaf. Lenin once summarized people's understanding of history, and pointed out the two chief shortcomings in all previous historical theories. In the first place, all previous historical theories at best examined the ideological motives in the historical activities of human beings, but without investigating the origins of those motives, without discovering the objective laws governing the development of the system of social relations, or ignoring the roots of these relations in the degree of development reached by material production. Secondly all previous historical theories did not embrace the activities of the masses. That is to say, all previous historical theories remained at the level of subjective motives of human beings, the subjective motives of great figures. Their fundamental shortcomings, as Lenin summarized, are consistent with the superficial characteristics which society takes on in the consciousness of the subject.

Thus, the materialistic understanding of nature predated that of society. If ontology and epistemology has experienced several forms of materialism, we can say it has been different in the historical sphere. Idealism had dominated this sphere before the emergence of the materialist conception of history. However, this does not follow that there is no change in the form of the conception of history, much less means that human understanding of history in the past has made no important progress at all and is merely a series of fallacies. Human understanding of history has also been progressive just like the objective history itself.

Concerning the Western cultural traditions with which Marx had a close relationship, famous historians appeared in the Greek and Roman times, such as Herodotus, Thucydides, Polybius, Quintus Fabius Pictor, Cato the Elder, Sallust, Livy, Tacitus and Plutarch, who wrote works about the ancient Greco-Persian Wars, the Peloponnesian War, the Greek history and the Roman history. They strove to save the accomplishment which humans had achieved from being buried and forgotten and explored the causes for certain historical events, which shows human beings' interest in and attention to their own activities. In terms of their understanding of history, the majority of them did not get rid of the bondage of God. They believed in destiny, and considered God as the supreme power governing the rise and fall of nations, the vicissitudes of life and the prosperity and decline of a people.

The theological conception of history which uses supernatural will and power to explain historical development and social life was predominant in the Middle Ages. They developed some ancient theological views of history into a system, just as Engels said, "The Middle Ages had developed out of raw primitiveness. It had done away with old civilization, old philosophy, politics and jurisprudence, in order to begin anew in every respect. The only thing which it had retained from that old shattered world was Christianity and a number of half-ruined cities deprived of their civilizations. As a consequence, the clergy retained the monopoly of intellectual education, a phenomenon to be found in every primitive stage of development, and education itself had acquired a predominantly theological nature. In the hands of the clergy, politics and jurisprudence, as well as other sciences, remained branches of theology, and were treated according to the principles prevailing in the latter."[3]

From Augustine to Aquinas, the active advocates of the theological conception of history, they preached that all orders on earth were arranged by God and ordained by Providence. Unless helped and inspired by God, man could never fully understand things about himself. This theological conception of history, by virtue of Providence, destiny and fate, had transformed the necessity of history itself and the causality of reality into the fatalism of theology.

---

3   Karl Marx and Frederick Engels: Collected Works, 1st Chinese Edition, Volume 7, p. 400, Beijing, People's Press, 1959.

Human understanding of history is subject to history itself. With the gradual development of the capitalist relations, especially the great geographical discoveries the historical horizon of human beings was greatly expanded. The bourgeois humanism, started in the Renaissance Period, which marks the transition from God to man. They gradually abandoned the theological conception of history, turned the celestial history into a secular history, explored the secrets of history in man himself instead of God's will, strove to turn the necessity of theology into that of history and raised the question of exploring the laws of history. This was a tremendous progress.

Herodotus of the ancient Greece is known as "the father of history", and Giovanni Vico, an Italian thinker in the 17th century, is called by Lafargue "the father of the philosophy of history". It is Vico who proposed to seek the common laws of historical development in his *The New Science, On Unifying Principle of Reasonable World Order* and other works.

Although Vico did not completely shake off the limitations of the theological conception of history, he did not use God's will directly to explain history like others did. He said, "Whoever reflects on this cannot but marvel that philosophers should have bent all their energies to the study of nature, which, since God made it, He alone knows; and that they should have neglected the study of the world of nations or civil world, which, since men had made it, men could hope to know."[4]

God made nature and only He alone knows it, while for the social sphere, society was made and could be known by man. Vico's distinction between nature and society is of course not scientific, but he stressed that man could know the society he has created, which is different from the tradition of the theological conception of history by Augustine to Aquinas.

A great achievement of Vico is that he emphasized the commonality of the laws of history. Although human history is complicated, and whatever their ethnic/national origins and geographical environments are, there still exists a unified process all nations experience

---

4   Vico: The New Science, quoted from Lafargue, The Origin of Ideas, p. 20, Beijing, SDX Joint Publishing Company, 1963.

in certain times. He said, "There exists an ideal and eternal history traversed by the histories of all nations, which will achieve civilization whether they proceed from barbaric, semi-civilized or wild (society) conditions."[5] It is because of his exclusion of God's interference with history that Vico had underlined the significance of the struggle of various social forces in social development.

Certainly, his understanding of the laws of history is not a materialistic one. He was incapable of seeking the inherent laws of society from itself, and instead put forward his theory of social development by making an analogy with that of human individual development. Just as an individual experiences childhood, youth and adulthood, the development of human society will experience the same process. The childhood of human society is the age of gods, when there is no state, people obey the priests and are completely ruled by religious views; the youth of human society is the age of heroes, which is the age of aristocracy; and the adulthood of human society is the age of mortals, which is the age of democratic republic or representative monarchy that guarantees the freedom of the bourgeoisie. Vico had an obvious political tendency. His consideration of the age of mortals as the highest stage of development of human society is purely related to his inclination to demonstrate the political ideals of the emerging bourgeoisie. Since he describes history according to the process of individual development, he is bound to land in such a predicament: Human society will die as a human individual does after childhood, youth and adulthood, or each generation restarts its life course, which runs in cycles and constitutes the continuous stream of life. Vico chose the latter and argued that human society would restart the same process after the three stages of development he described. In this way, human history falls into a cycle, moving back and forth in a closed circle.

The French Enlightenment made a step forward. They delved into the relationship between man and environment. The environment human beings living by was divided into two categories: Natural environment and social environment. The order of understanding them starts with the relationship of man to natural environment.

---

5   Ibid., p. 21.

The Spirit of Laws of Montesquieu attempts to seek the laws of social development in the natural environment indispensable to all human societies. In the preface, he says that he writes not to censure the various systems established in all nations but to expound them. Although there are various social laws and regulations, they are neither purely accidental nor determined by arbitrary acts, but have their own common laws. The history of any nation is an individual manifestation of the common principles, and the task of the researchers is to explore these common principles.

One of the common principles is that various constitutions and forms of laws are determined by natural environment on which human society depends, such as climate, geography, soil, etc. Montesquieu attached great importance to climate. He believed that cold climate rendered people healthy and brave, while hot climate rendered people effeminate and coward; southern nations were often enslaved, while the northern nations could maintain their independent freedom. Therefore, Montesquieu argued that servitude was closely related to the nature of climate. Some countries implemented despotism, polygyny and the system enslaving women, while other countries implemented republicanism and monogamy, which were both determined by climate. Even religious belief depended on climate, and that religion unsuited for the climate would not survive in that country. The reason why Buddhism was born in India was that the climate of India was hot. The excessive heat made people feel listless and weary, and thus tended to live in seclusion and do nothing.

Montesquieu also argued that the state constitution was determined by geography, i.e. and the size of territory. Republicanism is suitable for a small territory, monarchy for a territory of appropriate size, and despotism for state with a vast territory. The vast territory of Asia becomes a prerequisite for the establishment of a huge despotic empire. Montesquieu used the size of territory to explain the difference in European and Asian state forms. Monarchies of moderate size based on the rule of law were established in Europe due to the division of their natural territory, and if this state form was to be changed by men, they would tend to decline inevitably; on the contrary, the vast territory of Asia was suitable for the establishment of a huge despotic empires, and if the unified empire is divided into smaller units, this will contradict with that state's natural territory.

He also emphasized the dependency of social system on soil. In his view, nations without farming/farmers enjoy greater freedom than those agricultural nations, because nations with rich soil good for planting concentrate on farming instead of their liberties. Similarly when looking from the military perspective, fertile lands are easy to attack but hard to defend. Mountainous countries unsuitable for farming are easy to defend and will not become targets for conquest. Barren soil forces people to work hard and that cultivates their bravery and combat endurance. In contrast to those nations receiving gifts from nature and which obtain everything from nature, we see that their people are week, lazy and coward. Besides, the form of government varies with soil conditions. People living on mountains insist civilian rule; nations living on plains require a form of government led by some elites, while nations living in shores want a mixed form of the two.

There is no doubt that geographical environment influences human society, which is especially obvious in the early stage of human society, when the level of productivity is low. However, geological environment is not the decisive force effecting social development. Some nations which had created high level of civilization had declined, while we see some backward nations and regions have later advanced and stood at the forefront of historical development, and without any significant change in their geographical conditions. It is obvious that the geographical environment which changes slowly cannot be the reason for the relatively rapid changes in the life of societies. Facts have inevitably directed people to turn their eyes from external environment to human society itself.

This step was completed by the French materialism, which enters the relationship between man and social environment and leaves back the relationship between man and natural environment. The French materialists probed into social development not from such external factors as soil/land, climate and topography, but from the interaction between human views and social environment. For example, Helvetius objected to Descartes' concept of innate ideas, gave full play to Locke's materialistic principle and argued that man is the product of environment, and everything about man is the product of social environment. However, he did not understand the essence of social life. He considered social environment as a certain political system and legal system, believed that the character and wisdom of people of each nation varied with the form of government; even for the same nation, it was sometimes lofty, inferior, stable, ephemeral, brave, or timid because this nation practiced different forms of government. Therefore, when Helvetius explained why there were different social environments in different periods, he returned to man himself and sought determinants of social environment directly in the views of people living under that government. In his view, good laws and government will be established as long as there are real talented legislators, and the ignorant ones will produce flawed laws, which, in turn, will result in the aggravation of vices and social disasters.

The French materialists' argument of the interrelation between man and environment was clearly contradictory, but it is different from the contradiction in which the whale is on the water and the water is on the whale. The contradiction contained in the French materialist conception of history is not a logical contradiction that cannot be self-justified, but was a theoretical contradiction which people can encounter in their active exploration. To get out of this contradiction of mutual justification, further exploration was needed to be made.

Guizot, Thierry and Mignet, French historians of the French Restoration, tended to extricate themselves from this contradiction. They tried to get out of the circle of interaction, and shifted their focus on the environment. Guizot stated in *Introduction to the History of France* that "Most writers, scholars, historians or political commentators attempt to explain the specific state of a society, explain the degree and category of its civilization from its political system. It would be much wise to start with the study of society itself so as to recognize and understand its political system. The systems are firstly products before they become a reason; society first creates them and then society changes under their influence; the conditions of the people should not be judged according the form of government, instead they should be studied first and foremost in order to judge what their government should be and can be." Based on this,

Guizot also put forward that "Society, its components, different life styles of individuals with different social status, different class relations of each individual—in brief, people's civil life—undoubtedly, this is the first question that the historians who want to know how the nations had lived in the past and the political commentators who want to know how these nations were ruled in the past should pay attention to."[6]

There are two breakthroughs in the historical conception of the French Restoration historians. First, they no longer sought the basis of political institutions in people's views like the French materialists did, but explained political institutions with property relations in the society. For instance, Guizot studied the conditions emerging after the fall of the Western Roman Empire based on the principle mentioned above, and argued that for studying the history of this period and for understanding their political institutions, different classes in that society and their interrelations should be studied; and for understanding these different classes and their interrelations, the nature of land ownership relations should be studied. Second, they had already seen the facts related to class struggles. Guizot, Thierry and Mignet have observed the class struggle of the bourgeoisie against the aristocracy occurring in various forms of religious conflicts and partisan strife during their study of the British history and the French history.

However, the historians of the French Restoration could not attain the materialist conception of history. They have made a step forward by regarding property relations as the basis of political institution, and thus got out of the restrictions of the interaction between environment and people's views, but they could not solve the ultimate contradiction determining the political institutions.

When they attempted to answer the question related to the origin of property relations, and why there were different property relations in different periods, they again delved into human nature as the answer. In this way, although they stepped out of the restrictions of environment and peoples' views, they still remained within the big vicious circle of using human nature to explain history. Plekhanov once correctly summarized this point. He said, "When faced with

---

6   Quoted from Plekhanov: On the Development of Monistic Conception of History, p. 15, Beijing, SDX Joint Publishing Company, 1961.

the question of the origin of property relations, each of the historians of the time of the Restoration would probably have attempted, like Guizot, to escape from the difficulty with the help of more or less ingenious reference to 'human nature'." Similarly, Plekhanov pointed out that "[t]he view of 'human nature' as the highest reason/authority which decides all 'knotty cases; in the sphere of law, morality, politics and economics, was inherited in its entirety by the writers of the nineteenth century from the writers of the Enlightenment of the previous century."[7]

The further development of the conception of history has depended on whether the paradigm of explaining history with human nature could be surmounted. To explain history with human nature undoubtedly contains an unsolvable contradiction: How can the eternal human nature be the reason for the changes in history? If human nature is constantly changing, what, then, is the reason for the change in human nature? The French Enlightenment, the historians of the French Restoration and the three great utopian socialists of the 19th century were all flapped in this mire. Hegel saw this contradiction and tried hard to solve it. Hegel sought the driving force of history not in human nature but outside it, in his fictitious absolute idea, and used the self-development of absolute idea to describe the development of history. Hegel's idea on the laws of history is extraordinary, which systemizes and yet mystifies the ideas of the laws of historical development, which were explored ever since Vico. The traces of his predecessors can be found in Hegel's lectures and discourses on geological environment, his ideas on the necessity and accident in history, ideas on the role of vices (lust) in history and the role of historical figures. However, only such a genius as Hegel could weave all these ideas into the self-development of absolute idea by employing speculative logic.

Hegel regarded history as a process governed by laws, but the problem he faced afterwards was to solve the maze he had set and turn the law of idea into that of the development of history itself. This was not the requirement or product of pure thinking but a mission of the times. The person who fulfilled this great historical task is none other than Marx.

---

7   Ibid., p. 23.

II

If there were no Marx, would the materialist conception of history still appear?

If Marx were born a century earlier or later, would the materialist conception of history be established earlier or later accordingly?

If … In fact, we can come up with a series of "if(s)", but history, concerned with established facts, should be analyzed rather than hypothesized.

There is no doubt that the materialist conception of history is integrated with its founder, Marx. His natural talents, pedantic qualities, profound knowledge and spirit of thorough inquisition, and even his personal experiences and language style, has inevitably endowed his works on the materialist conception of history with his own characteristics. However, the materialist conception of history was not innate in Marx's mind, but rather the product of the times. It is history itself not the individual that has played a decisive role in the emergence of the materialist conception of history.

Engels, when discussing in his later years with W. Borgius on the interrelation between the necessity and accidental events in history, argued that a great man emerging at a particular time in a given country was of course a pure accident. However, cut him out of it, surely there will be a demand for a substitute, and this substitute will be found. The same applies for the establishment of the materialist conception of history. Engels said, "While Marx discovered the materialist conception of history, Thierry, Mignet, Guizot, and also all the English historians up to 1850 are the proof that it was being striven for, and the discovery of the same conception by Morgan proves that the time was ripe for it and that concept indeed had to be discovered."[8] Mehring made a similar statement that "the materialist conception of history is also subject to the law of historical movement it has formulated. It is the product of historical development, and could not have been conceived by any of the most talented minds in an earlier era. Only after reaching a certain height can human history reveal its own secrets."[9]

---

8 Karl Marx and Frederick Engels: Selected Works, 1st edition, Volume 4, p. 507, Beijing: People's Press, 1972.
9 Mehring: In Defense of Marxism, p. 3.

After human beings entered into the capitalist epoch, the contact and interaction among countries, especially among developed neighboring regions, cannot be matched and compared by the closed feudal society. If we can say that the German classical philosophy had spread beyond Germany and served the French Revolution as a German theory, this we can say is particularly true for the materialist conception of history. Like the whole system of Marxism, the materialist conception of history was not simply the product of Germany, but the common product of many European countries, including England and France. The intensification of the contradictions, peculiar to the capitalist epoch, has acted as the macro environment for the emergence of the materialist conception of history.

There are two major events in the capitalist epoch. Economically, one is the industrial revolution, starting in England and with the year 1825 as its turning point. Politically, the other is the bourgeois revolution in France, starting in 1789 and with the year 1830 as its turning point.

The industrial revolution began in England in the middle of the 18th century. Steam engines and cotton processing machinery were invented, and manual labour operation was gradually replaced by machinery-based production, and the place of manufacture was taken by the big, modern industry, which greatly promoted the development of the productive forces. Engels calls the industrial revolution "the storm and stress period", saying "[w]hilst in France the hurricane of the Revolution swept over the land, in England a quieter, but not on that account less tremendous, revolution was going on. Steam and the new tool-making machinery were transforming manufacture into modern industry, and thus revolutionizing the whole foundation of bourgeois society. The sluggish march of development of the manufacturing period changed into a veritable storm and stress period of production."[10]

The occurrence of the industrial revolution in England was not accidental, but a characteristic of the capitalist epoch. It would occur, sooner or later, in other capitalist countries in various ways. Alvin Toffler describes it as a "wave"—the Second Wave. Indeed, the

10   Karl Marx and Frederick Engels: Selected Works, 1st edition, Volume 3, p. 301, Beijing: People's press, 1972.

industrial revolution had a huge impact. It destroyed the mode of production based on agriculture and middle age manufacture, created new modes of production, changed social structure and class structure and impacted the traditional ideas and the ways of thinking, which provided objective possibilities for the materialistic and dialectic study of history.

The mode of production based on agriculture and manufacture was small in scale and limited people's horizon, while the capitalist mode of production based on large-scale machine industry not only formed a unified domestic market, integrated various production departments into a whole and established the social character of production, but also formed a world market, the development of which has built up closer ties between countries. The expansion of production scale was also accompanied with that change of people's horizon, and people were likely to surmount regional and national narrow-mindedness and began to carry out comparative studies on economy, history and culture of various countries from a macroscopic perspective.

The mode of production based on agriculture and middle age manufacture was characterized by slow gradual development. All the skills of producers and the source of life had depended on their "hands" and their labour "experience", and hence the revolutionizing of the instruments of production had deprived them from their original labour skills and experience, so the conservation of the old modes of production in unaltered form had become the primary condition of their existence. In contrast, in capitalist mode of production based on large-scale machinery, the iron law of competition had forced producers to use science and technology to improve the instruments of production so as to maintain their existence. "Constant revolutionizing of production, uninterrupted disturbance of all social relations, everlasting uncertainty and agitation distinguish the bourgeois epoch from all earlier ones."[11] Therefore, such a psychological state as being afraid of changes, and the fixed, conservative way of thinking that advocated traditions, formed on the basis of small-scale production, were just opposite to those formed in the rapidly changing large-scale industry age.

11   Karl Marx and Frederick Engels: Selected Works, 1st edition, Volume 1, p. 254, Beijing: People's press, 1972.

In the mode of production based on agriculture and middle age man-ufacture, the real cause for the development of history, the relations between economy and its effect on political and class struggles were hidden and confusing, concealed by some intermediate links. The division of social status of men as stipulated in laws had concealed the essence of class divisions; religious and ethical motives had of-ten covered up the economic nature of political struggles. However, such relations were relatively simplified in the mode of production based on large-scale industry. The capitalist mode of production has replaced that exploitation, previously veiled by religious and politi-cal illusions, with naked, shameless, direct and brutal exploitation. Here, any political struggle was launched obviously for economic interests, and political rights and slogans had become just means of realizing economic interests. The social consciousness of ego-ism and money worship, becoming prevalent in capitalist society, had compelled people to be aware of the critical role of economy in social life, generally all the time in the shallowest, rough and naked way.

The characteristics of the capitalist production based on large-scale industry, which distinguished it from the previous modes of pro-duction, were manifested gradually. The contradictions which were latent previously had developed into intense antagonisms only after the capitalist mode of production had developed and become domi-nant. The outbreak of the economic crisis of overproduction in 1825 with its shocking outward manifestations, has drawn people's atten-tion, to the inner contradictions of the capitalist mode of production.

This very first crisis of the capitalist world has shocked England, and was reported by many of its newspapers of the time, such as *The Times*, *Esquire* and *Almanac*. Williams Bank and a number of London-based companies, such as Iwalate Walker and Sykes Snash, closed down in succession.

"Many people and businessmen withdraw their money", "waiting with fear for new announcements of bankruptcy"; newspapers re-ported the rising unemployment of workers, the stoppage of numer-ous textile machines, "the current unemployment and poverty have never been seen over the past thirty years", "the situation is very terrible, the poor people are on the verge of starvation and all walks

of life are complaining about the disastrous time". They also reported that "the starving unemployed workers were so desperate that
riots have erupted". At that time, riots and rebellions broke out in
Blackbum, Accrington, Preston, Clitheroe, Rochdale, Manchester,
Bradford and Yorkshire.[12]

If the year 1825 marks a turning point of economy, the year 1830 is
a turning point of politics, which were closely related to each other.
Mehring wrote in his *The German History since the Late Middle
Ages*, that "since 1830, in the history of the world appeared a new
turning point, and the rise of the proletarian struggle which was of
world historical significance."[13] This is undoubtedly a correct view.

The year 1830 was a turning point, that the contradiction between the
proletariat and the bourgeoisie developed from a secondary contradiction into the main contradiction. From 1789 to July, 1830, the French
bourgeoisie underwent a complicated process of the revolution and then
the restoration, and eventually established its class rule. From then on,
the proletariat has begun to fight directly against the bourgeoisie.

The working class in France had actively participated in overthrowing the Bourbon dynasty, but the bourgeoisie stole the fruits of the
victory all for itself. The workers did not obtain real actual benefits
and saw their worsening situation, which had provoked widespread
discontent among the workers. Franz Liszt, a famous Hungarian music composer, once described his personal experience in Lyon in his
personal letter. He said, "I was caught in appalling suffering and
unbearable poverty upon setting my feet in Lyon; I was agitated and
deeply troubled by the unfair conditions, and my heart was full of
unspeakable grief"; "There was no peace and quiet for the old people, and no hope for the young people, and no joy for the children!
All of them were huddled in stinking slums"; "even those children
who have never seen smile on the lips of their mothers had to bend
over to operate the weaving machines, fixing their dull eyes on the
Arabic designs or decorative patterns on their hands for the pleasure
and enjoyment of high officials' children"[14].

12   See Selected Works of Documentary and Historical Materials of International
Communist Movement, Volume 1, p.p. 3-5, Beijing: China Renmin University Press, 1983.
13   Ibid., p. 27.
14   See Selected Works of Documentary and Historical Materials of International
Communist Movement, Volume 1, p. 27.

The workers of Lyon (Les Canuts) finally staged two massive armed uprisings in November, 1831 and April, 1834, joined by silk weavers as well as free masons, carpenters, shoemakers and printers, etc. The workers' uprisings in Lyon announced the end of the epoch of the third estate, and the proletariat was no longer fighting against the enemy of its enemy, but fought against is old ally.

Shortly after the failure of the workers' uprisings in Lyon, the British workers launched the Chartist movement, and the German textile workers started another important uprising in Silesia. These all marked the awakening of the European proletariat, signifying that the proletariat had stridden on the battle stage as an independent political force.

Engels took these struggles of the proletariat against the bourgeoisie very seriously, and regarded them as the decisive condition for the emergence of the materialist conception of history. He said that "[w]hilst, however, the revolution in the conception of nature could only be made in proportion to the corresponding positive materials furnished by research, already much earlier certain historical facts had occurred which led to a decisive change in the conception of history. In 1831, the first working-class uprising took place in Lyons; between 1838 and 1842, the first national working-class movement, that of the English Chartists, reached its height. The class struggle between proletariat and bourgeoisie came to the front in the history of the most advanced countries in Europe, in proportion to the development, upon the one hand, of modern industry [große Industrie], upon the other, of the newly-acquired political supremacy of the bourgeoisie."[15]

The principle that mature theories are compatible with mature class relations holds true for the establishment of the conception of history. When the contradiction between the proletariat and the bourgeoisie developed into the principal contradiction and the two classes were engaged in fierce struggles, when the British and French workers took to the streets and rose up against the bourgeoisie, these facts not only disclosed the distortions of the teachings of bourgeois political economy advocating the identity of the interests of capital

---

15   See Karl Marx and Frederick Engels: Selected Works, 1st edition, Volume 3, p.p. 65-66.

and labour, and the universal harmony and universal prosperity in the society as the consequence of unbridled competition, but also marked the bankruptcy of the illusions advocated by the British and French utopian socialism guided by the idealist conception of history. The idealist conception of history, which had failed to understand material interests and class struggles based on them, and ignored the decisive role of material production in social development, was in contradiction with the reality of class struggle in capitalist society. And for this reason, "the new facts had made imperative the new way of study of all past history", which had led to the discovery of the materialist conception of history.

Thus it can be seen that the discovery of the materialist conception of history in the 1840s was not an accidental event, but closely related to the economic crisis in 1825 and the new situation of class struggles in the 1830s. If we can say these conditions of that period can be regarded as the macro environment for the emergence of the materialist conception of history, the rapid development of capitalism and the intensification of class contradictions in the Rhine region of Germany was the intermediate environment, and Marx's family conditions and the related surrounding environment were the micro environment, of which the conditions or circumstances of the times had played a decisive role.

However, the analysis of the account of historical background alone is not enough, if we want to really understand the historical conditions for the emergence of the materialist conception of history; we must also know how Marx adapted himself to the rising demands of that times. Marx was chosen by history, but, more importantly, he had grasped that history. He established a real understanding of the times, reflected the requirements and desires of the proletariat, and converted the possibilities contained in the objective history itself into the scientific awareness and consciousness of history. Hegel had revealed the relationship between philosophy and times from the perspective of idealism. He wrote: "To apprehend what is the task of philosophy, because what is reason. As for the individual, everyone is a son of his time; so philosophy also is its time apprehend in thoughts."[16]

---

16   Hegel: Guidelines of the Philosophy of Right, p. 12, Beijing: The Commercial Press, 1961.

The relationship between the materialist conception of history and its historical circumstances or conditions is not simply one between the reflection and the reflected. The mechanism behind their relationship is complicated. It is impossible to have a materialistic and dialectic understanding of the essence of social life only based upon senses. In order to really grasp the essence and cause of historical process and the general laws of historical development, an analysis, dissection and study by going deep into society was required. This was an arduous scientific labour, and it can be unimaginable without motivation and passion. Marx's unremitting insistence in his explorations with the spirit of "self-sacrifice", though he suffered certain poverty and illness and persecution, was a proof of that.

We should attach due importance to the role of the subject of scientific research in the establishment of a theory, but we cannot therefore simply conclude that there would be no materialist conception of history without Marx. Where does the real motivation come from? It comes from the historical conditions itself, from the acute contradictions peculiar to every epoch. This contradiction, in theory, represents itself as a problem, i.e. the demands of or problem of the times. The genius of Marx lies in that he was keenly aware of the problem of the times in the face of reality, and had provided a scientific answer to it. Problem—the contradictions of the times; motivation—subjective intention to solve the contradictions; scientific answer—lies in the times itself. A problem contains its solution in itself, but the key is to study. Therefore, the times' circumstances was the objective condition for the emergence of the materialist conception of history, and this conception was Marx's theoretical awareness of the laws of history, formulated as his conscious adaptation to the needs of the proletariat which had stepped on the political stage, and he had seen through the openly appearing contradiction of capitalism which had developed to a certain acuteness. Or in Hegel's words, it was "its time apprehended in thoughts."

III

An era draws people's attention with its intensifying contradictions, and sets the scope and limits of human knowledge which could be achievable, but intensifying contradictions cannot alone spontaneously generate any theory. The creation of a theory is an intellectual production, and has its own special laws. One important law is that any theoretical thinking is premised on the thoughts and ideas of its predecessors. This which reflects the inheritance and continuity of human knowledge.

The materialist conception of history has its own theoretical sources. The difficulty lies not in the enumeration of the achievements in human understanding of history before Marx, but in illustrating how he had critically absorbed them. The theories that have not been studied by him cannot be considered as the sources of Marx's theory of history, just like the buried unexplored minerals do not constitute real wealth. Mehring had discussed the relationship between the German romantic historical school and historical materialism in his book *On Historical Materialism*. He commented on Lavergne-Peguilhen's ideas, a well-known representative of the romantic historical school, which he wrote in *Law of Motion and Law of History* in 1838: "The real and hitherto small progress in social sciences can be attributed to the fact that various economic forms are not divided clearly, and that people could not realize that the various economic forms constitute the basis of the entire society and basis of state organization. People have ignored that the content and development of production, product distribution, culture, cultural dissemination, state legislation and state form, are derived exactly from those economic forms; those social factors of vital importance arise inevitably from the economic forms and their proper use, just like products are the result of the interaction between productive forces, and the root of social morbidity observed in any place can usually be located and grasped in the contradiction between social form and economic form."[17]

This statement, with a strong resemblance to historical materialism, may be misjudged as the source of Marx's conception of history at the first glance. For this reason, Mehring had consulted Engels about it

---

17   Quoted from Mehring: In Defense of Marxism, p. 10.

and received a negative reply. Engels told Mehring that "in his Bonn and Berlin days Marx had read Adam Müller and Mr. von Haller's *Restauration*, etc.; he spoke only with considerable contempt of this insipid, bombastic, verbose imitation of the French romantics such as Joseph de Maistre and Cardinal Bonald. However, even if he had come across passages like the one cited from Lavergne-Peguilhen, they could not have made the slightest effect upon him at that time even if he understood at all what those people wanted to say.

Because, Marx was then a Hegelian and that passage from Lavergne-Peguilhen, was pure heresy to him. He knew nothing whatever about political economy and could not have had any idea about the meaning of a term like 'economic form'. Hence the passage in question, even if he had known it, would have gone in one ear and come out of the other without leaving a perceptible trace in his memory. However, I greatly doubt whether traces of such views could have been found in the works of those romantic historians, which Marx had read between 1837 and 1842."[18]

This shows that the sources of the materialist conception of history should indeed be what Marx had absorbed critically, and its basis is his works, especially his reading notebooks. Marx had formed the good habit of taking notes in his college days, making careful extracts as well as noting his comments and annotations. His *Bonn Notebooks*, *Berlin Notebooks*, *Kreuznach Notebooks*, *Paris Notebooks* and *London Notebooks* all provide us valuable materials about how Marx absorbed the cultural heritage of mankind. The index of Marx's manuscripts and notebooks, collected by International Institute of Social History, in Amsterdam, indicates that his readings cover the period from ancient Greece and Roman to the 1840s, including philosophy, economics, politics, history, religion, ethics, literature, art history, etc. From this we can detect the following characteristics of the sources of the materialist conception of history.

The first is the criticism and inheritance of all excellent cultural heritage of mankind.

---

18 Karl Marx and Frederick Engels: Collected Works, 1st Edition, Volume 38, p. 480, Beijing: People's Press, 1972.

Lenin is opposed to the view of Marxism as a rigid, fixed and closed system which is stalemate and refuses to advance, and he stressed that Marxism is not sectarianism, and rejects any departure from the road of world civilization: "Marxism has won its historical significance as the ideology of the revolutionary proletariat because, far from rejecting the most valuable achievements of the bourgeois epoch, it has, on the contrary, assimilated and refashioned everything of value in the more than two thousand years of the development of human thought and culture."[19] This conclusion is quite applicable to the materialist conception of history.

The materialist conception of history has multiple direct and indirect sources. Marx studied the ancient Greek and Roman philosophy, especially Aristotle, Democritus, Epicurus, Stoicism and Scepticism, read a lot of incomplete articles from relevant works of these thinkers and took notes. He studied contemporary history, the history of the French Revolution in particular, and the political theories of the bourgeois enlightenment scholars, especially the state theories developed by Montesquieu and Rousseau. He intensively studied the works of the French materialists of the 18th century and those of the historians of the French Restoration. He also studied the German classical philosophy, the British classical political economy, and the works of the three great utopian socialists of the 19th century and their predecessors and descendants. Indeed, as Lenin said, "He had critically reshaped everything that had been created by human society, without ignoring a single detail."[20]

The influence of his contemporaries should also be paid attention in examining the multiple sources, because the inspiration formed by interaction through scientific discussions cannot be neglected. When expounding that Feuerbach had stopped in the halfway and could not attain the materialist conception of history, Engels considered his rustication in a little village as an important reason for that, saying "this reclusion had compelled him, who, of all philosophers, was the most inclined to social intercourse, to produce thoughts out of his solitary head instead of in amicable and hostile encounters with other men of his calibre"[21].

---

19   Lenin Selected Works, 2nd edition, Volume 4, p. 362, Beijing: People's Press, 1972.
20   Ibid., p. 347.
21   Karl Marx and Frederick Engels: Selected Works, 1st edition, Volume 4, p. 227.

For Marx, it is a different story. Amid the vortex of boiling political life, Marx not only studied the cultural heritage of mankind, but also valued the accomplishments of his contemporaries. He admitted the influence of Engels, Hess and other people on him. It is generally acknowledged that Marx was inspired by Engels' *Outlines of a Critique of Political Economy*.

The second is the comprehensive absorption of the social theories in Western Europe in 19th century.

Lenin affirms that Marxism is the crystallization of the excellent cultural heritage of mankind in more than two thousand years, but emphasizes the sources of German classical philosophy, the British classical political economy and the three great trends of utopian socialism in the 19th century, believing that "Marx was the genius who continued and consummated the three main ideological currents of the 19th century, represented by the three most advanced countries of mankind". These two points are not contradictory, but further highlight the foremost important sources of Marxism, because they embody the highest achievement in human thought up to the first half of the 19th century. As far as the materialist conception of history is concerned, it does not simply originate in the German classical philosophy, but also absorbs, for example, the rational ideas of the historians of the French Restoration. However, concerning its major sources, it can be said that the materialist conception of history is the result of the combination of the German classical philosophy, the British classical political economy and the ideas of the three great trends of utopian socialism of the 19th century.

Hegel's philosophy is an important source of the materialist conception of history, which seems hard to understand and affirm. How can the idealist conception of history be the source of the materialist conception of history? In fact, it is not really surprising. The idealist conception of history can give birth to the materialist conception of history, just as Marxism had originated in non-Marxism. Intellectual production is quite different from physical production. The reproduction of human species with genes as the genetic material depends on the same species. But theoretical thinking can form brand new schools of thought or new theories through absorption, assimilation and recreation of the ideas of the predecessors. Engels made it clear that Hegel "was the first to try to demonstrate that there is an evolution, that there is an intrinsic coherence in history. Though some elements in his philosophy of history may seem very strange to us now, the grandeur of its basic conception still can be admired today, when compared both with his predecessors and with those who had followed him ventured to advance general historical observations. His monumental conception of history pervades through the *Phänomenologie des Geistes*, *Ästhetik* and *Geschichte der Philosophie*, and the material is everywhere set forth historically, in a definite historical context, even if in an abstract distorted manner. This epoch-making conception of history was a direct theoretical pre-condition of the new materialist outlook".[22]

The emergence of the materialist conception of history is unthinkable without dialectics. There is no doubt that the teachings of Hegel such as the necessity of history, that labour is the self-realization and self-creation of human beings, and that contradiction is a driving force of the development of things, etc.; all have provided an important guidance for Marx to uncover the dialectical process of history itself.

Feuerbach's conception of history was idealistic and metaphysical, but the materialistic humanism he advocated had then created favourable conditions for the emergence of the materialist conception of history. On the one hand this can be attributed to the fact that his materialistic ontology and epistemology had shortened Marx's shift from idealism to materialism, and on the other hand his views on the reality of man, the unity of man and nature and that the essence of man lies in social community had built a bridge which had led Marx to progress from the idea of absolute idea to the real man and his history. Engels wrote: "Because "with the theoretical equipment inherited from Hegel it was of course, not possible even to understand the empirical, materialistic attitude of these people."[23]

22   Karl Marx and Frederick Engels: Selected Works, 1st edition, Volume 2, p. 121, Beijing: People's Press, 1972.
23   Karl Marx and Frederick Engels: Collected Works, 1st Edition, Volume 3, p. 261, Beijing: People's Press, 1960.

In particular, Feuerbach, in his criticism of religion, sought the origin of religion in the depths of the alienation of the essence of man, and thus opened the door to the materialist conception of history through his analysis on the origin of religion. As Marx said, "owing to the fact that Feuerbach showed the religious world as an illusion of the earthly world, German theory too was confronted with the question which he left answered: how did it come about that people "got" these illusions "into their heads?". Even for the German theoreticians this question has paved the way to the materialist view of the world." This was exactly the fact. It is easy to find in his earlier works how Marx had attained the materialist conception of history by analyzing the secular (earthly) basis of religion.

The materialist conception of history is itself philosophy, but it had not originated in philosophy alone. Like the related breeding is harmful for the development of a species, a creative philosophical theory is bound to break through the limitations of several philosophies. The materialist conception of history was established by the assimilation of a wide range of achievements in fields other than philosophy. Here, the reshaping of the British classical political economy and the three great trends of utopian socialism had played a vital role.

The British classical political economy attaches importance to production, and shifts the studies on entire field of economics from the field of circulation to the field of production; the labour theory of value established by classical political economy was not only important for pure economics, but also had a philosophical significance, which recognizes labour as the self-creation ability of the subject in the form of economics.

The British classical political economy had also analyzed the class relations in the capitalist society from the perspective of economics. Although its giants had focused on the modes of distribution, and did not expose the essence of class divisions, it was undoubtedly a progress to analyze social classes from the perspective of economics instead of analyzing them from the aspect of judicial rights. Besides, many important categories of historical materialism, such as the mode of production, social-economic formation, productive forces, relations of production, economic base and superstructure, etc. were not borrowed from the German classical philosophy, but were the products of the studies in the sphere of political economy.

The conception of history of the three great utopian socialists of the 19th century was also idealistic, but contained some reasonable factors as well. In his *Letters d'un Habitant de Genève a Ses Contemporains*, Saint-Simon recognized that the French Revolution was a class war, not only simply between nobility and bourgeoisie, but between nobility, bourgeoisie and the non-possessors, which was the most pregnant discovery in the year 1802.

He also declared that politics was the science of production, and foretold the complete absorption and determination of politics by economics, thus expressing, in the embryo form, the knowledge that economic conditions are the basis of political institutions. Fourier's works contained much mysterious stuff, but they also cover many truly valuable elements thus constituted a philosophy of society with systematic ideas on it. His teachings that everyone—under a reasonable system—should work according to the direction of his own interests, that labour should be in proportion to enjoyment, in particular, his conception of history which divides social history into four stages of evolution—savagery, barbarism, the patriarchal society and civilization, were much more reasonable than the forced constructions of Hegel, who divided history in the light of the self-development of absolute idea. Also inspiring were Owen's views that human's character is the product of the combination of his heredity and the environment of the individual humans during their life. For him human's developing age (childhood and puberty) was very important. And Owen was quite brilliant when he advocated that reasonable conditions should be arranged and established to promote the all-round development of the character and intellect of human beings.

The above shows that just as the various parts of Marxism constitute a unified whole, the materialist conception of history had originated from more than one single theory. The achievements made by Marx's predecessors in philosophy, economics and politics have generated an integrated force, a theoretical composite force. If the highly developed capitalist mode of production in England and France had made up for the backward economy in Germany, and formed favourable conditions of the times for the emergence of the materialist conception of history, we could also say that the theoretical achievements of Marx's predecessors in different fields were mutually complementary, and produced a favourable theoretical environment for the emergence of the materialist conception of history.

The third is the combination of theory with practice. Shift of research focus.

Marx's criticism and absorption of his predecessors' ideas were not completed simply at one stroke but had experienced a process. Marx was unlikely to come into contact with various cultural achievements from the very beginning of his researches, but instead he kept expanding his horizon and research scope to solve the theoretical problems encountered by people in actual life. A careful examination of his notebooks and changes in his research focus can roughly outline the development of his thought and the formation process of his materialist conception of history. When he turned towards Hegel and joined the Young Hegelian movement in 1837, Marx read all the works of Hegel and most works of his disciples. When he criticized the absolute monarchy and religion of Prussia and argued for self-consciousness and freedom, he had studied intensively the ancient Greek and Roman philosophy; when he ran into those unfamiliar arguments about communism when editing the *Rheinische Zeitung* he worked for he turned his focus to studying the works of utopian socialists. Soon after he quitted the *Rheinische Zeitung* and focused himself on addressing the vexing problem—the relationship between civil society and state, he focused on readings on the exposition and criticism of Hegel's conception of state, he also studied the works of Feuerbach, besides history concepts and political theories of the bourgeois Enlightenment scholars; when he turned his attention to analyze civil society, he shifted his focus from philosophy to political economy, and read many works related to economics. This, of course, was not a linear, was not once-and-for-all process, but a repetitive one. For example, Marx had re-studied Hegel's works, especially his *Logic*, when he was writing *Capital*.

The historical conditions and theoretical sources of the materialist conception of history show that it is a conception of history having both class character and scientific character. This conception was established out of the needs of the proletarian class struggle, and thus has strong class character; but it is not, as some Western scholars have argued simply a class ideology, a class defence theory— a tool for arguing for the interests of a certain class. The materialist conception of history is a scientific conception of history, which has widely absorbed excellent cultural heritage of mankind, and truly uncovers the laws of history itself. The combination of class character with scientific character is its main characteristic as well as its merit. The materialist conception of history, as the crystallization of excellent cultural heritage of mankind, will maintain its scientific value, even if there occur radical changes in class structures and class relations in human society.

The argument we have suggested: The emergence of the materialist conception of history has its historical conditions and theoretical sources also applies for its development. If some philosophy in history had remained stagnant and withered after being respected—for a period—as an official philosophy, the materialist conception of history, which came to the stage with the victory of the proletariat, will not suffer a similar fate, because its principle of theory in consistence with practice ensures its infinite vitality.

It values new historical conditions and keeps studying new problems of the new times; it correctly values various theoretical sources and keeps assimilating new findings in social sciences and natural sciences. It will be definitely a mistake to turn the materialist conception of history into a closed ideology irrelevant to the times, i.e. attaching importance only to the historical conditions under which it was created and the theoretical sources at that time, and thus ignore the contemporary historical conditions and new theoretical sources.

IV

The development of the materialist conception of history is a never-ending process. History is created by man himself, and man keeps deepening his understanding of it. After Marx and Engels passed away, Lafargue, Mehring, Labriola, Lenin, Plekhanov, and the members of the Communist Party of China, with Mao Zedong as the main representative, all have made certain contributions to the development of the materialist conception of history, theoretically or practically. Deng Xiaoping has advanced the theory of building socialism with Chinese characteristics, and creatively applied the materialist conception of history to the practice of socialist construction. The period during which Marx established the materialist conception of history is relatively short when compared to the entire history of the development of the materialist conception of history. But this was a phase of vital importance, during which some basic categories and fundamental views of the materialist conception of history were established. Correctly answering the various questions theoretical development and contemporary reality poses to the materialist conception of history requires the study of Marx's thinking process when establishing this conception and his basic ideas. This "origin" or genetic method is very important.

For example, to answer the question whether the materialist conception is outdated, it is vital to explore why Marx established this conception. Some Western scholars argue that Marx's "theories bear the hallmarks of the capitalism in the British Victorian period", and argue that the general models he used to study society and history have already lost their value. Other scholars acknowledge the historical feats of Marx, but they emphasize that Marxism belongs to the old Second Wave—as a product of the industrial revolution. They argue that to diagnose the internal structure of today's high-tech society with Marxism would be similar to using a magnifier in the age of electron microscope. They simply ignore those conditions that urge the further application and development of the materialist conception of history, just as those for its establishment. It may well mean that they fail to completely understand its scientific character.

The materialist conception of history was established in the 1840s, *The German Ideology*, the classical work marking its establishment, was written between 1845 and 1846. This period was apparently distinct from our contemporary era, characterized by world-wide scientific and technological revolutions one after the other, and by enormous steps in terms of both the development of productive forces and the advances in science and technology. However, Marx had established the materialist conception of history not like a prophet, who attempted to give a detailed description of the future by cramming all the rich and varied contents of future human history into a fixed historical paradigm, but behaved as a scientist, who repelled from this attitude of the previous idealism, metaphysics and distanced himself from all forms of cyclic development theories those which used God's will, absolute idea, human nature and human will to explain history. On the contrary he provided us certain basic scientific theories and methods for the study of human society and history.

The completion of this task by him was absolutely possible if we carefully analyze the class related conditions when the proletariat stepped on the political stage in the 1840s, and read the intellectual records concerning the development of capitalist production from a certain developed level.

To date, no matter to what extent the productive forces, science and technology have been developed, there is no concrete evidence that can refute the teachings of the materialist conception of history; i.e. that the production of material goods is the basis of the existence and development of human society, that the productive forces are the ultimate decisive factor of social development, that class structure is determined by economic structure, that science and technology are productive forces, and the dialectical movement between productive forces and relations of production, between economic base and superstructure, are the contradictions that move the society forward.

On the contrary, in the absence of the materialist conception of history, it is impossible to correctly interpret the changes in the structure of productive forces, industrial structure, production management system and family structure of the society, which demonstrate themselves in the scientific and technological development, as well as in the way of life, human values and cultural psychology. Although several important theories of social history have been advanced after the establishment of the materialist conception of history, especially in recent decades, and although some of them have indeed raised some valuable questions and have offered remarkable new ideas, none of these schools could surpass or substitute the materialist conception of history, and their merry-go-round life cycle is a certain proof for that. We cannot oppose the scope of application of the materialist conception of history to the historical conditions for its establishment, because this conception has revealed the essence and the most fundamental laws of the history of human society. The content of the materialist conception of history needs to be enriched and developed, and also the topics of research of this conception need to be updated. However, these efforts should be carried out along the direction Marx had set; another "direction" will lead us to a blind alley, which is proven in intellectual history time and again.

Likewise, the understanding of the essence of the materialist conception of history is also inseparable from the study of the history of this period. In establishing the materialist conception of history, Marx began with criticizing religion, state and law, gradually shifted to explore its material origin in depth, and finally discovered that the production mode of material goods plays a decisive role. This is a process starting from the study of the phenomena of superstructure to that of economic base, this course of study is not only consistent with the law of knowledge building that human knowledge always develops starting from effect proceeds to the cause, but also related to Marx's historic mission of establishing the materialist conception of history: repel the idealist conception of history. Marx exerted all his strength at that time to find out the material force, which ultimately determined the outlook of the whole society and social development, and that material force which can rationally explain the various phenomena of superstructure, therefore he did not have the time and chance to expound the other aspect of this question. But Marx never denied the interrelations among the various elements of superstructure, nor ignored their reaction to economic base. This discovery can be observed in all the relevant works of Marx and Engels. The view that misconstrues the materialist conception of history as a vulgar "economic determinism", a theory which only recognizes the decisive role of economic factors, intentionally or unintentionally ignores the certain specific historical characteristics of the period when Marx had established the materialist conception of history.

Moreover, the process of Marx's thinking logic in establishing the materialist conception of history is one starting from estrangement to estranged labour, and then from estranged labour to the all-round establishment of this conception. It is in line with the process in which Marx started with superstructure, gradually went deep into labour process and the field of production, and lastly discovered the "ultimate reason" of history. It was a continuous, painstaking theoretical exploration process, including certain difficulties and contradictions and also efforts of self-sublation. To make appropriate evaluation of his achievements, raised questions by him and his development direction at each step, and to analyze Marx's thinking process historically and specifically will help us to correctly understand such controversial, important theoretical issues in the world as estrangement and humanism.

Marx did not start his theoretical works from studying such categories as human essence and estrangement in the abstract sense. On the contrary, his eyes were focused on the reality, first on the reality of Germany, and then on the working class movement in France and England. Marx had once compared the characteristics of his theoretical work with those of some members of the Young Hegelians, especially Stirner. He said, "With "Stirner", "communism" begins with searching for "essence". He added: "That communism is a highly practical movement, pursuing practical aims by practical means, [...] only perhaps in Germany, in opposing the German philosophers, can it spare a moment for the problem of "essence"."[24]

Certainly, this does not mean that Marx paid no attention to the question of estrangement and human essence. In fact, the opposite is true. In the process of establishing the materialist conception of history, Marx never strayed from this question from the criticism of religion, from the critique of state and laws to his analysis of civil society and to his analysis of "living labour" and estranged labour. This is not hard to conceive. The thinking process of Marx, who had started his theoretical exploration based on a certain historical premise, demonstrates the continuity of historical process and the power of theoretical traditions, which, of course, is not a "misfortune" of Marx. Without the process from God to man, which had begun and developed gradually since the Renaissance, it will be hard to expect that Marx could progress from the concept of abstract man to real man, and then proceed to the concept of material production activity of human beings in just a few years. Marx inherited and broke through the traditions of history concepts, and based his studies on human society and history, including his analysis of man, human

---

24   Karl Marx and Frederick Engels: Collected Works, 1st Edition, Volume 3, p. 236.

essence and estranged labour in capitalist society, on the materialist conception of history, which is the crux of the matter. Positing
the so-called young Marx in opposition to the old Marx, or reduce
the materialist conception of history to abstract humanism or argue
that historical materialism does not advocate humanism of any form,
these all would be one-sided views.

In Marxism, philosophy, economics and the theory of scientific socialism are inseparable and constitute an integrated whole, which
was particularly the case when Marx established the materialist conception of history. Marx did not establish the materialist conception
of history just for the sake of formulating a philosophy of history.
He gradually formed his theory of history when he was seeking the
way to completely emancipate the proletariat and scientifically define the historical mission of the proletariat. Likewise, if Marx did
not make those breakthroughs in the speculative thinking tradition
of the German classical philosophy, thus stayed within limitations of
pure philosophy, and if he did not turn his focus towards the study
of economics from that of philosophy, he, at best, would be nothing
but a speculative, Hegelian Marx, instead of being the founder of a
new scientific system. The establishment of the materialist conception of history, in turn, has provided scientific theories and methods
for establishing the political-economics and socialism theories of the
proletariat. Their relationship is one of mutual promotion and mutual complementation, instead of a single-track, chain-type causal
relationship.

We should never forget that Marxism is a unified whole, and the
removal of any part will cause it to lose its original character. For
instance, the debates on the prospects of capitalism in today's world
are focused, directly or indirectly, on this theoretical basis—the materialist conception of history. If the materialist conception of history were not a scientific conception of history, if history, as some
Western scholars have argued, was lawless and directionless, and
it was of pure self design and selection, or it was post-industrial
society, super-industrial society, information society, technological and E-society, etc. rather than capitalist society that will give its
way to socialist society, not only Marx's theory of socialist revolution will lose its basis determined by objective laws, but also human

understanding of history and society will again fall into the abyss of fatalism and voluntarism.

That "all history is contemporary history" is a famous remark by Croce. We certainly do not agree with this kind of relativism, but we have to admit that it is not easy to scientifically reflect the reality of history, especially the history of theoretical thinking. Excluding deliberate misrepresentation, incomplete literature and average competence will be enough to lead a researcher to draw wrong conclusions. To reproduce the correct process of Marx's establishing the materialist conception of history is a serious and difficult task and requires joint efforts. Good intentions may be understood in theoretical studies, but cannot serve as excuses to cover up mistakes. Criticism and correction are welcome.

CHAPTER I

CRITICISM OF RELIGION — GATEWAY TO THE ACTUAL LIFE

ON SELF-CONSCIOUSNESS AND FREEDOM

History does not repeat itself, but it does rhyme a lot. The process from God to man, which took a very long time in the history of Western Europe, was later reproduced in Germany in a condensed form. This movement did make its own special contribution, though it was not on such a magnificent scale and full of dedication as its counterpart was in history. For young Marx, it opened the door to the actual political struggle.

The anti-religious struggle also had a long history. It was a political struggle, whether in Italy, England, France or Germany. However, to criticize religion from the perspective of estrangement was the product of the German philosophy. Although religion was regarded as a phenomenon of estrangement by Hegel, Feuerbach and Bauer, their views contained different aspects. Marx was once a member of the Young Hegelian movement, and in his years in Berlin University he was a student of and had close contact with Bruno Bauer, a leader of the Young Hegelians. Marx also began to regard self-consciousness as the essence of man and used this concept to criticize religion, which was the central idea in his doctorial dissertation, *The Difference between the Democritean and Epicurean Philosophy of Nature*, and the series of notebooks on Epicurus' philosophy. This shows that Marx had inherited the tradition of the speculative dialectics in the German classical philosophy and thus highlighted the winning of self-consciousness of man.

1 ESTABLISHMENT OF THE PRINCIPLE OF SELF-CONSCIOUSNESS: FROM HUMAN MECHANICALNESS TO HUMAN ACTIVITY

The development of the bourgeois humanitarianism, which advanced gradually since the Renaissance, to the French materialism, undoubtedly contains a contradiction on the question of man: On the one hand, it sought to improve the status of man in society and elaborate systematically on the theory of freedom, equality and fraternity based on natural rights, but on the other, it denied the subjective status of man, belittled man and even view man as a machine evaluating him from the perspective of mechanism.

Engels has commented on the inclination to mechanism in England initiated by Hobbes. The mechanists subsumed all movement forms under mechanical movement, and even regarded every human passion as nothing but a mechanical movement which has a beginning and an end. So Engels said, "Materialism takes to misanthropy. If it is to overcome its opponent, misanthropic, fleshless spiritualism, and that on the latter's own ground, materialism has to chastise its own flesh and turn ascetic."[1]

This mechanist view is in opposition to human activity. If this is a characteristic of the British materialism, the same is also true for the French materialism. The emergence of the French mechanical materialists can be attributed to Descartes, who exhibits this inclination in his physics studies, and advances the idea that animals are machines. Julien Offray de La Mettrie further develops this doctrine, and puts forward that the man is a machine, and writes a book on it, *L'Homme Machine*. According to his view, the human body is a

---

1   Karl Marx and Frederick Engels: Selected Works, 1st edition, Volume 3, p. 383.

machine which winds its own springs, and the living image of perpetual movement; he wrote: "Man is not moulded from costlier clay;
nature has used but one dough, and has merely varied the leaven."
Therefore, man, in comparison with animals, has a few more wheels,
a few more springs, and his brain is relatively near the heart and
for this very reason receives more blood. Diderot had expressed a
similar view. In *Conversation Between D'Alembert and Diderot*, he,
in the form of a debate, stresses that there is no fundamental difference between a canary-organism and a canary, and between them
and man: The bird-organism is made of wood, and man is made of
flesh. The canary is made of flesh, and the musician is made of flesh
organized differently, but the two of them have the same origin, the
same formation, the same functions, and the same end. Of course
this kind of views have some rational elements, for they are against
spiritualism, dualism and religious mysticism of various forms, and
adhere to the principle of the material unity of the world, but they do
obliterate the special essence of man.

The shift from the French materialism to idealism of the German
classical philosophy is of dual nature: It is retrogression, a transition
from materialism to idealism in terms of the solution to the fundamental questions of philosophy, but it was a progress, a transition
from mechanism to dialectics in terms of the opposition between
dialectics and metaphysics. Marx thinks highly of the achievement
towards dialectics in the German classical philosophy, saying that
the "[s]eventeenth century *metaphysics*, driven from the field by the
French Enlightenment, notably, by French materialism of the eighteenth century, experienced a *victorious and substantial restoration*
in *German philosophy*, particularly in the speculative German philosophy of the nineteenth century."[2]

The dialectics in the German classical philosophy is distinguished
from the naïve dialectics of the ancient Greeks by such a characteristic as the former was largely not an ontological dialectics about
the objective world itself, but an idealistic, speculative one. From
Kant, through Fichte to Hegel, although their views on "subject"
are not exactly the same and can be divided into subjective idealism

---

2   Karl Marx and Frederick Engels: Collected Works, 1st Edition, Volume 2, p. 159,
Beijing: People's Press, 1957.

and objective idealism, they all emphasize the role of spirit and thus change the mechanistic view of man as a machine by the old materialism, and give first priority to the creativity of the subject from the idealistic aspect. In this way, "substantial" results were produced in at least two aspects:

First, from object to subject. The old materialists not only treated the material world and the objects of cognition as pure objects, but also considered man as an object. They did not see the essential difference between man and other objective things, and denied the subjective status of man. An achievement of the German classical philosophy was that it discovered subject, which is different from object and who creates object. In such propositions as Fichte's "the non-ego as the product of ego" and Hegel's "substance is subject", here both ego and subject refers to the spirit detached from matter, but they do, though in a reversed form, imply the subjective status of man.

Second, from passivity to activity. This aspect is associated with the first aspect above. The old materialism stresses the passivity of man, and regards man as a piano that must be played by nature to make sounds. It adheres to the materialistic theory of reflection, but this passive, intuitive theory of reflection reduces man to a passive position in the objective world and deprives him of his creativity. This relationship is inverted by the speculative dialectics of the German classical philosophy, which considers object passive and negative, and subject, i.e. the spirit, positive and active and as something created by ego.

The philosophy of self-consciousness of the Young Hegelians, represented by Bruno Bauer, is based on the tradition of the speculative German philosophy. It both bases itself on and somewhat deviates from the Hegelian philosophy.

The German classical philosophy reaches its zenith of idealistic dialects in the Hegelian philosophy. On the one hand, Hegel expresses, logically and speculatively, the activity of subject with his doctrine of absolute idea; but on the other, he includes in this absolute idea, both nature and man as the categories of substance and self-consciousness, and thus considers man and nature as the tools for absolute idea to realize its inner necessity. The Young Hegelians were not satisfied with this point. They adhere to Hegel's self-consciousness, and raise it to the dominant position from a subordinate level. The emphasis on the role of self-consciousness could have approached towards expressing the position of man in the whole world, but on the contrary it returns to Fichte's subjective idealism, because Bauer transforms self-consciousness from an attribute of man into an independent subject separated from both nature and man, into the sole creator of the world, creator of heaven and earth.

Indeed, the development of philosophical thinking is not linear, but infinitely approximate to a string of circles, to a spiral curve: The Seventeenth century metaphysical theory of the freedom of the will was driven out of the field by the Eighteenth century French materialism; then the speculative German philosophy rejected the Eighteenth century French materialism and revived the Seventeenth century metaphysics; Hegel rejected Fichte's subjective idealism and turned towards objective idealism, while the Young Hegelians, with Bauer as the representative, proceeded from Hegel but returned to Fichte's subjective idealism. It is after joining the Young Hegelian movement that Marx had commenced with his theoretical work and political activities, and he had also stressed the role of self-consciousness in the very beginning. Although Marx rejected Bauer's opposition between self-consciousness and substance, he did not go back to the idea of absolute idea as the unity of self-consciousness and substance. Instead, basing himself on the absorption of the rational ideas of Hegel, he gradually developed the idea of the unity of man and environment, that is, he apprehended the real man and real human species, and thus truly expounded the role and the position of man in nature and society, thus expressed the activity of man scientifically. Of course, the formulation of this view undergoes a process, of which Marx's doctoral dissertation was a prophetic, good start.

2 MARX'S EXPLORATION ON THE PHILOSOPHY OF SELF-CONSCIOUSNESS

Epicureanism, Stoicism and Scepticism are first considered as the philosophy of self-consciousness by Hegel, who wrote this evaluation in his *Phenomenology of Spirit* and *Lectures on the History of Philosophy*. But Hegel belittles these schools, and they are merely at a stage barely higher than sense certainty according to the Hegelian system. Seen from the history of ideology, this idea of Hegel contains some reasonable elements, but his belittlement of these schools is inconsistent with the spirit of the time, especially when the Young Hegelians fought for freedom.

Being a participant in the Young Hegelian movement, Marx had a keen interest in these schools. He refuses to view those philosophies since Aristotle as the decline of Greek philosophy, but fully evaluates their great importance for the history of Greek philosophy and for the Greek mind in general and emphasizes that "Only now the times have come in which the systems of the Epicureans, Stoics and Sceptics can be understood."[3]

Marx argues that Epicurus, the Stoics and Sceptics "are the philosophers of self-consciousness", and "these systems in their totality form the complete structure of self consciousness". His study of this philosophical system of "self-consciousness" is mainly motivated by the political needs for fighting against the despotic Prussian system, just as he said in a letter to Lassalle, "[Among the ancient philosophers]…Epicurus (him in particular), the Stoa and Scepticism, I had made them object of special study, but for [political] rather than philosophical reasons."[4] However theoretically, this attempt of Marx also deepens the principle—subjectivity and activity—established by the speculative German dialectics. Marx in his doctoral dissertation fully evaluates the active role of self-consciousness when analyzing, the difference between the Democritean and Epicurean philosophies of nature.

2.1 OPPOSITION TO MECHANICAL DETERMINISM

Democritus and Epicurus contradict each other on the question of the interrelationship between necessity and accident/chance. Democritus' atomic theory focuses on the empirical knowledge of natural science, so what it emphasizes is necessity. In his view, chance is incompatible with sound thinking, and human beings' creation of the illusion of chance is a manifestation of their perplexity. On the contrary, in Epicurus' philosophy, atom is not the physical

3   Karl Marx and Frederick Engels: Collected Works, 1st Chinese Edition, Volume 40, p. 286, Beijing: People's Press, 1982.
4   Karl Marx and Frederick Engels: Collected Works, 1st Chinese Edition, Volume 29, p. 527, Beijing: People's Press, 1972.

model of the material world, but a symbol of individual self-consciousness. Hence Epicurus rejects necessity and lays stress on accident, just as Marx said, "Accident is the dominating category with the Epicureans."[5]

It is because of his focus on necessity that Democritus emphasizes real possibility, because necessity reveals itself by means of the networks of conditions, reasons and causes, and is deduced from real possibility. In contrast, Epicurus emphasizes abstract possibility, the direct antipode of real possibility, because real possibility seeks to explain the necessity and reality of object, while abstract possibility is not interested in the object which is explained, but in the subject which does the explaining. The object needs only to be possible and conceivable. That, which is abstractly possible, that which can be conceived, constitutes no obstacles to the thinking subject, no stumbling-blocks. This shows that what Epicurus is interested in is not the object itself, nor the knowledge of nature, but "the ataraxy of self-consciousness".

Apparently, the opposition of necessity to accident, the insistence on the one and rejection of the other are both one-sided. However, Marx is inclined to Epicurus in their opposition, because Epicurus rejects necessity in order to combat mechanical determinism and fight for freedom. Epicurus believes that necessity is destiny and blocks the path to freedom, and that belief in necessity is worse than the myth about the gods, because this myth leaves hope for mercy if we do honour to the gods, while destiny is inexorable necessity. It is a misfortune to live in necessity, as a slave to the destiny. Therefore, the Epicureans extol their teacher, for by whom they are redeemed and "set free". Certainly, Marx does not reject necessity, and he acknowledges nature as being rational according to the Hegelian views, and expresses his idea, in its embryo form, to correctly settle the relationship between necessity and freedom.

---

5   Karl Marx and Frederick Engels: Collected Works, 1st Chinese Edition, Volume 40, p. 130.

2.2 THE DECLINATION FROM THE STRAIGHT LINE IS FREE WILL

The declination of the atom is a characteristic of the Epicurean philosophy, a fundamental difference between it and the Democritean philosophy of nature. Marx maintains that the declination of the atom from the straight line is not a particular determination which appears accidentally in the Epicurean philosophy, but goes through the whole Epicurean philosophy. It breaks the dominance of mechanical determinism and blind necessity, because the "*declination a recta via*" is the "*arbitrium* [free will]"[6].

For Marx, if the atom merely has the motion along the straight line, it is simply seen as a spatial point, and only has the spatial determination and lacks the principle of self-motion. While recognizing the motion along the straight line, Epicurus also proposes the declination from the straight line, and thus endows the atom with the principle of activity, making "motion established as self-determination", because the declination is negation of the motion along the straight line, and also affirmation is contained in this negation, namely, the being to which it relates itself is none other than itself. Equally an atom, the mutual repulsion and collision of many atoms take place because of declination. It is due to the atomic repulsion, impact and collision that the world is created, as is described vividly by Marx, he wrote: "As Zeus grew up to the tumultuous war dances of the Curetes, so here the world takes shape to the ringing war games of the atoms."[7] So Marx agrees to Lucretius' argument that the declination breaks "the fati foedera [bonds of the fate]", and believes that only the declination expresses the true soul of the atom, i.e. the absoluteness and freedom of self-consciousness.

Marx attaches great importance to the symbol of the pursuit of freedom contained in Epicurus' declination theory of the atom, but does not agree with his evaluation of freedom as the ataraxy of self-consciousness, separated from the external world. He further develops the declination theory of the atom. The declination of the atom from the straight line indicates that only by negating its relative existence,

6   Karl Marx and Frederick Engels: Collected Works, 1st Chinese Edition, Volume 40, p. 121.
7   Ibid., p. 123.

i.e. the motion along the straight line, and being related to other things (collision of atoms), can the atom realize the concept of the atom. So does man. Man ceases to be a product of nature only when he relates himself to the other human being. To be man as man, he must crush within himself his relative being, namely, self-reclusion and isolation, and relate himself to another human beings. Marx underlines that the Epicurean declination of the atom changes the whole inner structure of the domain of the atoms, and considers that repulsion is the first form of self-consciousness, both of which have this meaning. Hence, Marx argues that the inner freedom of an isolated subject "is freedom from being, not freedom in being"[8], and the true freedom lies in the contacts between men.

2.3 SELF-CONSCIOUSNESS TURNING INTO PRACTICAL ENERGY

Marx regards the Young Hegelianism as a philosophy of self-consciousness, just as he considers the Epicurean philosophy as a philosophy of self-consciousness. The relationship between the Young Hegelianism and the Hegelian philosophy, therefore, is nothing but the relationship between the realized philosophical system and its intellectual carriers, relationship to individual self-consciousness in which its progress appears. The Young Hegelians' opposition to the Hegelian system actually realizes an individual link of this system, i.e. self-consciousness.

Marx also lays stress on self-consciousness, but differentiates himself from Bauer. He does not return to Fichte's subjective idealism, nor is confined to self-consciousness itself, but focuses on the unity of self-consciousness and the external world. Self-consciousness as a power of the mind is inevitably manifested as will, and turns towards the external world, just as Marx said, "It is a psychological law that the theoretical mind, once liberated in itself, turns into practical energy, and, leaving the shadowy empire of Amenthes as will, turns itself against/towards the reality of the world existing without it."[9]. Marx had an objective idealistic understanding of practice at that time, he considered that practice was theoretical and it critically measured

---

8   Ibid., 228.
9   Karl Marx and Frederick Engels: Collected Works, 1st Chinese Edition, Volume 40, p. 258.

the individual existence and the particular reality on the basis of idea. However, by means of the category of practice, Marx establishes the relationship between self-consciousness and the worldly reality, and raises the question that the world becomes philosophical and philosophy becomes worldly, and maintains that it is in the process of becoming worldly, namely, turning into action that philosophy eliminates the flaws and errors inherent in its system. Thus it can be seen that the introduction of the category of practice suppresses the direction of self-consciousness towards voluntarism, and thus opens the way for correctly understanding the role of subjective activity.

3 RELIGION: ALIENATION OF SELF-CONSCIOUSNESS. HUMAN NATURE SUPERIOR TO DIVINITY

Alienation is a category widely used by the Young Hegelians. This trend of thought apparently influences Marx, who joined the Young Hegelian movement and frequently met the members of the Doctors' Club at that time. In his *Notebooks on Epicurean Philosophy* and his doctoral dissertation, he used the category of alienation to analyze the difference between Epicurean and Democritean philosophies on nature, especially when writing on Epicurus' anti-religious atheism. Although his views of estrangement then were idealistic, they are still significant for the full understanding of the development of his thought.

Marx puts forward the question of the alienation of concept when analyzing Epicurus' atomic theory. He argues that the atom, according to Epicurus, should not have properties. That the atom should have properties contradicts the concept of the atom, because properties are variable, properties mean variation, but the atoms do not change. Nevertheless it is a necessary consequence to attribute properties to atoms. Many of the atoms, separated by sensuous space, and mutually repulsive due to declination, are not immediately accordant with each other and also with their pure essence (i.e. the concept of the atom), but all are different from one another, and possess qualitative differences. It is "through these qualities" that "the atom acquires an existence which contradicts its concept; it is assumed as an *externalized being different* from *its essence*"[10].

---

10 Karl Marx and Frederick Engels: Collected Works, 1st Chinese Edition, Volume 40, p. 218.

Marx praises Epicurus, saying that he objectifies the contradiction between essence and existence, which is inherent in the conception of the atom. Because an atom is endowed with qualities, the atom is alienated from its concept, and it is because from repulsion and the ensuing conglomerations of the atoms, which has quality determination, that the world of appearance now emerges. Obviously, the world of appearance would have no way to emerge without the objectification of the contradiction between existence and essence. The atom, in this way, enters the world of appearance from the world of essence, and thus becomes the bearer of the world of appearance, which has manifold relations, while the world of appearance becomes the externalized form of the concept of the atom.

For this reason, Epicurus combines the world of appearance with the world of essence. However, Democritus does not see the contradiction of essence and appearance in the concept of the atom; he either blends one with the other, without seeing the difference between them, or separates one from the other and degrades appearance to the level of subjective semblance. Therefore, Marx underlines that "Epicurus was the first to grasp appearance as appearance, that is, as the alienation of the essence, activating itself in its reality as such: As an alienation."[11] There is no doubt that Marx regards the world of appearance as the alienation of the concept of the atom and explains Epicurus in full accordance with Hegel's views. However, it is here that the question of the contradiction between existence and essence is first time put forward, and treated as an important part of alienation, when we evaluate the development of Marx's thought. Marx also presents the alienation of nature in his *Notebooks on Epicurean Philosophy*. Man depends on nature for survival and nature is an indispensable life source for man. When the productivity was very low, nature was idolized by people, and in particular, some natural phenomena they could not explain, such as lightning and thunder, the waxing and waning of the moon, etc. turned into objects of deep fear. People often imagined that there was a supernatural power behind the natural phenomena. This dependence of human beings on nature was an alienation, just as Marx said, "Any reference to it [nature] as such is at the same alienation of it [nature]."[12]

---

11   Ibid., p. 231.
12   Ibid., p. 174.

Marx pays special attention to Epicurus' view on the relationship between man and the heaven, and he objects to the worship of the celestial bodies in the alienation of nature.

The worship of the celestial bodies is a cult practised by many Greek philosophers, and it is true of the Pythagoras, Plato and Aristotle. This worship is integrated with religious views, because the people assign the highest region—the celestial bodies—to the divine, and regard them as the dwelling places of the divine. All men have such an idea, then so-called barbarians as well as Hellenes, and in general, all who believe in the existence of gods. It seems to them that the divine is immortal, the celestial bodies are immortal, so the divine live in the heaven. The motion and position and eclipse and rising and setting, etc. of the celestial bodies, in this way, are ruled and ordered by a supreme and indestructible One. This supreme One is the divine.

Epicurus is opposed to the world outlook of the whole of Greek people, namely, against the worship of the celestial bodies. He believes that the greatest confusion of the human soul arises from the fact that men hold that the heavenly bodies are blessed and indestructible; he objects to explaining the phenomena of the heavenly bodies from the perspective of theological teleology, and believes that in and for itself the theory of the setting and rising of the sun and the moon, of the position and eclipse of the stars, contains no particular grounds for happiness, just because people see these things but do not understand them and they are terrified. So for Epicurus, any explanation of the heavenly bodies but not the religious one, is acceptable, and the point is to eliminate people's fears of the phenomena of heavenly bodies, and liberate them from their fears.

Marx argues that to remove the alienation of nature, man's fear of and dependence on nature, it is necessary to acknowledge that nature is rational/reasonable, "By the fact we acknowledge that nature is reasonable, our dependence on it ceases"[13].

But there are two kinds of reason: the so-called conscious reason, i.e. the divine, and the Hegel's reason, i.e. the universal mind. Marx took the side of Hegel at the time, and tried to draw an atheistic

---

13   Karl Marx and Frederick Engels: Collected Works, 1st Chinese Edition, Volume 40, p. 173.

conclusion from the Hegelian philosophy: "Only when nature is ac-knowledged as absolutely free conscious reason and is considered as reason in itself, does it become entirely the property of reason."[14] The consideration of nature as the manifestation of reason is cer-tainly idealistic, but it also contains a reasonable element—the de-velopment of nature is an inevitable process with its own laws. The fear and worship of nature can be dispelled and thus the alienation of nature eliminated, as long as the reason of nature is acknowledged and understood.

Marx expounds the idea of thorough militant atheism in his doctoral dissertation, and a major basis for his idea is the Young Hegelians' argument that religion is the alienation of self-consciousness.

The view that gods are created by man is quite old, but the develop-ment from naïve anthropomorphism to the theory of alienation un-derwent a long process. The ancient view on gods is naïve and intui-tive; it emphasizes "being similar in appearance" instead of "being alike in spirit", but it contains a profound idea: the image of gods worshiped by believers is created by man in his own image.

The atheism of the Eighteenth century French Enlightenment is more thorough, more profound and much richer, but one of its main ideas is still that gods are created by man. Yet, it goes beyond the argu-mentation from the image of gods, and goes deep into people' views on the concept and property of gods and their attitudes towards gods. For example, Holbach believes that gods are simply "exaggerated men", and "the various relations between these conceived, invisible things and them are always human relations". Those behaviours of people towards gods—respect, fear and flattery—are actually bor-rowed from the behaviours they take to make contact with a person of the similar kind they are afraid of and try to please. So Holbach says that human worship of gods, "i.e. the system of his behaviours towards a god, is inevitably in conformity with the concepts he has created for gods, just as this god itself is moulded according to his own feelings"[15].

---

14 Ibid., p.p. 173-174.
15 The Selected Readings of the Original Works of Western Philosophy, Volume II, p. 198, Beijing: The Commercial Press, 1982.

The German philosophers' doctrine of religion as the alienation of human essence assimilates the reasonable idea in the intellectual history that gods are created by man. Unlike the simple view of religion as a deception in the past, the German philosophy probes into religion from the aspect of alienation of human essence, and regards religion as an inevitable phenomenon. Although both regard religion as alienation, Feuerbach and Bauer have different views, which are determined by their different views on human essence. Marx, who was under the influence of Hegel's thought at that time, tended to agree with Bauer, and regarded religion as the alienation of self-consciousness, and used it to refute the various proofs of the existence of God.

Marx differentiates the role of gods from the existence of gods. Given that a God has a real, personalistic existence, it is non-existence, because every country, every nation has its own God. Go with your god to a country in which another god is worshipped, and you will find that your god does not exist. For a foreign and specific god, a given country, like a rational country for the common gods, is a place where the god ceases its existence. However, every god, pagan God as well as Christian God, has a real existence, in terms of the function of the God, and of the God as a power superior to and which is influential on human behaviours. The ancient Moloch dominated all, and Apollo at Delphi was a real power in the life of the Greeks, which shows that the concept of gods exerted a huge impact on human life.

Just because gods are impersonal existence, any proof of the existence of gods "is just a proof of the existence of self-consciousness of human essence, a logical explanation for the existence of self-consciousness"[16].

It seems to Marx that the most immediate existence is self-consciousness, and gods are the alienation of self-consciousness. Therefore, all proofs of the existences of gods are nothing but man's proofs of the conception of gods, which proves precisely the splitting of self-consciousness. So in this sense, all proofs of the existence of gods are the proofs of the non-existence of gods, and thus are refutations of all concepts of gods.

---

16   Karl Marx and Frederick Engels: Collected Works, 1st Chinese Edition, Volume 40, p. 285.

However, Marx was by no means an ordinary Young Hegelian who was sympathetic to some ideas of Bauer at that time. He adopted, but not limit himself to the argument of religion as the alienation of self-consciousness, and went further and investigated the cause for the emergence of religion from the world, nature and man himself. He emphasizes that gods exist because of the bad arrangement of nature; gods exist because of the existence of the irrational world; gods exist because of the non-existence of thought. In other words, the concept of gods will cease its existence, as long as the world and nature are arranged according the principle of reason and self-consciousness is made accordant to reason. Therefore, Marx is not entirely in agreement with Bauer. He does not confine the question of the negation of religion to self-consciousness, but extends it to the question of the arrangement of the world and nature, which establishes a general direction for him to investigate religion and the origin of religion from a truly materialistic perspective.

The relationship between man and gods was once a major issue in political life and the sphere of ideology in history. In the appendix to his doctoral dissertation, Marx makes the relationship between man and gods as an object of special study, and criticizes the attack of Plutarch on Epicurus' atheism. Concerning the relationship between man and gods, Marx did not set them in opposition at the very beginning, but stressed their union. For example, he discussed the necessity of the union of man with gods in a composition about religion problems, written by him in 1835. He said, "Our hearts, reason, history, the word of Christ, therefore, tell us loudly and convincingly that union with Him is absolutely essential, that without Him we cannot fulfill our goal, that without Him we would be rejected by God, that only He can redeem us."[17].

This certainly does not mean that Marx was a pious man, but his writing does show that he is influenced by the traditional religious morality. After involving himself in the Young Hegelian movement, Marx agreed with the Young Hegelians, and considered self-consciousness as human nature and that man was superior to gods, and human nature superior to divinity: "It will have none other beside", "human self-consciousness as the highest divinity."[18] This argument

---

17　Karl Marx and Frederick Engels: Collected Works, Volume 40, p. 820.
18　Ibid., p. 190.

clearly expresses the political stand and theoretical perspective of Marx's opposition to religion and the feudal autocratic system.

The superiority of gods to man had been the dominant relationship between the two since the ancient Greece and up to the Middle Ages. This not only refers to the power of church and the status of priests, but also means that gods have supreme authority in ideology. Many philosophers and theologians have endeavoured to prove the greatness of gods and the smallness of man, and that gods should govern man. For example, Anselm von Canterbury proclaimed that "[h]e who despises himself, is honoured by God. He who dislikes himself is liked by God. Therefore, be small in your own eyes so that you may be big in the eyes of God; for you shall be the more valued by God, the more contemptuous you are of men."[19].

Thomas Aquinas also stated publicly that theology was superior to philosophy, and all sciences should submit to the theological views, because the authenticity of theology "roots in the illumination of God", and "will not make mistakes"; "what theology explores is mainly what surpasses human reason and is supremely graceful, while other sciences pay attention only to what human reason can grasp"; but seen from its purpose, theology aims "at the eternal happiness, which is a purpose which all practical sciences aspire for as the final purpose"[20]. Gods, in this way, deprive man of the right to know truth, of the right and pleasure in and of a secular life.

Humanism, emerging in the Renaissance, marks the turn from gods to man. From human freedom and dignity, advocated by such earlier humanists as Pico, Vives, Erasmus and Montaigne, to the French Enlightenment's doctrine of liberty, equality and fraternity, based on natural rights, they have all emphasized that man should be the centre and superior to gods with respect to the relationship between man and gods. For instance, Dante says, "Human nobility, with respect to the number of the fruits it bears, surpasses that of the angels."[21].

---

19   The Selected Readings of the Original Works of Western Philosophy, Volume 1, p.p. 260-261, Beijing: The Commercial Press, 1981.
20   Ibid., p. 59 and p. 197.
21   The Collection of Bourgeois Writers and Artists' Views on Humanitarian Human Nature from the Renaissance to the Nineteen Century, p. 3, p. 11, Beijing: The Commercial Press, 1966.

Italian philosopher Petrarch overtly demanded earthly happiness, saying: "I do not want to become God, or live in eternity, or hold the heaven and earth in my arms. The glory which belongs to man is enough for me. This is all that I pray for, because I myself am a mortal, and I only demand mortal happiness." Shakespeare even praised man passionately: "What a piece of work is man! How noble in reason! How infinite in his faculties! In form and moving, how express and admirable! In action how like an angel! In apprehension, how like a god! The beauty of the world! The paragon of animals!"[22]. Rousseau laid stress on the study of man, saying, "The most useful and least perfected of all human studies is that of "man"".[23] It is a great historical contribution of the bourgeois humanitarianism to make man, rather than gods, stand out and place man over gods.

Marx inherits the historical tradition of man over gods in his doctoral dissertation. His stress on self-consciousness as the highest divinity and actually puts man over gods. In this dissertation, Marx praises Epicurus as "the greatest representative of Greek Enlightenment", just because he, in an era in which gods rule everything, dares to raise mortal eyes to challenge and fight against the heaven, and "denounce those who think man needs the heaven"; dares to deny the eternity of the heaven and make self-consciousness override the heaven and "the sound of his own voice drown the thunder and bolt out the lightning of the heavens".

In Marx's view, there are two kinds of persons in front of gods: one is anxiously buttoned-up and clinging into himself, servile and humble; the other is an "intrepid acrobat", fearless. The former refers to those fettered by the religious ideas of Plutarch, while the latter refers those who believe in the atheism of Epicurus and Lucretius, and are more moral and freer than theists. Marx said, "He, who would not prefer to build the whole world out of his own resources, to be a creator of the world, rather than to be eternally bothering about himself, has already been anathematised by the spirit, he is under an interdict, but in the opposite sense; he is expelled from the temple and deprived of the eternal enjoyment of the spirit and left to sing

---

22   Shakespeare: Hamlet, p. 61, Beijing: The Writers Publishing House, 1956.
23   Rousseau, Discourse on the Origin and Foundation of Inequality among Mankind, p. 62.

lullabies about his own private bliss and to dream about himself at night."[24]

Marx considers philosophy superior to theology, just because he puts man over gods. The first necessity for philosophical investigation is a bold, free mind, which enables man to obtain self-consciousness, while religion means the loss of self-consciousness.

Engels, who turned from the Young German movement to the Young Hegelian movement at that time, also highly praised self-consciousness. He poetically compared self-consciousness to the immortal "phoenix" when opposing to Schelling's irrationalism and obscurantism. He said, "The Idea, the self-consciousness of mankind, is that wonderful phoenix who builds for himself a funeral pyre out of all that is most precious in the world and rises rejuvenated from the flames which destroy an old time."[25].

There is no doubt that Marx's emphasis on self-consciousness and his view of religion as the alienation of self-consciousness is an idealist conception of history. However, it is easier to approach to the truth of history by highlighting self-consciousness and treating man as active subject, than regarding man as pure object governed by his natural instincts and as a machine.

4 FREEDOM: SPECIES-ESSENCE OF SPIRITUAL BEING. GENUS AND SPECIES OF FREEDOM

The criticism of religion was only a gateway to the actual life. What differentiates Marx from the theologian Bauer is that Marx does not focus his eyes on religion alone, but also on the most pressing problems of reality.

The first question Marx encountered is that of freedom of the press, when he turned his eyes towards the worldly life. This was a pressing problem of reality in the German political struggle of that time, which reflected the contradiction between the growing capitalist economy and the feudal despotism. In particular, this contradiction became more acute after the Prussian government issued a new

24 Karl Marx and Frederick Engels: Collected Works, 1st Chinese Edition, Volume 40, p. 112.
25 Karl Marx and Frederick Engels: Collected Works, 1st Chinese Edition, Volume 41, p. 268, Beijing: People's Press, 1982.

censorship decree on December 24, 1841. The fight for freedom of the press became the premise for the fight for all other freedoms in Germany; without freedom of the press, other freedoms would come to naught. However our focus here is not the political aspect, i.e. Marx's revolutionary democratic tendency to oppose the censorship and attack the despotic Prussian system, but on the philosophical aspect, i.e. his view on the estrangement of human essence which was embodied in his argumentation for freedom of the press.

The question of freedom is a general question, which the bourgeois of any country would definitely raise in its fight against feudalism and for its own dominion. But it would exhibit different characteristics in different countries due to the difference in the level of their economic development and specific class struggle. For example, in England with a highly developed capitalist economy, the question of freedom was more about economy, such as freedom of trade; in France typically and more intense as class struggles, what is frequently discussed was the political freedom. In France, liberty, equality and fraternity was a revolutionary slogan the bourgeois puts forward in its fight for domination. While in Germany, the question of freedom turned towards the realm of spirit, and realm of thinking, reason and consciousness and took the form of question of epistemology and ethics. Although the view of freedom of the German classical philosophy circuitously reflected the demands of the German bourgeois, it was limited to the realm of thinking after all.

The German classical philosophy was different from the French Enlightenment of the 18th century in the philosophical line, but this philosophy as an introduction to the German bourgeois revolution, it still yearned for the freedom won by England and France. Therefore, the principle of freedom also became an important principle in the German classical philosophy. In his *Lectures on the History of Philosophy*, Hegel regards Rousseau as one of "the two starting points of the German philosophy", and believes that his principle of freedom "furnishes the transition to the Kantian philosophy, which, if theoretically considered, made this principle its foundation"[26]. However, actually, Kant was very timid, for he opposed freedom to

---

26   Hegel, Lectures on the History of Philosophy, Volume 4, p. 234, Beijing: The Commercial Press, 1978.

necessity, moral law to natural law, opposed man being a sensuous being depending on experience to man acting as spiritual being, and he restricted the question of freedom to man himself being a cognitive and ethical subject, and regarded the freedom of will as the first postulation of ethics. He said, "Without…a freedom only which has innate practical power and without being true to its name, it is impossible to establish the moral law, and impossible to blame man according to this law."[27]. That is to say, if there is no freedom of will and man does not freely follow the moral voice, the moral law will lose its basis and meaning.

Fichte also stresses the significance of freedom with the influence of the French Revolution. In his book Reclamation of the Freedom of Thought from the Princes of Europe, he considers the freedom of thought as an unalienable right of man, and states that the monarchy has no right to limit people's freedom of thought. But Fichte regards freedom as a special property of "ego" in the light of his idealist world outlook, and thus turns the question of freedom into a question of speculative philosophy.

Hegel looks into the question of freedom from the perspective of objective idealism, and believes that freedom is the essence of Spirit. The essence of Matter is Gravity, while the substance or the essence of Spirit is freedom. All the qualities of Spirit exist only through Freedom; that all are but means for attaining Freedom; that all seek and produce this and this alone. Therefore, Hegel said, "'Freedom'" is the sole truth of 'Spirit'."[28]

According to Hegel, the history of mankind is that of the consciousness of freedom. The development of history is none other than the progress of the consciousness of freedom. The Oriental peoples have not attained the knowledge that Spirit—Man as such—is free, so they are not free. They only know the freedom of one, i.e. the freedom of a Despot; the Romans know only that some are free, not that everyone is free. Only the Germans know that man as man is absolutely free. Therefore, Hegel takes the consciousness of freedom as the driving force of history, as a criterion for the phased division

27   The Collection of Bourgeois Writers and Artists' Views on Humanitarian Human Nature from the Renaissance to the Nineteen Century, p.p. 632-633.
28   Hegel: The Philosophy of History, p. 55, Beijing: SDX Joint Publishing Company, 1956.

of the history of the world and an approach to investigate history. He said, "This sense of this existent principle has been an active force for centuries and centuries, and an impelling power which has brought about the most tremendous revolutions."[29]

Hegel's view on freedom was objective idealism but contained reasonable elements. He did not consider freedom unchanged, but understood it in the development of the world history and connected the progress in history and society with the development of human consciousness of freedom; he did not treat freedom from an individual perspective, but from the perspective of the entire history and society. In particular, Hegel objected to setting freedom against necessity, and believed that the view that freedom is necessity comprehended, and is undoubtedly dialectic.

Living in Germany, a country of philosophical traditions, Marx confined his views on and on basic ideas on man and human essence to Hegel's idealism around 1842.

What is a human being? Marx thinks that man is "spiritual being", a "rational being", or as he pointed out in his letter to Ruge, "As for human beings, that would imply thinking beings"[30]. This is certainly not to say that Marx did not acknowledge the natural reality of human body, but that he underlined the fundamental difference between human beings and animals: animal behaviours are governed by blind instincts, while human beings are rational beings and human behaviours are governed by reason, which constrains instinctive activity. It is right to use reason to distinguish human beings from animals on the one hand, but it is idealistic to regard it as the sole, decisive difference on the other. Consciousness, reason, religious belief or other things peculiar to human beings, all can separate man from animals, but what really distinguish them is the production of material goods. Marx remained within the realm of reason then, and thus could not discover the real decisive line between human beings and animals.

---

29 Hegel: Lectures on the History of Philosophy, Volume 1, p. 52, Beijing: SDX Joint Publishing Company, 1956.
30 Karl Marx and Frederick Engels: Collected Works, 1st Chinese Edition, Volume 1, p. 409, Beijing: People's Press, 1956.

Marx laid emphasis on the universal nature of human beings at that time. He asked: "Is there no universal human nature, as there is a universal nature of plants and stars?"[31]. This so-called universal nature is freedom, "freedom is after all is the generic essence of all spiritual existence"[32]. This view of human nature is the inevitable result of distinguishing human beings from animals by the aspect of reason, because the basic attribute of reason is freedom, and freedom is "a rational being"[33]. Therefore, reason as a criterion and freedom as a criterion were in fact the same thing, and freedom was sometimes used by Marx to draw a line between human beings and animals, for human beings can do what is free freely, "Otherwise what difference would there be between an architect and a beaver except that the beaver would be an architect with fur and the architect a beaver without fur"[34]. It is thus clear that his understanding of human nature was closely associated with that of human beings. As man is regarded as a natural being, the natural properties of man was emphasized; when man is seen as a spiritual being, the spiritual nature of man was be stressed. Only by regarding man as a social being, could the social nature of man be grasped.

Apparently, Marx had an idealistic understanding of man and human nature at that time. Freedom is not the freedom of spirit, and it cannot be apprehended as the freedom of self-consciousness, the freedom of thinking i.e., the freedom of reason. Those revolts against the unreasonable reality is not the self-awareness belonging to the nature of human freedom, but was determined by the real social relations. The slaves were treated as a talking tool and deprived of all rights in slave society; the serfs were tied to the land under serfdom, and they had no personal freedom, freedom of movement and political rights, but they did not put forward the slogan of fight for freedom. Their revolt against the rulers through sabotage, runaway, and even uprising, in fact was not resulted from the awareness of the nature of their freedom, but determined by their actual class status. The consideration of freedom as a true fighting slogan and consideration

---

31   Karl Marx and Frederick Engels: Collected Works, 1st Chinese Edition, Volume 1, p. 116.
32   Ibid., p. 67.
33   Ibid., p. 101.
34   Ibid., p. 77.

of freedom as human nature was the product of the rising capitalist economic relations, and was such a kind of self-awareness which declared that the shackles and bonds of the feudal system must be shaken off for the sake of the development of the capitalist economic relations. Marx was unlikely to reach this height then, but his idealistic understanding of human nature still contained some reasonable elements.

Marx regards freedom as a special property of spirit (reason), and holds that everyone has the right to show his spiritual outlook and to adopt his own style, i.e. way of expression. "Le style c'est l'homme" and it constitutes the form of the spiritual individuality of man. Therefore, the basis of freedom of the press is totally different from that of the basis of censorship. The freedom of the press is the embodiment of freedom of thought. Since freedom is inherent in man, the right of free press is inalienable; the censorship of Prussia, in contrast, is not the embodiment of freedom and is against that human nature. The opponents of a free press are not simply opposed to the freedom of the press, but also "question human freedom in freedom of the press"[35]. Here, Marx used human nature to judge and criticize the censorship and freedom of the press, which is revolutionary in terms of his political inclination, but idealistic from the perspective of the conception of history. But it is very important to notice that Marx also discussed the question of freedom with regard to the subject-object relationship, and argued that free expression was a right of both the subject and the object. He said, "Even if we leave, subjective side out of account, viz., one and the same object refracted differently as seen by different persons and its different aspects converted into as many different spiritual characters, ought the character of the object to have no influence, not even the slightest, on the investigation?...If the object is a matter for laughter, the manner has to seem serious, if the object is disagreeable, it has to be modest. Thus you violate the right of the object as you do that of the subject."[36].

---

35   Karl Marx and Frederick Engels: Collected Works, 1st Chinese Edition, Volume 1, p. 51.
36   Ibid., p.p. 8-9.

It is because he took into consideration the subject-object relationship that Marx did not treat freedom as the inherent property of the isolated subject. If freedom was seen as the inherent property of the subject, then attention would be focused on "ego", and thus ego and the environment, the inner nature of man and the external conditions would be separated from each other and would be in opposition. However, Marx did not do so. He underlined that freedom was the species-nature of man on the one hand, and emphasized the constraints on freedom, exerted by the interaction between the subjects, on the other. As early as in his doctoral dissertation, Marx showed his disagreement with Epicurus who saw freedom merely as the inner property of the subject (the atom as the symbol of self-consciousness), and pointed out, "abstract individuality is freedom from being, not freedom in being."[37]. In his first article about the debates of the Rhine Province Assembly, Marx criticized the German liberals, and censured their views that "freedom is honoured by being placed in the starry firmament of imagination instead of on the solid ground of reality", and that "any contact of the ideal of freedom with ordinary reality is a profanation"[38].

In his view, this was one of the reasons why freedom has remained a fantasy and sentimentality in Germany. By the beginning of 1844, Marx saw more clearly that human freedom was not animal "freedom" under the pure natural state. Some German liberals yearned for the freedom in nature, which was to seek the history of freedom of mankind in the ancient forests. Marx asked derisively, "But, what difference is there between the history of our freedom and the history of the boar's freedom if it can be found only in the forests?"[39]

In addition, although Marx stressed that freedom was human nature, he faced the reality and observed that only some few people had freedom under the despotic Prussian system. Freedom, in his view, was indeed inherent in man, and no one should be against it, or should anyone object, he objects to the freedom of other people

37 Karl Marx and Frederick Engels: Collected Works, 1st Chinese Edition, Volume 40, p. 228.
38 Karl Marx and Frederick Engels: Collected Works, 1st Chinese Edition, Volume 1, p. 84.
39 Karl Marx and Frederick Engels: Collected Works, 1st Chinese Edition, Volume 1, p. 454.

at best. For example, it is in their objecting to freedom that the opponents of free press realize their own freedom. However, the thing is that they view freedom merely as an attribute of some individuals and estates, and put in opposition the particular freedom of specific estate with the general freedom of human nature. Their so-called freedom is actually an estate's privilege. Marx bases his argument on human nature, but he does see the opposition between social estates through real the opposition between freedom and privilege, between the opposition of individual freedom and general freedom.

In order to combat the debasement of freedom of press to freedom of trade, and promote social and political writing, to break away from the bonds and temptation of money, Marx raised the question of the relationship between the species and genus of freedom. He called general freedom, namely the nature of human freedom, as the genus, and various specific freedoms, such as freedom of trade, freedom of property, of conscience, of the press, freedom of the courts as belonging to "all species of one and the same genus, of freedom without any specific name"[40]. On the one hand, these various forms of freedom govern one another, and whenever a particular freedom is put in question, freedom in general is put in question. Therefore, a particular form of freedom is not only a particular question, but "the general question within a particular sphere"[41]. On the other hand, the various forms of freedom were different from each other. Every particular sphere of freedom was the freedom of a particular sphere, and is subject to its own laws. Freedom of the press was a question of freedom of the spirit, and the publications are the most popular method for individuals to express their spiritual existence. Freedom of the press values reason, not the will of censors. Freedom of the press cannot be included in the sphere of freedom (freedom for-profit) the bourgeois trade. Marx said, "As you obey the laws of your sphere, so will I obey the laws of my sphere. To be free in your way is for me identical with being unfree, just as a cabinet-maker would hardly feel pleased if he demanded freedom for his craft and was given (to him) as an equivalent: The freedom of the philosopher."[42]. Although Marx's idea on the species and genus of freedom still

---

40   Ibid., p. 85.
41   Ibid., p. 95.
42   Ibid., p. 86.

contained a speculative character, he proposed that various forms of freedom had their own applicable sphere and own laws, which was a step forward for him to the specific analysis of freedom.

Marx's views on freedom in this period were tinged with distinctive revolutionary democracy, and directed at the despotic Prussian system. Marx argued that the slow development and the poverty of thought in Germany were due to its despotic system, which cultivated a group of pedantic, privileged individuals with stiff wig on head, who held tightly worthless, scholastic dissertations and who stood between people and spirit, between life and science, freedom and human being. The despotic system and the reactionary censorship made the German philosophy more speculative, for the latter could not and dared not to express its views openly, just as Marx said, "The sole literary field in which at that time the pulse of a living spirit could still be felt, but the philosophical field, ceased to speak German, for German had ceased to be the language of thought. The spirit spoke in incomprehensible mysterious words because comprehensive words were no longer allowed to be comprehended." So Marx asserts that "the censorship has undoubtedly influenced the development of the German spirit in a disastrous, irresponsible way."[43]

5 OPPOSITION BETWEEN PRIVATE INTEREST AND HUMANITY

When young Marx turned his attention from the question of freedom of the press to denouncing on the debates of the Rhine Province Assembly which debated on theft of woods, he began to enter the realm of material interests and gradually leave the realm of spirit, and turned consciously towards defending the material interests of the poor, those politically and socially propertyless, gradually leaving back the demands representing human spiritual nature. However, his views basically were still idealistic in his conception of history, though they contained the germ of some important thoughts.

---

43 Karl Marx and Frederick Engels: Collected Works, 1st Chinese Edition, Volume 1, p. 45.

For Marx, the feudal despotism, in a sense, was not a human society, but "the spiritual animal kingdom, was the world of divided mankind", in contrast to the human world.[44] Under the feudal caste system, everyone had a fixed caste like the separated boxes in a Chinese pharmacy, which is similar to the case in which t animals are born into a given species. The sole equality which could be found in the actual life of animals is the equality between one animal and other animals of the same species, and it is the equality of the given species within itself, but not the equality of the genus. The animal genus itself is seen only in the hostile behaviour of different animal species, which assert or force their particular distinctive characteristics one against another. Similarly, under the feudal caste system, equality is the equality of the given species (i.e. in the same caste), not the equality of the genus (i.e. man). There are fierce struggles between species (i.e. different castes). If animals are the animal kingdom as natural beings, the feudal caste society is a spiritual animal kingdom. Prussia is such a society. The Rhine Province Assembly attempts to include and judge peasants' gathering of fallen wood in theft, and attempts to aggravate the plunder of them by issuing the so-called the law on thefts of wood, and "they are in fact demanding instead of the human content of right, its animal form"[45], that is, right is turned into a means used by one species to plunder another species in the animal kingdom. Marx fought against those illegal lawless practices of the despotic Prussian system in the name of man.

During the debates of the Rhine Province Assembly, some people had argued for the inclusion of the gathering of fallen wood in theft with the pretext that in the forest areas of their regions, at first only gashes are made in young trees, and later when they are dead, they are gathered as fallen wood. Marx rebukes this view because it "makes the right of human beings give way to that of young trees". If this proposal is adopted, it is inevitable that many people not (in no way) of a criminal disposition will be casted into the hell of crime, and misery and infamy. Therefore, Marx cries loudly, saying, in this

---

44   Karl Marx and Frederick Engels: Collected Works, 1st Chinese Edition, Volume 1, p. 142.
45   Karl Marx and Frederick Engels: Collected Works, 1st Chinese Edition, Volume 1, p. 143.

way, "the wooden idols triumph and human beings are sacrificed!"[46] The forest owner, "in exchange for his piece of wood, receives what was once a human being", that is, he deprives, for the sake of wood, of those who "own nothing except themselves" of "life", "freedom" and "humanity"[47].

In contrast to the Rhine Province Assembly's sacrificing human beings for wood, Marx asserts that "the human being ought to have been victorious over the forest owner", that is, the Rhinelander people ought to have been victorious over the estate representatives of the forest owners, and the Assembly should entrust them with the representation of the general interests of the province. Why does the Rhine Province Assembly enact such a law on the theft of wood which "sacrifices human beings"? Marx investigates the question of private interest and the externalization of the essence of Assembly legislators.

Wood is the property of the forest owners. The law on the theft of wood safeguards the interest of the forest owners. "Interest has no memory, for it thinks only of itself. And the one thing about which it is concerned, itself, it never forgets."[48] True legislators, according to the requirement, ought to have no other motives but the opposition to illegal acts, and they ought to "exercise the utmost leniency"[49] formulate just laws to prevent crimes and avoid converting "theft" into a crime what only circumstances have caused to be an offence. However, when the legislators regarded private interest as the ultimate purpose and as their legislative basis, they have treated all those who violate the private interest as evil-doers, degraded the crimes and punishments specified by law, the life of the accused "to material means of private interest"[50], and also attempted to deal with them by enacting laws. Private interest is no more made capable of legislating by being installed on the throne of the legislator. But also the mute is produced which capable of speech by being given a speaking-trumpet. The essence of the legislators is estranged, and the laws they have enacted are unlikely humane, just because private

46   Ibid., p. 137.
47   Ibid., p. 172.
48   Ibid., p. 163.
49   Ibid., p. 148.
50   Ibid., p. 176.

interest serves as the motive for and the basis of their legislation. As Marx said, "Private interest, however, is always cowardly, for its heart, its soul, is an external object which can always be wrenched away and injured, and who has not trembled with the danger of losing heart and soul? How could the selfish legislator be human when something inhuman, an alien material essence, is his supreme essence?"[51]. This is to say that the legislator had lost his human essence, and his heart and soul are some inhuman material: Private material interest.

Therefore, Marx believes that private interests and humanity are in opposition, because they protect their interest by all means, regardless of their nature. For example, in Trier, Germany, the rulers had originally promoted religion vigorously and intensified the religious sentiment to safeguard their interests; later, prisoners were compelled to submit by reducing their food and driving with whips to labour. "Instead of prayer and trust and song, we have bread and water, prison and labour in the forest! How prodigal the Assembly is with words in order to procure the Rhinelander people a seat in heaven! How prodigal it is too, with words, in order that a class of Rhinelander people should be fed on bread and water and driven with whips to labour in the forest—an idea which a Holland planter would hardly dare to entertain in regard to his Negroes. What does all this prove? That it is easy to be holy if one is not willing to be human."[52] This shows that for Marx the religious inhumanity was consistent with and complementary to the inhumanity in the actual life.

Marx confronts the private interest of exploiters with humanity, and sees the inevitable inhuman character of this private interest. For instance, he considers dry twigs and branches as a gift of nature, as the mercy of nature to the poor. Nature also presents the antithesis between poverty and wealth in the shape of the dry, snapped twigs and branches separated from organic life in contrast to the trees and stems which are firmly rooted and full of sap. Human poverty and human wealth "sense this kinship" with natural poverty and wealth.

---

51   Karl Marx and Frederick Engels: Collected Works, 1st Chinese Edition, Volume 1, p.p. 149-150.
52   Ibid., p. 176.

If the trees and stems which are firmly rooted and full of sap belong to the forest owners, the dry twigs and branches, i.e. natural poverty, are the property of the poor. Therefore, Marx said, "In this play of elemental forces, poverty senses a beneficent power more humane than human power. The fortuitous arbitrary action of privileged individuals is replaced by the fortuitous operation of elemental forces, which take away from private property what the latter no longer voluntarily foregoes. Just as it is not fitting for the rich to lay claim to alms distributed in the street, so also in regard to these alms of nature."[53] Human society deprives the inadequacy to supplement the surplus, while the elemental forces deprive the surplus to supplement the inadequacy; natural law seems to be a more amiable force than humanity under the feudal system where one caste of people live over the life of another caste. Of course, Marx does not personify nature, nor does he consider that nature has conscious intentions, but his view of customary right, derived directly from nature and which is beneficial for the poor, is obviously the result of the influence of the natural rights idea of the French Enlightenment.

Marx despises private interest, calls it "abject materialism", and believes that "nothing is more terrible than the logic of selfishness"[54] Although he requires that there should not be a moment's delay in sacrificing representation of private interest to representation of general interest in case of their getting into conflict, in fact, the opposite is true. Private interest cares no more for the Rhein province than it does for the whole fatherland, and has no concern for local spirit, any more than for the general spirit. Its sole purpose is its material interests. Therefore, Marx said, "Wood remains wood in Siberia as in France; forest owners remain forest owners in Kamchatka as in the Rhein Province. Hence, if wood and its owners as such make laws, these laws will differ from one another only by the place of origin and the language in which they are written."[55]. Marx in those days expressed outrage over private interest, from the moral and emotional aspect, but now also began to see role of material interests theoretically.

---

53   Ibid., p. 147.
54   Karl Marx and Frederick Engels: Collected Works, 1st Chinese Edition, Volume 1, p. 160.
55   Ibid., p. 180

Before this, for example, in his first article about the debates in the Rhine Province Assembly, Marx regarded freedom of press as a spiritual demand; but after this, for instance in his article Justification of the Correspondent from the Mosel, he started to combine the question of freedom of press with that of material interests, and underlined that "the necessity for a free press follow from the specific character of the state of distress in the Mosel region"[56]. Because free press is both the product and the creator of public opinion, it alone can convert a particular private interest into a general one, and make the distressed state of the Mosel region an object of general attention and general sympathy, "the need for free press is actual need". This was a step forward, compared with the investigation of the question merely from the perspective of spiritual nature.

56   Ibid, p. 216.

CHAPTER II

MARX'S RESEARCH ON HISTORY IN KREUZNACH
FROM CRITICISM OF RELIGION TO EXPLORATION
OF THE STATE

Starting with the criticism of religion, through his struggle against the censorship and the law on the theft of wood, Marx gradually grasps the very core question of superstructure, i.e. question of the state. This was both an acute problem of reality and a major theoretical problem for Prussia of the time, and Marx could not move forward without making a breakthrough in this problem. It is based on his research on history in Kreuznach city that Marx wrote *Critique of Hegel's Philosophy of Right*, which preliminarily criticizes Hegel's idealistic views, and makes a breakthrough in the question of the relationship between civil society and the state.

But Marx's understanding of this question undergoes a certain process. Even in *Critique of Hegel's Philosophy of Right*, we can see the dual nature of his views on the questions of man, human essence and estrangement through his analysis of the question of the state, which contains the progress in his thought as well as his impurity based on Feuerbach's humanism. Marx was actually going through a "moulting" at that time.

1 OBSERVATION OF THE STATE THROUGH HUMAN EYES. HUMAN STATE AND INHUMAN STATE

The view on history goes through a transition from gods to man, so does the views on the state. In the question of the state, a major advance of the bourgeois humanism is that it objects to the theological conception of the state, and strives to look into the state from the perspective of man.

The political theories of theocracy, which looks into the state from the perspective of gods, had been occupying a dominant position for quite a long period. They derived the origin, nature and mission of the state from god's will, advocated the divine right of kings, the superiority of clericalism over the regime, and the obedience of monarch to pope. For example, Augustine preaches this theory in *The City of God*. He calls the Church as the City of God, the kingdom of God, but the state as the secular state, and argues that the City of God should be superior to the secular state. All power comes from God. The Church is the representative of God in earth, so the state must obey the Church. The task of the emperor is to serve the Church, to protect the canons and eradicate the "heresy". Thomas Aquinas combines some philosophical principles of Aristotle with the theology of Augustine, and preaches that the state is established according to God's will, and both its governance principles and its order come from God; human natural law and human positive laws are also derived from the eternal law of God, that is, they are a reflection of the requirements of the divine natural law. These rigid theological doctrines showed contempt for the secular life and reasonable demands of human beings, put gods over man and blocked the way to correctly uncover the nature and origin of the state.

An important change caused by the bourgeois humanism is that the state is dealt through human eyes. Just as Copernicus liberates natural science from the bonds of theology by overthrowing the geocentrism and challenging the theological doctrines, the observation of the state through human eyes also drives theology out of the social sphere and seeks to free the interpretation of the question of the state from the fetters of theology. Marx attaches great importance to this change. He said, "Immediately before and after the time of

Copernicus' great discovery of the true solar system, the law of gravitation of the state was discovered, its own gravity was found in the state itself." He also said, "Machiavelli and Campanella, and later Hobbes, Spinoza, Hugo Grotius, right down to Rousseau, Fichte and Hegel, began to study the state through human eyes and to deduce its natural laws from reason and experience, and not from theology."[1]

Although Marx includes Hegel in those who study the state through human eyes, this does not mean that Hegel and Rousseau have the same conception of the state. In fact, the conceptions of the state of the thinkers, whom Marx mentions in the above statement, are not the same. For instance, Grotius, Hobbes and Rousseau are theorists of social contract, who consider the state as the product of a pact into which people enter; while Hegel underlines that the state is the actuality of the ethical Idea, "the ethical spirit as substantial will, *manifest* and clear to itself", and he also says that "it is the *rational* in and for itself" and "the state is the spirit which is present in the world and which *consciously* realizes itself therein"[2]. So contrary to the theorists of social contract, Hegel emphasizes that the interest of individuals as such is not the ultimate end for which they are united. Concerning the relationship between the state and the individual, the mission of the state is not for the security and protection of property and personal freedom, instead, "only through being a member of the state" the individual himself "has objectivity, truth, and ethical life"[3].

Despite this difference, what they have in common is that they deduce the need of the state from human nature (reason and freedom) and reject divine intervention. They do not put gods over man, but vice versa. Human nature and needs become the centre in explaining the state. Hegel's absolute idea is objective Mind, which seems unrelated to man, but in fact, it abstracts human reason and makes it into something separated from man. Therefore, Hegel's conception of the state is also one that regards the state through human eyes, but appears in the form of absolute idea.

---

1 Karl Marx and Frederick Engels: Collected Works, 1st Chinese Edition, Volume 1, p. 128.
2 Hegel: Elements of the Philosophy of Right, p. 235 and p. 238.
3 Ibid., p. 254.

Marx's view on the state was basically a Hegelian idealistic one, when he edited the *Rheinische Zeitung* newspaper. He distinguished what the state ought to be from what the state actually is, but he did not involve himself in the absolute opposition between what ought to be and what is. Instead, based on this aspect, he inveighed against the despotic Prussian system, and expressed a radical political attitude through his longing for true state.

What is the nature of the state? For Marx, "the state should be the realization of political and juridical reason"[4]. So reason is the nature and foundation of the state. Since the state is the rational social existence, its true social function and way of educating its members is to make them members of the state, to turn the purposes of individuals into those of all, the barbaric instincts into moral intentions, the natural independence into spiritual freedom, and make individual and holistic life become one and the whole reflected in individual consciousness. Just because the nature of the state is the expression of rational freedom, the state ought to treat every member of the society equally without discrimination, for example, those who are accused of stealing wood ought to be treated with the state attitude, "the state will regard even an infringer of forest regulations as a human being, a living member of the state, one in whom its heart's blood flows, a soldier who has to defend his Fartherland, a witness whose voice must be heard by the court, a member of the community with public duties to perform, the father of a family, whose existence is sacred, and, above all, a citizen of the state. The state will not light-heartedly exclude one of its members from all these functions, for the state amputates itself whenever it turns a citizen into a criminal" (Ibid., p. 149). And just because that it is the expression of reason, the state is different from the government bodies and members. The despotic government organs may purport to embody the state reason, but they actually distort the nature of the state, and their frame of mind is not the frame of mind of the state, but that of the government members, in opposition to the nature of the state. A true state should support citizens when they rise up against this kind of government organs, "The *moral state* assumes its members to have *the frame of mind of the state*, even if they act in *opposition to an organ of the state*, when

---

4   Karl Marx and Frederick Engels: Collected Works, 1st Chinese Edition, Volume 1, p. 14.

they act against the government"[5]. The idealist conception of the state makes Marx fail to have a true understanding of the nature of the state, and the true relationship between the state and the government organs and members.

The state is closely associated with laws. There is no such a law whose implementation does not depend on the state, nor is there such a state who does not exercise its functions in the form of laws. Consistent with the idealized view of the state's nature, Marx also regards the true law as "the positive existence of freedom"[6], that is he affirms and recognizes freedom in the form of law. Laws are in no way obstructive and repressive measures against freedom, but are rather the positive, clear, universal norms, in which freedom has acquired an impersonal, theoretical existence independent of the arbitrariness of the individual. So Marx gives a general idea of law: "A statute-book is a people's bible of freedom."

A true state, a true law, is a measure, a standard, and a criterion to ascertain whether a state and its laws have reality. In Marx's view, actual things are different and varied, and thus cannot serve as the measure for reason; only reason can be a measure for things. So to regard reason as the measure is to make the concept of the state the measure, when he was discussing the question of the state. He said, "A true state, a true marriage, a true friendship are indissoluble, but no state, no marriage, no friendship corresponds fully to its concept."[7] Just as in nature's decay and death appear as themselves where an organism has ceased to correspond to its function, the world history has to decide whether a state deserves to continue its existence, if and when it has departed from the idea of the state. Based on this idea, Marx puts forward the question of human state and inhuman state.

A state which corresponds to the concept of the state is the true state. For Marx, the so-called correspondence to the concept, to reason, to human nature is the same, because reason and freedom are the connotation of the concept of the state as well as the basic content of human nature. When Marx says that "philosophy demands that the

5   Ibid., p. 17.
6   Ibid., p. 71.
7   Ibid., p. 184.

state should be a state of human nature"[8], he means a state which is the realization of rational freedom. Otherwise, "a state that is not the realization of rational freedom is a bad state",[9] namely, an inhuman state. Similarly, the true law is a "rational rule", i.e. a law that corresponds to "the nature of freedom". Where and when the law is the real existence of freedom, it is the true law. The law that suppresses freedom, i.e. in violation of human nature, is not the true law, but instead the public approval of illegality. So, actual law and formal law are as "different as arbitrariness and freedom"[10].

The theory and approach of Marx, which use human nature as a measure to distinguish human state from inhuman state, true state from bad state, are basically idealistic and not free from the influence of the abstract humanist conception of history. However, we see that two aspects of his views are really remarkable.

First, in contrast with Hegel's defence of Prussia and his view of it as the actuality of the ethical Idea, Marx draws the opposite conclusion from Hegel's above premise: the despotic Prussian system does not correspond to the concept of the state and it is not a true state. For example, seen from the attempt of the Prussian government to enact the law on the theft of wood and to include peasants' gathering of fallen wood in theft, it does not treat all of its members as the state and according to the mind of the state, nor act on its reason and universality. Prussia, a state in name only, actually violates the nature of the state and deviates from the convention, and turns into a servant and an instrument of the forest owner. All the organs of the state become ears, eyes, arms, legs, by means of which the interest of the forest owner hears, observes, appraises, protects, reaches out and runs. So what controls the soul of the state of Prussia is not reason and freedom, but private interest. This state which is degraded from the system of general interest to private interest, does not accord with the concept of the state.

The despotic Prussia is not a true state, also because "the state is based not on reason, but on faith"[11], that is, the state is based on religion, and regard the particular nature of a religion (Christianity) as

---

8   Ibid., p. 126.
9   Ibid., p. 127.
10 Ibid., p. 75.
11 Ibid., p. 14.

the measuring-rod of the state. This is to confuse political principles with Christian principles, the religious with the secular, and state with church. In a state there may be different religious sects, and the state should not reject one religion or advocate another. If so, this so-called state is not a state, but the church which is in contradiction with the nature of the state.

The laws of Prussia are not the true laws, for it does not correspond to the nature of the law, i.e. the security for and as the realization of freedom. In fact, "the very laws issued by the [Prussian] government are the opposite of what they make into law"[12]. For instance, the censorship executed by the despotic Prussian government aims at the punishment of freedom, so according to Marx, it is in the form of law, but it is "not a law, it is a police measure; but it is a bad police measure"[13]. Although the grounds of Marx's arguments are idealistic, his longing for true state, true law represents his attack on and hate for the despotic system, and his pursuit of a better system.

Second, and more importantly, Marx does not confine himself to the argumentation that the despotic Prussian system does not correspond to the concept of the state, but strives to investigate the roots of this deviation, and raises the question of private interest. Marx believes that private interest is extremely selfish, and it cares no more for the Rhein province than it does for the Fatherland, and has no concern for local spirit, any bit more than for the general spirit. Once private interest becomes the representation of the authority of the state and is of the status of legislation, actual state and actual law inevitably deviate from their concepts. In his *On the Commissions of the Estates in Prussia*, an article published in the *Rheinische Zeitung*, Marx says, "in a true state there is no landed property, no industry, no material thing, which as a crude element of this kind could make a bargain with the state; in a true state there are only *spiritual forces.*" And he believes that in a true state, "what is dominant is not matter, but form, not nature without the state, but the nature of the state, not the *unfree object* but the *free human being*"[14]. Although Marx is indignant against the determination of the state and law by private

12   Ibid., p. 18.
13   Ibid., p. 74.
14   Karl Marx and Frederick Engels: Collected Works, 1st Chinese Edition, Volume 1, p. p. 344-345.

interest, he cannot but admit this bare fact. This bare fact impels him to turn his eyes towards the question of material interests, and sets a direction for solving it correctly, in his later works.

2 MAN: ESSENCE OF ALL SOCIAL ORGANIZATIONS. MAN'S SOCIAL AND PHYSICAL QUALITIES

Since Marx proposes to regard the state through human eyes, it was inevitable for him to pay attention to the investigation of secular history. After he retreated from the editorial board of the *Rheinische Zeitung* in April, 1843, Marx investigated history in the city Kreuznach and left five Kreuznach Notebooks. His study is extensive, covering the period from the 6th century B.C. up to the 1830s, and many countries, including France, England, Germany, Sweden and Poland. Marx has compared the history of separated countries, and focused on a broad range of problems, such as property relations, production relations and political forms, change in the forms of the state, which are of vital importance for his criticism of Hegel's idealist conception of the state, and his discussions on the nature of the state.

In *The Leading Article in No. 179 of the Kölnische Zeitung*, written in June, 1842, Marx places Hegel and Machiavelli, Hobbes, Rousseau and others in the same category, who look into the state from the perspective of man. With his turn towards Feuerbach and after his thorough exploration of the history of mankind, Marx finds that Hegel's view on the state is not really from the perspective of man, but from a "logic, pantheistic mysticism", though his thought is more dialectic than the French Enlightenment of the 18th century.

The actual Idea, i.e. absolute idea, according to Hegel, acts according to a determined principle and towards a determined end. The Idea is given the status of a subject, and the actual relationship of family and civil society to the state is conceived to be its (The Idea's) inner imaginary activity, and family and civil society are distinguished from(The Idea) itself in the course of the movement. Therefore, for Hegel, what is important to recover in the state is not the human activities, but the so-called "the esoteric", i.e. "to recover the history of the logical Concept in the state".

When speaking of the constitution and the division of different state powers, functions and spheres of action, Hegel starts with the concept of "organism", and considers that the constitution of the state is an organism, and thus its different aspects and the different parts of powers is not inorganic, but rather interrelated. Hegel turns the moments of the constitution of the state into abstract logical moments, and the relationship among the moments must be rational, so the constitution of the state cleaves itself according to the nature of the Idea into three substantive divisions: the Legislative—the power to determine and establish the universal; the Executive—the power to subsume the spheres of particularity and individual cases under the universal; third the Crown—an individual unity into which different powers are bound, which is the apex and basis of the constitutional monarchy, the incarnation of the Idea, and the expression of ultimate decision of the will.

Thus it can be seen that in Hegel, the emergence and functions of the state, and the inner relations between its various institutions are all based on the Idea. Although his conception of the state is nothing but a German version of the bourgeois political practice, it is still considered to originate from the Idea, like Marx says in his comment on Hegel's views: "the constitution is rational in so far as its moments can be reduced to abstract logical moments. The state has to differentiate and determine its activity not in accordance with its specific nature, but in accordance with the nature of the Concept, which is the mystified mobile of abstract thought. The reason of the constitution is thus abstract logic and not the concept of the state. In place of the concept of the constitution we get the constitution of the Concept. Thought is not conformed to the nature of the state, but the state to a readymade system of thought."[15]

Hegel also talks about the activity of human beings, which is, however, seen subordinated to the activity of the Idea. Hegel believes that it is not actual persons who come to be a state but the state which must first come to be an actual person, and he does not regard the state as the ultimate reality of the person, but considers the monarch as "the existence of the Idea", "the ultimate actuality of the state".

---

15 Karl Marx and Frederick Engels: Collected Works, 1st Chinese Edition, Volume 1, p. 267.

Why does Hegel praise the Idea but disdain man? This does not mean that Hegel deviates from the historical tradition of the bourgeois humanism. In fact, Hegel wishes and imagines reproducing some achievements of the French revolution under the German conditions. But the thing is that Hegel disapproves of the bourgeois, humanistic conception of history which uses human nature to interpret history, but strives to seek this law outside human nature, i.e. in his fictitious absolute Idea, so history is seen as a law-governed process, and man and human activity become the instrument for the Idea to realize its immanent end. Hegel does so, first because he wants to write the biography of the abstract Substance, of the Idea, consequently human activity have to appear as the activity and result of something other than man; secondly because he wants to allow the essence of man to act for itself as an imaginary individual instead of acting in its actual, human existence. The consequence is that all real, empirical existence is converted dialectically into the moments of the Idea.

At that time, Marx began to turn towards Feuerbach and was under the influence of his materialistic humanism. His view on Hegel's objective idealism goes through such a process from doubt, vacillation and lastly to criticism. Marx objects to his consideration of family, civil society and state as being "determinations of the Idea", and emphasizes that they are the social forms of "man's existence", "the actualization and objectification of man's essence". So contrary to Hegel's view of the Idea acting as the inner esoteric of the state, Marx concludes that "Man then/thus remain what is essential within these realities"[16]. That is to say, the social forms are not the determinations and moments of the Idea, but the qualities immanent in man as actual subject, and appear as man's actualized universality. Without these social forms, man is abstract, unreal existence, a bare concept. Apparently, Marx's view of family, civil society and state as the organizational forms of man, as actual existence of man is more reasonable and closer to the nature of the problem than regarding them as the moments of the Idea and as pure, speculative, and logic categories. However, this statement that the essence of

---

16 Karl Marx and Frederick Engels: Collected Works, 1st Chinese Edition, Volume 1, p. 293.

all social organizations is man, the objectification of the essence of man, is clearly immature, compared with his later conclusion that the essence of man is the ensemble of these social relations, as he describes in the spring of 1845. Its remarkable achievement lies not so much in the content of the proposition itself but the achievement is in the direction of surpassing Hegel's idealism.

That man is the essence of all social organizations is clearly influenced with Feuerbach's humanism. If we can say Feuerbach had restored theology to the study of man, and believed that the mystery of religion lied in man and the essence of religion was human essence, Marx then also believed that the essence of social forms and social organizations lied in man and was the objectification of the essence of man. But Marx had then surpassed him in some aspects when compared with Feuerbach.

First, Marx considered family, civil society and state as the social forms of man's existence, as the social reality of man, which contained his objection to the view of man as a pure natural being, which separated from society. In fact, Marx had advanced the argument half a year later: Man is no abstract being squatting outside the world; man is the world of man, state, society, which was his deepening and development of the above idea.

Second, Hegel disdained the people. He argued that without the monarch, the government, the court, and the magistrates, the people were just an abstraction without determinations. According to this view, Marx pointed out that "as though the people were not the real state". But the fact is that "the state is an abstraction; the people is the concrete"[17]. The actual man, and the actual people is the "real ground" of the state. In terms of the relationship between man and the constitution, "it is not the constitution that creates the people but the people which creates the constitution."[18] In this way, Hegel proceeded from the state and put/made man into the subjectified state, while Marx turned the state into the objectified man. However, Marx did not see man as an isolated individual, "personality is merely an abstraction without the person, but only in its species-existence as

---

17 Karl Marx and Frederick Engels: Collected Works, 1st Chinese Edition, Volume 1, p. 279.
18 Ibid., p. 281.

persons is the person": the actual existence.[19] Third, and more importantly, Marx made a preliminary analysis of the question of the social quality and physiological quality of man, when he discussed the relationship between the functions of the state and human activity and criticized the prince's hereditary character advocated by Hegel. This reveals the new tendency which differentiates Marx from Feuerbach's humanism.

Although Hegel regards the state as the incarnation of the Idea from the standpoint of objective idealism, and analyzes the functions and activities of the state according to the pure logical requirements of the Idea, as a great thinker, he could not fail to see that the social sphere is a human sphere after all, and all social activities in their visibility are manifested as human activities, so Hegel acknowledges in *Elements of the Philosophy of Right* that the functions and activities of the state "are associated with the individuals who perform and implement them". But he emphasizes that what associates the individuals and the functions of the state is not "their immediate/ direct personalities but their universal and objective qualities", thus the link between these functions of the state and individuals "is external and contingent in character"[20].

In the Middle Ages, the functions and powers of the state were considered as private property, and an office or a governmental mission could be sold and inherited. For example, the seats in the French parliament were formerly sold, and in the English army officers' commissions up to a certain rank were sold, too. Hegel's emphasis advocating that the link between individuals and the functions and powers of the state is external and contingent, means that individuals are entitled to perform these tasks, or to exercise the functions of the state, not by nature but only by virtue of their objective qualities, i.e. according to the particular ability, skill and character of individuals, and they should be educated and trained for a particular occupation. This view of Hegel is of anti-feudal character in some way.

But the footing of Hegel's philosophy was objective idealism. He investigated the functions and activities of the state from pure logic and in the abstract, combined it with the Idea rather than human

---

19   Ibid., p. 277.
20   Hegel: Elements of the Philosophy of Right, p. 293.

activity. Marx opposed to this view of Hegel. According to Marx, what the functions and activities of the state embody is not the demand inherent in the Idea, but human functions. Only through individuals, namely, the individuals who hold public office can the state function. The relationship of the functions and activities of the state to individuals is not external and contingent, but internal and necessary, because man is the essence of all social organizations, and the state is the actualization and objectification of human essence, and it is the mode of activities and existence of man. Although there is something of Feuerbach's humanism in Marx's views, his investigation into the state from the perspective of human activity is much more reasonable than Hegel's placing the state in the realm of pure Idea. In particular, when elaborating this question, Marx posed the question of the two qualities of man (his physical quality and social quality), and pointed out that the human essence "is not his beard, his blood, his abstract *Physis*, but rather his social quality". When discussing that the functions and activities of the state were attached to individuals, he stressed, "not to the individual as physical but as political", "to the political quality of the individual", because the functions of the state are nothing but "the modes of existence and operation of the social qualities of men"[21]. Thus individuals "are to be considered according to their social and not their private quality".

Marx further expounded the view on the social quality and physical quality of man in the discussion of the prince's hereditary character.

Based on the view that the functions and activities of the state must be associated with individuals, Hegel proved that the state must have one individual as representative of its oneness, with this individual being the monarch. Hence the monarch is "personified sovereignty", "sovereignty become man". The whole "state-reason" and "state-consciousness" is the unique monarch with the exclusion of all others. Thus "he is to be person who is specified from the entire race of men, who is distinguished from all other persons", and "is conceived to be the existence of the Idea"[22].

---

21 Karl Marx and Frederick Engels: Collected Works, 1st Chinese Edition, Volume 1, p. 270.
22 Ibid., p. 267, p. 294 and p. 293.

Why the king is hereditary? According to Hegel, if hereditary succession, i.e. the natural inheritance is considered to prevent the formation of faction when the throne falls vacant, this is to make the consequence a reason, to be grounded not upon the Idea of the state, but on something outside it; similarly, if the monarchy is considered to be selected, because it is the concerns and interests of the people that the monarch looks after, and thus the people must be left to choose whom they wish to entrust their welfare to. And it is from this entrust alone that the right to rule arises. This view is "superficial". In fact, "elective monarchy is the worst of institutions"[23]. Hegel explains the succession of the throne by way of inheritance not by turning his attention to the objective history itself, but discusses it from starting the concept of the sovereign. He argues that "the hereditary character of the power of the sovereign is the moment inherent in the concept of the power of the sovereign"[24].

This is to say, the son of the king is born to be a king, the physical birth makes determinate individuals into the embodiments of the highest political tasks. The highest political activities coincide with individuals by reason of birth, just like an animal's position, character, animal's way of life, etc. are immediately inborn. This is the confusion of man's social quality with his physical quality. Birth gives man only an individual existence and establish him merely as a natural individual, whereas the functions and powers of the state are social products, not procreations of the natural individual, so there is no immediate identity, no sudden coincidence of man's physical quality with his social quality, or of the individual's birth with the individual as the bearer of a certain social dignity and social function, as Marx said, "I am man by birth, without the agreement of society; yet only through universal agreement does this determinate birth become peer or king. Only the agreement makes the birth of this man the birth of a king. It is therefore the agreement, not birth that makes the king. If birth, in distinction from other determinations, immediately endows man with a position, then his body makes him this determined social functionary. His body is his social right. In this system, the physical dignity of man, or the dignity of human

---

23   Hegel: Elements of the Philosophy of Right, p. 304.
24   Ibid., p. 308.

body (with further elaboration, meaning: the dignity of the physical natural element of the state), appears in such a form that determinate dignities, specifically the highest social dignities, are the dignities of certain bodies which are determined and predestined by birth to such dignity."[25]

Here, Marx explicitly distinguishes man's physical quality (birth) from his social quality (social dignity). There is no doubt that birth gives man life and physical existence, but this is not the inner cause and ground for the particular social right he has. Primogeniture (including the succession of the throne) is a political constitution, and based on private property. Therefore Marx wrote: "In the constitution, wherein primogeniture is a guarantee, private property is the guarantee of the political constitution. In the primogeniture, it appears that this guarantee is a particular kind of private property. Primogeniture is merely a particular existence of the universal relationship of private property and the political state. Primogeniture is the political sense of private property, private property in its political significance, that is to say, in its universal significance. Thus the constitution here is the constitution of private property."[26] Therefore, Marx criticizes Hegel for merely demonstrating that the monarch must be born, not that birth makes one a monarch. If an individual, as Hegel says, is raised to the monarch in an immediate, natural fashion, i.e. through his physical birth, then the sovereignty, the monarchical dignity would thus be born. Thus at the highest point of the state bare Physis rather reason would be the determining factor, and physical birth would determine the quality of the monarch as it determines the quality of cattle. There is no difference between men and animals: the horse is born a horse, and the king is born a king. Marx mocks, "That man becomes monarch by birth can as little be made into a metaphysical truth as can the Immaculate Conception of Mary."[27]

25 Karl Marx and Frederick Engels: Collected Works, 1st Chinese Edition, Volume 1, p. 377.
26 Ibid., p. 380.
27 Ibid., p. 286.

3 ESTRANGEMENT OF POLITICAL STATE AND DUALIZATION OF HUMAN ESSENCE

Marx's discussion of the question of the state in *Critique of Hegel's Philosophy of Right* proceeds from the unmasking of the holy form of human self-estrangement to the unholy forms of it, from the criticism of religion and theology to that of politics and state. Marx analyzed the relationship between the political state and civil society based on his absorption of Feuerbach's important ideas in *The Essence of Christianity* and his own personal experience and theoretical reflections when working for the *Rheinische Zeitung,* and in particular, his study of history in Kreuznach.

Hegel considered family and civil society as the spheres of the concept of the state, that the mind sunders itself into these two spheres, in order to rise above them and become explicit as infinite actual mind. Marx rejected this idea and differentiated the political state from non-political state. The so-called non-political state, also called as material state by Marx, actually refers to the civil society. He further expounded the relationship between civil society and the political state, and pointed out that "the rationality of the state has nothing to do with the division of the material of the state into family and civil society. The state results from both of them in an unconscious and arbitrary way. Family and civil society appears as the dark natural ground from which the light of the state emerges." Civil society is therefore conceived as the foundation, and the emergence of the political state is not the result of the mystified power of the Idea, but was an unconscious, i.e. objective, process.

Marx affirmed the dependence of the political state on family and civil society or their identity, and revealed their separation, i.e. "the aspect of alienation within the unity". Hegel also recognized this point, and argued that there was contradiction between the state as the system of universal interest and the family and civil society as the system of particular interests. But he attempted to reconcile this opposition through mediation, and claimed that "the strength of the state lies in the unity of its own universal end with the particular interests of individuals". In contrast, Marx had developed the aspect of estrangement, and in combination with his study of history, investigated the process of the political state estranging itself from civil society, he evaluated from the point of view of the development of history.

According to Marx, in the slave society of the ancient Greece, the constitution of the state was identical with the actual life of the people. That is to say, there is "the substantial unity" of the political state and civil society. The state did not adopt the fictitious formation of community which was superior to the classes. The aristocracy, free men were political classes and had political privileges; the public affairs of the state were their private concerns; the political state as such was the true and sole content of the citizen's life and their will. In the Middle Ages, i.e. the feudal society, this identity of the political state and civil society reached to the "peak". The classes of civil society in general had become the political classes. The serf owner, serf, feudal property, trade corporation, that is, property, trade, society and each single individual had determinate political status, and the sphere of civil society was the political sphere. Just as Marx said, "The peak of the Hegelian identity, as Hegel himself admits, was the Middle Ages. There, the classes of civil society in general and the Estates, or those classes which were given political significance, were identical. The spirit of the Middle Ages can be expressed thus: the classes of civil society and the political classes were identical because civil society was political society, because the organic principle of civil society was the principle of the state." [28]

The capitalist society is different. "The identity" of civil society and the political state "has disappeared" and they have become "two actually different spheres" and this manifests itself as the separation of the political state from civil society.

The emergence and development of the capitalist society transform the political classes of the Middle Ages into social classes, in other words, they have lost their political privilege and political character. Their position in civil society and their position in the political state do not coincide. Whatever estate (class) one belongs to, he has the same "equal" right formally. So in his political role the member of civil society rids himself of his class, of his actual private position.

---

28   Ibid., p. 334.

Even if you have nothing at all and live completely by your labour, the state acknowledges in law that you enjoy the same political right as the wealthy man. Thus individual difference in property, education and belief appears to be an external, unessential determination, and his sole determination is that he is a "man", a member of the state. In this transformation, the French bourgeois revolution plays a prominent role. According to Marx's view of the time, only the French Revolution completed the transformation of the political classes into social classes, made the class distinctions of civil society lose their original political significance and was transformed into social distinctions without political privilege.

In this way the political state was estranged from civil society. In capitalist society, the classes are unequal in actual life, but they seem to be equal in political life. In private life, the principle of individualism is predominant; everyone becomes an independent "atom"; individual existence is the final end, and labour, activity are merely means; while in political life, everyone is a "citizen" of the state, a social being. The political state appears to be a community that stands above classes and above opposite interests, it is the opposite existence detached from civil society and irrelevant to civil society, just like Marx said, "It was most difficult to form the political state, the constitution, out of the various moments of the life of the people. It was developed as the universal reason in opposition to other spheres, i.e. as something opposed to them." And "the opposite existence of the political state was nothing but the affirmation of the alienation of these particular spheres. The political constitution was until now the religious sphere, the religion of popular life, as the heaven of its universality in opposition to the earthly existence of its actuality. The political sphere was the sole sphere of the state within the state, the sole sphere in which the content, like the form, was the species-content, the true universal, but at the same time in such a way that, because this sphere was opposed to the others, its content also became formal and particular. Political life in the modern sense is the Scholasticism of popular life. Monarchy is the fullest expression of this alienation. The republic is the negation of this alienation within its own sphere."[29] Marx here compares the political state with

---

29　Ibid., p. 283.

religion, and regards it as the religious sphere in the political life. The bourgeois state is viewed in the political sphere as the equal heaven, as another "heaven" which is in opposition to the actual popular life, just as man alienates his essence into the divine, into the omnipotent God of mercy and love. This is estrangement. In fact, the state is determined by civil society. The bourgeois state is not the equal heaven, but an instrument which one class uses to oppress another class. The reason for its "equal" appearance seems to be that it puts aside the difference in property, education and belief, and grants people universal civil rights, which, however, consolidates and maintains precisely the actual inequality.

In capitalist society, the alienation of the state from civil society is concurrent with the dualization of human essence. A unified person becomes two-fold: The citizen of the state and the member of civil society. This dual identity is separated due to the alienation of the state from civil society, as is analyzed by Marx: "civil society and the state are separated. Consequently the citizen of the state and the member of civil society are also separated. The individual must thus undertake an essential schism within himself. As actual citizen he finds himself in a two-fold organization: [a] the bureaucratic, which is an external formal determination of the otherworldly state, of the executive power, which does not touch him and his independent actuality; [b] the social, the organization of civil society, within which he stands outside the state as a private person, for civil society does not touch upon the political state as such."[30] For instance, in the political state, a worker as a citizen enjoys formal equal rights given by law, while in civil society, the private sphere of economic life, he could be penniless poor. It is a satirical picture that his so-called equal political right is deviated from his actual unequal situation.

This case is different from the Middle Ages, which Marx calls as "the animal history of mankind". Not only does the estate based constitution of the feudal society display the separation of society, but constitution of the feudal society "separates man from his universal nature; it makes him an animal whose being coincides immediately with its determinate character"[31]. This, according to Marx's view-

---

30   Ibid., p. 340.
31   Ibid., p. 346.

point at that time, means that man loses his essence and degrades to the animal level. The physical birth and blood relationship of human beings determine their social positions and political rights, just as the natural quality of animals determine their habits and positions in nature. The fixed estate- based constitution of the feudal society makes an aristocrat an aristocrat by birth, the common people remain to be common people forever, and man thus becomes an animal whose being coincides with its natural determinate character. In fact, the estate privilege and hereditary system of the feudal society is a social system and determined by the private ownership of land. In the estate-based constitution and hereditary system, the bond of blood relationship as such is the requirement and manifestation of the private property system, rather being determined by the natural quality of man. And this point has been elaborated by Marx in his criticism of Hegel's view on the power of the sovereign (the hereditary monarchy).

In capitalist society, the blood relationship cannot endow people with political privilege. But there is another kind of estrangement because of the separation of the political state from civil society, and this is what Marx had said, "Modern times, civilization, commits the opposite mistake. It separates man's objective essence from him, taking it to be merely external and material. Man's content is not taken to his true actuality." Human economic life (including labour) is conceived to be the pure private sphere, as something that has nothing to do with human essence, while the abstract, political equal rights are viewed as the essential nature of man as a social being. In fact, what really makes man into man is precisely civil society, man's economic activity. Marx did not express this view explicitly and clearly at the time, but his view that man's objective essence, man's content is his "true actuality" shows a new direction he entered into, by looking into human essence, and potentially this direction contains some elements of the idea of estranged labour.

Marx had analyzed not only the estrangement of the political state from civil society but also the estrangement of the political constitution itself. For the former, he focused on analyzing how the political state and the material state (civil society) changed from their substantial unity to their separation; for the latter, he made various type of political constitutions an object of special study, he studied the relationship between monarchy, aristocracy, republicanism and democracy, and investigated the estrangement of the political form of the state from the aspect of their relationship with democracy.

For Marx, the state is the objectification of man. Just as it is not religion that creates man but man who creates religion, it is not the constitution that creates the people but it is the people who creates the constitution. The democracy precisely reflects this principle. Marx said, "In democracy the constitution itself appears only as one determination, and indeed as the self-determination of the people. In monarchy we have people of the constitution; in democracy we have the constitution of the people. Democracy is the resolved mystery of all constitutions. Here the constitution not only in itself, accords to essence, but accords to existence and thus actuality is returned to its real ground, actual man, the actual people, and established as its own work. The constitution appears as what it is, the free product of men." He also said, "Man does not exist because of the law but rather the law exists for the good of man. Democracy is *human exist-ence*, while in other political forms man has only *legal* existence."[32]

And for this reason, Marx highly praises democracy, and makes it the generic constitution, and evaluates other forms of constitution as "species", which are measured by democracy. Marx compares the relationship between democracy and other political forms to that between Christianity and other religions. Christianity is the religion *kat exohin*, deified man, and which is the essence of every religion. In the same way democracy is the objectification of man, and the essence of every political constitution. But in other political forms, such as monarchy, the people which created the state were subsumed under their political constitution and legal provisions, which is in fact an "accomplished alienation".

The alienation of the political state from civil society, the aliena-tion of the constitution from the species-essence of man must be eradicated. The historical task is to return the political state from the opposite world to the real world, i.e. to recover this unity, and democracy is this very constitutional form. The democracy here

---

32   Ibid., p. 281.

does not refer to the bourgeois democracy, for it does not eliminate alienation, but instead deepens it. The democracy in the mind of Marx recovers the true unity of universality (the political state) and particularity (civil society), recovers the unity of man and the state, and makes the constitution and law not in opposition to man, but "the self-determination and particular content of the people"; it eliminates the dualization of human essence and truly makes man into "socialized man". It is apparent that this idea of Marx about democracy is an obscure, unclear which longs for the future society. (ideal of communism)

How can the dualization of human essence be eliminated? How can the alienation of the political state from civil society be negated? Who can undertake this important historical task? Marx followed this line of thought after the completion of *Critique of Hegel's Philosophy of Right*.

CHAPTER III

ON THE WAY TO EMANCIPATE THE PROLETARIAT

COMBINATION OF THE THEORY OF ESTRANGEMENT WITH THE THEORY OF SOCIAL REVOLUTION

Marx's research on history in Kreuznach in 1843 plays an important role in establishing the materialist conception of history. The findings of this research were not only assimilated into *Critique of Hegel's Philosophy of Right*, helping Marx to preliminarily solve the relationship between civil society and the state, but were also applied in *On the Jewish Question* and *Contribution to the Critique of Hegel's Philosophy of Law: Introduction*. The study of the history of the French bourgeois revolution and the Declaration of the Rights of Man and the Citizen enabled Marx to discover the limitations of the bourgeois political emancipation and raise the question of the emancipation of mankind. This shows that the formation of the materialist conception of history was not isolated, but closely related to his exploration of the way of the complete emancipation of the proletariat and its historical mission.

Marx did not attain the materialist conception of history then, but he has used the idea of estrangement to expound his theory of social revolution. Based on man as the highest essence of man, the interpretation of human emancipation as the returning of the human world and relations to man himself were undoubtedly marked by the influence of Feuerbach's humanism. However, we should note that with the help of terms like, species, species-essence, individual, species' unity and other customary expressions, Marx not only elaborated the question of human emancipation and the mission of the proletariat, but also discussed the secular basis of religion, discovers the function of private property and money and puts forth the idea of abolition of the objective relations in which man is enslaved, which was a step forward to the materialist conception of history.

1 POLITICAL ANIMAL — MEMBER OF CIVIL SOCIETY — MAN

Man creates himself and distinguishes himself from other animals through labour, which is a leap for man as a species; then man consciously organizes and adjusts production, rids himself of the anarchic state and of the struggle for existence and brings himself out the life condition of animals into that of the real man through the eradication of private property and transformation of the old relations of production, which would be a big leap. This idea, which was in embryo in the early period and contained the characteristics of humanism, has been stated repeatedly by the founders of Marxism also in later period, but was supported by strict, scientific verification.

Marx uses the idea of estrangement to investigate the history of the Middle Ages in *Critique of Hegel's Philosophy of Right*, and concludes that the feudal estate-constitution separates man from his universal nature and makes him into an animal whose being coincides immediately with its determinate character. So Marx calls the Middle Ages "the animal history of mankind, its zoology"[1]. After applying this principle to Germany, Marx asserted that the then despotic Germany was the philistine world, i.e. a political world of animals. Under this constitution, the ruled are not human beings, but the property of their masters like a breed of horses; and those who

---

1   Karl Marx and Frederick Engels: Collected Works, 1st Chinese Edition, Volume 1, p. 346.

are called master are not human beings either, they are no less phil-istines than their servants; what they want is to live and reproduce themselves, like the animals do. This is precisely the characteristic of animals.

Just because the despotism is the political world of animals, the re-lationship between people in this type of constitution is not the true relationship between human beings, but one between animals, main-tained by brutality and inevitably incompatible with human nature. Hence Marx said that "despotism's sole idea is contempt for man, the dehumanized man", and "where the monarchical principle arouses no doubts, there human beings do not exist at all"[2]. Apparently, these were not scientific statements regarding the essence of despotism, but a moral struggle in the name of man.

Marx lashed out at the bourgeois liberals of the time, who "declare to make man into man" on the one hand, and attacked the despot-ism on the other, with the attempt to "realize the achievements of the French Revolution" in Germany. This was impossible. The new German emperor of the time appeared to be liberal on the surface, compared with his father William III, whose aim was actually to conceal his despotic nature. With the high-handed measures of this new emperor, "the mantle of liberalism has been discarded and the most disgusting despotism in all its nakedness is disclosed to the eyes of the whole world"[3]. Consequently, the basis of the old world must be destroyed for the sake of the transition from the political world of animals to the human world of democracy.

What is exactly the world of human beings? Marx was longing for the French bourgeois revolution at that time. Soon after he quitted the *Rheinische Zeitung*, he praised Holland in the letters to Ruge, written in March and May, 1843, "the most insignificant Dutchman is still a citizen compared with the greatest German". And he op-posed the French bourgeois revolution to despotism, saying that des-potism made the world "the *dehumanized world*", while "the French Revolution" "once more had restored man"[4].

---

2   Ibid., p. 411.
3   Ibid., p. 407.
4   Ibid., p. 407, p. 410.

But Marx changed this view after a period of research in Kreuznach. He thought that the French Revolution "once more had restored man", but later found that the bourgeois revolution did not restore man but separated man's objective essence from him, and that man's content was not recognized as his true actuality, so he proposed to differentiate between "rule by man and rule by private property"[5]. The French bourgeois revolution established the rule by private property, and it did not eliminate estrangement but carried it to an extreme. It is not man but the member of civil society that it had restored. The key to this change in this view is Marx's research on history in Kreuznach, especially on the history of the French Revolution.

The French bourgeois revolution exerted a huge impact, and it represented the era. The German theorists of the time paid great attention to the experiences, achievements and slogans of the French Revolution, but there were two different inclinations. One was manifested by such philosophers as Hegel, Fichte and Schelling. They in their youth yearned for the French Revolution and admired its achievements; they tried to turn the French revolutionary practice into a German theory, and used abstract, obscure philosophical ideas to reflect the requirements needed to develop capitalism. But later their attitude towards the French Revolution changed from acclamation to horror, and they felt hatred and disgust for the French Jacobins. In their view, the French Revolution went too far. Marx showed a different inclination. He was exploring "Whither" Germany should go, so he paid particular attention to the experience of the French Revolution in his research on history. He not only read the socio-political works of the French bourgeois revolutionists, but also studied the history of the French Revolution specifically. He read Ludwig's *The History of the Past Fifty Years*, Jacques Charles Bajeux's *Critical Analysis of the Posthumous Work of the Baroness de Staël*, Wilhelm Wachsmuth's *History of France in the Age of Revolution*, Jean C. Dominique de Lacretelle's *History of France since the Restoration*, Lancizolle's *On the Causes, Character, and Consequences of the July Days*, and also the *Memoirs of a Girondin leader, Jean-Baptiste Louvet*, Madame Roland's *An Appeal to Impartial Posterity*, *On The Revolutions of France and of Brabant (Belgium)*, co-authored by

---

5   Ibid., p. 417.

Camille Desmoulins' and Louis Marie Prudhomme. And also the *Declaration of the Rights of Man and of the Citizen* (1789) and *The 1793 Constitution*. After the study, Marx affirmed the world histori- cal significance of the French Revolution, but also saw its social and political limitations. Marx found that the bourgeois revolution was merely a political emancipation, and it did not transform man from the political animal into real man, but into a member of civil society. He took the opportunity of debating with Bauer on the question of the Jewish emancipation, and elaborated his research findings.

Bauer's solution to the Jewish question is in full accordance with the idealistic theory of estrangement. First, he reduces the question of the Jewish emancipation to a theological one, and makes the religious emancipation the premise of political emancipation. According to him, the Jew must demand that the Christian state should give up its religious prejudice, if he wants to be emancipated in the Christian state. But since the Jew holds to his religion, has he then the right to demand someone else to renounce his religion? The most rigid form of the opposition between the Jews and the Christians is the religious opposition; to resolve this opposition, Christian man must renounce his own religion, for the Jew who strives to be emancipated politi- cally, and fight for the Christian state which is to effect emancipation and is itself to be emancipated. Second, the abolition of religious be- lief is the return to self-consciousness. Bauer thinks that Christianity and Judaism are the different stages in the development of the hu- man mind. If man can be seen as a snake, then these two religious forms are different snake skins cast off by man himself; and if this understanding is reached, the relation of the Jew and the Christian is no longer religious but a human relation: "Only after the Jew and the Christian abandon the particular essence which separates them and makes them fall into permanent isolation, and recognize the uni- versal essence of man and regard it as the true essence, they are conceived to be human beings."[6]

Marx has a different view. He argues that Germany, the so-called Christian state, is a despotic state, in which "it is, indeed, estrange- ment which matters, but not man. The only man who counts, the

---

6   Quoted from Auguste Cornu: Karl Marx and Friedrich Engels, Volume 1, p. 594, Beijing: SDX Joint Publishing Company, 1963.

king, is a being specifically different from other men, and is, moreover, a religious being, directly linked with heaven, with God"[7]. Since
the religious spirit is not secularized, but closely associated with politics, in Germany the criticism of religion is the prerequisite of all
other criticisms.

But this does not mean that the renouncement of religion is the pre-
condition of political emancipation; these are two different questions. In terms of the realm of thought, the struggle against religion
is an indirect struggle against the old world maintained by religion,
and the criticism of religion can develop into the criticism of politics.
As Marx said, "It is the immediate *task of philosophy*, which is in the
service of history, to unmask self-estrangement in its *unholy forms*
once the *holy form* of human self-estrangement has been unmasked.
Thus, the criticism of Heaven turns into the criticism of Earth, the
criticism of religion into the *criticism of law*, and the *criticism of
theology* into the *criticism of politics*."[8] However, the complete abolition of religion is a different matter. In fact, political emancipation does not presuppose that everyone renounces his own religion,
but that the state casts off religion in general and abolishes the state
religion and religious privileges. When the state emancipates itself
from the state religion and the state as a state does not profess any
religion, but asserts itself as a state, the state emancipates itself from
religion according to its own law and in the manner according to the
characteristic of its own nature. Therefore, political emancipation,
i.e. the bourgeois revolution, just makes religion transfer from the
sphere of public law to that of private law, become personal religion.

Political emancipation does not and cannot eliminate religious estrangement. An individual can be a religious believer in the sphere
of private life, while in the political sphere he is viewed as a citizen,
equal with all others, regardless of his religion, due to the abolition
of the state religion and religious privileges. So it is not a complete
person but the schism of man that political emancipation attains.
Man is decomposed into Jew and citizen, Protestant and citizen, and
not only that, into merchant and citizen, day-labourer and citizen,

---

7 Karl Marx and Frederick Engels: Collected Works, 1st Chinese Edition, Volume 1,
p.p. 433-434.
8 Ibid., p. 453.

landlord and citizen, etc. In a word, man has one identity in civil society, and a different one in the political sphere. This situation indicates that under the domination of the bourgeois private property, man lives a twofold life—a heavenly and an earthly life. In civil society, man as a private individual, as an egoist in opposition to others, lives an earthly life; in the political sphere, man as a citizen, lives a heavenly life which corresponds to his "generic essence". Marx makes a deep analysis of this contradiction. He said, "Where the political state has attained its true development, man—not only in thought, in consciousness, but in reality, in life—leads a twofold life, a heavenly and an earthly life: life in the political community, in which he considers himself a communal being, and a life in civil society, in which he acts as a private individual, regards other men as a means, degrades himself into a means, and becomes the plaything of alien powers. The relation of the political state to civil society is just as spiritual as the relations of heaven to earth."[9] Thus, man as a real individual, lacks universality and is not a species-being, while on the other side, man as a species-being in political life, is deprived of his real individual life and has fictitious, unreal universality.

The emancipation of the state from religion is not the emancipation of the real man from religion. Political emancipation does not free man of religion, but on the contrary, it contains in self the basis of the production of religion. According to Marx, in the realm of thought, the estrangement of man's species-essence into God is consistent with the estrangement of man's essence into the state in the political sphere, the former being the reflection of the latter. As long as there is opposition between individual and species, and man is still not a real species-being, the existence of religion is inevitable. He said, "The members of the political state are religious owing to the dualism between individual life and species-life, between the life of civil society and political life. They are religious because men treat the political life of the state, an area beyond their real individuality, as if it were their true life. They are religious insofar as religion here is the spirit of civil society, expressing the separation and remoteness of man from man."[10]

9   Karl Marx and Frederick Engels: Collected Works, 1st Chinese Edition, Volume 1, p. 428.
10   Ibid., p. 434.

Thus it can be seen that political emancipation does not transform man from a political animal into the real man. Although man was regarded as the starting point and end-result by the bourgeois humanists since the Renaissance, Marx believed that this man was not the real man, but an egoist, a member of civil society. In Marx's words, that is to say, "it is man in his uncivilized, unsocial form, man in his fortuitous existence, man just as he is, man as he has been corrupted by the whole organization of our society, who has lost himself, been alienated, and handed over to the rule of inhuman conditions and elements—in short, man who is not yet a real species-being"[11].

Based on the above understanding Marx criticizes Bauer's view regarding the issue: the rights of man. In Bauer's conception, so long as the Jew is Jew and adheres to his religion, he cannot gain the rights of a man. Man has to sacrifice the privilege of religious faith in order to obtain the universal rights of man. Bauer considers the so-called human rights of the bourgeoisie as the expression of man's general essence, which is in opposition to the particular nature of the Jew.

Marx holds an opposite view. The so-called bourgeoisie human rights are divided into two parts. One part comes within the category of political freedom, i.e. the so-called civic rights, whose main content is the right to participate in the political community and in the activity of the state; the other part refers to the so-called rights of man, i.e. freedom of conscience, protection of his personality, his rights and property from infringement, etc. Man, here, is none other than the member of civil society; the so-called rights of man are the rights of a member of civil society. These rights not only do not accord with the essence of man, but also are separated from it; they do not go beyond egoism, but rather guarantee it. Marx wrote "None of the so-called rights of man go beyond egoistic man, beyond man as a member of civil society—that is, an individual withdrawn into himself, into the confines of his private interests and private caprices, and separated from the community. In the rights of man, he is far from being conceived as a species-being; on the contrary, species-life itself, society, appears as a framework external to the individuals, as a restriction of their original independence. The sole bond

---

11   Ibid., p. 434.

holding them together is natural necessity, need and private interest, the preservation of their property and their egoistic selves."[12] This shows that the positive result achieved by the bourgeois political emancipation is not the leap of man into the real man from a political animal, but a shift to a member of civil society. To resolve this contradiction and eliminate the schism of individual and species, the emancipation of mankind should be carried out forward.

2 RETURNING OF THE HUMAN WORLD AND HUMAN RELATIONS TO MAN HIMSELF

To transform man from a member of civil society into the real man, it is a must to combat against the extreme expression of man's self-estrangement, and return the estranged human world and relations to man himself, which is a conclusion Marx had arrived, in his analysis of the relationship between political emancipation and human emancipation.

According to Marx, the Jew still has right to demand political emancipation, without renouncing his religion. But the question of Jewish emancipation cannot be solved by political emancipation. In fact, the Jew has already emancipated himself in a Jewish way through his acquired wealth. In Germany, the Jew, adherent of Judaism, is restricted greatly in political rights and deprived of the right to be a state functionary, but he plays a significant role in the actual political life, which is also recognized by Bauer himself. For example, Bauer says in *The Jewish Question* that "The Jew, who in Vienna, is only tolerated, determines the fate of the whole Empire by his financial power. The Jew, who may have no rights in the smallest German state, decides the fate of Europe. While corporations and industrial guilds refuse to admit Jews, or have not yet adopted a favourable attitude towards them, the audacity of industry mocks at the obstinacy of the material institutions."[13] But Bauer treats this question idealistically, and argues that it is a "fictitious" state when in theory the Jew has no political rights, whereas in practice he has immense power. The contradiction between the practical political power of the Jew and his political rights is actually the contradiction between politics

---

12   Ibid., p. 439.
13   Ibid., p.p. 446-447

and the power of money. Although theoretically the political power is superior to money, in fact the political power is the slave of the financial power. Hence Marx said, "The Jew has emancipated himself in a Jewish manner, not only because he has acquired financial power, but also because, through him and also a part from him, the *money* has become a world power."[14]

Judaism fits with civil society. The basis of the Jewish religion is not religion itself. It has secular basis, namely, practical need and egoism. The secular icon of the Jew is huckster, and his worldly god is money. Practical need, egoism, money are also the principles of civil society, so the Jew is perpetually created by civil society from its own entrails. Seen from the perspective of historical necessity, the Jew, as a distinct member of civil society, continues to exist not in spite of history, but owing to history. So the emancipation of the Jew, in the final analysis, is the emancipation of mankind from Judaism, i.e. the emancipation of mankind from huckstering and financial power.

It is in this discussing the relationship of Judaism to the actual Jew and the secular basis of Judaism that Marx had elaborated his views on estrangement. Compared with *Critique of Hegel's Philosophy of Right*, Marx at that time had begun to shift his focus from the estrangement of the political state from civil society directly to civil society itself. Since practical need, egoism are the principles of civil society, and their concentrated expression is the need of money, Marx analyzed money specifically, and considered the rule of money as the extreme expression of man's self-estrangement.

According to Marx, money, or currency, is the estranged essence of man. "Money is the estranged essence of man's work and man's existence, and this alien essence dominates him, and he worships money."[15] Money is the supreme god, throwing all other gods in the shade. Lacking a thorough study of economics then, Marx failed to scientifically explain the origin, nature and functions of currency and its position and role in the commodity economy system, and still continued to use the concept of estrangement to explain them. But it is important to note that he did not regard currency as the

14   Ibid. p. 447.
15   Ibid. p. 448.

estrangement of self-consciousness, but connected it with man's labour, activity and man's products, which contains the simplest germ
of the advance of his former estrangement idea to the idea of estranged labour.

Marx translates the economic phenomenon in which currency serves
as a universal equivalent into the philosophical language, and asserts that money degrades everything worshipped by man and turns
it into commodity; money becomes the universal value of all things,
and it has, therefore, robbed the whole world, including both nature
and the human world, of its specific value. Under the domination of
private property and money, people show no respect to nature, but
disdain and degrade instead, because nature—from the animals to
the plants—has turned into property, into an object that people strive
to possess. Likewise, in this case, people also show contempt for
theory, art, history and for man as an end in himself. Everything is
commodity, and even the species-relation itself, the relation between
man and woman become an object of trade. The woman is bought
and sold. Thus under the domination of money, the products and activities of people are governed by their estranged essence—money.
And only in this way can they practically conduct their activities and
create things. This estrangement "sever all the species-ties of man,
and put egoism and selfish need in the place of these species-ties,
and dissolve the human world into a world of atomistic individuals who are inimically opposed to one another"[16]. This is called the
separation of the human world and human relations from man.

Marx goes deep into the secular basis of the Jewish religion, and
finds that Christianity and Judaism are actually unified, though in
opposition as religious forms. The Jewish spirit—pursuit for practical needs, egoism and worship of money—reaches its highest point
with the perfection of civil society, but it is only in the Christian
world that civil society attains perfection. Marx conveys this view
in speculative, philosophical language: "Christianity sprang from
Judaism. It has merged again in Judaism." "Christianity is the sub-
lime thought of Judaism, Judaism is the common practical application of Christianity", "the Jew is the practical Christian, and the
practical Christian has become a Jew again" , etc. Marx added: "This

---

16   Ibid., p. 450.

means that the Christian worships God in the realm of thought, but still pursues money in the actual life. The preaching of the Gospel itself and the Christian ministry chairs have become articles of trade, and the positions in the church have become a profitable vocation. The trader and the Gospel preacher can be inter-convertible. The trader whose business has failed can deal in the Gospel, just as the Gospel preacher who has some money at this disposal leaves the pulpit and goes into business. But the Jew worships money, and turns it into a god, a supreme god superior to all other gods. The difference lies in that Christianity is spiritualistic and elevates people's pursuit and need of the worldly life to the heaven and alienates man' essence as God, while Judaism makes God of the heaven into God of the worldly life, i.e., money. It is in this sense that Marx argues that although Christianity as a developed religion has completed in theory the estrangement of man from himself and from nature, Judaism "makes alienated man and alienated nature into alienable, vendible objects subjected to the slavery of egoistic need and to trading"[17].

Estrangement should be eliminated, which Marx shares with Feuerbach. But what Feuerbach aimed to eliminate was merely the religious estrangement; he returns the estranged species-essence of man to man himself and regards this as the way to eradicate all social ills. In this regard, Bauer's consideration of the renouncement of religion as the premise of political emancipation does not go beyond Feuerbach. Marx expresses a different view. He divides the elimination of religious estrangement into two questions on different levels. One is to emancipate the state from religion, i.e. the abolition of religious privileges and state religion problem, which is a question the bourgeois revolution tries hard to solve and is able to solve. The experience of France and North America had proved this point. The other is to free mankind completely of religious estrangement, which is a question which the political revolution cannot settle, and requires the elimination of the secular basis of religion. The existence of this inverted world outlook of religion indicates that the world which produces religion is inverted in itself. Therefore, not only should the estranged species-essence of man be returned from religion to man himself, but the fully estranged human world

---

17   Ibid. p. 451.

and estranged human relations should be returned to man himself, i.e. to eliminate the contradiction between individual sensuous existence and species-being from all spheres, to eradicate the egoistic state in civil society in which people are isolated and seek selfish interests. Only when an actual individual becomes a species-being in both political life and in his personal life, namely, in his labour and mutual relations, can the actual individual turn into the real man from a member of civil society. And this is the emancipation of mankind. So Marx said that "the philosophical transformation of priestly Germans into men will emancipate the *people*."[18]

3 COMPLETE EMANCIPATION OF THE PROLETARIAT ONLY THROUGH THE COMPLETE RE-WINNING OF MAN

Marx's criticism of Hegel's philosophy of right was the most consistent, richest, complete critique of Germany philosophy of the state and of law. This criticism was directed against German reality but not limited to it. On the one hand, it was the a criticism of the German status quo, i.e. the criticism of the past of such advanced nations such as England and France. Something of the past seems to suppress these nations, and constitutes the concealed deficiency of the modern state; on the other hand, this criticism exceeds the level of political emancipation and starts from a higher level question, namely, the so-called true human emancipation problem. And this question concerns both Germany and the whole world. Marx said, "Once *modern* politico-social reality itself is subjected to criticism, once criticism rises to truly human problems, it finds itself outside the German *status quo*."[19]

What Marx raises here is not an old question that whether Germany can achieve the political emancipation which has already taken place in England and France, but a completely new question, i.e. "can Germany attain a practice *à la hauteur des principes*—i.e., a revolution which will raise it not only to the *official level* of modern nations, but to the height of humanity which will be the near future of those nations"[20]. Marx was affirmative about this at the time.

---

18   Ibid., p. 461.
19   Ibid., p. 457.
20   Ibid., p. 460.

What was the truly human revolution? What is the revolution with the height of humanity? Political emancipation is not such a revolution. Although the bourgeois humanists considered themselves as the representatives of man, although Marx once called the French Revolution as it had restored the man, he now found that political emancipation turned man into citizen on the one hand, and into egoistic, independent individual on the other. This is not the emancipation of the whole society, but only that part: The civil society; this was not to make man have his essence all to himself, but to deprive man of his essence. The truly human revolution is the emancipation of mankind, and it focuses on restoring the estranged essence of man. So Marx said, "The only liberation of Germany which is *practically* possible is liberation from the point of view of that theory which declares man to be the supreme being for man." He also said, "The criticism of religion ends with the teaching that man is the highest essence for man—hence, with the *categorical imperative to overthrow all relations* in which man is a debased, enslaved, abandoned, despicable essence."[21]

"Man is the highest essence for man" was a view of Feuerbach, as an anti-theological and anti-religious proposition. The first "man" in this sentence refers to species, while the second "man" is the actual individual. That is to say, species is the essence of an individual. According to the religious and theological theories, God is the supreme existence of personality outside man, but Feuerbach inverts this view, asserting that God is the estranged species-essence of man, and thus man's God should not be outside man, but be man himself. He stated explicitly, "Homo homini Deus [the only God of man is man himself]". Feuerbach reduces theology to humanism, and seeks the mystery of God from man himself, but his theory of the contradiction between individual and species man could not really provide a scientific explanation for religion.

Marx approved of this proposition of Feuerbach then, but he did not repeat it exactly, for he saw Feuerbach's weaknesses. First, Feuerbach argued that man makes religion, religion does not make man as the theoretical basis for criticizing religion, but he abstracted man and saw him as a natural being. However, Marx argued that

21   Ibid., p. 467, p.p. 460-461.

"*man* is no abstract being squatting outside the world. Man is the *world of man*—state, society"[22]. For instance, when analyzing the nature of the Jews and Judaism in *On the Jewish Question*, Marx emphasized that "the nature of the modern Jew, and not as an abstract nature but as one that is in the highest degree empirical, not merely as a narrowness of the Jew, but as the Jewish narrowness of society"[23]. Second, Marx found that for Feuerbach, the criticism of religion "ends with" the proposition of man as the highest for man, which remained in the sphere of the opposition between man and gods. But Marx stressed that in Germany the criticism of religion was already completed, the indirect political struggle must turn to the direct one to overthrow all relations in which man was a debased, enslaved, abandoned, despicable essence. This, in Marx's words, would be "a *thorough* one", and will "breaking all forms of bondage"[24]. Yet despite all this, it is insufficient to argue for human emancipation with such a basis as "man as the highest essence of man". It is of humanistic character, for it derives the demand for revolution from the estrangement of the human world and relations from man, from their suppression and prevention of man from realizing his essence.

The most significant achievement, which Marx has attained in *Contribution to the Critique of Hegel's Philosophy of Right: Introduction*, is the elaboration of the historical mission of the proletariat. He considers the proletariat as "the heart", "the material weapon" of human emancipation, the key to the practically possible liberation of mankind.

After he came to Paris from Germany, Marx maintained exchanges with the leaders of the League of the Just and the secret societies of the French workers, and participated in the workers' rallies, which helped Marx have direct, perceptual knowledge of the modern proletariat, especially a more profound knowledge of theory. He had already recognized the internal relations of the proletariat to the capitalist society and the modern industry, and pointed out that the proletariat was "a class of civil society which is not a class of civil

22   Ibid., p. 452.
23   Ibid., p. 451.
24   Ibid., p. 467.

society", proletariat was "an estate which is the dissolution of all estates". The proletariat is a class of civil society, because it is a class within the capitalist society, for example, the Germany's proletariat was beginning to appear with the development of the capitalist industry in Germany; it was not a class of civil society, because it was "a class with *radical chains*", in opposition to the bourgeoisie which was the representative of civil society. Marx realized the all-round antithesis status of the proletariat to private property, and thus the most fundamental principle of the proletariat was to demand the negation of private property, and he also argued the identity of the emancipation of the proletariat with human emancipation, and that the proletariat could emancipate itself only if it effected the general human emancipation, etc. Meanwhile, Marx analyzed the class struggle in Germany, and compared the German bourgeoisie with the French bourgeoisie. He stated that in Germany, "the higher nobility estate (class) is struggling against the monarchy, the bureaucrat against the nobility, and the bourgeois against them all, while the proletariat is already beginning to find itself struggling against the bourgeois. The middle class hardly dares to grasp the thought of emancipation from its own standpoint although when the development of the social conditions and the progress of political theory already declare that its standpoint is antiquated or at least problematic"[25]. Therefore, the bourgeoisie played the role of emancipator in France, while in Germany, only the proletariat had the need and capacity for the general human emancipation because it was "forced by its *immediate* condition, by material necessity and its *very chains*"[26].

But we should also note that Marx's analysis of the class status and role of the proletariat was not yet based on the analysis of the capitalist mode of production, but from the perspective of the estrangement of human nature. According to Marx, the reason why the proletariat can and must shoulder this great mission was that proletariat is "the complete loss of man and hence can win itself only through the *complete re-winning of man*". The living conditions, situation and status of the proletariat in the capitalist society were opposed to its nature as man. The proletariat had lost what corresponds to human

25   Ibid., p. 465.
26   Ibid., p. 466.

nature, and only by re-winning its essence could it emancipate itself completely.

When Marx debated with Ruge upon the significance and roots of the Silesian weavers' uprising in 1844 in Germany, Marx refuted his depreciation of this uprising, and thus spoke highly of the revolutionary spirit of the German working class, and expounded the view that socialism must go through revolution, and the old ruling power must be overthrown and the old order dissolved. But Marx continued elaborating his view on estrangement as well. In his view, the outbreak of the French bourgeois revolution in 1789 was owing to the fact that people were isolated from the political community, i.e. in an isolated situation where they politically had no right, so this revolution was political emancipation and its very purpose was to abolish this situation and to make man into species-being in the political sphere. The proletarian revolution would be of a different kind. The community from which the workers were isolated was quite different from the political community, that is, they were not just politically rightless in general, but had lost their human essence. Marx said, "The community from which his own labour separates him is the life itself, physical and spiritual life, human morality, human activity, human enjoyment, human nature. Human nature is the true *community of men*." It is because that man is greater than being citizen and human life greater than political life that Marx called the proletariat revolution "a protest by man against a dehumanized life"[27].

Marx gave a substantial elaboration of both political emancipation and human emancipation by combining his idea of estrangement with the theory of social revolution. But his investigation into them merely from the view of the elimination of the estrangement of human essence could not really reveal their dialectical relationship, the objective, economic basis of their interrelationship and difference in a scientific way. Marx was right about the limitations of political emancipation, but was immature when thinking that the German realization of political emancipation was utopian dream. He evaluated Germany could "How can (Germany) it do a *somersault*, not only

---

27   Karl Marx and Frederick Engels: Collected Works, 1st Chinese Edition, Volume 1, p.p. 487-488.

over its own limitations, but at the same time over the limitations of the modern nations, over limitations which it must in reality feel and strive for as for emancipation from its real limitations? Only a revolution of radical needs can be a radical revolution and it seems that precisely the preconditions and ground for such needs are lacking."[28] "It is not the *radical* revolution, not the *general human* emancipation which is a utopian dream for Germany, but rather the partial, the *merely* political revolution, the revolution which leaves the pillars of the house standing"[29].

In fact, shortly after the full establishment of the materialist conception of history, Marx changed his view on the relationship between political emancipation (the bourgeois revolution) and human emancipation (the proletarian revolution), and expounded the position and role of the proletariat in the bourgeois revolution, and pointed out that the revolutionary movement of the bourgeoisie against the feudal estates and the absolute monarchy could accelerate the revolutionary movement of the proletariat, and the proletariat "can and must accept the *bourgeois revolution* as a precondition for the *workers' revolution*. However, they cannot for a moment regard it as their *ultimate goal.*"[30]

Whether in history or in the contemporary West, there are some scholars who grasp Marx's views on species, species-essence and elimination of the estrangement of human essence from man, and describe him as a "true socialist" thinker. This view is not correct and was refuted by Marx long ago. When talking about *On the Jewish Question* and *Contribution to the Critique of Hegel's Philosophy of Right: Introduction*, Marx wrote in these two articles, 'the traditionally occurring philosophical expressions such as "human essence", "species", etc., give the German theoreticians the desired reason for misunderstanding the real trend of thought and believing that here again it was a question merely of giving a new turn to their worn-out theoretical garment'[31]. Of course there is no doubt

28   Ibid., p. 462.
29   Ibid., p. 463.
30   Karl Marx and Frederick Engels: Collected Works, 1st Chinese Edition, Volume 4, p. 347, Beijing: The People's Press, 1958.
31   Karl Marx and Frederick Engels: Collected Works, 1st Chinese Edition, Volume 3, p.p. 261-262.

that some statements of Marx in this period possessed humanistic character because of the influence of Feuerbach, and thus have some similarities to the "true socialism" trend of thought which was based on Feuerbach's humanism. But, more importantly, we should notice that he appealed to the proletariat, combated against the teaching of love, and promoted the complete abolition of private property and transformation of old relations in an all-round way through the criticism of the weapon, which was fundamentally different from the "true socialism". But of course, it needed a process for Marx to completely overcome the influence of Feuerbach's humanism, for which a key factor was his later turn towards the study of political economy.

CHAPTER IV

COMBINATION OF PHILOSOPHY AND ECONOMIC STUDIES
FROM ESTRANGEMENT TO ESTRANGED LABOUR

If we say the research on history in Kreuznach in 1843 enabled Marx to preliminarily define the relationship of civil society to the state and see the necessity of human emancipation, then the economic studies in Paris in 1844 had impelled him to analyze civil society itself and go deep into the economic base and leave back the analysis of the estrangement of superstructure. So within just three years, Marx had carried out research in these two spheres—history and economy, and underwent such a process from religion then passing through the state and law towards civil society. The establishment of the materialist conception of history would be unimaginable without his economic studies.

The notebooks Marx composed in Paris—*Paris Notebooks* are mainly about economics, except for those about history and the socialist ideological trend. Marx read the writings of Smith, Ricardo, Say, Sismondi, Skarbek, Mill, Destutt de Tracy, MacCulloch,

Boisguillebert, etc. and made summaries and notes of those readings. This is the early stage of his economic studies, during which he put forward the theory of estranged labour, and used theory of estranged labour to criticize the bourgeois economics and offered new interpretations to the facts and those conclusions they had all arrived. *Comments on James Mill, Elements of Political Economy,* which is closely related to *Economic and Philosophical Manuscripts of 1844,* occupies a prominent position in his *Paris Notebooks,* and is an important book on the analysis of the estrangement of labour.

1 RESEARCH ON ESTRANGEMENT IN THE ECONOMIC SPHERE

ATTEMPT TO ESTABLISH THE METHODOLOGICAL PRINCIPLE OF EXPLAINING VARIOUS ECONOMIC CATEGORIES

Marx, who had shifted his position to the side of the proletariat and considered human emancipation as its great mission, were dissatisfied with the standpoint and method which the bourgeoisie used to study economics. Although Marx did not formulate categories unique to himself at that time, and although he did his study proceeding from the facts, materials and categories provided by the bourgeois politics, Marx tried his best to uncover the estrangement occurring in the economic sphere and strove to find the fundamental principle of expounding the various categories of political economy, which led him to establish and advance the theory of estranged labour.

Marx's idea of estranged labour certainly has its philosophical foundation, which is the theory of estrangement which was developed gradually by the German classical philosophy, but Marx broke through its speculative tradition, focused on the analysis of economic facts, and believed that the theory of estranged labour is an effective weapon to criticize the bourgeois political economy and solve the problems it could not solve.

In the 1840s, the question of private property was a fundamental theoretical and practical question, and was raised by the emerging labour movement as well as by all kinds of socialist ideological trends. Before he came to Paris, Marx had touched upon this question indirectly by discussing the question of material interests in his some articles on the debates of the Rhine Province Assembly; and in the polemical articles of Communism and the *Augsburger Allgemeine Zeitung* newspaper, he affirmed the necessity and rationality of the proletarian demand to possess the wealth of the middle class. During his research on history in Kreuznach after he quitted the *Rheinische Zeitung*, Marx paid close attention to the materials about the influence of ownership and its forms on political institutions, and discussed private property and its relationship to the political constitution through the analysis of primogeniture in *Critique of Hegel's Philosophy of Right*. Therefore, when he turned towards economic studies, he was opposed to the position of the bourgeois political economy which regarded the existence of private property as an established fact, and vigorously defended the capitalist private property. Marx criticized this basic limitation of the bourgeois political economy in his commentary on Say's works, pointing out that "private property is an undemonstrated fact, which is, however, the foundation of political economy. Without private property, there would be no property owners, and political economy in essence is a science of amassing great fortunes. Without private property, there would be no political economy. Therefore, the entire political economy is based on a fact which has no necessity."[1]

How could the historical or temporary nature of private property be proved? Could it be solved by looking into it in combination with labour? Historical experience proved this to be unworkable. For instance, it is from that the man's labour belongs to him that Locke, a British philosopher, concluded that individual ownership corresponds to human nature and thus is reasonable and eternal. He said, "Man mixes the thing he obtains from the objects nature creates and gives to him, with his labour, with something inseparable from and which belong to him, and thus makes it into his own property. When he acquires some object from that common wealth nature gives to him, he adds something to this object through his own labour, and thus excludes other people's common right."[2]

1   Karl Marx and Frederick Engels: Collected Works, 1st International edition (German), Part 1, Volume 3, p. 449.
2   John Locke: Selected Philosophical Writings, Russian edition, Volume 2, p. 19, 1960.

Although the British classical political economy established the labour theory of value, and changed the essence of private property from pure object into human labour, that did not stop it from advocating private property as an established fact, and saw the separation of capital, land and labour as a premise, because it regarded labour merely as a means of earning a living, separated the value the labour added to the raw material thus producing profit, rent, and also considered labour wages as a reasonable, natural mode of distribution which was conducive to the increase in the national wealth. It did not explore what kind of labour could serve as private property, but instead presupposed private property and took the interest of the capitalists to be the ultimate cause for defining the relationship between wages and the profit of capital.

Marx took a different approach, for he had concentrated on exploring the origin of private property. The theory of estranged labour was the theory and approach he used to investigate private property historically before he fully established the materialist conception of history and found the law of the dialectical movement between the productive forces and the relations of production. He treated private property as a historical phenomenon, an estrangement, "*private property* results from the concept of alienated labour, i.e., of *alienated man*, of estranged labour, of *estranged* life, of estranged man"[3]. It is this exploration of the origin of private property that caused Marx to shift from estrangement to estranged labour.

From its founder William Petty to its consummator David Ricardo, one of the greatest achievement of the British classical political economy was the labour theory of value. Ricardo overcame the lack of thoroughness, that confusion in Petty and Smith's labour theory of value, and specified clearly and thoroughly that the value of commodity was determined by labour time. But after Ricardo passed away in 1823, on the one hand the labour theory of value of the British classical political economy was vulgarized by its successors, and on the other hand some utopian socialists tried to draw from this theory a conclusion in favour of workers: They argued that since labour creates value, all products should belong to labourers. For

3   Karl Marx and Frederick Engels: Collected Works, 1st Chinese Edition, Volume 42, p. 100, Beijing: The People's Press, 1979.

example, Bray, a British utopian socialist, once said, "It is labour which bestows value [...] Every man has an undoubted right to all that his honest labour can procure him. When he thus appropriates the fruits of his labour, he commits no injustice upon any other human being; Because he interferes with no other man's right of doing the same with the produce of his labour ... All these ideas of superior and inferior – of master and man – may be traced to the neglect of First Principles, and to the consequent rise of inequality of possessions." Bray thus believed that under "a just system of exchanges", "the value of articles would be determined by the entire cost of product; and equal values should always be exchanged for equal values"[4]. But the relationship between the workers and the capitalists run counter to the labour theory of value, "The whole transaction, therefore, between the producer and capitalist is a palpable deception, a mere farce: it is, in fact, in thousands of instances, no other than a barefaced though legalized robbery"[5]. This attempt to apply the labour theory of value from the perspective of utopian socialism once had led some people to refute it. For instance, John Cazenove declared in 1832 that "That labour is the sole source of wealth seems to be a doctrine as dangerous as it is false, as it unhappily affords a handle to those who would represent all property as belonging to the working classes, and the share which is received by others as a robbery or fraud upon them."[6]

Marx not only disagreed with the attempt to draw a conclusion favourable to workers from the labour theory of value, but also criticized this s theory itself. In his view, the labour theory of value starts from labour as the real soul of production; yet to labourers it gives nothing, but to private property and the bourgeoisie everything. Therefore, Marx strives to reveal the estranged nature of labour in capitalist society and uses the theory of estranged labour to criticize the labour theory of value of the British classical political economy.

---

4 Quoted from Karl Marx and Frederick Engels: Collected Works, 1st Chinese Edition, Volume 4, p. 111.
5 Quoted Ibid., p. 112.
6 Quoted from Meek: Studies in the Labour Theory of Value, p. 137, Beijing: The Commercial Press, 1979.

Marx's criticism of the labour theory of value is certainly not a denial of the connection between the cost of production and value, but a criticism of Ricardo, who abstracts it from competition and the supply-demand relationship and who describes the cost of production as the only factor for determining value, and considers this as an impermissible abstraction. In commenting on Mill's view that the cost of production regulates the value of metal (gold and silver), as of other ordinary productions, Marx stated that "Mill commits the mistake—like the school of Ricardo in general—of stating the abstract law without the change or continual supersession of this law through which alone it comes into being. If it is a *constant* law that, for example, the cost of production in the last instance—or rather when demand and supply are in equilibrium which occurs sporadically, fortuitously—determines the price (value), it is just as much a *constant* law that they are not in equilibrium, and that therefore value and cost of production stand in no necessary relationship. Indeed, there is always only a momentary equilibrium of demand and supply owing to the previous fluctuation of demand and supply, owing to the disproportion between cost of production and exchange-value, just as this fluctuation and this disproportion likewise again follow the momentary state of equilibrium. This *real* movement, of which that law is only an abstract, fortuitous and one-sided factor, is made by recent political economy into something accidental and inessential."[7]

It was an incisive thought of Marx to emphasize the influence of the supply-demand relationship and competition on price, and the conditions in which the law takes effect; however, the most basic principles of the labour theory of value were negated in fact by separating value from exchange-value and concluding that the cost of production and value stand in no necessary relationship and therefore the labour theory of value elevates something abstract, fortuitous and one-sided and was elevated to a law based on the conditionality of the conversion of value to market price, and the role of the existing various factors.

---

7   Karl Marx and Frederick Engels: Collected Works, 1st Chinese Edition, Volume 42, p. 18.

Marx also exposes the inner contradiction of the labour theory of value to prove that the attempt to derive from this theory a conclusion favourable to the working class will not succeed. According to the labour theory of value of the bourgeois political economy, the whole product of labour belongs to the worker, but in the actual reality what the worker gets through the wages is the smallest and utterly indispensable part of the product, as much as is necessary for his existence: Not as a human being, but as a worker, and not for the propagation of humanity, but for the reproduction of the worker. According to the bourgeois political economy, all products are dead labour and capital is nothing but accumulated labour, so everything can be bought with labour, but in the actual fact the worker, far from being able to buy everything with his labour, must sell himself. According to the bourgeois political economy, it is solely through labour that man enhances and increases the value of the products of nature, but in the actual fact the rent of the idle landowner and the profit of the busy capitalist reach to the most of the product, and they lay down the law to the worker and are everywhere superior to him, and live a pampered, god-like life. According to the bourgeois political economy, labour is the sole unchanging price of things, but in the actual life there is nothing which is exposed to greater influence of the supply-demand relationship, nothing more fortuitous than the price of labour. In a word, concerning the bourgeois political economy, there is a fundamental contradiction between its value theory with labour as the starting point and on the other hand its standpoint which defended the interest of the bourgeoisie, also contradiction between the theoretical principle of labour theory of value and its reality. So the socialism based on the labour theory of value was nothing but a utopian dream. In fact, according to Marx, the thing is not to determine the quantitative relationship between quantity of labour and quantity of value, but to analyze the nature of labour, i.e. to uncover the fact that this kind of labour is estranged labour. The opposition of the labour which creates all products to those circumstances of the labourer, "this apparent contradiction is a contradiction between the estranged labour and itself". In this sense, the labour theory of value of the bourgeois classical political economy provides everything for the bourgeoisie, while Marx's theory of estranged labour tried to explore the root of the poverty of the proletariat and argued for the interest of the proletariat.

According to Marx, for the whole bourgeois political economy, from Smith through Say to Ricardo, these later economists had advanced further than their predecessors in their theories of the estrangement from man in a more thorough, more realistic, more active and more conscious way.

The worker without land and capital is inevitably conceived as a labourer, a labouring machine instead of as a human being by the bourgeois political economy according to its theories. Therefore, the lowest and the only necessary wages of the proletariat are that providing for the subsistence of the worker for the duration of his work and as much more as is necessary for the race of labourers not to die out and for them to support a family. The worker is in their eyes just a labouring animal, cattle that only has the essential physical need. What is important for a sum of money is not how many workers it can support but how much profit it can bring about.

When analyzing Ricardo's views on general income and net income, Marx attacks the bourgeois political economy's contempt for the proletariat. In Ricardo's view, wages are part of the cost of production, are expenditure, and only the increase in net income, i.e. the increase in rent and profit, is meaningful; the less the number of workers are, the more the increase in net income is, which will be beneficial to the state. This clearly shows his hostility to workers. Marx pointed out that "the abstraction of political economy reaches the climax of hypocrisy, owing to the fact that it denies all the important significance of general income, i.e. to deny the quantity of production and consumption regardless of surplus, and consequently it denies all the significance of life itself. Thus it can be openly said that 1) What political economy concerns is definitely not the interest of the state, not man, but net income, profit and rent alone, which are the ultimate aim of the state. 2) Human life has no value in and of itself. 3) The value of the working class, simply put, is the necessary cost of production, whose employment is only for net income, i.e. for the profit of the capitalists and for the rent of the landowners. They themselves still are and must be labouring machines, and it is enough to spend the capital necessary for keeping them in operation."[8]

---

8 Karl Marx and Frederick Engels: Collected Works, 1st International edition (German), Part 1, Volume 3, p.p. 514-515.

Marx also criticizes the school of Ricardo for considering the economic laws as "an average", disregarding everything fortuitous and real. According to Marx, the focus on "average" alone is an abstract movement with its focus on the investigation of materials, regardless of man, man's real life, and thus turns the material process which private property actually passes into general, abstract formulas. So Marx believed that "the average is the real insult and defamation against individuals." And he also said that "what the school of Ricardo cares about is the universal law. As for how this law is realized, whether millions of people go bankrupt because of it, it is of no significance at all for the law and political economists."[9] This view is also expressed by his comment that the labour theory of value is a theory antagonistic to man, a total denial of man realized under the semblance of recognizing man (man's labour).

In brief, Marx maintains that the bourgeois political economy is opposed to man. His comment that "Humanity is outside political economy, while inhumanity is within it" was his overall evaluation of this economic theory. But this is not a fault of the bourgeois political economy itself, and still less a fault of Ricardo. The bourgeois political economy is the "*scientific* creed" of the capitalists, the reflection of modern capitalist industry in consciousness, so the more real, more thorough it was, the more natural and more reasonable the estrangement of man was considered by it.

It is in criticizing the bourgeois political economy, in combating its basic stance, method and conclusion that Marx develops his theory of estranged labour. In his view, the economic studies should not presuppose the eternity of private property, and the separation of capital, landed property and labour to try to conceal estrangement, as the classical economic school does; instead, it must figure out the nature and origin of private property, and "grasp the intrinsic connection between private property, greed, the separation of the three: Labour, capital and landed property; the separation of the connection of exchange with competition, the separation of value and the devaluation of man, of monopoly and competition, etc.—the connection between this whole estrangement and the *money* system"[10].

9   Ibid., p. 557.
10   Karl Marx and Frederick Engels: Collected Works, 1st Chinese Edition, Volume 42, p. 90.

With respect to the theories and methods of economics, he wrote: The economic studies did not explain every economic phenomenon with greed and the war amongst the greedy capitalists—competition, this was what the classical economic school did. In contrast, Marx firmly grasped his private property and estranged labour theory, and with their help defined every category of political economy, and considered trade, competition, capital, money as a particular and developed his expression of these first factors.

This shows that it was inevitable for Marx to transit from estrangement to estranged labour when he entered into the analysis of economic base leaving back his superstructure analysis, and thus he had turned to analyzing civil society and criticizing the bourgeois political economy. This is a major turning point that Marx broke away from the perspective of examining labour merely from the quantitative determination, further analyzed the nature of labour in depth and acquired much valuable knowledge of the characteristics of the capitalist mode of production and the confrontation of proletariat with the bourgeoisie. But his theory of estranged labour could not gain a scientific form, for it contained something of Feuerbach's humanism and could not offer a theory and method for the entire political economy. This will be proved later by the development of Marx's thought.

2 MAN IS THE SUBJECT OF COMMUNITY, TRUE SOCIETY AND ESTRANGED SOCIETY

As we have said, the development of the humanism of the western Europe to the French materialism of the 18th century, undoubtedly contained a contradiction: On the one hand, the eighteen century materialism inherited the humanist traditions, emphasized that man was the starting point and destination, and put forward the theory of freedom, equality and fraternity based on man's natural rights, but on the other, it developed mechanism theory in philosophy, denied the subjective status of man, and developed Descartes' view of animals as machines into that theory of man as a machine. A contribution of the German classical philosophy to the theory of estrangement was the restoration of man's subjective status in the idealistic form. Only Marx could solve this question gradually and scientifically.

When discussing estrangement in the *Comments on James Mill, Elements of Political Economy* (*Comments* for short), Marx states that man is the "subject of community", and stresses that the man he refers to is not a concept, not the abstract kind disregarding and ignoring real individuals, but a "real, living, particular entity"[11]. The so-called man separated from this entity does not exist.

According to Marx, this real entity is not alone and isolated, but a "total being", a "species-being" as seen in Feuerbach's terminology. However, although Feuerbach believed that man is a species-being, and the essence of man is contained only in the community and unity of man and man, what he stressed was the needs between the sexes. Here, Marx's consideration of man as "total being" emphasizes the mutual need for the mutual products of labour, i.e. the mutual complementation of human activities and products in the process of production. The production activity is a social activity, as Marx indicated, "*Exchange*, both of human activity within production itself and of *human product* against one another, is equivalent to *species-activity* and species-spirit, the real, conscious and true mode of existence of which is social activity and *social* enjoyment."[12] It is because man is "total being", or species-being that Marx proclaims that "*human* nature is the *true community* of men".

Please note that the emphasis here is on the community of men, not on the natural connection between men, i.e. not on the connection of man as a species. Marx breaks through the limitation of Feuerbach who regards man as a natural species, and the essence of man as the abstraction of the common species-characteristics, and focuses on the community of men. Human beings are a species in form, but are actually isolated individuals seen from man's natural characteristics, while seen from the community of men, although they are seen as individuals, they are a totality in essence, i.e. they are social beings, because no individual can exist outside the community of men. If we can say Marx still stressed man's social quality from the relationship of man to the state in *Critique of Hegel's Philosophy of Right*, now here he began to shift his focus to production, stressing that the essence of man is the community of men in the process of production and exchange.

---

11   Ibid., p. 25.
12   Ibid., p. 24.

Therefore, the true community of men, as Marx said, is not the pure, emotional relationship, nor the ideal connection, but the real, objective relationship. It is formed when people actively manifest their social nature to satisfy their material needs. Marx made it clear that "this *true community* does not come into being through reflection, it appears owing to the *need* and *egoism* of individuals, i.e., it is produced directly by their life activity itself." The so-called egoism and the like were of course inexact words, for here it has nothing to do with morality, but his meaning is quite clear: The community of men comes into being in production, in human activity.

Marx makes a significant progress, compared with Hegel and Feuerbach, by viewing the real individual as subject, emphasizing the creation of the community of men by their production, the social character of man, and that the essence of man is his social nature. Hegel considers absolute idea as the estranged subject. Feuerbach regards man as the estranged subject, but the man Feuerbach refers to is a natural being separated from the given historical conditions and relations of production. From Hegel's absolute idea to Feuerbach's natural man and then to Marx's real man, these are the critical points in the transition from idealism further to the old materialism and then further to historical materialism.

However, that the real man is subject should not be an abstract proposition, but the reproduction of the unity of the specific diversity of the objective historical process in thought. So the scientific level this proposition by Marx could only be determined by his exploration of the laws of history itself and the correct handling of the subject-object relationship in the historical sphere. It was impossible for Marx to reach this height at that time, which was manifested clearly by his view on the relationship between human essence and production.

The theory of Marx, whose thought was in the process of formation, was still not an integrated whole, but contained several contradictions. On the one hand, he highlighted that the essence of man was formed in actively producing products which satisfied human needs, but on the other, he, on the basis of his idea on human essence, concluded that "Our products would be so many mirrors in which we saw reflected our essential nature"[13]. This statement is quite different from his later scientific proposition that the essence of man in reality is "the ensemble of the social relations".

The community of men is objective and necessary. Its existence does not depend on man's will, on which Marx laid a strong emphasis. He wrote: "It does not depend on man whether this community exists or not."[14] But what character this community has, whether it takes the form of estrangement or the form of man, would depend on the degree of the correspondence to human essence.

What is an estranged society? According to Marx's view at that time, "as long as man does not recognize himself as man, and therefore has not organized the world in a human way, this *community* appears in the form of *estrangement*", so the estranged society is one in which man is "estranged from his own nature"[15].

In this estranged society, "it is not man's nature that forms the link between the products we make for one another"[16]. Production has an obviously egoistic and selfish character, and its aim is to possess. I have produced for myself and not for you, just as you have produced for yourself and not for me. The result of my production has no direct connection with you, and vice versa. This is to say, our production is not the production for man as man, i.e. a social man, and each of us sees in his product the objectification of his own selfish need.

The ultimate purpose of production is to meet needs, and the products are to be consumed. Therefore, the product of a producer must be the need of another man and the object of his desire. Although my product is your need and it is the object of your desire, you do not have power over my product. It is not your need, not man's nature but your product that is recognized by my product. Your need, your desire, your will, are powerless as regards my product. Therefore, what we mutually recognize is the power of objects, and not that of human beings. Exchange is the medium for possessing the products of each other. People's connection and relationship take place

13   Karl Marx and Frederick Engels: Collected Works, 1st Chinese Edition, Volume 42, p. 37.
14   Ibid., p. 24.
15   Ibid., p. 24 and p. 29.
16   Ibid., p. 34.

through these objects; the relationship of object to object overrides that of between person to person. You can have an object only if you provide someone an object, which is a principle that cannot be breached. Hence Marx said, "The only intelligible language in which we converse with one another consists of our objects in their relation to each other. Thus we would not understand a human language and it would remain without effect. By one side it would be recognized and felt as being a request, an entreaty, and therefore a *humiliation*, and will be consequently uttered with a feeling of shame, of degradation. By the other side it would be regarded as impudence or lunacy and rejected as such. We are to such an extent estranged from man's essential nature that the direct language of this essential nature seems to us a *violation of human dignity*, whereas the estranged language of material values seems to be the well-justified assertion of human dignity that is self-confident and conscious of itself."[17]

In this way, man is degraded to the level of the instrument and the means of objects. You have to produce your own product in order to take possession of my product, and vice versa. We do not take each other as man, but as the instrument and the means for producing the objects of our mutual needs. In this case, the value of man is depreciated. The value of man is not in man himself, but in our objects, based on which we assess each other: "Our mutual value is for us the *value* of our mutual objects. Hence for us man himself is mutually of no value."[18]

In the estranged society, there is no real relationship of man to man, but that of property owner to property owner. It is the exclusive ownership of private property that both distinguishes between people and makes them enter into relations. It is by giving up his own exclusive object that through which each person can obtain other's exclusive object, hence what connects the two property owners with each other is not man himself, but the specific kind of objects, the private property of their own. At the same time they confirm private ownership, and each alienates a part of his private property to the other. The social connection or social relationship between the two property owners in this society is therefore "that of reciprocity in

17   Ibid., p. 24..
18   Ibid., p. 37.

alienation". Through the alienated private property, what people mutually possess are not the products of their own labour, but the products of others; the product of labour of a person moves away from himself and is possessed by others; and both sides regard each other as the representative of a different kind of private property. The relationship of man to man manifests itself as the estranged form of the relationship of object to object.

Marx contrasts the estranged society with the true society he imagines, and summarizes philosophically the characteristics of the estranged society in his *Comments*: "*man* is estranged from himself and the society of this estranged man are a caricature of his *real community*, of his true species-life, that his activity therefore appears to him as a torment, his own creation as an alien power, his wealth as poverty, the *essential bond* linking him with other men appears as an unessential bond, and separation from his fellow men, on the other hand, as his true mode of existence, his life as a sacrifice of his life, the realization of his nature as making his life unreal, his production as the production of his nullity, his power over an object becomes as the power of the object over him, and he himself, the lord of his creation, becomes as the servant of this creation."[19]

Marx criticizes the bourgeois political economy, just because he believes it affirms the estranged society, and takes everything as a normal phenomenon. For Marx, the community of men and the species-life of man are conceived by the bourgeois political economy in the form of exchange and trade. It seems to them that man is born as a property owner, and society is always a commercial society. For example, Tracy says, "society is a series of mutual exchanges", and Adam Smith says, "Society is a commercial society. Each of its members is a merchant". Hence Marx criticizes them for turning the relation of man to man into that of property owner to property owner, and criticizes them for starting from this relationship and defining "the estranged form of social intercourse as the *essential* and *original* form corresponding to man's nature".

---

19 Karl Marx and Frederick Engels: Collected Works, 1st Chinese Edition, Volume 42, p. 25.

If the estranged society is a society deviating from man's essence, then the true society is a society corresponding to man's essence, a society in which man recognizes himself as man and organizes it in a human way. In this society, the nature of man as a social being will be highly realized. The relationship between people will not be in the estranged form of money, exchange and trade; their mutual products will be no longer the power over himself and the other person involved, and the representative of an equivalent, but will satisfy the needs of man as man. Man's essence will form the link between the products we make for one another. "Human language" replaces "the estranged language of material values".

Marx also generalizes the true society from the philosophical perspective in *Comments* as he does the estranged society. He says, "Let us suppose that we had carried out production as human beings. Each of us would have *in two ways* affirmed himself and the other person. 1) In my *production* I would have objectified my *individuality, its specific character*, and therefore enjoyed not only an individual *manifestation of my life* during the activity, but also when looking at the object I would have the individual pleasure of knowing my personality to be objective, visible to the senses and hence a power *beyond all doubt*. 2) In your enjoyment or use of my product I would have the direct enjoyment both by being conscious of having satisfied a *human* need by my work, that is, by having objectified *man's* essential nature, and by having thus created an object corresponding to the need of another *man's* essential nature. 3) I would have been for you the mediator between you and the species, and therefore would become recognized and felt by you yourself as a completion of your own essential nature and as a necessary part of yourself, and consequently would know myself to be confirmed both in your thought and your life. 4) In the individual expression of my life I would have directly created your expression of your life, and therefore in my individual activity I would have directly *confirmed* and *realized* my true nature, my human nature, my *communal nature*."[20]

Marx's exposition of the true society and the estranged society contains many profound thoughts, for example, his views that estrangement is temporary and historical, that the relationship of man to man

20   Ibid., p. 37.

is manifested as that of object to object under private property, that the purpose of production is to satisfy needs in the true society, etc. which is in fact his ingenious conjecture of the opposition between the two social systems—the capitalist society and the communist society, which was expressed in undefined and unclear philosophical expressions. But it was not completely scientific, but clearly bears the stamp of Feuerbach's humanism, when evaluated from the basis and method of his argumentation. At that time, Marx did not know that it was not the essence of man that was objectified into the social relationship, but instead, it was the social relationship of men that formed the essence of man. Because the productive forces of each historical era, the social relationship conceived as estranged from or instead corresponding to the essence of man has their reasonable basis for their emergence and existence. The use of man's essence as the measure to distinguish the estranged society from the true society could not explain society in a scientific way, and was prone to become a moral condemnation.

3 ESTRANGEMENT IN "LABOUR TO EARN A LIVING" COMMENTS ON MONEY AND CREDIT

Marx preliminarily discusses the question of estranged labour in his Comments. Although people at home and abroad have different views on the order of the writing time of Comments and the First Manuscript of *Economic and Philosophical Manuscripts of 1844* (Manuscripts for short), in terms of their contents, Comments mainly analyzes the labour of general commodity production (i.e. the labour to earn a living), especially the estrangement of labour which appears after the transition from natural economy into commodity production economy, in which the relationship of labour to capital was analysed after the general commodity production had developed into the capitalist production, but it was not a focus. If we compare *Manuscripts* elaborates the estranged labour with the focus on the proletariat and the bourgeoisie. From the historical and logical perspective, *Comments* and *Manuscripts* are interconnected, the former being the preparation for the latter in theory and their material.

In *Comments*, in many places Marx repeats Mill's views, but he incorporates them into the theory of estranged labour, and sees the estrangement of labour as a historical process, developing gradually with the production and exchange of commodities.

According to Marx, under the barbaric, savage conditions, the amount of man's production was determined by the extent of his immediate need, i.e. to produce the object which directly satisfies his need. Man produces no more than he immediately requires; the limit of his need forms the limits of his production. This view of Marx is not complete. In fact, it is not the amount of need that determined the amount of production, but production in the first place determines the need. The poor need is obviously resulted from the backward production, though need inevitably reacts upon production. What matters here is not how to dialectically analyze the relationship of production to need, but that Marx uses the view of estrangement to discuss this question and argues that when demand and supply exactly coincide, the immediate purpose of production is one's need, and no exchange between products takes place, and therefore these is no estrangement, i.e. no such a phenomenon as the product of labour is separated from the labourer.

Things begin to change when there is surplus production. In "the crude form of alienated private property", i.e. in accidental barter, labour is the labourer's immediate source of subsistence, the active manifestation of his individual existence, but at the same the labourer exchanges with the other men the surplus of his production. Through this exchange process, labour therefore has become partly a source of income, and thus the purpose and nature of labour begin to change. The product of labour is no longer to meet the personal need of the producer alone, but is "produced as *value*, as *exchange-value*, as an *equivalent*"[21]. The surplus production is in appearance produced for each other's needs, but in the actual fact each possesses the other's product and tries to possess more with his surplus product.

---

21   Ibid., p. 28.

Marx sees exchange as a social connection, a social relationship, which, according to him, is not the relationship of men as man, but a relationship of private property to private property, as the reciprocal alienation of private property. The mutual complementation, the satisfaction of the mutual needs presented by exchange is a mere semblance, and is mutual plundering and mutual deception in essence. Therefore, Marx emphasizes that the social connection manifested by barter is opposed to the true social relationship of men. He said, "*Exchange* or *barter* is the social act, the species-act, the community, the social intercourse and integration of men with *private ownership*, and therefore the external, *alienated species-act*. It is just for this reason that it appears as *barter*. For this reason, likewise, it is the opposite of the social relationship."[22]

If estrangement is only partial in the mutual exchange of surplus products, the labour of man becomes the estranged labour in the labour realized to earn a living.

The so-called labour to earn a living is not to directly satisfy one's need, and nor used for the accidental exchange of surplus production, but it is the productive labour aimed at exchange. This actually refers to the commodity production. Historically it was inevitable to change from the accidental exchange into the labour to earn a living. The needs of individuals are diverse, whereas the activity of the producer is one-sided, and it is impossible for an individual to produce everything he needs, thus the labour of man inevitably becomes more and more, a labour to earn a living, namely, to acquire the means of subsistence by means of selling his product. What Marx started with in his study was mainly the estrangement in this kind of labour.

He said, "*Labour to earn a living* involves: 1) estrangement and fortuitous connection between labour and the subject who labours; 2) estrangement and fortuitous connection between labour and the object of labour; 3) that the worker's role is determined by social needs which, however, are alien to him and a compulsion to which he submits by the motivation of egoistic need and necessity, and which have for him only the significance of a means of satisfying his dire need, just as for them he exists only as a slave of their needs; 4) that to the

22   Ibid., p. 27.

worker the maintenance of his individual existence appears to be the *purpose* of his activity and what he actually does is regarded by him only as a means; that he carries on his life's activity in order to earn means of *subsistence*."[23] These four aspects Marx analyzed here are related to and different from the four aspects of estranged labour he theorized in *Manuscripts*. They are consistent in the view on labour, seen from their basic standpoints. Labour is man's *"free manifestation of life"*, man's *"true, active property"*, *"enjoyment of life"*, etc.. While the labour to earn a living is an estrangement, because it is not the realization of the labourer's natural abilities and spiritual aims, but it is for survival, it is for the acquisition of means of subsistence. It is motivated by the inner necessity (the nature of love for labour), but motivated by the external, fortuitous need (survival). This labour for the labourer is therefore not a self-"enjoyment", but a *"torment"*. These ideas were later developed further in *Manuscripts*. The difference is that Marx's exposition of the estrangement of the labour to earn a living focuses on analyzing the opposition between individual and society which results from the production and exchange of commodities: An individual becomes a slave of the social needs: What kind of labour the labourer chooses, what kind of products he produces depend on the social needs, instead of manifesting the natural abilities or hobby of the labourer. The social needs become the means of individual survival. But Marx's analysis of estranged labour in *Manuscripts* focuses on uncovering the confrontation between the proletarian and the bourgeois, and also on the bourgeois' possession of the labour and products of the proletarian.

Marx's these expositions on the estrangement in the labour to earn a living is clearly influenced by Feuerbach's humanism, for the social connection formed by the production and exchange of commodities is opposed to the essence of man. But its positive significance is that Marx investigates the development of economy from the view point of dialectics, describes the development process from natural economy→ further to general commodity production→ then further to capitalist commodity production, and takes the estrangement in the economic sphere as a historical phenomenon, which develops gradually with commodity production and exchange based on private

---

23   Ibid., p.p. 28-29.

property. This was actually an attempt to explore the deeper origin of estranged labour.

The theory of estranged labour was a basic theory and approach for Marx to study economics at that time. His analysis of money and credit in *Comments* is characterized by this philosophical feature.

Marx appreciates Mill's view on money as the medium of exchange, and asserts that Mill had "very well expresses the essence of the matter in form of a concept". However, Marx does not content himself with this point, and derives his estrangement ideas from money being the medium of exchange. He argues that the essence of money is not, in the first place, that property is alienated in it; it is but the product of the mediator. With money being the medium, the labour and product of man is not to satisfy the mutual needs, but aims to obtain money, and the human, social act (production) becomes the attribute of money. Money has power over man's will, activity and on his relation to other men, and money becomes the real God, and man is reduced to the status of slavery. Hence Marx said that "the complete domination of the estranged thing over man has become evident" in money.

The basic viewpoint which Marx expresses in the passage about money in *Manuscripts* is consistent with this view, but is more openly elaborated. He analyzes estrangement from the aspect of the function of money. At that time Marx had not studied comprehensively the various functions of money yet, so he focused only on one function, i.e. money as the means of circulation. Money has the property of purchasing everything, the property of appropriating all objects. With money, my wish, my need can turn from the thing of imagination into the thing of reality; without money, even if you have the need, it becomes unreal and unrealizable. The demand based on money is an effective demand, while the demand based on human nature is an ineffective demand. Only money can be the "procurer" between man's need and the object, between his life and his means of life. In this way, money, which appears initially as a means (the means of circulation), turns into a purpose—the purpose of life, and the pursuit of money becomes the aim of life. Anything except aiming for money has a limit. Limitlessness is the measure of money, and infinite quantity is the quantity of money.

This universal property of buying by money distorts the human and natural qualities. It can transform beauty into ugliness, ugliness into beauty, enemy into friend, friend into enemy, fidelity into infidelity, infidelity into fidelity, love into hate, hate into love, virtue into vice, vice into virtue, servant into master, master into servant, idiocy into intelligence, and intelligence into idiocy. Consequently, Marx remarked that "money, as the existing and active concept of value, confounds and confuses all things, money is the general confounding and confusing of all things—the world upside-down—the *confounding* and *confusing* of all natural and human qualities."[24]

Marx proceeds from the analysis of money to that of credit. If the mediating function of money makes man estranged, the emergence of credit appears to abolish this estrangement and appears to make man have once more human, more trustful relations to man. But Marx pointed out that "this abolition of estrangement, this *return* of man to himself and therefore to other men is only an appearance", and credit actually not only does not abolish the estrangement, but also is "the infamous and extreme self-estrangement"[25]

That a rich man gives credit to a poor is very rare. If any, it does not show the trust between people, because the life of the poor man and his talents and activity serve the rich man as a guarantee of the repayment of the money credited. Hence the death of the poor man is the worst possibility for the creditor, for it causes creditor to lose his capital and also the interest. This indicates that in this credit relationship the rich man estimates the value of the poor man in money instead of looking from the angle of human beings. Likewise, the reason why a rich man gives credit to a rich man is not that the latter is man, but that the latter is a rich man, a representative of some kind of wealth. So, credit here serves as a medium facilitating exchange, that is, now money itself is raised to a completely ideal form.

Thus it can be seen that for Marx in credit, money is not removed, but man himself is turned into money, and has become the mediator of exchange in place of metal or paper. In form, credit returns the medium of exchange from its material form to man, however, not to man as man, but as a man of existence as capital and interest. So, in

24   Ibid., p. 155.
25   Ibid., p. 21.

credit, "Instead of money, or paper, it is my own personal existence, my flesh and blood, my social virtue and importance, which constitutes the material, corporeal form of the spirit of money. Credit no longer resolves the value of money into money but into human flesh and into the human heart"[26]. For this reason, to counterfeit money requires material, while to obtain credit by cheating only needs one's own person, and man makes himself into "counterfeit coin".

Looking from the perspective of economics, Marx presented quite a few profound ideas in his analysis of money and credit. He studied the relationship of private property, exchange and money, discussed the inevitability of money to be produced under private property circumstances and considers the relationship of money to value, pointing out that money "is the real existence of value as value". Marx also criticized the monetarism school and the view of money of the bourgeois classical political economy, and held that the former was the "crude superstition" on money, while the latter was the "refined superstition". He analyzed the role of credit in deepening the antithesis between capitalist and worker, between big and small capitalists, etc. However, because he regarded money and credit as the estrangement of man's essence, Marx was inclined to give a negative evaluation instead of focusing on revealing the progressive role of development of commodity production, and also exchange, money and credit in human society, which shows the limitations of his using estrangement as a theory and method to analyze economic phenomena.

---

26   Ibid., p. 23.

CHAPTER V

ELABORATION OF THE THEORY OF ESTRANGED LABOUR

ESTRANGEMENT IN WAGE LABOUR

Marx comprehensively expounds the theory of estranged labour in *Manuscripts of 1844*, in which the question of estranged labour was discussed directly or indirectly from wage of labour, profit and rent also in his *First Manuscript* and also through his "the critique of the Hegelian dialects and philosophy" as a whole in his *Third Manuscript*. But his discussion in the section titled "Estranged Labour" was different which we will discuss this part specifically. Therefore, it is fair to say that the theory of estranged labour was the basic theory and method for Marx to analyze social problems and economic phenomena at that time.

However, compared with his *Comments on James Mill, Elements of Political Economy*, *Manuscripts* have such a significant characteristic that the labour which was analyzed there is no longer the general commodity production, but rather the wage labour; the opposition between the proletariat and the bourgeoisie (between capital and labour) under capitalism is the core of his analysis of estranged labour. In

Manuscripts (1844), it is after the analysis of wages of labour, profit and rent that Marx discusses intensively every aspect of estranged labour, and preliminarily uncovers the nature of this labour and the confrontations involved in it. He attempts to seek in labour itself the cause for the "dehumanization" of the proletariat under capitalism.

1 ROOT OF THE MISERY OF THE PROLETARIAT: EMPLOYMENT NATURE OF LABOUR

With the emergence and domination of the capitalist mode of production, the rapid development of production brings about a working class in extreme misery instead of general opulence. Soaring buildings are accompanied by slums, forming two worlds in one state. The condition of the working class is the acutest and most barefaced representation of all suffering in the capitalist society, and draws the attention of all kinds of socialists, and that of Marx and Engels in particular.

Engels focused on the actual investigation. Since his arrival in England from Germany in November, 1842, Engels spent twenty-one months on site observation and personal intercourse, and collected the complete materials which were confirmed by the official investigations for his in-depth study of the condition of the proletariat in England. In Engels' words, "What I have seen, heard and read has been worked up in the present book"—*The Condition of the Working-Class in England*[1]. In contrast, Marx mainly concentrated on philosophical reflections at the beginning. He used a very philosophical expression as "the *complete* loss of man" to describe the condition of the proletariat in Germany in *Critique of Hegel's Philosophy of Right*. And at the outset of his shift from philosophy to economic studies, "the complete loss of man" was still the base principle for him to examine the condition and status of the proletariat, but he strove to explain this question by utilizing the theories and facts provided by the bourgeois political economy, the materials offered by economics.

The bourgeois political economy concentrated its efforts on proving the superiority of the capitalist private property to the feudal property, ignoring the various negative consequences, the misery and poorly conditions of the proletariat under the capitalist system.

1　Karl Marx and Frederick Engels: Collected Works, 1st Chinese Edition, Volume 2, p. 278.

It regarded the impoverished life of the proletariat as the necessary and reasonable condition for advancing the national wealth, and thus explains the miserable condition of the proletariat from the interest aspect of the bourgeoisie. Therefore, it only emphasized the positive aspects of labour but obliterates its negative aspects to conceal the damages to the workers done by the capitalist factory system. Marx takes a different attitude. While affirming the positive effects of labour, he advances the theory of estranged labour, and focuses himself to reveal the status and condition of the proletariat under the capitalist system to seek explanation for its dehumanization. Hence the theory of estranged labour in *Manuscripts* (1844) is closely related to his endeavour to understand the nature of labour under capitalism, the situation and prospects of the proletariat.

Under the capitalist system, labour is separated from capital and landed property, which indicates the situation of labourers: they have neither capital nor rent of land, and live only by labour, to be exact, by their one-sided labour, which was splitted by the division of labour. The entire bourgeois political economy starts with this separation, and considers that capital produces profit, land produces rent, and labour produces wages, hence concealing the estranged nature of labour and distorting the origin of profit and land rent. Since Marx did not formulate the theory of surplus value then, Marx did not specify that both profit and rent of land came from the labour of the workers, and that living labour creates not only wages but also profit, interest and rent of land. But he did saw that the separation of capital, rent and labour was fatal for the workers. This separation puts the workers into such a position as being completely dependent on capital and landed property, and only by selling themselves can they realize the temporary combination (union) of labour with the means of production (with capital and landed property). Therefore, under the capitalist conditions, the worker is always a commodity, and "the worker's existence is thus brought under the same condition as the existence of every other commodity", and falls completely under the law of supply and demand. The existence of the worker depends on the social needs, which, in turn, depends on the movement of capital and landed property. Should the supply of the workers greatly exceed demand, a section of the workers degrades into beggary or starvation. So the worker needs to fight for material means of life as well as for a job, i.e. for the possibility and means of realizing his labour.

Just because labourers are commodities and because of the function of the economic laws as such, the workers can never shake off misery under the capitalist system. This is an important conclusion Marx arrives, when analyzing the condition of the workers in different periods of the development of the capitalist production.

Adam Smith does not deny that: when the wealth of society declines the worker suffers most of all, "*no one suffers so cruelly from its decline as the working class*". The decrease of social needs will cause the mass unemployment of workers and the falling wages, while the prosperity of society and the continuous increase in wealth will keep raising the wages of workers and improve their condition. According to this view, the misery of the workers is not determined by their social status and the nature of labour, but by the level of production development. The more developed the capitalist production is, the richer the worker would become. In this way, the interests of the proletariat become identical to those of the bourgeoisie.

This argument is rebutted by Marx, who takes the side of the proletariat. He argues that the demand for workers will exceed their supply in a society in which wealth is increasing, and thus is conducive to the raising of wages, but the raising of wages will give rise to over-time work among the workers. The more they wish to earn, the more they sacrifice themselves, completely losing all their freedom, in the service of greed. Thereby they shorten their lives. And the advance of the wealth of society means that the accumulation of capital expands, that the products of the worker are increasingly concentrated in the hands of the capitalist, and that the worker increasingly will depend on capital. Hence even in the condition of society which is most favourable to the worker, the inevitable result of the worker is premature early death due to overwork, decline to a mere machine, a bond as servant of the capital. Therefore, the impoverishment is the inescapable fate of the worker, just as Marx said, "in a declining state of society—increasing misery of the worker; in an advancing state—misery with complications; and in a fully developed state of society—there will be the static misery."[2]

---

2   Karl Marx and Frederick Engels: Collected Works, 1st Ch. Ed., Volume 42, p. 53.

Marx also quoted some arguments and statistical data to prove his view on the situation of the working class from Wilhelm Schulz's *The Movement of Production*, Charles Loudon's *Solution to the Problem of the Population and Livelihood*, Eugene Buret's *On the Misery of the Working Class in England and in France* and Pecqueur's *New Theory of Social and Political Economy or Studies of the Organization of the Societies*.

Why is the worker impoverished and dehumanized inevitably under the capitalist system? Why can the increase of the wealth of society not change the situation of the worker? Marx proceeds from here to the analysis of the nature of labour, pointing out that "when society is in a state of progress, the ruin and impoverishment of the worker is the product of his labour and of the wealth produced by him. The misery results, therefore, from the *essence* of present-day labour itself."[3] The so-called essence of present-day labour is the wage labour system of capitalism. However, Marx does not use this purely economic concept in his *Manuscripts of 1844* instead he uses a more philosophical concept—estranged labour, that is, it is estranged labour that makes the worker produce wealth for others, but misery for himself.

Starting with the condition of the proletariat under capitalism, Marx proceeds to analyze the nature of labour, and then further proceeds to expound the condition of the proletariat, closely combining the investigation of labour with that of the labourer. In analyzing the characteristics of classes in civil society in *Critique of Hegel's Philosophy of Right*, Marx had stated that "the lack of property, and the class in need of immediate labour, of concrete labour, forms less a class of civil society than the basis upon which the spheres of civil society rest and move."[4] This argument of immediate labour as the essential character of the labourer class is fully expressed in *Manuscripts of 1844*. The more deeply Marx analyzes the labourer's condition, the more he reveals the detestable, coerced character of labour and exposes the forced character of labour under capitalism and the situation and the status of the proletariat. And based on this, he criticizes sharply the separation of labour from the labourer by the bourgeois

---

3   Ibid., p.55-56.
4   Karl Marx and Frederick Engels: Collected Works, 1st Chinese Edition, Volume 1, p. 345.

political economy theory. It only studies labour, and does not study the labourer nor care his situation; it praises labour but depreciates the labourer and regards him as an instrument of production. Marx pointed out: "[i]t does not consider him when he is not working, as a human being; but leaves such consideration to criminal law, to doctors, to religion, to the statistical tables, to politics and to the poors-house overseer." He also says: "Political economy does not recognize the unemployed worker, the working man, insofar as he happens to be outside this labour relationship. The rascal, swindler, beggar, the unemployed, the starving, wretched and criminal work-ingman—there are *figures* who do not exist for *political economy* but only for other eyes, those of the doctor, the judge, the grave-digger, and bum-bailiff, etc.; such figures are spectres outside its domain."[5] His shift from labour to the labourer, this not only shows the distinct class nature of Marx's political economy, but also offers an approach to exploring the labourer's situation in labour, which, although immature in the beginning, it foretells a clue to understand history in labour.

2 FREE AND CONSCIOUS ACTIVITY: MAN'S SPECIES-ESSENCE

TRUE LABOUR AND ESTRANGED LABOUR

Marx's idea of estranged labour was the result of his shift to eco-nomic studies and the product of his integration of the speculative philosophy of the German classical philosophy with his own eco-nomic studies. His idea of estranged labour was different from the speculative theory of estrangement of Hegel and Feuerbach, but still retained then the characteristics of the estrangement theory of the German classical philosophy, i.e. to expound estrangement from the perspective of the essence of subject in opposition to man in inhu-manly conditions.

This estrangement theory was closely linked with the question of the subject-object relationship. Estrangement involves the question of subject, that is, what is estranged? And the question of object, that is, estranged into what? Estrangement can be divided as: The

5   Karl Marx and Frederick Engels: Collected Works, 1st Chinese Edition, Volume 42, p. 56, p. 105.

estrangement theory of spirit, the humanistic estrangement theory and estrangement theory of labour in terms of its subject, while a philosopher's attitude to and understanding of society can be judged based on its object, its manifestation and product. From Hegel to Feuerbach, they all connected the question of estrangement with the relationship of subject to object. Hegel's exposition of estrangement in the *Phenomenology of Spirit* is an elaboration of the speculative movement of how subject is alienated from object, and how the object, then, is superseded and returned into the subject. Feuerbach's uncovering of religious estrangement in *The Essence of Christianity* is fundamentally an exposition of how the subject objectifies its essence as God. Marx objected to turn estrangement into the abstract subject-object relationship, yet he also discussed estrangement from the angle of their relationship before his theory of estranged labour was advanced by him to the materialist conception of history. He made clear that "he [man] duplicates himself not only, as in consciousness, intellectually, but also actively, in reality, and therefore he sees himself in a world which he has created."[6] Therefore, each theory of estrangement had its own theory of subject and also its essence. The evolution of the idea of estrangement from Hegel through Feuerbach and then to Marx is prominently manifested in the change of the understanding of the subject of estrangement and the essence of man.

The estrangement theory of Hegel is an objective, idealistic estrangement theory of spirit, which is mainly represented by his consideration of absolute idea as the subject of estrangement. According to Hegel, substance is the subject. Absolute idea is the substance which is independent of any human thinking and is self-subsistent, but it is also subject, the solely active, creative force. The object is passive and negative, and is only used to confirm subject. Hence the whole process of estrangement and its supersession is the incessant revolving of absolute idea from its self-objectification to its return into itself. Absolute idea is the bearer and the subject of the whole process.

Based on this view, Hegel takes self-consciousness as the essence of man, as Marx said, "For Hegel the *human being—man*—equals *self-consciousness*. All estrangement of the human being is therefore

---

6 Ibid., p. 97.

nothing but estrangement of self-consciousness."[7] It is because Hegel sees self-consciousness as the essence of man that all confused reality of mankind is conceived as the specific form of self-consciousness, as the determination of self-consciousness, the real, objective expression of estrangement in the society with private property being dissolved into self-consciousness.

In fact, there is no absolute dividing line between human consciousness and self-consciousness, which are not two different kinds of consciousness. When the subject sees the external things as objects, this understanding is called consciousness, i.e. the consciousness of objects outside itself; when the subject sees the self as the object, this understanding is self-consciousness. So in the final analysis, self-consciousness, at its essence, is consciousness, nothing but the consciousness of being conscious of itself. The animals in general are not active, not conscious subjects. They have some mental activities or phenomena of consciousness, but no self-consciousness. Self-consciousness, in this aspect, is indeed a characteristic of man, but it is not the essence of man, nor the essential attribute which makes man into man and differentiates man from other animals. It is based on this view that Marx criticizes Hegel, saying that with him, "[t]he estrangement of self-consciousness is not regarded as an *expression*—reflected in the realm of knowledge and thought—of the *real* estrangement of the human beings. Instead, the actual estrangement—that which appears real—is according to its *innermost*, hidden nature (which is only brought to light by philosophy) nothing but the *manifestation* of the estrangement of the real human essence, of *self-consciousness*."

Feuerbach's humanistic estrangement theory has its own unique view on subject and the essence of man. Contrary to Hegel, Feuerbach considers man—the sensuous being, rather than self-consciousness, as the subject, and argues that self-consciousness cannot be separated from man and it is human self-consciousness, and proposes the proposition of "subject is man". This reverses the reversed Hegelian philosophy, but Feuerbach's theory of estrangement remains to be a theory about the estrangement and also return of human essence. For Feuerbach, man is the unity of the individual with the species. Any

---

7   Ibid., p. 165.

real individual is a physical, empirical and sensuous being as well as a species-being, because no individual can exist alone and independently, and they need each other. The species-essence connecting many individuals is the abstraction of the common, natural attributes inherent in each individual. Therefore, the species of Feuerbach is not society, and the species-essence is not the social essence of man, but man's natural essence. That the so-called essence of gods is the estrangement of human essence refers exactly to the self-splitting of man as subject, that is, his essence is objectified as a spiritual entity independent of man. Just because the man seen by Feuerbach is a pure, sensuous being, torn and separated from the given historical conditions, he is the abstract man, and the species-essence seen by him is an abstract essence. The estrangement theory based on this man and his essence is still idealistic evaluated from the perspective of the conception of history.

Marx's theory of estranged labour changes greatly in the views of both: On the subject and on the essence of man.

Marx concentrates on seeking the estranged, real subject in *Manuscripts* (1844), and he summarizes the history of economic theories from this point of view. Although Marx took a negative attitude towards the British classical economists' labour theory of value at that time, he saw its abstract philosophical significance, namely, the transfer of the subjective essence of wealth into labour, in the labour theory of value which was started by the physiocratic school and was completed by Ricardo. For Marx monetarism school and the mercantile school which look upon private property merely as a thing, as an objective substance, were fetishism, and in fact, "[t]he *subjective essence* of private property—*private property* as activity for itself, as *subject*, as *person*—is *labour*"[8]. However, the British classical economists did not really discover the subject, and they separated labour from the labourer and they only studied the labour.

For Marx, the British classical economists paid attention to labour but were hostile to man; Feuerbach discovered man but did not understand labour; Hegel grasped labour as the essence of man, but he understood it as abstract mental labour, i.e. the activity of

---

8   Ibid., p. 112.

philosophical thinking. Marx is different from all of them. The subject of his estrangement theory in *Manuscripts* is neither Hegel's absolute idea and Feuerbach's natural man, nor the labour in general in pure economic form, but the concrete person, namely, the labourer engaged in the production of material goods. Marx detects estrangement in the labour of this nature, and labour in estrangement and the subject—the labourer engaged in estranged labour.

Marx recognizes the labourer engaged in material production as the subject, but as long as estrangement remains his basic theory and method, its elaboration is bound to start with the quest for the essence of the subject. And Marx did not abandon this tradition completely at that time. Taking the essence of man as the medium, Marx discussed the essence of man in terms of the mode of activity, which distinguishes man from animals, and then this man is contrasted with the wage labour under the capitalist system, hence he set true labour and estranged labour in opposition.

Man was investigated by Marx as a "species" then, with the focus on revealing its "species"-character, i.e. species-essence. He believed that "[t]his whole character of a species, its species-character, is contained in the character of its life activity"[9]. The mode of human life activity differs from that of other animals. The animal is immediately one with its life activity, and its whole character is manifested in its life activity. The animal does not distinguish itself from its life activity. But man is different. His mode of life activity is a conscious activity instead of an unconscious and instinctual activity. Man makes his life activity itself, the object of his will and the object of his consciousness. That is to say, human activity is conscious and is governed by his consciousness. Hence Marx said, the "free, conscious activity is man's species-character."[10] The concentrated expression of this free, conscious activity is labour, which, by its very nature, should be free and conscious.

Marx's theory of estranged labour does not cast off the speculative tradition which analyzes estrangement from the perspective of the essence of subject, and it views the capitalist wage labour as estranged labour which confronts the essence of man, but his theory

---

9   Ibid., p. 96.
10 Ibid.

was based on the economic facts, rather than on the pure, logical deduction. Marx said repeatedly that he had "proceed[ed] from an actual economic fact", and his results "have been attained by means of a wholly empirical analysis based on conscientious critical study of political economy"[11]. Therefore, Marx considers the logical analysis of estranged labour inseparable from the analysis of economic facts. He said, "We took our departure from a fact of political economy—the estrangement of the worker and his production. We have formulated this fact in conceptual terms as *estranged, alienated* labour. We have analyzed this concept—hence analyzed merely a fact of political economy."[12]

What kinds of economic facts had enabled Marx to draw the conclusion of estranged labour? He analyzed the relationship of the worker to his products, the relationship to his labour and the relationship to the capitalist under the capitalist system.

The relationship of the worker to his products is the most immediate, visible objective fact. In the capitalist society, the labourer produces products, but cannot possess them. Instead, the more wealth the worker produces, the greater the power and the greater quantity of his products become, and the poorer he becomes. The more commodities the worker produces, the more he becomes a cheaper commodity. Marx indicated very indignantly that "the more the worker produces, the less he has to consume; the more values he creates, the more valueless, the more unworthy he becomes; the better formed his product, the more deformed becomes the worker; the more civilized his object, the more barbarous becomes the worker; the more powerful labour becomes, the more powerless becomes the worker; the more ingenious labour becomes, the less ingenious becomes the worker and the more he comes nature's slave."[13]

Marx found that the worker was related to the product of his labour as being related to an alien object, just as man is related to gods in religion. In religion, the more man puts into God, the less he retains in himself. The same is true of the relationship between the worker and the product in capitalist wage labour process. The more products

---

11   Ibid., p. 90, p. 45.
12   Ibid., p. 98.
13   Ibid., p. 92-93.

he makes, the more powerful becomes the alien world of objects which he creates over himself and against himself, the poorer his inner world becomes, and the less belongs to him as his own. This fact shows that the object which the labourer produces—labour's product—confronts the labourer—the subject of production as something alien, becomes as a power independent of the producer.

However, Marx discovered that the relationship between the product of labour and the labourer involved such two different aspects: Objectification and estrangement. Any product in the world is created by labour, and thus is labour which has been embodied in an object, which has become material. The realization of labour is objectification, which is the common characteristic of all societies with material production. All societies with material production are unimaginable without the objectified labour. But objectification does not necessarily result in estrangement. The capitalist private property is what links objectification and estrangement together. Under the condition of private property, objectification and estrangement are not two unrelated processes but two aspects of the same process (two aspects of the process of production). The labour's objectification not only means that the labourer creates the product, creates the external existence one after another, but also that he creates an alien power on its own which confronts him, which is estrangement. Marx put particular emphasis on this conditionality. Only "[u]nder these economic conditions", i.e. on the premise of private ownership, "this realization of labour appears as loss of realization for the worker; objectification as loss of the object and the bondage to it; appropriation as estrangement, as alienation"[14]. So objectification differs from estrangement, and it is estranged only under certain conditions. With the highly developed productive forces, with the advances of science and technology, the evils of the advanced western capitalist countries are exposed to a higher degree. The root cause for the unemployment of the workers and the loss of social morality lies not in objectification, i.e. not in the development of production, but in the private property itself.

---

14   Ibid., p. 91.

Marx proceeded from the estrangement of the product, i.e., the relationship of the labour's product to the labourer, and then to the study of the estrangement of labour—the relationship between labour and the labourer. According to Marx, estrangement under capitalism is manifested not only in the end result, in the products of labour, but also in the act of production, in the producing activity. The product is the result of life. The estrangement of labour's products is nothing but the summary of the estrangement of labour itself. If the worker were not estranging him from himself in the act of production, there would be no estrangement of labour's products from the labourer. In this way, Marx shifted from analyzing the external relation of labour's products to the labourer further to analyze the subject itself—the relationship of the labourer to his labour.

Seen from the perspective of the subject, labour is originally the essence of man, the expression of freedom of the will and creativity which is unique to man. But in wage labour, labour is external to the worker, and it does not belong to his intrinsic nature. His labour is not voluntary, but coerced, forced labour. This is a labour of self-sacrifice, of mortification. Therefore, in his work the labourer does not feel content but unhappy, does not develop freely his physical and mental energy, and ruins his body. The labourer feels a sense of relief when he is not working, and when he is working he feels extremely uneasy and unhappy.

The wage labour under capitalism is, in its form, a "free labour". The bourgeois does not force the worker to work by political coercion or a cudgel; concerning the relationship of the worker to the capitalist, there is no personal bondage, like the slave or serf who belongs to a master. But in fact, the wage labour is unfree labour; it is not direct, political coercion, but indirect, economic coercion, not the cudgel discipline but contains the hunger discipline. Although the worker does not belong to a capitalist, he belongs to the whole bourgeoisie. The worker's labour is therefore not the satisfaction of the nature of loving work, but only satisfies other needs external to labour, i.e. as a means of survival. As soon as no physical or other compulsion exists, labour is shunned like the plague. As a result, man only feel himself freely active in realizing his animal functions—eating, drinking, propagating; and in realizing his human function, i.e. the

function of labour which no animal has, he feels himself to be nothing but an animal. So Marx argued that a reversal occurred due to the
estrangement of labour: "animal becomes human and what is human
becomes animal."[15]

Since Marx considers the labourer as the subject, he calls the estrangement of labour from the labourer as self-estrangement, because what is discussed here is the relation of the worker to his
own activity. Here, what is estranged is the subject itself, instead
of something external to it: "the worker's own physical and mental energy, his personal life as an activity which is turned against
him, independent of him and not belonging to him."[16] The relation of labour's product to the worker is "the estrangement of the
thing", and is the relationship of the worker to his products and to
the object of his production, rather than to the act of production.
Marx puts "self-estrangement" in an important position. He had proposed that "[s]elling [*Veräußerung*] is the practical aspect of alienation [*Entäußerung*]" in his writing *On the Jewish Question*, which
he referred to religion and money at that time; and afterwards he
continued to develop this view in *Manuscripts* (1844) arguing that
the estrangement of the thing was realization of self-estrangement.
Without the estrangement of labour from the labourer, there would
be no estrangement of labour's products from the labourer; the estrangement of the thing in which the products of labour exercises
power over the labourer, results from the self-estrangement of the
worker in the process of production.

Marx notices that the question of estrangement is not just the question of the relationship of man to the thing (the estrangement of
products), nor simply the question of self-estrangement (the estrangement of labour). An isolated individual does not make much
of estrangement. The question of estrangement cannot be separated from the relationship of man to man, because in society "[t]he
estrangement of man, and in fact every relationship in which man
[stands] to himself, is realized and expressed only in the relationship
in which a man stands to other men"[17]. Therefore, both the estrange-

---

15   Ibid., p. 94.
16   Ibid., p. 95.
17   Ibid., p. 98.

ment of the thing and self-estrangement cannot be separated from the estrangement of man from man.

It speaks for itself. If the product of labour is alien to the labourer, if it is an alien power over the labourer, to whom, then, does the product of labour belong? If the activity of the labourer himself does not belong to him, but is an alien, coerced activity, who, then, forces him? Marx answered them in a very profound way: "If the product of labour does not belong to the worker, if it confronts him as an alien power, then this can only be because it belongs to some *other man than the worker*. If the worker's activity is a torment to him, to another it must give *satisfaction* and pleasure. Not the gods, not the nature, but only man himself can be this alien power over man."[18] Hence the power of the thing over man, the power of the worker's own labour over himself is, in the final analysis, the power of man over man. In this way, by starting from the fact that the immediate product visible to the naked eye does not belong to the worker, Marx further proceeded to analyze the subject itself in the process of production—the relationship of the labourer to his labour, and then to uncovering the estrangement of man from man, i.e. the exploitive relationship in which the bourgeois appropriates for free the surplus product and surplus labour of the labourer.

It is an objective fact that the products and labour of the worker do not belong to him but instead appropriated by the bourgeois under the capitalist system. But Marx was not satisfied with the mere description of these facts, and he wanted to clarify them. He, who was still under the influence of Feuerbach's humanism, took "the essence of man" as the medium, and used the theory of the estrangement of human essence to explain them. He advanced the proposition that "man's species-nature is estranged from him", which is seen as the summary of the estrangement of the thing and self-estrangement and which was as well as the intermediate link in the transition to the estrangement of man from man.

Of course, Marx's view on "species", "species-nature" differs from that of Feuerbach in his *Manuscripts* (1844). Marx regards the free, conscious activity as the species-nature of man, and production as

---

18   Ibid., p. 99.

the active, species-life of man, and the creation of a world of objects by his personal activity and his work upon nature as a proof of man as a conscious species-being. But his standpoint at that time was the difference between men and animals, so he had focused on revealing the opposition between human production and the so-called animal production: "animals also produce. They build themselves nests, dwellings, like the bees, beavers, ants, etc. But an animal only produces what it immediately needs for itself or its young. It produces one-sidedly, while man produces universally. It produces only under the domination of immediate physical need, while man produces even when he is free from physical need and only truly produces in freedom therefrom. An animal produces only itself, while man reproduces the whole of nature. An animal's product belongs immediately to its physical body, while man freely confronts his product. An animal forms only in accordance with the standard and the need of the species to which it belongs, while man knows how to produce in accordance with the standard of every species, and knows how to apply everywhere the inherent standard to the object. Man therefore also forms objects in accordance with the laws of beauty."[19] This discourse undoubtedly contains profound ideas, but it overlooks the most basic function of labour, considers labour as the internal need which is free from the restriction of the physical need, as the self-realized, self-created, free and conscious activity, and takes this as the measure of real labour. And this does not achieve the scientific understanding of labour.

Marx had "a third aspect of estranged labour which was deduced from the two already considered aspects"[20], that is, to subsume the estrangement of the thing and self-estrangement under the estrangement of man's species-nature from him. Because the estrangement of labour's products also means the estrangement of man from nature which man uses to realize his labour and in which he carries out labour activity and produces products, and estranged labour separates away from man the object of his production. The estrangement of labour means that the spontaneous, free activity of man is degraded to a means, a means of maintaining his physical existence. Therefore,

---

19   Ibid., p. 96-97.
20   Ibid., p. 95.

the estrangement of the thing and that of labour are, seen from the subject aspect, the estrangement of man's species-nature from him (human aspect). Marx said, "*Man's species-being*, both nature and his spiritual species-property, into a being *alien* to him, into a means of his *individual existence*. It [estranged labour] estranges from man his own body, as well as external nature and his spiritual aspect, his *human* aspect."[21] Man, in this way, loses the essence of man as man, i.e. being degraded to an animal, to the level of production as a means of maintaining his physical existence.

Marx also expounded the estrangement of man from man with the use of the idea of estrangement of man's species-nature from him: "the proposition that man's species-nature is estranged from him means that one man is estranged from the other, as each of them is from man's essential nature."[22] Obviously, since man has lost his species-essence, the relationship of man to man is not the true human relationship, but an estranged relationship. In this way, the estrangement of man from man, which takes the appropriation of the products of the worker's labour and of his labour by the bourgeois as the objective basis, was thus elaborated speculatively by Marx.

Thus it can be seen from the above that Marx's theory of estranged labour uncovers the employment nature of labour under capitalism, and the exploitive relationship between the bourgeois and the proletarian by analyzing the relationship of the products of labour to the labourer, and the relationship of the labourer to his labour, and the relationship of property owners to the proletarian. This was doubtless a tremendous advance in comparison with the "labour theory of value" of the British classical economists, which focuses on the quantitative analysis of labour, but there was something of Feuerbach's humanism in its philosophical explanation

Marx's theory of estranged labour could not shake off completely the German classical philosophical tradition which discusses estrangement from the essence of man, even though this essence was designated as a free, conscious activity—labour. However, since he proceeded from economic facts, he, unlike the German classical philosophy, did not take this estrangement as the abstract subject-object

---

21   Ibid., p. 97.
22   Ibid., p. 98.

relationship, but externalized it and used the concept of estrangement to expound the relationship between the labourer and the products of labour, and that between his physical and mental energy, in
his *Manuscripts* (1844). He said, "Estrangement is manifested not
only in the fact that *my* means of life belong to *someone else*, that
which I desire is the inaccessible possession of *another*, but also in
the fact that everything is itself something different from itself—
that my activity is *something else* and that, finally (and this applies
also to the capitalist), all is under (the sway) of in*human* power."[23]
Here "I" clearly refers to the proletarian and "someone else" refers
to the bourgeois. The essence of Marx's theory of estranged labour
is closely related to the exposure of the capitalist private property.
Therefore, although the estrangement in *Manuscripts* is mediated
by the essence of man, its most basic content is that the worker's
material and mental activity and their products have become an alien
power over himself. And this is a phenomenon unique to the capitalist society. We of course reject taking estrangement as the basic
theory and method, but we do not oppose to using of it as a concept
to express some particular phenomena (including certain phenomena governed by laws) of the capitalist society.

Concerning the objective basis of Marx's theory of estranged labour,
we should pay attention to the following aspects when discussing the
question of estrangement:

First, estrangement is an objective phenomenon instead of an experience of the subject, and is neither the unavoidable tension state
between human instincts and civilization nor the psychopathy due to
the suppression of the *id* by civilization as the Freudians have advocated. Marx saw estrangement under the capitalist system as "the *actual* estrangement—that which appears real", as "that of *real life*"[24].

Second, estrangement is associated with the activity of the subject,
and it is the domination of man's material and mental activity and
their products over him. Hence the question of estrangement and
that human action must obey the objective laws are not the same
thing. Human act has to obey and follow the objective laws in order
to achieve the desired purpose, which is a general law of cognition

23 Ibid., p. 141.
24 Ibid., p. 165, p. 121.

applicable to any society. Between man and the law, human act and will must abide by the law, and not vice versa, and it is true whether one has the knowledge of the law or not. The difference is that one follows the law consciously after he has known about it, and otherwise he is forced to follow it. Man's understanding and use of the laws always undergo the process from forced abidance to conscious abidance, which is also the process from necessity to freedom. Man cannot obtain knowledge of all laws, but we cannot say that he is in a permanent state of estrangement.

Third, estrangement should not be confused with contradiction. Estrangement is a contradiction, but contradiction does not equal to estrangement. Estrangement is a manifestation of contradiction, a specific contradiction between the subject and the object, which is formed by the subject and its creations (its production) under certain conditions. If estrangement is equated with contradiction, not only will the special content of estrangement be annulled, but the nature of contradiction will also be distorted. The relationship between these two sides of contradiction is the unity of opposites, rather than estrangement, one side being estranged from the other side of contradiction. The universality of estrangement cannot be derived from that of contradiction.

Fourth, estrangement occurs under certain historical conditions. It is conditional, not unconditional, and it is temporary, not permanent. It is a pessimistic view that estrangement occurs inevitably in any society, in any culture and historical period, and is the common fate of mankind.

When analyzing the question of estrangement under the capitalist system, Marx considered both the proletariat and property owners. He argued that "all is under (the sway) of inhuman power" manifested by estrangement, and this "applies also to the capitalist". But he distinguished property owners from the proletariat, and pointed out that "everything which appears in the workers as an *activity of alienation, of estrangement*, appears in the non-worker as a *state of alienation, of estrangement*."[25] The worker is a producer, so his estrangement is mainly manifested in his activity, that is, he is engaged

---

25   Ibid., p. 103.

in coerced, involuntary labour, and produces continuously the products confronting himself. The bourgeois are also in the state of estrangement, because they are governed by commodity and money as well. The fate of the capitalist depends on his commodity at the market; some of them inevitably sink into poverty and bankruptcy in capitalist competition. Furthermore, Marx indicated that "the worker's *real, practical attitude* in production and to the product appears in the non-worker who confronting him as a *theoretical* attitude." Marx reveals here the bourgeois nature of the British classical economics, and emphasizes that what it expresses is not the law of true labour, but that of estranged labour. These economists elevate the estrangement in the capitalist production, namely, the opposition between the products of labour and the labourer, between labour and the labourer, and the bourgeois' appropriation of the surplus labour and products of the proletarian to a theory in order to argue for the rationality of this situation. This suggests that theoretical attitude of the bourgeois to estranged labour and the practical attitude of the worker are in complete opposition.

More importantly, Marx already saw that although the capitalist society was an estranged society, the property owner and the proletarian in it were in different situations: "the non-worker does everything against the worker which the worker does against himself; but he does not do against himself what he does against the worker."[26] The property owners are the beneficiaries rather than the victims of the capitalist system. Although they also fall under the power of the thing, the production and appropriation of products, the selling of labour (force) and the possession of labour of someone else cannot be placed in the same category. And this idea was further elaborated by Marx in *The Holy Family*.

Thus the above shows that the theory of estranged labour directs all of its criticism at the capitalist system, and concentrates on uncovering the employment status of the proletariat under capitalism, thought was is not entirely scientific.

---

26 Ibid., p. 103.

3 PRIVATE PROPERTY AND ESTRANGED LABOUR
VARIOUS MANIFESTATIONS OF ESTRANGEMENT UNDER CAPITALISM

Marx considered private property and estranged labour as two basic factors, and that every category of political economy could be developed with their help, he wrote: "each category, e.g., trade, competition, capital, money only a *particular* and *developed* expression of these first elements"[27]. However, in terms of their relationship, estranged labour was more fundamental, around which Marx had critically discussed private property and other economic categories.

It is easy to understand that Marx paid great attention to the question of private property in *Manuscripts*. This, as I have mentioned earlier, was a fundamental question in the 1840s, which had been raised in the then labour movement, or dealt with by various socialist theories directly or indirectly. As early as in his editing days in the *Rheinische Zeitung*, Marx had posed the question of the rationality of the proletariat's demand to possess the wealth of the middle class based on the facts of labour movement in England and France in his polemical articles of *Communism and the Augsburg Allgemeine Zeitung*. When the question of human emancipation was analyzed later in On the Jewish Question, the question of private property was again discussed. But none of these discussions raised the question of the nature and origin of private property, which was later explored in *Manuscripts* after Marx shifted from philosophy to the political economy sphere.

According to Marx, the entire bourgeois political economy is based on private property and it regards it as a premise with no need for demonstration or explanation, as an established fact. "Political economy starts with the fact of private property; it does not explain it to us"[28]. However, the labour theory of value of the British classical political economy recognizes that labour creates value, and thus diverts the nature of private property into the subject itself. "Wealth as something outside man and independent of him, and therefore as something to be maintained and asserted only in an external

---

27 Ibid., p. 101.
28 Ibid., p. 89.

fashion, is done away with; that is, this external, *mindless objectivity* of wealth is done away with, with private property being incorporated in man himself and with man himself being recognized as its essence", "What previously was being external to oneself—man's actual externalisation—has merely become the act of externalizing—the process of alienating"[29]. Private property should therefore not be eternal, but have its own origin according to the theoretical logic of the labour theory of value. In order to get out this predicament, the bourgeois classical political economy confuses the product with commodity, the general nature of labour with its particular form (wage labour), and thus conceals the estranged nature of labour under capitalism and eternalizes private property.

Marx differentiates labour from estranged labour, focuses on studying the relationship of estranged labour to private property and strives to reveal the origin of private property. According to Marx, private property and estranged labour interact on each other and are in reciprocal causality. Private property is the product of estranged labour, and the means by which labour alienates itself, the realization of this alienation. This secret of this reciprocal relationship fully appears at the culmination of the development of private property, i.e. at the stage of capitalist private property. In the capitalist society, the cause for the estrangement of labour certainly lies in the private property, in the separation of the three: Capital, landed property and labour; in turn, private property is the accumulation of labour, the accumulation of estranged labour. Although Marx did not formulate the concept of surplus value, nor yet established the theory of the accumulation of capital at the time, he already saw by analyzing the estrangement of man from man, the fact that the worker's labour and products were appropriated by the capitalist, and that the worker produced in the production process not only products, also the opposition of his products against him, the opposition of his labour to him, but also the relationship of the other— the capitalist to his products (the appropriation of products) and to his labour (the possession of labour), as well as the relationship of the capitalist to him. In other words, the capitalist production was not only the production of material goods but also the reproduction of the relations of private property. Hence Marx wrote: "[t]hrough *estranged,*

29   Ibid., p.p. 112-113.

alienated labour, the worker produces the relationship to this labour of a man alien to labour and standing outside it. The relationship of the worker to labour creates the relation to it of the capitalist (or whatever one chooses to call: The master of labour). *Private property* is thus the product, the result, the necessary consequence, of *alienated labour*, of the external relation of the worker to nature and to himself."[30]

But Marx, who strives to reveal the origin of private property, does not settle here on this reciprocal relationship, and proceeds to explore the causality from their co-existence. So he affirms and argues that private property results from estranged labour, and not vice versa, with respect to the question of which one gives rise to the other. He argued: "True, it is as a result of the movement of private property that we have obtained the concept of *alienated labour (of alienated life)* in political economy. But on analysis of this concept it becomes clear that though private property appears to be the reason, the cause of alienated labour, it is rather its consequence, just as the gods are *originally* not the cause but the effect of man's intellectual confusion. Later this relationship becomes reciprocal."[31]

Marx put forward a difficult question which he could not answer then. If estranged labour precedes and creates private property, then why is labour estranged at first? Certainly, Marx who has a keen mind and loves to get to the deep bottom of things did not avoid but articulated this question. He wrote: "We have accepted the *estrangement of labour*, its *alienation*, as a fact, and we have analyzed this fact. We now ask, how does *man* come to *alienate*, to estrange, his *labour*? How is this estrangement rooted in the nature of human development?" But Marx did not answer it specifically, and it was unlikely for him to solve this mystery scientifically and in detail given his level of economics at the time, but it provided him with an overall direction for solving this question. He commented: "We have already gone a long way to the solution of this problem by *transforming* the question of the *origin of private property* into the question of the relation of *alienated labour* to the course of humanity's development."[32]

---

30   Ibid., p. 100.
31   Ibid.
32   Ibid., p. 102.

It is easy to see that Marx falls into the circular argument that es-tranged labour produces private property and private property gener-ates estranged labour when investigating their relationship from the aspect of their interaction. And when he gets out of this circular argu-ment and strives to explore the origin of private property, he believes the origin lies in estranged labour, he could not get rid of the general convention of man's self-estrangement completely. According to Marx, it is wrong to consider private property as something external to man and to speak of man himself only when it comes to labour. In fact, they all concern man himself. Private property is the prod-uct of estranged labour, and estranged labour is the manifestation of the estrangement of man's essence, and thus is actually the self-estrangement of man, seen from the subjective essence of private property. The "*material*, immediately *perceptible* private property is the material perceptible expression of *estranged human* life"[33]. In this way, Marx logically transforms the question of the *origin of pri-vate property* into the question of the relation of estranged labour to human development according to the process of his thought. As long as it is made clear why human labour is estranged in the course of human development, the reason for the emergence of private prop-erty will be discovered, because private property is nothing but the accumulation of estranged labour.

This answer was apparently immature, compared with his other argumentation for the origin of private property looking to it from the development level of productive forces and the development of division of labour and development of exchange. However, his ex-ploration of the origin of private property in estranged labour had contained several reasonable factors.

First, private property is not eternal but has its origin. This raises the question that the British classical economists carefully avoided, and thus removes a major obstacle to solving this problem in future.

Second, private property is not something unrelated to man, but it is the product of labour. The argument that estranged labour engenders private property purges the latter of its speculative element, and con-tains the idea that its origin must be sought in labour.

---

33   Ibid., p. 121.

Third, the root of estranged labour is not outside man but in the development of mankind itself, and thus the origin of estranged labour should be explored in the course of human development.

We indeed could "have already gone a long way to the true solution", if human essence as the medium were abandoned, the framework of "man's self-estrangement—estranged labour—private property" were also abandoned , and instead directly investigated the material origin of estranged labour and the relationship of the development level of labour to the emergence of private property.

Marx does not limit his analysis of estrangement to estranged labour in his *Manuscripts 1844*, and instead with it as the centre, he analyzes several economic categories under the capitalist system.

He reveals the nature of the capitalist wage, and criticizes the view of substantially improving the condition of the working class by increasing the wages, and also criticizes Proudhon's view of the equality of wages as the aim of the revolution through his study of private property and estranged labour.

According to Marx, "*wages* and *private property* are identical" under capitalism, and they are "a necessary consequence of labour's estrangement". The capitalist wage signifies the estrangement of labour:

First, the products which the worker creates cannot be owned by him, and only a part of them are returned to him, which is called the wage of labour. So the wage of labour suggests the free appropriation of some products of the worker.

Second, in the wage labour, labour does not appear as an end in itself but as the servant of the wage. That is to say, the purpose of this labour is to earn the wage, and not the internal need of man's life activity. Based on the analysis of the nature of wages, Marx affirms that an enforced increase of wages would be nothing but better payment for the slave, and would not win for the worker his human status and dignity. The level of wages under capitalism cannot change the employment nature of labour, just as the slave was always a slave at the slave market in the ancient times regardless of his price. Therefore, the nature of labour cannot be determined by the level of wages. The mere focus on the increase of wages will neither solve the fundamental problem of the workers, nor make them into "man". The equality of wages as proposed and imagined by Proudhon, that all people are paid equally, is nothing but the transformation of the relationship of the worker to his labour under capitalism, into the relationship of all men to labour; in the society where all men get equally paid, and thus society is conceived as an abstract capitalist. So Proudhon's imagination of the equality of all wages is an attempt to overcome economic estrangement within the scope of economic estrangement, and was a fantasy.

Precisely because Marx takes the wages as the manifestation of estranged labour, he advocates the elimination of wages. He said, "Wages are the direct consequence of estranged labour, and estranged labour is the direct cause of private property. The downfall of the one must therefore involve the downfall of the other."[34] In 1844, Marx did not develop the idea of distribution according to one's work, nor did he develop the idea of the two stages of the development of communism. He did not pose the question of what distribution form would be adopted for the individual consumer's goods after the abolition of private property, too. His argument that wages were the consequence of estranged labour is applicable to capitalism alone.

The adoption of wage system in the socialist society does not suggest that the labour force remains to be a commodity, and that labour is still estranged labour. The socialist wages as a form of the distribution according to one's work, is fundamentally different from the capitalist wages.

Marx also uncovers the nature of capital with the help of private property and estranged labour. According to Smith, capital is accumulated labour, but it is not the accumulation of the capitalist's personal labour, but that of estranged labour according to the Marx's theory of estranged labour. That is to say, it is not his labour but the exploitation of others' labour that makes the capitalist into a capitalist. Capital is the accumulation of estranged labour.

---

34   Ibid., p. 101.

Why does the capitalist have the right to appropriate other men's labour and products? What is the basis of this right? According to Say, by virtue of positive law, the question of the right of inheritance is a legal matter. But the right of inheritance can only stipulate who should inherit the property, and the right of inheritance cannot give capital the private property in the products of other men's labour. The governing power over the labour and product of the worker is the quality of capital. The capitalist possesses this governing power, not on account of his personal or human qualities, but inasmuch as he is an owner of capital. His power is the power of his capital, the purchasing power of his capital, which nothing can withstand. Hence capital for the worker is an alien power, the capitalist uses capital to exercise his governing power over labour, and the power of capital is not only over the labourer but "over the capitalist himself". Thus under the domination of capital, man is a machine for consuming and producing. Men are nothing, the product is everything.

Marx also talks about the question of estrangement when discussing the question of the rent of land. He considers that the domination of the land as an alien power over men is already inherent in the feudal landed property. On the one hand, the serf is the adjunct of the land, and bound to it for life; on the other, the lord of an entailed estate belongs to the land. Formally, the first-born son inherits the land, but in effect the land inherits him. So both the serf and the first-born son are the adjunct of the land and both of them belong to it. The domination of private property historically began with land. The possession of land constitutes the foundation of private property. The domination of the land as an alien power over men is actually the domination of private property.

But under the system of feudal lord, the rule of landed property does not appear directly as the rule of mere capital. When land is dragged completely into the movement of private property and becomes a commodity, the land ownership of the feudal lord is transformed into the capitalist ownership, and estrangement develops even further. On the one hand, the landed property, in the form of capital, exercises its domination over the working class, and the agricultural labourers depend not on the land but on capital; on the other, it dominates the proprietors of lands, because once the landed property is dragged into competition, it is governed by the law of competition like any other commodity. Sometimes it increases, sometimes it decreases, and it is transferred continuously from one person's hands into another's. Thus the proprietors of land are inevitably ruined or raised higher by the movement of capital. Therefore, Marx argues that as the landed property becomes a commodity, "The medieval proverb *null terre sans seigneur* is replaced by that other proverb, *l'argent n'a pas de maître*, wherein is expressed as the complete domination of dead matter over man"[35].

When analyzing the relations of private property, Marx strives to reveal the estrangement in it as well.

He analyzes two kinds of capital: one is the capital of the capitalist, and the other is that of the worker. How does the dispossessed worker have capital? The capital of the worker is himself, so his capital is himself in its subjective form and labour in its objective form. But the capital of the worker is different from that of the capitalist; it is a living and therefore an indigent capital. Labour for him is not his capital and he loses its interest—the wage, every moment he is not working, or he is unemployed. Hence man exists not as man but as a worker under the capitalist system. As a worker, his human qualities only exist insofar as they exist for capital alien to him, i.e. to maintain his physical existence through labour. So once the worker loses his work, and he is not working, he is not a worker. Without being a worker, he loses the right to life, and he will be impoverished, starve to death and be buried. So the worker, in the eyes of the bourgeois economists, is not a human being, but a machine, and the wage of labour is like the oil which is applied to wheels to keep them turning, the cost for the maintenance and servicing of the machines, and the death and substitute of the worker are similar to the updating of equipments and machines.

He also discusses the estranged nature of production under the capitalist private property. Production does not produce man as man, but "as a *commodity*, the *human commodity*, man in the role of *commodity*". This human commodity, though self-conscious and self-acting, is not a human being, but a commodity, "a *mentally* and physically dehumanized being"[36].

---

35   Ibid., p. 85.
36   Ibid., p. 105.

Marx goes deep into the nature of private property, and unmasks the opposition between capital and labour as the most basic private-property relationship. For the labourer, the producing activity which he conducts is an activity quite alien to itself, also alien to man and to nature, and to the free, conscious activity. Man in this production is "a mere *workman*", who does not create himself through labour, but "may daily fall from his filled void into the absolute void—into his social, and therefore actual, non-existence"[37]. The capitalist system of wage labour is like a devil, to which human blood is offered as a sacrifice. The worker is a producer, a labourer separated from capital and landed property, and therefore a "void". He is mentally and physically "filled void", when he throws himself into production at the outset, he keeps falling into "the absolute void", "into non-existence" due to the torture and damage in the work, like those young reeling workwomen we see in *Oh! The Nomugi Pass*. The fact was really similar to what is described in Marx's extract from Buret's *De la Misère*: "*the large industrial towns would in a short time lose their population of workers if they were not all the time receiving from the neighbouring rural areas constant recruitments of healthy men, a constant flow of fresh blood.*"

He also observes estrangement in the needs, production and division of labour in the capitalist society.

Human needs certainly have a natural basis, but the content and level of the needs depend not on man's natural essence and desire, but on production. Human needs appear as the social needs. Production and reproduction produce not only the products which satisfy the needs, but also new needs for products, which in turn drive production.

The socialist production and the capitalist production have different purposes. Marx believes that in the socialist society, human needs are plentiful and various, and the purpose of production is to gradually satisfy the plentiful, human needs, so a new mode of production and a new object of production are "a new manifestation of forces of human nature and they are the enrichment of human nature".

---

37   Ibid., p. 106.

It is reversed under the capitalist private property. The immediate purpose of the capitalist production is not to satisfy the needs but to seek profit. "Every person speculates on creating a new need in another, so as to drive him to fresh sacrifice, to place him in a new dependence and to seduce him into a new mode of enjoyment and therefore to economic ruin." For this reason, the more the capitalist production produces, the more powerful the thing which confronts and suppresses man becomes: "The increase in the quantity of objects is accompanied by an extension of the realm of the alien powers to which man is subjected to, and every new product represents a new *potentiality* of mutual swindling and mutual plundering."[38] The appearance of a new product is a means for the capitalist to overpower and abandon his competitors, contend for markets and gain more profit.

The estrangement of needs is represented by the fact that private property does not change crude need into human need, but into a fantasy, caprice, whim and mere enjoyment, and makes man a slave of "inhuman, sophisticated, unnatural and imaginary appetites". Just as the eunuch flatters his despot and uses despicable means to stimulate his dulled capacity for pleasure, so does the industrial eunuch, i.e. the capitalist. They take a need as a weakness which will lead the fly to the glue-pot so as to induce and catch "the golden birds", i.e. to empty the pocket of the consumer. So Marx said that "[h]e puts himself at the service of the other's most depraved fancies, plays the pimp between him and his need, excites in him morbid appetites, lies in wait for each of his weakness—all so that he can then demand the cash for this service of love"[39].

There are the needs of the poor, besides those of the rich in the capitalist society. The estrangement of needs produces the odd needs of the rich and the sophistication of the means of satisfying needs on the one side, and a bestial barbarization, crude, simplicity of need of the poor on the other. If man cannot afford the expensive rent, he has to live in a basement and thus returns to a cave dwelling. Light, air, even the simplest animal cleanliness cease to be a need for man. Marx stated angrily when describing the impoverished life of the

38   Ibid., p. 132.
39   Ibid., p. 133.

worker that "[i]t is not only that man has no human needs—even his animal needs cease to exist." "None of his senses exist any longer, and (each has ceased to function) not only in its human fashion, but in an inhuman fashion, so that it does not exist even in an animal fashion."[40] The indigent needs of the worker are even less than those of the animals.

Marx discovers profoundly that the needs of the rich and the poor are two aspects of the same question. It is the multiplication of needs and of the means of their satisfaction that breeds the absence of needs and the absence of means. But the bourgeois political economy, which represents the scientific creed of the capitalist, considers this estrangement in the needs normal and makes a strong defence for it. It reduces the worker's needs to the barest and most miserable level of physical subsistence, and declares that this life "is *human* life and existence"; it also counts the most meagre form of life as the standard, propagates that as far as possible, which, in fact, "turns the worker into an insensible being lacking all needs".

The phenomena of estrangement in the needs are actually the different modes of life determined by the mode of production. The mode of life of property owners, their food, clothing, shelter and transport, their various forms of enjoyment, are unmatched by those of the workers, qualitatively or quantitatively. With the sharp contrast between the needs of the rich and those of the poor, Marx brings to light the polarization between the bourgeois and the proletarian under capitalism. Of course, the living conditions of the contemporary western workers are not exactly the same with those in the early days of the development of capitalist industry more than a century ago, because the living standards of the whole society have changed. But we cannot conclude that the western workers' needs and the satisfaction of the needs tend to be identical with those of the bourgeois. The starting line of misery can be changed, but unemployment and misery are indestructible companions of the capitalist system. And in this lies precisely the positive significance of Marx's analysis of the estrangement of the needs.

---

40   Ibid., p. 134.

Marx's analysis of money also has distinctive characteristics. Money as a manifestation of estrangement has been discussed in combination with *Comments on James Mill, Elements of Political Economy*. Here we would like to point out that the analysis of money from the perspective of the estrangement of human essence is inevitably reduced to the moral evaluation of money. It cannot be expected to be a scientific analysis that the upside-down of the world, the loss of morality and the drowning of the relationship of man to man in the ice water of egoism can be attributed to money, and attributed to the estrangement of man's essence. As long as there is commodity, money will exist. The special status of gold and silver is neither the estrangement of the essence of man, nor depends on the subjective will of man, but is determined by the objective law inherent in the commodity and independent of man's subjective will. The emergence of money is the necessary consequence of the contradiction of commodity production, and was a progress forward. It breaks the limitation of barter in space, time and individual needs, facilitates the circulation of commodities and is conducive to the development of society. However, money deepens the contradiction of commodity production rather than resolving it. The so-called evil of money is not rooted in money itself, but in private property. Therefore, the function and nature of money varies with the ownership.

There are two different attitudes towards money. Some take the side of the self-sufficient, small-scale peasant economy, and attempt to restrict commodity production. They reject money and see it as the root of all evils, and believe that the people can return to their original simplicity, and become honest and warm-hearted, and all social ills will be solved so long as money is abolished. This view is reflected in the policy of physiocracy school and the restriction of business advocated by some dynasties of the feudal society in China. Some were even in favour of abolishing money, saying "the common aspiration of the people wavers, the less important things are run after, the tillers are less than half of their original number, the evils cannot be prohibited; and all these evils originate from money". The learned celebrities in the Wei and Jin Dynasties distained and did not spoke of money, calling money Aduwu to show their aloofness.

Marx is certainly different. He attacks the ills of capitalism from the socialist standpoint, but he fails to have an advanced scientific analysis on the function of money, due to the then his using estrangement theory as the basic theory and method, which easily makes him notice its negative aspects and thus sink into the moral evaluation.

In *Manuscripts*, Marx reaches a new height in his analysis of the situation and status of the proletariat, a new height on the antagonistic contradictions between the proletariat and the bourgeoisie and some economic phenomena under capitalism. But to have a truly scientific analysis of the mode of the capitalist production, attention should not just be paid to its bad results, but also to the exploration of its causes. And to do so, we needed to break the circle of the estrangement and idea of winning back the return of human essence and make the transition to the establishment of the materialist conception of history.

CHAPTER VI

INNER CONTRADICTION OF THE THEORY OF ESTRANGED LABOUR
NECESSITY AND INEVITABILITY OF THE TRANSITION TO THE MATERIALIST CONCEPTION OF HISTORY

The advancement of estrangement to estranged labour was undoubtedly a significant turn in the development of Marx's thought, but the theory of estranged labour was not the same with the materialist conception of history yet, and it contained inner contradictions. When Marx sees true labour as the essence of man and focuses on the subject itself, he cannot rid himself completely of the old paradigm which uses the estrangement and idea of return of human essence to describe history. And when he abandons the use of the true essence of man as a basis, considers estranged labour as an objective, historical phenomenon and concentrates on analyzing the objective relationships—between man and nature, between man and man—formed in labour process, he inevitably proceeded to conceive the development of society as a natural historical process, investigate the laws inherent in the development of history itself and thus move towards historical materialism. These two tendencies had coexisted in *Manuscripts of 1844*, indicating the contradictoriness and complexity in the development of Marx's thought. But the dominant tendency was his tendency to develop the materialist conception of history, which is closely related to his focusing on economic studies. In addition, we cannot underestimate the role played by the critical absorption of the positive elements of the Hegelian dialectics in the formation of the materialist conception of history.

1 HUMANISTIC ELEMENTS IN THE THEORY OF ESTRANGED LABOUR

The theory of estranged labour of Marx was superior to the estrangement theory of Hegel and Feuerbach. It contains some elements of the materialist conception of history, but is not the same with the latter. This theory still bears the traces of Feuerbach's humanism and has in a way the common defects specific to the theories which take estrangement as the basic theory and method.

When the essence of man is used as a measure and essence of man estrangement is used to explain history, the focus is necessarily placed not on the study of the objective historical process, but on the exploration of the essence of man to strive to discover an eternal, fixed essence which makes man into man, and take this as the starting point of history. The intrinsic nature of man is estranged from him at a certain development stage of human society, which causes the opposition between the objective existence of man and his essence. Thus the fundamental content of history becomes the contradiction between human existence and human essence; and the ultimate end of history is to make man regain his estranged essence and re-appropriate his essence.

The "return" or "regain" theory is the inevitable conclusion under the premise of the estrangement of human essence. This is true of Hegel. He starts with the self-estrangement of absolute idea and concludes with the return of the object into the subject and the realization of their unity. And so do Bauer and Feuerbach. Bauer regards religion as the estrangement of man's self-consciousness, and sees the supersession of religion as the return of religious consciousness into the self-consciousness of man. Feuerbach begins with religion as the alienation of man's species-essence, and ends it with that man re-appropriates his species-essence and becomes the perfect and true man. Although the essence of man is determined differently, they all conclude that this estranged essence must be returned into the subject itself. Estrangement and return (regain) constitute the two inseparable moments of the estrangement theory. Therefore, when used to explain and describe history, the theory of the estrangement of human essence is bound to fit the history of mankind into the triad of man—non-human—man, according to its own logic, and thus shrouds history in mysterious speculation and thus turns the real history into the "reflection" of the history of human essence.

It is evident that one has to concentrate on the exploration of the essence of the subject—man, and exclude the objective laws from his vision if he investigates history in this way. The essence of man is placed in a primary, dominant position in the development of history, and all aims at the realization of the essence of man and all must accord with the essence of man. So the fundamental contradiction of the whole human society is the contradiction between human existence and human essence, rather than that between productive forces and relations of production (appearing as class contradictions in class societies). And this contradiction reaches its peak at the point when man has lost completely his essence and lost all that corresponds to human nature, and then commences the historical course of the return of human essence. This conception of history distorts both the driving forces for the development of history and the course of history. The history of mankind is not the history of the estrangement of human essence and return of human essence. It is a fictitious triad to consider the unity of human essence with human existence as the starting point of history, the slave society, feudal society and capitalist society as the estrangement of human essence, and the future communist society as the return or regain of human essence. In fact, the primitive society was neither the golden age nor the Garden of Eden of mankind, and the class society was not the decline of mankind and the loss of humanity either. If the struggles against the Middle Ages are seen as restricting people's horizons, and the Middle Ages is conceived as the interruption and regression of history, and its great advances were therefore overlooked, then the same will happen if the historical role of the capitalist society is not analyzed by a correct conception of history. In fact, the history of mankind is developing, and the superseding of one mode of production by another mode of production signals the progress of history. Although there are contradictions and local regressions, history generally keeps moving forward. This is also valid for the development of production, the advances in science and technology as well as the change in morality. Even seen from the economic condition and political status of the labourers, changes have constantly occurred: From the slave who had no personal freedom and was treated as the instrument of production, to the semi-dependent serf and then to the worker of modern industry.

But, Marx's view on history in 1844 should not be confused with the above false conception of history. However, it was impossible for him, who was developing the materialist conception of history then, to completely shake off the influence of traditional thought. His investigation of history clearly has a speculative character due to the use of estrangement as a theory and method, which, in *Manuscripts*, is mainly represented by his view on communism.

He elaborates his view on communism in close combination with the transcendence of private property. This is his brilliance, but his approach to the question is still based on the essence of the subject. He said, "*Communism* as the *positive* transcendence of *private property* as *human self-estrangement*, and therefore as the real *appropriation* of the *human essence* by and for man; communism therefore as the complete return of man to himself as a social (i.e., human) being."[1] He dealt with this question in more detail in another place, arguing that "Just as *private property* is only the perceptible expression of the fact that man becomes *objective* for himself and at the same time becomes to himself a strange and inhuman object; just as it expresses the fact the manifestation of his life is the alienation of his life, that his realisation is his loss of reality, is an alien reality: so, the positive transcendence of private property—i.e., the *perceptible* appropriation for and by man of the human essence and of human life, of objective man, of human *achievements* should not be conceived merely

---

1 Karl Marx and Frederick Engels: Collected Works, 1st Chinese Edition, Volume 42, p. 120.

in the sense of *immediate*, one-sided *enjoyment*, merely in the sense of *possessing*, of *having*. Man appropriates his comprehensive essence in a comprehensive manner, that is to say, as a whole man."[2]

In the above discourse, Marx attributes private property to the self-estrangement of man, i.e. the essence of man confronting him based on the essence of man. This view was quite consistent around 1844. In *Contribution to the Critique of Hegel's Philosophy of Law: Introduction*, Marx sees religion as the holy form of human self-estrangement, and law and state as its unholy forms of human self-estrangement. In *The Holy Family*, shortly written after *Manuscripts*, he holds that the bourgeoisie and the proletariat "present the same human self-estrangement". Although the study of private property in *Manuscripts* shifts from the mere form of the thing, forward to the subject of creations, to the labour of man, but what it shifts to is the labour which he sees as the ideal essence of man and sees it separate from the restriction of the relations of production and this labour has no qualitative determinations. Limited to the subject itself, one cannot figure out why man is estranging himself from him, and why self-estrangement engenders private property, classes and state from the essence of man (even if human essence is defined as the free, conscious activity). To take self-estrangement as the basis actually presupposes a fact that has to be demonstrated. This way of thinking has some similarity with Feuerbach's reduction of religion to human self-estrangement, and this idea is barely halfway. If the focus is not shifted from human essence to the analysis of society which shapes and determines human essence, if the focus remains on man himself, rather than on the exploration of the origin of estrangement in society, then one is inevitably confined in humanism. Hence the truly scientific conception of history should proceed from a certain period of social economy, and shift the focus of study from the self-estrangement of human essence to the law of social development so as to really provide a scientific explanation for human essence and find out the cause for estrangement.

With this perspective, the particular contradictions under the various forms of private property are all reduced to the contradiction between inhuman life conditions and the intrinsic nature of man,

---

2   Ibid., p. 123.

because human essence is taken as the basis and the private property system is seen as the estrangement of human essence. Human nature becomes the standard for judging social relations and social systems, and a system is measured or criticized according to whether it corresponds to human nature or not. In fact, this is a subjective and arbitrary criterion , and as a standard, it only makes each person stick to his own argument for right and wrong. The British classical economists and the bourgeois enlightenment school maintain that the feudal system violates human nature, and only the capitalist system is the best system, because it accords with the selfish nature of man, while the utopian socialists argue that the capitalist system suppresses human nature, and only the communist system corresponds to the good nature of man. Everyone can conceive of a perfect system on the basis of his understanding of human nature, completely excluding the objective research of history. Even to this day, some people in the west still stick to this opinion. They claim that the capitalist private ownership plays a progressive role, just because it corresponds to, recognizes and affirms the selfish nature of man, gives full play to this nature, stimulates greatly people's passion for pursuing private interests and thus promotes the development of productive forces and promotes the advances in science and technology. This is actually to consider the so-called nature of man (selfish lust) as the driving force of social development. For them, it is not private property which generates private gains mentality, but vice versa; for them the historic progressiveness of capitalism lies not in its accordance with the requirements of the development of productive forces but with the selfish nature of man; it is not the capitalist competition generated by the capitalist commodity production but the selfish lust of man that impels them to risk their life and go all out in work. In fact, competition is the law of commodity production. The capitalist competition is the law of the capitalist commodity production, which is an economic law independent of human will, rather than being the law of human nature. The capitalist private property and its law of commodity production exercise power over people's actions, which, reflected in their consciousness, appears as the pursuance of private interests, just like Marx pointed out later in 1847: "The bourgeoisie must develop itself to the full, it daily expands its capital, daily reduce the production costs of its commodities, daily expand its trade connections and markets, daily improves its communications, *in order not to be ruined*. The competition on the world market compels it to do so."[3]

Certainly, the socialist enterprises should also advocate competition, because the socialist economy is a planned commodity economy and cannot abolish the general laws of commodity production. But in the socialist society, the purpose, nature, scope and means of competition are all different from those in the capitalist one. There is no doubt that the socialist competition is closely linked with individual material interests, but the concern for material interests is not equivalent to individualism. We advocate the correct handling of the relationship among the three: state, collective and individual. In the socialist society, the labourer's concern for his material interests does not originate in the selfish nature of man, but is determined by the development level of productive forces and the mode of distribution. The correct dividing line would always be missed and blurred, if the material interests are confused with the so-called selfish nature of man, as love is confused with fleshliness, and consumption with waste.

The theory of estranged labour is said to have humanistic elements, not because Marx used "human", "inhuman", "dehumanized" and other adjectives to assail capitalism at that time. As a denunciation of the capitalist system, these words intensify the emotional colour in certain situations. But the problem is that in Marx's theory of estranged labour the contradictions under capitalism are seen as the contradiction between human existence and human essence, i.e., the contradiction between the worker's life conditions and his human nature, which shows the tendency to use human essence to judge the rationality of a social system. This, if remained within this scope, is at best an impressive moral condemnation of the capitalist system instead of a scientific explanation. Following this theoretical logic, the transcendence of private property is inevitably viewed as the transformation from non-human to human, i.e., the re-appropriation of Man's lost essence and return to himself, to a *social* being (man as man).

---

3   Karl Marx and Frederick Engels: Collected, 1st Chinese Edition, Volume 4, p. 65.

It is true that many profound ideas are included in Marx's analysis of communism as he advances. For example, he objects that the crude equalitarian communism regards the transcendence of private property as the equal distribution of private property, criticizes that the direct, physical possession is seen as the sole purpose of life and existence, and instead Marx emphasizes the all-round development of man; he criticizes the equalitarian communism for viewing the transcendence of private property as asceticism which negates all material civilization and spiritual civilization and preaches indigence and lack of all needs, and stresses that all wealth of development until now should be preserved consciously, and human essence should be enriched, i.e., the appropriation of his essence in a comprehensive manner by man as a whole man. But still Marx fits the transcendence of private property and the all-round development of man into the paradigm of the return of human essence, because he presupposes the self-estrangement of human essence as the beginning. Man himself, or man as a real man, should be like this; but under the private property system, human essence is estranged, and man cannot appropriate his essence, let alone to appropriate it comprehensively, the individual is therefore in conflict with the species, and individual's existence conflicts with essence. Only communism which supersedes private property and eliminates self-estrangement can resolve these contradictions, and thus makes man really appropriate his essence in a comprehensive way, turns him from a non-human into a human, a whole man. In this way of thinking, the supersession of private property is not due to the highly developed productive forces, but based on the requirements of the return of human essence; it is not to develop new essence of man on the basis of the new relations of production, but to appropriate comprehensively the essence of man as man, which cannot be realized under the private property; it is not the high degree of development of production and the elimination of the old division of labour that require and promote the all-round development of man, but man as man will develop in an all-round way. The objective law of the development of history is converted into the law of the estrangement and return of human essence. This, of course, cannot be considered to be a scientific conception of history.

2 SURPASS FEUERBACH AND ADVANCE TOWARDS HISTORICAL MATERIALISM

Contradiction exists in things and in the realm of thought as well, especially in Marx who stood out from the German classical philosophical traditions then, which is clearly reflected by the achievements and limitations of his theory of estranged labour.

Although Feuerbach's influence on Marx is evaluated differently, there is no doubt that this influence did exist, and Marx and Engels themselves have discussed his influence explicitly and repeatedly. Marx was still under Feuerbach's influence until 1844. It can be seen that there is overestimate of Feuerbach and the exposition of some questions bear his traces in *Manuscripts*. No wonder Marx praised his *Principles of the Philosophy of the Future* and *The Essence of Faith according to Luther: A Supplement to the Essence of Christianity* in a letter to Feuerbach in August, 1844, saying that "[i]n these writings you have provided a philosophical basis for socialism and the Communists have immediately understood them in this way"[4].

But Marx was not a pure Feuerbachian. By 1844, although his theory of estranged labour still retained the influence of Feuerbach, it was this theory that constitutes an important link in his transition to the materialist conception of history.

It seems difficult to understand how contradictory things can be combined in one and in the same theory. Yet it is not strange in effect. When Marx restricts himself to the subject itself, and analyzes labour from the internal needs of man, he cannot break away from the speculative tradition which describes history with the estrangement and return/regain of human essence; when he regards labour as the basis of the existence and development of society and discusses various relations by going deep into the real labour process, he advanced towards historical materialism. Marx said that "Where speculation ends—in real life—there real, positive science begins: the representation of the practical activity, of the practical process of development of men."[5] The major achievement of *Manuscripts*

---

4   Karl Marx and Frederick Engels: Collected Works, 1st Chinese Edition, Volume 27, p. 450, Beijing: The People's Press, 1972.

5   Karl Marx and Frederick Engels: Collected Works, 1st Chinese Edition, Volume 3, p.p. 30-31.

is exactly that Marx takes the estrangement of labour as an objective social phenomenon, goes deep into the capitalist economic process and the private property, and has a deeper understanding of the role played by productive labour in the self-formation of man, and a deeper understanding of the relationship between man and nature, between man and man, and between nature and society and thus opens up the way to the materialist conception of history.

Feuerbach also calls himself a "communist", but his so-called communism is based on humanism. Starting with the unity of the individual and the species, he underlines that human beings are species-being, and they need and associate with each other, so communism for him is already contained in the essence of man. Marx has a different view. Communism is conceived by him as the return of human essence in *Manuscripts*, but it is derived not directly from human essence but from the law of the movement of private property by his study on the issue of private property. When Marx claimed that the entire communist movement "necessarily finds both its empirical and its theoretical basis in the movement of private property—more precisely, in that of the economy"[6], he rectified his preliminarily approach which argued for communism by the essence of man, and thus he found a support for the development of socialism from utopia to science.

Marx thus grasps the capitalist private property and construes the antithesis between the proletarian and the property owner as the antithesis between labour and capital. After the analysis of history, he argued that although there was antithesis between the property owner and the proletarian in ancient Rome, Turkey, it was not generated by the capitalist private property and appeared therefore as the antithesis between the rich and the poor. The proletariat in ancient times was supported by the society rather than proletariat supporting it, and was like something useless and waste, attached to the social organism, while it is a different story for the modern proletariat, who was produced by the capitalist private property. The antithesis between him and the property owner is manifested as that between labour and capital. On the one hand, there is the labour excluded

---

6 Karl Marx and Frederick Engels: Collected Works, 1st Chinese Edition, Volume 42, p.p. 120-121.

by property, i.e., the proletarian who himself possesses no means of production but creates wealth; on the other hand there is the excluded capital as labour, i.e., the capital which in itself does not work but is the accumulation of labour, and able to control and appropriate the labour of other men. This is a contradiction inherent in the capitalist private property. Hence the capitalist private property is both the root-cause for the antithesis between the property owner and the proletariat and the inherent basis of its solution.

Based on the law of the movement of the capitalist private property, Marx goes on to discuss the tendency of class relations being simplified in the capitalist society, that is, the society is increasingly splitting into two parts: The proletariat and the bourgeoisie. In industry, the middle classes keep dividing; in agriculture, the landowner is transformed into an ordinary capitalist, and the land, rent of land originally as the feudal property have lost their distinction of rank and been turned into capital and interest, so agriculture, like in industry, also appears as the antithesis between capital and labour. Just like Marx said, "the distinction between capitalist and land renter, like that between the tiller of the land and the factory worker, disappears and that the whole society must fall apart into the two classes—property owners and propertyless workers."[7] The simplification of class relations is also the intensification of class struggle, which, originally concealed and weakened by the complex estate system, now appears directly as the contradiction between the proletariat and the bourgeoisie, "this contradiction [between labour and capital], driven to the limit, is of necessity, the limit, the culmination, and the downfall of the whole private-property relationship"[8].

Marx also analyzes the situation of rural areas based on the law of the movement of private property. Because of its capitalization, the large landed property yields the utmost rent of land to the landowner, and the utmost profit for his capital to the tenant farmer, while on the other side it forces the wages of the agricultural labourers, i.e., the workers working on the land to the minimum. And due to the role played by the competition law, some landowners and tenant farmers go bankrupt and sink into the proletariat; and the wages of the

7   Ibid., p. 89.
8   Ibid., p. 106.

workers on the land, which have already been reduced to a mini-mum, is reduced yet further, to meet the market competition. This, as Marx concluded therefrom, "necessarily leads to revolution"[9].

It is because he regards the capitalist private property as the root-cause of the antithesis between the proletariat and the bourgeoisie that Marx objects to the approach which advocates to improve the condition of the workers by raising their wages, leaving the capi-talist private property untouched, which he calls "reformism". Doubtlessly, the economic struggle is necessary, which will compel the capitalist to raise the wages, and thus betters the workers' life within a certain range and in some measure, but it cannot substan-tially change their situation. The proletariat will remain to be wage labour as long as the capitalist private property exists, and this view of Marx is still quite valid today. Whatever new features the de-velopment of the contemporary capitalist society takes on, however greatly the conditions and content of labour change as production gets highly mechanized, automated and informationized, and what-ever increase occurs in the proportion of the white-collar workers, there will be no fundamental change in its basic class structure so long as the society is based on the capitalist private property. The working class remains to be the employed class. The distinction and antithesis between the proletariat and the bourgeoisie still exist and the contradiction is not resolved.

Marx's criticism of the equalitarian communism is also based on his understanding of the capitalist private property. Equalitarian com-munism is the earliest form of socialism in the history of social-ist thought. What it demands is not to abolish the capitalist private property, but to redistribute private property, so it does not overstep private ownership but is the generalization, consummation and the thorough manifestation of the relation of private property. It negates material civilization and spiritual civilization, spares no effort to de-stroy everything that is not capable of being possessed by all the people as private property, attempts to obliterate talent in an arbi-trary manner, denies individuality and culture and preaches poverty, crudeness and abstinence. This equalitarian communism not only fails to go beyond the level of the capitalist private property, but

---

9   Ibid., p. 87.

does not yet even reach it. It is not the real appropriation of the capitalist private property, but rather a kind of retrogression.

According to Marx, there are such two contradictory opposites as the material and spiritual as well as wealth and poverty in the capitalist private property. The positive transcendence of private property is never a negation of the material civilization and spiritual civilization created by mankind. Poverty is by no means socialism. We should discover and use all materials needed by the formation of a new society from the things created under the capitalist private property. We should move forward instead of backward. "Communism is no flight, no abstraction, no loss of the objective world created by man—of man's essential powers born to the realm of objectivity; they are not a returning to poverty to unnatural, primitive simplicity."[10]

It is also because he combined communism with the positive transcendence of private property that Marx raised the question of the communist action. Contrary to all utopian socialism and true socialism, Marx did not consider communism merely as propaganda, an appeal, but as a revolution. He said explicitly that "[i]n order to abolish the *idea* of private property, the idea of communism is quite sufficient. It undertakes actual communist action to abolish actual private property."[11] To resort to practice, to revolution, to action, is a significant conclusion drawn by Marx.

In Marx's theory of estranged labour, some elements of historical materialism were also included, which cover those important questions he analyzed when the estrangement of labour was discussed by him as an objective, economic phenomenon, such as the role of labour, the relationship between man and nature, between man and man in labour process, the relationship between estrangement in economy and ideology, etc. Marx initially identified a way to seek explanation for history and society in labour through the analysis of estranged labour.

What is history? Marx said that "the *entire so-called history of the world* is nothing but the creation of man through human labour, nothing but the emergence of nature for man." He also emphasized

10   Ibid., p. 175.
11   Ibid., p. 140.

that "[h]istory itself is a *real* part of *natural history*—of nature developing into man", "History is the true natural history of man"[12], etc. These ideas of Marx are inseparable from his analysis of the process of estranged labour.

There are antitheses between nature and man, between man and man in estranged labour, and man is not a real human being yet, but that man becomes a human being is the consequence of the whole history, the consequence of giving full play to his labour capacity through all human activities, including his activities in an estranged form. This view contains reasonable thought, though it does not cast off entirely the limitation of humanism.

First, Marx links labour with history, and considers that the history of mankind is created by man through human labour; second, nature and society are inseparable. The history of mankind is nothing but the transformation and appropriation of nature by man, the natural process of nature developing into man. Therefore, Marx censured the wrong tendency to value religion, politics, arts and literature as real human activities, but despised material production labour.

Although Marx views private property as human self-estrangement, he does not come to a standstill on it, and goes on to discuss the relationship of private property system to production and also the relationship of material production to spiritual production. He asserted that "[i]ts [private property's] movement—the production and consumption—is the *perceptible* revelation of the movement of all production until now, i.e., the realisation or the reality of man. Religion, family, state, law, morality, science, art, etc., are only *particular* modes of production, and fall under its general law."[13] The capitalist private property is seen by Marx as the perceptible revelation of the movement of all production in history until now, which suggests not only that capitalist private property is historic, but that he explores its origin in the process of production itself. Likewise, he discovers their real origin by taking the political superstructure and all kinds of ideology of the superstructure as the factors which are governed and determined by the general law of material production. Although it was a rather general approach to explain the entire superstructure directly with material

---

12   Ibid., p. 131, p. 128, p. 169.
13   Ibid., p. 121.

production, without probing into the inner structure of the process of production and the different functions of various elements of the base and superstructure, and though it lacks a scientific description of the mechanism and process of material production determining spiritual production, its overall direction was also correct.

Yat, Marx did not conceive the concept of social formation, nor develop a theory of social formation, but he found out two important moments in the development of society by analyzing the movement of private property. He elucidated the necessary victory of capitalism over feudalism, victory of capital over rent of land, of mobile over immobile property in his analysis of rent of land and the relations of private property. He argued that land becomes a commodity after the commodity economy penetrates the feudal landed property and this necessarily brings about the repartition and concentration of land, hereby inevitably leading to the emergence of the capitalist, large landed property, i.e., the large-scale capitalist agriculture. And the feudal landowners cannot escape this end, no matter how desperately they struggle. In addition, the rural bankruptcy leads to the migration of agricultural population to cities and its transfer to the industrial areas, which expands the power of industrial capital and helps capitalism defeat feudalism. So Marx said, "The real course of development results in the necessary (inevitable) victory of the *capitalist* over the *landowner*—that is to say, victory of the developed over undeveloped, immature private property", and asserts that any attempt to hold this tendency in check will be "in vain"[14].

He also considers the development of capitalism into communism as the real, necessary moment for the next future historical period. The private property is not eternal. Man "required *private property*" for the realization of his life activity—labour, but now he "requires the supersession of private property"[15].

The aforesaid discourse of Marx makes a rough outline of the development of mankind: feudal society→capitalist society→communist society. It has grasped the most important stages in the development of human history and offers the prospect for human development, though was it not complete.

---

14   Ibid., p. 110.
15   Ibid., p. 148.

In *Manuscripts*, Marx has not established the theory of the relationship between social being and social consciousness yet, but to a large extent, he came close to it when he discussed the movement of private property. For instance, when analyzing the history of economic theories, he sees the development as: From the mercantilist school to the physiocratic school and then to the British economic school as the reflection of the development of society itself in the realm of economic theories, rather than as a pure thinking process. When he comments on Quesnay, an important thinker of the physiocratic school, he says that physiocracy represents directly the decomposition of feudal property in economic terms; when he discusses Adam Smith, Ricardo, he believes that the British classical economists are the product of the real energy and the real movement of private property, the product of the modern capitalist industry. The theoretical contradiction of the British classical economists is a reflection of the inner contradiction of the capitalist industry itself. Marx distinguishes the ancient Greek fetishism of nature from the fetishism of money when analyzing the capitalist fetishism of money, because they had different social conditions. He said that "the sensuous consciousness of the fetish-worshipper is different from that of the Greek, because his sensuous existence is different."[16] Here the words used are the sensuous existence and the sensuous consciousness, but the idea expressed by these terms is very clear: existence determines consciousness.

Marx also considers directly the relationship of human consciousness to social life, to social community. He repeatedly stressed that "[m]y *general* consciousness is only the *theoretical* shape of that of which the *living* shape is the real community, the social fabric", and that it is not human consciousness that determines human existence, but rather the other way round: "In his *consciousness of species* man confirms his real *social life* and simply repeats his real existence in thought"[17]. Therefore, Marx opposes to setting thinking and being in opposition, highlighting that "Thinking and being are certainly *distinct*, but at the same time they are in unity with each other."[18]

---

16   Ibid., p. 139.
17   Ibid., p. 122, p. 123.
18   Ibid., p. 123.

Moreover, for Marx, religious estrangement occurs in the realm of consciousness, of man's inner life, while the estrangement of labour occurs in real life and it is economic estrangement. And the transcendence of estrangement embraces these two aspects. But unlike Feuerbach, who argues that the annulment of religious estrangement is the solution to all social problems, instead, Marx comes up with the conclusion that "the positive transcendence of *private property*", "is the positive transcendence of all estrangement"[19], which makes clear his view on the place of economic factors in the development of society.

The analysis of estranged labour under capitalism also deepens his understanding of classes and class struggle. The existence of classes and class struggle in modern society is not advanced by Marx. Before him, the bourgeois classical economists have done some analysis of each class economically. There are quite a few quotes from their views on the wage of labour, profit and rent of land in *Manuscripts*. The bourgeois classical economics has many reasonable elements, but it covers up the source of rent of land and profit and thus distorts the essence of the class relations in the capitalist society, when it treats profit as the earnings of capital, rent as the earnings of land, and wages as the earnings of labour. Although Marx did not develop the theory of surplus value at that time, he revealed the fact that the products and labour of the labourer were appropriated by the capitalist, through his analysis of the estrangement of labour's products from the labourer, and the estrangement of labour from the labourer. Therefore, Marx holds that the rule of the bourgeoisie appears as the rule of capital in the capitalist private property society, and "the relationship between proprietor and worker is reduced to the economic relationship of exploiter and exploited"[20].

The bourgeois economists see the capitalist society as a harmonious organism, while Marx emphasizes the antithesis between the classes. The capitalist and landowner, by virtue of capital and land, appropriate the majority of labour's products, while the "something more which the worker himself earns at the best of times amounts to so

---

19   Ibid., p. 121.
20   Ibid., p. 84.

little that of four children of his, two must starve and die"[21]. So in the capitalist society the struggle is centred on economic interests, just as Marx generalized, "We find the hostile antagonism of interests, the struggle, the war is recognized throughout political economy as the basis of social organization."[22]

Feuerbach is a materialist, but he does not deal with history. He fell into idealism in investigating history. He remained within his studies of human essence from the humanistic perspective and cut off his way to a scientific understanding of human society. Marx acted differently. Although he did not cast off the influence of Feuerbach completely then, he focused on analyzing the social, economic phenomena themselves, grasped the capitalist private property and its fundamental contradiction, and drew conclusions from the law of the movement of the capitalist private property. This helped him break through Feuerbach's limitations in many ways, and opened up a new way to understand the human essence scientifically, thus he dismissed and settled accounts with his Feuerbachian ideas thoroughly.

3 CRITICISM AND REFORMING OF HEGEL'S IDEA OF ESTRANGEMENT

DISCUSSION ON THE DIALECTICAL MOVEMENT OF HISTORY

It is by proceeding from Hegel and through Feuerbach that Marx establishes Marxism. At the outset, he absorbed Feuerbach's materialism to criticize Hegel's speculative idealism, and then going further he overcame Feuerbach's metaphysics and perception with Hegel's dialectics. In this way, the farther Marx was away from Feuerbach, the closer he got to Hegel, which seemed to be back to where he had started, but this was actually a materialist reform process of Hegel's dialectics at a higher level. Historical materialism is often seen merely as materialism, with its dialectics being overlooked, which is a one-sided view. Historical materialism embraces the historical dialectics, and it is the revelation of the dialectic laws of the development of human society. Without dialectics, historical materialism would not come into being. Marx critically absorbed

---

21   Ibid., p. 54.
22   Ibid., p. 76.

and transformed the German classical philosophy, Hegel's dialectics in particular, in developing his own materialist conception of history. Engels said that "the materialist conception of history and its specific application to the modern class struggle between proletariat and bourgeoisie was only possible by means of dialectics."[23]

For Marx, the most attractive part of the Hegelian philosophy was its dialectics, rather than its over-elaborate speculation and purely conceptual deduction. It is also because of the power of dialectics that Marx gradually returned to Hegel from being antipathetic to him at first. And in the unfinished work *Cleanthes, or the Starting Point and Necessity of Philosophy*, Marx follows the example of Hegel and tries hard to give "a philosophical-dialectical account of divinity", as it manifests itself as the idea-in-itself, as religion as nature, and as history. He speaks highly of dialectics and its power which nothing can withstand in *Notebooks on Epicurean Philosophy*: "dialectic is the inner, simple light, the piercing eye of love, the inner soul which is not crushed by the body of material division, the inner abode of spirit." He also compares dialectics to "the torrent", "which smashes the many and their bounds, which tears down the independent forms, sinking everything in the one sea of eternity"[24]. All is moving and changing, and nothing is absolutely stationary.

Marx's criticism and reform of Hegel's idealistic dialectics starts with the social sphere, rather than nature. Unlike Feuerbach who lays too much emphasis on nature, but too little on politics, Marx took the social reality very seriously. In *Critique of Hegel's Philosophy of Right*, he concentrates his criticism of Hegel's idealistic dialectics on the relationship between civil society and political state, that is, on the most disturbing question he faced when he was working for the *Rheinische Zeitung* newspaper. This was a critique of both his idealistic dialectics and idealist conception of history. Hegel regards civil society and family as the spheres of the concept of state, makes the absolute Idea into a subject and thus transforms the actual relationship of the two (family and civil society) with regard to the state, takes them as a relationship in the Idea itself. Marx reverses the

23   Karl Marx and Frederick Engels: Selected Works, 1st Edition, Volume 3, p.p. 377-378.
24   Karl Marx and Frederick Engels: Collected Works, 1st Chinese Edition, Volume 40, p. 144, p.p. 144-145.

relationship between civil society and the state, which not only has the significance of general materialism view (the reversed relationship between subject and predicate by Hegel is reversed again), but thus he also put forward an important principle of historical materialism. Marx's elaboration of these contradictions revolves exactly around the contradiction between civil society and the state, and the contradictions within civil society and within the state. He criticizes Hegel's idea of the reconciliation of contradictions by mediation, thus he advances the theory of the types of contradiction, which distinguishes those contradictions within the same essence and between different essences, and he especially emphasizes the study of the contradictions of the objective entity itself, "true philosophical criticism of the present state constitution system not only shows the contradictions as existing, but clarifies them, grasps their essence and necessity. It comprehends their own proper significance. However, this comprehension does not, as Hegel thinks, consist in everywhere recognizing the determinations of the logical concept, but rather in grasping the proper logic of the proper object"[25].

In *Manuscripts 1844*, Marx strives to carry out this principle put forward by him and grasps the particular contradictions of the special object (the capitalist private property) so as to unveil these contradictions and understand their essence and necessity. Marx combines the economic studies with the analysis of contradiction, because the in-depth analysis of the capitalist economy helps him to comprehend and reveal its inner contradictions, while his grasping of the inner contradictions of the capitalist society in turn facilitates his economic studies. It is by analyzing "civil society" that Marx further criticizes and inherits Hegel's idealistic dialectics, and to some extent he discovers the historical dialectics.

The return of Marx to the critical reform effort of Hegel's idealistic dialectics in 1844 is closely related to his economic studies. Marx not only sees the idealistic theoretical basis of the British classical economists, who explain the capitalist economic phenomena with greed and the war amongst the greedy—(competition), but also considers the methods used by them unscientific. These economists take what should be demonstrated and explored, such as the private property,

---

25   Karl Marx and Frederick Engels: Collected Works, 1st Chinese Edition, Volume 1, p. 359.

the relationship between the division of labour and exchange, as an eternal, established fact, instead of investigating how they came into being and developed; they have set necessity and accident in opposition, and explain competition fully with accidental, external circumstances, without clarifying "how far these external and apparently accidental circumstances are but the expression of a necessary course of development"; they oppose competition fact with monopoly fact, the guild with craft freedom, feudal property with the division of landed property, and do "not grasp the way in which the movement is connected", and fail to see that the latter is the necessary consequence of the development of the former. Furthermore, some of the British classical economists stress the identity of the interest of the landowner and capitalist with that of the entire society in order to conceal the antagonistic contradiction between the worker and the capitalist.

Unlike the British classical economists, Marx has dialectic thinking owing to the influence of the dialectics of the German classical philosophy. He concentrates his efforts on exploring the origin and development of the private property, thus analyzes its inner contradictions and investigates historically how the labourer and the means of production have developed from their direct or indirect unity into an antithesis. Marx does not regard the capitalist system as a harmonious organism either, instead he reveals the conflict between man and nature, between man and man, between objectification and self-confirmation, between freedom and necessity, between the individual and the species, between existence and essence, and considers the positive transcendence of private property as the solution to them. These arguments of Marx are all included in his theory of estranged labour. Therefore, we surely say the theory of estranged labour also contains the analysis of objective contradictions, in addition to the influence exerted by Feuerbach's humanism. Once the elements of Feuerbach's humanism are eliminated, these dialectic elements will be integrated with the materialism of history.

Marx, who was transforming and reforming Hegel's dialectics materialistically and tried to utilize it in his economic studies, was very unsatisfied with the attitude of the Young Hegelians, with Bauer as their representative. The Young Hegelians adhered to

self-consciousness idea in the Hegelian philosophy system, and regarded it as the premise of their philosophy. They kept their feet in
the mire of Hegel's idealism, and even repeated Hegel's views word
for word. They tried hard to avoid the relationship of the Young
Hegelians to its birthplace—the Hegelian idealist philosophy, and
there was "a complete lack of awareness about the *apparently formal*, but really *vital* question: how do we now stand as regards to
the Hegelian *dialectic*"[26]. Especially after Feuerbach published his
important works Provisional Theses for the Reform of Philosophy
and Principles of the Philosophy of the Future, they still clung to the
Hegelian idealism, and used Hegel's words and phrases to object
to Feuerbach's criticism of Hegel. By 1844, these Young Hegelians
had not yet realized that "the time was ripe for a critical settling
of accounts with the mother of Young Hegelianism—the Hegelian
dialectic"[27]. They called for criticism, but directed their criticism
against materialism, against the proletarian masses and took a completely uncritical attitude to the Hegelian idealism.

Marx did have some reservation about Feuerbach's attitude to Hegel
at the time. He praised Feuerbach and his serious criticism of Hegel,
and had assimilated his ideas, but he also noticed that Feuerbach
somewhat simplified the question of dialectics. For example, he reduced Hegel's view on the negation of the negation merely to such a
triad as religion—philosophy—the philosophy of religion, and overlooked its rich content and universality. As Marx said, "Feuerbach
conceives the negation of the negation only as a contradiction of
philosophy with itself—as the philosophy which affirms theology
(the transcendent, etc.) after having denied it, and which it therefore
affirms in opposition to itself."[28] Marx had discovered the essence
of the Hegelian idealism (the reversed relationship between being
and thinking), but this did not put him to give an end to the critical
discussion of the Hegelian philosophy and dialectics.

---

26 Karl Marx and Frederick Engels: Collected Works, 1st Chinese Edition,
Volume 42, p. 156.
27 Ibid., p. 157.
28 Ibid., p. 158.

Precisely because of this view, Marx deemed, when writing *Manuscripts* in 1844, that "a critical discussion of Hegelian dialectic and philosophy as a complete whole to be absolutely necessary, a task not yet performed"[29].

But unlike he did in 1843, Marx now chose *The Phenomenology of Spirit* as the target of criticism. Since he thought the criticism should now aim against the whole Hegelian philosophy and his idealistic dialects instead of a specific question, which he had done in his *Critique of Hegel's Philosophy of Right*. Now he thought the perfect target for criticism and discussion would certainly be The Phenomenology of Spirit which is seen as the birthplace and secret of the Hegelian philosophy.

Besides, Marx had advanced the theory of estranged labour in 1844 and around this writings he had probed into the capitalist private property and wage labour. Also to differentiate his theory of estranged labour from the idealistic estrangement theory of the German classical philosophy, The Phenomenology of Spirit should be critically analyzed, because it is in this book that Hegel elaborated his speculative doctrine of the self-estrangement and supersession of the absolute idea. Marx had unmasked the idealistic essence of Hegel's idea of estrangement, but as well recognized its positive achievements when discussing *The Phenomenology of Spirit* in *Manuscripts*, which promoted his understanding of the dialectic character of the course of history.

In *Hegel's Construction of the Phenomenology*, written by Marx in November, 1844, the first commentary is that "Self-consciousness instead of man. Subject—object."[30] This statement best generalizes the idealistic character of the estrangement theory in *The Phenomenology of Spirit* of Hegel.

Subject—self-consciousness, object—"thinghood" created by the alienation of self-consciousness. This is the manifestation of Hegel's paradigm of the self-objectification of the absolute idea and his idea on the supersession of estrangement in the realm of history. Hence, the opposition between subject and object which is generated by

---

29   Ibid., p. 46.
30   Ibid., p. 237.

estrangement is not the opposition between man and the real object which he creates, but the opposition between abstract thinking and real sensuousness within thought. For instance, when wealth, state-power are understood by Hegel as estrangement in *The Phenomenology of Spirit*, this does not refer to the objective, real wealth and state-power, and only happens in their form as thoughts, that is, they are dealt with as pure categories. The reason why self-conscious creates object is nothing but to achieve self-realization and self-knowledge through the process of subject→object, object→subject. Hence subject is active and positive, while object is passive and negative. For consciousness, the object is vanishing, and what it is posited is to do is to confirm the creative power of the subject. The supersession of estrangement is to supersede its objectivity and to resume object into subject. So in Hegel's The Phenomenology of Spirit, "[t]he whole history of the alienation process and the whole process of the retraction of the alienation is therefore nothing but the history of the production of abstract (i.e., absolute) thought—of logical, speculative thought"[31]. This idea of estrangement is surely idealistic, yet it is enlightening for the dialectical understanding of history (man and environment, subject and object in the realm of history) in that it stresses in abstract form the creative role of subject, the development of subject through the opposition between subject and object and the annulment of this opposition.

Marx notes that Hegel's idea of estrangement grasps the estrangement of man in the form of spiritual estrangement and it advocates the transcendence of estrangement, and therefore contains certain critical elements. For example, there is criticism of the entire sphere such as religion, state, civil society in The Phenomenology of Spirit, but Hegel's criticism is not revolutionary and practical, but merely apparent and false, as Marx said, "despite its thoroughly negative and critical appearance and despite the genuine criticism contained in it, which often anticipates far latter development, there is already latent in the *Phenomenology* as a germ, a potentiality, a secret, the uncritical positivism and the equally uncritical idealism of Hegel's later works—that philosophic dissolution and restoration of the existing empirical world."[32]

31   Ibid., p. 161.
32   Ibid., p.p. 161-162.

This uncritical, false criticism is mainly represented by the following two aspects. First, Hegel's transcendence of estrangement is not really to change the object through the actual practical activity, but rather conceived as the movement of understanding in pure thought, i.e., the understanding of its subjective essence from the object itself. Therefore, the supersession of religion, state and law in the Hegelian philosophy is not the supersession of real religion, state and law, but the supersession of dogmatics, political science, jurisprudence which have already become the objects of knowledge, and on the other side religion, state and law still exist in real life, just like Marx profoundly exposed, "this superseding in thought, which leaves its object remaining in existence in the real world."[33] Second, Hegel does not really supersede estrangement; instead he confuses objectification with estrangement and actually defends the existence of estrangement. Objectification for Hegel is the necessary moment for self-consciousness to realize and know itself. Self-consciousness should first objectify itself, and then only by superseding the objectivity of the object can it return into the subject itself. This is estrangement and its supersession, and also the self-confirmation of self-consciousness as well. The supersession of estrangement is therefore the confirmation of estrangement as the other-being of self-consciousness. For instance, "[t]he man who has recognized that he is leading an alienated life in law, politics, etc., is leading his true human life in this alienated life as such"[34]. This is a complete defence for the feudal constitution and laws of Prussia, there is a negation of the necessity to thoroughly change this constitution.

However, Marx also affirms the reasonable elements of the Hegelian idealistic dialectics from two aspects. One is the question is the affirmation of the role played by labour in the development of human history and the other is its dialectical view on the development of human history. Thus, he extends and develops some reasonable elements of the Hegelian idealism and approaches to the understanding of the dialectical process of history.

---

33   Ibid., p. 174.
34   Ibid., p. 172.

Marx points out: "Hegel's standpoint is that of modern political economy. He grasps *labour* as the *essence* of man—as man's essence which stands the test", and also underlines that Hegel "grasps the essence of *labour* and comprehends objective man—true, because real man—as the outcome of man's *own labour*". But on the other hand Marx writes: "For Hegel the *human being—man*—equals *self-consciousness.*" "The only labour which Hegel knows and recognizes is abstractly mental labour."[35]

Since self-consciousness is understood by Hegel as the essence of man, then why does Marx say that he takes labour as the essence of man? Since Hegel recognizes mental labour only, why does Marx say that he grasps the essence of labour? These two seemingly contradictory views show his understanding of the idealistic essence of the Hegelian philosophy, and the positive significance he has seen in it.

Hegel in fact does have an understanding of the role of labour, which is well expounded in his *Realphilosophie, The Phenomenology of Spirit* and *The Elements of the Philosophy of Right*. Especially in *The Phenomenology of Spirit*, his analysis of the relationship between master and slave is very profound. Hegel argues that the master becomes a slave of the slave because of his separation from labour, while a slave rediscovers himself and becomes a master of the master after he is engaged in labour. But what we would clearly like to point out that Marx does not mean this above idea of Hegel when saying : "Hegel regards labour as the essence of man", but rather Marx wants to underline that Hegel's consideration of self-consciousness as the essence of man evaluates labour as the essence of man, in an abstract form. The process from the self-objectification and estrangement of self-consciousness to the supersession of estrangement and return to the subject, in the process in which the subject is confirmed and developed, is actually a description of man's self-creation and the essence of labour. It is through the objectification and estrangement of labour and the constant overcoming of this estrangement of labour that the subject (man) itself is developed. If we replace Hegel's self-consciousness with man, his self-positing, self-annulling abstract action with man's actual labour, the estrangement of

---

35   Ibid., p. 163, p. 165, p. 168.

self-consciousness and its supersession with those of labour, all will be reversed, and we will get such a real process definition in which man creates himself through his labour. Therefore, Marx says that labour is understood by Hegel as the action of man's self-creation within the sphere of abstraction, and because Hegel reverses the relationship between thinking and being, this process appears "as a *merely formal*, because abstract, act, because the human being itself is taken to be only an *abstract, thinking being*, conceived merely as self-consciousness"[36]. The genius of Marx lies in the fact that he discovers the rational core from the shell of the Hegelian idealism and Hegel's description of the historical process of man developing himself through labour in a tortuous way, by means of the speculative form of the estrangement of self-consciousness and its supersession. As we see Marx is not narrating but reforming Hegel.

Marx also affirms Hegel's idea of historical dialectics. Unlike Feuerbach, who views the negation of the negation merely as a speculative game in which theology is affirmed later after having been denied, Marx detects its reasonable and general character. Hegel takes self-consciousness as the subject of history, and therefore is divorced from real man and real history, but the actual historical process of man is reflected in his view that the estrangement of self-consciousness and the supersession of estrangement will go through the process of the negation of the negation. Because Hegel abstracts from the real subject (man) and the real history (the actual labour of man), by him the real activity of man is abstracted and mystified, which is the absurd aspect of his view, but the reasonable aspect is that he "has found the *abstract, logical, speculative* expression" for the movement of history"[37].

Marx recognizes the universality of the negation of the negation as well. Hegel incorporates the rich, living, sensuous, concrete activity of man into the paradigm of the negation of the negation, and thus abstracts all of its content and turns it into an abstract form. This is certainly idealistic, but as a logical category, a thought form, this abstraction is reasonable. It becomes a general form pertaining and applicable to all and every content after abstraction, just as Marx said,

---

36 Ibid., p. 175.
37 Ibid., p. 159.

"one gets general, abstract *forms of abstraction* pertaining to every content and on that account indifferent to, and, consequently, valid for, all content—the thought-forms or logical categories separated from *real* mind and form *real* nature."[38] This general character as Marx said then was only valid within the Hegelian philosophy system, meaning that it was applicable to logics, the philosophy of nature and philosophy of spirit. It was the lever Hegel used to construct his system, and it was impossible for him to consider the negation of the negation as the general, objective law of nature, society and thought, as Engels had theorized this law later in his *Dialectics of Nature* and *Anti-Dühring*. However, to some extent, Marx confirms its universality by considering Hegel's negation of the negation as the pure logical form pertaining to all content.

Hegel's idea of estrangement was idealistic, but it had some positive elements, the criticism and reform of which was very beneficial to Marx's formation of historical dialectics.

---

38   Ibid., p. 176.

CHAPTER VII

MAN AND NATURE, MAN AND SOCIETY

In *Manuscripts*, Marx praises Feuerbach and argues that it is only with him that naturalist and humanist criticism begins. He sometimes calls it perfect or thorough naturalism and thorough humanism, and uses them to express his views on communism and some philosophical questions. As to some questions of man, nature and society, Marx was undoubtedly still under the lingering influence of Feuerbach then, yet he also surpassed him. These different ideas below, from Feuerbach's have constituted the positive factors which helped him advance forward to the materialist conception of history.

1 OBJECTIVE REALITY OF NATURE
ESTRANGED NATURE AND HUMANIZED NATURE

Feuerbach's philosophy is characterized by naturalism and humanism. He emphasizes the objective reality of nature, and sees nature as a material, sensuous being; he stresses that man is a product of nature, a part of nature. Feuerbach bases his philosophy on the unity of man with nature, and takes man, together with nature—which is the basis of man, as the sole, universal, and supreme object. His praise over man and nature displays his essence of combating religion and speculative idealism. However, he regards the relationship of man to nature as the relationship between two natural things, as the relationship of nature to itself, thereby he cannot really explain the relationship between man and nature scientifically.

Feuerbach stresses the objective reality of nature and makes it confront with Hegel's absolute idea. When nature is conceived by him (Feuerbach) as the primary entity, as the non-genetic, eternal entity, 'personality, "individuality", consciousness, without Nature, is nothing; or which is the same thing, an empty, unsubstantial abstraction"[1], And, Feuerbach adheres to materialism. But Feuerbach sees nature as the object of sensual perception rather than the object of practice. He inherited Spinoza's "self-caused idea", and tried to understand nature only from nature itself, and excluded man's practical activity from the relationship between man and nature.

Marx certainly recognized the objective reality of nature in 1844. But a new factor was added to his theory of estranged labour, that is, nature was investigated as an object of labour. According to Marx, the fundamental content of labour is objectification, that is, the labourer congeals his essential powers in the product, while objectification presupposes as premise: The objective reality of nature. "The worker can create nothing without nature, without the *sensuous external world*. It is the material on which his labour is realized, in which it (labour) is active, from which, and by means of which it produces."[2] Therefore, the relationship between the labourer and the product of labour is viewed by Marx as the relationship between man and nature as well, "the relation [of the worker] to the sensuous external world, to the objects of nature, as an alien world inimically opposed to him"[3]. Nature is seen as the object of labour and included into the labour process for study by Marx through his theory of estranged labour.

1   The Selected Works of Feuerbach's Philosophical Works, Volume 2, p. 122, Beijing: SDX Joint Publishing Company, 1962.
2   Karl Marx and Frederick Engels: Collected Works, 1st Chinese Edition, Volume 42, p. 92.
3   Ibid., p. 94.

It is just because Marx investigates nature as the object of practice that his criticism of Hegel's idealistic theory of the unity of subject with object is more profound than that of Feuerbach. Feuerbach uses nature to oppose the absolute idea, and emphasizes the objective reality of nature, but because he separates nature from the labour of man, this understanding of nature is abstract, and Marx writes: "*nature* too, taken abstractly, for itself—nature fixed in isolation from man—is *nothing* for man"[4]. In contrast, Marx affirms the objectivity of the object from the perspective of the dialectical unity of subject with object.

According to Marx, for man as the subject, objects independent of him exist outside him. These objects are objects that he needs—essential objects, indispensable for the manifestation and confirmation of his essential powers. The subject (man) can only express his life in real, sensuous objects. For example, hunger is a natural need of man; he therefore needs a nature outside himself, an object outside himself, in order to eliminate hunger. To draw a cake cannot satisfy hunger. Even the coarsest food which one has to settle for is also a material existence. Later in *The Holy Family*, when Marx criticized the Young Hegelians' absolute subjectivity and repudiated their objectivist, idealistic fallacy, he also illustrated this question by taking love as an example. Hence Marx said that "[a] being which does not have its nature outside itself is not a *natural* being, and plays no part in the system of nature. A being which has no object outside itself is not an objective being."[5]

Marx not only grasps the object from the perspective of the subject, viewing nature as the object of human labour and desire, as the objective object existing outside the subject, but also grasps the subject from the perspective of the object, seeing the subject as the conditioned, sensuous being.

Marx agrees with Feuerbach on that: Man is a natural being. Man is a real, corporeal, living material substance with his feet firmly on the solid ground and who exchanges with nature. But man is a living natural being, hence an active being. His vital powers, natural powers exist in him as the desire for and as pursuit of objects, so

4   Ibid., p. 178.
5   Ibid., p. 168.

man is a passionate being as well; but on the other hand, as a natural, corporeal, sensuous being he is a being conditioned and limited by the objective entities independent of him, thus man is a suffering being, like other animals and plants. For Marx, man has two kinds of nature: one is the nature of man himself, i.e., his physical existence and its special character, which is called by him the "organic body" of man; the other is the nature outside man, nature existing outside and independent of man, which is called by Marx the *"inorganic body"* of man.

It is based on the objective reality of man that Marx criticizes Hegel.

Man is seen by Hegel as a non-objective being, namely, man is independent of the objective entities. Because the essence of man is self-consciousness, all objects are posited by self-consciousness. The annulment of estrangement is the annulment of objectivity, which is the process of returning of the object into the self and merging into self-consciousness. Man becomes a monster without his own nature (human body) and object (external nature), a fleshless spirit. So Marx points out sharply that in Hegel "Man is regarded as a *non-objective, spiritual* being"[6].

There is no doubt that man has self-consciousness, but self-consciousness is human self-consciousness and depends on the material character of man. The self is nothing but the abstraction of man. Each person is the self, and his eye, his ear, every sense organ of his has this quality of selfhood, while self-consciousness is a quality of human nature—human sense organs, and will not exist if separated from human nature (sense organs). For this reason, Marx underlines that "man's *feelings*, passions, etc., are not merely anthropological phenomena in the (narrower) sense, but truly *ontological* affirmations of being (of nature)"[7]. That is to say, man perceives directly through his sense organs the objective world outside himself, the living, sensuous world, because each feeling has its corresponding objective existence, for instance, the existence corresponding to sight is the light wave, and the existence corresponding to hearing is the sound wave. It is the special character of the objective world itself which determines the different ways of feeling. And more than that,

---

6   Ibid., p. 164.
7   Ibid., p. 150.

man affirms the existence of the world of objects through his sense organs, and in turn, he affirms the subject itself and that man himself is an objective, sensuous being.

Marx would not surpass Feuerbach if he could only go so far, but he did not stay there His brilliance lies in that he not only objects to spiritualism, to the idealistic view equating man with self-consciousness, and emphasizes that man is an objective, natural being, but also underlines that man is a particular natural being, i.e., a human natural being: "man is not merely a natural being: he is a *human* natural being. That is to say, he is a being for himself. Therefore he is a *species-being*."[8]

Here "Species-being", a term of Feuerbach, was followed but was given different contents by Marx.

First, Feuerbach believes that human beings are not individuals independent of and isolated from each other, but they are a species and they belong to the human species. Man is a species-being, not only because he is a species objectively and has a common essence (species-essence), but because he is able to be aware of this, that is, he can go beyond his individual limits and realize that himself, the other—the you outside me, both of them belong to the human species. Man therefore can take both his individuality and the species as the object.

Marx is different. He also acknowledges that man has consciousness and can consider the species as his essence, or he can regard himself as a species-being. However, labour is the fundamental reason why man is a species-being. Marx reiterated that "[c]onscious life activity distinguishes man immediately from animal life activity. It is just because of this that he is a species-being." He also wrote: "[i]n creating a *world of objects* by his personal activity, in his *work upon* inorganic nature, man proves himself a conscious species-being"; "It is just in his work upon the objective world that man really proves himself to a *species-being*"[9], etc. This shows that Marx had already perceived that man related himself not only to nature but also to other men in the labour process. Any single, isolated individual could not

---

8   Ibid., p. 169.
9   Ibid., p. 96, p. 97.

work outside this relation, hence "production is his active species-life". Although Marx's view on labour was still rather abstract at the time, to seek the basis for man as a species-being in labour instead of in species-consciousness was the right direction.*

Second, for Feuerbach, man as a natural, sensuous being is identical with man as a species-being. The common essence of man as a species-being—his species-essence is the common attribute of man as a natural being, which is the purely natural attribute connecting individuals. Marx has a different view. He certainly does not deny the natural attribute of man, which he highlighted when he repudiated spiritualism and religion. But he argues that man is a human natural being, that is, his natural attribute is different from that of other animals, and is human, he has socialized natural attribute. In fact, eating, drinking, procreating for man are "genuinely human functions". Although they have something in common with the drinking, eating and propagating acts of animals, they embody human characteristics. Only separated from the sphere of all other human activity, and separated from their characteristics of the society and times, an when "turned into sole and ultimate ends, when taken abstractly, they are animal functions"[10].

Precisely based on this dialectical view, Marx criticized the community usage of women by the equalitarian communism trend. For Marx, the relation between men to women, the relation between the sexes is the direct and natural, and necessary relation between man and man. In this relation, man's relation to nature is immediately his relation to man, and in turn his relation to man is his relation to nature. The need for the opposite sex is a natural destination, but it is a human natural destination, so the overall development of man, the degree to which the natural behaviours of man has become human behaviours can be judged by this relation between opposite sexes. The community of women is nothing but an approach to women as the spoil and as the hand-maid of communal lust, in which is expressed the infinite degradation in which man exists for himself, the degradation of man to an animal.

---

10 Ibid., p. 94.

*) The nature outside man, nature existing outside and independent of man, is called by Marx the "*inorganic* body" of man.

Marx investigates the relationship between man and nature from the perspective of man as a human natural being, and thus overcomes, to some extent, Feuerbach's weakness of conceiving the relationship between man and nature merely as the relationship between nature and itself, as the relationship between animate natural things and inanimate natural things.

Marx affirms that man, like animals, depends on nature in the physical life. And man is more advanced than animals, the more universal is the nature on which he lives, the more is his dependence on nature. The cattle can live on water and grass, while man cannot. The more developed the society is, the greater is his dependence on nature. It did not matter whether there was petroleum or not in ancient times, but in the industrialized society petroleum becomes the lifeline of man. Man cannot be separated from nature, and can only live physically on nature. In spiritual life, man cannot be separated from nature, either, because nature is the object of both natural science and art. Therefore, Marx said that "[n]ature is man's *inorganic* body—nature, that is, insofar as it is not itself human body. Man *lives* on nature—which means that nature is his body, with which he must remain in continuous interchange, if he is not to die. That man's physical and spiritual life is linked to nature means simply that nature is linked to itself, because man is a part of nature."[11] That nature is the inorganic body of man and that man is a part of nature are used by Marx to highlight man's dependence on nature, his inseparable relation to nature. It is obvious that he wisely inherits and affirms the materialist principle in Feuerbach's naturalism.

Of course, Marx does not stop here. That man is seen as a part of nature is not an original idea of Marx. From the perspective of natural science, Huxley's *Man's Place in Nature* elaborates the relationship between men and animals, determines man's place in the animal kingdom, and advances for the first time that man and apes share a common ancestor from the aspects of comparative anatomy, embryology, palaeontology, etc. Philosophically speaking, what is repeatedly stressed by Feuerbach's philosophy is that man is a part of nature, and also the unity of man with nature. What was unique about Marx in 1844 was that he discussed the relationship between

---

11   Ibid., p. 95.

man and nature from the angle of the development of history, and included labour as a basic factor in the unity of man with nature by studying the process of nature from estrangement to its (nature's) humanization.

The humanization of nature is corresponding to the estrangement of nature, and they are associated with human labour. The estranged nature and estranged labour, the humanized nature and true human labour are inseparable.

In the estranged labour of Marx nature and man are in opposition. Nature as the condition of human existence should provide the labourer with both the means of labour and the means of subsistence, but in estranged labour, the more the workers possess the external, sensuous nature through their labour, the more they become a slave of their objects. The sensuous, external world, i.e. nature, provides neither the objects of labour nor the means of subsistence to maintain their physical existence for them, but confronts them as capital. So only in the form of estranged labour can the labourer make nature into the object of labour, and combine them. When private property is annulled, man becomes a real human being, and labour becomes true labour, nature changes from estranged nature to humanized nature. Here the opposition between nature and man is annulled, and nature no longer separates man from man as capital, but serves as the bond between people as the real object of labour. It is easy to see that Marx's expositions on estranged nature and humanized nature here is consistent with his view of the estrangement and return/regaining of human essence, the former being a part of the latter. If we remain within this scope, we will consider his idea on the humanized nature to be a reproduction of Feuerbach's humanism and fail to make a correct evaluation. Concerning this question, Marx's rationality is manifested in his integrating it with human activity when he studied both the estranged nature and the humanized nature, and also the transformation of the former into the latter, hence we can say he had studied nature by including it in the history of mankind.

There is no such thing as estrangement for nature itself. The estrangement of nature is about the relationship between nature and man, and it is related to human activity. Therefore, the relationship between man and nature appearing in estranged labour consists of two aspects: On the one hand, nature in the form of capital keeps man in bondage; on the other hand, man transforms nature and leaves his marks on nature, just as Marx said, "The nature which develops in human history—the genesis of human society—is man's real nature; hence nature as it develops through industry, even though in an *estranged* form, is true *anthropological* nature."[12]

The estrangement of nature, in this sense, is also the humanization of nature, and the estranged nature is the true anthropological nature. Nature which is closely linked to human activity is "man's product", "the nature created by history". The understanding of nature from the point of view of human activity is not only the epistemology of materialist dialectics, but also an important thought of the materialist conception of history. Later, Marx continued to develop this idea with the nature of history in *The German Ideology*. He said that "the sensuous world around [us] is, which not a thing given direct from all eternity, remaining ever the same, but instead the product of industry and of the state of society; and, indeed, in the sense that it is an historical product, the result of the activity of a whole succession of generations"[13]. The relationship between man and nature will be a mystery difficult to reveal, if the human nature is not understood from the development of history.

According to Marx, not only is the estranged nature the historical product, the product of human activity, but the real "humanization" of nature, i.e., the annulment of the opposition between nature and man "is only possible through the cooperative action of all of mankind, only as the result of history"[14]. Man as a real man is the result of his labour; nature as the humanized nature is also the result of his labour.

Although some statements of Marx still bear the traces of humanism, the inclusion of labour in the relationship between man and nature marks a significant progress. Only through labour can the relationship between man and nature could be differentiated from the relationship between other animals and nature.

---

12 Ibid., p. 128.
13 Karl Marx and Frederick Engels: Collected Works, 1st Chinese Edition, Volume 3, p. 48.
14 Karl Marx and Frederick Engels: Collected Works, 1st Chinese Edition, Volume 42, p. 163.

The animal is directly related to nature. It is a part of and acts upon nature through itself. The relationship between man and nature is mediated by labour, hence an indirect one. Man not only transforms nature by virtue of the instruments of production, but also can use the forces of nature to act upon it. This shows the subjective active role unique to man. For example, an earthworm can loosen the soil, but this is not its subjective activity but its biological habit, while that man utilizes this biological habit of the earthworm to improve soil clearly manifests the subjective activity specific to man.

The animal relies on and adapts itself to nature, while man transforms nature through labour and adapts nature to human needs. Man takes something from nature instead of waiting passively for the gifts of nature. Domestication is more characteristic for human labour than hunting, as is cultivation than picking fruits and vegetables.

The sphere of animal activity is determined by nature. It is and activity within certain sphere and does not try to go beyond it. But man is different: he keeps expanding his sphere of activity, which is not merely conditioned by nature, but in a large degree, depends on the level of production and science. With the development of production, science and technology, man continuously expands his sphere of activity, which can be proved by his entry into the space.

Just because the relationship between man and nature is different from that between animal and nature, a kind of danger lurks in this relationship, i.e., the destruction of nature. The animal itself is nature, and is a part of the ecological balance, whereas man may blindly destroy this balance. Therefore human transformation of nature should certainly create conditions conducive to his own existence and development, rather than destroying them; should protect and better his own living environment, rather than destroying the environment.

In today's world with the rapid advancement of science and technology, the transformation of nature is incomparable than ever before in both depth and width. But if man plunders nature and violates the laws of nature by virtue of the new achievements in science and technology, the contradiction between him and nature will be intensified inevitably. In recent decades, the environmental pollution and public hazards brought about by the industrial development have become a pressing concern. The events in which public hazards cause casualty and disease have occurred whether in the Meuse River valley industrial park in Belgium, or Donora in America, London in Britain, or in Yokkaichi, Toyama Prefecture and Minamata of Kumamoto Prefecture in Japan. In particular, in December, 1984, the world was shocked by the Bhopal gas tragedy, in which over 200,000 were injured and killed in Bhopal, the central state of Madhya Pradesh's (India) capital, by poison gas which leaked from Union Carbide India Ltd., an American transnational corporation. Of course, we cannot conclude that we should resist against the scientific and technological development, the transformation of nature and should return to the natural state. The American organization named "Nature Restoration Movement" has argued that the natural course should not be destroyed, and even rejected children's going to school and wearing clothes, and advocated eating raw meat. This trend of thought circuitously reflects people's protest against the capitalist reality, but it does not accord with the progressive trend of the times. The crucial issue is the social system; in addition, the study of human ecology should be conducted to explore the relationship between man and nature and its law so as to reach a positive equilibrium in the transformation of nature.

That labour is the bond which unites man and nature is an excellent idea of Marx. He does not regard nature as the object of sensual perception, but as the object of human labour, and emphasizes that through his labour, man makes nature appear as his work and reality, as "the objectification of his species-life", and sees man's power in the changes occurred in nature. However, we cannot conclude from this that Marx denies the objective reality of nature, and oppose Lenin's view to Marx's.

In his *Materialism and Empirio-criticism*, Lenin discusses specifically such a question: Did nature exist prior to man? And he makes it clear that the earth had already existed in such a state that no man or any other creature had existed or could have existed on it. This is not in contradiction to Marx's conclusion at all. Lenin is opposed to Mach and Avenarius, and the "principled coordination" idea, so he wanted to stress that the object and that the earth existed prior to man. What Marx discusses is the interaction between man and nature after the appearance of man, so he emphasizes the subject, the transformation of nature by man. Their discussion is from different perspectives. Lenin does not deny man's transformation effort of nature after his appearance on earth; conversely, Marx did not deny that the earth existed prior to man in 1844, either. Even when he elaborated the interaction between man and nature, Marx stressed the objective reality of nature, which can be supported by his opposition to the religious theory of creation and to Hegel's idealistic view on the annulment of estrangement defined as the annulment of object.

2 SOCIAL NATURE OF MAN
SOCIAL MAN AND NON-SOCIAL MAN

With respect to the question of the relationship between man and nature, Marx did not formulate the category of relations of production in 1844, and thus did not grasp that the sum total of the relations of production constitutes society, and constitutes a society at a certain stage of historical development. With human essence as his measure, the future socialist society is called by Marx "society", and the capitalist society based on private property "non-society". Nonetheless, his analysis on the transformation from the non-social man into the social man, especially the relationship between man and society in the so-called "social state", embraces many positive, reasonable elements.

What is man? According to Marx, man is not simply a single individual, but a species-being, a social being. And this opinion of him was reiterated in *Critique of Hegel's Philosophy of Right, On the Jewish Question, Contribution to the Critique of Hegel's Philosophy of Law: Introduction, Critical Marginal Notes on the Article "The King of Prussia and Social Reform, By a Prussian"*. The major difference between them and *Manuscripts of 1844* lies in that in the latter, Marx considers labour as the essence of man as a result of his economic studies, and combines the social nature of man with labour. In labour man connects himself to both nature and to other men. A single individual will be unable to work. Hence Marx argues that both the exchange of man's labour and the exchange of man's products in the production process are a "species-activity". In labour man is bound to social connections independent of the individuals' will.

The problem is that whether this social connection is the real human social connection is determined by whether it (social connection) and man's social nature are identical. For Marx at that time under the private property, man produces only for possessing. Production is not only utilitarian (to satisfy needs), but also individualistic, egoistic (to satisfy personal needs). This production is not the objectification of man's essence, but the materialization of his immediate, egoistic needs. The production under the private property is therefore not the social production, not the production for human needs. People produce seemingly to meet the needs of each other, but actually to resist the mutual possession of their products. So Marx believes that the bourgeois society is not the true community which is identical with human nature, it is not a society but a non-society.

Based on this, Marx criticizes the bourgeois political economy, which conceives the exchange and trade as man's species-life, the true human life, and thus regards society as a series of exchanges, as a commercial society, in which every man is a merchant. "*Society*, as it appears to the political economist, is *civil society* in which every individual is a totality of needs and only exists for the other person, as the other exists for him, insofar as each becomes a means for the other."[15] For Marx, this actually takes the estranged form of social intercourse as the form not corresponding to human nature.

Starting with the interest of protecting the capitalist private property, the bourgeois political economy considers the capitalist private property and its form of movement to be permanent and reduces all society to the bourgeois society; while Marx is against the capitalist private property and maintains that the bourgeois society is a non-society. This is two opposite standpoints. But Marx's view clearly bears the traces of Feuerbach's humanism. The essence of man is seen as a measure, and all societies that correspond to this essence are called a society; otherwise, it will be a non-society. This viewpoint is not so much an economic analysis as a moral evaluation.

---

15   Ibid., p. 144.

Individualism, egoism are the manifestations of the loss of man's social character. Hence, the bourgeois society for Marx is not a society, but a civil society, and man as the member of civil society is not a species-being, but an individual divorced from the society as a whole. Here, the sole bond connecting human beings and society is private interest, the personal protection of their property and egoism. Egoism is in opposition to man's social nature. "The greater and the more developed the social power appears to be within the private property relationship, the more egoistic, asocial and estranged from his own nature does man become."[16]

Marx's conclusion that the bourgeois society is a non-society and man in the bourgeois society is the non-social man is in conflict with his conclusion that man is by nature a social being. His "solution" to this theoretical contradiction was the theory of the estrangement of human essence. Man should by nature be a social being, but under the private property, human relations turn into non-human relations and human essence becomes non-human existence due to estrangement, hence man cannot realize his species-being, but instead loses his inherent essence. In this way, the opposition between human individual and the species, between existence and essence, are also the opposition between "should be" (what man should be) and "is" (what man actually is), between man and non-human. This way of thinking still had the character of Feuerbach's humanism.

If estrangement is dismissed as a basic theory and method, it should be said that the bourgeois society is not a non-society, but one of the social formations in history; it should be said that man does not lose his social nature in the bourgeois society, instead, the bourgeois society is more social than the previous societies, such as the primitive society based on blood kinship, the slave society and the feudal society based on agricultural production. The developed commodity relations and money relation has not only wiped off the barriers of feudalism and formed a unified domestic market, but also formed the world-market through the international trade. This point was later expounded in depth in *The Communist Manifesto*: "the need of a constantly expanding market for its products chases the bourgeoisie over the whole surface of the globe. It must nestle everywhere, settle

---

16   Ibid., p. 29.

everywhere, establish connections everywhere." And "the bourgeoi-sie has through its exploitation of the world-market given a cosmo-politan character to production and consumption in every country."[17] "And as in material production, so is also in intellectual production. The intellectual creations of individual nations become common property. National one-sidedness and narrow-mindedness become more and more impossible, and from the numerous national and lo-cal literatures, there arises a world literature."[18] The social character of the capitalist production combines people more closely.

Marx's argument that the capitalist system is "non-social" touches with an unscientific phrase: The contradiction between individual labour and social labour under the capitalist system, which he was not clear about yet. In the capitalist society, labour is social labour, and the labour of each property owner is provided/produced for the society and is part of the total social labour. On the other side, yet each commodity producer is a property owner, and the prod-ucts of labour belong to him, so this labour is also individual labour. Therefore, human labour is not immediately or directly manifested as social labour under the capitalist private property. It is mediated by money, and individual labour is manifested as social labour only through exchanges. Man does not lose his social nature and become a being in isolation from each other; instead, the relationship be-tween man and man is always linked to the things, and appears as the relationship between things, hence this conceals the relationship between man and man. The isolated, atomic individual is just a false appearance of this relationship.

It is based on this view on society and non-society that Marx had connected his understanding on society in 1844 with the idea of Feuerbach's species. He said in a letter to Feuerbach that "[t]he unity of man with man, which is based on the real differences be-tween men, the concept of the human species brought down from the heaven of abstraction to the real earth, what is this but the concept of *society*!"[19] The society here is the society in *Manuscripts*, in which the private ownership has been superseded, i.e., it is the communism

17 Karl Marx and Frederick Engels: Selected Works, 1st Chinese Edition, Volume 1, p. 254.
18 Ibid., p. 255.
19 Karl Marx and Frederick Engels: Collected Works, 1st Chinese Edition, Volume 27, p. 450.

as understood by Marx at that time. This is the realization of the species-essence of man, or the return of man to himself as a social being, as a real man. This is also Marx's solution brought to the contradiction between the individual and the species before 1844. Here in this society the species is no longer a power confronting the individual, and man has regained the human world and human relations to himself, and now man is a real species-being in labour process or in political life.

We should see not only the humanistic elements in the theory of estranged labour—the estrangement and return/regaining of human essence, but also the reasonable elements therein. Marx's idea of the series of changes after man has re-appropriated his essence and become a social being contains the important thoughts on property and man, man and society, nature and society as well as the relationship between subject and object under the communist system.

With a firm grasp on the capitalist private property, Marx combines the re-appropriation of his essence by man with the positive transcendence of private property, and regards the transcendence of the private property as the premise of all estrangement, including in the superstructure. Thus, he captures the crux of the problems in the capitalist society. Marx had intended to emphatically study the relationship between private property and the real human and social property relations in *Manuscripts*. The so-called real human and social property refers to the ownership established after the transcendence of private property. As to the form of this ownership, Marx was unlikely to know it yet at that time, but he proposed the replacement of one property relation (the legal term for the ownership, actually meaning ownership) by another one, which is quite different from the bourgeois classical political economy which eternalizes the private property and also different from equalitarian communism which advocates equal possession of private property.

In particular, here Marx poses the idea of association. He points out that the division of landed property negates the monopoly of property in land, after he analyzes the division of landed property in rural areas. But this negation only changes the form of monopoly—the concentration and scattering of land, does not change its essence—private property on the soil. For Marx, to prevent land from returning

again to monopoly in a still more malignant form, the private property in the soil must be abolished and the association should be implemented. He writes: "Association, applied to land, shares the economic advantage of large-scale landed property, and first brings to
realization the original tendency inherent in [land] division, namely,
equality. In the same way association also re-establishes, now on
a rational basis, no longer mediated by serfdom, lordship and the
silly mysticism of property, the intimate ties of man with the earth,
since the earth ceases to be an object of huckstering, and through
free labour and free enjoyment becomes once more a true personal
property of man."[20] Marx's idea of association (ed. a type of ownership form) designs a development path different from the private
property on the soil. As to the form of this association, we cannot
make excessive demand from Marx, which is a question that is to be
only be solved by the practice of socialism itself.

Marx also touches the relationship between man and production,
relationship between man and society. Under the private property,
through production the labourer not only produces himself as a commodity, but also reproduces the possession of labour and its products
by the capitalist, therefore, man through "his" labour produces the
physically and mentally degraded man. Whereas on the assumption of positively annulled private property, we can see: "how man
produces man—himself and the other man". Here the product is no
longer the estrangement of labour, but the manifestation of the individuality of the labourer himself; it is no longer a exchange value,
but the immediate satisfaction of other men's needs; people produce
for each other, i.e. for the society. It is in this type of producing activity which annuls private property, that man can achieve the unity
with society, "*just as society* itself produces *man as ma*n, so is society *produced* by him"[21].

It is also because of the annulment of private property that "[a]ctiv-
ity and enjoyment, both in their content and in their *mode of existence*, are *social*: they are *social* activity and *social* enjoyment" . This
not only means that the collective, communal labour in which many

20   Karl Marx and Frederick Engels: Collected Works, 1st Chinese Edition,
Volume 42, p.p. 85-86.
21   Ibid., p. 121.

people associate and are engaged is manifested as social activity, but also that even an activity which a person seldomly performs in direct community with others, such as the scientific research activity, is also a social activity. Because the material of the scientific activity is the product of society, as is even the language is the product of society on which the thinker is active, and in society the scientific research is for the society instead of for the individual.

Therefore, the society and the individual are in opposition under the private property. The society as the species-power is a power alien from the individual; the species-life (including the spheres of economy, politics and consciousness) is the abstract universality confronting the individual life. But for Marx that will change after the annulment of private property. "Above all we must avoid postulating 'society' again as an abstraction vis-à-vis the individual. The individual *is the social being*. His manifestations of life(even if they may not appear in the direct form of *communal* manifestations of life carried out in association with others)are therefore an expression and confirmation of *social life*."[22]

Under the domination of private property, nature as capital is also appropriated by some people, and is opposed to the labourer; it is not the manifestation of man's social essence, but the manifestation of his estranged essence; men are not linked to but isolated from each other in the process of the transformation of nature. However, the relationship between nature and man will change fundamentally after the annulment of private property: "The *human* aspect of nature exists only for *social* man; for only then does nature exist for him as a *bond* with man—as his existence for the other and the other's existence for him—and as the life-element of human reality. Only then does nature exist as the *foundation* of his own *human* existence. Only here has what is to him his *natural* existence become his human existence, and nature become man for him." Only after the private property has been annulled does man not really regard nature as the mere means of livelihood, but develops his talents to their fullest through the transformation of nature, that is, the estrangement of nature from man is eliminated. Hence Marx wrote: "*society* is the completely unity of man with nature—the true resurrection of

---

22   Ibid., p.p. 122-123.

nature—the consistent naturalism of man and the consistent humanism of nature."[23]

Marx had also considered the changes in the perceptive ability of the
subject—(man), from the perspective of the annulment of private
property. He said, "It is obvious that the *human* eye enjoys things
in a way different from the crude, non-human eye; the human *ear*
different from the crude ear, etc." He also said that "the *senses* of
the social man *differ* from those of the non-social man."[24] Here, the
crude, non-human, non-social man is the same, which means the
man under the private property, i.e., the man who has lost his social
nature; the so-called human, social man refers to man who has annulled the private ownership, i.e., the man whose social nature has
returned to him. This differentiation is certainly not scientific, but its
reasonableness lies in that Marx considers the change in the senses
of man not simply from the physiological structure of his sense organs, but from the annulment of private property, from the relationship between subject and object in the future society.

Under the condition of the private property, man as the subject becomes "stupid and one-sided". All physical and mental senses are
impoverished, reduced only to one sense—having or possessing; and
nature as the object only appears as the mere utility, and is treated as
the capital, or as the means of subsistence for eating, drinking, wearing and inhabiting. Man of this kind is the "non-social man". He has
ears, but he does not have the sense of music, and cannot feel the
melody; he has eyes, but he does not have the sense of beauty, and
cannot feel the beauty of form. "The *sense* caught up in crude practical need has only a *restricted* sense", "The care-burdened, poverty-
stricken man has no *sense* for the finest play; the dealer in minerals
sees only the commercial value but not the beauty and the specific
character of the mineral: he has no mineralogical sense"[25].

The transcendence of private property leads to the fundamental
change in subject and object and in their relationship. The subject
is the social man, namely, the man as real man, while the object
is no longer the strange object to itself, but the real human object.

23   Ibid., p. 122.
24   Ibid., p. 125, p. 126.
25   Ibid., p. 126

Man appropriates the object through his sensing, hearing, smelling, tasting, feeling, thinking, observing, experiencing, wanting, acting, loving, which is, however, not simply possessing, having, nor the immediate, one-sided enjoyment and consumption, but the full development and enrichment of his essence through the perceptible appropriation of the products created by him, appropriation of objective man, of human achievements. It is in this process that the perceptible wealth of man as the subject, such as the eye which feels the beauty of the form, the ear which has the sense of music, is gradually cultivated and brought into being. And it is in this sense that Marx wrote: "[t]he abolition [*Aufhebung*] of private property is therefore the complete *emancipation* of all human senses and qualities."[26]

Marx regards the positive transcendence of private property as the decisive critical moment in the transformation of the so-called non-social man into the social man, and combines it with the full development of man, the elimination of all evils under the capitalist private property, and the establishment of the new relationship between man and nature, between man and nature, which shows his full evaluation of the role of economic factors. However, he considers the positive transcendence of private property to be the demand and requirement corresponding to human essence, and individualism and egoism the basis for the capitalism which is the "non-society", which all indicates that his understanding of what society is, of what human essence is and his ideas on their relationship had not reached the height of the materialist conception of history.

3 FROM THE CATEGORY OF PRACTICE TO THE CATEGORY OF LABOUR

ON THE ROLE OF NATURAL SCIENCE IN SOCIAL DEVELOPMENT

A major achievement of *Manuscripts* of 1844 is that Marx combines labour, production with practice, breaks the limitation of practice to the theoretical critique and endows practice with the perceptive, material content, which paves for him a way for discovering the law of historical development by analyzing human activity in the material production.

---

26   Ibid., p. 124.

In the German classical philosophy, Hegel was a famous representative who emphasized the role of practice and labour in the idealistic
form. In *The Phenomenology of Spirit*, he conceives labour as the
moment in which the subject achieves its self-realization, self-confirmation through the creating and annulment of the object, while in
Science of Logic, he considers practice as the moment for achieving the absolute truth and evaluates the unity of subject with object
through the analysis of the process of knowledge. His understanding
of practice and labour conforms to his understanding of the active
role of the subject. But because the subject is conceived by him as
the absolute idea, and the object is conceived as the estrangement of
the absolute idea, the opposition between the subject and the object
manifested in nature and society is nothing but the opposition between the different forms of consciousness and self-consciousness
within the realm of pure thought, so practice and labour as the manifestation of the subjective activity, connecting subject and object, is
not the sensuous, material activity, but an abstract, mental activity.

After the death of Hegel, his students strove to shift from thought to
action and put forward the philosophy of action on account of their
dissatisfaction with the pure speculative nature of the Hegelian philosophy. This question was first raised by August von Ciezkowski,
a student of Michelet who belonged to the Old Hegelian group (Ed.:
right wing). In *Prolegomena to Historiosophie* published in 1838, he
declared that philosophy in future would "become a practical philosophy or rather a philosophy of practical activity, philosophy of
'praxis', exercising a direct influence on social life and developing
the future in the realm of concrete activity"[27]. But Ciezkowski did
not go beyond idealism. He viewed practice only as the theoretical
critique, rather than the revolutionary activity actually transforming society, and believed that the pure theoretical critique was capable of changing the existing system. Soon afterwards, the Young
Hegelian Hess wrote the *Philosophy of Action*, who, together with
Bauer, still construed practice as the theoretical critique itself. For
instance, Bauer stated in *Confessions of a Weak Soul* that "we have
so far believed that theory is practice"[28].

---

27   David McLellan: The Young Hegelians and Marx, 1982, p. 12.
28   Zvi Rosen: Bruno Bauer and Karl Marx, Beijing: China Renmin University Press,
1984, p. 190.

Marx's view on practice went through a process, which was closely related to the change in and development of his whole world outlook.

When Marx still took the side of Hegel, his view on practice was idealistic. In the dissertation *Difference Between the Democritean and Epicurean Philosophy of Nature* and the materials he prepared for it, he expounded the relationship between philosophy and the world, and underlined that philosophy should not focus its eyes to the external world to apprehend it, but as a practical person, it should relate itself with the world: "It is a psychological law that the theoretical mind, once liberated in itself, turns into practical energy, and, leaving the shadowy empire of Amenthes as will, turns itself against the reality of the world existing without it." However, for Marx, to turn theory into practice was manifested not as the actual activity of man, but as the critique of theory itself, so he said that "the *practice* of philosophy is itself *theoretical*. It is the *critique* that measures the individual existence by the essence, and the particular reality by the Idea."[29] Therefore this so-called practice remains within theory and cannot change the reality.

After Marx had changed from idealism to materialism, from the position of revolutionary democracy to communism, his view on practice underwent a significant change. He no longer limited practice to the realm of thought, and not considered the theoretical critique itself as practice, but viewed practice as the revolutionary struggle. He thought that his critique of Hegel's philosophy of right was a theoretical critique of the previous form of political consciousness, and after this critique he did not confine himself to theory itself, but had to concentrate on "those problems which there is only means of solving—the practice". Marx asked himself this question: "can Germany attain a practice *à la hauteur des principles*—i.e., a *revolution* which will raise it not only to the *official level* of modern nations, but to the *height of humanity* which will be the near future of those nations?" He deemed this possible then. Yet it should not rely on the theoretical critique alone, but on the revolutionary practice: "The weapon of criticism cannot, of course, replace criticism of the

---

29 Karl Marx and Frederick Engels: Collected Works, 1st Chinese Edition, Volume 42, p. 258.

weapon, material force must be overthrown by material force." [30] In this way, Marx distinguished practice from theory, and regarded practice as the material force solving social problems.

After he commenced studying economics in Paris, Marx combined labour and production with practice, and he thus discovered the most basic practical activity of man. He uncovered the characteristics of man's practical activity through the analysis of the relationship between man and nature, and he unified the history of nature, the history of mankind and the development of human knowledge through his analysis of labour. As long as he went deep into the labour process, Marx would eventually find a way to renounce humanism and lead himself to historical materialism.

Labour shows that the practical activity of man is a material activity. Material activity presupposes the existing objective entities and acts on the object. It is unlikely to have the real practical activity without the objective activity. Seen from the subject, man can transform nature through practice and create for himself a world of objects, because man himself is the living objective being, rather than self-consciousness. Labour as the basis of the unity of man with nature is the material exchange process between man and nature. Therefore, Marx emphasized that man "creates or posits objects, because he is posited by objects—because at bottom he is *nature*. in the act of positing, therefore, this objective being does not fall from his state of "pure activity" into a *creating of the object*: on the contrary, his *objective* product only confirms his *objective* activity, his activity as the activity of an objective, natural being"[31].

Labour shows that the practical activity of man is a social activity, i.e., it is the "species-activity". At that time, production for Marx was the active species-life of man, and it was in his work on the objective world that "man really proves himself to be a species-being". As a pure natural being, man could only be an isolated individual, or man relates to nature like an animal-like group. This so-called labour is actually the animal life activity, not the human practical

30   Karl Marx and Frederick Engels: Collected Works, 1st Chinese Edition, Volume 1, p. 460.
31   Karl Marx and Frederick Engels: Collected Works, 1st Chinese Edition, Volume 42, p. 167.

activity. In the transformation of nature, man conducts material exchange between him and nature on the one hand, and on the other hand exchanges labour and products with each other. There can be no relationship between man and nature outside society.

Labour process shows that the practical activity of man is a conscious, purposeful activity. The animal activity is an instinctive activity. Even if the animal life-activity can also have purposes, this can be attributed to the long-term natural selection, the adaptation to the environment, rather than existing as the subjective form in the animal itself. Human activity is different. Man makes his labour into the object with his will and consciousness. Man achieves his purpose while changing the objective, inorganic world, and transforms what exists in the Idea (at the outset of the labour process) into a material result.

It can be seen from the above that Marx's analysis of labour process and its factors reveals the most essential characteristic of practice, that is, practice is the sensuous, material activity in which man transforms the objective world.

Certainly, what Marx stressed in those days was the natural power of man himself, his essential powers, without analyzing the role of the instruments of production. In fact, human labour acts on the objects of labour mainly by means of the instruments of production instead of his natural organs. Man does not have particular organs which adapt to the natural environment. He is not necessarily better than other animals in terms of his physical strength, endurance, speed and sensitivity, but he is capable of making the instruments of production, and with their help he can transform nature and convert the adverse natural conditions into those conditions which are favourable for his existence and development. The analysis of labour was incomplete without considering the making of the instruments of production.

Nature has its own history. It develops and changes all the same without the involvement of mankind. However, man relates himself to nature through labour, and during the long development process, includes in depth and in width this immense nature, gradually and part by part into the sphere of human activity, thus man changes the pure nature into the nature with history, and in this way leaves his mark on nature. It is labour that establishes the actual, historical relationship between man and nature, between nature and society.

If man transforms pure nature into the nature with history through labour, then the history of mankind is the history of nature. It is inside, not outside, the relationship between man and nature that man created society and developed his own history of development. The emergence of nature for man was the formation of human history, and the basis for their unity of the two is labour. The most fundamental content of human history is the history of the production of material goods, i.e., it is the history of man transforming nature and acquiring the means of subsistence from it. There would be no human history if the relationship between man and nature is excluded from history.

Human history is the history of man transforming nature as well as the history of man transforming himself, because he keeps transforming himself in the process of transformation of nature. This includes changes not only the various social relations of man but also his capacity of knowledge. As far as Marx is concerned, he did not focus on the former change (the change of social relations), because he had not reach this level of understanding at that time, but he did present an insightful exposition of this change in the subject which is generated through labour.

Marx also recognizes man as a part of nature, but he emphasizes that man creates himself through labour. As everything which is natural has to come into being, man too has his act of origin—history—which is not his history of biology, but his history of social development. Therefore, the formation of human senses is inseparable from the society and human labour. Marx underlines that the forming of the five senses is the product of the entire history of the world from the beginning to the present, and he thus stresses the role played by the objectification of labour in forming abundant human senses.

In particular, Marx highlighted the function of industry based on the development of the then developing modern production. He said that "the history of *industry* and the established objective existence of industry are the *open* book of *man's essential powers*, the perceptible existing human *psychology*."[32] For Marx, industry here, in its broad sense, means all human activity, namely, labour. Marx links the history of labour and the products of labour with the development of human knowledge, and his evaluation of the products of labour as the knowledge in the immediate, direct, perceptible form was indeed very profound.

The entire history of human knowledge demonstrates that the emergence of the new products of labour, especially the upgrading of modern knowledge-intensive products, reflects not only the development level of productive forces, but also manifests the deepening of human knowledge. The appearance of each new product of labour is also an indication of the progress in human knowledge. Labour and the products of labour cannot be studied merely from their utility—not from the satisfaction of human material needs, we cannot separate them from the development of the subject's own capacity for knowledge. Thus Marx wrote: "A *psychology* for which this book, the part of history existing in the most perceptible and accessible form, remains a closed book, it cannot become a genuine, comprehensive and *real* science. What indeed are we to think of a science which airily abstracts from this large part of human labour and which fails to feel its own incompleteness, which such a wealth of human endeavour, unfolded before it, means nothing more to it than, perhaps, what can be expressed in one word—"need", "vulgar need"?" This statement of Marx summarizes the fundamental defect of those theories of epistemology in history and lays foundation for the scientific epistemology.

Precisely because he considers labour as the determinant for man to develop himself and also the determinant for the human history to come into being, Marx attaches great importance to the role of practice in human knowledge. It is in *Manuscripts* of 1844 that he gives top priority to practice, and points out that "the solution of theoretical riddles" "is the task of practice and effected through practice", "the true practice" "is the condition of a real and positive theory"[33]. Marx expressly resists to limit the solution of a theoretical antitheses to the realm of knowledge, resists to see a theoretical

32 Ibid., p. 127.
33 Ibid., p. 139.

antitheses merely as a theoretical problem, and argues that it should first be seen as a practical question, i.e., a question to be solved by the development of society itself: "we see how the resolution of the *theoretical* antitheses is only possible in a *practical* way, by virtue of the practical energy of man. Their resolution therefore by no means is merely a problem of understanding, but a *real* problem of life."[34] The basic reason why the philosophies in the past could not resolve this problem is that they remained within the realm of thinking and regarded the solution of the theoretical antitheses only as the task of theory itself, instead of resorting to practice.

Marx values labour and thus takes natural science very seriously. Although he did not see natural science as a productive force at that time, he fully estimated its role in social life.

Marx criticizes the opposition between natural science and philosophy. By the mid-19th century, natural science had developed enormously and had accumulated an ever-growing mass of scientific material. However, the opposition between philosophy and natural science, which started since the medieval scholasticism, was not solved yet. Philosophy was just as alien to natural science as natural science was alien to philosophy. The natural philosophy schools founded by some philosophers of the ancient past had attempted to unite them, this attempt was only a chimerical illusion. They could not unmask the relations/laws of nature from natural science, but had replaced the real relations/laws with imaginary ones. Although this previous natural philosophy had some reasonable conjectures, it was a speculative philosophy after all, instead of being a real unity of philosophy with natural science. This was also true for both Schelling and Hegel.

Marx affirms the utility and the enlightening role of natural sciences. Since the Renaissance, natural science had indeed, played a part in the fight against religion and the church. Quite a few great natural scientists had challenged the church with their discoveries, and consequently were burned at the stake or sent to the Inquisition. But Marx stresses that the role of natural science should not be limited to this. Marx thinks, in fact, through the medium of industry, natural

---

34   Ibid., p. 127.

science "has invaded and transformed human life all the more practically; and has prepared human emancipation, although its immediate effect had to be the furthering of the dehumanisation of man"[35] Here, Marx sees in a profound way that there is a contradiction inherent in the development and advance of natural science under the capitalist system. On the hand, it directly completes "dehumanisation", that is, the capitalist application of natural science serves and strengthens the exploitation of the workers, increases the rate of exploitation and enhances the competitive power of capital over labour; on the other hand, the development of natural science, its application to production, facilitate the development of production, improve the cultural level and skills of the workers and provide the material basis for human emancipation.

This important thought of Marx will guide us to correctly understand the relationship between the scientific and technological revolution and the social revolution in the developed capitalist countries. In recent decades, the scientific and technological revolution, marked by the microelectronic technology, bioengineering, optical fibre, new material, new energy, ocean development, astronavigation and other new technologies, has been gaining momentum. This development is far more dramatic in the advanced western capitalist countries, and has formed a wave. The development of the scientific and technological revolution inevitably changes the technical structure of the productive forces, changes the industrial structure, labour conditions and its content, and influences people's values, their daily life and cultural formation. According to Marxism, I disagree with the theory that the scientific and technological revolution will cause the contradictions of the capitalist society to disappear naturally, and bring about a society with general opulence and will increase the "integration" or convergence of the classes. The scientific and technological revolution cannot replace and abolish the social revolution. Although it brings relative stability and prosperity to some developed capitalist countries, its capitalist application, in the long run, will not ease, but rather exacerbate the contradiction between the developed capitalist countries and the underdeveloped countries, increase the struggle among the monopolies, and also the struggle between capital and

---

35   Ibid., p. 128.

labour. Science and technology itself will not and cannot automatically resolve the various kinds of basic contradictions of the capitalist society, but merely provides a more abundant material basis for the solution of these contradictions. Similarly, I am also opposed to this theory which goes against the tide of history, and which sets the scientific and technological revolution and the historical progress in opposition. The social evils, such as crimes, drug use, moral degeneration, the alienation between man and man, etc. exposed in the advanced western capitalist countries, do not arise directly from the development of science and technology, but are rooted in the social system itself. The essence of the question will be concealed if science and technology itself is not distinguished from their social application, and the evils of the capitalist society will be attributed to the scientific and technological revolution.

What's more profound is that Marx points out that "[n]atural science will in time incorporate into itself the science of man, just as the science of man will incorporate into itself natural science: there will be *one* science."[36] If we can say this was a prediction in the 1840s, the mutual infiltration between natural sciences and social sciences has become reality in modern times. The emergence of many interdisciplinary subject branches is narrowing the distance between natural science and social sciences.

---

36   Ibid.

CHAPTER VIII

THEORETICAL CHARACTERISTICS AND THE HISTORICAL STATUS OF ECONOMIC AND PHILOSOPHICAL MANUSCRIPTS OF 1844

The advancement from estrangement to estranged labour was a turning point in the development of Marx's thought. *Economic and Philosophical Manuscripts of 1844*, which elaborates the idea of estranged labour, holds an important place in the formation of the materialist conception of history. The evaluation of 1844 *Manuscripts* have been a constant, controversial subject around the world for more than half a century since its publication, which not only reflects the important position of Marxism in the political life of today's world, but also shows that various schools strive to seek in their own studies the "basis" for reinterpreting Marxism. The proper judgment of 1844 *Manuscripts*, especially the comprehensive evaluation of the theory of estranged labour, is of vital importance to a correct understanding on the formation of Marx's materialist conception of history.

1 THEME OF MANUSCRIPTS AND ITS PHILOSOPHICAL ARGUMENTATION

Why has *Manuscripts* become the heart of such controversy? Is it because it is an early work? Not exactly. *The Posthumous Writings of Marx, Engels*, which was edited and published by Mehring in 1902, is a collection of their writings in 1840s, made public for the first time Marx's doctoral dissertation paper *Difference Between the Democritean and Epicurean Philosophy of Nature*, which was completed in 1841, written earlier than *Manuscripts*. Besides, *Critique of Hegel's Philosophy of Right*, was first published in 1927, but was written in 1843 by Marx and this work was also before *1844 Manuscripts*.

Is it because it is immature? Not exactly. The *Manuscripts* was written after Marx had basically completed the two transformations in his ideas. It contains many valuable important ideas, though something immature in it. Compared with the years before 1844, Marx's thought in this work advances towards the materialist conception of history, rather than going backward.

The *Manuscripts* has become the heart of the controversy because of its theoretical characteristic, apart from several objective reasons. With estranged labour serving as the basic theory and method, its theme and philosophical argumentation were not well consistent, hence *Manuscripts* left some room for the explanation and interpretation of Marxism from different perspectives.

During the formation of Marxism, *Manuscripts* serves as such a work which discusses the questions of estrangement and man intensively and systematically. Yet, its theme is not an abstract speculation of the aforesaid two questions but the elaboration of the class status of the proletariat and the way to human emancipation. If we can say Marx had attempted to uncover "the mystery of the state" and resolve the most disturbing question—the relationship between civil society and the state in *Critique of Hegel's Philosophy of Right* of 1843, then we can say that he turned to analyzing civil society in *Manuscripts* of 1844 and attempted to explore the causes for the non-human status of the proletariat and the way of emancipation, he discusses the private property itself and its positive transcendence, i.e., to solve "the mystery of history" in the words of Marx.

Marx pays much attention to this theme in *Manuscripts*. Although he proceeded from the premises provided by the bourgeois classical political economy and used its language and laws, he did indeed elevate his thoughts above the level of political economy and raised two questions: First, what in the evolution of mankind is the meaning of this reduction of the greater part of mankind (proletariat) to abstract labour? This is actually a question about the status and mission of the proletariat under the capitalist system. Second, what are the mistakes committed by the reformism trend which either demands to raise wages to improve the situation of the working class, or regards equality of wages (as Proudhon had advocated) as the goal of revolution? This was actually a question about the goal of the proletarian revolution and the way of its complete emancipation. Therefore, what is studied in *Manuscripts* is not the abstract "man", but the confrontation between the proletarian and the bourgeois. Marx endeavours to reveal the confrontation between the proletarian and the proprietor class , and the situation and status of the proletariat under the capitalist system through his argument that the essence of the capitalist private property is the opposition between capital and labour, i.e., between the proprietor and the proletarian which is an "antagonistic confrontation"; that the separation of the three: capital, rent and labour is detrimental and fatal for the worker; that the worker cannot shake off poverty whether the capitalist production is on the decline or rise; and he had discussed the aspects of estranged labour. It was the proletariat that Marx devoted all his attention then.

Marx considers the complete emancipation of the proletariat instead of the emancipation of the abstract "man" as the goal in *Manuscripts*. In *Manuscripts* the universal human emancipation was elaborated and conceived as the result from the solution of the confrontation between capital and labour, and also from the annulment of private property, and these were discussed not as a goal overriding the emancipation of the proletariat. Marx pointed out expressly that "the emancipation of society from private property, etc., emancipation of society from servitude, is expressed in the political form of the emancipation of the worker; not that their emancipation alone is at stake, but because the emancipation of the workers contains universal human emancipation—and it contains this because the whole of human servitude is involved in the relation of the worker to production, and all relations of servitude are but modifications and consequences of this relation."[1]

However, *Manuscripts* features not so much the theme as the philosophical argumentation of the theme. Marx had begun to approach this theme in the *Deutsch-Französische Jahrbücher*, and followed and developed it further in *Manuscripts*. But a new factor appeared in 1844, that is, his turn to the study of political economy and wide reading of the British and French economists. Marx, who had basically completed the two transformations then and was seeking further scientific proofs for communism, was dissatisfied with the classical economists' standpoint and method, and with their attitude to private property and the worker, also was dissatisfied with the theories of utopian socialism. But what should be used as a weapon to criticize political economy, the capitalist private property and all kinds of theories of utopian socialism? His ideas from the traditional thought and the new ideas emerging in 1844 were in contradiction. On the one hand, Marx resorted to economics and proceeded from economic facts to reveal the essences of the capitalist private property and its contradictions; on the other hand, he pondered the economic facts philosophically with the help of the traditional philosophical categories.

This influence was also indicated by Marx in the preface of *Manuscripts*. Although there are different views on the degree, magnitude and time limit of this influence, it is hard to deny that Feuerbach's influence on Marx was still present when he was writing *Manuscripts* in 1844, despite that he had surpassed Feuerbach in many aspects. Marx wrote: "positive criticism as a whole—and therefore also German positive criticism of political economy— owes its true foundations to the discoveries of Feuerbach."[2]. In particular, he mentioned Feuerbach's work: *Provisional Theses for the Reformation of Philosophy* and *Principles of the Philosophy of the Future*, saying that they were the "writings since Hegel's

---

1   Karl Marx and Frederick Engels: Collected Works, 1st Chinese Edition, Volume 42, p. 101.
2   Ibid., p. 46.

Phänomenologie and *Logik* which contain a real theoretical revolution" . Moreover, Marx also listed the essays by Hess as the "original works of substance". Human essence and its estrangement are an important part whether in Hegel's *Phenomenology of Spirit*, Feuerbach's *Provisional Theses for the Reformation of Philosophy* or in Hess' essays.

There is no doubt that Marx attaches importance to the analysis of private property—the money system, and the goal which he sets for himself in *Manuscripts*: "To grasp the intrinsic connection between private property, greed, the separation of labour, capital and landed property; the connection of exchange and competition, of value and the devaluation of man, of monopoly and competition, etc.,— the connection between this whole estrangement and the *money* system"[3]. But because his materialist conception of history was still in the emerging phase, Marx did not yet affirm the dependence of man and his essence to the relations of production, instead he judged the rationality of the economic relationships on the basis of human essence, criticized political economy and the capitalist private property and expressed his pursuit of the emancipation of the proletariat, i.e., the pursuit of the ideal of true man, true society and true labour by distinguishing between true man and estranged man, true society and estranged society, true labour and estranged labour.

When summarizing the controversy over luxury and thrift between Lauderdale and Malthus on the one side, and Ricardo and Say on the other side, this division in the history of economic theories, Marx criticized the political economy and viewed it as "their scientific creed", because it was hostile to the worker and did not treat him as a human being. Marx said that political economy reduced "his activity to the most abstract mechanical movement; thus political economy says: Man has no other need either of activity or of enjoyment. Because it declares that this life, *too*, is *human* life and existence"[4].

It is because, for Marx, the worker under capitalism is non-human and has lost all human characteristics that his sole activity or sole characteristic is labour; and it is because political economy confirms and maintains this non-human status of the worker, turning the

3   Ibid., p. 90.
4   Ibid., p. 134.

worker into an insensible being lacking all needs and "turning man as non-essentiality into the essence"[5] that political economy is an anti-human theory. According to Marx, from Adam Smith through Say to Ricardo and Mill, the more consistently political economy as a whole develops, the more it is anti-human, because these economists advance in a positive sense constantly and consciously further than their predecessors in the estrangement from man.

Marx elucidates the idea of true society and estranged society in association with true man and estranged man.

The true society is one in which man as man organizes it in a human way, and man's essence, instead of commodity, money, forming the link between man and man. That is to say, the production of everyone is to satisfy "the needs of man", to create products that correspond to the essential needs of the other man; people attach importance to "man himself", "man's value", rather than to the things and to the "value of the things" possessed by man. Instead, for Marx at that time, the capitalist society mediated by commodity and money is an estranged society, because all social connections here are realized through exchange, commodity and money, and this society emphasizes the value of the things and disdains man's value. The language in which people converse with each other is also converse of the things, rather than a human language.

Marx takes labour very seriously, and the great achievement of *Manuscripts* is to treat labour as the origin of history and as the power of man's self-creation. But besides the real labour, a kind of true labour corresponding to human nature was conceived in *Manuscripts* and was used to confront estranged labour. According to Marx, labour as the free, consciousness activity is the character of human species, the character of human life, or his species-character: The species-essence. Therefore, true labour is only the labour which arises out of the inner necessity of man, serves as self-enjoyment and directly meets the essential needs of the other man, while on the other side the labour estranging itself from human essence, the estranged labour is the labour which arises out of external, fortuitous need and serves as a means of life. For Marx, the mistake of

---

5   Ibid., p. 114.

political economy is to reduce labour to the means of life and try to conceal the estranged character of labour under the capitalist private property.

It is not difficult to see that Marx's idea of the opposition between true man and estranged man, between true society and estranged society, between true labour and estranged labour, and his judgment of the latter by the former were not scientific. His views on commodity and money also exhibit the immaturity of his thought. However, the foresaid argumentation was the theme of *Manuscripts*. Marx seeks to unmask the class status of the proletariat under the capitalist system and the employment character of labour by analyzing estranged man, estranged society and estranged labour, and describe his longing for future society with true society, true man and true labour. The theme of *Manuscripts* which advocates that only by positively transcending private property can the proletariat emancipate itself and all humanity was correct, though its philosophical argumentation was imperfect and limited.

2 DIFFERENT UNDERSTANDINGS ON MANUSCRIPTS

It must be admitted that *Manuscripts* is quite a difficult work. It is natural to have different understandings on the expositions in it, to which a consensus may be reached through discussion. The *Manuscripts* is made more difficult to understand, especially due to the fact that its theme and argumentation are not completely classified but instead interwoven. But I will refuse to take *Manuscripts* as the basis for "reinterpreting" Marxism, hence refuse to oppose the young Marx to the old Marx.

Upon the publication of *Manuscripts* in the early of 1930s, some western scholars strove to use it as a basis for reinterpreting Marxism. In addition to Siegfried Landshut, the publisher of the German edition of *Manuscripts* in 1932, Herbert Marcuse also advocated this view, arguing that "[t]hese *Manuscripts* put the discussion of the origins and original meaning of historical materialism, indeed the whole theory of 'scientific socialism' on a new basis."[6] This view has not disappeared but spread more widely since the World War II.

---

6   Quoted from (An Anthology of) Studies of Economic-Philosophical Manuscripts of 1844, p. 298, Changsha: Hunan People's Publishing House, 1983.

E. Thier has particularly stressed that "the original work of Marx enables people to have the best and most well-founded concept of Marxism as understood by himself, without the help of the later works" in his comments on *Manuscripts*, Cologne edition of 1950[7].

In 1953, Siegfried Landshut maintained this view in the preface of the republished *Karl Marx: Die Frühschriften (Early Writings)*, saying that the publication of *Manuscripts* had made "the understanding of Marx acquire a completely new meaning" and argued that "all those ideas of Marx that are established" through Engels and Lenin "and which have authority over both Marxists and anti-Marxists should now completely be changed. A more comprehensive examination of his works up to 30 years old makes it clear what kind of limitation and 'materialistic' impoverishment into which the previous interpreters has made all wealth of Marx's spiritual world fall"[8]. I can well say that these writers have disregarded the theme of *Manuscripts* and took what they needed, in an attempt to reinterpret Marxism based on *Manuscripts*.

It is a mainstream attitude in the West to reinterpret Marxism with the abstract humanism principle. Whether they are the makers of two Marx or other who are the advocators of the unified Marx theory, they all endeavour to include Marxism completely in abstract humanism.

Marxism is not against humanism indiscriminately, but rather against abstract humanism and against the abstract humanist conception of history which abstracts the economic and political contradictions inherent in the capitalist society and views the realization of the essence of "man" as the ultimate goal of history. And this is what some western scholars tend to highlight. They one-sidedly grasp the humanist elements in the philosophical argumentation of *Manuscripts*, regard human essence and its realization as the theme and core of *Manuscripts*, and argue that *Manuscripts* "proceed from the philosophical idea, thus Marx attains the self-realization of man and the 'classless society' directly through human self-estrangement (capital

---

7 Quoted from Leonid Nikolayevich Pazhitnov: Tr. From Russian: Origin of Revolutionary Changes in Philosophy, p. 7, Beijing: China Social Sciences Press, p. 1981.
8 Quoted from (An Anthology of) Studies of Economic-Philosophical Manuscripts of 1844, p. 124.

and labour)." They also add that "the purpose of history is not to 'socialize the means of production', i.e., to eliminate 'exploitation' by 'depriving the exploiter'. All this will be meaningless unless we simultaneously strive for 'the realization of man'."[9] "The realization of man" is their main comment on *Manuscripts*.

H. Marcuse elucidated this view even more explicitly. He commented: "Marx has proposed to generally define human essence for the totality of human existence in two places of *Economic-Philosophical Manuscripts*", and "this is the real foundation of Marx in his critique and when he established his theories", "only on such a solid foundation (whose stability cannot be shaken by the pure economic arguments or political arguments) can the question of the historical conditions and the bearer of the revolution arise: The theory of class struggle and dictatorship of the proletariat. Any criticism, if focusing merely on this theory, —the theory of class struggle and dictatorship of the proletariat—without analyzing its real foundation, will miss the point and fail to grasp the crux"[10].

It is not only a view of some social democrats in the early of 1930s but also a characteristic of some contemporary "Marxologs" to consider human essence and its realization as the goal of history, as the basis of Marxism as a whole and thus to define Marxism as a kind of abstract humanism. E. Fromm attempted to incorporate Marxism into the humanist Western tradition. He stressed repeatedly that Marxist philosophy "is rooted in the humanist Western philosophical tradition, which starts from Spinoza then through the French and German enlightenment philosophers of the eighteenth century to Goethe and Hegel, and the very essence of which is concern for man and the realization of his potentialities"[11].

---

9   Ibid., p. 285, p. 294.
10   Quoted from (An Anthology of) Studies of Economic-Philosophical Manuscripts of 1844, p. 311, p. 327.
11   Quoted from the book Western Scholars on Economic-Philosophical Manuscripts of 1844, p. 15, Shanghai: Fudan University Press, 1983.

The argument of human essence and its realization is undoubtedly contained in *Manuscripts*, but the question is whether it constitutes the core of *Manuscripts*, and in particular, whether Marxism can be reinterpreted and conceived as the theory of human essence and its realization on this theoretical basis. The answers should be no.

The argumentation of the theme of *Manuscripts* for us is mainly based on the economic facts, namely, the analysis of private property and the contradiction between capital and labour. Marx analyzed the contradiction among the land owner, the tenant farmer and the worker on the land in agriculture, and indicated that the intensification of this contradiction "necessarily leads to revolution"; He analyzed the contradiction between the proletarian and the bourgeois, between the big capital and the small capital in industry, and revealed that the capitalist mode of production "incline to its necessary downfall" due to its inner contradiction. Marx would not avoid himself from unmasking the facts of the capitalist economy and drawing the above conclusions from those facts , even without his resorting to the idea of human essence and its realization. Nevertheless, Marx had not transcended the influence of Feuerbach, because he had just started with his deeper economic studies, which shows his then theoretical limitations.

It was an unscientific argumentation of Marx to see communism as the "realization", "appropriation" or "return" of human essence, but his ideas that only by abolishing private property can it be possible to completely emancipate the senses and special character of man, to enable man who will have an all-round development and striving to satisfy all human needs are positive and valuable. And these important points were later developed further by Marx on the basis of the materialist conception of history. It is false to think that Marxism is only based on economic analysis, and that Marxism is opposed to humanism in every sense, or even argue that it is anti-humanist, itself. The socialist revolution eradicating private property safeguards the fundamental interests of the majority of the people, takes every measure to eliminate and prevent anti-humanity, and its humane character cannot be matched by any bourgeois humanitarianism. However, what Landshut, Mayer, Marcuse and Fromm, etc. who employed the abstract humanist principle to interpret Marxism, advocate is not to transform man in the revolutionary transformation of the environment, but aims to regard human essence and its realization as the goal of history, as the essence and foundation of Marxism. Hence they have attempted to turn Marxism which includes the most general laws of the development of nature, society and human thinking merely into a speculative theory which seeks for the realization of human essence. Marxism is thus incorporated into abstract humanism and becomes one school of humanism. This will lead to the confusion of the boundary between the principles of these two different ideologies.

It is historical idealism to resort to human essence for everything, to do everything for the realization of human essence, and to derive the goal of history and the demand and the necessity of revolution from the estrangement and idea of return/gaining of human essence. On this basis, it would be impossible to establish scientific socialism, and that would only generate the "true socialism", which was proved by the later development of Hess' thought, who was a contemporary of Marx.

In Germany in the 1840s, the radicals among the Young Hegelians turned to socialism due to the ills brought about by the development of domestic capitalism and through their dissemination of the British and French utopian socialism. But they were unable to demonstrate socialism in a scientific way, and instead combined the German classical philosophy, Feuerbach's theory of the estrangement and return of human essence in particular, with the British and French utopian socialism. So did Hess, who considered socialism capable of eliminating the contradiction between the individual and the species and enable man regain his lost essence.

Unlike Feuerbach who paid attention only to religion, Hess had attached great importance to the role of money, yet his basic theory remained to be that of Feuerbach. Money was conceived by Hess as the estrangement of human essence. For him human essence is estranged into money in worldly life just as human essence is estranged into God in religion. This argument was repeatedly emphasized in his *Essence of Money*. He argued that "the actual atmosphere of man which in heaven is God, the superhuman good, is on Earth the extra-human, inhuman, touchable good, the things, the property, the product which has been taken from the producer its creator, the abstract essence of intercourse, money."[12]

Why is man estranged in this ways? It is because, according to Hess, human beings are in isolation, and they have to have a means with which they can engage in intercourse with each other, or which mediates between them: "they had to seek the unifying essence outside of themselves, i.e., an inhuman, super-human essence, since they were not men, i.e., they were not united. Without this inhuman means of intercourse they would never have entered into intercourse", and this means is money. And it is money that deprives man and his highest life and activity of value, and social life of value, expresses it in a dead mass. The more money one has, the more value he is of. "Money is human value expressed in figures".

It is from the view that money is the estrangement of human essence that Hess criticizes freedom, equality and the rights of man under the capitalist system. He argues that capitalism declares the independence and separation of man by seeing man as a single individual, by proclaiming the rights of man. This is in fact to replace the ancient direct slavery by the indirect slavery which makes all men free and equal—isolated and dead in effect.

For Hess, freedom corresponding to human nature is impossible in places where money exists, because man has to sell his life, his free life-activity in order to acquire the means of life, i.e., money so as to eke out his livelihood. So only by selling his own freedom can one buy the right of individual existence. It happens to both the proletarian and the bourgeois. In this estranged form of money, man cannot freely act out his life, nor can he create, instead he aims only at earning money. Thus everyone is turned into a cannibal, beast of prey, and bloodsucker. Hess therefore concludes that "where all intercourse from natural love, sexual relations, to the exchange of the thoughts of the fully educated world, is not feasible without money; where there are no practical men but cashed-in and sold-off men; where each emotion must first be converted into cash so as to be able to come into being", man can only be dehumanized.

---

12   Hess: "The Essence of Money", from Studies of the History of International Communist Movement, No. 7, p. 195, Beijing: People's Press, 1982.

Hess bases his position on these questions completely on Feuerbach's humanist theory of the contradiction between the individual and the species, he criticizes estrangement which he sees human species-essence being estranged from man, but applies it to a different sphere.

According to Hess, the individual and the species should be united. The species—the mutual exchange of individual life-activity, the intercourse, the mutual stimulation of individual powers, is the real essence of individuals. Individuals cannot realize, make use of, or cannot exercise, activate their powers, and they would die out, if they do not mutually exchange their life-activity in intercourse with each other. The animals in the natural world, when the individual and the species, i.e. self-preservation and self-creation, come into collision, would sacrifice the individual for the species-life. For example, the hen goes into an unequal fight to defend her chicks against attack, so does man. This suggests that nature is always only concerned with self-creation, with the preservation of the species-life, of the actual life-activity. Thus the estrangement of man lies in : "[t]he individual raised to an end, the species degraded to a means; that is the inversion of human and natural life in general." And this is exactly the case under the capitalist system.

Starting from this perspective, Hess considers the contradiction of the capitalist society as the contradiction between the individual and the species. On the one hand there is the species-essence of the individual, i.e., the development of the intercourse. And on the other hand there is the isolation of man; men grapple with each other for individual existence, see the species as the means, and waste their forces precisely through this struggle. So he believes that "we will only mutually ruin ourselves if we do not pass on to communism". But how can this transition be achieved? Based on Feuerbach's philosophy, love is conceived by Hess as a means to resolve the contradiction between the individual and the species: "At the stage of development where we are, we can only further mutually exploit and consume ourselves if we do not unite ourselves in love. Contrary to what the thoughtless liberals think, not centuries, not decades will elapse when the hundredfold-increased productive forces will precipitate into the deepest misery the great mass of people who have to work with their hands, because their hands will have become worthless; while a tiny minority, which is engaged in the accumulation of capital, will wallow in abundance and sink in disgusting dissipation, if they have not previously heard the voice and reason or if they have yielded to force."

It can be concluded from the above that it is from the estrangement of human species-essence that Hess derives the necessity of communism. He appeals to all men (including both the poor and the rich) to see love as a means to resolve the contradiction between the individual and the species so as to achieve the returning (gaining) of human essence. This theory has been proved by history to be unscientific and unfeasible. If the Marxist theory of socialist revolution is based again on the estrangement and return of human essence, and if socialism is seen as the realization of human essence, it will be a reversal from scientific socialism to the "true socialism".

Closely associated with the interpretation of Marxism with the abstract humanist principle is the interpretation of Marxism with the ethical principle, that is, to turn scientific socialism into ethical socialism.

Anyone who takes "man's essence", instead of the objective laws of history, as the basis, inevitably emphasizes the ethical motive of socialism and appeals to human nature, reason and conscience.

For instance, Henri de Man (Belgian socialist) stressed that Marxism "is by no means non-ethical", "Marxism (it) explicitly thinks that Hegel's idea that history is the highest realization of morality has an ethical goal", with difference only in that "the place where morality is realized is transferred from consciousness to existence". For him in *Manuscripts* "the idea of 'senses' (need and interest come from senses) is nothing but the incorporation of ethical evaluation into human needs. Man himself has his own standard and purpose", "man judges the 'environment' of the time by his talent which is not determined by this environment, but is part of his nature and guides him to face his mission". For this reason, Henri de Man believed that *Manuscripts* "reveal more clearly than any other work of Marx the ethical, humanitarian motive hidden behind his belief in socialism and behind the value judgment of all scientific writings in his life"[13].

---

13   Quoted from (An Anthology of) Studies of Economic-Philosophical Manuscripts of 1844, p. 369, p. 348.

This view has exerted a huge impact, though it was proposed in the early of 1930s, and to this day, some so-called Marxist scholars in the West still interpret Marxism according to this view. For example, Robert C. Tucker argues: *Manuscripts* demonstrates that Marx "is not an analytical sociologist he wants to be, but he is first and foremost a moralist or religious thinker and the like. The old idea that 'scientific socialism' is a scientific system is increasingly giving way to the idea that it is actually a system of ethical and religious views"[14].

Piere Bigo* also asserts that in *Manuscripts* "Marxist political economy is ethics", and does not contain the analysis of the objective laws of the capitalist society, but rather an analysis of "the status of man in the economic world" a system of human moral demands for the real world.[15]

M. Rubel even flatly declares that "Marx has achieved the proletarian movement through the ethical mission. He did not 'scientifically' attain socialism after grasping the material, historical conditions and the possibility of socialist revolution through long-term studies"[16].

This statement is incorrect. I think three different questions are involved here:

First, what was the role of moral elements in the change of Marx's thought.

Secondly, what were the relationship between economic analysis and moral evaluation in *Manuscripts*.

Thirdly, *Manuscripts* can serve as the basis for the ethicization of Marxism. And these questions are closely associated with the formation of Marx's materialist conception of history seen from the historical process.

---

14 Quoted from Soviet and Russian Marxist Teodor Oizerman: Marx's Economic-Philosophical Manuscripts and Its Interpretation, p. 119, Beijing: People's Press, 1981.
15 Quoted from Leonid Nikolayewich Pazhitnov: У истоков революционного переворота в философии (Origin of Revolutionary Changes in Philosophy), p. 15.
16 Quoted from Soviet and Russian Marxist Teodor Oizerman: Marx's Economic-Philosophical Manuscripts and Its Interpretation, p.p. 120-121.
*) See his book Marxismo eumanesimo, Bomplani, Milano 1963 (1954).

Man is a social being both with thoughts and feelings. Any objective condition must work through human brain and manifest itself as the motivation of behaviours, the desire. Under the same historical conditions, the understanding of everyone cannot be of the same depth and width, for understanding is significantly shaped by the subjective state, the values and the lofty moral ideal attitude of a person.

Marx undoubtedly had an advanced spirituality, since he was born into an enlightened professional/intellectual family. He lived in a developed and urbanized province of Germany, Rhineland, and was influenced by the French Enlightenment and humanism in his youth. He had written an ambitious and idealistic paper *"Reflections of a Young Man on the Choice of a Profession"* soon after his graduation from high school. Although this paper had a common theme— how to choose a profession, a common question faced by a young man who is about to graduate from high school, we can clearly see his enlightened background. Here, Marx had advocated welfare of whole mankind, the value of man and self-improvement of individual morality.

Young Marx had argued that two aspects should be considered when a young man chooses a profession: one is to choose that profession which mostly uplifts a man, which imparts higher nobility to his actions and to all of his endeavours, i.e. a profession that perfects oneself. The other aspect is to choose that profession which can offer us the widest scope to work for mankind, and help us to approach closer to the general aim—general perfection. The former is the perfection of the individual himself, while the latter is the perfection of his fellow men, i.e., the welfare of mankind. Marx highlights the integration of the two, and put priority on the welfare of mankind.[17]

Marx also values the worth of man. For him, "Worth is that which most of all uplifts a man, which imparts a higher nobility to his actions and all his endeavours, which makes him invulnerable, admired by the crowd and raised above it"[18]. He combines human worth with the independence of human acts, "worth can be assured only by a profession in which we are not servile tools, but in which we act

---

17 Karl Marx and Frederick Engels: Collected Works, 1st Chinese Edition, Volume 40, p.p. 6-7.
18 Ibid., p. 6.

independently in our own sphere". The professions which assure human worth should not be confused with the highest professions. The most lucrative professions with most social standing are the highest professions in the eyes of the secular people, but people who adopt them can have no independence and are slaves of their professions. Independent creation is the symbol of the worth of mankind.

Young Marx was brimming with the superiority feeling of being a human being. There is a poem titled *Human Pride* in his *Book of Love to Jenny*. It is not a merely passionate poem in which a young man who was in love pours out his innermost feelings to his beloved, but also an expression of his view on the worth of man as was also reflected in his *Reflections of a Young Man on the Choice of a Profession*. Marx despises the flattering, seemingly-giant bigwigs:

Shall I then revere these forms
Heavenward soaring, proud, inviolate?
Should I yield before the Life that storms
Towards the Indeterminate?
No! You pigmy-giants so wretched,
And you ice-cold stone Monstrosity,
See how in these eyes averted
Burns the Soul's impetuosity.[19]

Marx also proudly challenges the world in his poem, which may be resulted from the ups and downs in his love and marriage, and expresses his anger against the secular prejudice and tradition which value the ancestry and despise the populace. Marx, instead advocates his idea that man is God of the secular life, the real Maker as well.

He writes:

Then the gauntlet do I fling
Scornful in the World's wide open face.
Down the giant She-Dwarf, whimpering,
Plunges, cannot crush my happiness.
Like unto a God I dare
Through that ruined realm in triumph roam.
Every word in Deed and Fire,
And my bosom like the Maker's own.[20]

19   Ibid., p. 665.
20   Karl Marx and Frederick Engels: Collected Works, 1st Chinese Edition, Volume 40, p.p. 668-669.

We are not surprised by the profundity of the above ideas, because the welfare of mankind and individual perfection, human pride and human worth were the achievements of this era, but we are indeed surprised by the fact that all these ideas come from a teenager. This reflects not only that Marx had a rich inner world with uncommon brilliance, but also we can see that he has a developed level of morality.

However, we cannot conclude that all his later works were merely to expound and prove his moral ideal, or his works have replaced scientific judgment with value judgment. In fact, a lofty moral ideal can serve as the motivation for the behaviours of a person, and more possibly promote him more undertake some valuable task, but lofty moral ideals cannot be the ultimate reason for the emergence of a scientific theory.

Marxism is a science, and its theory of elimination of exploitation and realization of communism is a complete, well-knit scientific system including philosophy, political economy and scientific socialism. This theory was not the realization of Marx's personal moral ideal, much less the realization of his youth ideal, but was produced based on the critical inheritance of the outstanding cultural heritage of mankind and the summarization of experience of the European proletarian revolution. What drove Marx to achieve two transformations and establish Marxism is his active participation in the actual struggles of his time and his insistence in systematic scientific studies, rather than his moral ideal. The historical mission realized by Marx was to transform socialism from utopia to science, and this process is characterized precisely by the critique of utopian socialist theories, also those theories which attempt to explain socialism based on moral ideals, such as equity and justice.

At the beginning of 1844, Marx began to study political economy, and a significant achievement in his study was the *Manuscripts* which we have analyzed earlier. Can the socialism in *Manuscripts* be called ethical socialism? No. It is true that *Manuscripts* contain moral evaluation and moral censure, because it speaks of the value and degradation of man, the increase in value of the world of things and the devaluation of the human world under the capitalist private property, elaborates the confounding of right and wrong and the moral decay caused by money as the medium, and criticizes the ignorance of man in the bourgeois political economy, etc. However, in *Manuscripts*, the inevitable superseding of capitalism by a higher social formation is mainly based on the economic analysis. In *Manuscripts*, Marx does not treat man as an ethical subject, and does not take the relationship between man and man merely as a moral relationship, but instead emphasizes that "the relationship between proprietor and worker is reduced to the economic relationship between exploiter and exploited" and analyzes the hostile antagonism of interests, the struggle as the basis of social organization.[21] The facts in *Manuscripts*, prove that Marx saw socialism as the result of the contradictions and movement of private property, rather than merely as an ethical demand.

Marx also rejected "ethical socialism" as we see from the relationship between economy and morality discussed in *Manuscripts*, in this discussion he places morality and religion, family, state, law, etc. side by side as the factors governed by the general law of production, and expressly rejects to judge economic phenomena on the basis of morality. For example, when he refuted Michel Chevalier's critique of Ricardo for ignoring ethics in dealing with political economy, Marx wrote: "Ricardo is allowing political economy to speak its own language, and if it does not speak ethically, this is not Ricardo's fault. M. Chevalier takes no account of political economy insofar as he moralises, but he really and necessarily ignores ethics insofar as he practises political economy"[22].

Since economy and ethics belong to two different spheres, they have different standards and may thus be in conflict, but they are fundamentally in agreement: "The relationship of political economy to ethics, if it is other than arbitrary, contingent and therefore unfounded and unscientific relationship, if it is not being posited for the sake of *appearance* but is meant to be *essential*, can only be the relationship of the laws of political economy to ethics." In fact, "the opposition between political economy and ethics is only an *apparent* opposition and just as much no opposition as it is an opposition. All

---

21   Karl Marx and Frederick Engels: Collected Works, 1st Chinese Edition, Volume 42, p. 84, p. 76.
22   Ibid., p. 137.

that happens is that political economy expresses moral laws in *its own way*". In other words, the moral content of each society fundamentally conforms with the economic base.

Certainly, the establishment of the materialist conception of history has undergone an arduous exploration process rather than being accomplished in one move. Obvious immaturity exists before and even in *Manuscripts*. As we have analyzed above when discussing the theme of *Manuscripts* and its argumentation, Marx's critique against estranged society, estranged man, estranged labour and later his ideas on true society, true man and true labour bears the lingering influences of Feuerbach's humanism, and we can also see that he sometimes mixes economic analysis with moral evaluation. Yet we cannot conclude that his ideas in *Manuscripts* were ethical socialism, because therein we see, though imperfect, a text which concentrates on economic analysis and clearly declares that the entire communist movement "necessarily finds both its empirical and its theoretical basis in the movement of *private property*"[23], hence fundamentally denies ethical socialism.

In particular, it is necessary to point out that *Manuscripts* cannot be seen as the text of ethical Marxism on the ground that its argumentation includes certain degree of immaturity. *Manuscripts* text is not the finished form of Marxism, but a symbol of its formation in phases. Later, with the full establishment of the materialist conception of history, its defects have been overcome. For instance, in *The German Ideology*, Marx has derived communism from the contradictions and conflicts between the relations of production and the productive forces, and explicitly stated that "[t]he communists do not preach morality at all", "They do not put to people the moral demands: love one another, do not be egoists, etc"[24]. And this question was specifically dealt with by Engels later in his preface for the German version of Marx's *Poverty of Philosophy*. He had also noted that Marx did not base his communism upon the sense of morality, but "upon the inevitable collapse of the capitalist mode of production which is daily taking place before our eyes to an ever growing degree"[25]. The reason is clear: With

---

23   Ibid., p.p. 120-121.
24   Karl Marx and Frederick Engels: Collected Works, 1st Chinese Edition, Volume 3, p. 275.
25   Karl Marx and Frederick Engels: Collected Works, 1st Chinese Edition, Volume 21, p. 209, Beijing: People's Press, 1965.

the abstract moral demand as the basis, all exploitative social systems, all societies based on class antagonism and their development from one exploitative mode of production into another (to that with higher level) must be cast aside. This approach runs completely counter to historical dialectics.

We object to interpret Marxism with the moral principle, to turn Marxism into a moral precept, but we do not deny the significance of the moral ideal. Marxism has its own ethics and moral principles, which includes socialist humanist moral principle. However, moral principle is not the theoretical basis of Marxism, but just the opposite.

Estrangement has been a subject of much controversy since the publication of *Manuscripts* of 1844 especially after the WWII, due to important passages related to the theory of estranged labour in it.

It is natural to discuss estrangement as an academic question. But in particular, it is meaningful to study the role and evolution of the estrangement concept in the formation of the materialist conception of history, from the perspective of the history of development of Marxism. The progress from the idea of estrangement to estranged labour has also played a part in the formation of the materialist conception of history, the discussion of which, if well handled will enable us to clarify many questions. But I think the idea of estrangement cannot be used to interpret Marxism, and Marxism as a whole cannot be seen as a theory of estrangement. In fact this happens to be the prevalent view in the West. For example, Jean Hyppolyte argued: "the fundamental idea and, one could say, the germ of the whole of Marxist thinking is the idea of *alienation* borrowed from Hegel and Feuerbach. I believe that starting from this idea and defining *human liberation* as man's active struggle in the course of history against all alienation of his substance, in whatever form it may present itself, one could best of all explain the Marxist philosophy in its entirety and understand the structure of Marx's chief work, *Capital*."[26]

Jean-Yves Calvez has exactly repeated this view in his *La Pensée de Karl Marx*, and regarded the category of alienation as something which had remained unchanged and consistent all through the

---

26 Quoted from Soviet and Russian Marxist researcher Teodor Oizerman: Marx's Economic-Philosophical Manuscripts and Its Interpretation, p.p. 126-127.

process. He argued: "this philosophical category of alienation, inherited from Hegel by Marx in his youth, constitutes the framework
of this monumental work of his mature period." He also said that
"Marx has shifted the question of alienation to the sphere of political
economy. *Capital* is nothing but a fundamental theory of alienation
including the alienation in the realm of economic thought."[27]

The issue discussed here not only involves *Capital* but also concerns the nature of Marxism in its entirety. For example, M. Rubel
declared in *Karl Marx: Essai de Biographie Intellectuelle* that the
concept of alienation in the *Manuscripts* is "the key to grasping and
understanding all later works of this economist and sociologist"[28].

Fromm also believed that "[i]t is of the utmost importance for the
understanding of Marx to see how the concept of alienation was and
remained the focal point in the thinking of the young Marx, who had
written the *Economic and Philosophical Manuscripts* and of the old
Marx who had written *Capital*"[29].

It is hard to persuade people to agree with the above ideas which
consider alienation as the "key", or the "focal point" to interpret
Marxism, which derive theories of Marxist economics and socialist revolution, from alienation, thus turn Marxism into a theory of
alienation. If so, Marxism cannot be a scientific theory, but instead
a purely speculative construction based on the idea of alienation of
Hegel and Feuerbach. Everyone admits that Marx had spent 40 years
in writing his Capital and strove to reveal the laws of the capitalist
mode of production, he dedicated his life to explore the theory of
complete emancipation of the proletariat. All these studies are based
on objective facts and generalization of numerous materials he had
prepared in his studies.

The interpretation of Marxism based on the estrangement theory
could well lead to use human estrangement to conceal the contradiction between the proletariat and the bourgeoisie under the capitalist
system, thus to replace the theory of Marxist socialist revolution by
that of estrangement and goal of regaining of human essence. For

---

27   Ibid., p. 129.
28   Quoted from (An Anthology of) Studies of Economic-Philosophical Manuscripts
of 1844, p. 395.
29   Ibid., p. 394.

instance, Fromm, argued: "Marx believed that the working class was the most alienated class, hence that the emancipation from alienation would necessarily start with the liberation of the working class. Marx did not foresee the extent to which alienation was to become the fate of the vast majority of people, especially of the ever-increasing segment of the population which manipulate symbols and men, rather than machines. If anything, the clerk, the salesman, the executive, are even more alienated today than the skilled manual worker." Fromm therefore concluded that "the whole human race is today the prisoner of the nuclear weapons it has created, and of the political institutions which are equally of its own making."[30]

Marx's idea of estranged labour in *Manuscripts* was obviously distinct from the idea of estrangement of Hegel and Feuerbach. Marx not only advanced the idea of estrangement to estranged labour, but guided his criticism against the capitalist system, targeted the capitalist private property and revealed the antagonism between capital and labour, Marx has expounded the non-human status of proletariat under capitalism through the opposition between the worker and his products and his labour and through the relationship between the worker and the capitalist. And his progress from the idea of estrangement to estranged labour is only one part of the progress Marx made in his thought, and to evaluate this aspect from the whole progress will be inappropriate.

3 HISTORICAL STATUS OF MANUSCRIPTS

Any science is composed of two aspects: history and theory. Chemistry has chemical theory and chemical history; physics has physical theory and physical history, so do other sciences, such as biology, medicine, astronomy, geology, etc. because each science has its own unique categories and laws, and there has been process in which these laws were discovered. There is no science which has no history nor is there a history of science which has no science, when evaluated from the perspective of history of knowledge.

This is also true for Marxism, which has both theory and history. The history of Marxist philosophy is nothing but the process of establishment and development of the theory of Marxist philosophy.

---

30   Western Scholars on *Economic-Philosophical Manuscripts of 1844*, p. 68.

Without the theory of Marxist philosophy, there will be no development history of Marxist philosophy. Or conversely, the theory of Marxist philosophy is nothing but the summarization of natural sciences and experience of revolutionary practices by the founders and inheritors of Marxism and numerous Marxists of the world, it is the crystallization of their long-term theoretical exploration and studies.

The emergence of scientific Marxist theory would be out of question without the process of establishment, gaining maturity and further development. Therefore, theory of Marxist philosophy is inseparable from its history. It can be said that the history of Marxist philosophy is the theory of Marxist philosophy, the theory appearing in the form of history, i.e., the theory being formed; and every category, each principle of Marxist philosophy contains the history of Marxist philosophy, since they are not formed in one move but has undergone a process.

However, also differences exist between them. For example, to correctly study how the materialist conception of history was established by Marx, we have to reproduce the process in which Marx's thought had evolved from immaturity to maturity. And I think this process has a strict historical sequence and accurate sense of time. But theory is different, which puts aside those accidental factors in the historical understanding process, which eliminates those things which were immature, hence only deals with what Marxist theory has regulated, namely, its basic categories and laws. The knowledge which has been arranged in the theory has to be treated as a process in history, on the other side what is seen as a process in history has to be embodied in concepts, categories and laws. Thus emerges such a contradiction: In the theory things to be rejected as being immature has to be kept in history. Otherwise, it will be impossible to illustrate the development process of Marx's thought.

It is from this perspective that I evaluate *Manuscripts* of 1844. There is no doubt that *Manuscripts* is not a fully mature work, and contains ideas later rejected or completely revised by Marx, but it also contains many important thoughts. In analyzing *Manuscripts*, either its mature or immature aspects, to realize this analysis without ignoring the whole historical process is important for the correct illustration of Marx's thoughts in its development.

In the previous chapters I have discussed the immature aspects of *Manuscripts*, but I do not devalue the significance of this work. It is undoubtedly a major work in the formation of Marxism, and it is neither a deviation from the previous development stage nor the inspiration and fleeting spark of a genius thinker, but a necessary part in the development of Marx's thought: it marks the end of the two transformations, which began with his editorial work in *Rheinische Zeitung*, and it marks the beginning of the establishment of the Marxist ideology, embodying three components.

The *Manuscripts* makes progress on the basis of achievements attained by Marx at the previous stage, and in particular further develops his important arguments in *On the Jewish Question* and *Contribution to the Critique of Hegel's Philosophy of Law: Introduction*.

When commenting on the content of *Manuscripts*, Marx wrote: "in the *Deutsch-Französische Jahrbücher*, where also the basic elements of this work have been indicated by me in a very general way."[31] However, *Manuscripts* is a step forward compared with the articles published in the *Deutsch-Französische Jahrbücher*, which includes some changes of great importance. These changes not only include those important elements which manifest deepening of his thoughts but also deeper elaboration of some questions, also those important elements for the history of development of Marxism.

Marx's turn to materialism and communism and the establishment of the scientific system of Marxism are two stages which are closely related and differ from each other. His two transformations carry within themselves those important prerequisites and elements for the establishment of the Marxist ideology, but we cannot see them as the process of that establishment itself.

Marx engages himself in theoretical activities not for the establishment of an ideological system. Yet the transformation of socialism from utopia to science is a task involving several theoretical areas. The historical experience and the experience of Marx himself show that this task could not be fulfilled if it was restricted to the philosophical sphere only. The significance of *Manuscripts* is that this

---

31   Karl Marx and Frederick Engels: Collected Works, 1st Chinese Edition, Volume 42, p. 46.

work sublates the disconnection among the British classical political economy, the German classical philosophy and the French utopian socialism, and attempts to combine political economy, philosophy and the theory of scientific socialism to form a whole in which they justify and supplement each other. This attempt of combination was certainly incomplete, imperfect at the first step and contained contradictions, but contained a new direction.

Some scholars in the West consider the attempt for this combination as retrogression, and try hard to misinterpret this process or conceal this combination. They attempt to expel political economy from Marxism, simply try to retreat it to philosophy, to the philosophy which is greatly narrowed and distorted—"the theory of man", and transform Marxism into purely theoretical, abstract speculation about human essence, human value. Surely they base this view on the *Manuscripts* text. But the fact is that the characteristic and significance of *Manuscripts* lie precisely in this trinity combination, not in their disconnection.

Marx continued to develop the theme he raised in the *Deutsch-Französische Jahrbücher*, but he began to base his argumentation on economics, which really offered a solid foundation for the exploration of "theoretical application" of communism, which he elaborated in his work Communism and the *Augsburger Allgemeine Zeitung* in 1842. We attach importance to the guidance of philosophy as a world outlook and methodology, but the necessity of socialist revolution arises from the economic sphere, just as Engels wrote: "the ultimate causes of all social changes and political revolutions are to be sought, not in men's brains, not in their growing insight into eternal truth and justice, but in changes in the modes of production and exchange. They are to be sought, not in the philosophy, but in the economics of each particular epoch."[32]

The necessity of socialist revolution is rooted in economy, and is different from that socialist revolution is merely an economic revolution. Consequently it will be wrong to see socialist revolution as a purely objective process unrelated to human beings or human subjectivity. The annulment of private property and the transformation

---

32   Karl Marx and Frederick Engels: Selected Works, 1st Edition, Volume 3, p. 307.

of old economic relationships entail the revolutionary transformation of man, i.e., the creation of a new generation and the all-round development of man, but the foundation and ultimate cause of this interaction lie in economic facts. Despite the weakness of humanist elements in it, the argumentation of *Manuscripts* is based on economic facts and is an important part in Marx's shift to expound and prove communism economically. Therefore, we object to those views that ignore the economic features of *Manuscripts* and just reduce it to a philosophical work on "man". For instance, Fromm has stressed repeatedly that "Marx's *Economic and Philosophical Manuscripts*, his main philosophical work dealing with his concept of man, of alienation, of emancipation, etc.". He wrote:"Marx's aim, socialism, based on his theory of man", "follows from his concept of man"[33], etc., hence Fromm has evaluated *Manuscripts* in the same frame with the "true socialism" once prevalent in Germany.

There are humanist elements in the text of *Manuscripts*, but its development tendency was historical materialism rather than humanism. Although Marx was not fully aware of the great differences between him and Feuerbach at that time, he had actually surpassed Feuerbach on many important aspects. The *Manuscripts* includes further development of the idea that the state is determined by civil society, which Marx began to put forward in *Critique of Hegel's Philosophy of Right*, and a number of ideas he had produced through his analysis of civil society, i.e., his critique of the capitalist private property and political economy, the idea that labour is the essence of man and it is the fundamental difference between men and animals; the idea that the entire history is nothing but the creation of man through human labour. The text discusses the relations of production—compares the true man with estranged man, critically discusses the relationship of man to other man, and attempts to analyze the structure of society, i.e., the decisive role played by material production and its effect to all forms of superstructures, etc. And more importantly, the text emphasizes historical dialectics of private property and opposes to the classical economists' metaphysical approach which "because political economy fails to grasp the interconnections within the movement, (Ed. the movement of private property) it was possible for

---

33   Western Scholars on Economic-Philosophical Manuscripts of 1844, p. 23, p. 69.

them (classical economists) to oppose, for example, the doctrine of competition to the doctrine of monopoly, the doctrine of craft freedom to the doctrine of the guild, and the doctrine of the division of landed property to the doctrine of the great estate. Marx also expressed his dissatisfaction with Hegel's idealist dialectics, because "he has only found the *abstract, logical, speculative* expression for the movement of history"[34].

In *Manuscripts*, the idea of contradiction is utilized by Marx to analyze the essence of private property, to uncover the opposition between the proletarian and the proprietor, to discuss the historical process in which capital and labour has experienced from their direct or indirect unity to their opposition, the various contradictions under capitalism and their solutions, and to treat the process in which human society develops into a communist one as the negation of the negation, etc. which show that Marx tends to seek dialectics in the real history itself, despite there were traces of speculation in some parts of the text.

There is no doubt that immaturity exists in *Manuscripts*, and we can understand this, because Marx's philosophical thought, economic thought and his thought on scientific socialism do not develop in an absolutely balanced way. When writing *Manuscripts* in 1844, Marx had been studying philosophy for nearly ten years, but he had just started to study political economy. Therefore, it is impossible for him to immediately form a complete, well-knit and logically consistent whole in his attempt to combine them together, and contradictions and disharmony were inevitable. However, his later development is not a negative denial of *1844 Manuscripts*. Although his later development abandons some ideas in *Manuscripts* theoretically and methodologically, it incorporates what this work has achieved and follows the direction of seeking the historical roots in the productive labour, which was initiated in *1844 Manuscripts*. The full establishment of the materialist conception of history will be out of the question if this footing is not discovered. We should always remember that Marx was a serious scholar, an enthusiastic explorer, and his mature thoughts were not accomplished in one move. No

---

34 Karl Marx and Frederick Engels: Collected Works, 1st Chinese Edition, Volume 42, p. 90, p. 159.

matter how accidental its findings were, *Manuscripts* text was a necessary part of the development of Marx's thought, when we correctly evaluate its content. It would be very difficult to understand how Marx established the materialist conception of history in the absence of *Manuscripts* and the theory of estranged labour.

CHAPTER IX

CRITICISM OF BAUER'S THEORY OF ALIENATION ON HISTORY AND THE MASSES

Marx had expressed his readiness to criticize the Young Hegelians with Bauer as their representative in the preface of *Manuscripts*, and realized it in *The Holy Family*, co-authored by Marx and Engels. This polemic work is the first work co-written by them, and marks the beginning of the forty-year-collaboration between these two future proletarian revolutionary mentors.

It is still not hard to observe Feuerbach's influence in *The Holy Family*, but the idea of the estrangement and return of human essence does not occupy a central position any more compared with *Manuscripts*. *The Holy Family* carries forward the historical materialistic elements contained in *1844 Manuscripts*, and elaborates what is history, the origin of history, the great role of the masses, material interests and other questions. In particular, the idea of the relations of production is almost formulated through the analysis of Proudhon's economic ideas. Engels fully recognized in his later years the role played by *The Holy Family* in the formation of the materialist conception of history, saying that "The cult of abstract man, which formed the kernel of Feuerbach's new religion, had to be replaced by the science of real men and of their historical development. This further development of Feuerbach's standpoint beyond Feuerbach was inaugurated by Marx in 1845 in *The Holy Family*."[1]

1 FROM HEGEL TO BAUER. EXPOSITION AND CRITICISM OF BAUER'S NON-CRITICAL IDEALIST THEORY OF ALIENATION

History is complicated. The same class behaves differently in different countries, and takes on national characteristics conditioned by the developmental level of mode of production and the cultural traditions. The German bourgeoisie is distinct from the French bourgeoisie. The French bourgeoisie is in full cry and spares no efforts to fight with sword and pen for its interests, while the German bourgeoisie is dispirited, timid and overcautious, deft in abstract thinking. In France, all theoretical questions become social questions, while in Germany all social questions become philosophical questions. In Germany man becomes self-consciousness, and the pursuit of ideal becomes "conscience" and weak becomes "absolute order". And Rousseau's attack on the estrangement of private property, power and morality with a fighting posture is transformed into the opposition between abstract subjective and objective relationship in the German classical philosophy which only employs abstract thinking activity to accompany the development of modern states, without actively involving itself in the actual struggle of this development. In the German classical philosophy, the theory of alienation was philosophized especially by Hegel.

Fichte developed subjective idealism to an absurd extreme and led it to a dead end, so Hegel could not continue on the path of subjective idealism any longer and turned to objective idealism. He developed Fichte's theory of subjectivity, and put forward the proposition that "substance is subject", and considered absolute idea as the subject of estrangement. He said that "everything turns on grasping and expressing the True, not only as Substance, but equally as Subject."[2] He also succinctly stated that "substance is in itself Subject."[3]

---

1 Karl Marx and Frederick Engels: Selected Works, 1st Edition, Volume 4, p. 237.
2 Hegel: Phenomenology of Spirit, Volume I, p. 10, Beijing: The Commercial Press, 1979.
3 Ibid., p. 36.

It seems absurd, unreasonable, violation of common sense, to regard impersonal reason —absolute idea as subject, and the moments of development of nature, society and history as the alienation of this subject, but this is stipulated by Hegel's idealistic dialectics. Since Hegel believes that the whole universe develops and changes, this change must have a bearer; since all knowledge goes deep into the content of object and at the same time returns into itself, all content of knowledge should be nothing but subject's "reflection into itself"[4]. Only something ideal can serve this subject which governs and contains everything, and make Hegel offer his talents full play in the kingdom of speculation. As Marx said, "this process must have a bearer, a subject. But the subject only comes into being as a result. This result – the subject knowing itself as absolute self-consciousness – is therefore God, absolute Spirit, the self-knowing and self-manifesting idea."[5] It is based on absolute idea as subject that Hegel had built his large system of objective idealism.

Hegel certainly could not deal with alienation materialistically. He is the first philosopher in the history of philosophy to discuss alienation in detail from the idealistic perspective. He linked alienation and subject and formed the most fundamental meaning of the idealist concept of alienation: Object is split off from and it is in contradiction with subject. Hegel argued that "This Substance, as Subject", "is the bifurcation of the simple; it is the doubling which sets up opposition"[6]. "[T]he latter [self-consciousness] divests itself of its personality, thereby creating its world. This world it looks on as something alien."[7]

Object alienated from subject is a kind of movement, so subject itself cannot be fixed. Subject is not immediate but is presented as the movement of reflecting itself into itself. Like God in religion is seen as subject, the eternal, this is not the true subject, but "The Subject", "a meaningless sound, a mere name"[8]. Because this eternal, inert subject which has no content "is not only not the actuality of this

4   Ibid., p. 11.
5   Karl Marx and Frederick Engels: Collected Works, 1st Chinese Edition, Volume 42, p. 176.
6   Hegel: Phenomenology of Spirit, Volume I, p. 11.
7   Hegel: Phenomenology of Spirit, Volume II, p. 42, Beijing: The Commercial Press, 1979.
8   Hegel: Phenomenology of Spirit, Volume I, p. 14.

Notion, but it even makes the actuality impossible; for the antici-
pation posits the subject as an inter point, whereas the actuality is
self-movement" . Therefore, subject for Hegel is the movement, the
process. The alienation of subject into object is the unfolding of the
content of subject itself. The more we look into object, the more we
return into subject, because what we have perceived in the real world
is just the thought-content of this world, i.e. it is the thing which
makes the world into absolute idea and is gradually realized.

Absolute idea as subject is in constant movement, and is "a pure, *incessant* revolving within itself"[9], which is realized in the form of negation. Hence alienation and the supersession of alienation is actually the negation of the negation. For example, that absolute idea as
subject is externalized as the objective nature and on the other side
the society is a negation of itself, while the objective existence makes
absolute Spirit feel unfree, "because it values the other no more than
itself; its essential being is present to it in the form of an 'other', it
is outside of itself and must rid itself of its self-externality"[10], which
is actually a negation of the "negation", the return into subject itself.
In this way, the unity of subject and object is unlike Schelling's os-
sified, direct unity, but rather becomes a dialectic unity. In fact, the
whole of the Hegelian system is built according to this structure. For
instance, logical categories in his *Logic* are seen one by one as a negation, i.e., the externalization of human thinking, and then they are
seen as negation of the negation, namely, as the supersession of this
externalization, as the expression of the actuality of human thinking.

Negation becomes a moment and the driving force of movement in
Hegel's theory of alienation, because he deals with negation dialectically and combines negation with affirmation, i.e., preservation.
Affirmation itself contains negation, and affirmation without negation is in absolute identity with itself, and has no opportunity and no
element for development; negation also contains affirmation, and
negation without affirmation is the destruction of itself and the dis-
ruption of development. This combination of affirmation and negation constitutes supersession. Hegel criticizes the abstract concept

---

9   Karl Marx and Frederick Engels: Collected Works, 1st Chinese Edition,
Volume 42, p. 176.
10   Hegel: Phenomenology of Spirit, Volume I, p. 126.

of negation, which, he believes, makes "the unity split into lifeless, merely immediate, unopposed extremes; and the two do not recipro- cally give and receive one another back from each other consciously, but leave each other free only indifferently, like things. Their act is an abstract negation, not the negation coming from consciousness, which supersedes in such a way as to preserve and maintain what is superseded, and consequently survives its own supersession"[11].

Hegel's theory of alienation contains profound dialectics, but it has two fundamental weaknesses. First, his view of absolute idea as subject actually considers as subject the following: "Thought *sans** eyes, *sans* teeth, *sans* ears, *sans* everything", the "thought revolving solely within the orbit of thought" which runs counter to science and widely diverges from common sense.[12]

Second, although his theory of alienation contains critical elements, the supersession of this alienation does not touch its objects and is only the movement of the categories due to the idealistic essence of this theory. This supersession of alienation is therefore critical in form, but non-critical in reality and the preservation of the existing forms of alienation. Since then, the theory of alienation had evolved in two directions, as mainly represented by Feuerbach and Bauer.

According to Franz Mehring, between Feuerbach and Bauer "exists much difference. They stand not shoulder to shoulder, but back to back. Bauer spins the idealistic yarn until it breaks in his hand, while Feuerbach openly breaks with this philosophy, making the first step to defeat it eventually"[13].

The relationship between Feuerbach and Bauer on the philosophical line is vividly expressed by such words of Mehring as "not should to shoulder, but back to back". And one of its most important mani- festations is that they develop Hegel's theory of alienation along two different directions. In the history of philosophy, it is Feuerbach who first combined the theory of alienation with humanism.

---

11   Ibid., p. 127.
12   Karl Marx and Frederick Engels: Collected Works, 1st Chinese Edition, Volume 42, p. 178.
13   Mehring, In Defense of Marxism, p. 261.
*) sans (French) means without.

Feuerbach, first and foremost, fundamentally reversed the idealistic direction on the question of the subject of alienation, and concluded that "subject is man"[14]. He opposed his view to the idealistic tradition of the German classical philosophy and declared war against it, and expressly pointed out that "this philosophy has for its principle, not the Substance of Spinoza, not the ego of Kant and Fichte, not the Absolute Identity of Schelling, not the Absolute Mind of Hegel, in short, no abstract, merely conceptional being, but a real being, the true Ens realissimum—man; its principle, therefore, is in the highest degree positive and real."[15]

Feuerbach regarded man, the perceptual, corporeal man with various needs as subject to oppose Hegel, because absolute idea seen as subject by Hegel is nothing but to make human reason, thinking and ideas independent and separated from man and turn into a spiritual entity independent of man. This utterly reverses the relationship between being and thinking, just as Feuerbach criticized: "Thinking for Hegel is being, thinking is the subject and being is the predicate."[16] Concerning the question of subject, a great achievement of Feuerbach was the reversal of the subject and object relationship which was reversed by Hegel. Feuerbach considered this reversal as the path to truth, as the fundamental principle for transforming philosophy: "We only need always make the *predicate* into the *subject* and thus, as the subject, into the *object* and *principle*. He wrote: Hence we need only invert speculative philosophy and then have the unmasked, pure, bare truth."[17]

Feuerbach's argument that man is subject was directed at Bauer. As a Young Hegelian, Bauer emerged as a reformer of the Hegelian philosophy, but he did not go beyond Hegel, and remained within the frame of speculative philosophy, though he changed the subject of alienation from absolute idea into self-consciousness. According to Feuerbach, to really reforming philosophy firstly requires the change of subject, rather than putting the old wine into a new bottle. He wrote: "A new principle always makes its appearance with

14   The Selected Works of Feuerbach's Philosophical Works, Volume 1, p. 247, Beijing: SDX Joint Publishing Company, 1962.
15   The Selected Works of Feuerbach's Philosophical Works, Volume 2, p.p. 13-14
16   The Selected Works of Feuerbach's Philosophical Works, Volume 1, p. 144.
17   Ibid., p. 102.

a *new name*. That is, it elevates its name from a humble and lowly position to the princely rank, making its name the mark of the highest distinction." And he rebuked Bauer, saying that "If people translate the name of the new philosophy, i.e., the name of 'human being', with 'self-consciousness', then people would interpret the new philosophy in the sense of the old, placing it in the old perspective once again. Because the self-consciousness of the old philosophy, *separated from the human being*, is an *abstraction without reality*. The human being is the self-consciousness."[18] That is to say, self-consciousness is human consciousness, and only human being has self-consciousness, and the elevation of self-consciousness divorced from man to subject remains to be a copy of the old philosophy.

Contrary to Feuerbach, Bauer grasped one-sidedly and thoroughly elaborated Hegel's theory of self-consciousness. Hegel had emphasized the idea, but Bauer also praised self-consciousness. For example, he believed that a characteristic of the French philosophy, which was opposed to the status quo, opposed to the beliefs, and to all authorities which ruled mankind over thousands of years. This opposition of French philosophy was an opposition to what was alien to and incompatible with self-consciousness, or that in which self-consciousness could not find itself. Bauer had grasped this moment of the Hegelian system, regarded self-consciousness as subject and believed that it was the creator of all history. He wrote: "self-consciousness is the sole power of the world, while history has no other meaning except for being the variance and development of self-consciousness."[19] Self-consciousness has created the world, differences and the universe. Hence Bauer opposed self-consciousness to substance, put the former over the latter, and asserted that "substance is nothing but the evanescent flame, in which 'ego' burns its limitation and finiteness. Movement is not completed by substance but by self-consciousness; self-consciousness is really infinite"[20]. Only self-consciousness is the answer to the mystery of the Substance of Spinoza, the real reason itself.

---

18   Ibid., p. 117.
19   Auguste Cornu: Karl Marx and Friedrich Engels, Volume 1, p. 327.
20   Zvi H. Rosen: Bruno Bauer and Karl Marx, p. 77.

Just because Bauer believed self-consciousness was the subject, substance was just the alienation of self-consciousness and reflected the limitation and finiteness of self-consciousness and was something unstable and evanescent, whereas the existence of substance was an alien power for self-consciousness, an obstacle to its further development, the whole development process for him was nothing but the process in which self-consciousness created and continuously superseded objects,. In this process, "movement is completed not by substance but by self-consciousness, and only self-consciousness is really infinite and includes the universality of substance as its essence in itself"[21]. So Bauer's theory of alienation was a theory from self-consciousness to self-consciousness.

It is with this theory of alienation that Bauer had criticized religion. I have mentioned that Hegel also regarded religion as a form of alienation, but he superseded this alienation not for the transition to atheism and the annulment of religion but for the grasping of religion by reason, that is, to replace religion by philosophy of religion. In this respect, Bauer as a Young Hegelian was more radical than Hegel, and had somewhat developed the critical force included in Hegel's theory of alienation.

According to Bauer, religion is the alienation of self-consciousness, and is a fear, depression, that means, it is the manifestation of the repression of feelings which not only, does not believe in mankind, species and self-consciousness, but also lacks the courage of rising against the universality of self-consciousness, and consequently it is the manifestation of spiritual poverty and emptiness. So in his work the *Gospels* self-consciousness actually enters into a relation with itself. Although it is alienated and turned into an extremely funny imitation, it is the relationship of man to himself, i.e., to self-consciousness.

Bauer believes that religion is a power that confines human beings. Man considers his common power as an alien power confronting himself, in the face of which he trembles with fear and despises himself, and takes the Saviour as the guarantee for his existence. In fact, the so-called Revelation is nothing but the self-deceptive discourse

---

21   Auguste Cornu: Karl Marx and Friedrich Engels, Volume 1, p. 328.

of man about his mission; and the so-called atonement is nothing but the requirement of man to endure against the suffering caused by reality for the vain hope of future happiness. That is to say, we have to suffer hardships in real life for the sake of our future happiness; we have to become sinners, the irredeemable, hopeless sinner in advance for the sake of atonement. This teaching is as ridiculous as killing a man before saving him.

This form of religious alienation transforms man into a passive, poor, wretched and unfortunate man. Like those animals decorated colourfully for sacrifice, man offers himself as a sacrifice to the religious power. This religious form deceives him and makes him unaware of this misfortune. For example, Augustine declared that since the life of human beings was short and insignificant, it did not matter at all to live under whatever system, for man would die anyway. Bauer refuted this argument. He pointed out that religion intended to avoid the sufferings on earth and only rented out the heaven; in fact, the religious categories of the heavenly world and the human world, the category of supreme authority of the heavenly world over the human world, the category of strange changes happening when the heavenly world interferes in the human world, and the category of human obedience to the authority of the heavenly world, all of them were indispensable to religious consciousness to create its own world. Bauer advocated the supersession of religion and the return to self-consciousness, hence leading forward to atheism.

There is no doubt that Bauer's criticism of religion with the theory of alienation was of positive significance, and contributes to the studies of religion. However, due to the idealistic nature of his theory of alienation, he increasingly lost the progressiveness of the anti-religious struggle occurred at the beginning of the Young Hegelian movement, and later became the "dangerous enemy" of it.

Bauer denies substance and assumes that there is no substance in any field, which is actually a denial of any existence distinct from thinking, of any object different subject and of man himself and of any nature outside of man. What is left is the sole, rootless self-consciousness, the bodiless, fleshless soul. So Bauer and his companions resent the concept of object very much, because object means the sensuous object, the existence outside man, which is incompatible with the infinite, universal self-consciousness: "*Object!* Horrible! There is nothing more damnable, more profane, more mass-like than an *object—agrave*; *bas* the object! absolute subjectivity."[22]

This feature is clearly shown by the comment on love by of Edgar Bauer, the younger brother of Bruno Bauer. Love for him is a horror and abomination and excites his hatred and wrath, because love is the most materialistic thing. Love is a human passion and happens in the real, sensuous world and on the real individual. It needs a subject, a real subject as well as an object, a real sensuous object, so love really teaches man to believe in the objective world outside himself, which not only makes man into an object, but even the object into man. The Young Hegelians have objected to sensuous objects and to see love as the pursuit of sensuous objects. They abstract from the sensuous world and the sensuous objects and study love with the idealist conception of alienation, "making "*love*" a being apart, separate from man and as such independent. By this simple process, by changing the predicate into the subject, all the attributes and manifestations of human nature can be Critically transformed into their *negation* and into *alienations* of human nature."[23] The criticism here, like the use of hunger to demonstrate the objective reality of objects which satisfy hunger in *Manuscripts*, is basically not beyond Feuerbach. However, it is important to note that with love being the day-to-day fact that one human being makes another the external object of the emotion of his soul, Marx emphasizes "*objective importance*" instead of ego, simply.

Since self-consciousness is conceived by Bauer as subject, criticism is seen as its inherent attribute. Self-consciousness has to keep criticizing in order to remove and destroy all obstacles which prevent its development and hamper its return into itself. Therefore, Bauer's criticism, like the self-consciousness advocated by him, is a transcendental existence separate from the real subject, a spiritualistic phrase.

But Bauer knows that criticism is always done by man, therefore, they purport to be representatives of criticism, critical incarnates and critical criticism, whereas the masses are indolent, non-critical and the deadly foes of criticism. In this way, the criticalness contained in

---

22   Karl Marx and Frederick Engels: Collected Works, 1st Chinese Edition, Volume 2, p. 24.
23   Ibid.

Bauer's theory of alienation shifts its focus away from religion, and proceeds to complete opposition to the masses.

Proceeding from his idealist theory of alienation, Bauer limits criticism to pure thinking and only recognizes one criticism, i.e., theoretical criticism. This so-called criticism does not touch nor change real objects at all, and is merely an activity of pure thinking. Thus for him to eliminate alienation becomes a task of the theoretical criticism, and the so-called transformation of society is reduced to the cerebral activity of critical criticism, which fully indicates that this claimed criticism is actually a pernicious development of the non-critical element in Hegel's theory of alienation, that is, the supersession of alienation is not seen as the actual changing of objects but as a purely speculative movement.

According to this view, the capitalist private property, capital and wage-labour are not the reality of the capitalist society, but they are merely some categories. The reality will be changed so long as these categories are abolished in thinking. For instance, they will cease to be wage-workers if in their thinking they abolish the thought of wage-labour and cease to regard themselves as wage-workers; they can abolish real capital if they overcome in thinking the category of capital. The whole evil lies not in the reality of the capitalist society, but only in the workers' thinking. Therefore, the key is that the worker should abandon any actual political activity and he should focus on changing himself. As long as he changes "himself" in thinking, he can change his status, just as Marx wrote: "*Absolute Criticism* has learnt from Hegel's *Phänomenologie* at least *the* art of converting *real objective* chains that exist *outside me* into *merely ideal*, merely *subjective* chains, existing merely *in me* and thus of converting all external sensuously perceptible struggles into pure struggles of thought."[24] Like Don Quixote who fights against the windmills, Bauer called on the workers to turn the transformation of society into that of themselves.

This lie had already been refuted by the Chartist Movement in Britain and the Canut workers' uprising in Lyon, France, who had stood up and fought, and formed various associations, which showed that

---

24   Ibid., p. 105.

the workers in Manchester and Lyon were painfully aware of the difference between being and thinking, between consciousness and life. They knew that private property, capital, money, wage-labour and the like were not categories but very practical, very objective products of their self-estrangement. The workers were unable to argue away their masters and their own practical debasement by pure thinking, and had to act, that is, to abolish them by practical and objective struggles, in order to make themselves really become human beings not only in thinking, in consciousness, but in actual life.

Marx was a revolutionary. He not only criticized Bauer for turning the workers' revolutionary action which aimed to transform capitalism into pure speculation, but he also objected to the reformism, advocated by Eugène Sue in *The Mysteries of Paris*, "which ensures the well-being of the *worker without* prejudice to the *fortune of the rich*, which establishes links of sympathy and gratitude between these two classes and thus ensures tranquillity in the state *forever*"[25]. According to Marx, the abstract sense of good and evil advocated in the above novel causes Rodolphe, the hero, to travel incognito, uphold justice, save the good and punish the wicked, which is "a new theory to keep society upright by *rewarding the good* and *punishing the wicked*." In fact, the system of rewards for the good and punishments for the wicked is "the consecration of differences in social rank and the complete expression of a servile abasement"[26].

Marx advocated the abolishment of alienation under capitalism by revolutionary movement, and believed that the proletariat was capable of shouldering this mission. His analysis of the status and mission of the proletariat makes a step forward compared with that in *Manuscripts*, displaying more the feature of his historical materialistic analysis.

Two points still retain the influence of humanism in *The Holy Family*.

First, that "the propertied class and the class of the proletariat present the same human self-estrangement" was not a scientific formulation. It is obviously impossible to have a scientific understanding of the root cause for the emergence of the proletariat and the bourgeoisie,

---

25   Ibid., p. 251.
26   Ibid., p. 239, p. 240.

to understand the essence of their opposition and the necessity of eliminating this opposition by proceeding from human self-estrangement, without considering the mode of capitalist production. In fact, a scientific explanation is only possible when we start from the development of history itself and treat the opposition between the proletarian and the bourgeois as the product of the changes in the modes of production and modes of exchange.

Second, concerning the opposition between the capitalist private property and human nature. Marx pointed out that the bourgeois political economy accepted the relationships of private property system as human and rational, while Proudhon's achievement lay exactly in that he put an end to this view once for all. He took the human semblance of the capitalist economic relations seriously and sharply opposed them to their inhuman reality, and thus regarded the capitalist private property as real inhumanity. Based on this view, Marx analyzed the opposition between the humanistic nature of the proletariat and the capitalist private property, and he believed that under capitalism, in the proletariat itself is the abstraction of all humanity, even the semblance of humanity, was actually, practically completed, and the capitalist conditions of life for the proletariat were in their most inhuman form, the human nature of the proletariat was therefore in contradiction with the conditions which were the outright, resolute and comprehensive negation of that nature. This judgment on capitalist private property supported by the human nature of proletariat had ended the influence of humanism completely.

In addition to the above ideas, the analysis of proletariat in *The Holy Family* focused on analyzing capitalism itself and on uncovering the economic status of the proletariat so as to introduce its historical mission. Marx stated that "[i]t is not a question of what this or that proletarian, or even the whole proletariat, at the moment *regards* as its aim. It is a question of *what the proletariat is*, and what, in accordance with this *being*, will historically be compelled to do. Its aim and historical action is visibly and irrevocably foreshadowed in its own life situation as well as in the whole organization of bourgeois society today."[27] It is by analyzing the organization of bourgeois society today and the life situation of the proletariat that

---

27   Ibid., p. 45.

Marx expounded the historical mission of the proletariat from the organization of bourgeois society, instead of starting from the external "contradiction" (the contradiction between abstract species-nature and economic relations), hence has preliminarily displayed the scientific and revolutionary character of the principle of historical materialism.

Unlike Bauer and others, Marx did not seek the premise and basis for the opposition between the proletariat and the bourgeois outside their opposition, but considered them as the product of private property. It is the capitalist private property that restricts the proletariat and the bourgeoisie and makes them into the opposite parts of a single whole. More profoundly, Marx saw that it was not sufficient to regard them merely as two sides of a single whole, and the question was exactly what place each occupied in this antithesis. Precisely because of their different statuses, the bourgeoisie cannot abolish poverty nor the proletariat, but strives to maintain private property and thus inevitably preserves its opposite—the proletariat, while the proletariat has to abolish private property, which is the primary cause for it to become the proletariat in order to abolish itself as a dispossessed class. Therefore, the proletariat manifests itself as a negative factor in capitalist society and tries hard to change the present situation, while the bourgeoisie manifests itself as a positive factor and strives to maintain the present situation. Hence their different characters and aspirations are determined by their different economic statuses.

This kind of analysis helps him to reject the humanist elements in the theory of alienation. Although Marx had still considered the proletariat and the bourgeoisie as human self-estrangement at that time, he indeed highlighted their differences based on their different class statuses: "But propertied class feels at ease and strengthened in this self-estrangement, it recognizes estrangement as *its own power* and has in it the *semblance* of a human existence. The class of the proletariat feels annihilated in estrangement; it sees in it its own powerlessness and the reality of an inhuman existence."[28]

---

28   Ibid., p. 44.

There is also a change in Marx's view on labour. He had focused on elaborating the negative aspects of estranged labour in *Manuscripts*, the labourers' physical and spiritual sufferings caused by estranged labour; whereas in *The Holy Family* he highlights the education and cultivation of the proletariat by modern industrial labour, saying that "[n]ot in vain does it [the proletariat] go through the stern but steeling school of *labour*"[29]. Indeed, the proletariat in modern capitalist industry is different from craftsmen, apprentices in guilds or individual farmers. They have been tempered by modern industrial labour and are more powerfully organized, militant and united.

Here, Marx also dealt with the interrelation between the objectivity of the laws of history and subjective factors. He affirmed that "private property drives itself in its economic movement towards its own dissolution", which is "a development which does not depend on it, which is unconscious and which takes place against the will of private property by the very nature of things". However, capitalism will not bring ruin upon itself, but "only inasmuch as it produces the proletariat as proletariat, poverty which is conscious of its spiritual and physical poverty, dehumanization which is conscious of its dehumanization, and therefore self-abolishing"[30]. The proletariat is the executor of the sentence that history judges and pronounces on capitalism, but this task will not be fulfilled if they lack self-knowledge. Marx had praised the English and French proletariat of the time, because "a large part of the English and French proletariat is already conscious of its historic task and is constantly working to develop that consciousness into complete clarity"[31].

Marx expressly stated that "the proletariat can and must emancipate itself" based on his above analysis of the status of the proletariat in the organization of present bourgeois society. But contrary to Bauer's idealistic reduction of the proletarian emancipation to a pure thinking activity, Marx emphasized the need to abolish the objective conditions which produced the proletariat, "it cannot emancipate itself without abolishing the conditions of its own life".

---

29   Ibid., p. 45.
30   Ibid., p. 44.
31   Ibid., p. 45.

According to Lenin, Marx almost developed his ideas of the role of the proletarian revolution in *The Holy Family*, which should be attributed to his materialistic and dialectical analysis of the organization of bourgeois society. Although they bear the traces of humanism, Marx undoubtedly moved in the right direction to explore the historical mission of the proletariat and the way of its liberation by exloring capitalist society itself.

2 MATERIAL PRODUCTION: ORIGIN OF HISTORY

In *Manuscripts*, Marx had pointed out that the entire so-called history of the world is nothing but the creation of man through human labour, which is a summary comment on the role of labour in human history. He advances forward along this direction and further elucidates the origin and basic content of history and how to study history in *The Holy Family*.

Marx raises the question of the origin of history in *The Holy Family*, which is a fundamental issue in the conception of history, which was not correctly resolved by previous idealists.

Hegel considers that absolute idea is the origin of history, the entire history is nothing but the history of its self-development and mankind merely bearers its development with a varying degree of consciousness or unconsciousness. The empirical, exoteric history which people can directly see is an expression of the invisible, esoteric, speculative history. The history of mankind becomes the history of a spirit far removed from the real man.

Bauer criticizes religion, but he does not transform the history of the heaven into that of the secular world. He is hostile to nature and refuses to study nature and industry, and considers that self-consciousness is the origin of history and the sole power of history. History has no other meaning except for being the variance and development of self-consciousness.

Marx objects to this idealist conception of history by Bauer and stresses the role of material production. He argued: "Or does this Critical Criticism believe that it has reached even the *beginning* of a knowledge of historical reality so long as it excludes *from* the historical movement the theoretical and practical relation of man to nature, i.e., natural science and industry? Or does it think that it actually knows any period without knowing, for example, the industry of that period, the immediate mode of Production of life itself? Of course, spiritualistic, *theological* Critical Criticism only knows (at least it imagines that it knows) the main political, literary and theological acts of history. Just as it separates thinking from the senses, the soul from the body and itself from the world, it separates history from natural science and industry and sees the origin of history not in vulgar *material* production on the earth but in vaporous clouds in the heavens."[32]

This paragraph of Marx includes the following two important ideas.

First, there will be no history of mankind without the relationship of man to nature, and the basic content of history is the human activity of transforming nature, which he has discussed in *Manuscripts*. But Marx further developed it into the question of the origin of history, and argued explicitly that the origin of history was not in vaporous clouds in the heavens (the realm of pure spirit) but in material production on the earth. Thus material production is included by Marx in his conception of history as the focal point of investigating history, hence opening up a way to really reveal the law of historical development.

Second, Marx put forward the basic theory and method for studying history. The studies of political history, literary history and religious history are certainly important, but to really know any period in history, it is fundamental to study its mode of production rather than its ideology. All historical phenomena, the ideas and concepts or any historical period, can be explained reasonably so long as the social and economic conditions of this period in history are fully known.

Marx attacks Bauer's refutation of the article *On The Jewish Question* in *The Holy Family*, and launched a debate with him on the Jewish question once more. Marx not only reiterated his views in *On The Jewish Question*, but also raises the question of how to study history. He wrote: "Jewry has maintained itself and developed *through* history, *in* and *with* history, and that this development is to be perceived not by the eye of the theologian, but only by the eye of the man of

---

32   Ibid., p. 191.

the world, because it is to be found, not in *religious theory*, but only in *commercial* and *industrial practice*."[33] The so-called "eye of the theologian" and "eye of the man of the world" are actually point to two kinds of conception of history. The eye of the theologian refers to the conception of history of Bauer's idealist theory of alienation, which conceives Judaism and Christianity as two stages of the estrangement of self-consciousness, while "by the eye of the man of the world" is a method of materialist conception of history, which concentrates on the commercial and industrial practice, and is consistent with Marx's view that to know a period in history requires the knowledge of its mode of production.

Based on this view, Marx criticizes Bauer for seeing the Jewish question as a religious question and examining religion merely in a religious way. Marx argues that Bauer grasps only the religious essence of Jewry, but not the secular, real basis of that religious essence, therefore Bauer combats religious consciousness as if it were something independent. According to Marx, the real secular Jewry, and hence religious Jewry too, is being continually produced by the present-day civil life and finds its final development in the capitalist money system. The essence of the Jewish question cannot be understood without the investigation of the history of industrial and commercial development. Therefore, Marx argued that "Herr Bauer, therefore, dealt with the *religious* and *theological* question in the *religious* and *theological* way, if only because he saw in the "religious" question of the time a "purely religious" question."[34]

Bauer also opposes the state to religion. He images a modern state in which religious and theological tools are abolished, instead of studying the true relationship of the modern state to religion. Certainly, this was to examine the state by abstracting from the economic basis of the modern state, in an attempt to make the state the "executor of *Critical-theological* cherished desires". Marx examines the state in its relationship between the economic basis and the state, and believes that the bourgeois state will not abolish religion but instead recognize the freedom of religious belief, which is consistent with its economic basis. He wrote: "just as the ancient state had slavery

---

33   Ibid., p. 140.
34   Ibid., p. 142.

as its *natural basis*, the *modern state* has as its *natural basis* civil society and the *man* of civil society, i.e., the independent man linked with other men 'only by the ties of private interest and *unconscious* natural necessity, the *slave* of labour for material gain and of his own as well as other men's *selfish* need. The modern state recognises this as its natural basis as such stipulated in the *universal rights of man*. It did not create it. As it was the product of civil society driven beyond the old political bonds by its own development, the modern state, for its part, now recognised the womb from which it sprang and its basis by the *declaration* of the *rights of man*."[35] Therefore, the attempt to see the modern state in opposition to theology and religion and expect from the state to abolish the freedom of religious belief is tantamount to ask from it to stand up against the womb from which it sprang and stand up against its basis. This was clearly to consider the state with "the eye of the theologian", without knowing what the state was at all!

The state must meet the needs of its economic basis. Marx summarized the revolutionary experience in France after 1789, and demonstrated this point by his comment on the failure of Robespierre and Saint-Just. They were executed because they had confused the difference between the ancient democratic commonweal based on real slavery and the democratic representative state based on bourgeois society. On the one hand, they recognized and sanctioned in the rights of man the modern bourgeois society, the society of industry, of universal competition, of private interest pursuing its aims; on the other hand, they wanted to model the political head of the ancient state and eliminate the manifestations of the life inherent in this society. As a result, they themselves were sent to the guillotine. Marx criticized them for not knowing that man in bourgeois society was "a *man* who cannot be the man of the ancient commonweal any more, his *economic* and *industrial* conditions were not those of *ancient* times"[36]. They were completely mistaken about the times in their attempt to expect the ancient Romans and their political institution appear under the modern bourgeois economic and industrial conditions. In this regard, Napoleon was more realistic than them.

---

35   Ibid., p. 145.
36   Ibid., p. 156, p. 157.

He already discerned the real essence of the modern state and understood that it was based on the unhampered development of bourgeois society, on the free movement of private interest, etc. Yet at the same time Napoleon still regarded the state as an end in itself "and civil life only as a treasurer and his *subordinate* which must have no *will of its own*." Napoleon showed no more consideration for the essential material interests of bourgeois society, i.e., trade and industry, whenever they conflicted with his political interests, hence the same result—failure.

In addition, Marx elaborated the social nature of man in bourgeois society. If we can say that he considered that the man in bourgeois society is non-social, and has lost his social nature in civil life because of egoism and acts as a species-being only in political life in *Manuscripts*, then we can say he just rejects this view in *The Holy Family* when criticizing Bauer for seeing the members of civil society as individual atoms, which are held together only by the state.

Marx states emphatically that the members of civil society are not atoms. The specific property of the atom is that it has no properties and it is not necessarily connected with the external world. The members of civil society are different. Although they are egoists, they are not unrelated, self-sufficient, wantless, independent atoms. Each of man's senses compels him to believe in the existence of the world and of individuals outside him. Human needs can be satisfied only through the connection between them. "Therefore, it is *natural necessity*, the *essential human properties* however estranged they may seem to be, and *interest* that hold the members of civil society together; *civil*, not *political* life is their *real* tie. It is therefore not the *state* that holds the *atoms* of civil society together, but the fact that they are atoms only in *imagination*, in the *heaven* of their fancy, but in *reality* they are beings tremendously different from atoms, in other words, not *divine egoists*, but *egoistic human beings*."[37] So in bourgeois society man is a species-being not only in political life but also in civil society, only each person acquires the greatest freedom because of being free from the fetters of privileges of in the Middle Ages, and seems to be separate, independent, but actually connected with each other in economic life.

---

37   Ibid., p. 154.

The Holy Family not only regards material production as the origin of history, but also uncovers the relationship between man and history and criticizes Bauer's view of historical teleology.

Bauer advocated the so-called truth above history, and history above man. The real human individuals seem to him a mere means for history to achieve its aims, while history is the process in which truth arrives at self-consciousness. Thus, history has a definite aim, that is, to prove truth, which was a teleological view. According to the earlier teleologists, plants only exist to be eaten by animals, and animals to be eaten by men, while according to Bauer, man exists so that history may exists, and history exists so that the proof of truths can exist.

History does not have its aims, teleonomy is the characteristic of human activity. In history as an objective process, there is causal relationship between various phenomena. This definite causal relationship which keeps repeating appears as historical necessity which exits not outside but in human activity. Marx therefore asserted that "*[h]istory* does *nothing*, it "possesses *no* immense wealth", "it wages *no* battles". It is *man*, real, living man who does all that, who possesses and fights; "history" is not, as it were, a person apart, using man as a means to achieve *its own* aims; history is *nothing but* the activity of man pursuing his aims."[38] History is the history of man, real, living man. If the relationship between man and history is inverted, history is transformed into abstract subject, and man into a means of history to achieve its own aims, the idea of historical necessity will be mystified and made into historical fatalism.

Therefore it became possible to further discuss the interaction between people in material production because Marx now considered the production of material good as the original of history. It is in *The Holy Family* that Marx had approached the basic idea of his entire system, i.e., the idea of relations of production by criticizing Proudhon's "*equal* possession".

As a representative of petty bourgeoisie, Proudhon strongly attacked the capitalist private property, yet he strove to oppose the capitalist private property by "equal possession" to make each person possess private property equally, in order to eliminate the separation of

---

38   Ibid., p. 118.

means of production from man. This showed that Proudhon could not get rid of private property, but attempted to overcome private property within the frame of private property, thus realize human re-appropriation of the objective world in the form of equal possession.

Could equal possession abolish estrangement? No. Just as Marx indicated: "[t]he idea of "*equal* possession" is the economic expression and therefore itself still estranged expression for the fact that the *object as being for man*, as the *objective being of man*, is at the same time the *existence of man for other men*, his human relation to other men, the *social behaviour of man to man*. Proudhon abolishes economic estrangement *within* economic estrangement."[39]

The profundity of this argument lies in that Marx sees the equal possession of objects is not the relationship between man and objects, but a relationship between man and man which is realized through objects. Under the condition of private property, the social relationship of man to man takes an objectified form and appears as the relationship of object to object. It is thus clear that human equal possession of objects shows that the relationship of man to man remains to be that of between property-owner and another property-owner. The discovery of the social relationship of man to man which is concealed by the relationship of object to object is an important step towards the establishment of the materialist conception of history, a qualitative forward step from estranged labour.

3 HISTORY AND THE MASSES. ROLE OF MATERIAL INTERESTS

The development of the materialist conception of history involves two aspects: To reveal the role of production of material goods through labour and discover the objective laws of development of the system of social relations; to discover the great role of the masses by affirming the subjective status of man. These two aspects are interrelated to each other.

In *The Holy Family*, Marx and Engels proceed from the view that production of material goods is the origin of history, refute Bauer's idealist conception of history which despises the masses, and make a profound exposition of the great role of the masses in history.

---

39   Ibid., p. 152.

Bauer and his group had tried hard to elevate the role of self-consciousness and debase the significance of material production. They ignored the fact that the labourer was the creator of material wealth, and alleged that the worker created nothing, "To be able to create everything, a stronger consciousness is needed than that of the worker". They only consider the creations of their thought significant, as "everything", while the worker's labour is "everyday work", "is always individual, having as its object his most personal needs". They put abstract speculative activity above the activity of material production. *The Holy Family* denounces this "Phrase", and argues that "Critical Criticism creates nothing, the worker creates everything; and so much so that even his intellectual creations put the whole of Criticism to shame; the English and the French workers provide proof of this."[40]

Bauer and his group opposed truth to the masses. They scoffed that the masses think itself in possession of so many truths which seem obvious to it, but in fact, for them truth has nothing do with the masses. Truth proves itself, and the masses cannot know nor possess it. In this way, truth was put in opposition to the masses: "it addresses itself not to the empirical man but to the "*innermost depths of the soul*"; in order to be "*truly apprehended*" it does not act on his *vulgar body*, which may live deep down in an English cellar or at the top of a French block of flats; it "stretches" "from end to end" through his idealistic intestines."[41] The masses are ignorant, truth will be possessed by "Critical Critics", in whose idealistic intestines are hidden all the truth. However, the fact was that Bauer and his group knew nothing about truth, except the empty, the simplest, the self-evident, and the truth of history will be grasped in the end by "the quintessence of all truth"—man himself.

Bauer and his company also opposed the masses with the historical progress, and they regarded the masses not as the motive force of history but as the resistance to history, saying, "All great actions in the previous history were failures *from the start* and had no effective success because the mass became *interested* in them and were *enthusiastic* over them". For them, only thoughts were the decisive force for the development of history.

---

40   Ibid., p. 22.
41   Ibid., p. 102.

Contrary to Bauer's argument, Marx starts from the idea that material production is the origin of history and stresses the role of material interests in history. People are driven to fight not by abstract thinking principles but by real material interests. For example, it is not the slogan of liberty, equity and fraternity but the material interests of the bourgeoisie that played the decisive role in the bourgeois revolution in France. The mobilization and inspiration of this slogan lies precisely in its reflection of this material demand. "The "*idea*" always disgraced itself insofar as it differed from the "*interest*"."[42]

As for the majority of the non-bourgeois masses, their enthusiasm was inversely proportional to the process of the bourgeois revolution because the revolutionary principles (policies) of the bourgeoisie did not represent their real interests, and was not the revolutionary principles of their own, hence their enthusiasm was only momentary enthusiasm and only seeming *uplift*.

Likewise, material interests are also indispensible for judging whether or not a revolution is successful. The French bourgeois revolution was a success for the bourgeoisie, because it had concrete achievements and satisfied the material and political demands of the bourgeoisies in the end. It was a failure only for the non-bourgeois masses, because the real conditions for their emancipation were fundamentally distinct from those of the bourgeoisie. So contrary to the view of Bauer and his group, the French revolution was a failure not because the masses were interested in and enthusiastic over it, but because it represented an exclusive, limited masses rather than an all-embracing one, hence the enthusiasm of the most of the masses was only momentary and seeming uplift. Marx hereby drew such an important conclusion: "Together with the thoroughness of the historical action, the size of the masses whose action it is, will therefore increase."[43] Here the understanding on the activity of historical subject was elevated to a law.

The idea of Bauer and his group that the masses are the passive, spiritless material element and the Spirit, Criticism are the active element was nothing but a caricatured consummation of Hegel's conception of history, which, in turn, was nothing but the speculative

---

42   Ibid., p. 103.
43   Ibid., p. 104.

expression of the Christian philosophy: The antithesis between Spirit and Matter, between God and the world. Marx confronts this conception of history not with the idea of the estrangement and the idea of returning of human essence, but with the historical materialistic ideas that material production is the origin of history and that the masses are the creators of history. And this is a significant difference between *The Holy Family* and *Manuscripts*. From then on, Marx embarked on fully establishing the materialist conception of history by going deep into the origin of history and to uncover the law of motion governing the mode of production of material goods.

CHAPTER X

THEORETICAL PREPARATION PROCESS FROM "ESTRANGED LABOUR" TO FULL ESTABLISHMENT OF MATERIALIST CONCEPTION OF HISTORY

In *The Holy Family*, the influence of Feuerbach was greatly reduced, but the "worship" of him still existed; estrangement is no longer a dominant method, but human essence still served as the measure of the capitalist relations of production; whereas in *The German Ideology*, by proceeding from praising to criticizing Feuerbach, this time Marx fully established the materialist conception of history. Thus in *The German Ideology*, he abandoned interpreting estrangement from the point view of humanism. It seems difficult to understand this change, because he only in a short period, less than one year, passed from *The Holy Family* to *The German Ideology*, it was, however, not accidental at all. Marx's early thought was facing drastic changes. Since he was still exploring at that time, his thought seemed like the surging sea. After arriving in Brussels from Paris, Marx continued the study of both political economy and philosophy and fully grasped the major defects of Feuerbach's philosophy. He wrote An Article on Friedrich List's Book: *The National System of Political Economy* and *Theses on Feuerbach* in the spring of 1845, which provides us with those theoretical clues of this change which reflect his new economic and philosophical perspectives.

1 PRELIMINARY APPROACH TO THE PRINCIPLE OF THE DIALECTICAL RELATIONSHIP BETWEEN PRODUCTIVE FORCES AND RELATIONS OF PRODUCTION

Marx's intensive study on economics played a major role in the establishment of the materialist conception of history. If we can say the economic studies initiated in Paris in 1844 enabled Marx to break away from the speculative tradition of the German classical philosophy, and caused him to advance from estrangement to estranged labour, and discover the decisive role of labour in the formation of human history, hence opening up a path to the materialist conception of history, then we can say that the economic studies after his arrival in Brussels in the beginning of 1845 had offered him the theoretical preparation for his turn from estranged labour to the full establishment of the materialist conception of history. It is fair to say that his progress from estrangement to estranged labour and then to the full establishment of historical materialism is inseparable from his study on political economy, with the purpose of seeking scientific argument for the theory of communism.

Marx had migrated to Brussels in early February, 1845 due to the persecution of the French government. Here, he continued the study of political economy he had initiated in Paris, and read numerous works on political economy. He and Engels also made a trip to London and Manchester and studied various important literature. Our focus below will be on his comment on the First Book of *The National System of Political Economy*, written by the German economist F. List and published in 1841, to see how Marx began to approach the law of productive forces and relations of production.

Friedrich List was a German bourgeois vulgar economist. He advocated the system of protective tariffs and objected to free trade in order to meet the German bourgeois needs of developing industry, protect the German domestic market and thus guard against the competition from England. The First Book of his *The National System of Political Economy* was devoted to international trade, trade policy and the German tariff system. He emphasized the necessity of the protective tariffs in favour of Germany, and held that he would soon conduct a study on the essence of the errors in the theories of international trade and trade policy prevalent in political economy. But he did his utmost to conceal the essence of his theory under the so-called national interest cloak as if he did not represent the interests and desires of the German bourgeoisie. German bourgeoisie aimed to monopolize domestic market and enable the German industry reach the prosperity of England. Marx wrote: "He shrinks from speaking about the nasty exchange values which he covets and speaks about productive forces [*von Produktivkräften*]; he shrinks from speaking about competition and speaks of a national confederation of national productive forces; he shrinks from speaking of his private interest and speaks about the national interest."[1]

Both Engels and Marx intended to criticize List without prior consultation. In a letter to Marx, written in November, 1844, Engels said that he will write "a few pamphlets, notably against *List*". The aim of writing this pamphlet is the same with that of *The Condition of the Working Class in England* he was setting about to write. The Condition of the Working Class in England directly denounces the English bourgeoisie, but it attacks by innuendo the German bourgeoisie (*Auf Den Sack schlägt man, den Esel meint man*), expressing that the German bourgeoisie was the same with the English bourgeoisie, only it was not that courageous, thorough and ingenious in exploitation, while the pamphlet against List was a revelation of the essence of the German bourgeois protective tariff policy..

Engels and Marx had different focuses in their critique of List. Engels criticized List from the practical aspect, and clarified the practical conclusions of his economic thoughts. His speech in Elberfeld on February 15, 1845 included such an analysis. He investigated in detail the possibilities caused by the implementation of protective tariffs, and concluded that it necessarily led to the destitution of the proletariat and thus to revolution. Engels said, "substantiated also in detail what in the beginning, proceeding from competition in general, I set out in general terms — namely, that the unavoidable result of our existing social relations, under all circumstances, and in all cases, will be a social revolution. With the same certainty with which we can develop from given mathematical principles a new

---

1 Karl Marx and Frederick Engels: Collected Works, 1st Chinese Edition, Volume 42, p. 240.

mathematical proposition, with the same certainty we can deduce from the existing economic relations and the principles of political economy the imminence of social revolution."[2]

Contrary to Engels, Marx had focused his criticism on List's theoretical premises. He disclosed List's idealistic conception of productive forces, his pursuit of wealth under the pretence of concern with productive forces, and analyzed the relationship between the present-day industry and productive forces. Thus Marx was advancing his exploration on the most basic law of the development of history.

The German bourgeoisie was pursuing industrial wealth, the same as English and French bourgeoisie. But the English and French capitalists openly expressed this demand through their economists, and elevate wealth into a god and ruthlessly sacrifice everything else to it, including the sciences. Whereas the German bourgeoisie disavowed wealth while it was striving for it. It was creating for itself an "idealising" political economy, which had nothing in common with the profane French and English political economy, a new theory of wealth, in order to justify that they want to become wealthy. It uses empty, shallow, sentimental idealism to hide its pettiest, dirtiest, wealth-seeking shopkeeper's spirit. List's political economy was such a theory.

List placed productive forces in opposition to exchange values, and considered the former as a spiritual force, thus aimed to demonstrate that what he pursued was not the unrighteous material goods, not exchange values but the spiritual essence, i.e., the infinite productive forces. As Marx disclosed, "Productive force appears as an entity infinitely superior to exchange value. This force claims the position of inner essence, whereas exchange value claims that of a transient phenomenon. This force appears as infinite, exchange value as finite, the former as non-material, the latter as material—and we find all these antitheses in Herr List. Hence the supernatural world of forces takes the place of the material world of exchange values."[3]

---

2 Karl Marx and Frederick Engels: Collected Works, 1st Chinese Edition, Volume 2, p. 624.
3 Karl Marx and Frederick Engels: Collected Works, 1st Chinese Edition, Volume 42, p. 261.

In fact, productive forces are not the independent spiritual essence, nor the elusive phantoms, but material forces. Marx indicated that only by consulting any book of statistics can one read about water-power, steam-power, manpower, horse-power, all of which are productive forces. Although the bourgeois statistics took man as a force alongside horses, steam and water, thus expressing its contempt of man, it does "destroy the mystical radiance which transfigures 'productive force', thus showing that productive forces are genuine material forces.

The German bourgeois likewise wants to become rich, to make money, but it objects to exchange value, material wealth, and seems to be only interested in productive forces. List said, "The nation must sacrifice material forces in order to acquire spiritual or social forces. Raise protective tariffs for increasing its manufacturing power." He also said that "[t]he causes of wealth are something quite different from wealth itself; the force capable of creating wealth is infinitely more important than wealth itself." This was completely hypocritical. Marx argued that "List pretends that he is everywhere interested in productive forces for their own sake, quite apart from bad exchange values."[4]

In form, exchange value, money, always seemed to be an external aim, but productive forces were advertised as an aim which arose from the very nature of man, a self-aim. To be interested in productive forces was advertised as an interest in man himself, while the fact was: The German bourgeoisie was interested to increase its material wealth.

Was the German bourgeoisie, the factory-owner, at all concerned for the worker developing all his abilities, the worker exercising his productive capacities, fulfilling himself as a human being and thereby at the same time fulfilling his human nature? No. For them, if a crooked spine, twisted limbs, one-sided development and strengthening of certain muscles would make the worker more capable of working, then the crooked spine, the twisted limbs, the one-sided muscular movement would be the productive force. If the intellectual vacuity of the worker was more productive than his abundant intellectual activity, then his intellectual vacuity would be the productive

---

4   Ibid., p. 263.

force. If the monotony of an occupation makes the worker better suited for that occupation, then this monotony is the productive force. Therefore, the so-called productive force was nothing but "a means of wealth", "productive force of wealth". Hence Marx derided the German bourgeoisie, writing: they claimed to refuse "striving for unrighteous material goods, but strive for *spiritual essence*, for *infinite productive force*, instead of bad, finite *exchange values*. Of course, this spiritual essence involves the circumstance that the "citizen" ["*Bürger*"] takes this opportunity to fill his own pockets with worldly exchange values"[5].

List had distinguished the force which was capable of creating wealth from wealth itself to show his care for man. In fact, the effect and the cause should be inseparable. The nature of the effect is contained in the cause, and the cause carries with it some determining feature which manifests itself later in the effect. The bourgeois sees in the proletarian not a human being but a force capable of creating wealth. This "fine recognition" of man indeed "degrades" him. If the bourgeois considers an animal, a machine more favourable than manpower, they will replace man with an animal or a machine without any hesitation. List differentiates his view from the British classical political economy, and believes that the latter is built on exchange value, while his theory is based on productive forces. In fact, they are essentially the same. If the British classical political economy transforms man into a thing by characterizing him as an exchange value, then List's so-called theory of productive forces regards man as a cause of the creation of wealth, which sees man not as the true subject but as a machine creating wealth for the bourgeoisie.

For this reason, Marx argued that productive forces were not spiritual forces but material forces, which should not be abstracted from the social system when they are investigated. He stated: "in the present state of affairs productive force consists not only in, for instance, making man's labour more efficient or natural and social forces more effective, but just as much in making labour cheaper or more unproductive for the worker. Hence productive force is from the outset determined by exchange value."[6]

---

5   Ibid. p. 250.
6   Ibid. p. 263.

This fully shows that under capitalism, the development of productive forces suggests not only that human labour is made more effective but also that the exploitation of the worker is strengthened. And this point was repeatedly stressed later by Marx, who, in the *Inaugural Address of the Working Men's International Association* written in 1864, pointed out that in capitalist society, "every fresh development of the productive powers of labour must tend to deepen social contrast and point social antagonism"[7].

Compared with *Manuscripts*, Marx had made a step forward in his analysis of labour when he discussed List's views. In *Manuscripts*, he had abstracted labour from the form by which labour was realized, examined labour from the perspective of the subjective essence and defined it as a free, conscious activity, but here he argued: "[it] is one of the greatest misapprehensions to speak of free, human, social labour, of labour without private property. "*Labour*" by its very nature is unfree, unhuman, unsocial activity, determined by private property and creating private property."[8]

It is no doubt that it was a progress in Manuscripts to define labour as a conscious, purposeful activity and examine it from the perspective of the material exchange between man and nature which grasped the fundamental difference between men and animals, and analysed the fundamental character of labour—the objectification which is independent of any social form or applicable to all social forms. Yet *Manuscripts* had such a limitation: One cannot perceive the relations of production generated by mankind in a specific historical period from this labour alone, and is likely to see the real labour as estranged labour which confronts the labour as human nature. Although one may denounce and disclose the labour under capitalism by evaluating it as labour by its very nature, this perspective will restrict him from having a scientific understanding of it. Although general features of labour, abstracted from its various forms, can be summarized, its nature must be explained starting from the form by which it is realized (starting from definite relations of production) rather than from labour in general. When Marx emphasized

7   Karl Marx and Frederick Engels: Selected Works, 1st Edition, Volume 2, p. 130.
8   Karl Marx and Frederick Engels: Collected Works, 1st Chinese Edition, Volume 42, p.p. 254-255.

that labour under capitalism was an activity determined by private property and an activity creating private property, Marx had now turned to labour itself, leaving back his previous idea, which highlighted the opposition between human nature (true labour) and estrangement of human nature (estranged labour), Now he had started to examine labour by combining it with the form by which it was realized, hence a step forward in discovering the law of motion governing the contradictions between productive forces (as the relationship between man and nature) and the relations of production (as the relationship between man and man).

Marx began to approach this point in his analysis of the capitalist industry. He argued that industry could be considered from completely different point of views. One was to examine industry from the point of view of sordid huckstering interest, i.e., of the bourgeoisie.

For example, the German capitalists looked with greedy envy on the highly developed industry in England, and desired to reach this level in their own country. They flourished the whip of protective tariffs in order to install in their nation the spirit of "industrial education", certainly for the sake of the interest of the bourgeoisie.

The other point of view was to regard the development of industry as man creating for himself the conditions for human existence and creating the basis for human existence. For this reason, the system of present-day industry must be distinguished from the productive force that it (industry) creates against its will and creates unconsciously. The praise of the productive power of industry should not be transformed into praising and worshipping of the bourgeoisie, into praising of the capitalist private property. Marx wrote. "The forces of nature and the social forces which industry brings into being (conjures up), stand in the same relation to it as the proletariat. Today they are still the slaves of the bourgeois, and in them he sees nothing but the instruments (the bearers) of his dirty (selfish) lust for profit; tomorrow they will break their chains and reveal themselves as the bearers of human development which will blow him sky-high together with his industry, which assumes the dirty outer shell—which he regards as its essence—only until the human kernel has gained sufficient strength to burst this shell and appear in its own shape. Tomorrow they will burst the chains by which the bourgeois separates them from man and so distorts (transforms) them from a real social bond into fetters of society."[9]

This profound exposition differentiates the productive power of the capitalist industry from its condition (private property) in which it operates. It regards private property as the "chains", "outer shell", "fetters", and the development of the productive power of industry as the force which will "break", "burst" these "chains" and "fetters", and the proletariat as "the human kernel" who can master this productive power and make it appear in the form compatible with it. This revolutionary conclusion drawn from the inner contradiction (the productive power of industry and the form in which it operates) of the capitalist industry itself was undoubtedly more closer to historical materialism, and was about to be fully established in *The German Ideology*, which was a further step compared with the previous stage: The conclusions based on the contradiction between human essence and his existence.

2 ESSENCE OF SOCIAL LIFE. COMBINATION OF THE VIEW OF PRACTICE WITH THE CONCEPTION OF HISTORY

Roughly around the same time when *An Article on Friedrich List's Book The National System of Political Economy* was written, in these days Marx also wrote eleven theses on Feuerbach's philosophy, which is the famous *Theses on Feuerbach* (*Theses* for short). If we can say the evaluation on List was a reflection of how Marx approached historical materialism through his economic studies, then we can easily say that his thesis on Feuerbach was a summary of his major achievements by the spring of 1845 from the higher plane of a new world outlook.

The Theses involves two significant changes. First, Marx had changed from praising to criticizing Feuerbach in terms of their relationship. Marx had thus made it clear that he finally broke away from this "intermediate link" and moved towards the full establishment of dialectical materialism and historical materialism by regarding the criticism of Feuerbach as the major way to elucidate his theory. Second, accordingly, Marx had finally freed himself from the

---

9   Ibid., p. 258-259.

influence of Feuerbach's humanism: The idea of estrangement and return of human essence. He proceeded from self-estrangement to the division of society, from the species-essence of man to the analysis of the ensemble of the social relations, and scientifically uncovered the essence of social life and the material source of ideologies. But *Theses* did not come into being by accident and was still less a "breakage" of the development of Marx's thought. Only by carefully studying Theses can we easily find that many important ideas were previously raised in a scattered form in their embryonic forms in his works since *Critique of Hegel's Philosophy of Right*, especially in *Manuscripts* and *The Holy Family*. Yet all these ingenious ideas were interwoven with the influence of Feuerbach's humanism. But *Theses* is a different case, which, was directed against the fundamental defects of Feuerbach and the old materialism, was a summary, in the form of aphorism, manifested the profundity of Marx's thought by the spring of 1845, can be evaluated as the refinement of the quintessence of his previous thoughts.

The view of practice is the kernel running all through *Theses*. Marx introduced practice into the theory of knowledge and more importantly into the conception of history. The combination of the view of practice and the conception of history is a striking feature of *Theses*. Proceeding from the idea of labour as the essence of man to labour as the essence of social life, the door of the materialist conception of history was finally opened in examining human society, to examine it in human practical activity. For this reason, in 1888 Engels called *Theses* "the first document in which is deposited the brilliant germ of the new world outlook", and in a more specific way in 1893, he commented[10]: "the *genesis* of historical materialism".

What is the essence of society? Marx was not very clear about it before the spring of 1845. For instance, he regarded society as a community corresponding to the essence of man in *1844 Manuscripts*, so society referred to the state/stage in which private property will be annulled, while the society with private property was evaluated as non-social. In *Theses*, Marx investigates society from the perspective of practice and reveals the common essence of all social forms.

---

10   Karl Marx and Frederick Engels: Collected Works, 1st Chinese Edition, Volume 21, p. 412; Volume 39, p. 24, Beijing: People's Press, 1974.

He said, "All social life is essentially *practical*."[11] This conclusion of Marx is highly condensed and contains some important principles of historical materialism.

First, it reveals the origin and basis of society. Society differs from nature. Nature bases its existence on itself and exists independent of mankind, though it is made to change by human activity as well. Society is different. All social life is essentially practical and is the product of human activity. Society originates not from a contract as the advocates of contract theory believe but from labour. Labour creates human society as well as man, which are identical. Therefore, society is the sphere of human activity, an organic structure which is organized on the basis: On the definite activity of material production. Without the production of material goods, there will be no human society.

Second, it reveals the basic content of social life. Material production, as the most basic practical activity of mankind, is the basis of social being but it is not the sole content of social life. In addition to production activity, people conduct political activity, which mainly appears as class struggle in class society, and social activity as participating in the management of public affairs in non-class society, as well as scientific, artistic practices (experiments) and creative (artistic)activity. In a word, all social life is essentially practical, and it includes practical activities in various forms, without which social life would be unimaginable.

Third, it uncovers the characteristic of the law of social development. There are similarities and differences between natural laws and social laws. Natural law is the law of nature itself, and nature develops according to its intrinsic laws whether mankind participate/intervene in it or not; while society is the sphere of human activity, whose basic content is practical activity appearing in various forms, so social law exists not outside but in human practical activity, and appears as a force which eventually determines the outcome of human behaviours. Although everyone in the society has his own purposes and desires, the objective relations formed in their activity and the direction of their development are independent of their

---

11   Karl Marx and Frederick Engels: Selected Works, 1st Edition, Volume 1, p. 18.

individual will. For example, commodity is produced by mankind, but its movement in circulation is governed by its own law (the law of value) rather than by human will.

It is because all social life is essentially practical that Marx highlights his idea as. "[A]ll mysteries which lead theory to mysticism find their rational solution in human practice and in the comprehension of this practice" (The Thesis)

The idea that knowledge originates in practice is the fundamental principle of both Marxist theory of knowledge and the materialist conception of history, whose principles are identical, though they consider the issue from different perspectives. Shortly afterward, Marx and Engels had defined in *The German Ideology* historical idealism as "explain[ing] practice from the idea" and historical materialism as "explain[ing] the formation of ideas from material practice"[12], which show their emphasis on the role of practice in the conception of history.

To explain ideas from practice is, in the sphere of history, to explain ideologies with the social being of men, i.e., with the process of material production. Any vague, bizarre, mysterious ideology sees its "secret" not in the ideology itself but in human practice. Phenomena which seem incomprehensible at first sight can find a rational explanation in the scientific analysis of the practical activity in each definite era, especially in the activity of material production.

Marx had also undergone a transition from the analysis of human self-estrangement to the idea based on the inner strife in the society when criticizing Feuerbach's religious view. This was is s significant progress from man into human society.

Feuerbach started off from the fact of religious self-estrangement, from the duplication of the world into a religious, imaginary world, and a secular (worldly) one. His work consisted in resolving the religious world into its secular basis. For Feuerbach, religion was nothing but the estrangement of man from himself, the separation of human essence from man, he wrote: "Man objectifies his own secret essence in religion. It must therefore be shown that this opposition,

---

12   Karl Marx and Frederick Engels: Collected Works, 1st Chinese Edition, Volume 3, p. 43.

this dichotomy of God and man, which is the starting point of religion, is a dichotomy within man, dichotomy of man with his own essence."[13] Thus Feuerbach's secular basis of religion is not society but man, the abstract man, and for this reason Marx said, "the [earthly] world which in his writing appears is merely as a *phrase*"[14].

Unlike Feuerbach, Marx did not remain at the height that religion is the estrangement of man from himself, but strove to explore the question which was not answered by Feuerbach: Why did it come about that man got the religious illusions into his head? Marx claimed as early as in 1842 that religion itself had no contents, and it came from earth and not from heaven. Later, when studying the Jewish question in 1843 and 1844, he repeatedly stressed that the existence of the present-day Jew cannot be explained by his religion; but the tenacious survival of the Jewish religion could only be explained by practical features of civil society which were fantastically reflected in that religion. In the spring of 1845, in *Theses* Marx had advanced even further and pointed out that "'religious sentiment' is itself a *social product*", and raised the question of social contradiction, highlighting that "the fact that the secular basis lifts off from itself and establishes itself in the clouds as an independent realm can only be explained by the inner strife in it and intrinsic contradictoriness of this secular basis. The latter (that in the clouds) must itself be understood in its contradiction and then, by the removal of the contradiction, revolutionized."[15] Apparently, the secular basis here, according to Marx, is not the abstract man and the species-essence of man, but the real society. Although Marx did not specify what the inner contradiction of the society was, he affirmed the inner contradictoriness of "the secular basis" and proposed to annihilate the basis of religion by removing the social contradiction, which is entirely different from the explanation of religion from the aspect of the estrangement of human essence.

The idea that the aim of human knowledge is practice is not only an epistemological proposition, but also an important principle of historical materialism. When Marx said that philosophers had hitherto

13   The Selected Works of Feuerbach's Philosophical Works, Volume 2, p. 60.
14   Karl Marx and Frederick Engels: Collected Works, 1st Chinese Edition, Volume 3, p. 261.
15   Karl Marx and Frederick Engels: Selected Works, 1st Edition, Volume 1, p. 17.

only interpreted the world in various ways; the point was to change it, his focus was not on Nature but on society. He had devoted himself to social transformation at the time to get it "revolutionized in practice", and had further developed this argument in *The German Ideology*. Marx criticized Feuerbach, saying that he wanted, "like the other theorists, merely to produce a correct consciousness about an existing fact; whereas for the real communist it is a question of overthrowing the existing state of things." He also stated that "for the practical materialist, i.e., the communist, it is a question of revolutionising the existing world, of practically attacking and changing the existing things."[16] If the question of practice discussed here is merely limited to the theory of knowledge and excluded from the conception of history, the materialist conception of history will be transformed into an idealist conception of history.

Historical experience has proved that the conception of history which does not understand the role of practice in the social life of mankind can only be an idealist conception of history. The French enlightenment of 18th century advocated the proposition that man was the product of circumstances and education, but had remained within the idealistic frame of reason governing the world, because they neither realized that the change in the circumstances was consistent with human activity, nor that it was in the revolutionary practice that man changed himself while at the same time changing the circumstances. So did Feuerbach. Marx criticized him in *Theses* for regarding the theoretical activity as the only genuinely human activity, despising practice and not grasping the significance of revolutionary, practical activity. This critique was not simply directed at his epistemology, but more importantly at his humanistic conception of history. In terms of epistemology alone, Feuerbach somewhat voiced some reasonable views on the role of practice in knowledge, and for this reason, Lenin asserted in *Materialism and Empiro-Criticism* that 'Feuerbach also, like Marx and Engels, makes an impermissible—from the point of view of Schulze, Fichte and Mach—"leap" to practice in the fundamental problems of epistemology.' Lenin even argued: "Feuerbach makes the sum-total of human practice the basis

---

16 Karl Marx and Frederick Engels: Collected Works, 1st Chinese Edition, Volume 3, p. 47, p. 48.

of the theory of knowledge."[17] Once he went beyond epistemology and delved into the sphere of history, Feuerbach sank completely in idealism, which is easy to understand. It is impossible for one to be a materialist in the sphere of history, but he can still be a materialist without understanding the role of practice in the sphere of knowledge (epistemology), because all social life is essentially practical, without admitting the role of practice (of the production of material goods in particular) in social life, he cannot really grasp the relationship between man and nature, between man and man, and hence cannot have a scientific understanding of society and the law of its development. Marx wrote: "The highest point reached by contemplative materialism, that is, materialism which does not comprehend sensuousness as practical activity, is contemplation of single individuals and of civil society."[18] This was a summarized comment on why Feuerbach sank into historical idealism.

3 THE REAL ESSENCE OF MAN: THE ENSEMBLE OF SOCIAL RELATIONS

The idea that "it [the essence of man] is the ensemble of social relations", a fundamental proposition in Theses, marks the new level of Marx's understanding on the relationship between man and society in the spring of 1845.

In *The Holy Family*, Marx called Feuerbach's man the real man on the basis of nature, and praised him for completing the criticism of religion and sketching the basic features of the criticism of Hegel's speculative philosophy based on this. Yet, this time several months later Marx criticized him in *Theses*, for seeking the essence of man in the isolated individual, and underlined his new idea : The real essence of man as: the ensemble of social relations.

The question of the essence of man cannot be simply resolved into that of seeking the common nature of man in the individual (each single individual). One cannot surmount the limits humanistic perspective if he limits this question to the scope of the individual (concrete man) and the general (man as man). For historical materialism, the exploration of the essence of man is essentially a question of studying the relationship between man and society.

17   Lenin: Selected Works, 2nd Edition, Volume 2, p. 141, p. 142.
18   Karl Marx and Frederick Engels: Selected Works, 1st Edition, Volume 1, p. 18.

The limitation of Feuerbach's humanistic conception of history lay precisely in that he abstracted man from his social relations and the historical process, attempted to seek the essence of man in the isolated individual and resolved the essence of man into the question of relationship between the individual and the species. Although man was conceived by Feuerbach as a sensuous being made of flesh and blood, this human individual, who does not belong to any society and regarded outside the society, does not exist, hence the species based on these individuals, and the species-essence uniting them would certainly be unreal. Therefore with Feuerbach, human individual, the species, the species-essence were only some empty concepts.

There was already a difference in the views on man and the essence of man between Marx and Feuerbach even before *Theses* of 1845. Marx had emphasized the social character of man in *Critique of Hegel's Philosophy of Right*: that man is no abstract being squatting outside the world. And in *Contribution to the Critique of Hegel's Philosophy of Right: Introduction* he wrote: "man is the world of man, state, society." Later in *Manuscripts*, he regarded labour as the essence of man, all of which are manifestations of this difference. On the other side, before the spring of 1845Marx was still under the influence of Feuerbach on the two questions: The contradiction between the individual and the species, The estrangement question as the opposition of the species-essence of man to man himself.

In *Theses* Marx began to expound his theoretical differences with Feuerbach which meant he had transcended the influence of Feuerbach. In his argument against Feuerbach, Marx advanced his famous thesis: "The essence of man is no abstraction inherent in each single individual. In reality, it is the ensemble of the social relations". This argument not only scientifically defined the essence of man, but more importantly abandoned the Feuerbach's view on the individual, the species and the species-essence, thus removed the last obstacle to the full establishment of the materialist conception of history.

First, Marx's argument on the essence of man abandons the Feuerbachian human individual view. Undoubtedly, the real man appears as an individual, and man is inevitably an elusive, abstract being if abstracted from the individual. But human individuals in people's contemplation are not isolated from each other. Human individuals unrelated to each other only exist in imagination and are not real human beings, and the view based on this kind of human individual could only be a humanistic view.

That man as a social being was elaborated by Marx before *Theses*, but the sociality of man not only meant that man cannot be isolated from society but also that all human beings live in a definite social formation. And this is what *Theses* had emphasized. In criticizing Feuerbach's view of the "individual", Marx wrote: "The abstract individual that he analyses belongs in reality to a particular social form"[19].

All individuals are individuals who belong to a particular social form, but society is not a simple aggregate of individuals but the ensemble of the connections and relations which these real individuals enter among themselves. Therefore, the individuals belonging to a particular social formation exist in a definite social structure. For instance, in class society,the three: Individual—group (class)—society is united. The individual belongs to a definite group (class), which in turn constitutes or determines a definite society. So the relationship of human society contains the three: Individual—group—society, rather than individual—subordinate variety—species, and this latter formula was criticized by Marx: This approach means: "give history some hard clouts on the ear.

The solution to individual problems, in the final analysis, is determined by the fate of the class to which he belongs, while the future of a class is determined by the change in the social formation. In capitalist society, a worker can become a capitalist, a millionaire from a dispossessed person, but the emancipation of the proletariat as a whole cannot be realized by each worker getting rich. In fact, the future of a worker depends on the emancipation of the proletariat as a whole, which in turn depends on the resolving of the question of the entire society. It will be wrong to have the order reversed.

Second, his argument on the essence of man abandons Feuerbach's view on the individual and the species, and transforms the relationship between man and man from that between the individual and the species into that between man and society.

---

19 Ibid.

Before *Theses*, Marx did not have a clear understanding on Feuerbach's "species" idea. He sometimes equated "species" with society, which was evident is his letter to Feuerbach on August, 11, 1844. Confusion seemed that man as a social being and man as a species-being could replace each other, but this confusion was eliminated in *Theses* written in 1845.

Society and species are two different concepts. The "species" emphasizes the natural identity of individuals and treats them equally, while society refers to all connections and relations between active individuals. The ensemble of the social relations, as Marx said, refers to society, and he made this point even clearer in *Wage-labour and Capital*, writing: "[T]he relations of production in their totality constitute what is called the social relations, society, and moreover, a society at a definite stage of historical development, a society with peculiar, distinctive character."[20]

We can say it would be legal to see man as the relationship between the individual and the species in physiology, anatomy or physical anthropology, but this approach would not work in the true analysis of the society. It is of vital importance in the formation of the conception of history to transform the approach on man: From grasping man as the relationship between the individual and species to that between man and society. When proceeding from the first approach, one would inevitably focus his study on exploring the species-essence of the individual, i.e., seek for the eternal, constant essence of the individual. But starting from the latter approach one will necessarily study the relationship between man and man, i.e., society and the law of its development. When examining human individual from the perspective of species, one can only see the abstract identity— human beings are human beings, their differences are the differences within the same species: gender, colour of skin, age, etc. But examining man from the social perspective, one can see his social attributes, particularly, in a class society, his class attribute can be observed. In those societies with class antagonism, it will certainly contradict the materialist conception of history to see the slave owner and the slave, the capitalist and the worker, the landowner and the farmer merely as men. We can ask: Does man as man not have common

---

20   Ibid., p. 363.

nature? Are not parent-child love, love between man and woman, friendship, sympathy, pursuit of beauty prevalent in any times, any nation, and any country? Of course, we can observe those brilliant human feelings, the enthralling and touching praised by people and eulogized in poems and novels. Yet we can comfortably say that these are no abstraction of the attributes inherent in each single individual, but are rather formed in society. They are not the attributes of men as species, belong to men as social beings. Hence human nature will change as society changes.

Seen from the biological perspective, human beings belong to the same species, but they or their attitudes are not always treated on the basis of their "species" because they are social beings and in a class society there are different classes and antagonisms between the interests of political groups. The relationship between man and man (same species) is sometimes not as close as that between men and animals (between different species), which was also approved even by Feuerbach. Accordingly, he argued in *Towards a Critique of Hegel's Philosophy*: "[i]s man's relationship with animals only a despotic one? Do not the forsaken and the rejected find a substitute for the ingratitude, scheming, and unfaithfulness of their fellow human beings in the faithfulness of the animal? Does the animal not have a power that consoles and heals his broken heart?"[21] *Mumu*, a famous short story of Turgenev, presents two widely different relations, one between the serf owner and the serf, the other between the serf and the dog. In many parts of the world people enjoy keeping the so-called "pets", especially dogs. Human relationship seems so flimsy that people prefer to love dogs, instead. In a cemetery for dogs, one gravestone reads: "Here lies my dog Gill, who is more loyal to me than my three husbands." Another reads: "You were my loyal companion and sole friend in my lonely and painful life." Still another reads: "People kept disappointing me, but you were always sincere." I can list many and various epitaphs on this issue. This is no writing for killing time and astonishing readers, but society deserves some critique. I do not mean that man cannot develop a relationship with animals, nor that man should not love animals or ill-treat them, but reproach aims those who love dogs more than human beings.

---

21   Ibid., p.p. 46-47.

The co-existence of dog cafes, dog hotels, dog hospitals and dog dresses together with those people who are homeless and have great difficulties to earn a cup of soup, this phenomenon of caring for pets but no feeling for those suffering human beings is social morbidity. Of course this phenomenon cannot be understood if analyzed merely from the point of view approaching man as species, lacking the approach of historical materialism. Third, based on the previous two points, Marx has completely transcended Feuerbach who sought the essence of man in the isolated individual, defined the essence of man as the species, as the generality inherent in each single individual and who believed uniting individuals in a natural way. Thus Marx formulated his scientific conclusion: The essence of man, in reality, is the ensemble of the social relations. He had resolved the issue approaching from the relationship between man and society and placed man in a definite social form.

Perhaps some people might say that the essence of man is the qualitative determinant feature of man as man, which is applicable to everyone and which could only be the species-essence. For instance, labour is the essence of man, and it is independent from those changes in social relations, and is eternal and changeless; similar evaluation is possible when we say, man is a social being. It is valid for each era, each person; one is a social being as long as one is a human being. So the essence of man is less the ensemble of social relations than the fundamental attribute common to individuals.

In *Manuscripts*, Marx indeed, regarded labour as the species-character of man, as the fundamental difference between men and animals. Man is capable of conscious, purposeful labour, while animals in general act based on instincts; man is a social being, while animals in general are natural beings. But the thing is that a swarm of bees are actually a bee. The species-character of bees is the character of the individual bee. Man is different. Labour and sociality are not the characters inherent in human individuals. Man is a labouring animal not because everyone can labour; man is a social being not because everyone is a social being; on the contrary, man as an isolated individual does not have these characters. Labour and sociality are not and cannot be the abstraction of the attributes inherent in human individuals, of the species-character, but the social character of man. What social character generalizes is the basis of the existence of human society and the objective fact that all individuals belong to a definite social form. Therefore, the character of man as man could not be understood merely from the relationship between the individual and the species, without from the aspect of relationship between man and society.

It was a vital breakthrough that Marx evaluated labour as the essence of man and as the fundamental difference between men and animals, but his view to regard labour as the species-character inherent in man was is a reflection of the influence of Feuerbach's idea, view on the basis of the relationship between the individual and the species. In contrast, *Theses* discards the wording, species-essence. But that the essence of man being the ensemble of the social relations was not a negation of labour as the essence of man, but a step forward in this direction. I can also say that, the shift into the labour process to seek for the real essence of man in social relations was a progress from the difference between men and animals to that between man and man.

Society is the product of human activity, and all real individuals belong to a definite social form. Society is a kind of circumstances—social circumstances, which are the objective conditions which determine, restrict and shape human ideas and behaviours. The formation of the ideas, talents and concepts of anyone cannot be divorced from the society he is in. The difference between men in primitive society and slave society, between men in capitalist society and socialist society and, between people in the same social formation is not due to the physical character of man but to the society itself which is the ensemble of the social relations. In reality an individual is the product of the social relations of the time no matter how he conceives himself and though he imagines himself transcending the times and history. So in practical activity, the essence of man will change as the social relations of the society changes.

Theses thus serves as the theoretical preparation and outline for Marx to criticize Feuerbach and a crucial step to fully establish the materialist conception of history. It finally breaks the conventional view of the individual and the species, turns from the species-essence of man to human society and thus really achieves a scientific understanding of man.

CHAPTER XI

THE FULL ESTABLISHMENT OF THE MATERIALIST CONCEPTION OF HISTORY

In his *Theses*, Marx criticized Feuerbach's view of seeking the essence of man in abstract human individual and transformed the question of the relation between the individual and the species into the question of man and society. He further deepened his thought by going deep into society to reveal the law of its development, which was accomplished in *The German Ideology*.

By criticizing Bauer, Stirner and Feuerbach, Marx had summarized and further developed his previous achievements, expounded the basis and premises of the existence of human society and, its structure and evolution, and provided a scientific analysis of human society from the point of view of its cross section (social structure) and vertical section (replacement of social formations). Marx exposed and criticized Feuerbach's humanism and fully transcended this influence, and thus completed his leap from estranged labour to the materialist conception of history.

1 COMPLETION OF THE SHIFT AS THE STARTING POINT. FROM LABOUR AS MAN'S INNER ESSENCE TO LABOUR AS THE BASIS OF SOCIAL EXISTENCE

A correct starting point was necessary for the full establishment of the materialist conception of history. A great achievement of *The German Ideology* was that it thoroughly criticizes Feuerbach's abstract man and Stirner's idea "the Unique", scientifically expounds the premises of the materialist conception of history and uncovers the decisive role of the production of material goods in the development of human society.

To reveal the starting point of Marxism is a controversial issue, which a relatively correct answer, according to the author, requires a distinction between fact judgment and value judgment and a clear understanding on the meaning of the starting point.

There are two kinds of relations in terms of the relationship between subject and object. One is the question to what extent subject's knowledge reflects object, that is, whether subject's knowledge contains the content of the object independent of subject. To really reflect reality correctly, one must start from the objective entity and grasp as objectively as possible the law of development of the object itself. I argue this as the fact judgment. The other question answers why subject knows object, and to what extent this knowledge corresponds to the interest and wishes/will of the subject itself. This is value judgment. The former deals with the question of "what" the objective entity is, while the latter answers the question of "for what". They are related to but also different from each other. The judgment which corresponds to the interest and wishes/will of the subject itself may not be a scientific judgment.

As far as mankind is concerned, any kind of knowledge is closely associated with his interests, or for the sake of mankind itself. This is true for social sciences as well as natural sciences. The difference is that natural sciences have no class character, and its fact judgment is consistent with its value judgment; while in understanding society, value judgment penetrates the understanding of facts and tends to cover up facts and distort truth for the sake of narrow class interests. Only Marxism pursues a high degree of consistence between them.

Marxism has emerged out of the needs of the struggles of the proletariat. Certainly the purpose of Marxism is to emancipate the proletariat and mankind, this aim itself has served as the necessary condition for Marx to have a correct understanding of human society
because of the consistence between the interests of proletariat and
the law of social development, on the other hand this is not the reason why Marxism is a scientific theory. Marxism needed to correctly
reflect the laws of history itself in order to be a science.

Generally speaking, human cognition of history, has gone through
the theological conception of history, the bourgeois humanitarian
conception of history and the materialist conception of history, which
all favoured the interests of its own corresponding class seen from
their subjective aims. The theological conception of history was for
the interests of the slave owner and the feudal lord, the humanist
conception of history for the interests of the revolutionary bourgeoisie in terms of its origin, and the materialist conception of history for
the interests of the proletariat and all labourers. Therefore, they are,
in the most abstract sense, all for man, on the other side we should
say that matters irrelevant to mankind will not attract attention and
interest from people. Even the theological conception of history was
concerned with man in reality, with the interests of the slave owner
and the feudal lord, though in form it was for God.

The starting point we discuss here relates to the fact judgment, that
is, how to understand history, how to know the laws of history itself and attain a scientific understanding of history. In this sense,
different conceptions of history have different starting points. The
theological conception of history starts with God and sees god's will
as the ultimate basis for explaining historical changes and social
phenomena (wealth and poverty, life and death, weal and woe). The
bourgeois humanitarian conception of history proceeds from man,
that is, it regards the abstract human nature as the measure of society
and the basis for explaining history. This change from the theological conception of history to the humanitarian conception of history is
in essence a change of the starting point, i.e., a change in the guiding
principle for explaining history. There is no doubt that the bourgeois
humanitarianism made a great historical contribution. Seen from its
conception of history alone, it highlighted man instead of god and

explored the motive force for the development of history in man himself rather than in god's will, making a significant step towards unravelling the mystery of history. However, it remained within idealism in terms of its understanding history.

Value judgment can penetrate and influence fact judgment. Starting with the abstract man, the bourgeois humanitarianism in part reflects the fact (that the history is created by man not by god), but it is largely determined by its class interests. It is necessary for the rising bourgeoisie to represent its interest as the interest of all members of the society in order to achieve its aim and win over as many alliances as possible, as is indicated in *The German Ideology*: "For each new class which puts itself in the place of one ruling before it, is compelled, merely in order to carry through its aim, to represent its interest as the common interest of all the members of society, that is, expressed in ideal form: it has to give its ideas the form of universality, and represent them as the only rational, universally valid ones. The class making a revolution appears from the very start, if only because it is opposed to a class, not as a class but as the representative of the whole of society; it appears as the whole mass of society confronting the one class."[1]

In addition, the bourgeois humanitarianism is determined by the characteristic of the bourgeois revolution. The political practice and theoretical principle of the feudal society and the rule of church is the despised, the despicable, the dehumanized man. According to the theological conception of history, all men are born sinners no matter they are wise, foolish or unworthy. They preach that "[h]e who despises himself, is honoured by God. He who dislikes himself is liked by God"; "be small in your own eyes so that you may be big in the eyes of God"; "you shall be the more valued by God, the more contemptuous you are of men."[2] Before the feudal despot, all men, rich and poor, are subjects, or in Engels' words, all are equal—equally ciphers. Therefore, faced with the fight against the feudal system and the rule of church, the rising bourgeoisie inevitably regarded man as the starting point and destination in the idealistic form, confronted god with man and the right of kings with the rights of man so as to

---

1   Karl Marx and Frederick Engels: Collected Works, 1st Chinese Edition, Volume 3, p. 54.
2   Notes in Ludwig Feuerbach: Selected Philosophical Works, Volume 2, p. 53.

fulfill its historical mission of combating against the feudal system and establish the rule of the bourgeoisie. And it is from this perspective that Marx analyzed the reason for the bourgeois humanitarianism raising the banner of "man". He said, "Why is the member of civil society called "man", simply man; why are his rights called the *rights of man*? How is this fact to be explained? From the relationship between the political state and civil society, from the nature of political emancipation."[3]

The so-called "awakening of man", "discovery of man" means the progressive and advanced bourgeoisie's awareness of its own interests, which requires the removal of the estate system based on personal attachment and the system of privileges, and which requires satisfaction of its secular (worldly) desires. This represented the interests and demands of other oppressed classes to a certain degree. Therefore, the bourgeois humanitarianism the more abstract it makes man, and fights in the name of "man", the more it takes the opposition between man and god to extremes, and the opposition between the majority of the ruled and despotism. This act intensifies and reveals the contradictions between them, endows its attack against religion and despotism with an intense, emotional colour. The bourgeois humanitarianism had played an important, enlightening role and undertook the role of fermenter in cultivating political, moral, aesthetic views, besides literary and artistic creation which were generally more advanced than feudalism. During several hundred years a group of versatile, knowledgeable giants appeared in many fields and left numerous impressive, famous works, which are among precious treasure of human culture.

Although the bourgeois humanitarianism shifted the starting point from god to man, it contained unsolvable contradictions.

Theoretically speaking, it considers human nature as the measure of history and the good nature or reason of man as the driving force for the development of history. But how can the eternal human nature be the reason for the changes in history? The humanitarian conception of history was inevitably trapped in the problem of the relationship between history and human nature. In fact, the shift from god to

---

3   Karl Marx and Frederick Engels: Collected Works, 1st Chinese Edition, Volume 1, p. 437.

man, initiated by the bourgeois humanitarians, was merely an advance from divinity to human nature, but not to the real man yet, so it could not deal with history in a scientific way, just like Engels had commented when criticizing pan-Slavistic manifesto : "humanity", "freedom", "equality", "fraternity", "independence", "sound very fine, it is true, but *prove absolutely nothing* in historical and political questions"[4]. One is bound to exclude the objective laws of the development of history itself from his horizon when he merely relies on the nature of mankind instead of striving to seek the objective basis of history.

Practically speaking, there is a profound contradiction between the class character of the bourgeois humanitarianism and its abstract principle of man as the starting point. In theory, the bourgeois humanitarianism starts from the abstract man and human nature, advocates respect for the rights, dignity and worth of all men and promotes universal freedom and equality, etc.; but in practice it proceeds from the interests of the bourgeoisie, pursues the freedom and rights of the bourgeoisie and stands up for the dignity and worth of the bourgeois. This contradiction was latent and remained concealed at the outset and the common interest of combating the feudal system and the rule of church outweighed the class antagonism, which was long hidden behind the struggle for "man". However, when the bourgeoisie turned from an oppressed class into the ruling class, the capitalist system replaced the feudal system, the contradiction between the theory and practice of the bourgeois humanitarianism was clearly exposed. The reality and practice of the capitalist society was quite contrary to the abstract humanitarian principle: Marx wrote: "Trade developed more and more into swindling. The "fraternity" in that revolutionary slogan was realized in the chicanery and envy of the battle of competition. Oppression by force was replaced by corruption, the sword as the prime social lever was replaced by money. "The right of the first night" passed from the feudal lords to the bourgeois manufacturers."[5] The early bourgeois humanitarians indeed had sincere motivations, enthusiasm and advocated lofty ideals, and assumed that they were striving for everything of "man", but

---

4   Karl Marx and Frederick Engels: Collected Works, 1st Chinese Edition, Volume 6, p. 325, Beijing: People's Press, 1961.

5   Karl Marx and Frederick Engels: Selected Works, 1st Chinese Edition, Volume 3, p. 298.

the actual result was that some people dominated and oppressed others. This opposition between the ideal starting point and the actual destination was determined by the law of the historical development and independent of man's will.

To start with the abstract man is common to the bourgeois humanitarianism. This is true for the humanism which originated in Italy in 14th century, includes the French Enlightenment of the 18th century, and later the more abstract philosophical theory of man in Germany in 19th century. Feuerbach's humanism was a special form of the bourgeois humanitarianism. Feuerbach emerged as the opposite of Hegel in the chain of development of the German philosophy; for this reason, humanism and natural materialism were inseparable in his philosophy. Feuerbach's materialism was humanistic, that is, it elaborated the unity of body and spirit, unity of being and thinking with man as the centre; his humanism was materialistic, that is, it presupposed the sensuous reality of man. So Feuerbach's materialism had a humanistic character compared with the previous materialism, besides it was more materialistic than the previous humanitarianism.

But as a conception of history, Feuerbach's humanism also abstracted man similarly as the previous bourgeois humanitarianism. This was unavoidable, because he reproduced the process from god to man under the German conditions and always examined man in his opposition between man and god. He wrote that all his writings "have one aim, one will, one thought, one theme. This theme is religion and theology and whatever is connected with them", and that "[m]y principal theme is Christianity, is Religion, as it is the immediate object, the *immediate nature* of man."[6]

Feuerbach emphasized the sensuous reality of man and considered the essence of man as the "species", this was the abstraction he saw inherent in each single individual so that he could argue against the impersonal spiritual entity God and against Hegel's absolute idea. That "man is the highest essence of man" was an anti-religious proposition, a challenge against the theological doctrine of the despised and the despicable man. For man, man is God, and his highest essence is not in the god outside him but it is in man himself.

---

6   Ludwig Feuerbach: Selected Philosophical Works, Volume 2, p. 507 and p. 27.

Feuerbach's humanitarianism, appearing in the form of humanism, had its unique features. He merged several European bourgeois humanitarian traditions and the view of estrangement in the German classical philosophy, and thus established the theory of estrangement and return of human essence, in this way he designed humanitarianism and estrangement into the two aspects of one question: Here estrangement appears as the essence of man which is separating from him, of man becoming non-human, a slave of God and an egoist. On the other side the transcendence of estrangement will make man re-appropriate his essence and he transcends non-human state to turn into a real man. Feuerbach declared that he denied "the fantastic projection of theology and religion, in order to affirm the real essence of man", to transform men "from Christians into persons, into whole persons"[7]. In this way, the abstract humanitarian principle with man as the starting point was demonstrated in a more speculative and philosophical way by Feuerbach's theory of the estrangement and return of human essence.

If we can say that the abstract man as the starting point reflects the characteristics of the bourgeois revolution which combated against the feudal system, religion and theology, then we can say that Marxism which represents the proletariat needed to abandon this theoretical starting point in order to scientifically reveal the law of social development.

The historical mission of the proletariat is different from that of the bourgeoisie. The interest of the bourgeoisie requires it to conceal the nature of its revolution, while the proletariat is required to uncover the nature of its revolution; the bourgeoisie reduces the antagonistic classes to the abstract man, while the proletariat is required to discover classes behind "man"; the bourgeoisie advertises its particular interest as the general interest, while the proletariat is required to see through the fundamental opposition between its interest and the interest of the bourgeoisie in the vague view of the "general interest". Therefore, the proletariat can only be a class in itself and not a class for itself, if it cannot transcend the humanitarian conception of history which starts with the abstract man and, lift the amorous veil over the antagonistic classes. It is precisely out of this need that Marxism has emerged as a scientific theory.

---

7   Ibid., p. 525 and p. 786.

The proletariat entered the historical arena as an independent political force; the class relations in the capitalist society were increasingly simplified; and class struggles obviously revolved round the material interests; all these objective facts impelled Marx to re-examine the humanitarian conception of history which started with the abstract man, which provided him necessity and possibility for seeking out a new starting point. Yet the materialist conception of history being a scientific theory, its establishment needed to go through the thinking mind, i.e., the arduous theoretical exploration, which was a process of gradually overcoming the influence of Feuerbach.

In Germany in the 1840s, when the Hegelian philosophy was being disintegrated, Feuerbach was the philosopher who had the greatest influence on Marx. This influence involves two related and different aspects. One was humanism which was coupled by materialism, which helped Marx to transcend Hegel's idealism and criticize and reform his dialectics, the second was the theory of the estrangement and return of human essence, which meant that Marx still did not free his conception of history from the paradigm of the estrangement and return of human essence. In this period, we can see that his argumentation for the status and mission of the proletariat was tainted with certain humanistic character.

However, differences existed between Marx and Feuerbach at the very beginning, and Marx had been seeking a new starting point, though he was under the influence of Feuerbach. After elaborating the idea that civil society determines the state in *Critique of Hegel's Philosophy of Right*, Marx had gradually shifted his focus to the analysis of civil society and the study of political economy. In particular, in *Manuscripts*, the preliminary results of his economic studies, were demonstrated: Here Marx regarded labour as the essence of man, as the fundamental difference between men and animals, and discussed the role of labour in man's self-formation. This was a significant progress, which opened for Marx a way for seeking a new starting through man's labour process. But the analysis of labour in *Manuscripts* had an obvious limitation, because the text dealt with labour from the essence of the subject (man), considered it as a free, conscious activity, as the species-essence of man, contrarily the real labour was evaluated as estranged labour which confronted the species-essence of man. This understanding on labour posited as confronting the human essence and defined as estranged labour necessarily restrained Marx from having a scientific understanding on the role of labour.

THE GERMAN IDEOLOGY

In *The German Ideology* Marx regarded the production of material goods as the basis of the existence of human society. He dismissed the view of labour as the nature of man, labour as the intrinsic end of man, thus he rejected the idea which opposed labour to the maintenance of the physical being of man, His scientific analysis on the decisive role of the production of material goods in human society, finally led him to the correct starting point for the materialist conception of history. He argued: "We do not set out from what men say, imagine, conceive, nor set out from men as narrated, thought of, imagined, conceived, in order to arrive at men in the flesh. We set out from real, active men, and on the basis of their real life-process we demonstrate the development of the ideological reflexes and echoes of this life-process. The phantoms formed in the human brain are also, necessarily, sublimates of their material life-process, which is empirically verifiable and bound to material premises."[8] He also wrote: "The premises from which we begin are not arbitrary ones, not dogmas, but real premises from which abstraction can only be made in the imagination. They are the real individuals, their activity and the material conditions under which they live, both those which they find already existing and those produced by their activity. The premises can thus be verified in a purely empirical way."[9] This was not only a critique of Feuerbach but also an account-settling with his previous philosophical belief.

First, Marx replaced Feuerbach's biological, human individual with the real individual. Feuerbach's human individual does not belong to any social form, while Marx's real individual is not a human being isolated from the world but conditioned by the productive forces and by the form of intercourse and conducting material production under definite material conditions.

---

8   Karl Marx and Frederick Engels: Collected Works, 1st Chinese Edition, Volume 3, p. 30.
9   Ibid., p. 23.

Second, Marx replaced Feuerbach's view of man which was merely as sensuous object with man's sensuous activity. Feuerbach stresses the sensuous reality of man, but he could never arrive at the really active men, and stopped at the abstract man. So Marx criticized him, saying that "He says "Man" instead of "real historical man"."[10] In contrast, Marx emphasized that the man he meant was the real active man, the sensuous activity of man, not just the sensuous existence of man.

Third, Marx put the material production activity in the first place among all other human activities. He explicitly wrote: "[t]he fundamental form of this activity is, of course, material, on which depend all other forms—mental, political, religious, etc." activities,[11] because 'men must be in a position to live in order to be able to "make history". But life involves before everything else eating and drinking, a habitation, clothing and many other things. The first historical act is thus the production of the means to satisfy these needs, the production of material life itself"[12]. Marx stressed that "in any interpretation of history one has first of all to observe this fundamental fact in all its significance and all its implications and to accord it its due importance."[13]

Unlike the natural world, society is a sphere of human activity, and everything in the society involves man. But this fact can be generalized in two philosophical ways. One is to transform man into the abstract subject dispensed from all objective limitations, into a concept—"man". For example, this is what Stirner did. He regarded man as the active subject of all history, but man for him was only another name for the concept, the idea. This so-called man could neither be active in any practical activity nor create history, but was merely a spectre in the head of philosopher, which was a wrong generalization of the objective fact. Thus Marx criticized Stirner "Empirical relations, created by real people in their real intercourse and not at all by the holy concept of man, are afterwards interpreted, portrayed, imagined, consolidated and justified by people as a revelation of the concept "man"."[14]

---

10 Karl Marx and Frederick Engels: Collected Works, 1st Chinese Edition, Volume 3, p. 48.
11 Ibid., p. 80.
12 Ibid., p. 31.
13 Ibid., p. 32.
14 Ibid., p. 258.

In *The German Ideology*, the relationship between subject and object in the sphere of history was solved materialistically and dialectically. The real man active in practice is the subject of history. The various social relations are the product of the mutual activity of people. Therefore, history is not simply a stage provided for people's activity, but is their activity itself. Yet, in part, it provides each generation with the objective circumstances for activity, which are determinate, established and given. So, in general, man is both active and conditioned, the writer of and a character in the play. Marx wrote: " in [history] at each stage there is found a material result: a sum of productive forces, an historically created relation of individuals to nature and to one another, which is handed down to each generation from its predecessors; a mass of productive forces, capital funds and conditions, which, on the other hand, is indeed modified by the new generation, but also on the other prescribes for it its conditions of life and gives it a definite development, a special character. It shows that circumstances make men just as much as men make circumstances."[15] Therefore, historical materialism never studies man separating him from the historical circumstances of human activity, but bases the creative, active role of man on reality.

Historical materialism by no means rejects the study of man when regarding man's production of material goods as its starting point. The material production activity without human beings is just as unimaginable as human beings absent in material production. However, historical materialism rejects to start with the abstract man, rejects evaluating man and human nature in isolation. Society is neither the sum total of individuals nor a container which could be capable of accommodating any person, but a particular economic formation based on the sum total of the relations of production. It is not the essence of man that determines the nature of the mode of production, but it is the nature of the mode of production that determines the nature of man. What human beings are "coincides with their production, both with what they produce and with how they produce. The nature of individuals thus depends on the material conditions determining their production."[16] History has proved that it is because

---

15   Karl Marx and Frederick Engels: Collected Works, 1st Chinese Edition, Volume 3, p. 43.
16   Ibid., p. 24.

the materialist conception of history has established the new starting point that the understanding of man has reached new heights.

2 DEEP INTO THE PROCESS OF PRODUCTION: FROM THE RESEARCH ON THE CONTRADICTION BETWEEN THE INDIVIDUAL AND THE SPECIES TO THE DISCOVERY OF THE LAW OF SOCIETY

The change of the starting point was an epoch-making change. After he adopted this new starting point, Marx had completely abandoned the view of human essence as the measure of history, and instead analyzed the objective process of production itself, thus discovered the law of motion governing the productive forces and the relations of production. On this basis he revealed the inner structure of society and the successive replacement of social formations. As Marx himself wrote: "This conception of history depends on our ability to expound the real process of production, starting out from the material production of life itself, and to comprehend the form of intercourse connected with this and created by this mode of production (i.e. civil society at its various stages), as the basis of all history; and to show it in its action as State, to explain all the different theoretical products and forms of consciousness, religion, philosophy, ethics, etc. and trace their origins and growth from that basis." Marx also stressed only by proceeding from the production of material goods, can "the whole thing in its totality" and "the reciprocal action of these various sides on one another" could be described[17]. It is not difficult to imagine that to establish the whole theory of historical materialist view on the relation of the productive forces and the relations of production, the economic base and superstructure, social being and social consciousness, class and class struggle, state and revolution, etc. would be out of the question without this starting point.

Before the spring of 1845, Marx was still under the influence of Feuerbach's humanism, especially on the question of the relationship between the social form and human essence. On the one hand, he regarded family, civil society, state as the realization of human essence, and we see in some of expositions he evaluated them as the objectification of human essence. Hence the real social relations

---

17 Karl Marx and Frederick Engels: Collected Works, 1st Chinese Edition, Volume 3, p.p. 42-43.

became the quality inherent in the subject (man); on the other hand, he saw human essence as the measure of the rationality of human existence, i.e., the various social relations, and the unreasonable reality as the estrangement of the essence of man from himself. All these ideas were inverted by him in his six theses, included in his famous work, *Theses*.

Since the real essence of man is determined by the ensemble of the social relations, the essence of man cannot be in opposition to the social relations which generate it. But what, then, determines the social relations? This question was not answered in *Theses*. *The German Ideology* continued to elaborate and deepen the ideas accumulated in the critique of List's political economy, discarded the view that the social contradictions result from the suppression and distortion of human essence by social relations, and that the essence of man is estranged from man, now *German Ideology* was seeking the causes in the process of social production itself.

Marx went deep into the process of production and expounded the relationship between the productive forces and the relations of production from the relationship between man and nature, and between man and man. This double relationship was already dealt with in *Manuscripts*, but in *Manuscripts* there were differences in their expression and depth. In *Manuscripts*, the relationship between man and nature appears as the objectification of the essential powers of man, while the relationship between man and man was seen as the estrangement of human essence. This double relationship was mediated by human essence. But in *The German Ideology*, the focus was on the process of production itself. Marx indicated that the process of production appears as a double relationship: On the one hand as a natural, on the other as a social relationship. The relationship between man and nature is no longer evaluated as the objectification of the essential powers of man, i.e., objectification of the sense power, feelings and desires of man into products. Now this relationship means that man uses the instruments of production, offered/ produced by nature and especially created by civilization, thus transforms nature so as to meet his need of means of subsistence. The relationship between man and man is also not a mere form by which estrangement manifests, but a social relation, the shared, active,

material intercourse and material connection in the process of production: "By social [relationship] we understand the co-operation of
several individuals, no matter under what conditions, in what manner and to what end."[18]

Marx not only specified the two aspects of the process of production
more scientifically, but also further clarified their relationship. He
said that "the restricted relation of men to nature determines their
restricted relation to one another, and their restricted relation to one
another determines men's restricted relation to nature."[19] That is to
say, the productive forces and the relations of production condition
and promote each other, but it is the productive forces that ultimately
play the decisive role in their interaction: "the multitude of productive forces assessable to men determines the nature of society." With
the development of the productive forces, "in the place of an earlier
form of intercourse, which has become a fetter, a new one is put, corresponding to the more developed productive forces and, hence, to
the advanced mode of the self-activity of individuals—a form which
in its turn becomes a fetter and is then replaced by another"[20].

Here our focus is not on how the law of the productive forces and
the relations of production itself as well as Marx's concept of the
productive forces were formed, but we would like to explain how
he solved the issues left over by him and established the materialist
conception of history by starting from the production of material
goods and revealed the law of the dialectical movement of the productive forces and the relations of production.

First, the essence and driving force of history.

In *The Holy Family* progress is indeed made compared to *Manuscripts*
in which Marx conceived history as the creation of man through human labour. Now in *The Holy Family* explained the origin of history
and included the idea that wrote: history was nothing but the activity
of mankind pursuing his aims, but still the question of how history
developed remained unanswered.

18   Karl Marx and Frederick Engels: Collected Works, 1st Chinese Edition, Volume 3, p. 33.
19   Ibid., p. 35.
20   Ibid., p. 33, p. 81.

In *The German Ideology*, Marx proceeds from the idea that the multitude of productive forces determine the nature of society, emphasizes that the history of humanity must always be studied and treated in relation to the history of industry and exchange, and conceives history as the history of the development and change in the mode of production of material goods. History for Marx is nothing but the succession of separate human generations, they form—in the whole evolution of history—a coherent series of forms of intercourse. He writes: "Since these conditions correspond at every stage to the simultaneous development of the productive forces, their history is at the same time the history of the evolving productive forces taken over by each new generation"[21].

And precisely because of this, the transformation of the history of mankind from a local history into a world history is determined by the development of the productive forces. It is with the development of the productive forces that the separate nation' spheres of activity, which interact on one another, increasingly expand and their original isolation is destroyed and the universal intercourse between men is thus established. "From this it follows that this transformation of history into world history is not indeed a mere abstract act on the part of the "self-consciousness," the world spirit or of any other metaphysical spectre, but a quite material, empirically verifiable act, an act the proof of which every individual furnishes as he comes and goes, eats, drinks and clothes himself."[22]

The driving force of history is not something that exists outside or far above history, but lies in history. The driving force of history is in the inner contradictions of the mode of production which constitutes the basis and content of the development of history. Marx expressly stated: "all collisions in history have their origin, according to our view, in the contradiction between the productive forces and the form of intercourse."[23] This significant argument by Marx brings the "mechanism" of the development of history to light, that is, how the mode of production of material goods works. It not only answers "what" but also "why".

---

21   Ibid., p. 81.
22   Karl Marx and Frederick Engels: Collected Works, 1st Chinese Edition, Volume 3, p. 52.
23   Ibid., p. 83.

The relations of production must correspond to the nature and level of the productive forces, which was elaborated by Marx when he refuted the explanation of the transition from the slavery to the feudal system from the perspective of military invasion. He stressed that all depended to the productive forces of the nation which was conquered. "[T]he form of community adopted by the settling conquerors must correspond to the stage of development of the productive forces they find in existence, or, if this is not the case from the start, it must change according to the productive forces." Therefore, after the fall of the Roman Empire, the decisive force for the transition from the slavery system to the feudal system was , in the final analysis, determined by the development of the productive forces.

Marx also noted that a relation of production will not be abolished if it still could promote the development of the productive forces and if it did not become an obstacle to the development of production. He said, "private property is a form of intercourse necessary for certain stages of development of the productive forces; a form of intercourse that cannot be abolished, and cannot be dispensed with in the production of actual material life, until productive forces have been created for which private property becomes a restricting fetter."[24] To change the relations of production randomly according to our subjective will instead of considering the requirement of the development of the productive forces is bound to fail in the end, which young Marx already realized at that time. This point also indicates that his conception of history had attained its maturity.

Social sphere is a human sphere. The contradiction between the productive forces and the relations of production necessarily manifests itself in the relationship between man and man. In class society it appears as class struggle, and the most acute form of class struggle is revolution. Thus class struggle and social revolution are unavoidable in class society, and their necessity lies in the economic facts, just like Marx pointed out, "This contradiction between the productive forces and the form of intercourse necessarily on each occasion burst out in a revolution, taking on at the same time various subsidiary forms, such as all-embracing collisions, collisions of various classes, contradiction of consciousness, battle of ideas, etc., political

---

24   Ibid., p. 410-411.

conflicts, etc."[25] In this way, Marx further cleared how the contradiction between the productive forces and the relations of production, which acts as the decisive force of social development, was realized. The relations of production do not automatically meet the development requirements of the productive forces, and they are maintained or protected by the ruling class with all its strength no matter how decayed and backward they are. Thus the development of history would be unimaginable if class struggles and social revolutions are excluded from class society.

Nevertheless, the basis of revolution is not the absolute level of the development of the productive forces. Not a mere horizontal comparison, i.e., not the comparison of the development of the productive forces of one country with that of another country, abstracted from the concrete historical circumstances and national conditions of each country. Otherwise we will fail to understand the imbalances in the development of revolutions and the frequent occurrence of revolutions in those countries with less advanced productive forces rather than in those countries with the most advanced productive forces. Marx highlighted that all collisions in history had their origin in the contradiction between the productive forces and the form of intercourse, but he did not absolutize it. He wrote: "to lead to collisions in a country, this contradiction need not necessarily have reached its extreme limit in this particular country. The competition among industrially more advanced countries, brought about by the expansion of international intercourse, is sufficient to produce a similar contradiction in countries with a backward industry." Hence, Marx made a comparison between Germany and England: Germany lagged behind England in terms of the developmental level of the productive forces, while the capitalist private property was more advanced in Germany than in England in terms of ownership. However, the German bourgeoisie had an opposition by the feudal aristocracy and meanwhile afraid of the rising proletariat, it was attacked by both sides and faced with complex and acute contradictions. Marx pinned his hope on Germany, believing that the German revolution would precede the English revolution. Although this expectation did not occur, his method of analyzing problems is still instructive, and was proved by the victory of the Chinese revolution.

---

25   Ibid., p. 83.

Second, the multilayered structure of society and the relationship among various factors.

Marx distinguished between the productive forces and the relations of production from the production of material goods, clarified their dialectical relationship and thus revealed the structure of society. He analyzed society from the interrelation among the three: The productive forces, the relations of production and superstructure, and pointed out that "three moments, the forces of production, the state of society, and consciousness, can and must come into contradiction with one another."[26]

This is more scientific and accurate compared with his views before 1845, more accurate compared to his attempt in *Manuscripts* which to directly uses production to explain superstructure. To seek the root cause of the phenomena of superstructure in material production was the right direction, but it should not stop there. The production of material goods alone cannot explain why the development of production in capitalist countries does not change the nature of superstructure; why some countries with the low level of productive forces have more advanced social system and moral outlook than the countries with higher level of productive forces; or why the countries with the roughly same level of production have different social systems, and so forth. All these questions were scientifically answered by Marx in *The German Ideology* by differentiating the productive forces, the relations of production (mainly called by him as "the form of intercourse" then) and the superstructure, and regarding the relations of production as an intermediate link which is determined by the productive forces and which conditions the political and ideological superstructure.

The law of the structure of social organism (social formation) as revealed by Marx, deals with society as a complete system. He considered society as a whole in which various factors interacted with each other, and he analyzed the distinctive function of each factor. Marx was not a mechanical causal determinist, because he not only expounded the causal relationship among the productive forces, the relations of production and superstructure, but also noticed the reaction of superstructure, the reaction of the relations of production to

26   Ibid., p. 36.

INTO THE DEPTHS OF HISTORY

the productive forces. But Marx disagreed with the multifactor view which simply adopted the abstract concept of interaction to explain various factors related to society and thus denied the law of cause and effect in the sphere of history.

Third, social development evaluated as the process of natural history.

This issue was already raised by Marx in *Manuscripts*. He said, "History is the true natural history of man."[27] However, this argument by Marx refers less to the law of the development of history than to the content of history. That the content of history is the process of man transforming nature, a real part of nature developing into man. In contrast, when we evaluate his ideas from the perspective of successive replacement of social formations, Marx did not have a scientific understanding on the essence and law of successive replacement of social formations because he did not completely transcend the influence exerted by Feuerbach's theory of the estrangement and return of human essence yet.

In *The German Ideology*, while Marx on the one side, demonstrated different ideas on the classification of ownership into the tribal ownership, the ancient communal and State ownership, the feudal or estate property, the bourgeois property and the communist property in *The German Ideology*, on the other hand one thing is certain that Marx had discovered the law of movement of the productive forces and the relations of production, revealed the multilayered structure of society, and explained how the transition from one social formation to another more advanced social formation was realized in relation to the development of the productive forces. Hence he not only provided an objective standard for differentiating social forms but also an utterly scientific basis which evaluated this successive replacement as an objective process independent of human will. Thus Marx's theory of social-economic formation revealed the dynamics and mechanism of social development and thus expelled idealism from the sphere of history.

Some historians and sociologists in the West may deny the law of the development of history, and historical determinism and, preach nondeterminism. According to them, social phenomena, unlike natural

27   Karl Marx and Frederick Engels: Collected Works, 1st Chinese Edition, Volume 42, p. 169.

phenomena, are single, individual, non-repeated and fortuitous, and have no law to follow. They argue that "the belief that a certain law is the basis of social development, that the knowledge of this law provides foreseeable possibilities and thus defines the sphere of activity for the politicians, should be rejected, this is like superstition."[28] According to this view, the science of social history with objective significance does not exist at all. "History is contemporary history." Everyone reshapes history according to his own ideas and needs. In their eyes, Marx's theory of social-economic formation is a kind of mechanical "fatalism".

Specific historical events are single and non-repeated, but social phenomena are repetitive. The Franco-Prussian War in 1871 happened only once, but war as a social phenomenon occurs repeatedly; The French Revolution in 1789 will not be repeated, but revolutions in class societies are unavoidable. There will not be a second Robespierre or Danton in history, but the question of the role of individuals in history will recur. Similarly, although any country or nation has its own characteristics, unique language, cultural traditions, historical conditions, different historical figures and events, all societies are built on a definite mode of production and have a corresponding political and ideological superstructure. The productive forces determine and also are mediated by the relations of production, and ultimately condition the whole superstructure, which is a stable, repeated essential relation. This is the law, the general law governing the whole of human society.

Marx's theory of social-economic formation does not deny the diversity of the development of history. Every country has its particular historical circumstances, geographical conditions, cultural traditions and national mentality, and thus has different conditions. As far as feudal society is concerned, China differed from Europe as well as India. In Europe the feudal lord's land ownership was prevalent, in China the feudal land ownership dominated and in India land was owned by village community. The European feudal society bred capitalist society, while the Chinese feudal society remained stagnant for a long time and this society was finally reduced to a semi-feudal

---

28   Quoted from the book Categories of Historical Materialism), edited by N I. Dryakhlov, A.G. Spirkin and others. p. 246, Beijing: Beijing Normal University Press, 1984.

and semi-colonial society; As for Russia, Marx in his later studies even believed that there was a possibility of non-capitalist development for the Russian rural communities. All these were determined by their respective historical conditions. Marx objected to accept that the typical form of the capitalist development in West Europe as the road which all nations were destined to take regardless of their historical circumstances. It is true that history is not a military parade, but we cannot conclude that the development of history has no general law. All societies are governed by the general laws uncovered by the materialist conception of history, though there may be leaps, local/partial retrogressions or social anomalies in the historical sequence of their development. The production of material goods is the basis of the existence and development of society and society develops in the interaction of various factors inside it. The so-called "self-regulation" of the capitalist society is only relative, capitalist society cannot exist forever, which is an incontestable truth.

Social development is predictable, certainly not as accurate as the prediction of the solar eclipse, the lunar eclipse. The role of fortuitous factors is more complicated in social life than in the natural life. Under the guidance of the materialist conception of history, and with the use of some methods used by modern natural sciences, such as the system theory method, cybernetics, the theory of information and mathematical statistics, we can conduct qualitative and quantitative analysis on scientific and technological developments as well as several important aspects of social life, and thus it is possible to have an approximately proper judgment on the tendencies of social development. While it is hard to predict specific historical events, the tendency of the development of history is foreseeable, though existing conclusions can be revised and corrected continuously by the development of history. The flat denial of the possibility of predictability on history comes from the denial of the law of the development of history, which is a manifestation of certain agnosticism in the sphere of historical studies.

Therefore, we can be conclude from above that the materialist conception of history would not be established, if the focus was not shifted from the exploration of the inner essence of the subject itself, or from that contradiction between so-called human essence and social existence. Instead it was necessary to analyze the objective process of production to reveal the contradiction between the production forces and the relation of production in the process of production, and then based on this analysis, move to the scientific analysis of the cross section (social structure) and vertical section (replacement of successive social formations) of society.

With the establishment of the materialist conception of history enabled Marx to eliminate the remaining influence of Feuerbach's humanism.

Marx dismissed the view of opposing labour as the essence of man to labour as the means of maintaining human existence. In *Manuscripts*, he had considered the maintenance of physical existence as the symbol of dehumanization and degradation of man to an animal. While in *The German Ideology* he affirmed the following: "[T]he first premise of all human history is, of course, the existence of living human individuals. Thus the first fact to be established is the physical organisation of these individuals and their consequent relation to the rest of nature."[29]

There is no doubt that labour has multiple functions, including the creation of man himself, the development of human capabilities and the generation of pleasant sensation (pleasure at work), etc. But in any society the maintenance of human existence cannot be excluded from the purposes of labour. Even in communist society where labour is no longer a means of subsistence, the primary purpose of labour is still to meet the ever growing material and cultural needs of the entire society, on which depends the development and realization of its other functions. Hence Marx discussed this point in his criticism of Feuerbach's humanism. He argued that "[s]o much is this activity, this unceasing sensuous labour and creation, this production, the basis of the whole sensuous world as it now exists, „... if interrupted only for a year, Feuerbach would not only find an enormous change in the natural world, but would very soon find that the whole world of men and his own perceptive faculty, nay his own existence, were missing."[30]

---

29   Karl Marx and Frederick Engels: Collected Works, 1st Chinese Edition, Volume 3, p. 23.
30   Ibid., p. 50.

Marx also abandoned the idea: opposition between true man and estranged man he discussed in *Manuscripts*, and reinterpreted man's manly and inhumanly conditions according to the law of contradictory movement of the productive forces and the relations of production: "The positive expression "human" corresponds to the definite relations *predominant* at a certain stage of production and to the way of satisfying needs determined by them, just as the negative expression "inhuman" corresponds to the attempt to negate these predominant relations and the way of satisfying needs prevailing under them without changing the existing mode of production, an attempt that this stage of production daily engenders afresh."[31] Or more generally, when the relation of production corresponds to the requirement of the productive forces and people are satisfied with it, it is "human"; when it severely hinders the development of the productive forces, endangers the entire society and engenders circumstances which are not conducive to human development, it is inhuman and against human nature. Marx gave a metaphor: for a whale taken from the ocean and put in the Kupfergraben aquarium, its living environment changed, if whale possessed consciousness, it would declare this situation created by unfavourable circumstances to be unwhale-like. Hence Marx asserted: "The nonsensical judgment of the philosophers that the real man is not man is in the sphere of abstraction merely the most universal, all-embracing expression of the actually existing universal contradiction between the conditions and needs of people."[32]

Human, inhuman, humane, inhumane are not expressions that cannot be used and that should always be rejected, the problem with them is their philosophical basis. The view will be humanistic, if it abstracts from the inner contradiction of society, and if it takes the intrinsic nature of man as the measure and regards all evil things as the estrangement of human nature. We often use "inhuman savagery" to denounce Fascism, and praise "an act corresponding to human nature" to emphasise a person's noble act, etc., which are two different cases. Therefore, we should differentiate between the humanistic philosophical views and evaluation based on the code of ethics of man.

---

31   Ibid., p. 508.
32   Ibid., p. 505.

And this distinction was carefully made by Engels in *German Socialism in Verse and Prose* refuting Herr Grün's misinterpretation of Goethe. He wrote: '[Herr Grün's] transformation of Goethe into "the poet of all that is human" was incidentally facilitated by the fact that Goethe himself had a habit of using the words "man" and "human" with a special kind of emphasis. Goethe, it is true, used them only in the sense in which they were applied in his own day and later also by Hegel, for instance, the attribute "human" was bestowed on the Greeks in particular as opposed to heathen and Christian barbarians, long before these expressions acquired their mystically philosophical meaning through Feuerbach. With Goethe especially they usually have a most unphilosophical and flesh-and-blood meaning."[33] We quote this passage to make clear that the study of the development of Marx's thought should focus on the change of his thoughts rather than focusing on certain words in an isolated manner. Even if Marx used the words "most favourable to human nature" and similar phrases after *The German Ideology*, it by no means indicates that his views remained unchanged, compared to those before the spring of 1845. Some disputes and debates arise on Marx's ideas precisely by not distinguishing his philosophical ideas from common words.

3 NEW UNDERSTANDING ON ALIENATION. FROM EXPLAINING DIVISION OF LABOUR WITH ALIENATION TO EXPLORING ALIENATION IN DIVISION OF LABOUR

With the transition from the theory of alienated labour to the full establishment of historical materialism, the status and the function of alienation in Marx's thoughts has changed radically, as historical materialism becomes the only guiding principle of Marx in analyzing social history. Thus, only by persisting in historical materialism can we make scientific explanation on the phenomenon of alienation.

The theory of alienation was not any specialty exclusively prevalent in Germany. It didn't emerge as any abstract theory of speculation, but as an attempt to explain social phenomena. Historically speaking, as an idea its origin has blood connection with the bourgeois

---

33   Karl Marx and Frederick Engels: Collected Works, 1st Chinese Edition, Volume 4, p. 255.

humanism that gradually developed since the Renaissance. The newly emerged bourgeoisie advocated starting from man, took liberty, equality, dignity, and human value as the nature of man and as the inalienable, natural rights of man, and strongly attacked the feudal system to replace liberty with slavery, equality with old privileges and criticized trampling on human rights and dignity. Yet, why and how did man lose their intrinsic rights and lose their dignity and lose his nature as a man? As a conception of social history, alienation was generated as an answer to this "question". Though Rousseau didn't use the concept of alienation, he discussed the so-called antagonism between impersonal reality and human nature with his theory of transfer of rights which contained the bud of the theory of alienation later.

As a bourgeois enlightenment thinker and a humanist, Rousseau's social contract theory is closely related with his humanism. Rousseau advocated that "love all men, even those despising the others", "man, can by no means speak ill of the mankind"[34]. Rousseau sharply criticized that the feudal, autocratic government is "an iniquitous and absurd system which degrades humanity and dishonours the name of man"[35].

According to Rousseau, man was born free and independent, but in the society at his time, man was not only controlled by the whole nature but also controlled by his own kind and lost his liberty. To renounce one's liberty is to "renounce being a man, to surrender the rights of humanity and even its duties" and "Such a renunciation is incompatible with man's nature"[36]. What he wanted to explore was: why would a man disobey his own nature and "transfer his nature", or in other words, alienate his nature? He said, "Man is born free, and everywhere he is in chain", and "How did this change come about? I do not know. What can make it legitimate? That question I think I can answer."[37]

---

34 Rousseau: Emile: on Education (Émile: ou De l'éducation), Volume 1, p. 311, Beijing: The Commercial Press, 1978.
35 Rousseau: *The Social Contract (Social Contract or Political Rights Principle)* (hereinafter referred to as Social Contract), p. 121, Beijing: Law Press China, 1958.
36 Ibid., p. 13.
37 Ibid., p. 6.

In Rousseau's mind, in order to transcend the natural state, men make contracts with each other, they never want to transfer their liberty but pursuing to guarantee it. In the natural state, because those obstacles in the way of the survival of the mankind show their power much greater than men's resources at the disposal. Thus each individual suffered hard for maintenance under these circumstances. Under those circumstances because pure natural condition could no longer subsist; and because human race would perish unless it changed its manner of existence. Thus, men wanted to "find a form of association which will defend and protect with the whole common force the person and goods of each associate, and in which each man, while uniting himself with all, may still obey himself alone, and remain as free as before"[38]. Therefore, Rousseau thought sovereignty is unalienable, untransferable, because "Sovereignty, being nothing less than the exercise of the general will, can never be alienated, and that the Sovereign, who is no less than a collective being, cannot be represented except by himself: the power indeed may be transmitted, but not the will"[39]. In this way, he criticized Thomas Hobbes's theory of absolute monarchy that the subjects of a feudal ruler must give up their sovereignty and absolutely submit to the ruler, and Rousseau mocked at this theory for it seemed to change men into herbs of sheep and cattle, "who keeps guard over them for the purpose of devouring them"[40].

However, a theory is nothing more than theory, while facts are always more powerful than theory. According to Rousseau's theory of social contract, the people do not alienate their sovereignty; officials are the servants of the people, and the government, —the executor of the Sovereign citizen—should perform according to the general will. As long as the Sovereign citizen desires, he can restraint, modify or take back the entrusted power, he has offered. However, in fact, the State or the Government are far above the Sovereign, take away their liberty and become "their master". Rousseau saw this contradiction and criticized "the abuse of government and its tendency to degenerate": "sooner or later the prince must inevitably suppress the Sovereign (Ed.: citizen) and break the social treaty. This is the

---

38   Ibid., p. 19-20.
39   Ibid., p. 35.
40   Ibid., p. 8.

unavoidable and inherent defect which, from the very birth of the body politic, tends ceaselessly to destroy it, as age and death end by destroying the human body."[41]

So from the moment the government usurps the Sovereignty, the social contract is broken and all private citizens are then forced, but not bound, to obey the government. Herein the "alienation" as Rousseau described is the alienation of power in the feudal society, which totally deviates from the desire and will of men when they made the "social contract".

Any theory must have a basis to make a point. If we evaluate it from the perspective of speculation, the state of alienation must presuppose the state of non-alienation, the two of which contrast each other and can thus form a picture in order to evaluate the realty at that time. That's how Rousseau did. He assumed there were two kinds of men: "natural men" and "civilized men", the former representing the natural state of mankind while the latter the civilized society, and starting from this contrast, he designed his theory of social contract. This method, more or less, had some effects on the theory of personal and impersonal (societal) alienation later.

As Rousseau considered, in the primitive natural state, men lived their life according to their own nature and obeying their nature. The "natural men" were satisfied with their own shabby cabins, made clothes of fur with thorns and fishbone and dressed themselves up with feathers and shells. They lived in a free, healthy, kind and happy life without any horrible consequences of our civilized society. This kind of view was very common at Rousseau's time and had nothing special. Marx once said, "According to a fiction current in the eighteenth century, the natural state was considered the true state of human nature. People wanted to see the idea of man through the eyes of the body and created men of nature, Papagenos, the naivety of which idea extended even to covering the skin with feathers. During the last decades of the eighteenth century, it was supposed that peoples in a state of nature possessed primeval wisdom and everywhere one could hear bird-catchers imitating the twittering method of singing of the Iroquois, the Indians, etc., in the belief that by these arts the

---

41   Ibid., p. 18.

birds themselves could be enticed into a trap. All these eccentricities were based on the correct idea that the primitive state was a naive Dutch picture of the true state."[42]

However, in association with the germination of Rousseau's thought of alienation, the novelty of this description about natural state lies in that it sets up a standard to evaluate the reality. Rousseau also knew that this natural state was not real, so he repeatedly called it as "a hypothesis based on human nature". He said, "The investigations we may enter into, in treating this subject, must not be considered as historical truths, but only as mere conditional and hypothetical reasoning, rather calculated to explain the nature of things, than to ascertain their actual origin; just like the hypotheses which our physicists daily form respecting the formation of the world."[43]

Rousseau actually took his ideas about the natural state as the hypothesis in natural sciences. He needed this hypothesis because "it is, nevertheless, necessary to have true ideas, in order to form a proper judgment of our present state"[44], which indicates that his real purpose has not much to do with the primitive natural state. He was using the past to satirize the present and to express his anger at his current society and his longing for liberty and equality, so he didn't praise the natural state or asked to go back to the natural state unconditionally. He refuted this opinion by asking satirically: "Must societies be totally abolished? Must meum and tuum be annihilated, and must we return again to the forests to live among bears?" He clearly pointed out that, we "can no longer subsist on plants or acorns, or live without laws and magistrate"[45]. Rousseau, was not sentimentally reminiscing the past, but had turned his eyes at the present. He didn't simply see changing the reality (sublating alienation) as a return to the natural state, instead his view was dialectic.

Rousseau recognized the situation that the contractual society deviated from the will of the Sovereign (citizen) in a relatively comprehensive way. Besides the alienation of power mentioned above, i.e. the usurpation of sovereignty and degeneration of government, he also discussed about the issues of morality and property.

---

42 Karl Marx and Frederick Engels: Collected Works, 1st Chinese Edition, Volume 1, p. 97.
43 Rousseau: Discourse on the Origin of Inequality, p. 71.
44 Ibid., p. 64.
45 Ibid., p. 166.

What made Rousseau a prominent figure and brought him great reputation was his first work—*Discourse on the Arts and Sciences*, which was a sound dissertation debating whether the advance of sciences and arts contributed to the refining of moral practices. Rousseau in his essay which was awarded with the prize of Academy of Dijon, France, flatly denied that the advance of science and arts could promote and perfect morality but on the contrary it corrupted the public morals and degenerated morality. He wrote: "Our souls have become corrupted to the extent that our sciences and our arts have advanced towards perfection", and "virtue flies away to the extent that their lights have risen over our horizon".[46]

He also illustrated many nations which had advanced science and arts but were conquered by "barbarian" nations because of corruption, and gave special attention to China under the feudal system, and wrote: "There is in Asia an immense country where literary honours lead to the highest offices of state. If the sciences purified morals, if they taught men to shed their own blood for their country, if they inspired courage, the people of China would become wise, free, and invincible. But if there is no vice which does not rule over them, no crime unfamiliar to them, if neither the enlightenment of ministers, nor the alleged wisdom in the laws, nor the multitude of inhabitants of that vast empire was capable of keeping it safe from the ignorant and coarse yoke of the Tartars, what use have all these wise men been to them? What fruits has it reaped from all the honours lavished on them? Could it perhaps be the reward of being an enslaved and wicked people?"[47]

As a bourgeois enlightenment thinker who should have publicized science, chanted praises of culture, Rousseau's speeches seem to "go off the rails". But his opinion arguing for the inverse proportional relationship between the progress of science and technology and morals is much more complicated than words to express his resentment and cynicism about the world and the reality, but he has a sight on the phenomenon of alienation in the moral field: On one side, it was the progress of science and technology; on the other side, it was the fickleness of the world, the degeneration of morals, full of doubts,

---

46   Rousseau: Discourse on the Arts and Sciences, Beijing: The Commercial Press, 1963.
47   Rousseau: Discourse on the Arts and Sciences, p. 13-14.

suspicion, indifference, hatred, duplicity and evil tricks among man and man. He saw this contradiction but failed to correctly understand it. Indeed, Rousseau tried to find an intermediate link between the two sides, which is luxury. He said, "Luxury rarely comes along without the arts and sciences, and they never develop without it." "While the commodities of life multiply, while the arts perfect themselves, and while luxury spreads, true courage grows enervated, and military virtues vanish—once again the work of the sciences and all those arts which are practiced in the shadows of the study"[48]. The progress of sciences brings about luxury and dissolution of morals, which is Rousseau's formula. Of course, we shouldn't blame him for not knowing the distinction between objectification and alienation or for not really understanding the relation between science and morals, because that is determined by the limitation of his conception of history. On the contrary, we should say that it is quite outstanding and profound that Rousseau, with his intelligent thought and sharp insight, saw this contradiction as well as the phenomenon of alienation in the field of morals, and put forward his questions.

Especially he really made much account of private property. For example, when speaking of the relationship of private property and morality, he said, "In a word, there arose rivalry and competition on the one hand, and conflicting interests on the other, together with a secret desire on both of profiting at the expense of others"[49]. When speaking on the alienation of powers, he also associated it with private property. It is because of the private property, the rich made contracts with the poor by cheating them and thus originated the society and the law, "which bound new fetters on the poor, and gave new powers to the rich; which irretrievably destroyed natural liberty, eternally fixed the law of property and inequality, converted clever usurpation into unalterable right, and, for the advantage of a few ambitious individuals, subjected all mankind to perpetual labour, slavery and wretchedness"[50].

In his *Discourse on the Origin of Inequality*, Rousseau quoted the wise axiom of Locke: "There can be no injury, where there is no property" and expressed one of his important conclusions. Though

---

48 Ibid., p. 18 and p. 22.
49 Rousseau: Discourse on the Origin of Inequality, p. 125.
50 Ibid., p. 128-129.

his idea on the origin of private property hasn't broken away from the chains of idealism, it is still a very ingenious thought as he high-lighted "metallurgy and agriculture were the two arts which produced this great revolution"[51].

Above I have tried to demonstrate that there are some reasonable ideas contained in Rousseau's social and political theory, especially in his historical dialectics, but to expound the society with alienation (transfer of power) was an idealistic conception of history after all.

The German Classical Philosophy had turned alienation into a speculative theory. Though each philosopher had his different opinions on the nature of human, all of them agreed on one common point, which is to explain the opposition between the impersonal reality (such as religion and state) and human nature by the alienation of human nature. At first, Marx also started his course along this road, but gradually he abandoned it and encountered a radical change especially starting with *The German Ideology*.

In *The German Ideology*, Marx criticized Stirner's idealistic conception of alienation and this critique was the continuation and extension of his criticism on Hegel's and Powell's conception of alienation in his *Manuscripts* of 1844 and *The Holy Family*. However, the difference of the text of *The German Ideology*, lies in that Marx hadn't completely surpassed the influence of Feuerbach in the works above (*Manuscripts* of 1844 and *The Holy Family*), so in some parts of his critique against the idealistic conception of alienation, he still kept the view that the human nature alienated from human itself. Thus he had used the self-alienation of human to explain the antagonism of the proletariat and the bourgeois; but his criticism against Stirner in *The German Ideology* was completely established on the basis of historical materialism.

Stirner formally abandoned the abstract man of Feuerbach and stressed on the "ego" as the "single person". Actually his "ego" was not the empirical or real person but was an "ego" getting rid of all relations with others, which was just an alias of the abstract man. Based on this "ego", Stirner carried out his idealistic conception of alienation, called everything other than the ego as "non-ego". This

---

51   Ibid., p. 119.

"non-ego" had so many different names that it could be expressed as pure logical concepts like "being-in-itself" and "alien-existing", or as concrete conceptions like people and state. But what really mattered was not Stirner's description about the non-ego but important was the way how he saw everything as the non-ego opposite to the ego; in his mind, non-ego is what was different from ego, thus the relationship of ego and non-ego was the relationship of alienation. In this way, he pre-announced all practical relations and practical individuals as alienated and turned all these relations and individuals as completely abstract nouns about alienation. So when Marx refuted Stirner, he said, "Thus instead of the task of describing actual individuals in their actual alienation and in the empirical relations of this alienation, purely empirical relations, the same happens here—the setting forth is replaced by the mere idea of alienation, of the Alien, of the Holy"[52].

Obviously, Marx didn't generally oppose to use the concept of alienation but opposed to turn alienation into a mere, empty noun, so he replaced the alienation of man with the actual alienation of actual individual, besides he replaced the abstract subject-object opposition with his studies on those empirical conditions in which alienation is generated. Accordingly, in *The German Ideology*, he scientifically uncovered the nature and origin of the alienation under the conditions of private property through his discussion on the relation between the old labour division and alienation, he got out of the "dilemma" of his circular reasoning in *Manuscripts* and further materialized the knowledge about the law of the dialectic movement of productive forces and relations of production.

In *Manuscripts*, Marx had made his initial contact with the issue of labour division through his studies on the British classical political economics. In *Manuscripts*, he had made several quotes from Adam Smith, Jean Baptiste Say, Skarbek, and Mill on division of labour and exchange and also commented on them; Marx had commented on the essence of division of labour, "The political economists are very vague and self-contradictory about it"[53].

---

52   Karl Marx and Frederick Engels: Collected Works, 1st Chinese Edition, Volume 3, p. 317.
53   Karl Marx and Frederick Engels: Collected Works, 1st Chinese Edition, Volume 42, p. 144-145.

On the other side since he had just started to study on economics, he didn't also understand division of labour quite clearly. He said, "The division of labour is the economic expression of the social character of labour within the estrangement. Or, since labour is only an expression of human activity within alienation, of the manifestation of life as the alienation of life, the division of labour, too, is therefore nothing else but the estranged, alienated positing of human activity as a real activity of the species or as activity of man as a species-being"[54].

It was certainly correct to say that division of labour is the expression of the social character of labour. The social character of man is basically the social character of labour. If labour could be practiced completely independently, no material communicative relation would be established among man and man. The division of labour shows man's labour is social labour, and men are mutually related to each other by the use of division of labour and of exchange closely bounded up with it in labour process. In addition, Marx also paid attention to the views of the British classical economists on division of labour: Such as division of labour could improve proficiency of labour, increase the products of society, but it also restrained the capability of individual and degenerates it; the difference in men's capabilities is more a result of division of labour than being a reason of it; division of labour and exchange can form social productive forces, and so forth, all of which had played a positive role for Marx to further analyze division of labour. However, Marx had considered division of labour as the expression of alienated labour and explained division of labour with alienation, thus failing to truly expose the reason and essence of division of labour.

But this time in *The German Ideology*, Marx analyzed the division of labour by closely relating it with the forces of production and the production relations, and analyzed alienation as arising from the old division of labour.

Division of labour is determined by the state/degree of productive forces. The extent to which the productive forces of a nation are developed shows itself most manifestly by the degree to which the division of labour is elevated. Marx pointed out, "Each new productive

---

54   Ibid., p. 144 - Ed. See Manuscripts of 1844.

force causes a further development of the division of labour"[55]. At first, the division of human labour was spontaneously formed according to the differences of gender and physical power; later, the division of labour was developed as the separation of industrial and commercial labour from agricultural labour, then later by the separation of commercial labour from industrial labour, and later the more and more detailed division of labour among the individuals working together in the same department of labour; and for Marx, all of these changes had originated from the development of productive forces.

Division of labour is also closely related with the relations of production. The different stages of the development of division of labour actually are the different forms of ownership. Marx said, "The division of labour implies from the outset the division of the conditions of labour, of tools and materials, and thus the splitting-up of accumulated capital among different owners, and thus, also, the division between capital and labour, and the different forms of property itself"[56]. When Marx analyzed the division and replacement of the different forms of property, he highlighted that they all fit into the certain degree to which the division of labour is developed.

Therefore, according to Marx, contradictions were bounded to arise among the three: Productive forces, relations of production, and superstructures, as the result of the existence of the old division of labour.

Because the division of labour not only boosts up the development of productivity (productive forces) and not only produces surplus products, but also enables some men to occupy the products of some others through the distribution of production means and products, in this way, material activities and mental activities, enjoyment and labour, production and consumption, get split up. That's why Marx said, "The only possibility of their not coming into contradiction lies in the negation in its turn of the division of labour"[57]. The division of labour negated herein of course refers to the old division of labour related with private property.

---

55   Karl Marx and Frederick Engels: Collected Works, 1st Chinese Edition, Volume 3, p. 24. Ed. The German Ideology.
56   Ibid., p. 74-75.
57   Ibid., p. 36.

Based on this understanding, Marx no longer took alienation as the self-alienation of man or the separation of the species nature of man from man itself, but realized that it is rooted in the mode of production. He said, "Within the framework of definite modes of production, which, of course, are not dependent on the will, alien practical forces, which are independent not only of isolated individuals but even independent of all of them together, always come to stand above people", and clearly made out that this power is "a power created by intercourse, and is transformed into social relations from the personal behaviours of individuals, into a series of powers which determine and subordinate the individual"[58].

Just because of the division of labour, the social activity of man is fixed, and everybody is restricted within an exclusive sphere of activity. This sphere is imposed to him, and he can by no means go beyond this sphere: "He is a hunter, a fisherman, a herdsman, or a critical critic, and must remain so if he does not want to lose his means of livelihood"[59]. Yes, individual's submitting to the division of labour and to some activity he is forced to do can improve the proficiency of his labour, but it also can mislead him into a way of one-sided, twisted personal development. The antagonism between mental labour and physical labour results in such a situation in which some people works only with physical power while others only with mental power; while the antagonism of city and country turns some people into constrained city animals, the others into constrained county animals. The more developed production and division of labour become, the smaller the range in which man's activities are confined. The division of labour boosts up the development of production and finally creates conditions for the full development of man, but within a certain historical period, it is also a power enslaving man.

Division of labour and exchange are inseparable. For individuals living within a certain fixed sphere of activity, they become related with each other through exchange and thus transform their individual labour into social labour. In this way, the labourers get separated from their own product and mutually occupy that of others, labour gradually becomes the means to earn one's living and

58   Ibid., p. 273-274.
59   Ibid., p. 37.

breeding and thus promotes the emergence of capitalist commodity production from simple commodity production. Human's activities become more and more supervised and dominated by the power of market. Marx said, "Separate individuals have, with the broadening of their activity into world-historical activity, become more and more enslaved under a power alien to them, a power which has become more and more enormous and, in the last instance, turns out to be the world market"[60]. Commercial economy transcending and replacing the natural economy marks the progress of history. A more developed commodity production always corresponds with a higher state of production. However, the capitalist commodity production established on the basis of highly developed division of labour and exchange forms such a blind power, the market which men cannot control, throwing the fate of commodity producers into the hand of commodity and money.

The transformation from individual power to material power, due to the division of labour also manifests itself as the formation of social productive forces. Individual powers are separated, opposed to each other, which can only become a real power, i.e. social productive forces, through division of labour and cooperation, through intercourse and mutual relation of individuals. This power, under the conditions of private property, is manifested as a thing that is totally independent of individuals and isolated from them, as a special world coexisting with all individuals. Men cannot fully control or utilize the productive forces as they desire but on the contrary, they become controlled. Just as Marx pointed out, "The social power, i.e., the multiplied productive force, which arises through the co-operation of different individuals as it is determined by the division of labour, appears to these individuals, since their co-operation is not voluntary but has come about naturally, not as their own united power, but as an alien force existing outside them, of the origin and goal of which they are ignorant, which they thus cannot control, which on the contrary passes through a peculiar series of phases and stages independent of the will and the action of man, nay even being the prime governor of these[61].

---

60   Ibid., p. 41-42.
61   Ibid., p. 38-39.

Thus we can tell it is not the alienated which labour leads to division of labour but it is the division of labour leads to the alienation of labour. Development of productive forces—development of division of labour—generation of property, this is the historical process described in *The German Ideology*.

Of course, the division of labour discussed by Marx in *The German Ideology* is the old division of labour integrated with private property. This division of labour tied workers up with one certain career for their whole lives, leading to one-sided development of men and gradually forms—through the exchange process—a material world in which commodity, money and capital dominate men. In socialist society there also exist the division of labour, exchange, commodities and money, but the socialist commodity production is a properly planned commodity production, and what the socialist division of labour, exchange, commodity and money reflect is the socialist relations of production. We spare no efforts to develop the socialist commodity economy, at the same time apply the law of value and arrange the relation of demand and supply to regulate production, and gradually push exchange, production, and the relation of the two under our control, which is quite different from the bourgeois society blindly controlled by the power of market and manipulated by the relation of demand and supply.

4 FROM REALIZATION OF HUMAN ESSENCE TO MAN'S ALL-ROUND DEVELOPMENT

Historical materialism has nothing similar with structuralism, because it starts from the mode of material production to uncover the inner laws of social development but pays much attention to researching the questions about men.

Any influential theory may be faced with critiques from a bunch of different aspects. With regard to this point, Lenin's comments on the critiques against Kant, Dühring, and Dietzgen is quite inspiriting and profound. Lenin said, "Marx and Engels always "talked with contempt" about those bad socialists, but we should infer from that: what they really want is a correct, scientific socialist theory rather than a dramatic leap from socialist views to bourgeois views. Marx and Engels always rebuked the bad materialism (mainly the anti-dialectic ones) but based themselves on the more advanced and more developed dialectic materialism instead of on the doctrine of Hume or Berkeley.[62]

It would be the least advisable for us to take the stand of feudalism to oppose to the bourgeois humanism, to negate its historical progressive role and some of its reasonable factors. Marxism had abandoned the abstract humanist conception of history with man as its starting point but not the rational factors of the bourgeois humanism. As an atheism, Marxism, though treasures very much the religion-themed mural paintings and statues in European churches and in the Dunhuang Caves (in Middle China), and still tries to understand them limited within the sphere of arts; thus we could certainly tell that Marxism opposes to take abstract man as starting point but doesn't negate the achievements that the bourgeois humanism has made in politics, morals, aesthetics, and arts. The bourgeoisie was once an oppressed class too, and some slogans it raised in the fights against the feudal system also reflected the progressive trend of social development. It couldn't be more wrong to think that we would be entitled to care about no man and be indifferent about man just because we criticize those theories taking abstract man as their starting point; or we could pay no respect to the personality and dignity or the liberty and equality of man because we criticize abstract liberty, equality and fraternity, and that we criticize abstract values and dignity of man; criticizing abstract humanism never means we don't need humanism in any sense. Socialist society is humane society, and socialist humanist principles should be embodied in dealing with the relationship among man and man.

As Lu Xun (a famous Chinese writer) said, "One merciless hero may not be a real hero." A real revolutionist ought to be very merciful and love the masses from the bottom of his heart. Marx is such a revolutionist who has the most sincere sympathy and love for millions of labourers and who devoted all his life to exploring the truth for the proletariat and the mankind in spite that he was ill and poor himself and was continuously disturbed by the counterrevolutionaries. However, Marx never took his humanistic feelings as the basis of his theory, just as a magnificent doctor who can bring the dying

---

62   Selected Works of Lenin, 2nd Edition, Volume 2, p. 244.

to life never replaces his diagnosis with his feelings toward his patients. In *The German Ideology*, Marx criticized the "true socialists" those who take the realization of the essence of man as the ultimate goal of history, but at the same time, he also paid great attention to the free and comprehensive development of individuals on the basis of historical materialism.

"True socialism" was a petty-bourgeois utopian socialism popular in the 1840s in Germany. And the true socialists used the German classical philosophy, especially Feuerbach's theory about the alienation and restoration of the essence of man to understand and interpret the French utopian socialist books. They judged everything with the essence of man, saw money and wage labour as the alienation of the essence of man but socialism as the requirements or demand of the realization of the essence of man. For example, Herman Zemeckis had considered the haves and the have-nots as the alienation of the essence of man in his article "Communism, Socialism, Humanism" also as the alienation of the essence of man, while socialism was describes as the necessary result of truly understanding the essence of man. He said, "Nowadays, our society has been so barbarized that some people (the rentiers) jump on the labour products of others so greedily like a beast and make their inherent essence corrupt because of their idleness; what this situation will inevitably lead to will be that other people (the proletarians) will be forced to produce like a machine; and their properties (their inherent essence of man) are lost not as a result of idleness but of excessive weariness." "The natural, necessary result of the understanding of the essence of man has already been the real human life"[63].

Rudolph Matej had also claimed in his article "The Cornerstone of the Socialism": "to admit that everyone is born equal and has the right to live is based on the consciousness of the essence of man that is common and shared by all"[64].

Before the spring of 1845, Marx had also remained in the argumentation paradigm of alienation and restoration of the essence of man in some aspects, especially in his *Manuscripts of 1844*; while in *The*

---

63   Research Materials of International History of Communist Movement now named as Contemporary World & Socialism, Issue 7, p. 226 and p. 228.
64   Ibid., p. 237.

German Ideology, he took the interactions between productive forces and the relations of production as basis and launched critiques against Stirner and "true socialism", in this process he had also criticized and corrected his previous philosophic beliefs.

Marx abolished the viewpoint that sees communism as the realization and restoration of the essence of man. He said, "With "Stirner", "communism" begins with searching for "essence"". He corrected: "communism is a highly practical movement, pursuing practical aims by practical means"[65]. Communism is the product of the mode of intercourse, and its deepest root lies in the bourgeois mode of production: "In the development of productive forces there comes a stage when productive forces and means of intercourse are brought into being, which, under the existing relationships, only cause mischief, and are no longer productive but destructive forces (machinery and money); and connected with this a class is called forth, which has to bear all the burdens of society without enjoying its advantages, a class which is ousted from society, is forced into the most decided antagonism to all other classes; a class which forms the majority of all members of society, and from which emanates the consciousness of the necessity of a fundamental revolution, the communist consciousness, which may, of course, arise among the other classes too, through the contemplation of the situation of this class"[66]. The last sentence actually confirms the effects of the intellectuals who were not born to the working class but who clearly understand the situation and mission of this class. Contradiction of the mode of production—antagonism of class—consciousness of communism, this mode of argumentation is completely accordant with the materialistic conception of history.

Marx had specially highlighted the importance of the development of productive forces. Only through the high development and enormous growth of productive forces can the power of the proletariat be strengthened and can the contradiction between the proletariat and the bourgeoisie be intensified; in the same sense, the high level development of productive forces is also an absolutely necessary practical premise to guarantee socialism to be a real wealthy society.

---

65   Karl Marx and Frederick Engels: Collected Works, 1st Chinese Edition, Volume 3, p. 236.
66   Ibid., p. 77-78.

Otherwise, the so-called equality would only be the generalization of poverty but poverty is by no means, equals socialism.

Marx also paid much attention to the question of individuals' liberty, but he was against Stirner's view that deduces liberty from the concept of man and believes the extent of liberty should depend on the extent to which it coincides with the concept of man. Liberty is neither the essence nor the species nature of man, but a concrete, historical concept that is determined by the mode of production. Marx said, "Never did men gain their liberty within the range determined and allowed by their ideals of men but within the range determined and allowed by the current productive forces"[67]. This judgment has important significance both relating to nature and to the society.

With regard to the relation between man and nature, man's understanding and applying the laws of nature rest on the extent that productive forces have developed. With the development of productive forces, the mankind is gaining more and more liberty from the natural world.

With regard to the relation between man and society, the situation may be more complicated. The possibility that individuals can obtain a certain degree of free development in the social field directly depends on the nature of the relations of production. Man can never live without society; only in the community can personal freedom be possible. However, there are two kinds of collectives. One is the false community, or the illusory community as Marx called, for example, in class society, personal freedom has existed only for the individuals who developed within the relationships of the ruling class, and only insofar as they were individuals of this class; on the contrary, for the individuals of the ruled class, this illusory community not only can't guarantee their personal freedom, but is a new fetter as well. Why does this happen? One of the direct reasons is the division of class, but the division of class corresponds to the extent that the social production has developed. Therefore, Marx thought that in the social field, the issue of freedom is also tightly tied up with the development of productive forces. He said, "It is the limited productive forces that play the role as the basis of all the freedom gained

---

67   Ibid., p. 507.

before; production that is limited by the productive forces and which cannot meet and embrace the whole society ties up the development of men in such a form: Thus some men meet their needs by relying on others, so a few men (the minority) grasp the monopoly rights of development; while some other men (the majority) who frequently have to struggle for meeting their most urgent needs, thus lose the possibility of any development temporarily (before the new revolutionary force comes out). It is shown that up to now, the society has been developing within antagonism, the antagonism between freemen and slaves in ancient times, that between aristocracies and serfs in the middle ages, and that between the bourgeoisie and the proletariat in the modern times"[68]. The antagonism of class restrains the freedom of the oppressed class, making freedom something conditionally and exclusively owned just by a few people.

Marx wasn't against liberty at all but against this so-called liberty at the cost of sacrificing the liberty of a part of people; he believed the free development of individuals should be the conditions of the free development of all men. To realize this goal, the conditions of survival in the old societies must be abolished, so is the phenomenon that individuals must belong to a certain class; a new association must be established, which is communism. "In a real community the individuals obtain their freedom in and through their association." To achieve this point, we must be "based on the developed productive forces"[69].

In the same sense, the possibility and necessity of the full development of individuals is also rooted in the mode of production. In the previous history, the fact that individuals are subject to the division of labour corresponds to a certain definite state of productive forces and to the nature of the relations of production. Though the high development of capitalist productive forces demands their labourers to be equipped with certain scientific knowledge and educational level so as to meet the needs and the capital transfer of the capitalist industrial development, and the "law of the transformation of labour" also requires labourers with diverse skills, the capitalist private property and the antagonism of class both still limit the possibility

68   Karl Marx and Frederick Engels: Collected Works, 1st Chinese Edition, Volume 3, p. 507.
69   Ibid., p. 84 and p. 85.

of individuals' all-around development. However, the communist mode of production, taking over the place of the capitalist mode of production, opens up a road for the full development of individuals: "Only at this stage does the self-activity coincide with material life, which corresponds to the development of individuals into being complete individuals and the casting-off of all natural limitations. The transformation of labour into self-activity corresponds to the transformation of the earlier limited intercourse forward into the intercourse of individuals as such"[70].

Of course, the full development of man is also relative. The so-called abolishing the subjection of individuals to the division of labour is mainly to abolish the previously existing antagonism between physical labour and mental labour, city and town, as well as the separation between labour and enjoyment, production and consumption, and to abolish the situation in which individuals are forced to engage in some kind of labour, rather than abolish all divisions of labour. The division of labour is an inevitable requirement of the development of productive forces and the socialization of production. Marx's hypothesis that "in communist society, where nobody has one exclusive sphere of activity, but instead each can become accomplished in any branch he wishes, society regulates the general production and thus makes it possible for me to do one thing today and another tomorrow, to hunt in the morning, fishing in the afternoon, rear cattle in the evening, criticize after dinner, just as I have a mind, without ever becoming hunter, fisherman, herdsman or critic" is quite idealized. However, under communist conditions, men work not because they are forced to but because they like to, hope to and are able to; and because of the extension of non-production time, men have enough time and energy to work in any department they like to cultivate and develop all their abilities. This kind of new communist man is determined by the nature of the communist relations of production and by the highly developed productive forces.

Marx started from the mode of material production to examine the all-around development of man and abandoned the view that sees the all-around development of man as the realization of the essence of man. When criticizing Feuerbach, he pointed out, "The individuals,

70   Ibid., p. 77.

who are no longer subject to the division of labour, have been conceived by the philosophers as an ideal, under the name "Man*". They have conceived the whole process which we have outlined as the evolutionary process of "Man", so that at every historical stage "Man" was substituted for the individuals and shown as the motive force of history. The whole process was thus conceived as a process of the self-estrangement of "Man", and this was essentially due to the fact that the average individual of the later stage was always foisted on to the earlier stage, and the consciousness of a later age on to the individuals of an earlier. Through this inversion, which from the first is an abstract image of the actual conditions, it was possible to transform the whole of history into an evolutionary process of consciousness."[71]*

In *The German Ideology*, Marx reversed this inversion completely: he didn't study the abstract man or the abstract nature of man but the practical conditions, i.e. the human activities of material production, and on this basis, he studied real man and its real essence and thus made a scientific description of the individual liberty and full development of man.

---

71   Ibid.
*) Man written with big M letter.

CHAPTER XII

COMBINATION OF HISTORICAL MATERIALISM WITH LABOUR MOVEMENT.

A BRIGHT ANALYSIS OF HISTORY OF CAPITALIST SOCIETY AND SOCIAL STRUCTURE

The German Ideology only represents a comprehensive elaboration of the principles of historical materialism rather than the end of historical materialism. Publishers could prevent this masterpiece from publication and bury this pearl into dust, but they could neither block a thinking mind nor take away the achievements Marx had already made. On the contrary, after *The German Ideology*, Marx mounted to a broader political stage with his new historical viewpoints.

If we can say in *The German Ideology*, Marx still focused on Germany and set up his own theories by clearing his old philosophical beliefs and criticizing the "True Socialism" sweeping over Germany like a plague, then after he had also finished the arduous engineering of establishing historical materialism by and large, he was faced with the task to promote his views among workers, make the European proletariats believe they were right so that they could oppose all the mistaken ideological trends severely influencing the labour movement at that time, which thus started the glorious time combining historical materialism and labour movement.

In *The Poverty of Philosophy*, by criticizing the economic and philosophical points of Proudhon, Marx had further advanced and developed some principles which were established in *The German Ideology*. Especially in *The Communist Manifesto*, he analyzed the structure of capitalist society by historical materialism and made a scientific program for the working class in the world. *The Communist Manifesto* is an excellent example of applying historical materialism to analyze the modern history, the history of capitalism's emergence and development. It unquestionably proves that once the historical materialism is applied in reality, it will develop infinite power.

1 VIEW OF SOCIETY AS A WHOLE AND ULTIMATE REASON FOR HISTORICAL DEVELOPMENT

Marx is a very diligent and studious scholar as well as a great fighter, who has spent his whole life fighting against all kinds of mistaken ideological trends and developing his scientific theories. When Marx made himself clear on "True Socialism", his dispute against Proudhon rose to a more highlighted place.

Proudhon had his own historic status, but his scientific theory was inferior. This Frenchman, in front of his country fellowmen, seemed to be a philosopher good at German speculation; while on the other side in front of Germans, he acted as an excellent economist. Actually, he was neither. To Marx who had known him since 1844 and who had excelled both at German classical philosophy and British and French classical political economics, wrote: "Mr. Proudhon is a downright petty-bourgeois philosopher and economist"[1]. Proudhon's book— "The System of Economic Contradictions, or Philosophy of Poverty" published in 1846 is such a historical-idealism-centric counterfeit that has vulgarized Hegelian dialectics and Ricardo's labour theory of value

---

1   Karl Marx and Frederick Engels: Collected Works, 1st Chinese Edition, Volume 27, p.487-488.

In Marx's letter to Pavel Vasilyevich Annenkov on December 28, 1846 and later in *The Poverty of Philosophy*, he refuted Proudhon's economic viewpoints, philosophical viewpoints, and reformist social political viewpoints, and in this debate, he stated a series of important theories in a positive way among which the most leading one was the historical materialism. F. Mehring thought very highly of *The Poverty of Philosophy* and considered "this book is not only a milestone in Marx's life, but is also a milestone in the history of science"[2]. His focus was also on the historical materialism.

When Marx refuted that Proudhon treated all kinds of economic relations linking to each other only as successive relations, he emphasized, "The production relations of every society form a whole"[3]. This view of Marx taking society as a whole, which is also a conception of holism considering all components of society interact with each other, is quite important and profound. Proudhon sorted the different social relations of a society in time sequence, one-sidedly emphasizing on their chronological order and blotting out their concurrent interdependent and interactive relations. In fact, this single-track and chronological arrangement segmented all the aspects of a unified society and turns them into different social stages in which one produces another. Transforming a unified and organic dimensional social structure into a disunited ad non-living plane graph was quite a distortion of the organism of human society. When criticizing Proudhon, Marx pointed out: "In constructing the edifice of an ideological system by means of the categories of political economy, the limbs of the social system are dislocated. The different limbs of society are converted into so many separate societies, following one upon the other. How, indeed, could the single logical formula of movement, of sequence, of time, explain the structure of society, in which all relations coexist simultaneously and support one another?"[4].

Marx considered the society as a whole but he didn't believe that all the factors constructing the society were just independent systems that depended on each other and performed the same functions.

---

2 F. Mehring: Karl Marx, P159, Beijing: People's Publishing House, 1972.
3 Karl Marx and Frederick Engels, 1st Chinese Edition, Volume 4, p. 144.
4 Ibid., p. 145.

When surveying the society, Marx objected to stay only and alone on the abstract graphs of the interactions of all factors but supported to distinguish the relations of different layers and explored the decisive factor of historical development.

Proudhon was a historical idealist, who ignored the objective reality of history, denied the chronological realistic history, treated abstract logical categories as the basis of realistic history and argued that the practical economic relations were the embodiment of economic categories. In this way, the objective history is just the decorative pattern on the base cloth of logical category.

Marx was against this view. In his opinion, economic category is a kind of logical structure existing in scientific thinking instead of an independent entity; it is derived rather than being native; it is the theoretical expression of relation of production, i.e. scientific abstraction. The fact is far from that economic relation adapts to and embodies an economic category, but it should be the other way around. In the productive process, people not only produce relation sof production, but also create corresponding principles, conceptions and categories according to their own social relations. Therefore, the order of economic categories in a thinking mind should reflect the internal relations of production. Otherwise, however well the order of logical categories is, it will be no more than the so-called order in an extremely chaotic mind. This kind of order is no scientific system but fiction.

The logical system of economic categories is not an absolutely closed system but is a logical system depending on relations of production. Then what decides relations of production? Marx did not go in circles from relations of production to economic categories, but went further starting from the relations of production to productive forces. Marx said, "Social relations are closely bound up with productive forces. In acquiring new productive forces men change their mode of production; and in changing their mode of production, in changing the way of earning their living, they change all their social relations. The hand-mill gives you society with the feudal lord; the steam-mill, a society with the industrial capitalist."[5] He also

---

5   Ibid., p. 144.

clearly stated that productive force and relations of production not only have coexisting and interdependent functional relation, but also have causal relationship, and productive force is the final decisive factor: "the mode of production, the relations in which productive forces are developed, are anything but eternal laws, but that they correspond to a definite development of men and of their productive forces, and that a change in men's productive forces necessarily brings about a change in their relations of production"[6]. In Marx's letter to Annenkov, he repeatedly highlighted this point. Though it is a complex process of productive forces' deciding and restricting relations of production and though its internal mechanism still awaits further studies, this kind of causal relation undoubtedly exists, which can be proved by the whole human history.

Productive force determines relations of production and they are indivisibly bound to each other. However, productive force itself forms a comparatively independent system. In *Manuscripts of 1844* ("Manuscripts" for short), Marx proposed that the concept of human's essential power embodies the content of productive force, which means the natural power owned by human such as desire, passion and labour is an objectified power. In *The German Ideology*, he emphasized on the functions of means of production and divided the means of production into two kinds: the means produced by nature (e.g. earth, water, etc.) and the means created by civilization (all kinds of instruments of labour); in *The Poverty of Philosophy*, apart from means of production, he paid special attention to the functions of the subject of labour—workers, and pointed out that "Of all the instruments of production, the greatest productive power is the revolutionary class itself"[7]. Thus, human and tools constitute the two basic factors of a productive force system.

However, a productive force is an organic structure rather than a mechanical combination of human and tools. Merely human and tools are just possible productive forces instead of real productive forces. In the practical process of production, productive force exists in a certain structure mode. This structure can be classified into two: The social structure and technical structure. The social structure is a

6   Ibid., p. 155.
7   Ibid., p. 197.

social mode combining human and tools, which includes ownership, division of labour and cooperation. Technical structure is the nature of the means of production and includes the level of labourers' using tools, for example, in manual labour, it is labourers who use tools, so the experience and skills of the labourers are a symbol of the level of productive forces; while in machine production, it is workers who operate and control machines, so science and technology are directly transferred into productive forces. Therefore, even with the same means of production, because of the differences in social structure and technical structure, the level of productive forces will also be different. Productive force is constantly developing, so the modes of structure of the factors of productive forces also keep changing. The functions of labourers in the process of production also change accordingly, from using more physical strength to using more intelligence and from directly participating in production to controlling and supervising machines, but we couldn't thus make a conclusion that the claims of Marx that human is the subject of production and that the most powerful productive force is the workers' class itself have already been obsolete ideas. In fact, no matter how completely robot takes over the direct labour of labourers, robot cannot be the subject of production at all but is merely the means of production and is the intermediate between labourer and the object of labour. A scientific and technical revolution only changes the technical structure of productive forces. It doesn't and also can't change the subject position of human.

Marx considered the society as a unified organic whole based on the inner contradiction of production mode. This point of view is totally different from the theory of social organism advocated in the western sociological theories. Some western sociological schools also treat the society as an organism, but they understand the human society according to the concept of biological organism, considering it as a self-regulating system like a biological organism and comparing all kinds of social systems to the organs and functions of an organism. For example, the sociologist E. O. Wilson from Harvard University combined sociology and biology together and explained social life with the New Darwinian evolution theory, directly applying the principles of biological evolution into society. Here natural selection and struggle for existence became important principles to explain social evolution. Undoubtedly, human society is the result and the supreme form of the development of organic lives, playing a very special role in the natural world. Anthropologically speaking, human beings are also faced with the problem to adapt to natural environment. However, different from animals, we humans neither passively rely on the nature nor adapt to the nature by changing our physical structure; we change the nature by labour and make the nature meet the demands of human existence. Therefore, social laws are different from biological laws, and social organisms are different from biological organisms. The society itself contains the opportunity and the source of motion and development. The social organism is the unity of contradiction, based on the inner contradiction of the mode of production rather than on the biological adaptation of human to nature.

Thus, in Marx's conception of history and in his investigation of history, social contradiction plays the leading role. The society develops and advances itself by solving the contradictions inside it. Marx commented on the capitalist society and said, "The production relations in which the bourgeoisie moves have not a simple, uniform character, but a dual character"[8]. And he also further pointed out, "The very moment civilization begins, production begins to be founded on the antagonism of orders, estates, classes, and finally on the antagonism of accumulated labour and actual labour. No antagonism, no progress. This is the law that civilization has followed up to our days. Till now the productive forces have been developed by virtue of this system of class antagonisms."[9] So any self-regulating function of social formations which are based on antagonism can only be to a limited degree. Though a social formation or a self-regulating function can regulate through all kinds of social controllers (political, legal, and moral), it could only ease the contradiction but couldn't get rid of the social contradiction. When the social contradiction gets intensified to a certain extent, the society will be out of control, brake valve will be ineffective act, and no regulation will be of any help. To over-exaggerate the self-regulating functions of

---

8   Ibid., p. 155.
9   Ibid., p. 104.

the society and absolutize the relative stability of western capitalist countries means that we could only see the temporary peace but not the latent undercurrents.

Marx criticized Proudhon's metaphysical historical views. Proudhon usually praised himself as an expert in dialectics proud of showing off his knowledge of Hegel dialectics, but actually he was a metaphysician, who mechanically divided the capitalist economic categories into two aspects: the good ones and the bad ones, trying to retain the good aspects and eliminate the bad ones by dialectic integration, which he thought was a dialectic motion. In fact, it isn't motion at all, and on the contrary, it is the end of motion. Proudhon applied this theory of contradiction conciliation into the field of politics and absolutized social balance. Just as Marx said, "He is exactly like the political doctrinaire who wants a king and a chamber of deputies and a chamber of peers as integral parts of social life, as eternal categories. Only he seeks a new formula with which to balance those powers."[10] Marx also criticized the bourgeois humanism and philanthropism according to dialectic historical conception for they both denied social contradiction, and they were "willing to preserve those categories expressing bourgeois relations rather than find the nature constructing these categories and admit the confrontations inseparable with these categories"[11].

In Marx's opinion, society is an organism containing inner contradictions and he studied this organism from the perspective of social structure. Relations of production is a kind of structure—the way in which humans combine and interact together; productive force is a kind of structure—the way in which the means of production and human beings combine together; similarly, all the super structures including all kinds of ideologies have their own specific ways of existence. However, Marx didn't treat the social structure as a pure form but as a way of being of human actions. He opposed Hegel's view that people were the self-realization tools of absolute ideas and he also opposed Proudhon's view of treating people as the tools of the self motions of laws, principles and categories, which was just a vulgarized copy of Hegel's view. Marx thought that Proudhon's

---

10   Karl Marx and Frederick Engels: Collected Works, 1st Chinese Edition, Volume 27, p. 486.
11   Karl Marx and Frederick Engels: Collected Works, 1st Chinese Edition, Volume 4, p. 157.

view was a theory of Manifest Destiny and in this mysterious theory, God's will becomes his engine driving the self motions of all economic categories.

As Marx stressed, history is the product of human activities. When studying history and on the historical realities of each era, we shouldn't put human activities aside or treat human beings as the passive tools of history; what we should do is to treat men "both as the authors and as the actors of their drama"[12]. This is an important idea put forward in *The Poverty of Philosophy* and is the fundamental principle to survey the subject-object relationship in history materialistically and dialectically.

Men are the authors of history. There is nothing in the human society that isn't the product of human actions. Relations of production are the product of human interactions, while productive forces are the capability of human to transform the nature; and others like science, literature and art are all created by human. It is impossible to imagine a history without human actions.

However, men are also the actors in this drama, which means in terms of the mode of human activity, he is active but the consequences of his activity is unpredictable and his acts are restrained. Just as the character in a play whose personality, behaviours and results are restricted by the play plot (the interactive relationship among the play's characters), human activity also has its passive side. All generations live and act under their given historical conditions. The stage of history is formed by the activities of the last generation, established and given. The existentialist theory strongly advocates "free choice", but actually this choice still has certain limits.

Marx asked, "Is man free to choose this or that form of society? By no means." Social forms always correspond to the existing level and nature of productive forces. "If you assume a given state of development of man's productive faculties, you will have a corresponding form of commerce and consumption. If you assume given stages of development in production, commerce or consumption, you will have a corresponding form of social constitution, a corresponding organization, whether of the family, whether of the estates or of the

---

12   Ibid., p. 149.

classes—in a word, a corresponding civil society. If you assume this or that civil society, you will have this or that political system, which is but the official expression of civil society."[13]

Are men free to choose a definite productive force? The answer will also be no. "Man is not free to choose his productive forces—upon which his whole history is based—for every productive force is an acquired force, the product of previous activity. Thus the productive forces are the result of man's practical energy, but that energy is in turn circumscribed by the conditions in which man is placed by the productive forces already acquired, by the form of society which exists before him, which he does not create, which is the product of the preceding generation"[14].

Therefore, social development has its own law which is independent of man's will. Individual's behaviours are purposeful and conscious, but the history formed by man's behaviours is purposeless and unconscious. As for human action, we can ask about the purpose; but as for social history, we can't ask about the purpose but only about the reason. The relations among social phenomena are not purposeful relations but causal ones. Each one's social behaviour reflects their purpose, but the results of the interaction of social phenomena always go beyond or violate people's purposes. We do researches on social history not to explore the purposefulness of history but to find the regularity of history itself. Of course, we humans are not the slaves of laws, which is also applicable to the field of history. To make use of laws, we must follow the laws. The subject who is not restricted by laws is only the imagined "ego" that could neither think nor act.

It is true that people are both the authors and the actors in the play, which, in the mind of metaphysicians is a "hard walnut" difficult to bite open. So it was for Proudhon, and as well as to the people in the contemporary western world who attack the historical materialism as economic materialism and historical determinism.

---

13   Karl Marx and Frederick Engels: Collected Works, 1st Chinese Edition, Volume 27, p. 477.
14   Ibid., p. 477-478.

2 HISTORY AND HUMAN NATURE. CRITERION FOR HISTORICAL EVALUATION

As in the mode of production, the ideology of each epoch also has its own features. The abstract humanistic conception of history rising step by step in the 14th century has widely spilled over into the fields of literature, art and morality and has played a leading role for quite a long time. Proudhon's view of history doesn't jump out of this circle though he tried hard to explain Ricardo's theory with abstract conception of equality and thereby drew conclusions to the benefit of labourers.

In *The Philosophy of Poverty*, Proudhon hypothesized the God did exist and assumed there was an unknowable power leading asterisms and atoms and rotating the whole universe; he even asserted that he "needs to establish the authority of social science by the assumption about God". In fact, Proudhon didn't allow the God to interfere in the mortal world. As other humanists in history, in terms of the problems about human and god, Proudhon also emphasized on the contradiction between human and god: "God is contradictory of man, just as charity is contradictory of justice; as sanctity, the ideal of perfection, is contradictory of perfectibility; as royalty, the ideal of legislative power, is contradictory of law, etc." Thus he put forward that "The true remedy for fanaticism, in our view, is not to identify humanity with God, which amounts to affirming, in social economy as communism, in philosophy as mysticism and the status quo; it is to prove to humanity that God, in case there is a God, is its enemy"[15].

Proudhon asserted: "I do not contradict humanism; I continue it"[16]. He abandoned his hypothesis about the existence of God in the preface of *The Philosophy of Poverty* and stated "henceforth to reproduce the theological hypothesis is to take a step backward in science. We must confine ourselves strictly to society, to man"[17]. In order to attest that his humanism is different from the abstract humanism, Proudhon even criticized the theory of original evil of human

---

15   Proudhon: The Philosophy of Poverty, Volume 1, p. 371, p. 380. Beijing: The Commercial Press, 1961.
16   Ibid., p. 371.
17   Ibid., p. 370.

nature believing human is born evil and argued against Rousseau's view that man is born good and against his idea that society and civilization make people degrade. He was also arguing against assuming people as abstract existence isolated from the reality, which he thought is "they abandon the reality to seize a projection; the true man is not the real man; to find the veritable man, the human ideal, we must leave time and enter eternity."[18]

In fact, Proudhon didn't go out of the range of abstract humanistic conception of history. He elaborated his theory of value by human and human needs. With careful investigation, it is easy for us to find that the human and needs that Proudhon mentioned are printed with obvious marks of abstract theory of human nature.

Proudhon paid great attention to the theory of value and considered "value is the corner-stone of the economic edifice", and "The fundamental idea, the dominant category, of political economy is value"[19]. In *The Philosophy of Poverty*, he used a whole chapter (Chapter 2) to explain the contradiction of value and thus started his exposition of the whole book. Proudhon divided value into three categories: value in use, value in exchange and comprehensive value (or named it social value). Pushed by self contradiction, useful value produces exchangeable value; they two interpenetrate and mutually absorb from each other, producing comprehensive value. And the motive power of useful value's transforming to exchangeable value is need.

From Proudhon's point of view, the needs of humans are quite various, but "Since, then, of the objects which I need, a very large number exist in Nature only in moderate quantities, or even not at all, I am forced to assist in the production of that which I lack; and, as I cannot turn my hand to so many things, I propose to other men, my collaborators in various functions, to yield me a portion of their products in exchange for mine. I shall then always have in my possession more of my own special product than I consume; just as my fellows will always have in their possession more of their respective products than they use. This tacit agreement is fulfilled by commerce[20]. According to the thinking process explained here, the

---

18   Ibid., p. 374.
19   Ibid., p. 62, p. 107.
20   Ibid., p. 63.

starting point is the isolated individuals cut off from the society. These Robinson-type individuals have many kinds of demand, then from these demands is division of labour derived and from the division of labour is exchange derived. However, the problem is: Away from the production of material goods and away from division of labour and exchange, why would an isolated person have so many needs? How are these needs produced? Taking this kind of need as his starting point, Proudhon went back to his old road: To natural man and taking man's nature as starting point.

Marx didn't deny the importance of people's needs. To eliminate people's demands from the historical materialism is equal to drive people away from the society, which is impossible to imagine. Made of flesh and blood, humans have some similarities with other animals, which are the needs to maintain the survival of human body. In *Manuscripts*, Marx affirmed this point. He said, "Hunger is a natural need; it therefore needs a nature outside itself, an object outside itself, in order to satisfy itself, to be stilled."[21] However, the natural needs of human are humanized (socialized) needs; both their contents and the modes to meet them are all determined by the state of production development and they are all the product of social and historical development.

What is especially important is that during the process of social and historical development, man keeps having new needs which are not determined by the nature of human but are the products of new production and living conditions. Production keeps producing needs for products. Therefore studies on needs shouldn't start from the nature of an isolated person. We should focus on production and on the development level of labour division and exchange so that the problems that how the various needs of mankind produce and how these needs react up on production can be explained; also we should study on relations of production, because by studying on the different positions of people in relations of production can we understand why different people have different needs. Thus, in *The Poverty of Philosophy*, Marx refuted Proudhon's view of proceeding from abstract needs and stressed that needs are "determined by his social

---

21 Karl Marx and Frederick Engels: Collected Works, 1st Chinese Edition, Volume 42, p.168.

position which itself depends on the whole social organization. True, the worker who buys potatoes and the kept woman who buys lace both follow their respective judgments. But the difference in their judgments is explained by the difference in the positions which they occupy in the world, and which themselves are the products of social organization." Marx also raised another question: "Is the entire system of needs on estimation or is it on the whole organization of production?" and then he gave a rather clear answer, "Needs arise directly from production or from a state of affairs based on production."[22]

If say need isn't determined by human nature but by the state of production development, then so does exchange. Proudhon tried to explain the origin of exchange was historical materialistically trying to explain it by the individual's suggestion to other people, but he couldn't make it clear how this single individual, "this Robinson, suddenly had the idea of making "to his collaborators" a proposal of the type known and how these collaborators accepted it without making the slightest protest"[23]. Actually, exchange doesn't originate from the suggestion of an individual to other people to meet his various needs; indeed, it depends on the level of production and labour division. Exchange has its own history and has gone through different stages. Once upon a time, for example, in the Middle Ages, only the surplus goods were exchanged because men produced more than they could consume; not until the capitalist society are all products put inside the range of commerce and even morality, love, belief, knowledge and conscience all become something that could be sold and bought..

Proudhon also treated competition from the view of the abstract theory of human nature.

Proudhon's views on competition did have their unique and excellent features. He saw the negative parts of capitalism—competition causes poverty, leads to civil wars, destroys freedom, and corrupts morality, but he also admitted the positive role competition plays and recognized the necessity of competition. He thought that as long

---

22   Karl Marx and Frederick Engels: Collected Works, 1st Chinese Edition, Volume 4, p. 86-87 and p. 87.
23   Ibid., p. 79.

as one product is sold by the only one manufacturer, the real value of this product will be a secret forever either because the manufacturer conceals the knowhow of the product, or the manufacturer doesn't pay adequate attention to or he just can't decrease the cost to the minimum, so, anyway, the privilege of production is a real loss to the society. And the publicity of industry, as competition between labourers, was a necessity, and all the Utopias ever imagined or any imaginable plans cannot escape this law. Proudhon even put forward an assumption to prove the necessity of competition.

He said, "Ordain that, beginning by January 1, 1847, labour and wages are guaranteed to all: immediately an immense relaxation will succeed the extreme tension to which industry is now subjected; real value will fall rapidly below nominal value; metallic money, in spite of its effigy and stamp, will experience the fate of the assignats; the merchant will ask more and give less; and we shall find ourselves in a still lower circle in the hell of misery in which competition is only the third turn."[24]

He even had an argumentation with some Fourierists about whether there would be competition in the future socialist society. According to Fourierists, there is a useful, praiseworthy, moral competition, a competition which enlarges the heart and the mind, a noble and generous competition, —it is emulation; and there is another competition, pernicious, immoral, unsocial, a jealous competition which hates and which kills, —it is egoism. Thus, emulation and competition are different. Proudhon didn't agree with this point of view, and he said, "They say: emulation is not competition. I note, in the first place, that this pretended distinction bears only on the divergent effects of the principle, which leads one to suppose that there were two principles which had been confounded." And he stated clearly that "Emulation is nothing but competition itself."[25]

Proudhon didn't deny the positive effects of competition and also predicted that competition would still exist in a socialist society, which is very inspiring. However, he mechanically divided competitions into good ones and bad ones, trying to eliminate the bad side of competition and keep its good side. This view is quite metaphysical

24   Proudhon: The Philosophy of Poverty, Volume 1, p. 186.
25   Ibid., p. 184.

especially when Proudhon didn't see competition as the peculiar economic phenomenon of commercial production but as an eternal category, hoping to find out the origin of competition from the nature of humans that will never change. He said, competition is "a principle of social economy, a decree of destiny, a necessity of the human soul", "man's life is a permanent war, war with want, war with nature, war with his fellows, and consequently war with himself"[26]. Proudhon used this view to explain the French bourgeois revolution against the trade associations, guilds and chamber of commerce in the Middle Ages, which had opposed all feudal privileges and advocated free competition. This view that boils down to the inner requirements of "human soul" was a kind of abstract theory of human nature.

In The Poverty of Philosophy, Marx objected Proudhon's view of competition. He said, "Mr. Proudhon, not understanding that the establishment of competition was bound up with the actual development of the men of the 18th century, makes of competition a necessity of the human soul, in partibus infidelium [literally, territory of the infidels; here, meaning, beyond the realm of reality]"[27]. What is worthy of mentioning is that Marx refuted Proudhon's views that reverse history and human nature and treat competition as an eternal human nature, putting forward the famous statement that "all history is nothing but a continuous transformation of human nature"[28].

Competition doesn't originate from the egotistic nature of human but is an economic phenomenon inherent in commodity economy. This secret won't be revealed until commodity production develops to its highest stage—the capitalist commodity production that sweeps up everything. In the capitalist market economy, competition is an objective law that is independent of man's will and has nothing to do with human nature. Whether moral or immoral, kind or cruel, greedy or generous, man or women, young or old, as long as this person doesn't abandon himself/herself to go bankrupt, he/she must compete in the capitalist market economy. This is the requirement of capital gain. Undoubtedly, to survey on its subject, capitalist

26 Ibid., p. 188 and p. 192.
27 Karl Marx and Frederick Engels: Collected Works, 1st Chinese Edition, Volume 4, p. 175.
28 Ibid., p. 174.

competition must go through the self awareness of private interest, showing itself as greed, desire and pursuit of profits, or in short, behaving as extreme egotism which is the inner demand of "human soul" as Proudhon said. Actually this so-called human nature is the refraction of history just as coin is poured out of its mold. Therefore, though in the commodity economy of socialism does exist competition, it no longer shows itself as greed, desire and extreme egotism but acts as self awareness of socialist economy laws that is the conscious pursuit of socialist economic benefit and of the interests of the whole; the partial and personal interests of direct operators are eventually included in the interests of collective. That is the transformation of history rather than that of human nature and that is the result of the changes of relations of production.

Marx also criticized Proudhon's idealistic conception of history which measures history with abstract concepts of equality.

In terms of cognitive subjectivity, there must be levels of measurement to measure things, and so is to evaluate history. However, it is far from enough to evaluate history with a single measure of value, that is, the extent to which objective historical phenomena accord with the interests and demands of cognitive subject (class and individual), and the most fundamental one is the law of history itself. In this way, the standards of measuring history are basically the views of history which highlight the nature of the conception of history.

As a representative of the thoughts of petty bourgeois, Proudhon is a contradiction himself, and so is his conception of history. He strongly opposed to use abstract moral views to evaluate economic relations, objected to "continually interject fraternity, charity, sacrifice, and God into the discussion of economic questions", and denounced fraternity, charity and sacrifice as "mysticism"[29]. However, he had never jumped out of the circle of idealistic conception of history. As he said, "For social order is established upon the basis of inexorable justice, not at all upon the paradisiacal sentiments of fraternity, self-sacrifice, and love, to the exercise of which so many honourable socialists are endeavouring now to stimulate the people"[30]. It is of no help to change the nature of the problem by replacing love and

29   Proudhon: The Philosophy of Poverty, Volume 1, p. 232.
30   Ibid., p. 86.

selflessness with justice and equality just like replace meter with inch.

As early as in 1840 when Proudhon published What Is Property, he assailed property with the basis of equality. "Property is theft" the very agitative slogan challenges what is considered eternal and sacred by bourgeois political economy. He did express his profound and sincere wrath to the evil of capitalist system, but his argument basis is wrong. No scientific exposition is made to explain the historical necessity of capitalist private property and the reasons why it must be replaced by attacking the private ownership of capitalist with equality and justice. Just as Engels said, "Proudhon uses the standard of 'Equality' to measure all social, legal, political and religious principles in all his works, and he spurns or admits these principles according to whether they accord with his so-called 'equality'"[31]. That does not explain history, but humiliates history by sweeping the whole history of human's private ownership to dump with the broom of "equality" so as to welcome the coming of the heaven of equality.

The view above gets further developed in Proudhon's The Philosophy of Poverty published in1846. The difference lies in that here he combined his conception of equality with the theory of value from the perspective of economics with the attempt to explain the labour theory of value of Ricardo in an equalitarian way to draw out the conclusion of establishing a new society on the basis of equal exchange. He repeatedly stressed that "equality alone is our rule, as it is also our ideal"[32] and considered equality as the equality in exchange and as the elimination of the contradiction embodied in value. So he said, "The theory of the measure or proportionality of values is, let it be noticed, the theory of equality itself"[33]. As long as all producers produce in strict accordance with the so-called correct proportionality relationship and exchange at a fair price which means to trade products for those of equal labour, then the society can be established on the basis of equality and justice. That day will surely come. Like a traveller who climbs from a deep valley to the summit along a leaning and winding road so bravely, unremittingly and persistently,

31   Karl Marx and Frederick Engels: Collected Works, 1st Chinese Edition, Volume 18, p. 306, Beijing: People's Publishing House, 1964.
32   Proudhon: The Philosophy of Poverty, Volume 1, p. 109.
33   Ibid., p. 86.

history is also advancing towards its goal of equality and justice after having gone through so many difficulties and inequalities.

Proudhon's measure of history with fairness, justice and equality, as the measure of abstract rationality or conception of kindness and evil, belongs to the abstract humanistic conception of history only in a different way of expression, which is a subjective measure and requires that history should be in accordance with its conception of morality and legal right. It discusses more about what history should be than about what history is. He believed he has found an eternal measure for history, but in fact people's conceptions of kindness and evil, justice and injustice, fairness and unfairness are extremely relative and constantly changing. And the basis of their changes is just the very object they measure.

Measure is comparison. To measure history is to compare history, so the measure of evaluating history must reflect the real process of history development. The history of human is first of all the history of the mode of production, which requires that the measures of history development could only be the development of production and production mode and the development of corresponding society, politics, culture, science and education, which could never be the abstract human nature or the eternal ideas of morality and rights. In *The Poverty of Philosophy*, taking an example of automatic workshop system, Marx illustrated this point. He said, "The automatic workshop opened its career with acts which were anything but philanthropic. Children were kept at work at the whip's end; they were made an object of traffic and contracts were undertaken with the orphanages. All the laws on the apprenticeship of workers were repealed, because, to use M. Proudhon's phraseology, there was no further need for synthetic workers. Finally, from 1825 onwards, almost all the new inventions were the result of collisions between the worker and the employer who sought at all costs to depreciate the worker's specialized ability. After each new strike of any importance, there appeared a new machine. So little indeed did the worker see in the application of machinery a sort of rehabilitation, restoration—as M. Proudhon would say"[34]. However, in the sight of

---

34 Karl Marx and Frederick Engels: Collected Works, 1st Chinese Edition, Volume 4, p 169.

Marx, that is a progress of history which cannot be washed away by the abstract conceptions of equality and justice, so he assailed that Proudhon, not understanding the revolutionary side of the automatic workshop so he should suggest workers take a step backward, "To sum up, M. Proudhon has not gone further than the petty-bourgeois ideal. And to realize this ideal, he can think of nothing better than to take us back to the journeyman or, at most, to the master crafts-man of the Middle Ages"[35]. The result of this case will necessarily be like this. To take the abstract conception of equality as a measure, he must embrace some romantic missing feelings about the past his-tory; and his yearning for the future is just an idealized painting with the yet lost equality as its blueprint.

After criticizing Proudhon in 1846, Marx conducted a debate with Karl-Heinzen in 1847. Marx refuted the idealistic conception of history of Heinzen and continued to make use of his achievements made in *The Poverty of Philosophy*.

Heinzen, who used to be a minor official of the Liberals, had already imagined the progress within the law and attempted to realize some kind of revolution within the Constitution in 1844. Forced to leave Germany because of publishing *The Prussian Bureaucracy*, he went to Switzerland and met Lugar there. Through Lugar, Heinzen accept-ed the abstract humanism of Feuerbach, the idealism of Hegel and the thoughts of Stirner. Heinzen's conception of history is idealistic.

Heinzen, transforming from the Liberals to the Radicals, combined the tradition of American Revolution and that of France in 1793 with the revolutionary measures he stole from communists and suggested that a German Democratic Republic similar to Switzerland should be founded in Germany. In order to glorify the imagined German Democratic Republic, Heinzen put it into the vulgarized humanistic framework of Feuerbach, declaring the republic would be the com-ing "kingdom of man". Heinzen even dreamt that without changing production mode or exchange mode, people could freely change and adjust their property relations and their right of inheritance; he ad-vertised that morality is the measure of history and propagated that society should be established on the basis of nobility, justice, moral-ity and other eternal truths.

---

35   Ibid., p. 172.

Heinzen's conception of history stands on the opposite side of the historical materialism established by Marx. In September 1847, Heinzen published an article on the *Deutsche-Brüsseler-Zeitung* attacking the communists. Immediately Engels wrote an article— "Communists and Karl-Heinzen" to refute him. Then Heinzen rudely flung abuses to Engels with the paper—"'One Representative' of Communists". For this reason, Marx wrote the paper "Moralizing Criticism and Critical Morality" which is neither a regular polemical article nor simply to fight off Heinzen's attack to Engels. Just for this case, then Heinzen's paper is worthy of no serious answer. What Marx wanted was to take advantage of this opportunity to give positive expositions to some important issues in historical conception such as the moral evaluation of history and the problem of human nature through analyzing the moralizing criticism and critical morality expressed in Heinzen's papers and Heinzen's prescription that "humanizes the society".

Marx refuted Heinzen's view that history and morality are opposites and historical development is betrayal in morality. To Marx, history is always advancing. All developments, whatever they are, can be seen as a series of different stages which are linked together by one negating another. Development inevitably contains negation, which is to negate the old form that has already been out of date. It is rather ridiculous to measure history with some obsolete moral views and to consider the development of history and the negation of new things to old things as betrayal.

The development of history itself will inevitably cause the changes of view of values and view of morality. With different moral standards and contents, there must be a different evaluation. A thing that is moral and noble in the eyes of the advanced class might be immoral and mean to the downfallen class. Especially when history faces a period of rapid change, derogatory words such as "moral degradation", "depravity of human hearts" and "moral bankruptcy" always become the moral basis on which the downfallen object to reforms. Thus Marx strongly criticized that Heinzen treated development as denying morality and called him as a "worthy philistine". Marx said, "*Denying!* With this catchword the philistine as critic can condemn any development without understanding it; he can solemnly set up his undevelopable undevelopment beside it as moral immaculate-ness. Thus the religious phantasy of the nations has by and large stigmatised history, by transposing the age of innocence, the golden age, into *pre-history*, into the time when no historical development at all took place, and hence no negating and no denying"[36]. If one stubbornly evaluates history with obsolete moral standards, then not history but his moral meanness—the protection of outdated social relationship will be reflected in the mirror.

Also Marx objected to Heinzen's view of reversing property relation and political power relation and using so-called equality and justice to measure property relation. Heinzen boiled the property relation under capitalist system whether it is just that one man possesses eve-rything while another man nothing down to "similar simplistic ques-tions of conscience and clichés about justice"[37].

In fact, the question of property has not much to do with equality, justice or morality, but it has always been the "vital question" for a particular class closely related with their material interests. With the development of production, under different historical conditions, the question of property will be expressed in very different forms. For example, In the English as well as the French revolution, the ques-tion of property presented itself in such a way that it was a matter of asserting free competition and of abolishing all feudal property relations, such as landed estates, guilds, monopolies, etc., because these relationships had been transformed into fetters for the industry which had developed from the 16th to the 18th century. Therefore, the abolition of feudal property relations was the vital question for the bourgeois class. Similarly, the abolition of bourgeois property rela-tions is a vital question for the working class. The question of prop-erty is a major social problem. Escaping from the field of economy to the field of morality, even if he had fired all his shells of moral outrage, he still couldn't make any scientific explanation of the na-ture and solutions of property relations.

More ridiculously, Heinzen thought "injustice in property relations is only maintained by power". He only focused on one side of the problem that is political power's protection to property relation, but

---

36   Karl Marx and Frederick Engels: Selected Works, 1st Edition, p. 169.
37   Ibid., p. 174.

he ignored that a certain political power appears on the basis of a certain ownership relationship, and its nature, function and its limits of effects is fundamentally decided by economic relationship. As Marx pointed out, "Incidentally, if the bourgeoisie is politically, that is, by its state power, 'maintaining injustice in property relations', it is not creating it. The 'injustice in property relations' which is determined by the modern division of labour, the modern form of exchange, competition, concentration, etc., by no means arises from the political rule of the bourgeois class, but vice versa, the political rule of the bourgeois class arises from these modern relations of production which bourgeois economists proclaim to be necessary and eternal laws"[38]. No matter how a bourgeoisie country adjusts and makes its administration "scientific", it will never maintain the property relation of capitalism forever. It could only ease the contraction for a while but couldn't settle it. As long as the economic conditions of implementing socialism revolution become mature, the day when the political rule of bourgeoisie is overthrown will soon come.

Marx also refuted Heinzen's abstract theory of human nature of eliminating class struggle by human nature. Heinzen attacked that communists made class struggles, inciting people to oppose each other. He said, "'The 'narrow-minded communist view' which only treats people in terms of 'classes' and incites them against one another according to their 'craft', is something I must confess I have been innocent of in my revolutionary propaganda, because I make allowance for the 'possibility' that 'humanity' is not always determined by 'class' or the 'size of one's purse'"[39].

This is a series of fallacies.

Class contradiction is not a matter of the size of purse not to mention the quarrels of crafts. The occupational division of labour is not the division of class. The size of purse is just a quantitative difference which could be the distinction within the same class; similarly, the distinction of class is by no means on the basis of crafts. The division of labour creates different types of work within the same class. And it is perfectly possible that what individual persons do is not always determined by the class to which they belong. Some members from

---

38   Ibid., p. 171.
39   Ibid., p. 182.

different classes can even join into the opposite camp, which is especially so in times of historical changes. For example, in the French bourgeois revolution time, a few noblemen transferred to the third estate. However, this fact couldn't change the nature of class struggle, because though these few noblemen betrayed their class, they didn't go beyond the class struggle but threw themselves into the struggle against the decayed noblesse led by the revolutionary class at that time—the bourgeoisie.

Heinzen, obliterating all class differences, emphasized on common humanity and persisted in making the opposite classes vanish in humanity, which is naturally fantasy. As Marx said, "However, if Herr Heinzen believes that whole classes which are based on economic conditions independent of their own will and are forced into the most virulent contradiction by these conditions, can by means of the quality of "humanity", which attaches to all men, shed their real relationships, how easy must it be for one particular prince to rise by the power of "humanity" above his "princely condition", above his "princely craft"[40]! Heinzen even tries to establish a man-oriented party that represents neither bourgeois nor proletariats—"party of man". How ridiculous the abstract theory of human nature has driven him!

Heinzen's remedy of "humanization of society" exposes his idealistic conception of history in a very intensive way. He opposed the French Bourgeois Revolution and condemned the Committee of Public Safety and the Jacobins supporting them as cold-blooded mobs, but boasts his assumed measures humanizing the society as a glary road to found the "best republic" for man, for good man, for humane man. Among all these measures, the most critical one is to properly adjust property relations on the basis of morality and justice.

To Heinzen, the capitalist property relations are unreasonable. Many people have nothing and even some basic necessities to survive, while some people accumulate millions of dollars of filthy lucre like a nobleman by plundering scantily-clothed proletariats. To make the society humane, one person could neither possess too much nor

---

40   Ibid., p. 183.

too little. Therefore, the minimum property and the maxim property of each citizen should both be guaranteed. It is this fair moral measure that Heinzen uses to settle all economic contradictions and humanize the society, which shows he knows nothing about political economy. Marx states, the private ownership of capitalism is anything but a simple relation, but the sum total of all bourgeois production relations, of which the most fundamental one is class relation, so to abolish private ownership is to eliminate class and to radically change the bourgeois production relation. It is a titanic historic change and is the product of all social activities. It is indeed more like an idiot's nonsense to achieve this great change by morally and automatically adjusting property relations. No wonder Marx would satirize him that "It is to the 'Incas' and 'Campe's Books for Children' that the great Karl Heinzen owes his recipes for the "humanization of society"[41]. Say his words can only coax kids.

3 PRODUCTION RELATIONS AND CLASS RELATIONS. DISCUSSION OF THE MATERIAL BASIS OF CLASS STRUGGLE

Besides criticizing Proudhon and Heinzen, Marx pays close attention to the wrong trends of thought in labour movements and follows the publicity activities among workers, elaborating his scientific views to workers in a positive way. *Wage Labour and Capital* includes several speeches Marx makes in the Association of German Workers. Though this book was serialized in the *Neue Rheinische Zeitung* in April 1849, its basic ideas still belong to 1847.

The establishment of historical materialism is inseparable with Marx's economic researches, which is well expressed in *Manuscripts*, *The German Ideology*, and *The Poverty of Philosophy*. Though *Wage Labour and Capital*, is one of his books of 1840s, some views in it are different from those in books written after 1859, and compared to his books later, some phrases or even whole sentences are improper and even incorrect such as mixing up selling labour and selling labour power, it is undeniably the first time that Marx positively and plainly publicizes and elaborates his economic views, and especially combines economic views with historical materialism, in

41 Ibid., p. 189.

which book Marx "portrays the economic conditions which form the material basis of the present struggles between classes and nations" by "examining more closely the economic conditions themselves upon which is founded the existence of the capitalist class and its class rule, as well as the slavery of the workers"[42]. With this book, He discusses about what is society, production relations and class relations as well as the nature of class struggle on the economic basis and deepens some important ideas of historical materialism.

When we examine any society, we see a network with an extreme number of human activities and relations. It is so bizarre and motley that our eyes are easily dazzled. However, as long as we go deeper into it, we could find out all these complex relations can be divided into two categories by and large: relations between man and nature, relations between man and man, while the core and basis by which to connect the two kinds of relations is material production. Marx said, "In the process of production, human beings work not only upon nature but also upon one another. They produce only by working together in a specified manner and reciprocally exchanging their activities. In order to produce, they enter into definite connections and relations to one another, and only within these social connections and relations does their influence upon nature operate, i.e., does production take place"[43]. Therefore, material production is the skeleton and ground-floor upon which the entire social edifice is built.

Marx seizes the decisive factor of the whole society. Different from the previous social outlooks either equating society with country, or seeing the society as the enlargement of family, or considering the society as a simplistic set of individuals, Marx grasps the essence of the society. He said, "We thus see that the social relations within which individuals produce, the social relations of production, are altered, transformed, with the change and development of the material means of production, of the forces of production. The relations of production in their totality constitute what is called the social relations, society, and, moreover, a society at a definite stage of historical development, a society with peculiar, distinctive characteristics.

---

42   Karl Marx and Frederick Engels: Selected Works, 1st Edition, Volume 1, p. 351 and p. 350.
43   Ibid., p. 362.

Ancient society, feudal society, bourgeois (or capitalist) society, are such totalities of relations of production, each of which denotes a particular stage of development in the history of mankind"[44]. This excellent elaboration of Marx not only reveals the common nature of different societies, but also uncovers its specific essence. However, both its commonality and its specificity are closely related with the analysis of production relation itself. Of course, this doesn't mean that to study the totality of production relations only can generalize the entire society with no need to examine other kinds of relations, such as political relations, moral relations, family relations, thought relations, and so on, but means to understand what is society and to master the nature and face of the society by and large, we must study the totality of its social relations. Except this way, there is no one available.

Just because Marx grasped the production relations, his examinations on man and objects all arise to a new scientific height and no longer stays at abstract humanism and fetishism. When he refutes escaping from the production relation and mixing up Negro and Negro slaves, he points out, "A Negro is a Negro. Only under certain conditions does he become a slave. A cotton-spinning machine is a machine for spinning cotton. Only under certain conditions does it become capital. Torn away from these conditions, it is as little capital as gold is itself money, or sugar is the price of sugar"[45]. This point of view, compared to the *Manuscripts*, is obviously a great leap.

In *Manuscripts*, Marx considered the alienation of men as the species-being estranged from man and man losses his human aspect because of alienation. Here, he stressed on the constraints of production relations. The reason that Negros became slaves falls into a certain production relation. Therefore, to explore the reason of Negros becoming slaves is not to explore his human nature but to study on the production relation at the specific historical stage. Only within the range of definite social relations and social connections could scientific explanation for this social phenomenon be made.

---

44   Ibid., p. 363.
45   Ibid., p. 362.

Similarly, in terms of the physical expression forms of capital, it is a form of substance including raw material, instruments of labour and means of subsistence, but its nature is still a social relation. Because the production material, the instruments of labour, and the raw material that constitute capital are all produced and accumulated within a definite production relation and under definite social conditions and will also proceed new production within the certain production relation and under the social conditions. The final product of all material production will be necessarily expressed as objects and as the totality of some material products, the process of which can reflect the nature of the social relation upon which the product is produced. It is a social property and has nothing to do with the natural property of the product. The physical expression of capital varies a lot, for example, we can replace wool with cotton, wheat with rice, railway with steamboats, but the nature of capital will be changed in the slightest. So Marx said, "Capital also is a social relation of production. It is a bourgeois relation of production, a relation of production of capitalist society."[46] The examined substance estranged from social relations is not the "substance" of historical materialism.

In the society, man can by no means be isolated since he must live within some social relations and social connections. As we have directly observed, man is individual, but indeed, man is collective, for it forms different groups. In a class society, this large social group is class. Class, as a kind of social group, different from the family relationship bound up with the ties of blood and also different from the neighbourhood relationship based on regions, is a group in which people combine with each other according to their different positions in their production relations. A certain production relation must have its corresponding class relation. The nature and structure of production relation determine the class structure of the society. In *Wage Labour and Capital*, grasping this fundamental point, Marx conducts an examination to the most basic class relations constituting the society of capitalism.

Workers are labourers. Labour is the life activity of a worker and is also the active expression of the worker's own life, but not all labourers are workers. According to Marx, labour is not always

---

46   Ibid., p. 363.

wage-labour and labour (power) is not always commodity. The slave did not sell his labour-power to the slave-owner, any more than the ox sells his labour to the farmer. He slave, together with his labour-power, was sold to his owner once for all. He is a commodity that can be sold on a market and can pass from the hand of one owner to that of another. He himself is a commodity, but his labour power is not his commodity. Serf, though selling part of his labour power to the land owner, can't get any wage but also have to pay tributes. A wage-labourer is different. He does not belong to any owner or to the land; he is free. He can and must sell his very self and that by fractions, selling some hours in his everyday life to the capitalists. He gets rid of the relationship of personal bondage and is a labourer free in form.

Also, capitalists are private owners, but not all private owners are capitalists. Slave owners and feudatories are owners, but they don't have any commodity exchange relation with their slaves or serfs. A capitalist is a capitalist not only because he is the owner of production material, but because he, through the relation of commodity, makes the active labour of workers as the means of maintenance and appreciation for the yet accumulated labour.

Like the South Pole and the North Pole of magnetic field, wage labour and capital, workers and capitalists, constrain each other and cannot live without each other. They are the products of the same production relation and are two opposite social groups formed due to their different positions in the production relation. Therefore, the relation between workers and capitalists are anything but the relation of individual to individual, but a class relation. Though their relation is always expressed through individuals, they don't interact with each other as individuals but as the members of a certain class. As Marx points out, "The worker leaves the capitalist, to whom he has sold himself, as often as he chooses, and the capitalist discharges him as often as he sees fit, as soon as he no longer gets any use, or not the required use, out of him. But the worker, whose only source of income is the sale of his labour (in the edition of 1891, labour was changed as labour-power), cannot leave the whole class of buyers, i.e., the capitalist class, unless he gives up his own existence. He does not belong to this or that capitalist, but to the capitalist class;

and it is for him to find his man – i.e., to find a buyer in this capitalist class"[47]. The modern bourgeois class eagerly advertise the creed of "love your family, love your factory" and spare no effort to cultivate a homey and intimate feeling of workers for capitalists, which may make the class relation less shrill for a while but could never change this relation radically. Capital will never represent labour. It is even harder to build a unified feeling and relation between these two than to make peace between a tiger and a lamb.

Through production relations, Marx not only finds the basis upon which capitalists and workers exist, but also finds out the origin of their antagonism, i.e. the material basis of their struggle. By analyzing the relation of wage and profit, Marx discovers that the antagonism between capitalists and workers are the antagonism of their fundamental interests and thus refutes the various viewpoints that advocate the consistent interests between capitalists and workers.

At that time, Marx hadn't made a clear distinction between labour and labour power, and hadn't formed the concept of surplus value or seen wage as the price of labour, but he had already seen that wage is the workers' labour income and is opposite to the profit relying on capital income. An outstanding expression of the antagonism is the inverse proportion relationship between wage and profit.

Marx divided wages as nominal wages and real wages. Nominal wage is the money price of labour (power), while real wage is the amount of commodities which are actually given in exchange for the wages. The problem is that the rise of nominal wage can cover the fall of real wage, and that neither nominal wage nor real wage can exhaust the relations which are comprehended in the term wages, because wages above all is determined by their relation with the profits of capitalists. Even if the real wage keeps the same or even gets a rise, the wages of workers, compared to the profits they create, still fall and the distribution of social wealth between capital and labour become even more unbalanced. "Profit and wages remain as before, in inverse proportion"[48], because if the proportion that capital covers, i.e. the profits, grows, the proportion of labour, i.e. the wages, will fall, vice versa. When the profits grow, then the wages fall; and

47   Ibid., p. 356-56.
48   Ibid., p. 370.

when the profits fall, then the wages grow. This is an antagonistic contradiction. That's why Marx said, "We thus see that, even if we keep ourselves within the relation of capital and wage-labour, the interests of capitals and the interests of wage-labour are diametrically opposed to each other"[49].

Marx also refuted many theories that blot out the opposition between capital and labour. Though the viewpoints were once popular a hundred years ago, his criticism of them still has important theoretical and practical meanings. In the modern world, the views refuted by Marx still keep appearing in various forms and still can confuse many people especially because the capitalism is in a relatively peaceful and stable time.

First, "the fatter capital is the more will its slave be pampered"[50]. According to this claim, the interests of capital and the interests of labour are consistent and the growth of productive capital and the rise of wage are mutually coordinated, which are strongly objected by Marx. He emphasized that the more productive capital grows, the more it extends the division of labour and the application of machinery; the more the division of labour and the application of machinery extend, the more does competition extend among the workers, the more do their wages shrink together. Especially because of the increase of productive capital and the fierce competition, the capitalists are compelled to exploit the already existing gigantic means of production on an ever-increasing scale, and for this purpose to employ all the credit agencies, which as a result makes economic crises more and more frequent, in the midst of which a large number of workers just like the ancient poor slaves buried together with their owner's corpse will be dragged into the tomb of the crisis due to unemployment and hunger.

It is true that with the increase of productive capital and the development of productive force, social wealth, social needs and social pleasures will grow accordingly. The quality and the quantity of the consumer goods that workers get can also have some change compared with the past, but this couldn't prove the consistency of the profits of capital and labour. As Marx stated, "Our wants and pleasures have

49   Ibid., p. 371.
50   Ibid., p. 373.

their origin in society; we therefore measure them in relation to society; and we do not measure them in relation to the objects which serve for their gratification. Since they are of a social nature, they are of a relative nature."[51] For example, no matter how small a house is, it can always satisfy people's needs for a residence when all the houses around it are of the same small size; but once a palace towers aloft near the small house, the petty one will shrink to the size of a poor bothy. Therefore, even the production develops itself, the things that the workers can get still decrease than increase compared with what the capitalists get and with the average social development state. "If, therefore, the income of the worker increased with the rapid growth of capital, there is at the same time a widening of the social chasm that divides the worker from the capitalist"[52]. The views that claim the workers have an interest in the rapid growth of capital only mean this: the more the workers augment the wealth of the capitalists, the larger the scraps will be which fall to their mouths. This is the "improvement" of the life of slaves. An enlightened worker will by no means sing the praises of his own slave position.

Second, "those labourers who have been rendered superfluous by machinery find new venues of employment"[53]. There is nothing like that in the reality. Unemployment is inevitable in the capitalist system. The workers who find new jobs are not all the laid-off workers but are always the young workers who are new into the labour market. Even the machinery industry that accommodates the largest number of labourers also began to force its workers out because of its increasingly extensive application of machinery, not to mention the constant supplement of the bankrupt people from other ranks and classes. Thus the hands stretching out and begging for jobs become denser and denser as a large forest, but the hands themselves become thinner and thinner. As the flowing water needs a "reservoir", the flowing labour of capitalist society also needs a "man reservoir"— an army of the unemployed. It is still the same nowadays. It is nothing but a myth that the workers forced out of the so-called "sunset industries" can all find jobs in the so-called "sunrise industries"— the newly emerging industries.

---

51   Ibid., p. 368.
52   Ibid., p. 372.
53   Ibid., p. 378.

Third, "the profit of the capitalist may also rise through improvements in the instruments of labour, new applications of the forces of nature, and so on"[54], which means that it is not labour but the new instruments of production and the application of scientific technology that create value and bring more profits for the capitalists. Marx had already refuted this view long time ago. He said, "The improvements of machinery, the new applications of the forces of nature in the service of production, make it possible to produce in a given period of time, with the same amount of labour and capital, a larger amount of products, but in no wise a larger amount of exchange values." "Whatsoever proportion the capitalist class, whether of one country or of the entire world-market, distribute the net revenue of production among themselves, the total amount of this net revenue always consists exclusively of the amount by which accumulated labour has been increased from the proceeds of direct labour."[55] However great science technology develops, whether it realizes automation or informatization, it could only change the proportion of the spent physical strength and intelligence in workers' labour, but couldn't overthrow the scientific conclusion that labour is the only source of value. In this way, the application of scientific technology in production under the capitalist system, though advancing production and beneficial for the progress of the society, still intensifies exploitation rather than reduce it.

It can be indicated from the above that the antagonism between the bourgeoisies and the proletariats is rooted in the essence of the bourgeois production relation, and is expressed through the contradiction of profits and wages as the antagonism of material profits, which can never be solved by any kind of empty moralization. It is a historical materialistic point of view, diametrically different from the idealistic conception of history that blots out material interests from history and excludes the class struggle based on the antagonism of material interests.

---

54 Ibid., p. 370.
55 Ibid., p. 371.

INTO THE DEPTHS OF HISTORY

4 HISTORICAL MATERIALISM: CORE OF THE COMMUNIST MANIFESTO

The Communist Manifesto is the scientific program made by Marx and Engels for the Communist League and written from December 1847 to January 1848, which highly embodies the important achievements of Marx and Engels in philosophy, economics, and scientific socialism in the late 1840s, among which the most especial one is historical materialism.

As Engels has pointed out many times, the fundamental idea consistent in *The Communist Manifesto* is historical materialism. The first Italian Marxist Antonio Labriola also laid stress on this point. In Antonio's famous essay in memory of *The Communist Manifesto*, he said, "The vital part, the essence, the distinctive character of this work are all contained in the new conception of history which permeates it and which in it is partially explained and developed. By the aid of this conception, communism, ceasing to be a hope, an aspiration, a remembrance, a conjecture, and expedient, found for the first time its adequate expression in the realization of its very necessity, that is to say, in the realization that it is the outcome and the solution of the struggles of existing classes"[56]. It is true that in *The Communist Manifesto*, Marx realized an excellent application of historical materialism to study all the modern history, and to analyze the structure of capitalism society. He got rid of abstract moral laws, divine rights, eternal rationality and the eternal truths of equality, justice and fairness, explaining the laws of history from history itself. *The Communist Manifesto* expresses the scientificalness and practicalness of historical materialism in an extremely vivid, evident and unanswerable way, indicating that it is the only scientific conception of history and methodology.

Marx firmly held that the major economic productive mode and the exchange mode of each era and the social structure definitely produced by which are the basis upon which the political history and the spiritual history of this era are established. He sought for the reasons of the bourgeoisie's emergence and development through the changes of the mode of material production, pointing out that

---

56 Antonio Labriola, Historical Materialism, p. 5, Beijing: People's Publishing House, 1984.

"the modern bourgeoisie is itself the product of a long course of development, of a series of revolutions in the modes of production and of exchange"[57].

Marx, when trying to figure out why the original chartered burghers would spring from the serfs in the Middle Ages and why the first element of the bourgeoisie would emerge from the burgesses, kept holding economy as the leading clue and closely combines it with the development of production, the increase of demands, and the extension of the world market, due to which reason, the gigantic modern industry took over manufacture, steam and machinery revolutionized industrial production, and the place of the industrial middle class was taken by the industrial millionaires, the leaders of the whole industrial armies. What is worthy of special attention is that Marx noticed the function of geographical factors and affirms the significance of the discovery of America and the sailing bypassing Africa to the development of capitalism in the Western Europe. However, different from the determinism of geographical environment, he didn't consider the geographical environment as an existing factor that can determine the society from outside, but examined the functions of geographical factors from the perspective of social development. The reason why the discovery of America and the sailing route bypassing Africa are possible and can influence the development of capitalism is that they both fit in with the needs of the newly emerging bourgeoisie to open up new activity places. It is not the geographical conditions but the development of industry that establishes the world market well prepared by the discovery of America.

Marx hadn't ignored the effects of politics, but he insisted on historical materialism and considered that the expansion of political force and the strength of economic power are inseparable. Each step in the development of the bourgeoisie was accompanied by a corresponding political advance of that class in accordance with its economic status. For example, it was an oppressed class under the sway of the feudal nobility, an armed and self-governing association in the medieval commune in Italy and France, a counterpoise against the nobility in a hierarchy monarchy or in an absolute monarchy, and even the

---

57   Karl Marx and Frederick Engels: Selected Works, 1st Edition, Volume 1, p. 252.

main foundation of a large monarchy. Of course, there is no absolute balance between economy and politics, and between the two always lurk contradictions, but the condition that the bourgeoisie rules the society in economy but is ruled in politics won't last long. In the end, the economic force will destroy the dated political force. Once establishing gigantic industries and world markets, the bourgeoisie will dethrone the feudal nobilities, set foot on the palace of the so-called bourgeois republic and become the dictator.

Marx used the historical materialism to analyze the structure of the capitalist society when refuting the various blames of the bourgeoisie to the communism.

Instead of being established on the basis of the general ownerships, the capitalists was established on the basis of the capitalist private ownership of class antagonism and some people exploiting the other part. The educational system, family relationship, and all the conceptions of religion, morality, philosophy, politics and laws in the capitalist society all fit in with this relationship.

When someone said to eliminate the bourgeois education was to eliminate all educations, Marx showed his objection to this view. He emphasized that education is determined by the society and by the social relation by which men use to educate. The bourgeois education, to most people, just trains man to be machine. Also, the nature of family relationship relies on social relations. In the capitalist society, the modern bourgeois family is based on capital and on private property; while all the family relations of the proletariats have been destroyed by the development of great industry and their children gradually become commerce objects and the instruments of labour. The so-called freedom in the capitalist society is the free within the bourgeois relations of production in the final analysis and is the reflection of free competition in the field of thought. The bourgeois relations of production with core of the private ownership of production material, like a light, shine in every aspect of the capitalist society and paint the society with its specific colour. That's why Marx said, "Man's ideas, views, and conception, in one word, man's consciousness, changes with every change in the conditions of his material existence, in his social relations and in his social life"[58]. When he replied to those separating the bourgeois conceptions about freedom, education and law from the bourgeoisie society, he said, "Your very ideas are but the outgrowth of the conditions of your bourgeois production and bourgeois property, just as your jurisprudence is but the will of your class made into a law for all, a will whose essential character and direction are determined by the economical conditions of existence of your class"[59].

Does Marx hold a negative attitude to the entire capitalist society? No. Marx sees the communist revolution as a clean break with the traditional ownership (private property) and traditional conception (conception of private property), so it is totally understandable of his emphasizing on the capitalist social evils, but his analysis of the capitalist society is not only materialistic but also dialectic. The conception of historical materialism itself contains dialectics, i.e. the historicism attitude to history. Lenin praised that *The Communist Manifesto* "has done a great job of describing a new world outlook thoroughly and outstandingly, narrating the thorough materialism including social life, and elaborating dialectics—the most comprehensive and most profound development theory"[60].

Marx affirmed "the bourgeoisie, historically, has played a most revolutionary part"[61]. Engels thought the comment "does full justice"[62]. If to examine from the process of history development, the bourgeois system does have exerted significant positive effects on the development of human history.

First of all, "The bourgeoisie, during its rule of scarce one hundred years, has created more massive and more colossal productive forces than have all preceding generations together"[63]. Yes, the capitalist society taking the place of the feudal society greatly emancipated the productive forces. With subjection of Nature's forces to man, machinery, application of chemistry to industry and agriculture,

---

58   Ibid., p. 270.
59   Ibid., p. 268.
60   The Complete Works of Lenin, 1st Chinese Edition, Volume 21, p. 30, Beijing: People's Publishing House, 1959.
61   Karl Marx and Frederick Engels: Selected Works, 1st Edition, Volume 1, p. 253.
62   Ibid., p. 249.
63   Ibid., p. 256.

steam-navigation, railways, electric telegraphs, clearing of whole continents for cultivation, and gigantic productive forces slumbered in the lap of social labour, the capitalist society was like a relieved Prometheus. At that time, the bourgeoisie was an advanced class and of all bourgeois classes, the industrial bourgeoisie played the leading role.

Second, the bourgeoisie started its process of "worldlization", subjecting the country to the rules of town, the agricultural nations to the rule of industrial nations. In a word, "it creates a world after its own image"[64].

When developing its industry, the bourgeoisie has created enormous cities and made city population dramatically outnumber rural population, which is the process that countries went bankrupt and got plundered by cities, full of pain and cheat. However, just as for its objective functions, thanks to it, a quite large number of residents got rid of the ignorance of rural life and were thrown and involved by the torrent of industrial civilization. It is preordained by the history that to enter in "the heaven", human must go through the suffering of "the purgatory".

The bourgeoisie also started The Crusades to open up its markets in the world with not only cannons but also cheap commodities as its weapons. The bourgeoisie was not the peace envoy who spread science and "civilization'; the colonial history of capitalism is a piece of ugly history full of blood and fire, but it unintentionally broke up the regional and national self-sufficiency and self-seclusion state in the past and strengthened both the material communication and spiritual communication among different nations, outdating the one-sidedness and boundedness of the nations. Therefore, the rise of capitalism opened up the real "world history", which, seen from the perspective of historical development, is a progress of the time.

Third, the bourgeoisie replaced the outdated feudal values with its values. The bourgeoisie, wherever it has got the upper hand, has put an end to all feudal, patriarchal, idyllic relations. It breaks the big family structure where generations live together to pieces, tears off the sentimental veil of family, and reduces the family relation

---

64   Ibid., p. 255.

to a mere money relation. It makes money as the universal measure value, drowns the feudal ethical ideas in the ice water of egoism. It sweeps the concept of feudal scholar-officials that "to be a scholar is to be the top of the society" and degrades the scholars who have been respected for generations as the labourers that can hired with money.

The bourgeoisie also developed the conception of free competition, which is determined by their relations of production. Adhering to past practices, sticking to traditional rules, afraid of reformations, conserving the old mode of production without any change, these are all the features of small producers, the bourgeoisie couldn't survive unless they constantly revolutionize the instruments of production and thereby their production relations and even the entire social relations. Just as Marx described, "Constant revolutionizing of production, uninterrupted disturbance of all social conditions, everlasting uncertainty and agitation distinguish the bourgeois epoch from all earlier ones."[65]

It is the most common law in the universe that things that oppose each other also complement each other. All comments are comparatively spoken. The historical advancement and revolutionary functions of the bourgeoisie couldn't stand away from its relation to feudal systems. The victory of the bourgeoisie against the feudal class is the victory of rationality against superstition, science against ignorance, bourgeois jurisdiction against feudal privilege, free competition against feudal guide, accumulation against extravagance, avarice against indulgence. However, in the advancement of the bourgeoisie contains irresistible contradictions, because the capitalism's taking the place of the feudalism is one exploiting system taking over another and is "for exploitation, veiled by religious and political illusions, it has substituted naked, shameless, direct, brutal exploitation"[66].

The greatness of Marx lies in that he conducted a historical evaluation of the bourgeoisie rather than an unprincipled praise. To describe the past is to describe the present. Marx examined the bourgeoisie from the whole process of its emergence, development and doomed death

---

65 Ibid., p. 254.
66 Ibid., p. 253.

and treated its historic function as a link out of a whole process, which is real historicism and thorough historical dialectics. Based on this conception of history, through the analysis of the inner contradictions contained in capitalism itself, Marx got the conclusion that "its fall and the victory of the proletariat are equally inevitable"[67].

The historical materialism in *The Communist Manifesto* is also evidently expressed in Marx's criticism of all kinds of socialism ideological trends. It is more than the criticism of one political theory against another, but the opposition of two conceptions of history.

All the socialisms will inevitably criticize capitalism as the common feature by which they are called socialist ideological trends. However, with different stands and starting points, they thus have different measures to evaluate the capitalist society. Actually they are more like measures scaling themselves than measures scaling objects. Through the measures, instead of the real process of history, what we can see are various backward idealistic conceptions of history.

The feudal socialism and the petty-bourgeois socialism are all backward conceptions of history that measure the capitalist production mode with feudal or petty-bourgeois scales. The feudal nobilities defeated by the bourgeoisie pretended to care about the worker class and denounced the bourgeoisie in order to win sympathy. But in their articles that were "half lamentation, half lampoon; half an echo of the past, half menace of the future", they boasted of the superior of feudal exploiting mode and how their exploiting mode was different from the capitalist ones. They took the emergence of the revolutionary proletariats as a reason why capitalism must go back to feudalism. The petty-bourgeois socialism "uses, in their criticism of the bourgeois régime, the standard of the peasant and petty bourgeois"[68]. The petty-bourgeois socialists were squeezed out by big industries and were constantly thrown into the troops of proletariats. Sometimes they could also incisively analyze the contradictions in modern relations of production, but they attempted to recover the old production material and exchange means so as to recover the old ownership system and old society, or tried to force the modern

---

67   Ibid., p. 263.
68   Ibid., p. 276.

production material and exchange means into the frameworks of the old ownership system that had already been broken. The two socialist ideological trends mentioned above have different political meanings, but historically speaking, they are all backward.

The Critical-Utopian Socialism and Communism bear different political and historical significances. The originators of these systems were revolutionary in many respects, and many of their active suggestions and practical measures about the future society were valuable genius conjectures, but, from the perspective of historical conception, they completely developed the rationalism of the French Enlightenment School in the 18th century and thinking comprehension became the only standard evaluating all, man's brain and by which the principles were discovered were claimed to be the basis upon which all human activities and the society were combined together. Just as *The Communist Manifesto* pointed out when criticizing their conception of history, "Historical action is to yield to their personal inventive action; historically created conditions of emancipation to fantastic ones; and the gradual, spontaneous class organization of the proletariat to an organization of society especially contrived by these inventors. Future history resolves itself, in their eyes, into the propaganda and the practical carrying out of their social plans."[69]

What's worthy of special attention is that Marx considered German or "true" socialism as "meaningless speculation about the true society and about realizing the essence of man"[70]. Marx disproved their historical conception with the standard of human essence and criticized that they saw money relation as the "Alienation of Humanity" and the criticism of the bourgeois state as "Dethronement of the Category of the General", and that they claimed to represent "not the interests of the proletariat, but the interests of Human Nature, of Man in general"[71], and so forth. It is a clear side-taking of Marx after *The German Ideology* to take humanity as standard of history and to explain socialism with the estrangement and regression of humanity.

---

69   Ibid., p. 282.
70   Ibid., p. 277.
71   Ibid., p. 278.

5 HOLD THE KEY TO HISTORY OF CLASS SOCIETY

Engels spoke highly of class struggle as a great historical law, believing the class struggle is to the history of class society what the law of conservation of energy to natural science and considering the class struggle as the key to understand the whole history of class society. One of the most outstanding contributions of *The Communist Manifesto* to historical materialism is that it revealed this law by concluding history and especially the history of capitalist society and rose to the height most allowable under that history conditions in 1848.

Marx was not the first one who found class struggle. He affirmed the economic analysis of class of the English classical economists and admitted the efforts of the French historians in the Restoration time of realizing class struggle and using it to understand French history. Marx spoke highly of Thierry and called him as "the Father of Class Struggle of French historiography". However, none of their achievements can be paralleled to Marx's. Only Marx could examine class and class struggle from the production mode and exchange mode of each era and the social structure thereby produced and transform the theory of class struggle as scientific conception of history and methodology. Undoubtedly it had to go through a long process. From pleading for the poor peasants in *Rheinische Zeitung* to explaining the historic tasks of the proletariats in *German-French Annals*, from *Manuscripts*, *The Holy Family*, *The German Ideology*, to *The Communist Manifesto*, the theory became more and more profound. Though a few individual judgments in *The Communist Manifesto* are not perfect yet, with its analysis on class struggle both from history and reality, it not only unfolded a grand picture of class struggle history, but also gave a careful description of the features of the class struggle in the capitalist society, pointing out a leading clue for man to understand the complicated and confusing history and reality.

From the perspective of historical development, Marx conducted a longitudinal investigation on class struggle, pointing out, "The history of all hitherto existing society is the history of class struggles"[72]. Later this statement was corrected by Marx and Engels. In the end

---

72   Ibid., p. 250.

of 1847 when they were writing *The Communist Manifesto*, the pre-history of society, the social organization existing previous to recorded history, still kept unknown. Since then, August von Haxthausen (1792-1866) from Prussia discovered the common ownership of land in Russia, Georg Ludwig von Maurer (1790-1872) proved it to be the social foundation from which all Teutonic races started in history, and, by and by, village communities were found to be the primitive form of society everywhere from India to Ireland. Not until the outstanding American scholar Morgan (1818-1881) found the real nature of nation and its relation to tribes and discovered the typical form of the inner organizations of primitive communist society was the fact laid bare that only with the dissolution of primitive communes did the society begin to be divided into the unique and mutually opposite classes.

The mistakes of the judgments mentioned above in *The Communist Manifesto* don't exert much influence on Marx's analysis on class struggle. It has been proved that Marx does make significant achievements in the historical investigation on class struggle.

Firstly, Marx declared, "Freeman and slave, patrician and plebeian, lord and serf, guild-master and journeyman, in a word, oppressor and oppressed, stood in constant opposition to one another, carried on an uninterrupted, now hidden, now open fight, a fight that each time ended, either in a revolutionary reconstitution of society at large, or in the common ruin of the contending classes"[73]. Here Marx briefly and concisely made clear the relation between social structure and class structure—each social form has its own specific basic classes; uncovered the nature of the opposing classes—oppressor and oppressed; uncovered the driving force that makes the whole society revolutionized—class struggle; revealed the laws of class struggle—the intensification of contradictions has a process from hidden fight to open fight, and so forth.

Secondly, Marx differentiated class and social rank. He said, "In the earlier epochs of history, we find almost everywhere a complicated arrangement of society into various orders, a manifold gradation of social rank." For example, in ancient slave society, there were

---

73   Ibid., p. 251.

patricians, knights, plebeians, slaves; in the Middle Ages of feudal society, feudal lords, vassals, guild-masters, journeymen, apprentices, serfs. Classes can't be equated with ranks. Class is determined by the different economic positions of people in their social relations, while ranks are the groups ordered by laws that have different identities and rights. In almost all of the slave societies and the feudal societies, again, there were subordinate gradations. The strict hierarchy built a trapezoidal frame inside the society and thereby covered class relations. Marx's distinction and relationship between classes and ranks enable us to see class from the distinctions of ranks and see ranks from the distinctions of class, providing a clear and definite class picture of the complicated relationships of affiliation in the slave societies and the feudal societies.

Thirdly, Marx showed us the common features of the ideologies in class societies. According to Marx, the history of all past society has consisted in the development of class antagonisms, and each epoch has its own special class relations in which lies the differences of class societies. "But whatever form they may have taken, one fact is common to all past ages, viz., the exploitation of one part of society by the other. No wonder, then, that the social consciousness of past ages, despite all the multiplicity and variety it displays, moves within certain common forms, or general ideas, which cannot completely vanish except with the total disappearance of class antagonisms"[74]. Marx offered us the guidance to investigate the history of ideology with the views of class and elaborated why some forms of social ideology, religious conceptions, and private ownership conceptions will transform into an ineradicable "tradition", which is not because of the commonality of human nature but because private ownership and class oppression are the common historical environment of the human societies for the past thousand years.

Marx not only studied on the class struggles in the history longitudinally, but also made special efforts on analyzing the reality of the bourgeois class struggle. By taking into serious consideration the inner contradictions existing in the bourgeois production mode, he did a historical materialistic analysis of the features, the laws and the final result of the class struggle of the capitalist society.

---

74   Ibid., p. 271.

In Marx's mind, the modern capitalist society spouting from the ruins of the feudal society hasn't eliminated class antagonism, but he highlighted that the capitalist society "has but established new classes, new conditions of oppression, new forms of struggle in place of the old ones"[75]. And the researches on the new classes, new conditions of oppression and new forms of struggle are consisted in the unique contents of Marxism about the bourgeois class struggle.

The class relation of the capitalist society rids itself of the rank features of the previous slave societies and feudal societies and is directly expressed as class antagonism. And the class relation of the capitalist society is also being simplified gradually, "society as a whole is more and more splitting up into two great hostile camps, into two great classes directly facing each other—Bourgeoisie and Proletariat". The previous middle class has also been split up. Failing to compete with the larger capitalists, the lower part of the middle class including petty industrialists, small merchants and rentiers, handicraftsmen and peasants joined in the team of the Proletariats. The simplification of class relation means the intensification of social contradiction.

Marx settled the revolutionary status of the Proletariats through comprehensively analyzing the conditions of each class in the bourgeois society. He distinguished the Proletariats with the lumpenproletariats, and claimed that the latter one as the passive and rotting part in the lowest layer of the old society, may here and there, be swept into the movement by a proletarian revolution; but attributed to their conditions of life, they were more willing to play the part of a bribed tool of reactionary intrigue. He also analyzed the conditions of the middle class—petty industrialists, small merchants and rentiers, handicraftsmen and peasants, exposing their contradictions with the bourgeoisie and their dual characters of revolution and conservation. He said, "The proletariat alone is a really revolutionary class. The other classes decay and finally disappear in the face of Modern Industry; the proletariat is its special and essential product"[76]. His judgment was in relation to the Western European countries with relatively developed bourgeois production at that time. For China

---

75   Ibid., p. 251.
76   Ibid., p. 261.

with the agricultural population as the majority, it is by no means advisable to underestimate the revolutionary power and functions of the peasants as the allies of the Proletariats.

Furthermore, Marx, through analyzing the different stages that the Proletariats have gone through against the bourgeoisie, uncovered the laws of the Proletariats transforming from class-in-itself to class-for-itself. The Proletariat opposing the bourgeoisie started from individual workers, then the workers of a factory, then the workers of the same labour department in a certain place, and by and by became national fights; developed from dispersed unorganized struggles to organizations and even a class and then founded parties; from breaking down machines, burning factories to realizing their own fundamental rights and thereby seized the power. That is the common law of the labour movements of different countries; however, after the birth of Marxism, this process has been greatly shortened, so not every country must repeat the long arduous road the Western European workers went.

In *The Communist Manifesto*, from the perspective of occurrence, Marx did not realize the correlation between the emergence of class and a certain stage of production development but saw the whole human history as the history of class struggle. But he had already seen that class won't exist forever and when the Proletariats, by use of their political supremacy, wrest all the capital of the bourgeoisie step by step, concentrate all means of production in the hand of the State, i.e. the proletariats organized as the ruling class, and increase the total productive forces as rapidly as possible, the class difference will disappear: "In place of the old bourgeois society, with its classes and class antagonisms, we shall have an association, in which the free development of each is the condition for the free development of all"[77]. Marx's ideas that take "to to increase the total productive forces as rapidly as possible" as an important condition to eliminate class and consider the rise of the proletariats to be the ruling class as the transition to a classless society are quite profound, which contain the famous viewpoints in his letter to Joseph Wedemeyer in 1852.

---

77   Ibid., p. 273.

The theories about class and class struggle in *The Communist Manifesto* are still right in its basic ideas. Though after the WWII especially in the past few decades, the major capitalist countries have seen a rapid development of science and technology and thus brought along some new features of class relations, but this fact doesn't refute but prove the theories of Marx about class and class struggle.

According to Marx's views, production relation determines class structure. Each society has its basic classes determined by its production relations. Of course, in capitalist societies, the members of each class or each rank won't keep fixed. With the rapid development of modern productive forces and the intensifying competition, this flowability becomes more and more obvious, but it can't be used to blot out the class antagonism in capitalist societies. In fact, in a capitalist society, occupations and the types of works within the same class flow much more than those between classes. Even the flowing among the class members can't and won't lead to the change of social class structure. In the capitalist society based on bourgeois private ownership, there must consist in the antagonism and struggle between the bourgeoisie and the proletariats. To take a certain worker's legend of becoming a millionaire as the show window of the fantasy that every worker can ascend to the status of the bourgeoisie by "flowing" is nothing but to cover the real class antagonism with an abstract possibility.

The class relations of the capitalist society become simplified and the law of its splitting up into two opposing classes doesn't change. The popular viewpoints in the western world are untrue that the capitalist society is faced with the expanding trend of the "middle class" and by the trend, class antagonism will be eliminated. Undoubtedly, the development of scientific technology will change the industrial structure and the occupational structure, e.g. the decrease of "blue-collar" workers simply doing in physical labour and the increase of skilled technical workers (the so-called "white-collar" workers) and the managerial stratum appearing because of managerial modernization and scientification, and so forth are all a new kind of social phenomenon deserving our attention. But there is no reason to replace the division of class with the types of occupation, and pure income.

No scientific theory could advocate the division that separates the employed and high-income physical labourers and mental labourers from the class of workers. Scientific development hasn't changed the basic class structure and the general development trend of the capitalist society. Capitalists are still the owners of production material (whether they directly run and manage the companies or not), and workers are the employed labourers (however much they earn, however high their education level is and whatever type of work they are involved with). Production automation deduces the demand of blue-collar workers but increase the number of white-collar workers. The size of work force is cut down because companies are scattered and their size shrunk down, but the development of the entire society constantly "creates" new workers. The development of the capitalist production is the expansion of work force, which is an iron law that can never be overthrown or changed.

The publication of *The Communist Manifesto* in February 1848 declared the birth of Marxism to the whole world. *The Communist Manifesto* is an immortal work. Though it couldn't exhaust the knowledge of capitalism, the scientific conception of history and methodologies it provides are still our guiding lines of analyzing the modern capitalist society.

CHAPTER XIII

THE REVOLUTIONS OF 1848 AND DEVELOPMENT OF THE MATERIALIST CONCEPTION OF HISTORY.

MARX'S SUMMARY OF THE EXPERIENCE OF FRENCH AND GERMAN REVOLUTIONS

When *The Communist Manifesto* was published, the Europe was seeing a storm of revolution which swept over the Continent of Europe till the border of Russia. It is a bourgeois revolution but not a copy of the past French bourgeois revolution. This revolution has its special features and expressions no matter in its allocation of class power, its revolutionary tasks, or the figures and parties performing in the political stage. Marx himself took part in this revolution, which is not only the most highlight in his cause but also forms an important period of the development of historical materialism.

If say, in *The Communist Manifesto*, Marx focused on the "modern history" of his epoch, i.e. the process of how the capitalist society was bred and developed in the womb of the feudal society, then his important political comments published in *Neue Rheinische Zeitung* and his books like *The Class Struggles in France: 1848 to 1850*, and *The Eighteenth Brumaire of Louis Bonaparte* focused on the "contemporary history", i.e. to explain and interpret "the political events of the day". By summing up the revolutionary experience of France and Germany, Marx further developed historical materialism in the issues about social revolution, class struggle and the State, the dialectic relationship of the subjective and objective factors in social development, and how to evaluate historic figures. His analysis, judgment and prediction of the events that have happened, are happening, and will happen not only express his genius insight, but also eloquently prove the cognitive value of historical materialism as scientific conception of history and methodology.

1 THE REVOLUTIONS OF 1848 AND THE SHATTERING OF THE PRINCIPLE OF ABSTRACT HUMANITARIANISM

In 1848, France is the country with the most intense, most typical and most drastic political struggles all over the Europe. The February Revolution of France in 1848 became the signal shell triggering the flames of revolutions in Germany, Austria, Hungary, and Czech.

The February Revolution of France, as a bourgeois revolution, is the revolution in which the industrial bourgeoisie fought against the arbitrary rule of the financial aristocracy. The workers of Paris joined in this revolution, but it was the bourgeoisie who had the fruits of victory all to themselves. The provisional government who nominally ruled wasn't a "socialist republic" as the workers expected but was a bourgeois dictatorship decorated with Louis Blanc and Arber.

What Marx focused on was not only the bourgeois nature of the February Revolution but its imagination of ideology. The February Revolution wrote liberty, equality and fraternity on its banner, in which the opposing bourgeoisie and proletariat seemingly fought together to answer the call of fraternity. Fraternity—a slogan declared by the revolution, was written with large capitals on the gables of Paris, on each prison and on each barrack. People seemed to go back to half a century ago and return to the France of 1789. Indeed, the February Revolution in 1848 is different from the French Bourgeois Revolution in 1789. The one in 1789 is more like a revolution of the Europe than merely a revolution of France; it is more than the victory of a certain social class, but is the victory of political system in the new European society, declaring the success of the capitalist society against the feudal society. As for the whole world, it not only reflects the requirements of France but also reflects the development trend of the world. That is the progress of the epoch. At that time, liberty, equality and fraternity were an advanced banner, a banner that mobilized all oppressed classes to rise and fight together. The revolution of 1848 was different. The bourgeoisie, fighting against the feudal system, also felt the powerful threat of the proletariat. Between hammer and anvil, the bourgeoisie wanted to use the people as the lighting conductor of the king and use the king as the lighting conductor of the people. Under the banner of freedom, equality and fraternity, it instigated the proletariat to pull chestnuts out of the fire and got itself well prepared to suppress any proletariat daring to propose their own demands at any time.

It was proved when France moved on from the February Revolution to the June Revolution. When the bourgeoisie seized the political power in the February Revolution, on the battlefield only left the bourgeoisie and the proletariat. The bourgeoisie made great efforts to establish its own military power and drove large numbers of workers to national factories in the name of succour. When the workers tried to protect the rights they had obtained, the bourgeoisie would savagely crack them down. In the June insurrection of Paris proletariat, the proletariat was brutally persecuted, over 110 thousand people were slaughtered, more than 250 thousand imprisoned, exiled, and put at hard labour, with Paris overwhelmed by their blood. Facts prove that "fraternity" exists only when the interests of the bourgeoisie and the proletariat are combined together and when the proletariat isn't a threat of the bourgeoisie's interests at all. Once the proletariat, as a single class that has its own interests and demands, dares to oppose it, the bourgeoisie will make replace the inscription of Liberté, Egalité, Fraternité, with the unambiguous words: infantry, cavalry, artillery[1].

That isn't the unique feature of the French bourgeoisie but is determined by the time conditions. It is especially so with the German bourgeoisie. When the February Revolution of France took place,

---

1   Karl Marx and Frederick Engels: Selected Works, 1st Edition, Volume 1, p. 640.

Germany was also going through the March Revolution. However, the bourgeoisie that was sent to the peak of the state's power by the revolution compromised with the German feudal forces right away and turned back to suppress the proletariat. If say, in France, the bourgeoisie showed up with its mask of an antirevolutionary leader only after the February Revolution and after it had wiped out all obstacles in front of its way of ruling the country, while in Germany, the bourgeoisie, even not having obtained the freedom of its citizens or the basic conditions for its control, but became the tail of the feudal system. In France, the bourgeoisie acted like a tyrant and implemented its anti-revolution; while in Germany, the bourgeoisie came out like a servant who served for the interests of its tyrant and fought against the revolution. In France, the bourgeoisie got the success and then brought the masses under control; while in Germany, the bourgeoisie couldn't be more pleasant to serve the feudal forces just not to let the people win. Compared with the French bourgeoisie in 1789, compared with its ancestors, those unworthy descendents were just dwarves.

How can one expect the bourgeoisie of 1848 would seriously hold the banner of liberty, equality, and fraternity and fight together with the proletariat? When Ruge said "So far, no revolution that swept the world was greater than the revolution of 1848", Engels exposed the nature of the "human" slogan of the Revolution of 1848. He said,

"As regards its principles, it is the most humane revolution" for these principles have arisen as a result of the glossing over of the most contradictory interests."

"It is the most humane revolution as regards its decrees and proclamations", for they represent a compendium of philanthropical fantasies and sentimental phrases about fraternity produced by all the feather-heads of Europe.

"It is the most humane revolution as regards its actuality", that is the massacres and barbarities in Posen, the murderous incendiarism of Radetzky, the ferocious cruelties committed in Paris by the victors of June, the butcheries in Cracow and Prague, the rule of brutal soldiery everywhere—in short, all the outrages which constitute the "actuality" of this revolution today, September 1, 1848, and which have spilled more blood in four months than was spilled in 1793 and 1794 taken together.

The "humane" Citizen Ruge![2]

According to Marx, it is the epoch's illusion to still be indulged in the slogans of 1789 at the year of 1848; these so-called revolutionists sticking to the French bourgeois revolution are just pedants; those petty-bourgeois socialists who had blind faith in "peace in class", begged the bourgeoisie for alms to the people and tried to hypnotize the proletariat with tedious cliché of fraternity were just utopians. They lost their memories and their period feel: "The majority quite rightly greets with catcalls those hapless utopians and hypocrites guilty of the anachronism of still using the term fraternity, brotherhood. The question at issue was precisely that of doing away with this term and with the illusions arising from its ambiguity"[3]

History itself is the most powerful. Though in the February Revolution, the proletariat in Paris were intoxicated in the widespread atmosphere of fraternity, generosity, and mercy, though Lamartine called the provisional government as "une gouvernement qui suspends ce malentendu terrible qui existe entre les différentes classes [a government that removes this terrible misunderstanding which exists between the different classes, from Lamartine's speech, 24 February 1848]", when the merry fireworks of Lamartine changed into the gunfire of Cavaignac and when Paris was burning, groaning and bleeding, the proletariat finally woke up in the illusion of "fraternity". Just as Marx concluded, "What succumbed in these defeats was not the revolution. It was the pre-revolutionary traditional appendages, results of social relationships which had not yet come to the point of sharp class antagonisms—persons, illusions, conceptions, projects from which the revolutionary party before the February Revolution was not free, from which it could be freed not by the victory of February, but only by a series of defeats"[4]. The proletariat got grapeshot, lost illusions. This is a victory, a victory paid by blood. The defeat in barricade battles got double compensation

---

2 Karl Marx and Frederick Engels: Collected Works, 1st Chinese Edition, Volume 5, p. 425, Beijing: People's Publishing House, 1958.
3 Karl Marx and Frederick Engels: Selected Works, 1st Edition, Volume 1, p. 302.
4 Ibid., p. 393.

from the victory of getting rid of the old traditional conceptions and ideologies.

Based on the experience of the Revolution of 1848, especially on the political evolution that France went through from 1848 to 1851, Marx made excellent elaborations on the emergence of ideology, the social functions of traditional ideology and its changes, and the features of intellectual production, which all significantly enrich historical materialism.

It is no accident that the traditional bourgeois ideology—abstract humanism principles constitute the illusive motive of human actions in the February Revolution of 1848. Men all act under existing historic conditions which are more than merely material conditions, but also include traditional conceptions. As Marx summed up, "The tradition of all dead generations weighs like a nightmare on the brains of the living. And just as they seem to be occupied with revolutionizing themselves and things, creating something that did not exist before, precisely in such epochs of revolutionary crisis they anxiously conjure up the spirits of the past to their service, borrowing from them names, battle slogans, and costumes in order to present this new scene in world history in time-honoured disguise and borrowed language. Thus Luther put on the mask of the Apostle Paul, the Revolution of 1789-1814 draped itself alternately in the guise of the Roman Republic and the Roman Empire, and the Revolution of 1848 knew nothing better to do than to parody, now 1789, now the revolutionary tradition of 1793-95"[5].

The tradition of ideology is an enormous power, but it plays different roles under different historical conditions. The representatives at the rising period of bourgeoisie like the heroes of Camille Desmoulins, Danton, Robespierre, St. Just, and Napoleon, put on Roman costumes, spoke in Roman phrases, but performed the task of their time that was to unchain the bourgeoisie, establish new social systems and set up an appropriate environment meeting the requirements of the time in the Continent of Europe for the French bourgeoisie. They turned to Rome because they wanted to find the essential ideals, art forms and illusions from the highly strict traditions of the Roman

---

5　Ibid., p. 603.

Republic to fulfil the bourgeois historical mission and to cover their revolutionary and narrow-minded bourgeois nature, so as to keep their own passion at the great height of historical tragedy. This is not a deliberate deception but a true belief. When some of their men were sent to the guillotine, they were still full of self-sacrifice and heroic spirit, sincerely believing they had devoted themselves for all mankind. It is thus clear that to resurrect the dead in the upswing time of bourgeois revolution is to glorify new struggles, and to magnify the meaning of some given imagined task. When the revolution purpose is achieved, a new ideology adapting to the new economic foundation from form to content will surely be established: "Once the new social formation was established, the antediluvian colossi disappeared and with them also the resurrected Romanism—the Brutuses, the Gracchi, the publicolas, the tribunes, the senators, and Caesar himself. Bourgeois society in its sober reality bred its own true interpreters and spokesmen in the Says, Cousins, Royer-Collards, Benjamin Constants, and Guizots; its real military leaders sat behind the office desk and the hog-headed Louis XVIII was its political chief. Entirely absorbed in the production of wealth and in peaceful competitive struggle, it no longer remembered that the ghosts of the Roman period had watched over its cradle"[6].

That isn't hard to understand. The capitalist society after all isn't the slave society and the bourgeoisie not the slaveholders either. Though the burgeoning bourgeoisie revived the "Renaissance" movement and could find the treasures they wanted from the lost literatures of Ancient Greece and Rome; though men who bore these emotions and opinions via tradition and education would think these emotions and opinions were the real motives and starting point of his actions, actually, what determines the ideologies of any class are the material conditions and the forms of property by which they live. When analyzing the reasons of the antagonism between Legitimists and Orleanists, Marx pointed out, "Upon the different forms of property, upon the social conditions of existence, rises an entire superstructure of distinct and peculiarly formed sentiments, illusions, modes of thought, and views of life. The entire class creates and forms them out of its material foundations and out of the corresponding social

---

6   Ibid., p. 604.

relations"[7]. This important statement provides the scientific comprehension of the nature and origin of ideology.

As Marx highlighted, any ideology, in terms of its origin and the content it reflects, must be related to a definite class and a form of property, but as for its creators and embracers, they may not all belong to the class, which is an important feature of intellectual production. Intellectual production is a relatively independent department. The mental workers and authors engaged in mental production may come from different classes. They "produce" theories, views, and ideologies for all classes to make the psychology, emotions and needs of the reflected classes systematic and theoretic. What makes intellectual production the representation of a certain class is not its class origin, but is its product—intellectual product, and the practical class interests and demands reflected in its intellectual products. When analyzing the petty-bourgeois democracy in the French Revolution of 1848, he laid emphasis on this point and said, "Just as little must one imagine that the democratic representatives are indeed all shopkeepers or enthusiastic champions of shopkeepers. According to their education and their individual position they may be as far apart as heaven and earth. What makes them representatives of the petty bourgeoisie is the fact that in their minds they do not get beyond the limits which the latter do not get beyond in life, that they are consequently driven, theoretically, to the same problems and solutions to which material interest and social position drive the latter practically"[8].

The functions of the social ideology of a class won't be permanent. Its effects and social functions will vary with the changes of the material interests and position of the class it relies on. In the French bourgeois revolution of 1789, liberty, equality and fraternity were the banner of revolution and advancement. Though the humanist principle showing up in an abstract and universal form was still illusory, its social functions were revolutionary. To a certain extent, it also reflected the interests, hopes and demands of the oppressed labourers and mobilized them to fight against the feudal system. However, in the revolution of 1848, it passivated and concealed the

7   Ibid., p. 629.
8   Ibid., p. 632.

effects of the antagonism between the proletariat and the bourgeoisie or played the role as Marx said "to lull the proletarian lion to sleep"[9]. This change of ideological functions reflects the change of class relation and class contradiction.

More profoundly, Marx keenly saw it was not the humane principles like liberty, equality and fraternity that betrayed the bourgeoisie, but it was the bourgeoisie who succeeded betrayed its original ideal. When they could continue to use "humanity" as camouflage and protect their own interests with abstract liberty, equality and fraternity, they wouldn't give up these catchwords. In the 1860s, as Marx had exposed for many times, the bourgeoisie's strategy was to exploit humanity, liberty and other catchwords to fight. In his paper "The Washington Cabinet and the Western Powers", he said, "in fact, the manifesto in 1856 hides huge inhumanity behind its charity words. In principle, it changed the war of people of different countries to the war of their government. It endowed inviolability to property but little to man. It warded off the terror of war for trade so as to protect the bourgeoisie in industry and commerce from this terror. Besides, evidently, the human excuse of the manifesto of 1856 was only meant to show for the European audience, which is exactly the same with the religious excuse of the Holy Alliance"[10]; in the paper "English Humanism and America", he also said, "Humanity in England, like liberty in France, has now become an export article for the traders in politics." "But Cato the Censor himself could not watch over the morals of the Roman citizens more anxiously than the English aristocrats and their ministers over the "humanity" of the war-waging Yankees!"[11]: once they feel their interests are threatened, they will decisively abandon it. Just as Marx argued, "the bourgeoisie has correctly understood that all the weapons it forged to oppose to the feudal system have turned back and targeted itself; all the educational means it created have turned around to object its own civilization, and all the gods it creates have deserted it"[12]. To the bourgeoisie, all that invades and goes against its rule is bad,

9   Ibid., p. 300.
10   Karl Marx and Frederick Engels: Collected Works, 1st Chinese Edition, Volume 15, p. 452, Beijing: People's Publishing House, 1963.
11   Ibid., p. 538.
12   Karl Marx and Frederick Engels: Selected Works, 1st Edition, Volume 1, p. 644.

"whether it is sentimentally crying for the pains of the mankind, or it is advertising the millennium kingdom and fraternity of Jesus, or it is rambling about spirit, education and freedom with a humanistic attitude, or it just vaguely makes up a system in which all classes could live harmoniously and happily" It is indicated that to analyze the social functions of the abstract humanist principles, we must distinguish whether it is the deliberate deception or struggle strategy or the bourgeoisie and its politicians, or the protest of the progressives who haven't get rid of the idealistic conception of history against the inhumane bourgeois system.

The lesson learnt from the revolution of 1848 shows that the proletariat should have its own ideology which not only represents the interests and wishes of the proletariat, but should also reflect the objective course of history scientifically. The bourgeois revolutions could play revolutionary dramas in Roman costumes, but the proletariat can't and it must figure out its status and mission in the capitalist society. As Marx pointed out, "The social revolution of the nineteenth century cannot take its poetry from the past but only from the future. It cannot begin with itself before it has stripped away all superstition about the past. The former revolutions required recollections of past world history in order to smother their own content. The revolution of the nineteenth century must let the dead bury their dead in order to arrive at its own content. There the phrase went beyond the content – here the content goes beyond the phrase"[13]. The proletariat shows respect to all the outstanding cultural heritages of human beings including all the achievements made by the bourgeoisie, but it decisively breaks the chains of the fossilized, obsolete historical traditions; it always looks back at the previous history but looks forward to the future; it doesn't change social systems on the old basis but firmly stands on the basis of the reality. This is the proletariat and this is the proletarian ideology.

---

13   Ibid., p. 606.

2 HISTORICAL PROGRESS AND SOCIAL CHANGE. INEVITABILITY AND NECESSITY OF SOCIAL REVOLUTIONS

Social revolution is both a problem of conception of history and a practical social problem. Marx had been exploring this issue during the process of his thinking transformation. In *The Communist Manifesto*, Marx had already made exposition in principle of the problems of social revolution from the new conception of history; in *The Germany Ideology*, Marx had already found that all historical conflicts are rooted in the contradiction between productive force and communication form; the intensifying of the contradiction will inevitably lead to the explosion of revolution. He also highlighted, "The motive force of history and that of religion, philosophy and any other theory are revolution rather than critique." In end of *The Philosophy of Poverty*, he exposited enthusiastically the relationship of social evolution and political revolution. As for *The Communist Manifesto*, the great program which could even be seen as the revolutionary declaration of the proletariat, it declared the purpose of the proletariat revolution and drew up the strategies and measures of proletariat parties in the revolution by analyzing the inner contradiction of the bourgeois mode of production and the antagonism between the proletariat and the bourgeoisie. However, until the publication of *The Communist Manifesto*, Marx hadn't witnessed any revolution himself or personally joined any. What really gave the chance to Marx to examine and develop his theory of social revolution at the height of historical materialism was the Revolution of 1848 in which he experienced himself. Engels once highlighted this point, and said, "The inquiry into, and the exposition of, the causes, both of the revolutionary convulsion and its suppression, are, besides, of paramount importance from a historical point of view"[14].

Compared with the nature, the changes of society are much more obvious. In all class societies since slave society, the turmoil and uprising of the oppressed and the changes and successions of regimes have been directly recognizable facts, thus people always focus on the field of political struggle and treat revolutions just as changes of regime and as simple political revolutions, failing to explore its

---

14   Ibid., p. 501.

profound economic origin and its abundant significance, while Marx broke this narrow mentality. Undoubtedly the primary problem of any revolution should be state power. The transfer of the state power from one class to another is the primary symbol of a revolution. However, not all changes of regime can be called revolution. A real political revolution ought to be a social revolution. It is a political action in which a definite class, with wresting political power as intermediary, destroys the old relations of production and consolidates the new ones, breaks the old superstructure and establishes the new one. Therefore, revolution is the reform of the society and its deepest origin exists in the social contradiction itself. The grand and spectacular Revolution of 1848 is a revolution like this, only an unsuccessful one. It is very idealistic to attribute the occurrence of this revolution to the malicious incitement of the minority or to find all the reasons of its failure from a few leaders' occasional motives, advantages, disadvantages, mistakes or apostasies. By use of historical materialism, Marx studied on the reasons of the inevitable outbreak and the doomed failure of this revolution from the overall social conditions and the living conditions of the country where this revolution happened, and refuted various idealistic conceptions of history.

It is no accident that the February Revolution took place in France and then evolved into the June Revolution. After the Revolution of 1789, France went through unprecedentedly fierce struggles for the next 40 years, but on the eve of the February Revolution of 1848, it was no longer the bourgeoisie but one of its groups that governed the country: bankers, exchange magnates, railway magnates, owners of coal mines and forests and a part of land owners related to them, i.e. the so-called financial aristocrats. So the industrial bourgeoisie had contradictions with the financial aristocrats. At the same time, the bourgeoisie and the proletariat also had contradictions. Those contradictions were complicatedly weaved together. The domination of the financial aristocrats caused strong objection and dissatisfaction of the people, which got even more severe due to the occurrence of two economic world events in 1845 and in 1846—one is the potato blight and the crop failures and the other is the general commercial and industrial crisis in Britain that significantly influenced

France, pushing the angry complaints to explode as armed uprisings, which finally resulted in the outbreak of the February Revolution. However, the provisional government coming out in the barricade wars in February was after all a government representing the bourgeoisie. In June, the proletariat was forced to recapture their weapons, but it still turned out to be a failure. In Marx's mind, the February Revolution and the June Revolution of France originated deeply in economy and the inevitability of its failure was also rooted in the economy. He said, "Given this general prosperity, wherein the productive forces of bourgeois society are developing as luxuriantly as it is possible for them to do within bourgeois relationships, a real revolution is out of the question. Such a revolution is possible only in periods when both of these factors – the modern forces of production and the bourgeois forms of production – come into opposition with each other"[15]. According to his analysis, the basis of the bourgeois social relations in 1848 was still so consolidated that any attempt to stop the development of the bourgeoisie will be necessarily crushed down by this basis. But as long as the economic conditions generating revolution become mature, the revolution will arrive anyway. "A new revolution is only a consequence of a new crisis. The one, however, is as sure to come as the other."

As France, the March Revolution of Germany and the evolution after it were determined by the overall situation and class structure of the German society. It is the development of the bourgeois mode of production of Germany that determined that the bourgeoisie must oppose to the feudal system; and it is the congenital dysplastic bourgeois economy that determines the German bourgeoisie would become so weak, craven and quail. However, even not induced by the February Revolution of France, the economic contradiction and the political contradiction inside Germany itself will also trigger the revolution anyway.

Marx not only analyzed the necessity of the Revolution of 1848 from the contradiction of the bourgeois mode of production and the feudal mode of production and from the contradiction of the bourgeois mode of production itself, but also refuted those theories that used idealistic views to misrepresent the Revolution of 1848 by the book review

---

15   Ibid., p. 488.

commenting on the brochure of Guizot and G.Fr. Daumer published on the *Political Economic Review of Neue Rheinische Zeitung*.

Guizot is a famous politician and historian in the Restoration period of France, one excellent contribution of whom to the field of history theory is to study on class and class struggle. However, even "the most intelligent person" "the genius historian" under the "ancient régime" (ancient regime) "got addlebrained" by the February Revolution of 1848 "so that he couldn't understand history completely"[16]. In "Why Is the English Revolution Successful: Discussion on the History of the English Revolution" (Pourquoi la révolution d'Angleterre a-t-elle réussi? Discours sur l'histoire de la révolution d'Angleterre) published in 1850, Guizot made an idealistic explanation of the revolution. He went backward from the theory of class and class struggle that he had once supported but thought "all revolutions are caused by the malevolence and religious fanaticism of a few troublemakers not satisfied by the general freedom"[17]. The reason that France had the February Revolution should be attributed to the character of Frenchmen, "nothing but the mean character of Frenchmen should be blamed for the shameful bankruptcy in 1830 of the July Monarchy which had gone through 18 years of hard time but couldn't last as long as the English Monarchy since 1688"[18]. He also treated the bourgeois republic as "a small thing made out by some ambiguous, fanatical, impulsive and spiteful people"[19]. Guizot felt quite sorry that France lost the balance of all political powers and admired the "tranquil and pastoral" England very much. Indeed, the English society was also suffering from sharp class contradictions at that time, and "witnessing extremely severe conflicts and profound reformations"[20]. All of these indicate that the theorists who had used the views of class struggle to examine the bourgeois revolution against the feudal class could never objectively consider the reality of the class struggles in the capitalist society. They got the conclusion that the revolution against the feudal system was inevitable, but the revolution against the bourgeoisie was occasional and was the malicious incitement breaking political balance. It's no

---

16   Karl Marx and Frederick Engels: Collected Works, 1st Chinese Edition, Volume 7, p. 247.
17   Ibid., p. 250.
18   Ibid., p. 247.
19   Ibid., p. 250.
20   Ibid., p. 251-252.

wonder that Marx said, "not only the king should go away, but the capacities of the bourgeoisie should go away either"[21].

In his "Critique of Georg Friedrich Daumer's "The religion of the new epoch: an attempt of founding combinatorial aphoristic"", Marx refuted Daumer's idealistic conception of historical conception. Daumer evaluated the 1848 Revolution as "the deviant behaviours of the citizens", as the product of "jealousy, anger and admiration of the lower class to the upper class" and as the product of the "fight of vulgarity against 'civilization'"[22]. Thus he couldn't explain class struggles and social revolution based on the existence conditions of classes evaluated the emergence of the revolution by the nature of some malicious men playing dirty tricks, attempting to misuse ordinary people and inciting them to oppose the civilized class. Daumer turned the class struggle based on material interests into a moral and cultural strife between "civilization" and "savagery".

More ridiculously, Daumer put religion over revolution, argued that revolution would produce no practical effects and only the foundation of a new religion could change the world. He wrote: "Only by a new religion can a brand-new world order and new social relations be produced. The Christianity and Islam are perfect examples for their contributions in this regard. Abstract and single politics is weak and incapable and useless, which can be well proved by the revolutionary movements carried out in 1848"[23]. Certainly these ideas reflected total ignorance about the course of history. In no way was it the new religion that produced new world order but just the other way around. Take Christianity for example; it was established after the collapse of the ancient "world order" and was the result of this collapse. Commenting on the relationship between social revolution and religious transformations, Marx pointed out, "obviously, along with each spectacular historical reform of social system, men's ideas and conceptions will change accordingly, which means their religious conceptions will change as well"[24]. Men can reveal the ultimate secret of social reform or revolution in the socio-economic life rather than in religious life.

---

21   Ibid., p. 253.
22   Ibid., p. 237 and 238.
23   Ibid., p. 239.
24   Ibid., p. 240.

The deepest reason of social revolution is rooted in the fundamental social contradiction of the society. Thus social revolution is the external expression of this contradiction which gets extremely intensified, and also the social tool to solve this contradiction. Social revolutions play such huge social functions and promote social development because it releases—in the form of mass struggles—those revolutionary forces which can solve the contradictions that have accumulated for a long time in so called peaceful days. Affirming this view, Marx wrote: "Revolutions are the locomotives of history"[25].

All the representatives of reactionary classes defame social revolutions. They evaluate the sluggish development of the old system as a normal phenomenon or existence, but evaluate social revolutions as a social malady which blocks the development of productive forces, which is of course deeply prejudiced.

It is no wonder that social revolutions cause certain destruction. It destroys old production relations, old superstructures and obsolete conceptions, in one word, it destroys old social order. Also in revolutionary wars, the productive forces are also damaged to a certain extent. But the essence of revolution is not merely destruction but construction. It establishes and consolidates new production relations and superstructures, aims to create favourable economic and political circumstances for the rapid development of productive forces. Revolutions release real powerful engines for social and political progress, which enables a society in just five years of such a turbulent period, accomplish those development tasks which couldn't be completed in one hundred years in normal circumstances. Ideologists who exclude social revolutions from the history of class societies aim none than see the society, its lively organism, into a lifeless fossil to serve the ruling class dominate forever. The revolutionary changes and turbulences in history constantly crush this dream. Marx opened the way for the proletarians themselves to grasp this law and fought to elevate their consciousness to the height of the revolutionary historical conception, which was indeed a great contribution.

---

25   Karl Marx and Frederick Engels: Selected Works, 1st Edition, Volume 1, p. 474.

Marx also summed up the historical practices beginning with the French bourgeois revolution in 1789 to the European revolution in 1848, and classified bourgeois revolutions into two types. Due to their different economic and political development courses, France and Germany went through a different course of bourgeois revolution during 1848 Revolutions, but their revolutions both belonged to the early bourgeois revolutions, only being different types.

In the French Revolution of 1789, the bourgeoisie was the progressive class that practically led the revolution. In the course of the revolution some bourgeoisie parties becoming more and more revolutionary grasped the helm of the state one after the other. Following the Constitutionalists, ruled the Girondins, and the Jacobins overthrew them for their own rule. The latter was always more radical than the former. "Each of these parties rely on the more progressive party for support. As soon as it has brought the revolution far enough to be unable to follow it further, still less to go ahead of it, it is thrust aside by the bolder ally that stands behind it and sent to the guillotine. The revolution thus moves along an ascending line"[26].

The Revolutions of 1848 were different. Not only the weak German bourgeoisie betrayed its allies after the victory of the March Revolution, but the tougher French bourgeoisie also turned its guns against the proletariat after it grasped the fruits of the February Revolution. This time, in France, those political groups that retreated and became milder and milder and even assuming reactionary positions wrested the political power. They constantly suppressed those parties more radical than themselves with the pretext to protect private property, family, religion and order. Marx wrote: "The revolution thus moves in a descending line. It finds itself in this state of retrogressive motion before the last February barricade has been cleared away and the first revolutionary authority constituted."

In the long-term struggles of bourgeoisie to seize and consolidate its political power, it is not a coincidence that bourgeois revolutions move in two opposite lines: The ascending line and the descending line, instead the base for two opposite lines is determined by the circumstances bourgeois mode of production gradually ascended to

---

26   Ibid., p. 625.

the dominant position and second basis is the changes in the class relations and the balance of class power caused by these changes. Challenging the bourgeoisie stands the proletariat with shabby clothes, full of hatred, strong and powerful, and making the bourgeoisie full of fear. The bourgeoisie can't promote revolutions; the petty-bourgeois liberals can't embark revolutions on their own either. However, summing up the experiences of the 1848 Revolutions, Marx saw another possibility, i.e. the proletariat should carry the democratic revolution to the end and transforms it to a socialist revolution, which is Marx's thought known as permanent revolution and was elaborated by Marx in "The Class Struggle in France, 1848-1850" and in his "Address of the Central Committee to the Communist League". Though his thought of permanent revolution wasn't realized under the conditions of that time, his ideas about the dialectic relation between bourgeois democratic revolution and socialist revolutions, and his ideas on the struggle strategies of the proletariat in democratic revolutions and socialist revolutions are rather profound and significant which were correctly inherited and developed by Lenin and Mao Zedong in Russian and Chinese revolutions.

3 EXAMINATION OF STATE ISSUE FROM THE PERSPECTIVE OF HISTORICAL MATERIALISM

State issue falls within the category of politics, but on the other side how to examine and understand the nature of state falls within the category of conception of history. State issue is the core issue of political struggles. Marx paid substantial attention to the state issue which was also the breakthrough point in his building historical materialism. Indeed it was through his clearing and criticizing Hegel's idealistic conception of state that Marx opened the door to historical materialism.

As early as in his first *Rheinische Zeitung* period, in 1843* "Justification of the Correspondent from the Mosel", Marx had already argued his objection to explain state with the individual will of the rulers and highlighted that it was essential to study the objective aspects of all the relations that determine the essence of state.

---

*) In the second period (1848-1849) the name of the newspaper was changed as *Neue Rheinische Zeitung*.

In his *A Critique of Hegel's Philosophy of Right*, Marx criticized Hegel's theory of state and proposed the principle that the civil society determines the state, laying the first cornerstone of historical materialism. And in *The German Ideology*, he completely reached the materialistic understanding on the essence of state. He not only uncovered that the state appearing in the form of representing the general interests of the community was a mistaken view, but also theorized the nature of historical evolution of the state systems with the view of class struggle, stressing that all the struggles inside a state like the struggles of democracies, aristocracies and monarchies and the struggles for the right of universal vote, and so forth were after all the struggles of different classes. In *The German Ideology* his judgments including his conclusions about the previous historic experience of France lacked enough verification and explanations based on practical facts. However, this crucial blank was surpassed by the summation of the experiences of the 1848 European revolution. Especially this summation included his thoughts arguing for the dismantling the bourgeois state apparatus and expounding the historic missions to be undertaken by dictatorship of the proletariat which had promoted the Marxist theory of state to a new stage.

Political system is the core of those superstructures founded on a certain social economic base. Political system both reflects the class property of a regime and possesses the form with which the ruling class uses to achieve its control. By summing up the experience of the 1848 Revolution, Marx made excellent elaborations on the evolution of the latter one, i.e. on the forms of bourgeois political systems. In these works he examined the bourgeois state system from the aspect of class struggles and from the aspect of dynamics of changes in the balance of class powers. Marx called the period of the French February Revolution from February 24th to May 4th, 1848 (from the violent fall of Louis-Philippe to the opening of the Constituent Assembly) as the prologue of the revolution and as a "Universal-brotherhood swindle". During this period, the hastily founded provisional government (the February Government) included the representatives of all classes such as the opposing faction of the monarchist bourgeoisie, the monarchist-Republicans, the petty-bourgeoisie Democratic Republicans, and the worker movement representatives as Socialist Democrats, had their seats. Each of these parties evaluated the role and mission of this provisional government according to their own opinions and interests. For example, the workers party assuming the victory as the product of their struggle declared it a socialist republic, but in fact this provisional government had a bourgeoisie class nature. However, due to the dynamic balance of class powers of the day, the government appeared as a political coalition representing all the classes who overthrew the July Monarchy together compromised with each other and jointly shared the fruits of common success.

When the proletarians in Paris were still intoxicated with the feelings of complete success and were indulged with the illusion of "social republic", the political forces against the proletariat were arranging their forces, as soon as they were ready they attacked them. This second period, starting from May 4th 1848 when the National Constituent Assembly was convened to December 10th when Louis Bonaparte was elected as president, was called by Marx as "the dictatorship of the pure bourgeois republicans". This Constituent Assembly publicly announced to establish a republic, but not the "social republic" as imagined or expected by the proletariat in the February Barricade War, but a bourgeois republic. Marx wrote: "The republic proclaimed by the National Assembly, the sole legitimate republic, is a republic which possesses no revolutionary weapon against the bourgeois order, but rather its political reconstitution, the political reconsolidation of bourgeois society; in a word, a bourgeois republic"[27]. This bourgeois republic established upon the dead bodies of the June proletariat insurgents was nothing but the rule of the whole bourgeoisie "acting in the name of people" and its task was to consolidate domination of the capital and enslave the labourers. In this way, the transformation of the February provisional government which was once imagined as "a social republic" to a bourgeois republic clearly manifested the changes in the class relations and changes in the balance of class powers, briefly to say proletariat had changed from an ally to an opponent and the winner of the February Revolution was now the loser of the June Insurrection.

---

27   Ibid., p. 413.

However, the dictatorship of the pure bourgeois republicans didn't last long. Because of their suppression of the proletariat and their issuing of the heavy taxes and financial policies damaging the benefits of the petty bourgeoisie and peasants, they fell down to the inferior position in the fight against the Royalists supporting the monarchy. They lost and Louis Bonaparte became the president, and finally captured the throne of king by a coup and restored the monarchy. It wasn't accidental that the bourgeois parliamentary republic retreated to monarchy, instead this change was a clear reflection of bourgeoisie's fear from the people, "Their instincts taught them that the republic, true enough, makes their political rule complete, but at the same time undermines its social foundation, since they must now confront the subjugated classes and contend against them without mediation, without the concealment afforded by the crown, without being able to divert the national interest by their subordinate struggles among themselves and with the monarchy. It was a feeling of weakness that caused them to recoil from the pure conditions of their own class rule and to yearn for the former more incomplete, more undeveloped, and precisely on that account less dangerous forms of this rule"[28]. It was neither the reminiscence of the past or nor their attachment to the old dynasty for royalists which motivated them to attempt for restoration the monarchy, but the practical needs of their class interests. The class of squires and the big bourgeoisie needed the crown and were bound to realize their rule under the crown. For them it didn't change the nature of the thing at all, whether the crown was not put on the head of a Bourbon Dynasty (the dynasty of the big landed property) member or on the head of Orleansists (the dynasty of money) or it was seized by the Corsican Louis Bonaparte.

Marx combined the analysis of the changes in the political forms of the bourgeois dictatorship during 1848 with the analysis of the descending line of this revolution. Changes from the "social republic" of the February Revolution to the bourgeois parliamentary republic and then to the Second Empire of Louis Bonaparte, all these successive changes in political forms were the place where class struggles took place and these political forms were also the result of class struggles. Each political form was the aggregate of the changes in

---

28   Ibid., p. 630.

the balances of class powers. Through summing up the experience of the French Revolution of 1848, Marx further developed his previous thought that the civil society determines the state and it constitutes the intermediate through which the production mode determines the state.

Marx also revealed the development laws of the bourgeois state power through his studies on the experience of the French Revolution.

First, expansion of bureaucratic and military apparatus: The bourgeois state is developed upon the basis of the inheritance of the feudal state. It further develops the centralism practiced by the autocratic monarchy and greatly expands the limits, the attributes, and the agents of the governmental power. For example, in France, an enormous bureaucratic and military (apparatus) organization had already been formed in the autocratic monarchy age which possessed a sophisticated and ingenious state apparatus. This apparatus employed officials numbering half a million, besides an army of more than half million men. After the victory of the revolution, the bourgeoisie didn't eliminate this bureaucratic machine but further developed it so as to realize its rule. Without army, police, prison, officials, huge administrative machinery, and military forces, the bourgeoisie can never realize its dictatorship. The bourgeois society is based on class antagonism. This antagonism of class interests and the fundamental nature of the minority ruling over the majority determine the inevitable trend of expansion of bureaucracy and military apparatus of the bourgeois state political power.

Second, restraining the legislative power of the parliament and expansion of the executive power: The parliament indeed played a positive role in the bourgeois fight against the feudal autocracy, but when the bourgeoisie established its own domination, the parliament became the form of the bourgeoisie's realizing its rule. The legislative parliament and the executive power are all parts of the bourgeois state machinery. Since the day of its foundation, the Constituent Assembly founded after the French February Revolution in June, suppressed the proletariat and aimed to realize the rule of the bourgeoisie. However, the real power of the bourgeois dictatorship does not lie in the parliament but the executive power. The decision making for it policies and their implementation are executed by the government (executive power). The law of development of the bourgeois states is to enlarge executive power and restrain parliamentary power as much as possible and try to degrade the parliament to a decorative place where much empty talk is made. For example, in France at that time, the executive power employed and governed more than half a million officials, by which it ruled, controlled, instructed and monitored the entire society, which was everywhere and saw everything; while the parliament was just some place for debates. Though the deputies seemed so "passionate and eloquent in the National Assembly", they were actually "unproductive." It was natural that Marx criticized "parliamentary cretinism", i.e. a malady that people have superstition about parliament, people generally put parliament over executive power and believe parliament can control and govern those holding the executive power. He said, "Peculiar malady which since 1848 has raged all over the Continent, parliamentary cretinism, which holds those infected by it fast in an imaginary world and robs them of all sense, all memory, all understanding of the rude external world"[29]. That, of course, doesn't mean that the proletariat should reject parliamentary struggles but means that they should grasp the essence of the bourgeois parliament and be conscious about the limits of parliamentary struggles.

Third, the expansion and contraction of democracy: True enough, the bourgeois dictatorship can adopt different forms of state, but that shouldn't to the conclusion that "revolutionary struggle for a form of polity (state) is meaningless, illusory and futile?" In fact, for the revolution of the proletariat, "the best form of polity (Ed.: state) would be the form in which these contradictions can reach a stage of open struggle in the course of which they are resolved."[30] This form of polity is the bourgeois democratic republic state because the freedom and democracy it provides is favourable to train, and organize the proletariat in its fight and also for publicity work.

The bourgeois liberty and democracy, though limited and incomplete, are still a huge progress compared to feudal autocracy. The development of the bourgeoisie itself needs liberty and democracy, but they are also weapons for the proletariat to oppose bourgeoisie.

---

29 Ibid., p. 655.
30 Ibid., p. 303.

In *The Eighteenth Brumaire of Louis Bonaparte*, Marx wrote: "The bourgeoisie had a true insight into the fact that all the weapons it had forged against feudalism turned their points against itself, that all the means of education it had produced rebelled against its own civilization, that all the gods it had created had fallen away from it. It understood that all the so-called bourgeois liberties and organs of progress attacked and menaced its class rule at its social foundation and its political summit simultaneously."[31] Therefore, the bourgeoisie tried every means to constrain and shrink liberty, on one side, it "advocated liberty and democracy, and on the other hand, fearfully minded out the proletarians" and "exploiting" this liberty. For example, in France, as stipulated by the Constitution of 1848, the personal liberties, freedom of publication, speech, assembly, education and religion, and so forth, were designed as the indivisible rights of French citizens, but the laws always contained supplementary stipulations which noted those rights can be used unlimitedly so far as their use do not limit the freedom rights of others and so far as they do not threat the public safety. Another supplementary stipulation noted that these freedoms could also be restricted by laws. "Each paragraph of this constitution contains its own antithesis" with "liberty in the general phrase, abrogation of liberty in the marginal note"[32]. Also the bourgeoisie can totally quarantine "public safety" (which is actually the safety of the bourgeois society) or restrain the freedom of others with the pretext of their violating laws. Therefore, when the bourgeoisie tries to limit and reduce the liberties and democratic rights of citizens, the proletariat strive to increase them. This kind of struggle constitutes an important aspect of the struggles between the proletariat and the bourgeoisie.

Furthermore, Marx reached an extremely important conclusion for the proletarian revolution in his glorious work *The Eighteenth Brumaire of Louis Bonaparte*. Therein he analyzed the changes in the political forms of the French bourgeois dictatorship during 1848 Revolution, especially focused on the expansion of the bureaucratic and military machine after the coup of Louis Bonaparte. He concluded the previous revolutions had all perfected the bureaucratic state machine instead of diminishing it. In 1848 all the French political

31   Ibid., p. 644.
32   Ibid., p. 616.

parties fighting to conquer the helm of the state considered the capture of this giant state machinery as the major war trophy for their victory, to "transfer the bureaucratic-military machine from one hand to another", but the task of the proletarian revolution should be to smash the bourgeois bureaucratic-military machine. This statement to smash the bourgeois state machinery is a basic element of the Marxist theory of state, which scientifically solved the problem of how to replace the bourgeois dictatorship with the proletarian dictatorship.

Marx's judgment to smash the bourgeois state machinery wasn't based on voluntarism or anarchism, but on the view of historical materialism and on analysis of bourgeois states. What Marx opposed was huge expansion of bureaucracy and military apparatus of the bourgeoisie state machinery as well as its class property of guarding the interests of the minority, at the same time suppress the labourers. For Marx, the centralism carried out by bureaucracy attached to bourgeoisie state still has the nature of a low-grade vulgar form which was even—to a certain degree—opposed by the feudal system. The *first* French Revolution, (ed. February 1848) with its task of breaking all separate local, territorial, urban, and provincial powers in order to create the civil unity of the nation, was bound to develop what the monarchy had begun: The centralization, but at the same time develop the limits, the attributes, and the agents of the governmental power. Napoleon completed this state machinery. "The centralization of the state that modern (Ed.: Bourgeoisie) society requires arises only on the ruins of the military-bureaucratic government machinery which was forged in opposition to feudalism."[33] Instead the centralization implemented by the dictatorship of the proletariat is on the basis of expanded democracy for the people and its state form includes a system which combines democracy and centralization.

For Marx smashing the bourgeois state machinery doesn't mean totally repudiating the administrative and executive experience accumulated by the bourgeois states, which undertake some certain social functions. State is the tool of class oppression but it also plays

---

33   Karl Marx and Frederick Engels: Selected Works, 1st Edition, The Eighteenth Brumaire of Louis Bonaparte. Karl Marx 1852, Volume 1, p. 699.

to a certain degree a social/administrative role in managing social life and social economy. These two different properties of it are mutually related and interact with each other. All previous states in human history possessed these two properties. In "The British Rule in India" written by Marx in 1853, he narrated the economic functions undertaken by the ancient Asian states such as realizing common public works, building agricultural water supply systems and building irrigation canals , etc. Similarly, contemporary bourgeois states also must carry out certain social and economic functions. After smashing the bourgeois state machinery, the proletariat critically absorbs the experience of the past, and uses appropriate elements when establishing and consolidating its own political power.

The proletarian dictatorship is a new kind of state. As a state, it naturally has the oppressive function, i.e. the dictatorship over enemies. However, the oppressive function is by no means be the only function of the proletarian political power and it should also undertake certain economic functions and other social management functions in order to create those conditions for the future transition towards communist society. Marx has never treated the proletarian dictatorship as the purpose in itself.

Marx clearly put forward the concept of the dictatorship of the proletariat for the first time, in his work *The Class Struggles in France: 1848-1850*. Also herein, he carefully defined the tasks of the proletarian dictatorship: "the class dictatorship of the proletariat is the necessary transit point to the abolition of class distinctions generally, to the abolition of all the relations of production on which they rest, to the abolition of all the social relations that correspond to these relations of production, to the revolutionizing of all the ideas that result from these social relations"[34].

Later in his letter to Joseph Weydemeyer on March 5, 1852, Marx took a further step in expounding his conclusions after summing up the lessons of the 1848 Revolution. He wrote: "I do not claim to have discovered either the existence of classes in modern society or the struggle between them. Long before me, bourgeois historians had described the historical development of this struggle between

---

34   Ibid., p. 479-80.

the classes, as had bourgeois economists their economic anatomy. My own contribution was: 1. to show that the existence of classes is merely bound up with certain historical phases in the development of production; 2. that the class struggle necessarily leads to the dictatorship of the proletariat; 3. that this dictatorship itself constitutes no more than a transition to the abolition of all classes and to a classless society."[35] Here we see that, Marx preliminarily corrected his formulation in *The Communist Manifesto* that evaluated the entire human history as the history of class struggles, instead he highlighted the internal relationship between the emergence of classes and certain degree of relatively sufficient development in production level. He wrote: "2. that the class struggle necessarily leads to the *dictatorship of the proletariat*; 3. that this dictatorship itself constitutes no more than a transition to the *abolition of all classes* and to a *classless society*". In certain historical phases, and under certain circumstances the state power of the proletariat rule needs to be strengthened, in accordance with the fundamental interest of all citizens. But it should neither unrestrainedly enlarge the organization, power and limits of the governmental body nor one-sidedly emphasize the dictatorship aspect of the state. Instead it should scientifically consider the mechanisms and functions of the socialist state machinery, find ways for scientific decision making and scientific management, and efficiently mobilize state's social roles so as to vigorously develop productive forces and also to promote the task of material and spiritual civilization. Evaluating political power merely as the power of oppression is a historical idealistic conception. Even a state dominated by an exploiting class would never maintain its existence merely by oppression or violence.

4 SUBJECT AND OBJECT OF HISTORY. EVALUATION OF HISTORICAL FIGURES

Revolution period is the most active period of classes as well as their political representatives. Among those figures we saw on the front stage of politics, there are both brave earthshaking revolutionary fighters and insidious treacherous politicians; there are both great heroes who pushed the history forward and who will be remembered

---

35 Karl Marx and Frederick Engels: Collected Works, 1st Chinese Edition, Volume 28, p. 509, Beijing: People's Publishing House, 1973.

forever, on the other side there are crafty sycophants blocking the historical progress who will remain as infamous names in history for the future thousands of years. These sophisticated struggles among classes and their representatives, their successes and failures, draw numerous dramatic historical tableaus.

So was the 1848 French revolution. Different classes actively struggled for their victory, among them the proletariat was suppressed in the June Revolution, the bourgeoisies believed they would certainly win, the petty bourgeoisie was the greatest talker but least doer, the peasants were struggling to protect their small backward and undeveloped lands, and big landlords and the big bourgeoisie attempted to restore the old dynasty. These different factions had their own representatives, such as Louis Auguste Blanqui, Armand Barbès and François-Vincent Raspail were the figures fighting on behalf of workers; Alexandre-Auguste Ledru on behalf of the petty bourgeoisie; Louis Blanc who claimed to represent workers but who was indeed a petty bourgeois socialist. On the other side we see those bourgeois politicians as fishers of fame and credit, those councillors, bankers who gathered around the newspaper called *The National*: Their leaders were Louis Eugene Cavaignac and Armand Marrast. However, like a mockery of the history, France finally fell into the hands of Louis Bonaparte after encountering flood of revolutions. Louis Bonaparte was elected as president in December 1848, and later launched a coup on December 2, 1851 and dismissed the Legislative Assembly. A year later, he imitated his uncle and restored monarchy, ascended to the throne.

Louis Bonaparte's coup like a bolt from the blue shocked the whole political world. Some people, from the aspect of morality, loudly shouted to condemn him. Observers were confused, felt helpless to grasp the essence of the problem, as we see in Victor Hugo's two evaluations: *Napoleon le Petit* and Proudhon's *Coup d'Etat* (full name as The Social Revolution Demonstrated by the Coup d'Etat of the December 2nd) both published in 1852.

Victor Hugo condemned Louis Bonaparte with mean but witty critique. However, he was unable to analyze the class relations of France and couldn't grasp the circumstances leading Louis Bonaparte's coup to a success, instead he considered the coup as a personal violent behaviour. As if Louis Bonaparte, merely by virtue of his own will and power, had changed the historical process of France all by himself within one single day. Hugo tried hard to expose the ugly acts of Bonaparte as an adventurer, on the other side he one-sidedly exaggerated his personal subjective power as unprecedented in the world history, he painted him as a great hero instead of a mere nobody.

In his work *The Social Revolution Demonstrated by the Coup d'Etat of the Second of December* Proudhon evaluated the events from just the opposite view, fully contrasting Hugo's world outlook. Proudhon was fully entangled by pure objectivism thus tried hard to seek the causal relationship of the coup in history alone and described the coup as a kind of historical inevitability, as the result of the previous historical development. Thus Louis Bonaparte was no more than a puppet and/or tool of historical inevitability. As Marx wrote: In this way, "his historical construction of the coup d'etat becomes a historical apologia for its hero"[36].

Among those numerous evaluations written on the coup of Louis Bonaparte, only Marx's *The Eighteenth Brumaire of Louis Bonaparte* written in 1852 offered an excellent historical materialistic analysis. Marx analyzed the circumstances of the class struggles of the epoch, and also analyzed in detail the whole process of events after the February Revolution and circumstances caused by it; he examined the acts of Louis Bonaparte in certain historical background, examined his personal characteristics as well as all his rogue means and dirty tricks, and thus explained what on earth had "made it possible for a grotesque mediocrity to play a hero's part"[37].

After the coup that just happened, Marx made excellent comments and forecasts and discussed on some important issues related to the relationship between subject and object in history, and the role of historical figures.

These two related issues above are not the issues only faced in the field of epistemological studies, I can comfortably say that in the conception of history also exists the issue of relationship between subject and object. When we look more closely the content and logic

---

36   Karl Marx and Frederick Engels: Selected Works, 1st Edition, Volume 1, p. 599.
37   Ibid., p. 601.

of the above issues in these two different spheres of study, seem crossed and overlapping but we should carefully differentiate them.

If we look into the subject, we see that the subject of cognition and the subject of history are the same subject, i.e. the practicer, practical man. If we look into the object, not only the object of history is the object of cognition, but also nature as the object of cognition and object of transformation also become historical factors through material production and thus nature becomes the bond linking man and man. Therefore no nature, no human society and of course, no human history either. However, the two study fields focus on different perspectives. Epistemology mainly studies the laws of subject's cognition, i.e. tries to answer through what kind of cognitive process, approach and means can the subject reach the truthful recognition of the object, while the conception of history focuses on the laws of societal development, focuses on the object created by human activities. In epistemology, we can't abstractly say no subject, then no object; but in the sphere of conception of history, it is fair to say: No human activity, then no society or history. However, we can't thereby affirm such a conclusion that there is no object but only subject, only man and man's activity in the conception of history. Thus the analyses of Marx in *The Eighteenth Brumaire of Louis Bonaparte* all started from solving the subject-object relationship in the field of history materialistically and dialectically. He wrote: "Men make their own history, but they do not make it as they please; they do not make it under self-selected circumstances, but under circumstances existing already, given and transmitted from the past"[38].

"Men make their own history", means Marx affirms, men are the subjects of history. It is neither any abstract conception nor God's will and His standards that make history, but men themselves. Thus men compose their own "Song of History" by their own activities.

Different from epistemological studies focusing on men's thinking structure and cognitive structure, historical materialism analyzes men's social structure in which they live. Marx, when summarizing the French history between 1848-1851, analyzed different classes, different parties, political factions, and different type of figures. He not only examined the relations between classes, relations between

38   Ibid., p. 603.

parties and their representatives, but also examined their different positions and roles in historical development. Thus, the judgment that "men are the subject of history" doesn't envelop the real history in abstract philosophical principles or deprive history from the roles of individuals; on the contrary, it truly reveals epochal characteristics of history and real contents of human activities.

Indeed, history is created by men, but men can't make history at their own will. All acts of men must go through their thinking minds, which are expressed as passion, desire, will and purpose, but men's acts and motivations are socially restricted. And these restricting conditions are the social environment and the historical stage on which men act. Among all these conditions, the one that plays primary decisive role is the economic condition, i.e. the mode of material production; and the second to it is the political conditions, i.e. the class structure and political system determined by the mode of production and the mental/ideological tradition existing in men's mind. For all generations of men, these conditions are not self-designed but appears as the result of the activities of the last previous generation, which already exists, which is given and inherited. Men can neither freely choose any productive force or production relation nor determine their class at their will; even the mental/ideological tradition of the dead forefathers also confuses or entangles the living minds of our current age like a nightmare.

Marx fully recognized the historical subject position possessed by men as well as men's creativity, but on the other side he also scientifically revealed the limits of their thoughts and actions and studied on the general laws which determine the process of historical development. Laws of history is not independent of men's actions but exists inside their actions, thus they (laws) open up a road for themselves by the effect of the conflicts and contradictions occurring among numerous single wills and actions. Marx's conception of history is materialistic and dialectic; he combined the consideration of both the historical subject position of man and the objectivity of laws of history, thus he both rejected fatalism and voluntarism.

In *The Eighteenth Brumaire of Louis Bonaparte*, Marx expressed his basic opinions about how to analyze and evaluate historical figures through his analysis on how such figures like Louis Bonaparte came into being, and their historical roles, the reasons of the temporary success of the coup, and he made forecasts about the result of his coup from the aspect of the conception of history.

When analyzing the class struggle in France from 1848 to 1850, he said, "Every social epoch needs its great men, and when it does not find them, it invents them, as Helvétius says"[39]. This statement not only emphasizes that positive prominent figures exert significant effects on the progress of history, but also emphasizes that those negative figures block the development of history. Louis Bonaparte was such an example. Though he was extremely arrogant as if nobody on the earth could beat him, he had no idea about the real reasons that made him the "indispensable man" but saw himself in the giant's mirror. Marx went straight to the heart of the problem and said, "While his party had sufficient insight to ascribe the growing importance of Bonaparte to circumstances, he believed that he owed it solely to the magic power of his name and his continual caricaturing of Napoleon"[40].

Those circumstances mentioned in the above sentence of Marx is the social environment at that time, i.e. the class struggles in France in 1848 and the political situation formed by the descending line of revolution. The ruling dynasty of France was overthrown by the 1848 February Revolution; next, the proletariat was brutally suppressed in the June Uprising, later the bourgeois republicans and the petty bourgeois democrats were defeated by the Party of Order acting on behalf of the big landlords and the big bourgeoisie. France sank into constant political turbulences. The bourgeoisie cried out, "Rather an end with terror than terror without end!" Due to this feeling reflecting their weakness, they retreated from their rule, in other words they gave up their bourgeois republic, and "yearned for the former more incomplete, more undeveloped, and precisely on that account less dangerous forms of this rule"[41]. That's why they needed someone just like Louis Bonaparte.

---

39 Ibid., p. 450.
40 Ibid., p. 496.
41 Ibid., p. 630.

The emergence of a historical figure depends on the needs of the epoch, so he must be equipped with the characteristics of his own epoch and his own class. When studying a historical figure, comparative examination may be appropriate or possible but not any superficial historical comparison which ignores the epoch and class character of each historical figure and which only focuses on some superficial similarities. Because of class struggles and the differences in the economic conditions of fighting parties, political figures produced by theses struggles are by no means the same. Marx paid special attention to this point, and said, "I hope that my work will contribute toward eliminating the school-taught phrase now current, particularly in Germany, of so-called Caesarism. In this superficial historical analogy the main point is forgotten, namely, that in ancient Rome the class struggle took place only within a privileged minority, between the free rich and the free poor, while the great productive mass of the population, the slaves, formed the purely passive pedestal for these combatants....With so complete a difference between the material, economic conditions of the ancient and the modern class struggles, the political figures produced by them can likewise have no more in common with one another than the Archbishop of Canterbury has with the High Priest Samuel"[42].

When analyzing the figures in the French Revolution of 1848, especially Louis Bonaparte, Marx firmly held on this dialectic materialistic method. He debunked Bonaparte's tricks and fantasies of intentionally copying his uncle and taking the name of "Napoleon" as the garland on his own head, and discussed on the differences of the two Bonapartes. In this context Marx developed a view of Hegel on history. Hegel believed all great historical events and figures in the world appear twice, and Marx added that the first time they appear as a tragedy while the second time as a farce. For example, in the French bourgeois revolution, there were two Napoleons claiming to be an emperor, the first one was the uncle—Napoleon I, and the second, half a century later, the nephew—Napoleon III. Different epochs determined their different historical positions and roles. Although the nephew imitates the uncle, they were quite are two kinds of different people. Napoleon I was the representative of

---

42   Ibid., p. 599-600.

the revolutionary bourgeoisie, the destroyer of the old feudal system, whose rule was violent and brutal but much milder that the
aristocracies he defeated. He attempted to promote and consolidate
the bourgeois system by war, destroyed the Holy Roman Empire and
promulgated the *Codes Napoleoniens*. The failure of Napoleon I was
the downfall of a hero, which was a tragedy. However, Napoleon
III was the representative of the bourgeoisie which was scared of
carrying out a radical anti-feudal revolution; he suppressed the past
revolutionary achievements of democracy, and blocked the revolution which consequently led to those circumstances unfavourable for
the labourers. Louis Bonaparte's becoming an emperor was nothing
but a historical parody.

Contrary to Hugo's view, Louis Bonaparte did not lead the successful coup because he had unprecedented subjective powers, but due
to objective historical conditions. At that time, all other political
powers were exhausted during long class struggles, the power of
executive organ of the state power had expanded dramatically, the
power of legislative parliamentary organ had dramatically faded, under these circumstances Louis Bonaparte seized the executive power
in his own hands. Apart from these above, he also got the support
of small size farm owners (peasants), which constituted the largest
population of France. Marx pointed out, "Insofar as there is merely
a local interconnection among these small-holding peasants, and the
identity of their interests forms no community, no national bond,
and no political organization among them, they do not constitute a
class. They are therefore incapable of asserting their class interest in
their own name, whether through a parliament or a convention. They
cannot represent themselves, they must be represented. Their representative must, at the same time, appear as their master."[43] Because
Napoleon I was the representative figure in the French Bourgeois
Revolution, and fought against the feudal system, this historical
legacy gave rise to peasants' belief in a miracle, this man named
Napoleon would bring all glory back to them. Legacy of the uncle led those peasants to a full fantasy and high expectations from
the nephew. Of course, the nephew didn't represent revolutionary
peasants, but conservative peasants; not the future of peasants, but

43   Ibid., p. 693.

their past. However, the above political attitude of the small-holding peasants, secured Louis Bonaparte's victory in his conspiracy and eventually led him to the throne.

However, Marx didn't place objective historical conditions and individual's historical role in contradiction. He recognized the important role played by certain special properties of Bonaparte, his personal nature. Marx carefully analyzed his political and moral qualities, thus proving that there were some certain personal reasons that Bonaparte was the right man, and somebody else could not play this role. Marx called Bonaparte as the "chief of the lumpenproletariat", "dirty man" "an old, crafty roué", he was "a man who does not decide by night in order to execute by day, but decides by day and executes by night"[44]. Marx wrote: "Bonaparte, bought the scum of society with whisky and sausage, his dirty tricks were countless". Morality problem is just a personal quality issue for ordinary men, but for historical figures, morality would be an important factor that would affect critical political events, and they will be remembered with this event. Just as a marriage by ordinary citizens will be a private issue of them but a political marriage between two top members of dynasties might be a critical political issue in the history of Europe. Historical materialism doesn't ignore the analysis of the personal qualities of historical figures and also their ideas including the effects of their qualities. But certainly the effects of these personal properties and individual's role play their part jointly in interaction with historical laws. No individual can change historical laws. Marx once said, "When the imperial mantle finally falls on the shoulders of Louis Bonaparte, the bronze statue of Napoleon will come crashing down from the top of the Vendome Column"[45]. And history has proved his prediction.

---

44   Ibid., p. 658.
45   Ibid., p. 599.

CHAPTER XIV

IN-DEPTH COMBINATION OF THE MATERIALIST CONCEPTION OF HISTORY WITH ECONOMIC STUDIES. SYSTEMATIC ANALYSIS OF THE CAPITALIST SOCIAL FORMATION

The 1848 European Revolution, the largest and most far-reaching one in the 19th century modern world history, finally ended. The proletariat didn't act according to Marx's assumption of permanent revolution, but they accumulated rich practical experience in this revolution. In the preceding epoch the proletariat began to establish stronger organizations and accumulate strength. After the Revolution of 1848, the capitalism entered an epoch of relatively steady development.

In the late half of 1849, Marx arrived in London, the centre of the capitalist world. Leaving from the violent barricade wars in Germany, he turned to another battlefield and resumed his economic studies interrupted by the revolution. This meant an extremely hard job for him, seeking to expose the objective laws that would inevitably lead capitalism to death, which needed a systematic analysis on the forms of capitalist economy. Besides writing political comments for *New*

York Daily Tribune as a correspondent, Marx spent nearly all his efforts to prepare his book *Capital*. Nothing could stop his passion for researches and writing, whether it was illness, poverty, or the misfortune of his family. Thus he left us a large quantity of manuscripts on economics and achieved to publish the first volume of *Capital*. Through these economic studies he accomplished his second great discovery—the theory of surplus value, besides he enriched and developed historical materialism.

1 THE NEW PROGRESS ON THE MATERIALIST CONCEPTION OF HISTORY

The thought history of Marx proves that his historical materialism and economic studies are inseparable. Historical materialism established scientific theories and methods for studying economics; in turn his studies on economics enriched and promoted the development of historical materialism. The prosperous epochs in economic studies were often development days of historical materialism as well. For example, the research achievements on economics by Marx in Paris in 1844 were included in his *The Economic & Philosophic Manuscripts of 1844* and *The Holy Family*; and later his economic studies in Brussels in 1845 were reflected in *The German Ideology*, *The Poverty of Philosophy*, and *The Communist Manifesto*.

However, not until 1848 had Marx done a comprehensive, and systematic analysis of the capitalist society, but just prepared components for this great project. In *1844 Manuscripts*, he analyzed the nature of private properties throughout the history and the alienation of labour, but he laid particular stress on the distribution relations and tried to reveal the relation between property owners and workers by analyzing wage, profit and rent. In *The Communist Manifesto*, he analyzed the structure of the capitalist society, its production relations, class relations as well as the family, education, law and others in the bourgeoisie society, but these analyses were still rough and basic. We can say, the masterpiece in which Marx really treated the capitalist society as a living organism, revealing its production relations in full scale, the concrete expressions of its inevitable class struggles, the bourgeois political superstructure supporting and guarding capital's domination, the bourgeois ideologies such as liberty and equality, and even discussing the bourgeoisie family relations was *Capital*, where he demonstrated all its inner relations in an integrated logical system.

It is no exaggeration to say that Marx devoted his whole life to create his work *Capital*. On the basis of his achievements before 1848, he started his comprehensive preparatory works in the 1850s. Not long after he moved to London, Marx turned his research focus on the basic theories of political economy, made numerous readings on the history of national (country) economics and on the practical situation of the capitalist world, collecting and gathering materials he needed among the works of bourgeois economists, official files and journals, this initial studies of him, which includes, extracts, marginal notes, statistics, comments constituted his *London Notes* on economics. Later, he wrote another important parts of his drafts for *Capital*: *Economic Manuscripts: 1857-1858*, *Economic Manuscripts: 1861-1863*, and *Economic Manuscripts: 1863-1865*, and his published work (published in 1859) the first fascicule of *A Contribution to the Critique of Political Economy*. Thus, while establishing the proletarian political economy, Marx has also deepened and developed the historical materialism. In this context both his famous text *Preface* and his *Introduction* for the work *A Contribution to the Critique of Political Economy* have significant meaning in the history of historical materialism.

According to the time order, his Introduction for the work *A Contribution to the Critique of Political Economy* ("Introduction" for short is earlier than his *Preface* of the work *A Contribution to the Critique of Political Economy* ("Preface" for short). The Introduction was written from the end of August to the middle of September in 1857 but in the academia there are different opinions about the time when it was actually written. The Former Soviet Union scholar, D. Riazanov doesn't agree with the date confirmed in *Marx and Engels Collected Works*. He argued: "As it is proved by several researches, there is no adequate evidence to confirm the Introduction was written between the end of August (23th) and the middle of September. Probably Marx finished it only in a few days by the end of August." That problem may be important for textological studies, but concerning the content of the theory, I think this difference of half a month won't make any practical effect. The Introduction which specifically discussed the objects and methods of economic studies was still a philosophical article. Besides including research methods and reasoning methods, historical analysis methods and logical analysis methods, the relation between abstract and concrete, the relation between analysis and comprehension, questions about epistemology and dialectic logic, it also specifically discussed the important issues of historical materialism.

In the Introduction, Marx expressly discussed the issues about material production. He elaborated the social nature of production process, the general and specific forms of production, the interactions among the elements included in production relations, the determinate effect of material production on intellectual/ideological production and the interactions between the two. Thus the text included a brief but consistent elucidation on the views of the historical materialism related to material production, and also included idealistic historical views of Rousseau, Smith, David Ricardo, Bastiat, Carey, and Proudhon.

Material production is the basis upon which the human society exists, is a viewpoint Marx advocated since he began building historical materialism. Through his studies on the history of economy and the history of society in the 1850s, Marx was firmly convinced that any society , if ceased material production, not to mention one year, maybe just for a few weeks, would cease to exist, this truth was simple common sense for all. However, Marx was not satisfied with this affirmation, and tried to develop a theoretical-philosophical analysis of this fact as well.

In Marx's mind, any production is the "appropriation (create, shape) the products of nature by individuals (members of society) in the very social formation they live in. Production can't do without individuals; on the other side production is not merely the production of an individual. As Marx said, "Man is a Zoon politikon [political animal] in the most literal sense: he is not only a social animal, but an animal that can be individualized only within society. Production by a solitary individual outside society—a rare event, which might occur when a civilized person who has already absorbed the dynamic social forces is accidentally cast into the wilderness–is just as preposterous as the development of speech without individuals who live together and talk to one another"[1]. Since the nature of production, above all, is *social* production, thus men acting for production is bound to be social men. It is not the human nature that determines the social nature of production, but the social nature of production determines that man can't live and labour isolated. The social nature of production is the key to understand human nature.

By virtue of this fundamental view, Marx criticized the social philosophy of Rousseau and his social contract theory which argued that the mutual relations and connections among the naturally independent subjects were established through contracts. In fact, the relations among men are formed, not via contracts among individuals, but in the process of production. Marx also criticized Smith and Ricardo about their ignorance on the social nature of production and their view which led them to take single solitary fishers and hunters as the starting point when examining production, which should fall under the unimaginative fictions in Robinson Crusoe books in the 18th century. However, in the 19th century, the American economist Carey, the French economists Bastiat and Proudhon introduced this absurd view of the 18th century to economics again, attempting to make a historic and philosophic explanation of the origin of economic relations, which indeed demonstrated their superficiality. All these prove that Marx's discussions about the social nature of production in the Introduction was quite critical both for the conception of history and proletarian economics.

That is the fundamental viewpoint which Marx repeatedly discussed in his efforts of building and developing historical materialism. Years later, he argued on this issue again in his book review written by Adolf Wagner—a textbook on political economy. In the first volume of this textbook on the general principles of national economics, Wagner abstractly talked of man, his needs and value which he disconnected from social production, thus considered value as the natural desire of man. He argued: since man has to evaluate if he wants to clearly cognize the relationship between the property outside and his needs; for Wagner through this evaluation, the property or the material from the outside world is given a value. Criticizing

---

1   Karl Marx and Frederick Engels: Selected Works, 1st Edition, Volume 2, p. 87.

this view, Marx incisively pointed out: "'Man', if here it refers to the category of 'general man', then he has no needs at all; if it refers to a solitary man standing alone in front of the nature, then he should be seen as a non-social animal; if here he is a man living in whichever social formation—as Mr. Wagner presumed, because his 'man' who may not take a university education can at least speak—then the starting point is, he should be equipped with the certain property of social man, i.e. the certain property of the society he lives in, because herein, production, i.e. the process of his obtaining his means of subsistence, has already had this or that social property"[2]. Obviously, all of these notions explained by Marx will hardly be grasped without acknowledging the social nature of production.

Marx also affirmed the necessity to comprehensively study the material production functioning as the basis of social existence and social formation. Any production is inevitably the production at a certain social stage, but throughout all the ages' production and production process inevitably shares some common marks and common rules; otherwise, no production can be done. Therefore, to abstract the general features of production by comparative study of all ages was of great value for us to understand the common properties of production. Marx said, "Production in general is an abstraction, but a sensible abstraction in so far as it actually emphasizes and defines the common aspects and thus avoids repetition"[3]. For example, any material production process contains the subject-object relation, as Marx wrote: "the very fact that the subject, mankind, and the object, nature, are the same" Material production is a process between man and nature, a process of material exchange (metabolism) between man and nature caused, adjusted and controlled by the activities of man. This kind of material exchange (metabolism) is an eternal natural condition of human society and shared by all the social formations (societal forms) in the history of human social life.

Marx warned, we cannot "ignore the essential differences existing among them despite their unity"; that we should research "the relation between the general categories of production at a given social

2   Karl Marx and Frederick Engels: Collected Works, 1st Edition, Volume 19, p. 404-405, Beijing: People's Publishing House, 1963.
3   Karl Marx and Frederick Engels: Selected Works, 1st Edition, Volume 2, p.88.

stage and the particular forms of production in each stage", which emphasizes researching the integrated history of the relations of production, from these two aspects. For example, instrument of production, it is the inevitable general condition of any production process. Without instruments of production, without the past, accumulated labour, (dead labour) any production is impossible. However, the instruments of production gaining the form of capital is not a general, eternal natural relation or an essential link in the relation between subject and object (man and instruments of production). Only in a certain mode of production occurs that the instruments of production or the previously accumulated, dead labour become capital. Therefore, Marx said, "There are categories which are common to all stages of production and are established by reasoning as general categories; the so-called general conditions of all and of any production, however, are nothing but abstract conceptions which do not define any of the actual historical stages of production"[4].

That was an extremely important methodological principle proper for both economics and philosophy. Marx points to dual aspect of the research on material production This means: we not only should study the general categories of production and the relation between man and nature in production process, but on the other side we should study the specific form in which this production is realized in each societal stage and also study the concrete forms of relations between *man and man* in each societal stage in history. Evaluating production, by disconnecting its commonality (unity) and difference, or putting its universality and specificalness apart, or talking merely on general production without examining the specific form of production in each historic stage, will definitely turn "the general categories of production" this reasonable and rational abstraction into rigid dogma that can barely explain anything.

Production isn't any isolated individual act but has a social nature, which demonstrates itself intensively as: Production is an integrated economic process consisting of four elements: Production (production in its narrow sense), distribution, exchange and consumption. Marx went deep inside this integrated process of production and expounded the dialectic relations among each element part therein, and

---

4   Ibid., p. 91.

further enriched the materialist conception of history which treats production relations as an organic whole.

Holism view is an important view of the historical materialism. Any complicated thing or system must contain different parts that constitute its unity as a whole, which is true both for the natural world and also in the social world. In *The Poverty of Philosophy*, Marx has already pointed out that "The production relations of every society form a whole"[5]. In the Introduction, he reemphasized this opinion and wrote: "There is an interaction between the various aspects. Such interaction takes place in any organic entity."[6] However, in his several decades' of careful research, Marx didn't restrict himself with expounding on general principles of production, instead he researched into the concrete content and function of each element (part) of production constituting the whole, were realized.

Marx thought highly of consumption, thus he expounded the dialectic relation between production and consumption. He analyzed the three expressions of the dialectic identity between production and consumption and affirmed the positive effects of consumption to production. The product only attains its final consummation in consumption. For example, a railway on which no one travels, which is therefore not used, not consumed, is potentially but not actually a railway; a house which is uninhabited is indeed not really a house. A product different from a simple natural object will manifests itself as a product, will become a product, only in consumption. And because consumption creates needs for new production, it provides the conceptual, intrinsic motive reason for production. However, in the interactive relation between the two, it is the production that plays the primary or decisive role, for it provides materials and objects for consumption, determines the patterns of consumption (the quality and quantity of consumption and lifestyle), and stimulates the needs of consumers by the products it supplies. And "production is the point where the realization begins and thus also the decisive phase, the action epitomizing the entire process"[7]. Reasonable consumption would be beneficial for production, while ignoring the status of

---

5   Karl Marx and Frederick Engels: Collected Works, 1st Chinese Edition, Volume 4, p. 144.
6   Karl Marx and Frederick Engels: Selected Works, 1st Chinese Edition, Volume 2, p.102.
7   Ibid., p. 97.

production and pursuing exaggerated consumption will only hamper production and finally lead to the withering of consumption.

Marx's analysis of relations between production and distribution, production and exchange, —concerning its guiding principles and methods—, is parallel with his analysis on the relations between production and consumption. Although Marx's guiding examination method considers the interactions among different factors, he does not skip to multi-factor causality theory, thus he does not ignore that production plays the decisive role. When he talked about distribution, he highlighted, "The structure of distribution is entirely determined by the structure of production. Distribution itself is a product of production, not only with regard to the content, but also with regard to the form."[8] As for exchange, which is the medium between distribution and consumption, it is either directly contained in production or determined by it.

Having analyzed all the above four links of production, Marx made a significant conclusion. He said, "The conclusion which follows from this is, not that production, distribution, exchange and consumption are identical, but that they are links of a single whole, different aspects of one unit. Production is the decisive phase, both with regard to the contradictory aspects of production and with regard to the other phases. The process always starts anew with production process. That exchange and consumption cannot be the decisive elements is obvious; and the same applies to distribution in the sense of distribution of products. On the other side distribution of the factors of production, on the other hand, is itself a phase of production. A distinct mode of production thus determines the specific mode of consumption, distribution, exchange and the specific relations of these different phases to one another. Production in the narrow sense, however, is in its turn also determined by the other aspects."[9] In the history of the historical materialism, this conclusion by Marx shows us a clearer picture of the interactions of all the elements in the material production process as well as its operating mechanism.

---

8   Ibid., p. 98.
9   Ibid., p. 102.

Having made above analysis, Marx started out by analyzing the functions of material production in the whole society. In the fourth part of the *Introduction*, he made an outline of the principle points (as title) which he prepared to discuss about: "Means of Production and Conditions of Production. Conditions of Production and Communication. Political Forms and Forms of Cognition in Relation to the Conditions of Production and Communication. Legal Relations. Family Relations" Though he didn't develop his views according to this outline, he still mentioned many significant opinions, such as, the dialectic relation between productive forces and relations of production, the expression of the relation of productive forces and relations of communication in armies, the relation of cultural history (religion history and political history) and history of reality, the relation between the necessity and contingency in history, the influences of transportation on historical process to evolve it towards the history of the world, and so forth. What's worthy of specially attention in his remarks is the unbalanced development between material production and artistic production, which is truly an important problem in the historical materialism.

Marx thought some of the peaks in arts history by no means correspond to the general development of society; nor do they therefore correspond to the material substructure, the skeleton as it were of its organization. In the history of artistic creations, certain important branches of art were only possible at an early stage in the development of art. For example Greek mythology. All mythological narrations subdue, controls, and visualize the forces of nature in imagination and through imagination; thus they disappear when these forces of nature are actually controlled. In the epoch of capitalism, there is no way to reproduce these epoch-making classic epics and Greek mythology that can bring us aesthetic pleasure and are in certain respects regarded as a standard and unattainable ideal by some ideologists. This idea doesn't contrast historical materialism, because the art creation in Greek epics and mythology "does not conflict with the immature stage of the society in which they originated. On the contrary its charm is a consequence of this and is inseparably linked with the fact that the immature social conditions which gave rise, and which alone could give rise, to this art cannot recur"[10].

---

10   Ibid., p. 114.

He also emphasized, "The concept of progress is on the whole not to be understood in the usual abstract form"[11], because there is no absolute balance between material production and intellectual production. The high development of the capitalist social productive forces does not necessarily bring corresponding progress in the field of literature and art; on the contrary, the capitalist production will confront some spheres of intellectual production such as art and poetry. This judgment of Marx is proved by the reality of the modern western world. Of course, this doesn't mean in the capitalist society, literature and art can no way to make any progress but just means there is not a simple linear relationship but a series of intermediate layers between material production and intellectual production, thus their development is not in complete synchronization. Thus the view that twists the historical materialism as some vulgar economic determinism is totally wrong.

If we can say the *Introduction* focuses on discussing the sociality of production and the structure of production relations, then the famous *Preface* written in 1859 is very different from it, for the latter one makes an overall generalization of the materialistic conception of history from a macroscopic level.

In the thought development process of Marx, he gave a general summarization of the materialistic conception of history twice, first in *The German Ideology* which sums up the achievements by 1846; the other in "Preface of *A Contribution to the Critique of Political Economy*" (Preface for short) which concludes the achievements by 1859 among which the experience of the Revolution of 1848 and the economic research results in the 1850s especially from 1857 to 1858 have special effects. If we conduct a comparative study of the two conclusions, we can recognize the progress Marx made in the materialistic conception of history.

In *The German Ideology*, when generalizing the historical materialism, Marx stated, "This conception of history depends on our ability to expound the real process of production, starting out from the material production of life itself, and to comprehend the form of intercourse connected with this and created by this mode of production

---

11　Ibid., p. 112.

(i.e. civil society in its various stages), as the basis of all history; and to show it in its action as State, to explain all the different theoretical products and forms of consciousness, religion, philosophy, ethics, etc. etc. and trace their origins and growth from that basis"[12].

However, in 1859, Marx made a more complete and accurate interpretation of the historical materialism in the Preface. Having briefly described his process of exploring historical materialism, Marx said, "The general conclusion at which I arrived and which, once reached, became the guiding principle of my studies can be summarized as follows. In the social production of their existence, men inevitably enter into definite relations, which are independent of their will, namely relations of production appropriate to a given stage in the development of their material forces of production. The totality of these relations of production constitutes the economic structure of society, the real foundation, on which arises a legal and political superstructure and to which correspond definite forms of social consciousness. The mode of production of material life conditions the general process of social, political and intellectual life. It is not the consciousness of men that determines their existence, but their social existence that determines their consciousness. At a certain stage of development, the material productive forces of society come into conflict with the existing relations of production or—this merely expresses the same thing in legal terms—with the property relations within the framework of which they have operated hitherto. From forms of development of the productive forces these relations turn into their fetters. Then an era of social revolution begins. The changes in the economic foundation lead sooner or later to the transformation of the whole immense superstructure. In studying such transformations it is always necessary to distinguish between the material transformation of the economic conditions of production, which can be determined with the precision of natural science, and the legal, political, religious, artistic or philosophic—in short, ideological forms in which men become conscious of this conflict and fight it out. Just as one does not judge an individual by what he thinks about himself, so one cannot judge such a period of transformation by its consciousness, but, on the contrary, this consciousness

---

12   Karl Marx and Frederick Engels: Selected Works, 1st Edition, Volume 1, p. 43.

must be explained from the contradictions of material life, from the conflict existing between the social forces of production and the relations of production. No social order is ever destroyed before all the productive forces for which it is sufficient have been developed, and new superior relations of production never replace older ones before the material conditions for their existence have matured within the framework of the old society. Mankind thus inevitably sets itself only such tasks as it is able to solve, since closer examination will always show that the problem itself arises only when the material conditions for its solution are already present or at least in the course of formation. In broad outline, the Asiatic, ancient, feudal and modern bourgeois modes of production may be designated as epochs marking progress in the economic development of society. The capitalist mode of production is the last antagonistic form of the social process of production—antagonistic not in the sense of individual antagonism but of an antagonism that emanates from the individuals' social conditions of existence—but the productive forces developing within bourgeois society create also the material conditions for a solution of this antagonism. The prehistory of human society accordingly closes with this social formation."[13] Herein, Marx didn't use the concepts in *The German Ideology* such as "civil society" and "form of intercourse (Verkehrsform)", but adopted the categories like mode of production, productive forces and relations of production, economic foundation and superstructure, social formation, and economic development of society to make a more concise generalization of the basic laws of the development of human society.

The biggest achievement of the *Preface* is its holistic view, not the holistic view on social events but the holistic view on laws. Instead of talking about the laws of social development one by one separately, it discusses them from the whole of their interactions. It both uncovers the unique content and function of each law and exposes their mutual relations and mediums. No law could play its part alone without other laws. Marx laid special stress on uncovering how the change of one element would lead to the change of another and therefore cause the evolution of the social formation, which functions like a chain. In order to master a certain law, we could break

---

13   Karl Marx and Frederick Engels: Selected Works, 1st Edition, Volume 2, p. 82-83.

this whole in our thought process and focus on one particular, but in the practical social life, they are inseparably interwoven together. Therefore, Marx considered the human society as a rather complicated historical process which is full of contradictions and affected by the interactions of all kinds of laws.

However, Marx didn't entangle himself in the empty discussions on abstract interactions and interrelations. In the *Preface*, he tightly grasped the decisive link among all the interrelated factors and starting from this link, carried out his examination. Marx classified the relations of production as part of the social structure and found the repeatability and regularity of social events; furthermore, he closely evaluated the relations of production to productive forces and found the primary decisive element of history. If we grasp productive forces as the primary link of the chain, then it means we have grasped the decisive link of social historical development. Only when analyzing the status of productive force at a certain stage can we find the basis upon which a certain relation of production exists and changes; also, only the productive force can provide us the objective standard to distinguish whether any relation of production conforms with it or not. Without referring to the contradiction between productive forces and the relations of production, one could hardly understand why economic base and superstructure would come into conflict or comprehend the deepest root of social revolutions. In one word, only by grasping the role of productive forces and lifting our view on the relations of production to the height of examining them by the criterion of productive forces can there be solid scientific basis to see the development of social formation as a natural and historical process. Marx's dialectic theory about social development is established upon this basis of materialism. If the principle that productive forces play the final decisive role were taken away, this theory would again fall into idealism, i.e. quasi dialectic theory of multifactor interactions (causality) theory.

True enough, the *Preface* has significant effects in the history of the historical materialism, but it also reflects the features of its epoch, i.e. the epochal characteristics of Marx's discussion of the historical materialism. Starting from productive forces, the *Preface* makes a sequencing examination as: productive forces → relations of production → superstructure → social revolution → replacement of the social formation, but pitifully it doesn't make any alternative scenario. But, Marx has never negated the impacts of superstructure and the relations of production on productive forces, but did not discuss this scenario as the main aspect at that time, which was in conformity with the properties of the epoch than a deficiency of his theory.

2 SOCIAL FORMATION AND MAN

In the history of historical materialism, the founders of Marxism have mainly analyzed two social formations with great efforts: one is the primitive clan society, and the other is the capitalist society. The master work for the former is *Origin of the Family, Private Property, and the State* written by Engels based on the works of Morgan and the notes of Marx, and that of the latter is *Capital* of Marx. The two works are closely related to each other. If we can say *Origin* (for short) emphasizes on exposing how private property, classes and the state emerge, then *Capital* proves they will inevitably perish by dissecting the anatomy of the capitalist society. Marx analyzed the capitalist society as the last social formation with class antagonisms.

It is not abstract man but social formation that is the research object of *Capital*. Just as Marx said in the preface of the first edition of *Capital*, "In this work I have to examine the capitalist mode of production, and the conditions of production and exchange corresponding to that mode"[14]. Through his analysis of the bourgeois production process, circulation process and the general process of production, Marx represented the emergence, the development, and the inevitable trend of capitalism towards perishment as natural historical process in a logical analysis form, which, nevertheless, does not lead to the conclusion that *Capital* excludes or separates men's activities from economic laws. Marx said, "Man himself is the foundation of his material production as well as that of all the other kinds of production"[15]. If no man and no material exchange between man and nature, then no human society or the so-called laws of social

14 Karl Marx and Frederick Engels: Collected Works, 1st Chinese Edition, Volume 23, p. 8, Beijing: People's Publishing House, 1972.
15 Karl Marx and Frederick Engels: Collected Works, 1st Chinese Edition, Volume 26, p. 300, Beijing: People's Publishing House, 1972.

development either. True enough, Marx analyzed the capitalist social formation far from ignoring the subject or apart from men's activities of material production, but what he focused on was not the
men's wills or their desires or pursuits, but the objective relations
formed in the process of production independent of human consciousness as well as how these relations develop according to their
own laws. He examined the objective process strictly according to
the development status of productive forces and the corresponding
production relations, and never sought help from the abstract nature
of man, whether in his analysis of the transition from commodity
to money and then to capital, from simple commodity production
to capitalist commodity production, from simple coordination/coop-
eration in labour process to coordination/cooperation in workshops
and then further to capitalist factory production, or in his analysis on
the production of absolute surplus value and production of relative
surplus value, and the appropriation and transformation of surplus
value. He revealed the relations between man and man through the
relations between object and object. Therefore, in *Capital*, the analysis of man always insists on starting from society, placing man into
a certain social formation and examining man as the performer of
a definite relation of production. It is a fundamental aspect in the
historical theory of Marx to analyze man from the perspective of
society.

In the *Economic Manuscripts: 1857 to 1858* as the first draft of
Capital, Marx analyzed the development of man in three major social formations in human history. He pointed out, "Relations of personal dependence (entirely spontaneous at the outset) were the first
social forms, in which human productive capacity develops only to
a slight extent and at isolated points. Personal independence founded
on objective dependence is the second great form, in which a system of general social metabolism, of universal relations, of all-round
needs and universal capacities is formed for the first time. Free individuality, based on the universal development of individuals and on
their subordination of their communal, social productivity as their
social wealth, is the third stage. The second stage creates the conditions for the third. Patriarchal state, and ancient (feudal) state thus
fall down with the development of commerce, luxury, money and

exchange value, while modern society arises and grows in the same measure"[16]. It isn't that difficult to discover that what Marx advocated is the principles of historical materialism that productive forces determine the relations of production and the social status constituted by the totality of the relations of production determines the position of the individual (man) as we see in the above paragraph.

In ancient times, the individuals practicing production were subordinated to a larger collective: patrilineal clan or matrilineal clan, and were later subordinated to various communes emerging due to the conflicts and fusion among clans. Each person acted as a member of some tribe or community. "These individuals have the corresponding qualities necessary to form this certain community"[17], such as their special "religions", the "limited characteristics" of individuals in these societies, the consciousness and views of people in the primitive society, and so forth. Of course these features don't originate from the nature of man, but "correspond to the limited development of productive forces, which is limited in principle"[18].

If human originally acted as species in groups, if tribal groups, social animals, and communities bonded by blood lineage, then with the development of production and exchange, the existence of these type of groups (bonded by blood lineage) became unnecessary and disintegrated, people becoming isolated. In the past, this blood relationship made individuals be the appendage of a certain narrow group, but later, the individuals surpassing the natural relations appeared as social "atoms" isolated from each other. In fact, this kind of isolated men is not the starting point of history, but the result of history, as the result of the breakdown of the old common ground bonded by blood relationship. In the 18th century, this view of isolated individual rose to its peak. Actually, "the epoch that produced this view of isolated person is the epoch that has the most developed social relations by now."[19] The highly developed capitalist commodity

16 Karl Marx and Frederick Engels: Collected Works, 1st Chinese Edition, Volume 46a, p. 104, Beijing: People's Publishing House, 1979.
17 Karl Marx and Frederick Engels: Collected Works, 1st Chinese Edition, Volume 46b, p. 35, Beijing: People's Publishing House, 1980.
18 Karl Marx and Frederick Engels: Collected Works, 1st Chinese Edition, Volume 46a, p. 497.
19 Ibid., p. 21.

production further strengthened the relations between man and man in which the needs of one man can and must be satisfied by the products of another man, and vice verse. They may not know each other at all, and be indifferent and even hostile in perception, but the differences in production and differences in need inevitably place them in a certain social relation. However, this relation is objectified in commodity and money, so the relation between man and man is intermediated with object and concealed by the relation between objects too. In fact, "the dependent relation of object is nothing but the independent social relation opposite to the seemingly independent individuals, i.e. the independent relation of production among these men and opposite to themselves"[20].

Thus it can be seen that the individual/isolated person emerging in the capitalist social formation is the expression of the community breaking down the blood bond and sublation of the narrow relationships of personal bondage and personal ties, but they still to a degree remain to live within certain social relations. The capitalist system manifests such a contradiction as follows: On one hand, the relations of people are tighter than any other societies in the history; on the other hand, people are estranged, distant and isolated from each other in perception and in emotion. This situation is naturally not caused by the changes of human nature but originates in the contradiction between the sociality of production and the privacy of property, which means it is rooted in the essence of the capitalist mode of production.

Just because Marx placed man into certain relations of production and analyzed man from the perspective of society, thus in *Capital*, his examination of man is closely attached with the capitalist relations of production. He said, "I paint the capitalist and the landlord in no sense couleur de rose [i.e., seen through rose-tinted glasses]. But here individuals are dealt with only in so far as they are the personifications of economic categories, embodiments of particular class- relations and class-interests. My standpoint, from which the evolution of the economic formation of society is viewed as a process of natural history, can less than any other make the individual responsible for relations whose creature he socially remains,

---

20   Ibid., p. 111.

however much he may subjectively raise himself above them"[21]. When talking about the distinction between capitalists and workers, he highlighted, "The principal agents of this mode of production itself, the capitalist and the wage-labourer, are as such merely embodiments, personifications of capital and wage-labour; definite social characteristics stamped upon individuals by the process of social production; the products of these definite social production relations"[22].

The view above of Marx contains abundant and significant thoughts.

Firstly, man is the bearer of certain class interests and relations, of course when in class societies. In this kind of class societies, individuals are the bearers of certain class relations and interests, each of whom are subordinated to their specific class and have particular interests. The most essential relation among them is class relation. The individuals of a certain class can transfer from one class to another (such as a worker can ascend to be a capitalist, while a capitalist may go bankrupt and descend to be a worker, thus they both change their class positions and interests), but the class distinctions won't cease to exist because of the class transfer by any individual member. The structure of classes is relatively stable. A certain type of production relation based on private property inevitably has one basic class structure corresponding to it and involves certain individuals corresponding to class divisions of this specific (type of) production relation. That individuals must belong to a certain class is an undeniable objective fact existing in class society. An "individual" who belongs to no class, has no specific interests and is free from class is impossible to exist in the world.

Secondly, man is the personification of economic categories. One person owns his capital not because he is a capitalist, but he becomes a capitalist because he owns capital. In the same way, he doesn't sell his labour force because he is a worker, but he becomes a worker because he sells his labour force; a usurer becomes a usurer because he uses money as his capital to gain interest and there is no usurer

21   Karl Marx and Frederick Engels: Collected Works, 1st Chinese Edition, Volume 23, p. 12.
22   Karl Marx and Frederick Engels: Collected Works, 1st Chinese Edition, Volume 25, p. 995, Beijing: People's Publishing House, 1974.

in the world without any money capital. Therefore, the identity or the social quality and status of a person is not determined by his natural properties but is the embodiment of the regularity (laws) of the social relations or regularity of economic formations upon which he depends. Outside the bourgeois relations of production exists no distinction between capitalist and wage-labourer. This distinction is combined with wage labour and capital, and is the mode of individual's social existence.

This judgment of Marx is totally different from Hegel and Proudhon who vulgarized Hegel. Proudhon considered the economic categories as a basis to ignoring men's role as subjects and evaluated man's all economic activities as the self motions of economic categories, which was already refuted by Marx in *The Poverty of Philosophy*. The economic categories mentioned by Marx here above are not ideological (thought) forms but are the relations of production, those objective and practical relations formed in the process of production and exchange, which determine the social properties of human beings. For example, he analyzed the impacts on men's relations which commodity causes in the circulation process with the same view. He said, "The commodity-owners entered the sphere of circulation merely as guardians of commodities. Within this sphere they confront one another in the antithetical roles of buyer and seller, one personifying a sugar-loaf, the other gold. Just as the sugar-loaf becomes gold, so the seller becomes a buyer. These distinctive social characters are, therefore, by no means due to individual human nature as such, but to the exchange relations of persons who produce their goods in the specific form of commodities"[23].

Since capitalists are the personification of capital, so they have some distinct characteristics as persons, not stemming from any abstract human nature, but reflecting the characteristics of capital. For example, different from the idleness, laziness, parasitism and luxury peculiar to the feudal aristocracies living on land rent, the individual characteristics of bourgeois rooted in the capitalist mode of production, which is mainly expressed as their enthusiastic pursuit for the appreciation of value, their extreme desire for wealth, egoism, as

---

23   Karl Marx and Frederick Engels: Collected Works, 1st Chinese Edition, Volume 13, p. 85, Beijing: People's Publishing House, 1962.

well as pinching each penny in business and the unconventional progressive spirit. Law of free competition as the external driving force dominates each bourgeois, forcing them to maintain his own capital by constantly accumulating and expanding capital. If the personal characteristics of a bourgeois don't fit into the characteristics of capital, he will never be a "qualified" capitalist and will be to go bankrupt.

Thirdly, man is the product of various kinds of social relations. The nature doesn't create slave owner and slave, capitalist and worker, or any other different kind of division among men. It is the mankind itself that creates itself. The material production and re-production not only produce material products or the relations of production and reproduction, but also reproduce man itself. Herein, it includes both the reproduction of the population and the reproduction of the bearers of production relations, which means reproduction of individuals in certain relations of production. As early as in 1844, Marx had already seen through this point. He highlighted in the *1844 Manuscripts* that the bourgeois production not only produces products, but also produces man as commodity man, as man with the law (regularity) of commodity, produces him as dehumanized existence spiritually and in bodily. He often mentioned this basic view in *Capital*. His descriptions, whether of capitalists, workers landowners or of industrial capitalists, commercial capitalists and money capitalists, were always closely linked with their positions in the relations of production, relations with capital, wage labour, land rent, industrial capital, commercial capital, and money capital. What he wanted to uncover is not the eternal human nature, but the individual's social characteristics formed by the relations of production.

Marx always examined man within certain social formations, so his theory about the all-round and comprehensive development of man in the communist society is completely established on the basis of historical materialism. The all-round and integrated development of individuals neither means the all-round realization of the essence of human nor moral ideals based on abstract humanistic principles; but argues that the new mode of material production will surely create a new generation of communists corresponding to it. That is an objective law of historical development, but only in the ideological forms sphere it is expressed as the ideal and hope about the future development of man.

Marx repeatedly highlighted: "Universally developed individuals… are no product of nature, but of history"[24]. He also wrote: "Not an ideal or imagined universality of the individual, but the universality of his real and his ideal relations….For this, however, necessary above all that the full development of the forces of production has becomes the condition of production; and not that specific conditions of production are posited as a limit to the development of the productive forces"[25].

First, communism embodies the full development of the forces of production. As a social formation in the history of human development, the significant historical contribution of capitalism lies in that it forms universal social and material exchanges, abundant various needs and relatively developed forces of production. Although the labour division in the capitalist society represses the workers' comprehensive aspiration, their interest and ability of production, and they develop one-sidedly and abnormally by being intentionally and one-sidedly educated or trained, the application of scientific technology in the production process still requires improvement in workers' educational level. On the basis of big automated industry, all kinds of polytechnic schools, agricultural schools and occupational schools have emerged and have developed greatly. This phenomena manifest that the enormous development of productive forces embodies in itself the objective requirement and objective trend of combining physical and mental labour. Also, the development of productive forces and free competition constantly change the allocation of capital and labour, which requires those workers who can adapt to the constantly changing circumstances of labour market. The development of productive forces and free competition also replaces those workers who can only shoulder partial or single social function with those workers who are more developed and can take different social functions in as many as alternative conditions. Under the capitalist conditions, the law of labour force transformation plays

24 Karl Marx and Frederick Engels: Collected Works, 1st Chinese Edition, Volume 46a, p. 108.
25 Karl Marx and Frederick Engels: Collected Works, 1st Chinese Edition, Volume 46b, p. 36.

a rather blind role, which brings disasters to workers but at the same time forcefully constrains the workers to work in a certain department of labour process.

Of course, it is far from enough when only the forces of production are developed it is also critically essential to reform the relations of production accordingly. The capitalist society has advanced productive forces, but it is a society based on class division and confrontation. Therein, the occupational education of workers is relatively quite limited; the improvement in productive forces do not lead to the shortening of necessary labour time, instead often workers are laid-off. The capitalist relations of production not only hinder the development of productive forces, but also block the realization of this objective trend which is embodied in productive forces themselves.

Marx's assertion about the full development of individual is designed according to ideal man, but is rooted in his analysis of the capitalist mode of production. Through the reality high developed productive forces and the objective trend of capitalist productive forces, he predicted the necessity and possibility of full and all-round development of individuals in the future communist society. In the future communist society, due to the significant development of productive forces and of the extinction of classes, "The surplus labour of the population ceases to be the condition for the development of general wealth, just as the non-labour of the few, for the development of the general powers of the human head. With that, production based on exchange value breaks down, and the direct, material production process is stripped of the form of penury and antithesis. The free development of individualities, and hence not the reduction of necessary labour time so as to posit surplus labour, but rather the general reduction of the necessary labour of society to a minimum, which then corresponds to the artistic, scientific etc. development of the individuals in the time set free, and with the means created, for all of them"[26].

With that above, we could see that Marx did place man into a certain society and examine the changes of man in that certain social formation. It is determined by the development of the mode of material production that man develops from the narrowly developed man as the

---

26   Ibid., p. 218-219.

first step, to the partially developed man in the capitalist society and then to the fully developed man in the communist society. However, this doesn't lead to such a conclusion that man's adapting to a certain mode of production is passively and spontaneously formed. In fact, when people are establishing a new mode of production and forming new productive forces and new relations of production, they are also changing the subjects—themselves, and during this process, the links in the superstructure especially the educational system play a very important role in changing the subjects. But how on earth does the mankind shape itself and the objective feasibility and necessity of its self-moulding? And spontaneously on the other side how come that the limits men can reach in this self-moulding are determined by the development status of productive forces and by the nature of the relations of production rather than any ideal model for man which was so enthusiastically advocated by some thinkers. This is a basic issue solved by historical materialism and is also the fundamental view and method *Capital* adopts in examining the development of man.

3 RE-EXAMINATION OF ALIENATION IN THE CAPITALIST SOCIETY

In the development process of the theory of the historical materialism of Marx, there is a remarkable phenomenon: From his doctoral dissertation and the preparation materials for the doctoral dissertation to the *Manuscripts* in 1844, the alienation theory appears to become more and more prominent; but during a rather long time after his founding historical materialism in *The German Ideology* and criticizing the idealistic alienation theory of the Young Hegelians and the "True Socialists", he hadn't used the concept and term "alienation". However, in the several drafts of *Capital*, such as *Economic Manuscripts of 1857-1858*, *Economic Manuscripts of 1861-1863*, and *Economic Manuscripts of 1863-1865*, we again see a large number of places where this concept alienation was used. Even the officially published *Capital* still often uses the concept of alienation to expound the fetishisms of commodity, money and capital. The concept of alienation that once had disappeared later returned to the economic works of Marx. His thought seems to go around a circle: ascend from labour of alienation to historical materialism, and then go back to its starting point, to the alienation theory. This phenomenon confuses many people and causes intense debates.

It will be a kind of formalistic practice if we boldly assert that alienation is the core of Marxism as well as the consistent—without any changes—idea of Marx just relying on the fact that Marx still used the concept of alienation in *Capital* and in the preparatory works for it. Therefore we will prefer to examine the development of the concept of alienation or changes in it. I think, whether Marx ever used the concept of alienation in his late books is insignificant, what really matters is what significance and meaning he gave to this concept in these works. Was the basic theory and method of his analysis of the capitalist system historical materialism or the alienation theory? Ignoring these fundamental questions but only evaluating the superficial phenomenon will lead to anywhere but a correct conclusion.

After ascending from the theory of alienated labour to historical materialism in *The German Ideology*, Marx no longer took alienation as his fundamental theory or method. In *Capital* and its preparatory works, though he still used the concept of alienation, the basic theory and method had become the historical materialism (also the dialectic materialism). The "Introduction to *A Contribution to the Critique of Political Economy*" he wrote in 1858 and the "Preface to *A Contribution to the Critique of Political Economy*" in 1859 are specifically written to expound the objects and methods of political economy studies, thus they can be seen as the guiding thoughts used when writing *Capital*, but there is not even one sentence mentioning alienation in these two texts. If the alienation theory is really the fundamental view and method of all his later economic works, there is no way he talked nothing about it. On the contrary, in the *Introduction* and especially in the *Preface*, what people can see is the classic expression of historical materialism, which is no accident. Just as Engels commented when talking about the economic researches of Marx: "Only the establishment of the Customs Union enabled the Germans to *comprehend* political economy at all". "The essential foundation of this German political economy is the materialist conception of history whose principal features are briefly outlined in the "Preface" to the above-named work"[27].

---

27   Karl Marx and Frederick Engels: Selected Works, 1st Edition, Volume 2, p. 116-117.

We can easily recognize that point if we make a rough comparison of the *Manuscripts* and *Capital* with its drafts. The *Manuscripts* in 1844 is an important work in which alienation concept of Marx ascends to alienation of labour. By researching on labour, Marx not only discovered some essential ideas of historical materialism, but also put forward his profound opinions about the nature of private properties appearing in human history, about wage, interests, land rent and money. However, he didn't pay due attention to the social forms in which labour was realized, instead examined labour as the species nature of human, accordingly considered the labour of workers under the capitalist system as the alienation of human nature, thus considered the capitalist system as a system antithetical to the species nature of man (human). With this theory as a starting point in examining the capitalist system, maybe it can be possible to raise sharp refutation and condemnation against capitalism, but it is impossible to reach any scientific understanding on the nature of the capitalist mode of production, and the objective economic basis of its emergence and extinction. His analysis in 1844 *Manuscripts* doesn't completely surpass the frame of the concept of alienation and re-winning of human nature.

Yes, some people might say that it can be totally possible to examine man's labour without taking into consideration the social forms in which labour is realized, relying on the argument that labour is the universal act in which man enters into material exchange (metabolism) with nature; that this is shared by all social men, and is not restricted to any definite social form. Actually, there are two different questions here. One is about the general elements of labour shared by labour of any nature. Just as we can abstract "general production", we can also abstract this general labour, i.e. labour of any nature. And it can expound the process of labour, how the subject (man) acts on the object of labour via instruments of labour. This aspect of study is very necessary. In *Capital* and its drafts, Marx has often discussed this aspect of the problem. The other aspect (true labour versus real labour duality) puts the social form of labour aside, evaluates the true labour as the essence of man and as a consequence measures and evaluates the real labour with the essence of man as criterion, which will lead to see real labour degrade into the frame of historical aspect. This view embodies the duality of the aspects of alienation/re-winning aspect and the historical aspect. It is proved by facts that without considering the social form in which labour is realized and without considering the basis upon which this social form exists, it is impossible to make a correct evaluation on the nature of labour.

But *Capital* and its drafts are different, which embodies the guiding thought as the principles of historical materialism expounded in the "Preface to *A Contribution to the Critique of Political Economy*". It examines economic phenomena, not from the aspect: alienation of the species nature of human, but from the interactive relations between the forces of production and the relations of production. In the *Economic Manuscripts of 1857-1858* in which the concept of alienation is used more often, it is the principles of historical materialism that guides all the content of analysis. For example, Marx's analysis in the chapter on Money in the *Economic Manuscripts of 1857-1858* is not the same as in the *1844 Manuscripts*. In the *Manuscripts* in 1844, he saw money as "the alienated ability of mankind", and the divine power of money "lies in its character as men's estranged, alienating and self-disposing species-nature"[28]; while in the *Manuscripts of 1857-1858*, he laid more stress on examining the essence and functions of money from its relations with commodity and value form. He criticized the theory of "labour money" of Proudhon and his follower Alfred Darimon, analyzing value and use value of the commodity and the contradiction between the two values, emphasizing that money is the inevitable result of the development of the commodity form of product. Marx said, "As value, commodity itself is money." "The exchange value of a commodity, as a separate form of existence accompanying the commodity itself, is money; the form in which all commodities equate, compare, measure themselves; into which all commodities dissolve themselves; that which dissolves itself into all commodities; the universal equivalent.)[29] Therefore, money is not explained as the alienation of the species nature of human, but as the result of production development. If without the development of production and the development of exchange, and

28 Karl Marx and Frederick Engels: Collected Works, 1st Chinese Edition, Volume 42, p. 153.
29 Karl Marx and Frederick Engels: Collected Works, 1st Chinese Edition, Volume 46a, p. 85-86.

without transformations from simple *product* production to *commodity* production, there would be no money either.

Likewise, when examining capital in the chapter titled as Capital, Marx also focused on the development of production. He said, "It must be kept in mind that the new forces of production and relations of production do not develop out of nothing, nor drop from the sky, nor from the womb of the self-positing idea", "production resting on capital and wage labour differs from other modes of production not merely formally, but equally presupposes a total revolution and development of material production"[30]. He illustrated this issue with the example of the ownership of land. The ancient proprietor of land transforms himself to the modern farmer both changing the form in which he obtains his revenue and the form in which the labourers are paid, but "this is not, however, a formal distinction, but presupposes a total restructuring of the mode of production (agriculture) itself; it therefore presupposes conditions which rest on a certain development of industry, of trade, and of science, in short, of the forces of production"[31].

In his *Capital*, as the brilliant model of applying and developing historical materialism, Marx considered the capitalist social formation as a natural historical process and revealed the laws of its emergence, development and inevitable perishment analyzing through the inner contradictions of the capitalist mode of production. The alienation and re-winning of human nature concept left behind, Marx tightly held the rope the concept of relations of production and evaluated the forces of production as its causal source. In his debate against Mikhailovsky, a Russian Narodnik, Lenin specially highlighted the guiding principle of "two attributes" in *Capital* and spoke highly of the comprehensive analysis of capitalist social formation in *Capital*, praising this work as the bright demonstration of historical materialism.

In fact, in the 1850s, the biggest achievement of Marx's economic researches is the establishment of the theory of surplus value of which the theoretical and methodological principles come from historical materialism. The concept of alienation used and applied in *Capital* and in its preparatory works helps to describe the antagonistic nature

30   Ibid., p. 235.
31   Ibid., p. 234.

of capitalist production relations which was already revealed by historical materialism and theory of surplus value. No way, it would be possible to reach such a height by taking alienation as the fundamental theory and method. We can comfortably say that without historical materialism or surplus value theory, there wouldn't be *Capital* and it would be impossible for us to grasp the antagonistic nature of production relations of capitalism also wisely described by Marx with alienation. In this way, it is reasonable to believe that it is appropriate to summarize the development process of Marx's historical materialism as ascending from the concept of alienation to the concept of alienation of labour, and then from the concept of alienation of labour further to the full establishment of historical materialism.

The re-introduction of alienation into the economic manuscripts of 1850s and 1860s and into *Capital* doesn't mean that Marx skirted *The German Ideology* and went back to the ideas of *1844 Manuscripts*. The issue we discuss here means that, not only that the role of alienation concept in Marxism did change but so did its content. In 1844, by analyzing the regularity of alienated labour process, Marx revealed the antithesis between products of labour and labourer, between labour itself and labourer, between man and man, but he saw this antithesis as the separation of the species nature of human from human himself and from this theory he deduced the antithesis between man and man. Though he had already seen the antagonistic relation between capital and labour, his opinion on alienation was still painted with some colours of Feuerbach.

Capital, together with its preparatory works, is not completely the same as the *1844 Manuscripts*. *Capital*, absorbed and added the economic and philosophic achievements made in the latter period into the alienation analysis, but it also cleared the influences of humanism in it. Herein, Marx didn't explore the alienation of human nature through the relation between the products of labour and labour itself, but analyzed the characteristics of the capitalist relations of production and elucidated how the capitalist relations of production, through objects and expressed as objects, create the false appearance, that objects dominate man.

As Marx considered, the capitalist society is a social formation which can be characterized as: the dependence on the object. The social relations of people formed in their process of production, with object as medium, are expressed as relations between object and object. Commodity, money, capital, are all expressed in forms of object, but their true nature isn't object but they are certain social relations embodied in objects. Truly object doesn't enslave man. For example, machines don't exploit workers and they enslave workers only if they are possessed by capitalists as capital. That's why Marx said, "The emphasis comes to be placed not on the state of being objectified, but on the state of being alienated, dispossessed, sold; on the condition that the monstrous objective power which social labour itself erected as opposite to itself as one of its moments belongs not to the worker, but to the personified conditions of production, i.e. to capital"[32]. He also said, "The worker's propertylessness, and the ownership of living labour by objectified labour, or the appropriation of alien labour by capital—both merely expressions of the same relation from opposite poles—are fundamental conditions of the bourgeois mode of production, in no way accidents irrelevant to it"[33]. By analyzing the alienation of labour, the separation of the conditions of labour from labourers, the antithesis of capital and labour, the social consequences brought by application of science to labourers, Marx revealed the essence of the bourgeois relation of production and its antagonistic nature. Commodity fetishism, money fetishism, and capital fetishism are the objective features of the objectified bourgeois relations of production, while the "trinity" formula (land—land rent; capital—interest; labour—wage) advocated by the vulgar political economy only stays on the level of phenomena, thus remains desperate, could neither see the origin of surplus value and nor see the cognitive wisdom to elevate the relation between man and man to the relation between object and object.

It is one characteristic of the capitalist relations of production to enslave men with the production relation expressed in objectified form. This is the product of productive forces as they develop to a certain extent and form/create universal material exchange circumstances

---

32   Karl Marx and Frederick Engels: Collected Works, 1st Chinese Edition, Volume 46b, p. 360.
33   Ibid., p. 361.

and universal social relations and this is also the manifestation of the fact that the productive forces aren't developed sufficient enough to radically force a change in the relations of production. It is inevitable but not eternal. Its final origin lies in the mode of material production instead of the disconnection of human's species nature from human himself. Marx specially emphasized this point. When talking about the alienation phenomena in the capitalist society, he said, "But obviously this process of inversion is a merely historical necessity, a necessity for the development of the forces of production solely from a specific historic point of departure, or basis, but in no way an absolute necessity of production; rather, a vanishing one, and the result and the inherent purpose of this process is to suspend this basis itself, together with this form of the process"[34]. If to analyze the capitalist social formation and its forces of production and relations of production without historical materialism, the so-called man enslaved by object ("this form of the process" as mentioned by Marx, will become a magic power, an unpredictable and unsolvable "deadlock".

4 MARX'S RESEARCH ON RUSSIAN RURAL COMMUNITY. SUCCESSION AND SKIPPING PHENOMENA IN THE REPLACEMENT OF SOCIAL FORMATIONS

The most important content of the historical conception of Marx is about the class nature of social development and the law (regularity) of one social formation transiting to another. As early as in the *Manuscripts*, Marx had already commented on the two essential links of historical development: from immovable property to movable property, and second from the capitalist society with private property to the abolition of private property, in which he described the transformation from feudal society to capitalist society and that from capitalist society to socialist society in a less accurate way.

It is in *The German Ideology* that Marx really made specific classification on the social formations seen in the world history and put forward the theory about the changes of social formations for the first time. According to the forms of ownership, Marx distinguished

---

34 Karl Marx and Frederick Engels: Collected Works, 1st Chinese Edition, Volume 46b, p. 361 or p. 831-832 from Grundrisse.

between tribal ownership, ancient commune ownership, state ownership, feudal ownership, bourgeois ownership and communist ownership, and based on the laws he discovered about the interaction between forces of production and forms of communication, he roughly described the basic features of each social formation and the inner mechanism of their transformation process. In the *Economic Manuscripts of 1857-1858*, he made a specific discussion about all the modes of production before the capitalist production. In the "Preface to *A Contribution to the Critique of Political Economy*" in 1859, he abstracted all his previous research results into a formula, "In broad outline, the Asiatic, ancient, feudal and modern bourgeois modes of production may be designated as epochs marking progress in the economic development of society"[35]. His argument about the historical divisions and evolution of social formations indicates that he considered the human's historical development as a regularly advancing movement according to certain laws.

The question is: should each stage (epoch) or nation evolve go through all the five social formations in a successive order as Marx classified above? Till the publication of the first volume of *Capital*, he still gave no direct answer yet. And this question was solved between the late 1870s and the early 1880s.

The meticulous work *Capital* makes a very careful and thorough analysis of the capitalist social formation, which mainly takes England with the most developed and typical industry at that time as example. However, Marx didn't limit his research in England. After publishing the first volume of *Capital*, he deeply researched on the economic circumstances of many other nations, especially of Russia. In order to make a correct judgment of the Russian economy, in his fifties (which is quite old when compared with today) and very busy as he was, he even learned Russian by himself, examined the Russian rural communes and the Russian Reforms of 1861 and its consequences. He reviewed many official publications of Russian government and other materials related to Russia. Marx's findings during this research further enriched and developed historical materialism in two aspects.

---

35   Karl Marx and Frederick Engels: Selected Works, 1st Edition, Volume 2, p. 83.

First, the peoples or nations living under the same social formation have their own characteristics.

Marx divided historical stages according to different modes of material production, deduced the development of the world history into several social formations and thus revealed the repetitiveness and regularity of social phenomenon, but he didn't negate the certain specific characteristics of each people or nation. For example, in the *Economic Manuscripts of 1857-1858* and in the "Preface to *Contribution to the Critique of Political Economy*", he put forward the Asian mode of production, and commented on the features of the mode of production of various ancient Asian countries. Later, in the third volume of *Capital*, Marx raised this analysis to a general theoretical principle and pointed out that "This does not prevent the same economic base – the same from the standpoint of its main conditions—due to innumerable different empirical circumstances, natural environment, racial relations, external historical influences, etc. from showing infinite variations and gradations in appearance, which can be ascertained only by analysis of the empirically given circumstances"[36]. His scientific judgment here is completely proved by history. Though all belonging to the feudal social formation, China was different from Europe; all belonging to the capitalist social formation, England, America and Japan still possess unique characteristics of their own. It is unadvisable to neglect this particularity when studying the history of each nation.

However, the research on the national particularity can't negate Marx's theories about social formations. This particularity is the characteristics under the same social formation, which inevitably have many essential things in common and are dominated by the general laws exposed by historical materialism. Therefore, when Marx talked about their difference, he emphasized, "It is always the direct relationship of the owners of the conditions of production to the direct producers—a relation always naturally corresponding to a definite stage in the development of the methods of labour and thereby its social productivity—which reveals the innermost secret, the hidden basis of the entire social structure and with it the political form of the relation of sovereignty and dependence, in short, the

---

36 Karl Marx and Frederick Engels: Collected Works, 1st Chinese Edition, Volume 25, p. 892.

corresponding specific form of the state"[37]. With similarity included in differences and on the other side, differences included in similarity, as the two aspects, that is an important law of historical dialectics.

Secondly, there is discontinuity, or in another word, skipping possibility in the succession of the replacement of social formations.

Not only seen horizontally, different nations and peoples living under the same social formation have their different characteristics; but even we look vertically from the process of historical development, the successive replacements of social formations—in different nations—also manifest differences. The general laws of the world historical development don't repel the specific characteristics of the development of each nation or each people. When analyzing the future development prospect of the Russian rural communities, Marx made an excellent analysis about this issue.

On the 10th issue in 1877 of the Russian magazine—*Otecestvenniye Zapisky*, an article named—"Karl Marx before the Tribunal of M. Shukovsky" written by Mikhailovsky, a Russian Narodnik, was published which mistakenly interpreted *Capital*. For this reason, Marx wrote a letter to the editorial staff of the *Otecestvenniye Zapisky*, and for the first time declared his thoughts about the question that "whether Russia must begin by destroying the village commune in order to pass to the capitalist regime, or whether, on the contrary, she can without experiencing the tortures of this regime appropriate all its fruits by developing the particular historic conditions already given to her"[38]. He answered this question in a rather strict scientific attitude, not simply confirming or denying from abstract principles but putting "conditions" in the first place. He said, "Thus events strikingly analogous but taking place in different historic surroundings lead to totally different results. By studying each of these forms of evolution separately and then comparing them, one can easily find the clue to this phenomenon, but one will never arrive there by the universal passport of a general historic-philosophical theory, the supreme virtue of which consists in being super-historical."[39]

---

37   Ibid., p. 891-892.
38   Karl Marx and Frederick Engels: Collected Works, 1st Chinese Edition, Volume 19, p. 129.
39   Ibid., p. 131.

He clearly thought this could be the basis for considering two pos-sibilities. He said, "If Russia continues to pursue the path she has followed since 1861, she will lose the finest chance ever offered by history to a nation, in order to undergo all the fatal vicissitudes of the capitalist regime."[40]

This letter wasn't sent off. A few years later, Vera Ivanovna Zasulich, on behalf of the Russian revolutionists, asked Marx for his opinions about the fate of Russian rural communes and the future prospects of Russian history, especially about the theory that all the nations in the world, due to the historical necessity, must go through the capi-talist stage. Marx wrote a letter back and also made out three drafts for this letter of reply, in which he in a more detailed expounded and developed his previous views raised in 1877.

Marx took a firm stand on the historical dialectics, combined his analysis for the future prospects of the Russian rural community with the analysis of surroundings it was in at that time, he refuted to examine the rural community in abstract separation. Thus he meant, the analysis of the capitalist social formation in *Capital* contained neither the evidence for the Russian rural community still had vital-ity in itself, nor any evidence against that, and the key to decide that would lie in the analysis of surrounding conditions, Marx wrote: "either the element of private property which it implies will gain the upper hand over the collective element, or the latter will gain the up-per hand over the former. Both these solutions are *a priori* possible, but for either one to prevail over the other it is obvious that quite different historical surroundings are needed. All this depends on the historical surroundings in which it finds itself."[41]

Based on this view, Marx didn't negate the possibility of a non-capitalist path that Russia might take, the surrounding conditions of which are proletarian revolutions. "If revolution comes at the oppor-tune moment, if it concentrates all its forces so as to allow the rural commune full scope, the latter will soon develop as an element of regeneration in Russian society and an element of superiority over the countries enslaved by the capitalist system"[42]. Later in the pref-

40   Ibid., p. 129.
41   Ibid., p. 435.
42   Ibid., p. 441.

ace of the Russian edition of *The Communist Manifesto* in 1882, he reaffirmed this viewpoint that if the Russian revolution could give a signal of start to the western proletariat revolution and the two could supplement each other, then the Russian commune based on the public ownership of land could be the starting point for the development of communism.

He also mentioned the other possibility, a quite practical one, i.e. the dissolution of commune and the development of capitalism in Russia, because in the Russian villages at that time, a rural middle class including wealthy farmers had already emerged and the communes were faced with the threat of dissolution by the extortion of the Tsar government, the plunder of merchants, the exploitation of landlords, and the destruction of usurers from inside out: "what is threatening the life of Russian commune is neither the historical necessity nor any theory, but the oppression of the State and the exploitation of the capitalists who have penetrated deep inside the communes and are bred by the State through sacrificing the interests of the peasants"[43].

History realized the latter possibility in the end. After abolishing the serf system in 1861, the capitalism in Russia, first of all, the industrial capitalism was developed. Russia finally didn't skip the capitalist development stage but faced and manifested the general law of capitalism in its unique way.

However, this doesn't lead to the conclusion that Marx's assumption about the possibility of the non-capitalist path for Russia was mistaken and meaningless. On the contrary, his prediction about the historical prospect of Russia embodies valuable thoughts for the discontinuity of historical development stages, which greatly supplements the theory of the five social formations he established. The victory of Chinese revolutions and the development of many Chinese national minorities all prove the correctness of his judgments.

The problem is that we shouldn't, like some western scholars, counter pose the two aspects –the discontinuity of historical development and the general laws on the replacement of social formations put forward by Marx, or negate the latter by the former, or consider that

---

43   Ibid., p. 446.

the historical development of each nation is like a fallen broken vase scattered randomly without any certain direction. That would be a non-determinist conception of history. Just as Lenin pointed out later, "the general laws of the world's historical development, not at all repel the particularity of any individual development stage expressed in its developing form or sequence, but presuppose that."[44]

Firstly, the division of social formations by Marx is exactly right. The semi-feudal and semi-colonial society in the old China was not an independent social formation, but a variant as the combination of capitalism and feudalism. As for the so-called "information society" and "post-industrial society" in the western world, they are neither independent social formations, but still capitalist society. We don't know and also can't know what the development after the communist society will be, but this doesn't matter. What really matters is that till today, though we can observe many variants of a certain social formation, there is still no social formation beyond the five social formations mentioned by Marx.

Secondly, the sequence of the world historical development elucidated by Marx is right. Even though not every society or nation evolves exactly according to this sequence, but their development direction is consistent with the general sequence of the world history. It is impossible to presuppose that a nation develops from primitive society to slave society, while another nation starts from slave society and then "develops" from slave society to primitive society; or when we observe that the capitalist society of a nation matures in the womb of feudal society, while in another nation, the feudal society in the womb of the capitalist society. All as such actually has never happened yet. The development of history is winding and sometimes it will even go backward for a period, but the course of its development is directed. The historical development of a nation can surpass a certain historical stage, but the path of its history can by no means be a backward motion contrasting the historical laws uncovered by Marx.

---

44   Selected Works of Lenin, 2nd Edition, Volume 4, p. 690.

Thirdly, the exposition of Marx about the inner contradiction of the mode of production and its law of motion is quite correct. The core of the evolution theory of the five social formations is to underline the conditioning functions of productive forces for the relations of production and to expound how the development of productive forces finally cause the transformation of one social formation to a higher one. Any nation that skips over a certain historical stage due to its internal and external conditions doesn't prove the invalidity of the law above, but it realizes it in a different way.

One historical stage (i.e. a social formation in which a certain relation of production plays the dominant role) can be skipped, but we should never ignore the productive forces of the skipped stage, in such a case. The orderly change of social formations can be skipped in order to move to an advanced one, but the corresponding development level of its productive forces (of the advanced one) is absolutely essential and it is never possible to build and consolidate a socialist society based on feudal productive forces. When Marx assumed that Russia need not have to go through the capitalist development stage (as a possibility under certain conditions), and when arguing that possibility he considered the form of its ownership instead of the level of its productive forces and scientific achievements. Because, in the eyes of Marx, the Russian rural commune and the western capitalist production shared the same historical stage of the world history*, "it is thus able to appropriate its (Ed.: Western capitalist production) fruits without subjecting itself to its *modus operandi* (mode of operation)", and "allows Russia to incorporate into its communes all the positive acquisitions devised by the capitalist system without passing through its Caudine Forks**"[45]. It is thus clearly indicated that the world history, as a whole, can't skip beyond any historical stage, but only some certain parts of it, such as a

45 Karl Marx and Frederick Engels: Collected Works, 1st Chinese Edition, Volume 19, p. 436 and p. 438.

*) Caudine Forks, a metaphor used by Marx, borrowed from Roman history, points to humiliating, exploitive and suppressive realities as one aspect of capitalism.

**) Ed. Marx, following strict scientific manner, in order to argue for this possibility, ignored the weak and stagnant development of capitalism in Russia and only considered the condition of external western capitalism. In the later decades the capitalism in Russia began to develop much faster.

nation or a certain society in a region can skip it, because such a nation may leap beyond the average level of whole mankind by virtue of its more abundant and higher development of productive forces in the same epoch.

The complete materialistic and dialectic conception of history as a whole is indeed the unity of the uniformity and diversity of the world historical development. As for the standpoint of some western scholars who negate that capitalism will be replaced with socialism in the end and try to find a third road according to the so-called "multi-linear" development theory of history, we can say that this view obviously falls within the capitalist theory of defence permeated with class interests. The socialist revolution has proved and will continue to prove that this theory is mistaken.***

5 MARX'S "ANTHROPOLOGY" NOTES IN HIS LATER YEARS AND HIS DISCUSSION OF PREHISTORIC SOCIETY

In the late half of the 19th century when Engels concentrated on the writing of The Dialectics of Nature and Anti-Dühring and devoted himself to expound the dialectic materialistic conception of nature and systemize Marxism, Marx focused on the studies of primitive society and oriental society, during which he wrote five reading notes on this subject from 1879 to 1881: Conspectus of Kovalevsky's *Communal Ownership of Land, Reasons, Process and Result of Its Dissolution*, Conspectus of Lewis Morgan's *Ancient Society*, Conspectus of Maine's *Legal Lectures*, Conspectus of Lubbock's *Origin of Civilization and the Original State of Man*, Conspectus of Phil's *Aryan Village Communities in Hindu and Ceylon*. The theories developed in the above mentioned letters to the editorial staff of the Russian magazine—*Otecestvenniye Zapisky* and to Zasulich were not any sparks of talent occasionally erupted, but were the fruits of these researches, especially the researches on the communal system of land in the Orient.

***) In The German Ideology Marx correctly saw that humankind was moving towards the world history, leaving back regional and national histories.

Both Chinese and foreign scholars pay much attention to the relationship between Marxism and anthropology and highlight the special role anthropology played in the formation and development of Marxism. Some scholars even think the path of Marx's thoughts started by philosophical anthropology in his early days and then developed to empirical anthropology in his late years. However, these writings that are called "notes on anthropology" are neither philosophical anthropology nor sociological anthropology, but actually historical researches in which Marx applied historical materialism to study primitive society and oriental societies. The research object of them is not the mankind itself but the society. They research on the pre-capitalist social formations, especially the law of development of primitive society.

Marx spent his whole life for the researches on the capitalist society. It took him 40 years to prepare for and write *Capital*. Furthermore, he also paid great attention to examine the pre-capitalist social formations, which is very essential to more profoundly analyze the capitalist society. However, for a long time, due to insufficient scientific historical materials, he wasn't quite aware about the circumstances of prehistoric human societies.

In *The German Ideology*, he called the tribal property as the first form of property in the human history, and considered it as a "prehistoric state" of the mankind indeed. He described this "prehistoric state": "The social structure is, therefore, limited to an extension of the family; patriarchal family chieftains, below them the members of the tribe, finally slaves. The slavery latent in the family only develops gradually with the increase of population, the growth of wants, and with the extension of external relations."[46] He also said, "This latent slavery in the family is the first property" "where wife and children are the slaves of the husband"[47]. Obviously, in Marx's eyes, in the tribal property latently exists family slavery, and the social structure was patriarchy which was the extension of family. This illustrates that Marx wasn't very clear about the distinction and relations between matriarchy and patriarchy, between individual family and clan, public property and slavery, therefore evaluated the slavery in the family as the first social formation in history.

46 Karl Marx and Frederick Engels: Collected Works, 1st Chinese Edition, Volume 3, p. 25.
47 Ibid., p. 36-37.

In the *Economic Manuscripts of 1857-1858*, Marx conducted a study on the different ownership and production mode forms before the capitalist production mode. When talking about the form of ownership in Asia, he wrote: "In the first form of this landed property, an initial, naturally arisen spontaneous [naturwüchsiges] community appears as first presupposition: family, and the family extended as a clan, or [a clan formed] through intermarriage between families, or combination of clans." "They relate naively to earth as the property of the community, of the community producing and reproducing itself in living labour. Each individual conducts himself only as a link, as a member of this community as proprietor or possessor."[48] Just because of this, in the "Preface to *A Contribution to the Critique of Political Economy*" written in 1959, Marx treated the Asiatic mode of production as the part of first social formation in human's social development and used this thought to correct his previous idea in *The German Ideology* (*social formation based on* tribal property was mentioned as the first form in *The German Ideology*) and wrote: "the Asiatic, ancient, feudal and modern bourgeois modes of production are the epochs marking progress in the economic development of society" which manifests that Marx started believe that the public ownership of land was the starting point of history, the earliest ownership relationship of the mankind.

However, till then, Marx still didn't have a clear understanding of the conditions of the primitive society. In fact, not only Marx, the whole academic society at that time also lacked sufficient knowledge about the primitive society.

An important turn happened in the 1860s. Within about a decade, many great works studying on the family, marriage, clan, matriarchy and patriarchy in the primitive society were published one after another, for example, Bastin's *Mankind in History*, Maine's *Ancient Law*, Bachofen's *On Matriarchy*, McLennan's *Primitive Marriage*, Tyler's *The Primitive History of Human*, Lubbock's *Origin of Civilization and the Original State of Man*, Morgan's *Blood System* and *Ancient Society*, and so forth.

---

48 Karl Marx and Frederick Engels: Collected Works, 1st Chinese Edition, Volume 46a, p. 472.

Of all the above books, the Ancient Society of Morgan possessed a significant scientific value. Through his long-term and tiring investigations and researches, Morgan discovered important aspects of the social structure in the primitive society, proved *matriclan***** was the basic unit of the primitive society, explained the evolution law of family forms, expounded the function and role of family forms and marriage forms in the primitive society, and consequently evaluated that the emergence of private property had led to the appearance of monogamous family and the establishment of civilization. Engels said, "First, to the history of primitive society, the key to which was provided by Morgan only in 1877"[49]. Marx also thought very highly of Morgan's *Ancient Society*. In his notes, he changed the original system structure argued by Morgan, corrected some of his mistaken viewpoints, but on the whole, absorbed many valuable parts and facts. By studying *Ancient Society* and these recent valuable works, Marx achieved a relatively profound research on the primitive society and made up for the blank parts in his previous studies.

Marx affirmed the objectivity of the blood relationships in the primitive society. When refuting Grote's argument that the blood relationship as a conceptive relation, he said, "Dear Sir! Not conceptive but material, or *Wollust* in Dutch!"[50] Blood relationship is different from kinship system, which was recognized by Morgan. Morgan thought family was an active factor which never remained still, while the kinship system was passive which escorted the progress of the family during long ages and which only changed radically when family changed radically. Marx agreed with Morgan's above view and further developed it. In this way, Marx put the blood relationship in a very special position in the primitive society. Marx also changed his previous opinions about the relationship between individual family and clan and about the sequence of matriarchy and patriarchy in the primitive society. At first he believed that the monogamous individual family emerged earlier than clan and clan was a collective of families and an extension of the families; and that the patriarchal

49   Karl Marx and Frederick Engels: Selected Works, 1st Edition, Volume 3, p. 50.
50   Karl Marx and Frederick Engels: Collected Works, 1st Chinese Edition, Volume 45, p. 503, Beijing: People's Publishing House, 1985.
****) A clan, with membership determined by matrilineal descent from a common ancestor.

family emerged as the earliest family in history and the family members were under the control of paternity as slaves. After deeper readings Marx indeed absorbed the reasonable and correct ideas in Morgan's work, affirmed that the basic unit of the primitive society was the clan, not the individual family; clan emerged earlier than the individual family; the matriarchal clan preceded the patriarchal one. When refuting Grote's mechanical application of the characteristics of Roman families into the Greek families at the Homeric age, he wrote: "according to origin, clan is earlier than monogamous and pairing family; it is something roughly at the same time with Punalua family, but none of these family forms is the basis of clan" and "once clan is produced, it will continue to be the unit of the social system"[51].

Marx also expounded the origin and nature of state through his research on the primitive society. He refuted Maine's thoughts as follows: "Unfortunately even Maine himself knows nothing about that: in the place where a state (after primitive communes), a society politically organized exists, the state will by no means be the primacy of matter; it just looks so." When talking about morality, he said, "as for their moral existence, they are always derivative, of secondary quality, by no means of the primary."[52]

In these notes, Marx also abandoned his previous view in the 1844 *Manuscripts*, evaluating communism as the re-winning of human nature, at the same time emphasized that it will repeat the characteristics of the primitive communist society on a higher stage, "the collapse of society will become the end of the process with wealth as the only ultimate goal, because this process contains self-destructive elements [...] this (a higher social system) will be a resurrection of the freedom, equality and philanthropy of the ancient clans, but in a more advanced form."[53]

The development of the men's individuality isn't the needs or the self-realization of human nature, but restrained by economic conditions. Marx profoundly expounded this principle through the history of the primitive society and its dissolution. He said, "At first,

51   Ibid., p. 646.
52   Ibid., p. 397.
53   Ibid., p. 398.

the individuality sheds off the shackles that were not dictatorship at the beginning (as Maine, the fool understands) but are the bonds of satisfaction and fun brought by the collective, the primitive community—thus that is just one-sided development of individuality. However, as long as we analyze the content of this individuality, i.e. its interests, its real nature will show itself up. And then we will find that these interests, such as class interests and so forth, at the same time are the special interests of a certain social group as well. So this individuality itself is the individuality of the class, etc. and after all they are on the basis of economic conditions"[54]. This shows that Marx's notes of "anthropology" in his late years have nothing to do with the abstract humanism.

Besides, by researching on the organization structure of primitive society, Marx found that the public ownership of land is the common feature of primitive society while the private ownership of land was the distinct feature of the age of civilization, which sublates his previous view that the entire history of mankind was the history of class struggles.

On March 14, 1883, Marx left the world forever. Many of his glorious ideas that hadn't been published yet were later included in Engels' book—*Origin of the Family, Private Property, and the State*, becoming a constituent of the whole Marxism system.

Marx advanced along the road of mankind's exploring historical laws. Dedicating himself to research, he finally saw through the surface of history—the consciousness and self-consciousness of man and stepped into the depth of history, discovering the general laws controlling the development of human society.

Marxism develops itself through struggles. In accordance with the tortuosity of the revolutionary road of the proletariat, Marxism has also gone through ups and downs in its development and progress. In Marxism, it is the historical materialism that suffers the most criticisms and attacks. Some bourgeois scholars and the western "Marxology" either twist the historical materialism as vulgar economic determinism, and as abstract theories of alienation and humanism; or try to replace and supplement the historical materialism

---

54   Ibid., p. 646-647.

with technological determinism, multi-factor causality theory, psychological determinism, etc. The history will eventually prove that all these attempts will end up in vain and the great achievements Marx made in the field of history will never lose their value. Marx revealed the truth of history but doesn't end the history of truth, so we will certainly keep advancing along the road opened up by Marx.

APPENDIX I

SELF-DESCRIPTION OF ACADEMIC COURSE

A few years ago, perhaps in the spring of 2001, I was in hospital and wrote two poems when resting in bed, and below is one of them:

Hair has gotten white when it was once black
Talent has slipped away when it once flowed like a river
Illness is a friend of me and visits a lot more frequently in my old age
So I am too lazy to recall the old days and dreams
Prose I love the ones with thunderous momentum
Friends I respect are the ones who can stand together regardless of wind and storm
The scholar is now too old to carry the weapon
But he will devote his life to pursuing truth anyhow.

This poem was written for over ten years. Now the scholar gets even older, but his will of pursuing for truth is still as firm as he was young. I majored in Marxist Philosophy and have spent my whole life in "seeking for truth", learning and studying Marxism, even though I was not a student with quite satisfying marks.

In 1953, I graduated from the Department of History of Shanghai Fudan University and then I was assigned to study in the Marx and Lenin Research Class in Renmin University of China. In 1956, I graduated from the class and stayed in the Department of Philosophy of Renmin University of China. Actually, in the nearly twenty years from my first day of work to the downfall of the Gang of Four in 1976, I didn't get much time to research and hadn't written much either. It is since 1980s that I really settled down to do my research. When people ask my age, I always answer "two eights": my physical age is nearly 80 but my academic age is only 28, and they are the "two eights".

After the Gang of Four was crushed, my first paper was "Comment on the Status and Function of Feuerbach in Marx's Early Thoughts" published in the Journal of *Philosophical Researches* in 1981, criticizing the popular view of the time that explained Marx with abstract humanism. Then, I wrote "Two Transitions of Marx's Alienation Theory" published in the 2nd issue of 1982 of *Social Sciences in China*. I put forward that the alienation theory of Marx has two transitions: "from alienation to alienated labour", and secondly "from the contradiction between individual and class to the contradiction between productive forces and relations of production", and made a historical and concrete examination on the alienation theory of Marx. Not long after, I published another paper named "Comments on the 'New Discoveries' of Marxology", refuting various views of Marxology twisting and misunderstanding Marx's thoughts of alienation. These two papers all involved the question about how to treat humanism. Yes, the illegal, brutal, inhuman acts in the ten years' of Great Cultural Revolution should be condemned, and the socialist humanism should be recognized, but the abstract humanism is by no means the remedy for our mental trauma. "Scar"* can be denouncement of literature but it can't be a philosophical view concluding the history. In my mind, we need to promote the socialist humanism, reject the abstract humanism and truly hold our ground on Marxism, conducting a historical reflection on the ten years of the Great Cultural Revolution with the thoughts and methods of Marxism.

*) Scar literature or literature of the wounded is a genre of Chinese literature which emerged in the late 1970s, soon after the death of Mao Zedong, portraying the sufferings of cadres and intellectuals during the tragic experiences of the Cultural Revolution and the rule of the Gang of Four.

Before long, *Research on the Early Thoughts of Marx* co-written by Jin Huiming and me was published as one of the earliest books studying on the early thoughts of Marx in China, and instantly attracted the attention of the academic circle the day it got published. In 1987, I had my personal monograph—*Into the Depth of History* published. This book breaks through the range of Marx's early thoughts and takes a systematic and comprehensive research on his conception of history. I did have a reason to name this book studying on Marx's conception of history as "Into the Depth of History". Some scholars take the structure of cultural mentality, the structure of self-consciousness or the subjectivity of man as the deep structure of history, which in fact may fall back to the idealistic conception of history through different sort of paradigms. In this book, I focused on how Marx found the laws of historical development. To me, subjectivity, self-consciousness and the structure of cultural mentality, true enough, are important to understand history, but they still belong to the upper layer of history; what the materialistic conception of history means to solve is something profound and behind the upper layer—to uncover the deep structure deciding culture and man's consciousness and expose the regularity of the development of social history. The formation and realization of social laws can never do without the actions of subjects, but the formation and realization of social laws is the law of objective relations, formed in human activities. Social law is not determined by man's will, but on the contrary, it is a kind of joint force coming from the mutual repulsion and conflicts of numerous wills. We ought to differentiate the logical statements on laws from objective laws. Scientific laws produced in research are pure and contain mono-meaning, while objective laws are the deepest thing that plays the ultimate decisive role in a series of accidents and all kinds of errors. This book combined the historical conditions in which Marx lived, the situation of labour movements, and the thinking experience of Marx himself, and reproduced the thinking and logical process of Marx's finding historical laws, wherein it makes a detailed analysis of the important categories and the ideological and theoretical value of *The Economic and Philosophic Manuscripts of 1844*, alienation and humanism, and Marx's views about man and nature, man and society. It conducted some valuable explorations on the internal contradiction and the leading trend in the thought process of Marx and on the inevitability of how Marx headed for the historical materialism through overcoming his theoretical contradictions. The book has exerted relatively large impacts on the fields of Marxist philosophy and the history of Marxist philosophy, being chosen as the reference book for the postgraduates of Marxist Philosophy and of History of Marxist Philosophy by some Chinese universities and having received pretty high comments in many book reviews. In addition, it has won lots of awards, such as the Outstanding Winner of Philosophic and Social Science Works of Beijing, the First Prize of China National Excellent Researches on Humanities and Social Science issued by Ministry of Education (Education Commission), the First Prize of Outstanding Science Researches of Renmin University of China, and so forth.

In 1989, I, cooperating with two of my students, published *An Overview of Philosophy of Karl Marx and Frederick Engels*. In August 1990, I published *The Dismembered Marx*, a book which had been prepared in my mind for a really long time. It was a theoretical book, a work about the history of Marxism, carrying out a critical investigation on all the modern western theories and viewpoints that try to dismember Marxism, for example, the antagonism between two Marxes, i.e. the young Marx and the old Marx, the antagonism between Marx and Engels, and the humanization, alienation and religionization of Marxism. Several students of mine helped me to complete this job. This book once won the First Prize of "Wu Yuzhang Scholarship" Award.

Before that, in 1982, I, together with some colleagues in the former Institute of History of Marxism and Leninism, published the *History of Ideas of Marx and Engels*, which is the first monograph in China comprehensively studying the ideas of Marx and Engels and tried to uncover the history of Marxism from the interaction of the three components of Marxism. That is a very meaningful theoretical construction and attempt, because the integrity problem is the key to the scientificalness of the Marxist system and it is feasible to study Marxism respectively from philosophy, economics and scientific socialism, which helps us to research on this science more specifically and more profoundly. However, it is unadvisable to turn them into three disciplines independent of each other and having no mutual relations or cut the complete scientific system of Marxism apart into three large separable plates. In 1988, *A Course in the Basic Principles of Marxism* chiefly edited by me was published. One of its features was to explain Marxism as a whole. If we can say *History of Ideas of Marx and Engels* emphasizes on historical investigation, then A Course in the Basic Principles of Marxism focuses on the interpretation of theories.

In the past two decades, I have published more than 170 essays in *Social Sciences in China*, *Philosophic Researches*, *Qiu Shi* (truth seeking), *People's Daily*, *Guangming Daily*, *Journal of Renmin University of China*, *Journal of Teaching and Research*, and many other influencing newspapers and magazines. These essays involve a very wide range, not only containing the basic principles of Marxism and the important problems of the history of Marxism, but also concerning the issues about culture and traditional Chinese culture. In these articles, I have always expressed my views on some practical and theoretical problems, especially on the important ones in relation to historical materialism. I have two papers—"Emphasis on the Status and Functions of Humanities in Cultural Construction" and "On Marx and Marxism" which respectively won the seventh and the ninth Award of "Five 'One' Project (a good book, a good TV series, a good play, a good film, a good article)" of The Propaganda Department of CC of the CPC. Also, some of my papers won the Excellent Essay Award of *Hong Qi* (red flag) magazine, the first prize of *Philosophical Research*, the Excellent Essay Award of the Research Centre of Social Science Development of Ministry of Education, the Philosophy and Social Sciences Research Achievement Award of Beijing, and other awards. Some papers were reprinted by *Xinhua Digest*, and even more were reprinted by the Social Science Information Centre of Renmin University. Afterwards, the China Renmin University Press compiled my monographs and most of my essays into *The Collected Works of Chen Xianda* (6 volumes) and published it. In 2004, Beijing Normal University published my book named *The Philosophy of the Gap* listed as one of the *Contemporary Chinese Philosophers Anthology*.

In my life, I am easy to get pleased with myself in relation to academics: I focus on the reality and on the philosophic problems which have significant practical and theoretical meaning. Seldom or never, do I write any scholastic article which I can't understand it myself and don't want others to either; nor do I play philosophical games from one concept to another, not because I don't want to write, but because I really don't have that ability of speculation or that kind of "philosophical interest". My papers, in the eyes of some scholars, may be too shallow and have no depth to study. However, as I always believe, to us scholars on Marxist philosophy, philosophy is the "sophisticated" knowledge but also can be popular philosophy, the functions of which can only be realized and developed by publicizing it to the masses and edifying them. Those articles that can only be understood and appreciated by a very few people or only understood and appreciated by their narcissistic writers are the "fatal injury" of the works related to Marxist philosophy. Actually this rule also goes for many other things far more than Marxist philosophy, and even to Kant, the philosopher who is famous for his obscure philosophy, who also advocated that articles should be plain and popular. He didn't pretend to be profound and he even felt sorry his works were so difficult to understand. I have quoted his words many times, for example: "the lack of popularity is a fair accusation raised by the public for my writings. In fact, any philosophical work must be able to be popularized; otherwise, it may just be full of meaningless twaddle covered by a seemingly esoteric smokescreen." How well he said! Even the great philosophers like Kant had pursued for popularity, not to mention us the apprentices taking Marxist philosophy as lifelong cause. I always argue for that the articles we write should be as popular and easy to understand as possible, the less rare and abstruse words the better; and we'd better not choose sentences like any sealed book with nobody knowing its meaning. It is kind of bluffing to claim those articles no one can understand as good ones. The sense in an article can be profound, but the words should be readable. One of the standards of evaluating papers should be "profound meaning in simple words". If the articles written by the Chinese philosophical workers couldn't be understood by their counterparts, then they wouldn't be any easier for common readers either. However good its sense is, this kind of article is also a waste of paper, for a currency that can't be circulated is also like a waste paper however high its nominal value is".

In my old age, I have become more inclined to the olive-type short essays of which the words are milder and simple but the meaning is profound and worthy of deep thinking. I used to like writing long essays, each one of 10 thousand characters at least, but now I only write such a long one when I get adequate time and energy. However, I do like short ones better. A long article may seem very "complicated", "academic" and "splendid", but its writer must have a rather large knowledge reserve and have done many in-depth researches, otherwise, this long essay of thousands of words without any heartfelt experience or pertinent opinions of the writer will be just a combination of empty words like the foot wrappings of some lazy women in the ancient China, intolerably bad smelling and long-winded. Therefore, my writing style of my old age has been changed a bit, and I like short essays which tell something, may about a man, a thing, a reason, a feeling or just some words worthy of chewing and savouring, or even just one of these above will be enough as well.

Of all my works in my whole life, my favourite is the series of "Chen Xianda's Essays on Philosophy": *Reverie and Ramble*, *Night Talking in the Garden of Peace*, *Philosophic Gnosis*, and *A Return to Life*. I spent nearly ten years on writing and publishing these four books. They are all written in my old age, of more than one million characters, all flowing out from my heart. Whether good or not, these are my words spoken by myself and expressing my own ideas.

I have a reading habit that whenever I have some new thought, I will write it down. Sometimes it is a complete paragraph and quite like a pre-article which just needs some modification; sometimes, it is just a few words, or an inspiration suddenly coming out and needing to be further processed and developed. Each book I write is always the rewriting and abstraction of the tiny drops of my ideas accumulated in years. I like to compare composing my books to building houses. In usual times, the needed wood, bricks and tiles are piled in the yard, i.e. written on the notebook, and when they are accumulated to a certain amount, the house needs to be built; I will move them out one by one. To me, to make reading notes is a dull method to learn, but is also an extremely useful one. Human has limited capacity of memory, let alone me who just has a mediocre intelligence. If I don't write them down at all times, I am afraid I wouldn't remember much of what I have read, not to mention to write a book within a short time. Intuition is transitory, and inspiration is fleeting. Without gifted intelligence, I think we'd better not place our hopes on intuition or inspiration but ought to really come down to earth and make some "dull" efforts like reading notes.

I also think that the level of a philosophical article isn't measured by its quotes, its length, or its obscurity. An article with some special flavour, no matter how long it is, must say something, tell something. And this so-called "something" is what you want to pass on to the readers, which may be your ideas, your feelings, your inspirations or the sparks of your mind. As long as it flows from your own thinking mind, more or less, deep or shallow, it is far better than the thing you copy from others.

To be honest, my "Essays" mentioned above are just like some black bread that couldn't be served in a fancy feast. However, to man, all his own geese are swans, which makes no exception for me either. However bad these little books may be, they are still typed by me, the old man, letter by letter. I like them and maybe a little too much like an old man who likes his youngest son most. Also my readers like this kind of articles. One book review called—"An Excellent Work Blending Philosophy, History and Literature together" had once praised these philosophic essays of mine as follows: "The essays involve almost all the frontier questions argued by the contemporary philosophic circle, which, as shown in the book, are many in-depth observations imbued by common sense of life. The writer expresses Marxist philosophy in a very attractive and popular way with the plainest language."… "he writer combines the profoundness of philosophy, the elegance of literature, and the abundance of history together so well that professional philosophy workers won't think it is shallow and non-professionals will also be attracted by philosophy". These over-flattering words, for my work, are a kind of comfort to the lifelong hard work of an aged man.

Truly, I am old, for I have been feeling more and more urgent in recent years. I really appreciate that the China Renmin University Press has listed my old book in "The Contemporary Chinese Humanities Series", which is quite an encouragement for me. Of course, I would like to write something new, if God allows and I also work hard enough myself. Luckily, I am not any guy hopelessly accepting his oldness; though I am aged, I never get slack at studying and it seems like I will work and study until my last day. Nearing the end, I would like to finish this "personal statement" with two of my poetries in the old style:

I.

My hair gets white like frost falls on my head
Autumn comes when all leaves turn yellow
One should know death and life better when he gets older,
Since one is weak, he'd better climb more stairs
Coldly I look at the officialdom and down upon the corrupt officials
Who are the kings of the world in the sunrise but prisoners in the sunset?
All people say life is like a drama
On which rate will my writing life be?

II.

All my past eighty years are like a dream
Full of bittersweets of life
A goose walking in a snowfield still leaves its footprints
How could one's life vanish like passing clouds?
Ashamed of selling myself for a bubble reputation,
For no reward I write what I like
The articles written in the first half of my life are old papers now
But I will still write a lot more, old as I am!

Written in the sweltering summer of 2009 in Yi Garden

APPENDIX II

ON THE ESSENCE AND CONTEMPORARY VALUE
OF THE MATERIALIST CONCEPTION OF HISTORY*

Materialistic conception of history, as the most important constituent part of Marxist philosophy, its establishment was the key of Marxism when realizing the revolutionary changes in philosophy. Without the materialistic conception of history, Marxist philosophy would still be a halfway materialism, a reprint of the old one. However, even if the materialistic conception of history wasn't surnamed Marx, not founded by Marx or Engels, some of the regularity factors therein will still be found sooner or later, of which the clues had already shown up in the thought history of the Western Europe in the first half of 19th century. It is already manifested that the core problem of historical materialism is a problem of social and historical laws, thus the excellent thinkers at the same epoch might provide similar ideas in different aspects to different extents. However, the materialistic conception of history also contains historical values reflecting the standpoints and social ideals of its founders.

*) Article first published in the Journal of Theoretical Front in Higher Education, 2002(5).

The bourgeois historians could recognize the existence of class and class struggles, but they could only get conclusions beneficial for the bourgeoisie against the feudal aristocracies; the British classic economists saw the relationship of labour and value and the important functions of material production and wealth growth to the development of society, but what they got were the conclusions merely favourable for consolidating and developing the capitalist system. In Marxist philosophy, historical materialism and scientific socialism are inseparable, the whole historical materialism takes fighting for the emancipation of the proletariat and the mankind as its supreme mission, so only Marx and Engels as the representatives of the theories of proletarian revolution were likely to establish a both scientific and revolutionary, systematic and complete conception of history.

Of course, ever since Marxist historical materialism was established, debates and arguments around Marxist Philosophy, especially about historical materialism have never stopped, all kinds of "additions" and mistaken misunderstandings or attacks have emerged every now and then. It was quite reasonable that some of our theorists have expressed their dissatisfaction to the dogmatism in the Soviet philosophy textbooks and pursued to expound the historical conception of Marxism comprehensively and correctly; in addition, they also raised some difficult problems and hot issues, which is in great favour of deepening the researches on materialistic conception of history. But we really ought to avoid fully negating the most basic principles of historical materialism under the slogan of objecting traditional text book historical materialism and under the banner of returning to the Marxist conception of history. If that happened, it would definitely cause confusions and disorders in theory and put us in a self-contradictory dilemma. What leads to the mistaken understanding above may be a wrong understanding of the essence of historical materialism or a failure to distinguish between the difference and relationship in the logical expression, theoretical interpretation and the practical application of historical laws. For this reason, I would like to raise some of my opinions and hopefully they can attract other respectable scholars to give their valuable contributions to this topic.

1 IF THE BASIC LAWS OF SOCIAL DEVELOPMENT ARE NEGATED, HISTORICAL MATERIALISM WILL NO LONGER EXIST.

1.1 DON'T NEGATE HISTORICAL MATERIALISM BECAUSE OF THE DEFICIENCIES IN TEXTBOOKS

"Dialectic Materialism and Historical Materialism" written by Stalin, included in the book "*A Concise Course of Soviet Party (Bolshevik)*" has deficiencies; the Soviet textbooks with Stalin's works as model also have deficiencies. That is needless to say and also very understandable, but it will be incredible that a philosophy textbook written more than 70 years ago should have nothing to criticize, to supplement or to develop. Engels once said the later generation would criticize our mistakes more than we have criticized the past generation. This is a truly wise judgment of a thoroughgoing materialist. But when we make comment on the philosophy textbooks of Stalin and Soviet Union, it is likely to result in a full negation of historical materialism if we fail to distinguish what the basic principles of Marxist conception of history are and what inadequate or even mistaken points limited by historical conditions are, instead sweep them off in the same way.

What is the traditional materialistic conception of history? To this question, different people have different answers. In the western world, some theorists consider Marx's conception of history marked by the *Economic and Philosophic Manuscripts of 1844* is a humanistic conception of history, but consider that Engels' conception of history is an economic-determinist conception of history, and that the latter one was a deviation and counterfeit of Marx's conception of history. Engels' conception of history is an orthodox historical conception that has been playing a leading role in the Marxist theories for a really long time. And there are the so-called two Marx theory and the so-called antagonism between Marx and Engels which we are familiar with. Before the dissolution of the Soviet Union, the historical conceptions of Lenin, Stalin and Mao Zedong, and those in Soviet and Chinese philosophy textbooks have all followed Engels' conception of history, which are all traditional economic-determinist conception of history, different from that of Marx. And that's the discourse above why there comes the problem of Marx and the re-construction of historical materialism.

In the Chinese theoretical circle, there is seldom this kind of intense and extreme opinions, but there are a lot different opinions about the description and discussion on historical materialism in the text-books. Some of the opinions are reasonable and worthy of great at-tention and further study, for example, the subjectivity of social life, the position of practice in historical conception, the mechanism and implementation model of social laws, the relationship between the objectivity of laws and the selectivity of human activities, and the epistemology and axiology issues in historical materialism. Given this situation, it is very essential for us to re-read the original works of Marx and Engels, to enrich and develop the principles of histori-cal materialism based on the experience of contemporary practices and on the new achievements of scientific researches.

If it is just a problem concerning the deficiencies in philosophy text-books, then it is worth the least argumentation; but if someone to-tally negates the social laws expounded in the philosophy textbooks and thinks that productive forces and the relations of production, economic base and superstructure, social existence and social con-sciousness, are purely speculative categories and don't exist at all, then it will no longer be merely a problem about how to treat the textbooks, but following this sense, it becomes a problem of prin-ciple concerning how to understand and even protect the Marxist philosophy. Also, the so-called critique of the deficiencies in the tra-ditional historical materialism theories actually becomes the critique of the Marxist conception of history, because to negate the laws above is to abandon historical materialism in full scale. What makes historical materialism a great discovery of Marx and Engels lies in that they discovered the laws of social development including the general laws above. Yes, the historical materialism of Marxism will never exhaust social and historical laws, but without the laws above, historical materialism will be an empty shell with nothing in it. If the three laws above were negated, then the new historical conception which is so-called a return to Marx, or the slogan of "new material-ist and dialectic historical conception, based on practice", would be nothing but empty talks.

Also, we can't praise over highly the censure of some western philosophic ideological trends advocating the "man absence" existing in the Marxist historical materialism, but should go down to earth and analyze the essence of this problem. Our philosophic textbooks haven't done a good job in expounding man and also man's subject position in social life, which is a deficiency of the textbooks but this is not an evidence proving that the Marxist conception of history doesn't pay due attention to the issue of man. On the contrary, the foothold of Marxism when realizing the transformation of historical conception is just on a most adequate estimation of the functions of real man and the practical activities of the mankind in social life. We could be very clear about this point in *The German Ideology* and *The Holy Family* in which Marx and Engels had highlighted: "Our starting point is man engaging in practical activities", "history is anything but some special individuality taking man as a tool to reach its goal" and "it is man, real, living man" that creates history. However, to make the Marxist historical materialism a scientific theory, it is far from enough to only focus on "man", because even Vico knew that history was created by man. In his masterpiece named New Science (Scienza Nuova), he said that history was created by man and thus man could know history. We can say that the Renaissance started the transformation from the theological conception of history to the humanistic conception of history, and the transition of theory from God creates history to man creates history, gradually and step by step. As for Marx and Engels, they not only transformed the idea of abstract man taken as foothold and core by the humanistic conception of history, and turned their eyes into real man, but more importantly, they went further from the level of human's consciousness, motivations and personal actions, and found historical laws through man's activities and in man's activities. That is called "into the depth of history".

Historical materialism naturally should study man, but it is much more than a theory of man. It is quite farfetched to comment on and evaluate Marxist philosophy according to the contemporary existential philosophy, philosophy of survival, and philosophy of life. The mission of Marxist historical materialism is to overthrow the idealistic conception of history which had always ruled in the history and to uncover historical laws through deeply studying the activities of men. The greatest discovery of Marxist historical materialism is not the discovery of man, but that of social laws. Engels said, "Just as Darwin discovered the law of development of organic nature, so Marx discovered the law of development of human history"[1].

Therefore, the essential content of materialistic conception of history is inseparable with some basic laws of human society it uncovers. Obviously, if we negate the historical laws uncovered by Marx and Engels, stay on the level of man's consciousness and his motivations and try to please those views so-called "discoveries on man" and "man creates the history" advocated on these bases, then what we could get would be merely an idealistic conception of history, not better than going back to the humanistic conception of history before Marxism and there would be no reforms in the Marxist conception of history at all.

1.2 CORRECTLY UNDERSTAND THE RELATIONSHIP OF THE SUBJECT AND OBJECT OF HISTORY AND THE SOCIAL STRUCTURE

There is one point of view advocating that man is the subject of social life and all the social life and social structure apart from man are all the objects created by man. Everything in our society is object created with consciousness and purpose, thus the subject is the decisive element of the society. Therefore the choice theory is the only correct historical theory, and any theory that emphasizes that social development has its own rules and especially that there are objective laws independent of man's will is mechanical determinism and it is the negation of man as subject. If following along this thinking way, then we could go nowhere but to historical idealism again: man takes the place of God, and the worship of man, of that of God.

Marxist conception of history naturally pays much attention to the subject-and-object relationship, but Marx's conception on this issue is much more than such a simple dichotomy. Marx had once criticized the abstract antagonism between man and society: That man is the subject and all the other things in the society are the objects created by the subject. If we abstracted man away from productive

---

1   Karl Marx and Frederick Engels: Selected Works, 2nd Edition, Volume 3, p. 776, Beijing: People's Publishing House, 1995.

forces, then the productive forces would become merely dead means of production and dead material of labour, which would have no effects on society or man, and which would not be practical productive forces any more but only be some historical remains of the productive forces that once showed up in history; if we abstracted man away from all kinds of social relations, the social relations would become the social environments of pure material. If one believes that all is determined by the subject, then he will also believe that all secrets of the society are hidden beneath human nature, which is not historical materialism at all. The essence of historical materialism is to enter into a deeper social structure through the activities of man, between man and man, through the subject-object structure of social life and enter to examine man, the subject of social activities, by putting the subject into a certain social structure: "Once man has emerged, he becomes the permanent pre-condition of human history, likewise its permanent product and result, and he is pre-condition only as his own product and result"[2]. Only in this way can there be the contradictions between man's initiative and passivity, between the consciousness of individual activity and the unconsciousness of collective, between the purposiveness of man's activity and the non-purposiveness of activity's result, and also can there be the contradiction between the objectivity of laws and the selectivity of human activities, and only in this way can we produce the solutions to correctly deal with these contradictions under the guidance of historical materialism.

Everything in the society is created by man, but man can't do the so-called creation as freely and as unconditionally as he likes just because he is an active thing with consciousness and purpose. Man creates under certain historical conditions which are fixed and given, thus man's activities are conditioned as well. The conditionalness of man's activities is actually the passivity of man itself. The answer to the question what man is, doesn't depend on man itself, or man's subjective wishes or the abstract human nature, but depends on the society he lives in and on the mode of production. Marx said that men are what their productions are, and consistent with the both:

2 Karl Marx and Frederick Engels: Collected Works, 1st Chinese Edition, Volume 26c, p. 545, Beijing: People's Publishing House, 1974.

What and how they produce. If no slave mode of production, no slaves or slave owners; and if no capitalist private property, no capitalists or wage labourers either. Yes, we can say that the slavery system is created by the slave owners, and capitalist private property by the capitalists, but history has proved that each form of property and social relation all go through the nurture process in the womb of the old system. This process is spontaneous and will turn/transform to the spontaneous creation of a certain group only if the society develops to a definite extent or to definite phase, which indicates that social development has its own laws, or as Marx said, social development is a natural historical process in which the subject is man and which also has aspects independent of man's will. This law is both a law of human activities and a law of society, both sides of which are in accordance with each other: In terms of its origin and its way of realization, it is a law of human activities; on the other side in terms of its (this law's) dependence on society and dependence on social relations and in terms of its control over social development, it is a law of society. What historical materialism means to discover is this very law that can enable it to correctly deal with the subject-and-object relationship in social life and the relationship between man and environment, and historical materialism guides it not to swing to any side of them. Therefore, only on the basis of admitting social laws can the subject-and-object relationship of history be rightly processed. Marx's description that man is both the writer and the actor in the drama is a very vivid explanation of the subject-and-object relationship based on laws.

Marx said, "All social life is essentially practical. All mysteries which lead theory to mysticism find their rational solution in human practice and in the comprehension of this practice."[3] Herein, it actually means that the "mysteries" can only be reasonably explained in the social structure formed by practice. Marx criticized Feuerbach of not understanding that it is the self-division of the secular basis that leads to the appearance of religion. Though Feuerbach knew religion was created by man, he didn't fully understand the social basis which generated religion, so he still failed to expose the nature of religion. Social production is the basis of social existence and

3   Karl Marx and Frederick Engels: Selected Works, 2nd Edition, Volume 1, p. 60, Beijing: People's Publishing House, 1995.

development, and the laws of the mode of material production and of the development of social structure are some most basic concepts of historical materialism. When speaking of historical materialism, Marx and Engels repeatedly highlighted, "This conception of history depends on our ability to expound the real process of production, starting out from the material production of life itself, and to comprehend the form of intercourse connected with this and created by this mode of production (i.e. civil society in its various stages), as the basis of all history; and to show it in its action as State, to explain all the different theoretical products and forms of consciousness, religion, philosophy, ethics, etc. etc. and trace their origins and growth from that basis"[4]. Can we imagine: what kind of historical materialism would be left if we drove out all the laws and theories on the movement of basic social contradictions from it?

Actually, in Marx's historical conception, the view of insisting on the historical materialist theory of society and social structure is consistent with the view of insisting on practice. That's why Marx and Engels made this further explanation after raising to the understanding above, "different from the idealistic conception of history, this conception of history explains the formation of concepts by starting from material practice". To explain concepts from material practice is to explain the relationship between economic base and superstructure from the view of social structure; whereas, to hold to the historical materialist concepts about material production and social structure is to hold to the view of explaining concepts with practice. Any theory that negates the movement of basic social contradictions and social structure by one-sidedly emphasizing the importance of practice it will be not incomprehensible, since neither exist disassociated: Both the human practical activities excluded from basic social contradictions nor the basic social contradictions excluded from human practical activities.

It is manifested both by theory and facts that the subject-object theory related to society can only be a scientific theory only if it goes deep into the social structure and uncovers the basis and movement laws of the social history. In this sense, Lenin considered the "two attributes", i.e. to attribute social relations to the relations of

4   Ibid., p. 92.

production, and to attribute the relations of production to the development state of productive forces, he saw these as the basis of the scientificalness of the materialistic conception of history. But any understanding concerning social structure and social laws couldn't do without correctly dealing with the subject-object relationship in the social life. A subject-object theory drifting away from scientific grasp of social structure and laws will always incline to subjectivity theory and selectivity theory; while behind those concepts on social structure and laws which mistake or abolish the social subject-object relationship always hide theories of mechanism and determinism. Lots of our debates and mistakes in conceptions of history have much to do with this problem.

2 LOGICAL EXPRESSION, THEORETICAL INTERPRETATION AND PRACTICAL APPLICATION OF THE BASIC LAWS OF HISTORICAL MATERIALISM

2.1 LOGICAL EXPRESSION

The logical expression of theories is totally necessary, which equally applies to natural science, social science and philosophy. Logical expression marks the maturity of a theory. If one theory couldn't express its understanding of the nature of its subject with theorems or formulas, then we can say it still stays at an empirical stage; and if the content of a philosophy couldn't be expounded in concepts or categories, then we can say the philosophy itself hasn't reached the understanding of the essence of objects. As a scientific conception of history, Marxist historical materialism surely can be abstracted and summarized in a logical way. In the Preface to *A Contribution to the Critique of Political Economy*, Marx described the principles of historical materialism in a purely logical way, by applying the most basic categories of historical materialism to expound the most basic principles of historical materialism in a highly concise and systematic way. In this Preface there were not a single law of historical development but a group of laws of historical development, which has nothing similar with the self motion of absolute ideas as what Hegel wrote in his *The Logic of Mind* and *The Phenomenology of Mind* or with the fake Hegelianist Proudhon who saw categories as the self-motion of impersonal reason. Marx thought, "Economic categories are only the theoretical expressions, the abstractions of the social relations of production, M. Proudhon, holding this upside down like a true philosopher, sees in actual relations nothing but the incarnation of the principles, of these categories, which were slumbering—so M. Proudhon the philosopher tells us—in the bosom of the "impersonal reason of humanity"[5].

Marx made a logical expression of historical materialism different from the purely logical expression of Hegel. Though we haven't directly seen any reference to human activity in Marx's logical expression, we can't thus say it was purely speculative, because it presupposes human activities and is abstracted from them, as an upgrade of the laws of human activities. This logical expression not only shows the consistency of theory and practice, but also embodies the consistency of history and logic, for it presents in a logical way the basic contradictions and the intensification and solution process of the contradictions of each society as well as the changes of social formations and the future development direction of history.

All scientific expressions of laws have no subject. Natural laws are the laws of material movements and material is the subject of all changes, but the expressions about natural laws can totally be formulas and theorems looking as if the subject itself is abstracted, which actually affects the least of its scientificalness. In the same sense, the laws of historical materialism are the laws of society as well as of human activities in which the laws exist and through which they realize themselves. However, it doesn't mean that we should add subject to each law of historical materialism when designing their logical expression; if not, its expression will look like as follows: The contradictory movement laws of man's productive forces and man's relations of production, man's economic base and man's superstructure, man's social existence and man's social consciousness, laws of man's class struggle or the changes of man-subjected social formations. I suggest such expressions are really repetitious and needless, because the starting point of historical materialism, and Marx's principle that history is nothing but the activities in which men pursue their own goals, and the summary of all human historical activities

5   Ibid., p. 141.

in the basic principles of historical materialism have already built the strongest dam to prevent the historical materialism of Marxism from becoming the self movement of categories and laws. If not mistakenly or intentionally misinterpreted, it is impossible to take the basic laws and categories of historical materialism as impersonal, and as purely conceptive movement.

It is very necessary to expound the basic principles of historical materialism by categories and scientific laws; without this abstraction, it will be unlikely for historical materialism to rise to a scientific conception of history or develop its effects of theory and methodology, which is why the expressions about the basic laws of historical materialism in Marxism, especially Marx's theoretical exposition in the Preface to *A Contribution to the Critique of Political Economy*, have permanent theoretical charm. It contains the power of theory, of laws, and of logic.

2.2 THEORETICAL EXPOSITION

The logical expression of the principles of historical materialism can never take the place of theoretical exposition. In the logical expression of laws, we see nothing concrete, because Marx has already gone from the concrete to the abstract and discarded the basis by which he got the conclusions. In fact, his logical expression about the laws of social history is the quintessence of all his previous researches. However, if he hadn't theoretically developed the logical expression of laws or correctly expounded it, he might turn it into a dogma or twist its original meaning. Actually our researches are quite insufficient on Marx and Engels' discussion of the functions of laws of historical materialism and the ways by which they function. One of the shortcomings of our past Marxist philosophy teaching is that we always stay on the logical expression of the basic laws of historical materialism and just mechanically apply mere generalities like action, reaction or interaction but not focus to fully analyze them or concretely expound the mechanism and characteristics of the social laws. However, this shortcoming in expounding shouldn't be the reason to negate the laws of Marxist historical materialism and the logical expression of the laws.

It will be very bold and opinionated to judge that the law that the forces of productive determine the relations of production is purely speculative and never exists in history. Human society couldn't live without production. To keep producing and reproducing, there must be relation of man and nature and relation of man and man. Neither any production without productive force nor any production without any certain relation is possible, which has already been proved by the production in history and in reality.

What the scientific law of the contradiction movement of productive forces and relations uncovers is not a quantitative relationship of the two in which they are like screws and nuts exactly fitting each other. It is a macroscopic law exposing the essential and necessary relationship between productive forces and relations. This relation is not a self movement of productive forces and relations of production without any man involved, but is a selection of a certain group of people (class or group) under certain conditions for their own interests. Interest is not a third power besides the mode of production and is determined by the different positions and situations of man in productive forces and relations of production. When the relations of production fits into with the property (nature) and the level of the productive force, it means the present nature and relation of distribution not only do good for the owners of the means of production but can also bring more profits to the direct producers than the old nature. On the contrary, when the contradiction between relations of production and productive forces gets intensified and becomes the shackles of the development of productive forces, then it means to continue to protect this property is only in the interest of old owners of the means of production instead of the new owners. Any attempt to change the old relation of production will be resisted by the ruling class or the vested interest groups who are inseparable with the old relation of production. The contradiction of the productive forces and relations in a class society is shown as the contradiction in class interests, while in socialist society as the contradiction of interest distribution within the masses. If abstracting man out of productive forces and relations of production and turning the interest relationships as a third party without anything to do with productive forces and relations of production, the contradictory movement of productive forces and relations of production will become quite incomprehensible.

Besides, the participation of man and the intermediary function of interest don't and also can't change the nature of the contradictory movement of productive forces and relations of production. The interest relationship itself is an embodiment of the nature of the contradiction between productive forces and relations of production, thus different interest relationships are embodied in different relations of production and the different positions of human therein, and also embodied in the different modes of the combination between human and instruments of production under different conditions of production: The contradictory movement of productive forces and relations of production realizes itself just by use of men's struggles for their own interests. This truth has been revealed by Engels when he said it was the dirty lust of man that became the lever of historical development ever since the emergence of classes. The thing deep behind the lust of man is the contradiction movement of productive forces and relations of production, which may not be necessarily recognized even by the participants, because it is the spontaneous function of this law.

The realization of man's interests can by no means violate the contradictory movement law of productive forces and relations of production, but on the contrary, man could satisfy his own interests only by realizing this law. As Marx said, man can't freely choose any productive force because it is an existing force of history; man can't freely choose any relations of production but only can choose one that corresponds to the nature of and the development level of the productive force, which manifests the objective demand of this law. Since ancient times, for the benefit of the masses, many thinkers have tried to choose a fair and reasonable property form, but none of them succeeded. All the experiments of the utopian socialists had failed; Mao Zedong tried to implement the commune system which will have "large-scale and high-level of socialization" for the benefits of all people, impulsing no interests but hunger and poverty only, which indicates that interest is concrete rather than abstract and that the interests of any class can never be realized by choosing an ideal relation of production which surpasses the development level/ nature of the existing productive forces. Man, under certain conditions, can only select the relation of production that is favourable for the development of productive forces and favourable for the subject of interests. This is the law; anyone violating it will be punished anyway.

Interest also plays an intermediary role between productive forces and relations of production that should never be ignored; not being pushed by interests, the relations of production won't be changed. However, what deserves equal attention is the condition of the instruments of production because the instruments of production are an important part in the system of productive forces. Marx paid much attention to the role of the instruments of production in productive forces. He described the instruments of production as an indicator of the relations of production and said, "The hand-mill gives you society with the feudal lord; the steam-mill, society with the industrial capitalist"[6]. People may ask, does the instrument of production itself ask for any certain relation of production? Of course not. The instrument of production is object, with no language, no desire, and no subjectivity, but it is controlled and used by man to produce. Man not only needs certain instruments of production to improve productivity/productive forces and will also choose a certain ownership form to better combine labourer and instrument of production. Therefore, as long as the instruments of production are not exhibited in a museum but being practically utilized, they will be asked to fit into their relation of production and utilize and develop the best of its effects. The socialized mass production and the application of machine require the combination mode of capitalist property, while the simple hand tools only fit to the small property of individual owners. It is the utilization of certain means/instruments of production that enables the emergence and existence of certain relations of production possible. Since the socialist relations of production couldn't live without the modern instruments of production, thus it looks a fantasy to attempt to build a long-term socialist public property on the basis of hand tools. As long as we do not deny the history, we could discover that the evolution of social formations is always accompanied with the changes of the system of production instruments. Sooner or later, the mankind will choose an ownership corresponding to the nature of the instruments of production so as to

---

6   Ibid., p. 142.

fully develop the effects of the instruments of production and thus to meet its own interests. We are against the simple deterministic view regarding the instruments of production, but we are also against the practices taking the instruments of production as mere objects that can't talk, ignoring their functions, and not able to judge how to distinguish the instruments of production in the production process and these instruments as historical fossils.

The contradictory movement of productive forces and relations of production is a complicated process. To establish a relation of production fitting for the productive force is truly a process of choice, but it is the state/nature of the development of productivity that finally decides which relation of production that people choose, because it is the need of the existence and development of the interest subject. Marx once took the example of Rome's conquest by the so-called German barbarians, in order to illustrate that any conqueror will set up a social system sooner or later based on the state of the productive forces of the conquered people. He wrote: "the form of community adopted by the settling conquerors must correspond to the stage of development of the productive forces they find in existence; or, if this is not the case in the beginning, it must change according to the productive forces"[7].

In the history of China, the Mongols invaded and took over the central plain of the ancient China, but they still couldn't turn the whole China into pastures and on the contrary, they had to adapt to the demands and conditions of the productive forces that had already been developed and decided to develop agriculture, which shows that in the interactive relationship of productive forces and relations of production, the choice of man is after all made on the basis of the state and development demands of the productive forces. It is the demands of this law that plays the final role as well as where the interests of the representatives of the advanced productive forces of each epoch lie.

We can't just explain the connotations of social existence and social consciousness or their interactive relationship at will. It is a core question when distinguishing between two conceptions of history. Social existence is man's social existence instead of man's existence;

---

7   Karl Marx and Frederick Engels: Collected Works, 1st Chinese Edition, Volume 3, p. 83.

social consciousness is the consciousness of the society instead of any subjective consciousness of an individual. The relation between social existence and social consciousness can't be boiled down to the relation between man's flesh and soul. Social existence cannot live without the activities of man and it is the actual living process of human; while social consciousness is man's social consciousness instead of the consciousness of any individual person. However, in relation to its essence, the individual's consciousness is also a social consciousness, but the individualization of the latter; it is also dominated by the law of the interactive relation between social existence and social consciousness.

Social existence and social consciousness are distinguished in relation to the overall social structure, and they are two essential parts in any society. Social consciousness, truly enough, is also a kind of existence, only the existence in this sense is not philosophical term of historical materialism to divide social structure, but it is a life term. It shows nothing but that consciousness is neither nothingness nor non-existence. Where does social consciousness exist? In human's mind, and in the cultural connotation which takes language and words as its carrier. This existential way with material as its carrier doesn't change its essence as social consciousness at all. Engels once criticized Dühring's clumsy tactics of attempting to obliterate the distinction between material and consciousness, which is the mistake that we should never make again.

If we want to stick to historical materialism, we must then stick to a dialectic and materialistic view in terms of the relation between social existence and social consciousness. One of the major mistakes in Lukacs' theory is that he doesn't distinguish social existence and social consciousness in the overall theory of social existence, but one-sidedly stresses that social consciousness is social existence and all is included in the totality of social existence, thus obscuring the boundary between the two and deviating from historical materialism. In the social structure of a society, social existence determines social consciousness; the social consciousness can only be an existence that is being aware of this and besides this, it has no other source. Yes, I admit that the influence of a nation's historical and cultural tradition is very important, and so is the influence of the ideas of different people in the same society, and that influence of the foreign ideas,; this interaction function in the field of consciousness becomes even more important especially in the current trend of economic globalization. However, all these above can only be attributed to the field of ideology and ideas, not to the sphere of social existence. We ought to distinguish between the source and the flow of social consciousness. The theory that social existence determines social consciousness solves the problem of the source of consciousness, which uncovers why there are different social consciousnesses under different social formations; while the historical and cultural tradition and interaction in the field of consciousness solves the problem of its flow, i.e. solves how under similar social conditions, how an individual's consciousness or a society's social consciousness changes because of the influences of historical tradition and foreign ideas. The flow can't live without the source, because in the final analysis, how people treat and comprehend their tradition and treat foreign cultures depends on the state of social existence and on their (people's) different positions therein.

It is the least advisable to misunderstand that social existence determines social consciousness as that the "dead" material determines the "living" ideas of man, and thus to objectify the social existence as a dead, impersonal, social material environment. Machines cannot determine man's thoughts but can determine the way of using machines, i.e. man's practice can. Money cannot determine man's thoughts. It is always believed that the quantity of money dominates a man's mind and people are inclined to think the richer one is will be worse in morality, and the poorer is one, will be better in morality; what determines man's thoughts is the way he earns his money, the way of his wealth accumulation, because the way of wealth accumulation falls within the mode of production and money is the objectification of the relations of production. Once an object gets away from human activities, it can only be an existence of material rather than a social existence as historical materialism advocates and concerns. Therefore, the relation between social existence and social consciousness is always the relation between the existence and consciousness of real man in real activities. Also because of that, Marx considered social existence as the processes of man's actual life and processes of man's practical activities, and man's social conscious-ness as the reflection and echo of their practical life.

Man is the subject of society in which everything is created by man. But no one can thus say that man can create whatever social exist-ence and whatever social consciousness he wants. If things happened that way, the law that social existence determines social conscious-ness would be a false one. Man is both producer of material and in-tellectual products. When Marx criticized Proudhon, Marx said men not only made cloth, linen, or silk materials in definite relations of production, but also established social relations in conformity with the material production; and he wrote: "the same men also produce principles, ideas, and categories, in conformity with their social rela-tions." "Thus the ideas, these categories, are as little eternal as the relations they express. They are historical and transitory products."[8]

The transformation from the logical expression to the theoretical in-terpretation of historical materialism contains arduous theoretical re-search works, not only because the difference in comprehending the classic books demands us to go back to the original ones whenever necessary, but also because there are different comprehensions about the principles as well. And it is still an important task of philosophy workers to correctly interpret the principles by combining the expe-rience of practice both in the history and in the reality. No one could claim that his understanding is absolutely right. Concerning this is-sue, we should stick to the "Double-Hundred Guiding Principle" (a principle raised by Mao Zedong about literary and art creations and academic researches), but shouldn't counterpose the theoretical in-terpretation of historical materialism and the logical expression of it.

2.3 PRACTICAL APPLICATION

If we can say the process from the logical expression of histori-cal materialism to its theoretical interpretation still falls within the sphere of theory and belongs to the range towards the abstract from the concrete, ,then we can say the application of historical material-ism goes back to the concrete from the abstract, from theory to prac-tice, which is an essential part of historical materialism to develop its functions and also a more sophisticated and more difficult question.

8   Karl Marx and Frederick Engels: Selected Works, 2nd Edition, Volume 1, p. 142.

Without this link, historical materialism will again go back to the old level of historical philosophy which it had transcended. Marx and Engels thought very highly of the application of historical materialism and they highlighted again and again that their conception of history isn't any dogma to tailor history, but is a method to observe history and reality. They are not only the founders of historical materialism but are also its most excellent users. As long as we read some of their works, such as *The Communist Manifesto, The Eighteenth Brumaire of Louis Bonaparte, The Peasant War in Germany, Origin of the Family, private Property, and the State*, and also *Capital*, and so forth, we can recognize how they had adhered to historical materialism. In these books, there are no formulas or conventional talks, but only profound theoretical analyses based on understanding the basic social contradictions and insisting in class analysis methods. So are the works of Mao Zedong. His works, especially several famous comments about the white paper issued by USA, are of grand momentum and well organized, fully manifesting the value of the methodology of historical materialism.

We couldn't understand the real value of the methodology of historical materialism if we get rid of the logical expression and theoretical interpretation of historical materialism. Without a correct understanding of the principles of historical materialism, it will be very easy for us to make mistakes of dogmatism, pragmatism, and mislabelling, like some of the ridiculous arguments we made before, such as advocating that the practice of "poor transition to communism" and practice of "large-scale and high-degree socialization" will accord with the law that the relations of production correspond to the forces of production; on the other side advocating the practice of destroying "the four olds (old ideas, old culture, old custom, and old habits)" in the Great Cultural Revolution period and advocating that implementing the total proletarian dictatorship accord with the law that the superstructure must fit into with the economic base, and so forth.

The correct application of principles needs to expound the principles comprehensively and correctly. A wrong understanding won't lead to the correct application of the principles. Since the western developed countries possessing highly developed productive forces are still at the capitalist stage, while China with relatively backward productive forces has established socialism already, someone may ask: doesn't this worldly situation indicate that the law that the relations of production must fit into with the nature and state of productive forces is fictitious? This is a question worthy of great attention. As early as half a century ago, Mao Zedong put forward this question when reading the Soviet textbooks of political economy. He said why revolutions first succeeded in those countries with lower level of capitalist production and smaller population of proletarians like Russia and China instead of the western countries with higher level of capitalist production and larger population of proletarians, and he thought great attention should be paid to this question. However, we did not pay due attention to studying it. As a result, the drastic changes in Eastern Europe became an important sally port to oppose socialism and historical materialism.

It is a rather complicated theoretical problem, which I think concerns the overall grasp of materialist principles at least. What the historical materialism uncovers is groups of laws rather than single functioning laws; no law can function without its corresponding social and historical conditions or the cooperative/combined functions of the laws closely related to it. Whether the production force demands/requires to change the relation of production does not depend on the absolute state of the productive force but on the degree of the contradiction between the two. A certain relation of production will not die out when it still can accommodate and promote the development of the productive force. Neither can we split the basic social contradiction, nor can we ignore the regulating effect of the capitalist superstructure to the relations of production. In fact, the welfare policies and relatively advanced social insurance system in the western world do play an important role in consolidating the capitalist system and easing its contradiction between productive forces and relations of production. However, it was a quite different situation in the old China before the victory of revolution. The productive forces in old China was at a lower absolute level than the western countries, but it had a sharper contradiction with the relation of production, because the ownerships of imperialism, bureaucrats and compradors and the feudal ownership of land extremely fettered the productive forces and left no room for their development; what's worse, the whole superstructure, especially the old regime's exploitation and tax policies that kill the goose that laid the golden eggs deprived the masses' means to live and caused boiling public anger. The people had no other way out but revolution. This really shows that the law of the contradiction movement of productive forces and relations of production comes into effect in an interactional relation with the law of the contradictory movement of economic base and superstructure. No Marxist has ever said that the absolute level of productive forces is the only reason or the only symbol of revolution. To break ourselves away from the overall movement of the two basic social contradictions but to examine the level of productive forces alone is anything but historical materialism.

There is also a problem concerning the right application of the theory of contradiction between economic base and superstructure. It is undoubted that economic base determines superstructure. It is obvious that it is the ruling class in the relations of production that grasps the state power and stays at the dominant position in the ideological field. The so-called state power is actually the owners of the means of production who have greater economic power; and their position in the economic base, in the relations of production, endows them with the power. That's why the democratic elections in the capitalist society can never select any president who truly stands for the people. As Engels said, no bayonet is sharper than cotton and economic power will beat violence in the end. It is completely right that economic base determines superstructure.

The union of certain economic base and certain superstructure classifies societies into different social formations, but that doesn't negate that in the same social formation exist concrete differences and diversity. All nations have their own special national cultures, which are different from each other whether seen from their cultural traditions or their practical cultural conditions. Even in the capitalist society, there are also different political systems from presidential system to constitutional monarchy, with queen and even Mikado. The emergence of this kind of phenomenon can't be simply attributed to economic base. Engels once said, "Without making oneself ridiculous it would be a difficult thing to explain in terms of economics the existence of every small state in Germany, past and present, or the origin of the High German consonant permutations, which widened the geographic partition wall formed by the mountains from the Sudetic range to the Taunus to form a regular fissure across all Germany"[9]. Therefore, concrete historical research always requires deep analysis of concrete situations; it is the least advisable to simply and mechanically apply some known conclusions.

For social sciences including history, historical materialism provides theory and method only. Its significant meaning lies in that it overthrows the explanation of history made by the idealistic conception of history, but it doesn't set what any social science should or shouldn't research. Human society is an extensive field which can be studied from all kinds of perspectives and which has all kinds of questions to study. There isn't any question breaking through the vision of historical materialism at all, whether to study on the history of society, of human development and of culture or on the other aspects of the social life, such as the history of secret societies, of the prostituting, and of beggar. It is very unreasonable to prove historical materialism has theoretical deficiencies by extending the field of historical researches.

There are differences among the logical expression, the theoretical interpretation and the practical application of historical materialism, but there is not any theoretical contradiction among them and they should be consistent with each other in relation to basic theories. However, what the practical application faces is reality and practice, and the failures of application caused by the misunderstanding of theory aren't rare in socialist practices. With those failures, we can sum up the experience of our practice with both positive and negative sides, enrich and develop the principles of historical materialism, and correct the mistaken explanations and theoretical "additions".

---

9   Karl Marx and Frederick Engels: Selected Works, 2nd Edition, Volume 4, p. 696-697, People's Publishing House, 1995.

3 CONTEMPORARY VALUE OF HISTORICAL MATERIALISM

3.1 HISTORICAL MATERIALISM IS UNPARALLELED IN OUR CONTEMPORARY TIME

Engels considered historical materialism as one of the two greatest discoveries of Marx and spoke highly of its effects in transforming socialism from utopian to scientific one in the revolutionary practices of proletarians. He said, "Marx helped the worker class with historical materialism. He proved: "all the concepts of man like law, politics, philosophy, religion and so forth all come from their economic conditions, their means of production, and their modes of product exchange, thus generating the world outlook suitable for the living conditions and struggle conditions of the proletariat"[10]. During the one and half century since Marx and Engels founded the materialistic conception of history, historical materialism has shown irresistible persuasion in both spheres of theory and practice because of its strict scientificalness and its firm standing for the benefits of all labourers in the world, which no conscientious scholar should deny.

In the *Main Trends in History*, a project result of UNESCO, its project director, the famous British historian Geoffrey Barraclough, fully acknowledged the enormous effects Marx's materialistic conception of history had exerted on historiography and highlighted that "in the Marxist historiography, there is no cluttered subjective concepts such as liberty, personality, nation and religion arbitrarily selected by idealistic historians as standards". Even the German philosopher Habermas advocating to reconstruct historical materialism didn't dare to negate the laws of historical materialism but positioned the "reconstruction" at the recombination of the existing theories. He wrote: "Revival seemingly means to update a kind of yet abandoned tradition during this period. Marxism needs no revival. The reconstruction we said is to disassemble a theory and recombine it in a new way so as to better reach the goal established by this theory. That is a normal attitude towards a theory of which some aspects need to be corrected but the potential encouraging power hasn't gone exhausted yet."[11]

10   Karl Marx and Frederick Engels: Collected Works, 1st Edition, Volume 21, p. 548.
11   Habermas: Reconstruction of Historical Materialism, p. 3, Beijing: Social Sciences Academic Press.

Marxist philosophy has gone through the spring-up and spread in the 19th century, enjoyed prosperity in the early half of 20th century and the ups and downs in the late half, and now it has entered the third century after its foundation. The 21st century is now seeing more rapid and more complicated social development than all the previous epochs. Faced with the trend of economic globalization and the new world pattern after the dissolution of the Soviet Union, we also meet more questions like how to observe the development direction of human society, how to observe the contemporary capitalism, and how to observe the future and fate of socialism; to answer these questions above scientifically, we must stick to the theory about the basic contradiction of human society in historical materialism. None of the humanistic conceptions of history, the cultural history of the clash of civilizations, the metaphysic conception of history on the end of history, convergence theory, or the eclectic conception of history that two systems co-exist permanently, can correctly explain history, so the researches based on these theories can lead to nowhere but to mistaken conclusions.

3.2 THE SCIENTIFIC THEORY AND METHOD TO OBSERVE THE CONTEMPORARY WORLD

Economic globalization is one of the major trends of the contemporary world. If one researcher isn't equipped with any historical materialistic insight of the world history or abandons the theory of the basic social contradictions, he won't be able to understand the historical necessity and the internal contradiction of economic globalization. The statements of Marx and Engels in *The German Ideology* and in *The Communist Manifesto* about the transformation from human history to world history and about the inevitable capital expansion trend of the capitalist socialized production provide us with the basic theory and method to observe the contemporary globalization.

The revolution of science and technology in the late half of the 20th century extended the expansive nature of capital that had been slow and had lasted for a long time after the birth of capitalism to the maximum extent. Without the high level development of productive forces and the high socialization level of production, in no way could occur the global allocation of resources, enormous increase of information, enormous increase of world trade or international division of labour, etc. Since the forces of production and the relations of production are inseparable, thus in the process of the modern economic globalization, the international companies and international monopolies in the western developed countries do play a very essential role. However, the contemporary world is no longer the epoch as the early stage of the capitalist development when the bourgeoisie had "made barbarian and semi-barbarian countries dependent on the civilized ones, nations of peasants on nations of bourgeois, the East on the West"[12]. Many developing countries are also trying to develop themselves by participating in the process of economic globalization. Development has been an important theme of the times. Therefore, cooperation and contradiction coexist with each other in the economic globalization among developed countries and developing countries, rich countries and poor countries, and countries with different social systems and among countries at different levels of development. When dealing with economic contradictions, the superstructure of each country, mainly the state or government must take part in, which is shown as that each government makes its own countermeasures to handle the economic globalization. If we erase the theory of the basic social contradictions, we would put ourselves in a predicament when observing this situation of the world.

By no means can we deduce political globalization and cultural globalization from that of economic globalization. This deduction may seem to accord with the theory that in historical materialism, economy determines politics and culture, but it is actually an abstract deduction deviating from the method of class analysis. Economic globalization isn't equal to economic integration, because the nations in the world are different from each other in their nature of ownership forms, their nature of political power and system, and in their national tradition of culture as well as their national culture. In a world with nation as unit, the contradiction between productive forces and relations of production, between economic base and superstructure, is concrete, which forms the existing social formation of a nation. There is no possibility that the whole world would share a unified economic base, not to mention a unified superstructure.

---

12 Karl Marx and Frederick Engels: Selected Works, Edition 2, Volume 1, p. 277.

The so-called economic globalization has a limited connotation and conditioned functions. Thus, economy can be globalized, but polity should be multi-polarized, and culture should also be diversified. Though economic globalization affects the political situation, for example, the socialized mass production and market economy do require democracy/democratization and rule of law in politics; though convenient cultural communication in the economic globalization is beneficial for the mutual absorption of cultures and brings about some similarities in cultural phenomenon, we cannot thus equate this with integration. This doesn't violate the determinist principle of the relationship between economy and politics and culture, because economic globalization doesn't change the nature of each country's economic base upon which they build their superstructures and upon and by which they make favourable policies for their own country.

We should also examine the capitalist society with the view of basic social contradiction, not the theory of the end of history which is based on the assumption that the bourgeois private property is the perfect system best fit for the human nature and that there is no basic social contradiction at all. In fact, the contemporary reality can't prove the superiority of private property. Except the socialist countries, most of the countries in the world are on the basis of private property, but how many countries are there as America? The capitalist private property in the overwhelming majority of the countries hasn't shown its superiority and their development rate is far slower than the socialist countries. In addition, even in the wealthy countries like America, there is also poverty, a huge gap between the rich and the poor, and all kinds of social problems bothering them a lot. The deepest reason of these social problems is the basic social contradiction, rather than the mere cultural crisis and the loss of human spirit as is said. Only the theory of historical materialism about the basic social contradiction can help us analyze the modern capitalist society and provide us with the scientific theory and method.

3.3 THE FUTURE AND FATE OF SOCIALISM

The future and the fate of socialism are also determined by whether the basic social contradictions in the socialist society can be correctly dealt with. In his early days, Stalin stressed that the productive forces in the socialist society should be in complete accordance with the relations of production; in his late days, though he admitted that the two had contradiction, he didn't thoroughly deal with it, so the social contradictions in the Soviet Union had built up more and more. Later, the leaders of the Communist Party which were at the core of the superstructure, instead of regulating the contradictions by improving the socialist reforms, have intensified the contradictions through their mistaken line and policies. They claimed to dismiss the Communist Party, abolish the leading position of Marxism, and promote private property, which, as a result, caused the dissolution of the Soviet Union and the restoration of capitalism. The failure of the Soviet Union's socialism quite typically manifested the interactive effects of the basic social contradictions. If the Communist Party, the ruling party in the superstructure, had adjusted the contradiction between productive forces and relations of production via a correct line, and could coordinate the relationship of productive forces, relations of production, and superstructure, the Soviet Union might not have ended in dissolution. However, the fact is that the contradictions among them were so sharp that the productive forces were bogged down and the masses of people lived in a miserable and poor life, thus the collapse of the original system became an inevitable historical necessity.

The accomplishments that China has made since the reform and opening up should be credited to China's correctly dealing with the basic contradictions of the socialist society. As early as in 1956, Mao Zedong raised his theory about the basic contradictions in the socialist society, which was a great contribution to the theory of socialist construction, but pitifully, he made several mistakes in dealing with the basic contradictions. In the contradiction between productive forces and relations of production, he focused on changing the latter and constantly tried to modify the system of ownership; regarding the contradiction between economic base and superstructure, he emphasized on the so-called continued revolutions in superstructure;

while in the spheres of superstructure, he mainly emphasized on building the ideological sphere but ignored the construction of culture and law of the superstructure, which wouldn't do any good for the development of productive forces, the prosperity of socialist culture, the perfection of legal system, or the improvement of the living standard of the people. Deng Xiaoping accepted Mao's theory about the basic contradictions in the socialist society and kept going along the road of the localization of Marxism in China opened up by Mao Zedong. But when dealing with the contradiction between productive forces and relations of production, he paid much attention to developing productive forces; and regarding to the spheres of superstructure, he laid much stress on perfecting legal system and education and the culture of the superstructure. His theories on the essence of socialism and on the "Three Favorables", basically, were centred on developing and emancipating the productive forces and aim to reform all the systems, both those in economic base and superstructure that fail to fit or even restrain the development of productive forces; this has been a correct road that could make socialism keep self-improving by correctly dealing with the basic social contradictions. As for the important thought of "Three Represents" of Jiang Zemin, in its essence, it is also based on the theory of correctly dealing with the basic socialist contradictions. To represent the development requirements of advanced productive forces and to represent the orientation of advanced culture, both were in fact aimed to represent the requirements of the orientation of the basic contradictory movement of the socialist society; while to advocate representing the basic interests of the masses was the starting point and end result of correctly dealing with the basic contradictions of socialism. The "Three Represents" thought of Jiang Zemin solved a significant problem in the socialist superstructure, i.e. what kind of a party should be constructed and how to construct the party?

The construction issue of the ruling party actually concerns the big question about which route line should be taken to deal with the basic contradictions in socialist society. If the party changes, the upper structure of the party changes and the route of it will also change, thus the party not only couldn't properly handle the basic contradiction of socialism but would also be overwhelmed by the contradiction, which is one of the bitter lessons learned from the international socialist movements. Jiang Zemin put forward that we should study the laws of human society development, of socialist society development, and the laws of the ruling parties, and raised four questions about how to understand these laws. None of the researches on these questions could be solved without historical materialism, especially without its theory of the basic contradiction in social development. The historical materialism provides scientific theory and method to observe the contemporary world, socialism and capitalism, which is the major embodiment of its contemporary value. If historical materialism, especially its theory of basic social contradictions, was negated, our party would definitely lose the theoretical basis to correctly design our lines , guiding lines and policies; all the policies of the reform and opening up as well as the important thoughts from "Three Favorables"** to "Three Represents" would lose their theoretical fulcrum; all our social science workers would lack an excellent and effective tool of theoretical study. This problem goes far beyond the sphere of historiography, thus it surely attracts the attention of the whole circle of theory including the circle of philosophy.

**) "Three Favorables": In the reform and opening period Deng Xiaoping proposed an idea to measure if a reform would be favourable or not. He suggested three criteria: Firstly, any reform should promote development of productive forces; secondly, any reform should be favourable to increase the aggregate power of the country; thirdly, any reform should be favourable to better the living standarts and the well being of the majority of people.

APPENDIX III

ON THE MATERIALISTIC CONCEPTION OF HISTORY IN THE SOCIALIST PRACTICE*

Ever since the victory of the October Revolution in Russia, the relation between the materialistic conception of history and socialism has been transformed from the theoretical relation based on capitalist society into the relation of practical operation based on socialist practices, which means that the materialistic conception of history has been taken as the theoretical basis to make general lines, principles and policies in the socialist construction. Thus the socialist practice has begun testing and developing the theories of historical materialism, and whether we can comprehensively and correctly apply the materialistic conception of history and stick to it is quite an essential question concerning the rise and fall, birth and death of the socialist cause. Therefore, whether we can adapt to this transformation is of great significance.

---

*) The article was originally published in Theoretical Front in Higher Education, 2000(12).

To construct socialism, we must correctly and properly deal with the relation between the materialistic conception of history and socialism. If we can say, in the epoch of Marx and Engels, without the materialistic conception of history, there will be no scientific socialist theory; then in our contemporary times, we can say that without the materialistic conception of history, there won't be the correct, effective socialist practice, which truth has already been proved by the rise and dissolution of the Soviet Union, and the practices and achievements of the new China in constructing the socialism with Chinese characteristics in the last fifty years especially in the last two or three decades.

PART I

When the democratic revolution had succeeded in 1949, China stepped into the period of socialist transformation and socialist construction. The socialist practice itself kept putting forward new questions different from those in the period of democratic revolution.

1 THE RELATION BETWEEN ECONOMIC DEVELOPMENT AND CLASS STRUGGLE

Before wresting the political power and in the preparatory time of revolution, the proletariat needed to put efforts to fight against the vulgar theory of productive forces , because if they did not o oppose the vulgar theory of productive forces, they can't establish their confidence that the revolution must prevail, and can't take any revolutionary stride either. However, having taken the political power, they have changed their role from the offensive to the defensive, from the destroyer of the old moribund, corrupt things to the builders of a new country, so they shouldn't advance along the road of fighting against the vulgar theory of productive forces any more, but they should shift their emphasis on developing the productive forces and criticize the mistaken ideas that ignore the importance of productive forces; otherwise, no progress in the construction the country can be made. This is a fundamental change taking place after wresting the regime, which the application of the materialistic conception of history must adapt to.

In the certain periods of the Chinese revolution, Mao Zedong had made great efforts against the vulgar theory of productive forces and against the theory of second revolution (waiting for a proletarian-led revolution in China coming (second) after capitalist reform or revolution is accomplished). His famous theory of new democracy is one of the innovative developments in the Marxist theory of scientific socialism in China. Mao Zedong and the CPC took advantage of the favourable, mature revolutionary situation and finally won the victory of the democratic revolution led by the proletariat in such an economically and culturally backward country. Anyone who just sits back and waits for the development of productive forces and thus misses the crucial revolutionary opportunity is carrying out an opportunist line, and is the sinner of history.

When leading the Russian revolution, Lenin also sharply fought against the vulgar theory of productive forces of Eduard Bernstein, Karl Johann Kautsky, and the Russian opportunists. In the Fourth Party Congress of the R.S.D.L.P. (Russia) in 1906, Plekhanov said: Any creation of the masses could never change the nature of the bourgeois revolution we had experienced. What are we pursuing for? A bourgeois republic. As for taking the control of the regime, it should be the task of the future subsequent proletarian revolutions. Lenin was extremely opposed to this view and eventually won the victory of the October Revolution in Russia.

Lenin was surely aware of the backwardness of the economy and culture in Russia, but as he said in "Our Revolution" in 1923, when replying to the denouncement of N. Sukhanov: If a definite level of culture is required for the building of socialism (although nobody can say just what that definite "level of culture" is, for it differs in every Western European country), why cannot we began by first achieving the prerequisites for that definite level of culture in a revolutionary way, and *then*, with the aid of the workers' and peasants' government and Soviet system, proceed to overtake the other nations?

You say that civilization is necessary for the building of socialism. Very good. But why could we not first create such prerequisites of civilization in our country by the expulsion of the landowners and the Russian capitalists, and then start moving toward socialism? Where, in what books, have you read that such variations of the customary historical sequence of events are impermissible or impossible?

And Engels in "The Peasant Question in France and Germany", criticized the view that advocated to wait for the proletarianization of peasants first and then revolutionize them. He said, "It will serve us nought to wait for this transformation until capitalist production has developed everywhere to its utmost consequences, until the last small handicraftsman and the last small peasant have fallen victim to capitalist large-scale production"[1].

Concerning the materialistic conception of history, what on earth is the boundary between the vulgar theory of productive forces and the scientific theory of productive forces? In my opinion, the vulgar theory of productive forces is mechanical productivity determinism which considers productive forces as the only decisive power in isolation; while the scientific theory of productivity is dialectic determinism, which examines the ultimate, decisive effect of productive forces to the contradictory movement of both productive forces and the relations of production, and also to economic base and superstructure. For example, all revolutions need certain economic conditions, which are impossible to happen or last long without certain economic development, and which of course will never succeed; a social revolution of mass character cannot be any conspiracy of a few people, which is one law of historical materialism. Marx said, "A radical social revolution depends on certain definite historical conditions of economic development as its precondition"[2]. But the development state of productive forces can only be the precondition of revolution rather than the only decisive factor. There are countless examples where the productive forces are highly developed with no revolution exploding. What's more, the growth of economy can always ease the discontent of the masses and thus contributes to consolidating the political power of the ruler. As a complicated syndrome combining multiple contradictions related to economy, politics, and ideology or ideas , a revolution will take place when the ruler is unable to rule the country in the old way and the ruled people refuse to live in the old way too, which are formed as the result of the combination of both domestic and foreign conditions. As long as these conditions are there, any tiny spark may trigger a

---

1   Karl Marx and Frederick Engels: Selected Works, 2nd Edition, Volume 4, p. 500.
2   Karl Marx and Frederick Engels: Selected Works, 2nd Edition, Volume 3, p. 287.

revolution. As for productive forces, it won't be a rapidly developing period at all but will be a shrinking period. Because of brutal wars, agricultural lands are deserted and the people have no means to live. When the old relation of production severely hinders the development of productive forces but the old superstructure especially the state power still spares no efforts in protecting the old relation of production, the basic social contradiction will be greatly intensified and usually a revolution will break out. In his famous Preface to *A Contribution to the Critique of Political Economy*, Marx analyzed social revolutions just in this way. For example, the old feudal China saw a weaker development of productive forces than any western country, but it also suffered from more complex social contradictions than them. The corrupt character of the old political power and the old relations of productions such as the exploitation of imperialism, feudalism, and bureaucrat-comprador bourgeoisie over Chinese people especially over Chinese peasants had dramatically intensified the basic social contradictions in China, leaving no possibility to boost up any further development of the productive forces in China. There were only two roads in front of the Chinese people to choose: Either to miserably live in a colonial and semi-colonial society and suffer slavery forever, or bleed and fight for the existence of the Chinese nation without fear of death. One and a half centuries later after the Opium War, the heroes of China, especially the Chinese Communists, chose the second one. This road was the only road the Chinese society needed to take to liberate itself, which was not determined by the absolute development level of the productive forces, but instead by the deepening level of the basic social contradiction in China. Only by/through this contradiction could the certain development degree of Chinese capitalist economic elements, certain level of its productive forces, and certain number of the working class in China had produced those effects which were far stronger than their absolute level and their numbers could do.

A country with a relatively low level of productive forces, can also be revolutionized and also wrest the political power when the revolutionary opportunity matures. It is certainly right to oppose to the vulgar theory of productive forces in the preparatory and proceeding period of the revolution, which means Lenin and Mao Zedong were also right in terms of this question. In October 1977, in his conversation with the American professor Lin Daguang, Deng Xiaoping said, "when Lenin criticized Kautsky's vulgar theory of productive forces, he said that the underdeveloped countries can also wage socialist revolutions. We are also against the vulgar theory of productive forces, but we have adopted a different way from the October Revolution, which was to conquer the cities beginning from the countryside. At that time, there had already been an advanced proletarian party and a preliminary level of capitalist economy in China as well as appropriate conditions outside China, so in such an underdeveloped China could struggle for socialism be waged and developed, which is the same as what Lenin talked about when opposing the vulgar theory of productive forces"[3].

However, after taking over the regime, how to deal with the relation between productive forces and class struggle will manifest itself as a new question. It is proved by the historical experience that a new relation of production can be seen as superior because it can boost up the development of productive forces after its establishment. The rapid development of the bourgeois productive forces didn't take place in the 17th and the 18th century when Britain and France were going through bourgeois revolutions, but in the 19th and 20th century after they had taken power, especially in the late half of the 20th century. Therefore, after the success of the proletarian revolution, it should be a paramount subject and importance to make use of the newly established socialist relations of production and social system, and shift the focus on developing productive forces. In the revolutionary wars period, we ought to oppose the vulgar theory of productive forces, otherwise, we would have no chance to promote the revolution deepening. But, after taking the power if we still place class struggle on the focus of our work with the pretext of opposing the vulgar theory of productive forces the economy will not be developed so rapidly, the poverty won't be shaken off, and the socialist society will stay backward and underdeveloped for a really long time, without displaying the superiorities of the new socialist system. It is fair to say that after the victory of the democratic revolution, Mao

---

3   A Chronicle of Deng Xiaoping's Thought from 1975 to 1997, p. 46-47, Beijing: CCCPC Literature Press, 1998.

Zedong did pay much attention to developing China's production. In his speech on the Second Plenary Meeting of the Seventh CC of the CPC in 1949, he mentioned: "after the success of the revolution, we must restore and develop our production as quickly as possible, and fight against the foreign imperialism, so as to steadily transform China from an agricultural country into an industrial country and to construct China into a powerful socialist country"[4].

He also specifically instructed to mobilize all forces to restore and develop production, which should be treated as the key sphere of all our works and as the central task of the Party. After 1956, because of some changes happening both at home and abroad and because of the excessive estimations about this change, class struggle was gradually was placed to central position and taken as a key link and later even all works were subordinated to class struggle. That deviation gave us quite a hard lesson and it was also a rather expensive historical price we had paid for the progress of Chinese socialist construction.

2 HOW TO DEAL WITH THE RELATION BETWEEN PRODUCTIVE FORCES AND A REASONABLE STRUCTURE OF OWNERSHIP

The fundamental purpose of the proletarian revolution is to eliminate the bourgeois private property, eliminate exploitation, and realize distribution according to work and in the end proceed to a distribution mode which is according to one's needs, which has been reaffirmed many times by Marx and Engels in *The Principles Of Communism* and *The Communist Manifesto* and in many other works, and which is also the common view of all communists in the world. However, it is a new subject and practical problem which Marx and Engels had never faced about how to determine the type of ownership that fits to and conforms to the nature and level of the productive forces in a country after the success of revolution. For example, with regard to the question of ownership, shall we proceed from the above stated general principle, change all the previous types of ownership forms as early as possible and rapidly and thus cause a new disharmony between the productive forces and the

4   Selected Works of Mao Zedong, Volume 4, p. 1437, Beijing: People's Publishing House, 1991.

relations of production, or shall we adapt our ownership reforms to the new situation of the productive forces and set up new relations of production gradually, step by step? With regard to the question of distribution, shall we adopt the form of distribution that is favourable for the development of the productive forces or shall we simply pursue for fairness and equality under the prevalent circumstances of undeveloped productive forces? In my mind, absolute equalitarianism will lead to the generalization of poverty, and this general poverty will lead to a resurgence of all that is old and outdated.

3 THE RELATION BETWEEN THE PARTY AND THE MASSES

Before taking the political power, the CPC and the masses were as inseparable as fish and water; otherwise, the CPC wouldn't be able to survive, not to mention take the power. Lenin had stressed this important point for many times. He said, " Open political struggles compel the party to maintain a closer relation with the masses; because without this relation, the party will be of no use at all"[5].

The party can succeed nothing without any connection with the masses. The danger of being isolated from the masses will be easy to occur after the victory of revolution because in the new period after the party conquers the rule to the relation between the party and the masses is added a new relation which is between the governor and the governed. The CPC undertook the role as the ruling party and began to appoint the officials at all levels, it can be estimated that these officials could quite easily forget where their power came from, mistakenly think that they only need to be responsible to their superiors, assuming that the power was assigned to them by their superiors. By this token, it would be hard for these officials to correctly integrate their responsibilities to their superior and to the masses simultaneously. But shouldn't it be that the responsibility to the masses must be their supreme standard. This problem among the official cadres— especially in the leading positions—if not correctly handled will severe the relations of the party with the masses and they will never learn how to serve the masses.. Estimating this problem arising from

---

5   Collected Works of Lenin, 2nd Edition, Volume 17, p. 325, Beijing: People's Publishing House, 1988.

old and long feudalism of China the party and Mao Zedong have always emphasized the line of "from the masses, to the masses" as the leadership style and launched many intense struggles against bureaucratism, but this question was is still a fundamental question we have faced for long time after taking the ruling power.

4 THE RELATION BETWEEN THE LEADER AND THE MASSES

Before taking the ruling political power, personality cult lacked the conditions and its soil to grow so strong. In the hard struggles to seize the regime and defeat the enemy forces, it was impossible not to practice democracy within the party or without democracy it was impossible to concentrate and mobilize the strength of all people around us. Besides there could not occur a situation for lifelong tenure of a leader especially in this period of revolutions and wars, since the setbacks and defeats of the revolution had always caused the replacement or loss of the party leaders. As our experience has proved, a party leader should not lead by virtue of others' worship but by virtue of his personal excellent skills and collective teamwork spirit. When the revolution is won, the personality cult for the leader might gradually spring up because of the masses' sincere admiration and due to the supreme popularity and authority enjoyed by the new regime, which is a common case in the eastern countries with a backward economy and culture, small peasants constituting the majority of the population.

Marx once talked about this issue, when analyzing the coup of Bonaparte in France, he wrote: "the peasants are incapable of asserting their class interest in their own name, whether through a parliament or a convention. They cannot represent themselves, they must be represented. Their representative must at the same time appear as their master, as an authority over them"[6]. In this sense, it is quite a serious problem to preventing and oppose personality cult possibly occurring in the eastern countries when the proletarian revolutions are won.

---

6   Karl Marx and Frederick Engels: Selected Works, 2nd Edition, Volume 1, p. 677-678.

5 THE PROBLEM OF STATE

The state is an important problem of historical materialism as well as a practical problem faced by the proletariat after the success of revolution. Historically speaking, the appearance of state was a progress in history, and the managerial function of the state over economy and cultural and educational undertakings can be favourable for the progress of society as well. However, the nature of state is not merely limited to its managerial functions, and it indeed works as the tool of class oppression. In all the previous class societies, the state power was originated and generated from the society, but stayed above the society and gradually drifted away from the society. It employs officials, armies and police forces by tax and national debts, consumes the sweat and toil of the labourers, in order to maintain its rule. Thus, some classical Marxist writers called the state as "social superfluousness" attached to the organism of the society. What's worse, because the functions of the state are always performed by some men who are governmental officials and social managers at the same time and who can spoil the advantage of the power which is entrusted to their hands, it becomes easy for them to "transform themselves from the servants of society into the masters of society".

Engels wrote: these men who "transformed themselves from the servants of society into the masters of society" "can be seen, for example, not only in the hereditary monarchy, but equally also in the democratic republic. Nowhere do "politicians" form a more separate, powerful section of the nation than in North America. There, each of the two great parties which alternately succeed each other in power is itself in turn controlled by those people who make a business of politics, who speculate on seats in the legislative assemblies of the Union (Federal State) as well as of the separate states, or who make a living by carrying on agitation for their party and on its victory are rewarded with positions"[7].

That is a brief elucidation on how political power becomes corrupt by Engels. It is no exaggeration that no political power ruled by an exploiting class could avoid the problem of corruption, and the progress of society and the development of economy could not eradicate

---

7   Karl Marx and Frederick Engels: Selected Works, 2nd Edition, Volume3, p. 12.

corruption either. Though every political power in every society opposes corruption for the long-term interest of its class rule, none of them could solve the problem radically but all, in the end, meet their death through corruption. That's the so-called periodicity of regime change, a doomed destiny of all regimes of exploiting classes.

After the success of revolution, the proletarian will and must rule in the form of state, and will also grant the social management function to a group of few men, which is quite necessary. We are not anarchists and cannot dream that the victory of revolution will make the state perish; but we need to keep a cool mind and vigilant that even a socialist state power may breed corruption. How to treat the problem of corruption is so important a problem that it can even disturb or break our socialist cause and also has a direct bearing on the birth and death of our ruling party. This profound historical truth and has been recognized before the CPC moved to Beijing. For example, in Yan'an, Huang Yanpei asked Mao Zedong the question about how the communist party could avoid the cyclicity of history; and Mao Zedong has answered him, CPC's moving into Beijing would be an exam for that. The proletarian regime doesn't absolutely bring about corruption, and extremely harmful is the view that considers the proletarians and the labourers should give up revolution forever and renounce to wrest political power because power will inevitably cause corruption. But we have to admit that a power without supervision will corrupt easily and even more easily when it is in the hands of a few people who aren't restrained by efficient laws or legal institutions or supervised by the masses. It is wrong to one-sidedly emphasize on the "elitistic politics". True, to run a country needs outstanding knowledge, capability and experience, but the view which excludes people's supervision and mystifies running a country or state is just something that the rulers have produced to fool the people, scare the people and attempt to rule forever. The classical Marxist writers have criticized this political view many times. The socialist country is a country where the people are the masters of the society and where the people can govern their country and state in all kinds of effective ways. Mao Zedong compared democracy as the therapy to prevent against the periodicity because he hoped the people could take part in governing the state and supervise the cadres effectively. Anti-corruption struggle is a long-term war, but is also a war that must keep bearing fruits. Anti-corruption becomes an increasingly serious problem proletariat has to face after taking power, especially when the storm of revolution have just faded away and the society begins its economic construction in the mode of market economy.

6 THE QUESTIONS ON IDEOLOGY

Any revolution need to contain fights in the sphere ideology and the class rule in any society inevitably contains the rule of ideology. From the Renaissance era to the foundation of bourgeois republics in France and England, the bourgeois revolution has gone through hundreds of years of struggles against feudal thoughts. When the bourgeoisie begins to rule, its ideology begins to rule too. The bourgeoisie keep training its talents of ideology for its own class. Marx once clearly wrote: in the capitalist society, "the dependence of the ideological, etc., classes on the *capitalists* was in fact proclaimed", and the bourgeoisie "has likewise given recognition to the ideological professions as flesh of its flesh and everywhere transformed them into its functionaries, of like nature to itself"[8]. The socialist revolutions should pay more attention to ideology; especially when the power has been conquered, the battle of ideology does not end because we make achievements in our economic construction or because the direct political resistance of the counter revolution weakens. All the previous revolutions were done within private property, with one form of private property replacing the other. But socialist revolution is a revolution that completely and radically breaks with the traditional private property, so in the field of ideas, it must break with the traditional ideas of private property as well. This can be a very long process, in which the battles in the field of ideology also rise and fall every now and then. In this process, we proletarians not only should avoid the "left" mistakes in the work of ideology, the "left" mistakes turn the struggles against the bourgeois and feudal ideologies into struggles against traditional cultures and against intellectuals and harm them; but also we should avoid the "right" mistakes, which allow the bourgeois and feudal ideologies to spread as

---

8   Karl Marx and Frederick Engels, 1st Edition, Volume 26, p. 168-169 and p. 315.

freely as they like and even enable the bourgeois ideological trend of liberalism gain popularity among the masses. In a socialist country, once the guiding position of Marxism is shaken off, the westerniza-tion ideological trend of the west and the liberal ideological trend of China will ally and become an extremely destabilizing factor en-dangering the social stability. The field of ideas and theories is such a crucial fortress that if the proletariat doesn't secure it, then the bourgeoisie will do that, which is a steel powerful law independent of anyone's will. Therefore the theorists of a socialist country ought to research ideological questions from the perspective of historical materialism, and truly, correctly, and fruitfully develop the guiding role of Marxism in the field of ideology.

7 THE QUESTION OF THE INTEGRATION OF MARXISM WITH THE LOCAL SOCIALIST PRACTICE

All the questions above can boil down to one thing, that is, the in-tegration of Marxism with the local practices, or localization of Marxism. This problem has been partly solved if the political power is conquered; if not, the revolution could not have won the victory. However, this solution isn't something you achieve once and for ever. That they two were integrated correctly in the democratic revo-lution stage doesn't mean the same will also happen in the social-ist revolution and construction stage, because the two stages have their own unique characteristics. In terms of complexity, the integra-tion of historical materialism with socialist revolution and socialist construction practice is much more difficult than the revolutionary struggles of the revolutionary stage. The period of democratic revo-lution didn't have many complex goals, the supreme one of which was to conquer the regime; but the socialist building period after the revolution is quite a complicated process which includes reforming the whole society including the people, this involves all the aspects of the social life and needs a systematic engineering. An ancient Chinese sage said it will be much harder to maintain a business than to start it. Socialism is not to maintain the business but involves to start a new business which also includes the consolidation of the political power, which is more difficult and more significant than the former stage. In his report to the Second Plenary Meeting of the Seventh CC of the CPC, Mao Zedong said, "With this success, we just finished the first step of the new Long March and it's quite a small thing to be proud of, because we will have many more to be proud of in the future too"[9]. It is proved both by history and is the reality that not many proletarian countries can consolidate their power for a really long time although quite a many have won it. If the problem of integrating Marxism with the domestic realty is not solved, all theoretical and practical problems would be quite difficult to handle.

More similar questions can be put forward. But I suggest, these above questions are the fundamental ones from the aspect of materialistic conception of history, i.e. the relation between economy and politics, the relation between productive forces and the relations of production, the interrelations among class, party, leaders and the masses, and the relation between the common laws of socialist development and the unique characteristics of each nation, and so forth. They have all existed in China as well as in the Soviet Union. The Soviet Union has proved with its 70 years of history from rise to dissolution that these relations and the way in which they are handled can either prosper or abandon socialism.

Before the revolution, Lenin had made keen efforts to criticize N.N. Sukhanov and some other supporters of the vulgar theory of productive forces in Russia, and led Russia with backward economy and culture to win the socialist revolution for the first time. However, after the October Revolution, Lenin didn't continue to oppose the so-called vulgar theory of productive forces but laid stress on developing productive forces and clearly recognized that highly developed productive forces would be the main guarantee for the new society to beat the old one, strategically. Generally speaking, his New Economic Policy, was the policy that aimed to use every possible means to develop the productive forces of the country. Within a certain period, Stalin has also paid much attention to develop the productive forces. If fairly evaluated, under Stalin's leadership, the economy, scientific technology and the national defence capacity of the Soviet Union were dramatically developed, making it the second strongest nation in the world. However, after 1930s, Stalin had over emphasized the importance of inner-party struggles and class

---

9   Selected Works of Mao Zedong, Volume 4, p. 1438.

struggles, excessively expanded the magnitude of suppressing and elimination of counterrevolutionaries, and even artificially created, incited some class struggles; and later, he went farther and farther from the law regulating the relation between economic base and politics in historical materialism.

As for the relations between the party and the masses, between the leader and the masses, he abandoned socialist democracy but allowed or even promoted personality cult.

As for the relation between productive forces and the relations of production, he abolished Lenin's New Economic Policy and pursued for the monolithic public ownership in the industry and agriculture.

In the struggles of ideological sphere, he adopted some "left" policies, specifically in the late 1940s when criticizing literature, arts, and philosophy. The Soviet Union was not so successful in solving the problem of integrating Marxism with its socialist construction, but often mechanically and dogmatically followed Marx's and Engels' assumptions on socialism, established a highly centralized planned economy based on monolithic public ownership and a distribution system with mono mode which only included according to work and ignored other distribution modes which could be favourable for the development of the productive forces and favourable for socialist construction.

Stalin even denied there was any contradiction in the socialist society and thus blocked the studies which could correctly understand the unique nature of socialist society, consequently adaptation of correct measures to handle the basic contradictions were impossible. After Stalin passed away, his successors, when correcting his mistakes, went into another way which led to the restoration of capitalism.

If we can say that Stalin has just deviated from some principles of historical materialism, then we can say that his successors have betrayed the fundamental principles of historical materialism gradually, step by step. None of the contradictions generated and developed in the era of Stalin was settled, but they got even worsened in the right direction. With the pretext of objecting personality cult, the successors, completely negated the historical role and effect of the outstanding individuals in history, they retrogressed to the vulgar theory of productive forces once again, thus advocated that the productive forces of Russia cannot promote socialism at all, so they tried hard to develop economy by promoting private property, abolished the leadership of the communist party, abandoned the guidance of Marxism which are the core spheres of the superstructure. What did they get? Nothing, but only have ruined the fruits of the October Revolution.

China has gone along a different road when compared to Soviet Union. Of course, we also made some similar mistakes of the Soviet Union which violated the historical materialism. For example, in the past, we have also boosted personality cult, ignored the decisive function of productive forces in socialist construction but instead blindly pursued "large-scale and high-level of socialization", negated market economy but worshipped planned economy as the only economic system, and even abolished the principle that production mode decides distribution, thus practicing petty bourgeoisie equalitarian distribution and general poverty, and so forth. However, there is one fundamental point in which we were different from the Soviet Union: the CPC has adhered to its good tradition of integrating Marxism with the Chinese practice and followed the principle of integrating historical materialism with socialist practice, drawing lessons from the past, correcting mistakes bravely, thus seek the right direction.

THREE DIFFERENT STAGES OF CHINESE HISTORY

The over fifty years' history of the new China is undividable, though in which there are three different stages—the first 17 years before the Great Cultural Revolution, the 10 years of the Great Cultural Revolution, and the more than 20 years since the reform and opening up, which have some distinctions and even some significant distinctions. They are still unified within fifty years of socialist construction, in which the socialist practice kept advancing yet in turns and twists. In these fifty years of socialist practice, the Chinese philosophers may have a more profound understanding of the relation between historical materialism and socialist practice than ordinary people. If we didn't return to the major principle of historical materialism that the relations of production must adapt to the nature and state of productive forces, or the principle that the development of productive forces play the ultimate decisive role in the development of the society, or the principle of the relation between economy and politics, or the principle of the mutual interrelation between individuals and the masses, and so forth, we wouldn't have those achievements after 1976 or keep following the socialist road, but we would possibly retrogress and negate the past thirty years under the pretext of correcting mistakes and thus negate socialism.

Deng Xiaoping is praised as a great and wise man because he creatively stood on the side of Marxism, applied the principles of historical materialism to sum up past experiences, criticized personality cult but also fully defended and protected the historical status of Mao Zedong; he rebuked the policy of "large-scale and high-level of socialization", applied historical materialism correctly by adjusting the ownership system and the realization of ownership forms so that they fit to the development requirements of the productive forces but also maintained the dominant position of public ownership.

He discovered the idea of "Three Favourables" as the criteria when making judgments when developing the productive forces, but also highlighted the socialist orientation of our modernizations in the four spheres. He suggested being alert to both "Left" and "Right" type of mistakes and interruptions. In my opinion it isn't difficult to recognize the inner relations between the laws of historical materialism and Deng Xiaoping's theories of socialism building, specifically in his theory of building socialism with Chinese characteristics** and in his theory of the primary stage of socialism, in his theory on the essence and the fundamental task of socialism, in his theory on the basic economic system of socialism in the primary stage, his grand policy socialist reform and opening up, and several others which are as important as those I have mentioned. .

We could certainly say that Deng Xiaoping's theoretical system of building socialism with Chinese characteristics is an outstanding manifestation of the integration of historical materialism with Chinese socialist practices. The contents of the ideological line of emancipating the mind and seeking truth from the facts advocated

---

**) This theoretical system after further theoretical studies by the later generations includes 15 sub theories or sub-systems.

by him actually has promoted correct study of all fundamental questions about historical materialism. That is the summary of the experience of China's socialist practices in the past fifty years from both positive and negative sides. Without the combination of historical materialism and socialist practice, there wouldn't be such a favourable and progressive situation full of vigour in China today.

PART II

The fundamental difference between Marxism and all the previous philosophies including the modern era western philosophy lies in its concerns about the radical emancipation of the mankind and about the prospects of social development. It is different from the religious philosophy preaching the ultimate end of "liberation", and also different from the humanist philosophy which only cares about individuals or species. Marxist philosophy really concerns about the emancipation of the proletariat and the labourers and tries to replace the capitalist society with the socialist society. This nature of Marxism was quite accurately and vividly manifested when Marx defined philosophy as "the head of this emancipation" emancipation of men and proletariat, and emphasized the work of education of the educators for the communist cause.

In this sense, the Marxist philosophy never aspires to set up a metaphysical speculative system but throws itself into practical revolutionary movements taking with philosophy as weapon. The nature of the Marxist philosophy determines that in the history of Marxist philosophy, the Marxist philosophers should also be revolutionists at the same time, who will take part in the battles to overthrow the old world in all possible means, which equally applies to many famous Marxist theorists from Marx, Engels, Lenin, Stalin and Mao Zedong to the many respectable theorists of the First International and in the Second International.

After the proletarian took the political power, proletariat faced a new task of Marxist and communist education which relates to ideological, ethical and social consciousness spheres of the superstructure. After the October Revolution, the Soviet Union has cultivated a large number of Marxist educators, teachers and theorists, and so did China, because this was the indispensable requirement in order to construct and consolidate socialist political power and guarantee our leadership in the ideological sphere. In the past fifty years, the party and the government have educated large quantities of teachers of Marxist philosophy including researchers specialized in historical materialism. The specialization and professionalization in Marxist philosophy researches and the expansion of the Marxist ranks both contribute to popularizing and researching on Marxism. An individual educator of Marxism seems not very essential, but a collective troop of them can play an essential role; our job may be ordinary, but our work is closely related with the leadership of socialist ideology in social consciousness, which is critical for the cause of building socialism.

The maturity in theory marks the maturity of a party. Without well educated thousands of Marxist theoretical troops, the socialist society can't develop orderly, and can't last for long. Thus it is an important task to develop Marxist theoretical troops with unwavering stand, clear banner, high theoretical level and proficient in relating themselves with practice. As early as in the 1950s, Mao Zedong had strongly suggested this task. He said we should make out a plan to form thousands of such well educated theoretical troops, and warned that our problems could not be all settled only by socialist industrialization, socialist transformation, modernizing national defence, or atomic energy researches.

During the past fifty years, the Chinese researchers of historical materialism have explored and discussed about many important principles about historical materialism, among which some were related with the questions faced and raised in the socialist construction, and on the other side some purely theoretical, axiological, paradigmatic debates. For example, the debates on the relation of the whole economic base and the whole superstructure, on the contradiction between advanced relations of production and backward productive forces, about class and class struggles in the transition period, on the transition period itself, about humanism and alienation, about the starting point of historical materialism, and so forth. Certainly all these debates had obvious social and political backgrounds. There are some other debates which can be mainly classified as falling within academics and theories, such as the debates about the object and nature of historical materialism, about the logical starting point of historical materialism, and about whether economic base is equal to social existence, whether superstructure belongs to social existence, and whether economic base contains productive forces, and the debates in recent years about the five social formations and three major social formations discussed by Marx, about multi-line determinism theory and single-line determinism theory, and about theory of historical laws and the theory of choice, and whether man or the masses are the creator of history, and so forth, most of which are related to some basic principles of historical materialism.

During the past fifty years, the Chinese researchers on historical materialism have more profoundly understood and more comprehensively mastered historical materialism in the two aspects when compared to the period before the Great Cultural Revolution and even when compared to the period before the reform and opening up. For example, their understanding of the object of historical materialism has gone beyond historical ontology, breaking through the old paradigm that considered historical materialism only as studies on the common laws of social history, beginning to notice the importance of the researches on historical epistemology and historical axiology; breaking through the western views that place speculative historical philosophy and critical historical philosophy in opposition; thus they have obtained more profound knowledge about the effects of the mode of production in social development and its relation with class struggles, and researches on the scale, the standard and the final decisive function of productive forces; they have understood the relation between the objectivity of social laws and the subjective choice of man more comprehensively. And some other issues such as the unity and diversity of social development, the diversity of approaches in socialist construction, the stages of social development, and the importance of superstructural spheres such as socialist ideological and ethical progress, socialist cultural construction, social sciences and education, were intensively studied. I can say researches on man and on the quality of man were also quite abundant. It is proper to say that the researches on historical materialism in the new China for the past fifty years are rather outstanding.

Of course, there are still lots of questions to study and debate, many of which are questions concerning basic principles. For example, in terms of how to treat the Marxist theory of class and class struggles, some scholars have criticized Mao Zedong and evaluated his view that "class struggles, some classes triumph, while others are eliminated; such is history, such is the history of civilization for thousands of years. To interpret history from this viewpoint is historical materialism; standing in opposition to this viewpoint is historical idealism"[10]. I think to reject this ideo of Mao is distorted historical materialism which was the theoretical basis of the ultra-Left trend of thought.

On the other hand, some of those who objected "taking class struggle as the key link", have extended this objection to such an extent that they suggested in all class societies, the examining of questions should never emphasize on class views or class analysis method, which was of course false. Even in our society, the examination of questions can't completely abandon the method of class analysis, otherwise, we would be unable to explain why America and some other western countries still try with every possible means to restrain socialist countries and point their finger at China after the dissolution of the Soviet Union; or explain why the political turmoil of 1989 would happen in China and why "Fa Lun Gong" such a political fundamentalist heresy could be formed in China and even agitate its believers to siege Zhongnanhai*** headquarters, and so forth.

What's more, whether the nature of a society is determined by the dominant relation of production or not is self-evident when evaluating from the perspective of historical materialism; but some of our theorists have suggested that the issue of ownership is unessential, for them what really matters is to develop productive forces, and as long as the social equality is guaranteed and living standards of the masses are improved, it is socialism.

Some scholars misinterpreted the idea that science and technology constitute the primary productive forces, obscured the boundary between historical materialism and technology fetishism, and treated

---

10   "Cast Away Illusions, Prepare for Struggle" (August 14, 1949), Selected Works of Mao Zedong, Vol. IV, p. 428.
***) Zhongnanhai is the office where the current China's leadership works.

science and technology as the only decisive power of social development in isolation. Some other scholars took the pretext of science and technology being the primary productive force and of the so-called information technologies to advertise the new heroic conception of history and believed that man creating history is only the man providing information while on the other side it is the man who has the master of science and technology that determines the development of society.

Some scholars took the contemporary science and technology as basis to negate Marxist theories of labour value and surplus value, negated that the private property of the means of material production is the origin of exploitation, also negated the law that productive forces determine the relations of production, but instead they have advocated that science and technology is the source of surplus value.

Some people even denounced the objectivity of social laws, and the two inevitabilities, i.e. the inevitable historical trend for capitalism to perish and inevitable trend for socialism to succeed. Some people couldn't differentiate scientific and vulgar conceptions of productivity, and denied the possibility and necessity of socialist revolutions in economically backward countries; some theorists even placed social laws and subject's choices in opposite positions, believing that the possibility of subject's choice only exists within the possible space outside of the sphere of necessity, while within the sphere of necessity, the subjects are not free, thus they have attempted to overthrow the "traditional view" of Marxism about the relation between freedom and necessity, and so forth.

There are indeed quite a lot of questions of debate, many of which are matters of principle concerning the survival of Marxist historical materialism, so we must figure them out. In the letter to Conrad Schmidt, Engels asked them to be good at analyzing theory, because only by clear theoretical analysis can the correct road could be pointed out through the complicated facts. Faced with the new practices in China and with so many theoretical questions raised in the reality, we do have to shoulder heavy responsibilities and have a long way to go as the researchers of historical materialism, and must make more arduous efforts in the future.

We are now standing on the turning point between two centuries. The 20th century was a great epoch, in which significant changes have happened in China in the past hundred years. In the last five decades, or especially in the more than two decades since reform and opening up, our social life, in every aspect including thoughts and ideas, has seen unprecedented changes in the whole history of China. However, faced with the coming new century, we will embrace larger opportunities but larger challenges as well, which also applies to the researches on historical materialism. We ought to have a quite clear understanding of the experience and lessons we've learnt about the historical materialism in China's socialist period in the past fifty years.

Undoubtedly, during the fifty years of the socialist revolution and construction, historical materialism has seen much new developments and has been involved with larger ranges and further questions. However, looking at the future development, we still have many deficiencies. In the epoch of democratic revolution, the researchers and the revolutionists of the Marxist historical materialism were united as one, who studied theories in order to solve the practical problems for the revolution, recognized the needs of reality, and paid attention to studying on the history and reality of China applying historical materialism. The situation was quite different after the foundation of the New China that our Marxist researchers and historical materialism researchers have been professionalized as a specialized team and they have taken the research as their job career in colleges and universities and in research institutes. We have expanded the range of research and deepened the researches of some questions, but we can easily ignore the needs and voices of practice but only focus on the studies in a purely academic way. Therefore, within the questions we have been studying and debating, there have been more debates about concepts, categories, and definitions while our studies lack profound researches on practical questions. Also due to this reason, among those researches on historical materialism, there aren't many works of historical materialism which include significant practical and theoretical properties. We have produced many textbooks among which there are some quite good ones. Textbooks are important, but only textbooks are obviously far from enough. We ought to realize that practical problems are the most important aspect of historical materialism. Lack of practicalness, historical materialism will have no vitality, no soul. In fact, it is of paramount importance to know how to apply historical materialism to analyze the problems we are faced with, for example, the working class's status as masters of society under the conditions of market economy, the questions about how to protect and keep the leading status of public ownership, when it is in coexistence with diversified form of ownerships, including the development of privately owned economy, the question of the guiding position of Marxism, and Marxism being in coexistence with other multiple ideological trends in the ideological field and under the conditions of market economy, and the question of the origin and prevention of corruption, and so forth, all of which are essential problems related to the prospect and fate of Chinese socialism. If the theorists of historical materialism weren't interested in any of them, then what they study couldn't be historical materialism any more but would go back to a general historical philosophy, a theory that explores the metaphysical questions of social history from the most abstract perspective. I am afraid I won't admit that it would be a correct direction for the studies on historical materialism.

In the coming century, we surely should continue marching forward along the road of the localization of Marxism in China opened up by Mao Zedong and developed by Deng Xiaoping. The researches on historical materialism ought to be integrated with those studies on the socialist construction practices having Chinese characteristics, making the former one gain more Chinese characteristics too. With such a large and outstanding professional research team, we have every qualification to do better than the present situation and we also need to train another batch of historical materialist theorists.

Some people think these Marxist philosophy workers are quite the same like a thousand men with only one face and have no specific individuality, because their works share the same principles, which couldn't be more wrong. In fact, when we look deeper, all the masters in the history of Marxist philosophy are of distinctive personalities. No need to mention Marx or Engels, but Paul Lafargue, August Bebel, Lenin, Plekhanov, Mao Zedong, and Deng Xiaoping, they all have their own distinctive characteristics. A theory that has distinctive characteristics isn't equal to an absurd or heretic theory, but to the development of truth with creation. Where there is development, there is an essential characteristic; and development must stand on the reality instead of on the theory itself. Reality itself has essential characteristics as it changes and develops constantly, so different realities generate different problems. Even if the Marxist philosophers may share common principles, they are faced with different realities and have to solve different questions, in addition they will have their different level of applying the theory, so the conclusions they draw will be different as well. Thus different Marxist philosophers are naturally equipped with their own characteristics and specific personalities. Thus individualization of Marxist philosophy is at the same time nationalization, or the localization of Marxism in China, since this theoretical individualization is the fruit of the specific characteristics of China's reality. It is deeply rooted in China and can't live without China. It is born Marxist but also absolutely has Chinese characteristics. We are looking forward to cultivate such kind of Marxists in the field of historical materialism researches.

PART III

In the modern world, all kinds of socialist ideological trends exist from the Occident to the Orient, from developed capitalist countries to developing countries. We can easily discover that each ideological trend has its corresponding philosophic basis, especially a corresponding conception of social history. Naturally, a certain kind of conception of social history leads to a certain kind of socialist ideal and scheme it deserves.

From the foundation of scientific socialism by Marx and Engels to the contemporary socialist practice in China, within the one and a half centuries, socialism has gone through the process from theory to movement and to system, having different focal points in different epochs. In the epoch of Marx and Engels, they stressed on the scientificalness of socialist theory, and argued mainly on the inevitability of socialism, and emphasized the class struggle basis of socialist theories. They once criticized the Right opportunism within the party in Germany and said that "When the class struggle is pushed on one side as a disagreeable "crude" phenomenon, nothing remains as a basis for socialism but "true love of humanity" and empty phraseology about "justice""[11]. In Marx's letter to Friedrich Adolph Sorge in October 1877, he brought up this kind of criticism again on the communist party in Germany, he wrote: "A rotten spirit is making itself felt in our Party in Germany, not so much among the masses as among the leaders (upper class and "workers").

The compromise with the Lassalleans has led to compromise with other half-way elements too; in Berlin (e.g., Mr Most) with Dühring and his "admirers," but also with a whole gang of half-mature students and super-wise doctors who want to give socialism a "higher ideal" orientation, that is to say, to replace its materialistic basis (which demands serious objective study from anyone who tries to use it) by modern mythology with its goddesses of Justice, Freedom, Equality and Fraternity."[12].

Lenin was the leader of the Russian socialist revolution and was also the first practitioner who turned socialism from a movement to system. What Lenin had emphasized was the practicalness of socialism because he led the socialist practice in Russia and shouldered the historic mission of building socialism practically. After the success of the Russian October Revolution, Lenin said, "For Russia, the time in which we argued about socialist principles based on books has passed away and gone forever as I deeply believe, so today we could only talk about socialism according to our experience"[13]. When talking about what socialism is, he said: "the bricks of which socialism will be composed have not yet been made. We cannot say anything further, and we should be as cautious and accurate as possible.....It will be suspected that our Programme is only a fantasy. The Programme describes what we have begun to do and the succeeding steps that we wish to take. We are not in a position to give a description of socialism and it was incorrect that this task was formulated."[14].

As Deng Xiaoping lived in another time of socialist construction, he had the experience of socialism in both positive and negative sides,

---

11 Karl Marx and Frederick Engels: Selected Works, 2nd Edition, Volume 3, p. 684

12 Karl Marx and Frederick Engels: Selected Works, 2nd Edition, Volume 4, p. 627.

13 Collected Works of Lenin, 2nd Chinese Edition, Volume36, p. 466, Beijing: People's Publishing House, 1985

14 Collected Works of Lenin, 2nd Chinese Edition, Volume 34, p. 60-61, Beijing: People's Publishing House, 1985

and deeply realized that we hadn't yet made clear about what socialism really is, so he paid special attention to highlighting the essence of socialism and the China's road of socialism building. Inheriting Mao Zedong's unfinished cause of exploring the Chinese socialist construction road as well as his experience and lessons learnt from this previous exploration, Deng Xiaoping put forward the theory of building socialism with Chinese characteristics and thus elevated the theory of scientific socialism to a new level.

I think it is impossible to figure out what socialism is or how to construct socialism being limited in the theoretical stage. In the establishment stage of the theory of scientific socialism, what was required from it was: It should be demonstrable in theory and consistent in logic; on the other side in the sphere of pure theory, socialism was expounded and discussed as a social formation (with its basic forms) in the development of human societies and was described within the framework of five social formations and as a stage which will replace the capitalist society and would be highly advanced compared with its former, in every aspect. This kind of definition of socialism as a social formation was abstract and purely theoretical.

However, the socialist society in practice is no abstract socialism but is generally a concrete social existence within a specific state (definite stage) or nation; having certain degree or level of productive forces, a society with certain degree of culture and education among its masses, and the ethical ideas in this certain society may be far from the level that Marx and Engels had expected to reach in their purely theoretical elucidation. Therefore, it is of paramount importance not to see the construction of socialism based on the abstract principles of socialist societal formation but based on the actual conditions of one's own country. In this sense, in the stage of socialist practice, the socialist theories and principles must be combined with the countries' reality and should be operable and have relevance. In real socialist practices, if the expected purpose is not reached, productive forces are not developed in a long-lasting, steady and in a fast pace, people's living standards are not improved significantly, and the democratic and legal system of this socialism is far from being orderly functioning, it will definitely mean that we haven't totally made clear what socialism is and how to build socialism. And for this failure neither Marx and Engels nor our forefathers should be blamed, while their task was just to expound the general characteristics of socialism and scientific demonstration of socialism from the height of the general laws of social development.

As for how to realize, transform or break through these principles in a concrete way, it should be the business of the later generation. Marx and Engels have highlighted this point many times and they carefully avoided explanations which will constrain the minds or hands of the later generations with their socialist conceptions. However, the scientificalness of socialist theories stressed by Marx and Engels, the practicalness emphasized by Lenin, and the national characteristics of the socialist construction road highlighted by Mao Zedong and Deng Xiaoping are basically consistent. A theory must be scientific so that it can direct practice; and since practice is always concrete, therefore it must have national characteristics. Therefore, in the theories of scientific socialism, three aspects: *scientificalness, practicalness and national characteristics* are inseparable, each of which may draw different level of attention under different conditions. Furthermore, they are all based on historical materialism and are different way of expressions of combining historical materialism with socialism in certain epochs.

There is another so-called socialist road opposite to scientific socialism based on the materialistic conception of history, that is, the democratic-socialist road based on abstract humanism. This socialist road specially and one-sidedly emphasizes on the humanistic character of socialism, i.e. socialism is a society of humanity, a society with liberty, democracy, humanity, equality and justice as supreme principles, and thus puts the question of value at the highest place as the essence of socialism. In the time of Marx and Engels, this trend which attended to replace historical materialism with abstract humanism as the theoretical basis of socialism gradually became an important school among socialist movements, and one of its most important representatives was Bernstein, a leader of the Second International. In his mind, the success of socialism would not be determined by its inner economic necessity but it should only be evaluated as an ideal, so he put forward the slogan—"Go back to Kant", thus turning socialism into a pure value goal. Since then, under the significant influence of Bernstein, three ideological trends were gradually formed: The democratic-socialism ideological trend in western developed capitalist countries, the humanist ideological trend of western Marxism, and the humanistic-democratic social- ism ideological trend in socialist countries mainly represented by Mikhail Gorbachev, all of which are the extension and variation of the thoughts of Bernstein. The result was quite obvious. The west- ern developed countries are still capitalist societies, neither got hu- manized as the democratic socialism expected nor became social- ist; because to realize socialist values on a capitalist basis is more likely to happen in the Arabian Nights. On the contrary, some certain countries that were once socialist went towards capitalism through the effect of democratic socialism. Though Gorbachev worked so hard to publicize democratization and openness and to agitate that the interest of the whole mankind is higher than that of nation and of class, his abstract humanistic principles had inevitably failed to make the Soviet Union prosper and solve its crisis, instead led it to further disaster and disintegration.

After the disintegration of Soviet Union and the dramatic changes in the Eastern Europe, the question what socialism is, became a dif- ficult problem for the whole world. The leaders of some western democratic-socialist or social-democratic parties and workers par- ties as well as some leaders of the communist party had once held a discussion with theme "what will be the future socialism like?" and founded a magazine named *Future Socialism*, in which many articles were propagating the theory of democratic socialism and even some articles had deliberately distorted the relation between Marxism and scientific socialism and put forward the demagogic slogan that socialism didn't need Marxism. The article of Jean Ellen Stain—"Marxism is Dying, Marxism Died, Long Live Socialism!" was such an example, in which the writer repeatedly argued: "so- cialism is not a mode of production. It represents a new attempt to endow our technology and civilization with conscience and morals." "We have nothing related with revolution, with the proletarian dicta- torship or with class struggles", and "socialism is neo-humanism," it is "the contemporary humanism", and so forth[15].

---

15   See p. 449 and p. 451 in Future Socialism, Beijing, 1994

This ideological trend of the abstract humanism was once also emerged in China, but it was sharply criticized by Deng Xiaoping. We can keep walking on our socialist road uninterruptedly and keep winning concrete achievements in building socialism with Chinese characteristics because the Central Committee of the party led by Deng Xiaoping had insisted s on building socialism under the guidance of historical materialism, always considered the correct handling of the basic social contradiction of socialism as the central issue, advocated dominant position of socialist public ownership in the economy. And our leadership insisted that we should reform all kinds of systems which contradict the essence of socialism, so that only in this way we can emancipate and develop the productive forces.

True enough, we on the one side highlight the necessity and practical feasibility of socialism both socially and economically, but on the other side we pay equal attention to the importance of socialism as ideal, value and belief. As a system different from capitalism, socialism contains socialist principles of equality democracy, justice and humanity itself. One of the important aspects of the superiority of socialist society is to build a democratic state governed by rule of law and principles of virtue.

In our past socialist practices, some people have one-sidedly emphasized the merits of class struggles in the socialist society, thus violated the socialist principle of rule by law and socialist human rights, which has severely damaged the authority of socialism. Luckily, these "Left" mistakes were corrected. The value system of socialism we advocate is one indispensable part of our socialist system, but which are based on certain socialist economic and political systems. Without the development of socialist economic base or without having a consolidated socialist political system, all fancy words, within capitalism, about equality, justice and humanism will be nothing but empty talks and lies. Even in the socialist society, the value system of socialism is unlikely to be realized by itself spontaneously either without the correct leadership of the Communist Party, or without the stable dominant position of public ownership. Just for this reason, in the past when we have opposed and fought hard to correct the "Left" mistakes, we have also opposed to abstract humanism and placed to develop economy and efforts to consolidate socialist system at the first place. I think this was the correct way to really make sure the realization of socialist value system, based on a highly-developed economy and an efficient system ruled by law and virtue. If we replace historical materialism with the theory of abstract humanism as our theoretical, if we ignore to combine historical materialism with the practice of socialism and advocate for some kind of abstract freedom and democracy, we may follow the same disastrous road occurred in the Soviet Union.

In a certain sense, the future development of Chinese socialism, will depend on the theory, we will follow as the basis of our socialist theory and practice. I think we will always be able to follow our correct socialist orientation although there is a volatile and complicated international circumstance as long as we stick to historical materialist views. Here I would like to repeat them: The view that the laws of social development is in consistent with the purposefulness of human activities and that the historical necessity and inevitability of socialist society's establishment in China are consistent with its socialist value system, and ultimate goal of building advanced socialism, i.e. communism. As long as we adhere to Deng Xiaoping's theory on the essence of socialism and his theory of building socialism with Chinese characteristics. I should also mention that the essence embodied in the practice and lessons we have learnt in the fifty years' socialist practice of the New China is our correct orientation of combining historical materialism with socialism.

APPENDIX IV

MARXIST THEORY OF SOCIALIST FORMATION AND CONSTRUCTION OF HARMONIOUS SOCIETY*

Truly enough, we can seek for the resources of thoughts and theories to construct the harmonious society from human cultures, especially from the traditional Chinese culture, but the factual basis to construct the harmonious society lies in the reality of the contemporary socialist construction in China, based on Marxism and especially the Marxist theory of social formation as its guiding theory and methodology.

1 FOCUSING ON REALISTIC CONTRADICTIONS AND FACING PRACTICAL PROBLEMS

The important theoretical and practical problems in the socialist movements all have practical features. To construct a harmonious society, neither as a purely logical deduction of the relationship between harmony and antagonism, nor as a modern version of the social ideal in historical literatures or ancient classics, should be a

---

*) Article was first published in Studies on Marxism, 2006(9).

scientific conclusion drawn from focusing on the reality and solving the problems of overall significance we are faced with, and should be based on the Marxist theory of social formation and with the law of the unity of opposites as the method of contradiction analysis.

In this sense, we could say that to construct a harmonious society turns Deng Xiaoping's theories about what socialism is and how to build socialism into instructive, feasible principles and policies. To construct a harmonious society not only indicates a new road of constructing the socialism with Chinese characteristics but also enlightens the light of ideal for the prospect of the mankind in the world.

From the perspective of contradiction, harmony is very likely to exist as a definite state in which the two struggling parties of the contradiction haven't developed as totally incompatible and the two contradictive parties can still coexist harmoniously. However, the harmonious society is quite different, which is the fundamental nature of society, deduced from a general grasp based on the nature and type of social contradictions, the economic, political and cultural systems as well as their organic relations established by all social members on the basis of co-existence, co-prosperity, mutual cooperation and common fundamental interests, and also based on the circumstances and living state of man. It not only involves the harmony between man and man, but also between man and nature, as an overall judgment of the degree and the range that the social harmony has reached, which is the essence of the social structure of a new social formation in human history that is likely to emerge only after going through the societies with class antagonism.

Therefore, in my opinion, the construction of a harmonious society contains problems in two aspects. The first one is in which kind of social formation can a really harmonious society be established, which is a question about social formation. It would be easy for us to ignore the distinctions between social formations and call the pursuit of harmony as a universal value that any society can realize, take the standpoint of moral determinism and cultural determinism, thus w can even deviate from the theory of historical materialism and social reality, if we didn't take social formation or the fundamental nature of social relations into account but only discussed this question within the moral and legal realm of fairness, justice, liberty and equality, or within the philosophic concepts about the relation between contradiction and harmony or within the sphere of discourse..

The second problem is how to construct a harmonious society, which falls within the basic lines, principles, and policies of the ruling party in a socialist society. How to deal with this problem, whether to insist on "taking class struggle as the key line" to strengthen and intensify contradictions, or to adopt correct methods in order to ease and resolve contradictions and make all social members of the society be the beneficiaries of the social system through the achievements of socialist construction step by step, concerns what kind of thoughts and theories we take as the guiding principles of constructing the harmonious society.

Considering from the perspective of social formation, if we ask whether there is any possibility to build a harmonious society, and ask under which social formation may a harmonious society be built; how to build it, what kind of route, principle and policy should we adopt, and whether the construction of harmonious society can be realized or not. These are all questions concerning the fundamental system of socialism and the exertion of its advantages, both of which are absolutely indispensible in the practice of constructing a socialist and harmonious society. This combination of the selectivity of man's subject(ive) behaviour and the possibility provided by the definite social formation is actually about the relation between the purposiveness and the lawfulness of man's behaviours.

2 HOW CAN THE CONSTRUCTION OF A HARMONIOUS SOCIETY BE POSSIBLE?

I never object to trace to the root of the matter or to seek for the support of thoughts and theories for the harmonious society from the perspective of culture. Many great thinkers and philosophers including many utopian socialists, both in East and West, all have quite a lot of thoughts about harmony and social ideals about constructing a harmonious society. And this kind of thoughts about harmony and peace are especially abundant in the traditional Chinese culture. However, there is one point we must keep in mind that though there is the culture of "harmony" in ancient China, the previous Chinese societies had never seen any overall harmony for even once and no

harmonious society had ever shown up. The struggles of oppression and anti-oppression, exploitation and anti-exploitation, rule and
anti-rule, had always existed in the whole feudal society of China.
Of course, the feudal society had also seen some relatively stable
periods and prosperous periods, for example, the Reign of Emperor
Wen and Emperor Jing (in Han Dynasty, 179B.C.-141B.C.), the
Governance of the Zhen'guan Reign (in Tang Dynasty, 627A.D.-
649A.D.), the Flourishing Kaiyuan Reign Period (in Tang Dynasty,
713A.D.-741A.D.), and so forth, but all the stable periods added
together could not make the feudal society a harmonious society,
because in that time, its basic contradictions were class struggles
and oppression relations that can by no means be harmonious. So
many famous Chinese poets in the past feudal dynasties had written
all kinds of poems to pay their sympathies to the poor peasants, such
as the "On the Faults of Qin Dynasty " and "Strategies for Public
Security" written by Jia Yi; Du Fu's "three poems about officials
" and "three poems about farewell"; Bai Juyi's "The Old Charcoal
Seller "; Pi Ri Xiu's "Complaints about Corrupt Officials", "The
Ballad of Peasants ", and "Poor Long People ", which all expose the
miserable situations of the peasants in the so-called those flourishing ages to different extents. Please don't read the official history
books only, but read more unofficial ones and more poems, from
which you could easily understand and experience the point above.
Even the legendary epoch of Yao, Shun and Yu (the three best kings
in the primitive society of China) was no harmonious society at all,
but it was the prehistoric state in the primitive society when there
hadn't emerged any class division yet. In the "Horse Hoof" written
by Zhuang Zi, he described, "In the supreme moral society, men live
together with animals; the mankind is no different from other kinds
of creatures in the world; no distinction exists between gentlemen
and villains!" This seems to be an ideal world, in which man and
man, man and nature, all get along harmoniously, but it is in fact a
stage without complicated social relations and in which man is in
absolute dependent to nature.

In the pre-capitalist society with low level of productive forces, it
was impossible to form a harmonious society, either in slave society
or in feudal society. In terms of the relation between man and nature,

the so-called idyllic scenery is only the nature in the eyes of literati, not in the eyes of the peasants who work hard all day long in the fields. It was more the constraint of earth on man and the dependence of man on the nature than the harmony between man and nature. As for the relation between man and man, it contained a pyramid-like hierarchical structure, with rule and absolute obedience existing in the seemingly simple and plain interpersonal relations. The social members were, like the Chinese medicine put in the drawers of a shop of traditional Chinese medicines, put and fixed forever in the drawers of hierarchy by the social relations.

In the modern capitalist society with highly developed productive forces and scientific technologies, it is also impossible to build a harmonious society. The basic class relation and basic social contradictions in the capitalist society determine that it is unlikely to construct a harmonious society within the capitalist social formation. The capitalist harmonious society can exist nowhere but in the historical fantasy prepared by the bourgeois scholars and theorists in their theories of eternal capitalist system and regarding the end of capitalist society. In the developed countries all over the world, like U.S.A., Britain, Japan, France, and Germany and so on, they are all bothered by various contradictions, e.g. contradictions between man and himself, and contradictions of that society including class relations, race relations, and foreign policies, etc.. The bus workers strike in New York, the students parade in France, the flight attendants strike in Britain, and others, all indicate that even if the productive forces of a country are quite developed, as long as it is still a capitalist society, it cannot be a capitalist harmonious society in terms of its social nature and class relations. As for the developing countries, such as some countries and regions in Africa, Latin America, and Asia, it is even more impossible for them to build a harmonious society when suffering from poverty, corruption, turmoil, and civil war.

In the theories and practices of building socialist harmonious society, we ought to distinguish harmony, social stability, and harmonious society, because if we didn't clarify these three, we might turn this special historical mission of today's socialist society: The building a harmonious society, into such a state that might already exist or actually had existed in all social formations, which not only goes against the Marxist theory of social formation, but also doesn't conform with historical facts.

As a philosophic category, harmony uncovers a relationship of the two contradictory parties commonly existing in a definite stage of development. The harmony of contradiction will show up when the struggles of the two parties of contradiction stay in the quantitative phase, or after the new unity taking the place of the old unity. The existence of the harmony is inevitable but also relative, because when the contradiction develops to a certain stage, one contradictory party will adopt different methods to break the original harmonious relation and then build a new unity of opposites that is both antagonistic and harmonious, which is a universal law of the development of nature, society and thought.

As a category of social history, social stability expresses the degree and the state that the social contradiction is intensified. From the perspective of social development, social stability is a state that the social operation is relatively orderly, the social economy and culture are relatively developed, and the antagonistic emotions among all social members haven't been completely open or public. In such a state, the ruler can rule his country in the old way, while the ruled emotionally and factually admit the legality of this rule and are willing to accept it as well. Undoubtedly, in the whole development process of a society or a country, sometimes it may develop a little faster, sometimes it may be in an economic stagnation or in a period of revolution, and sometimes its class contradiction will be eased. Revolution, rebellion, or the oppression on the ruled don't always exist in any stage of social development, therefore, any social formation of any (whichever) nature is likely to see its period of social stability. Otherwise, this social formation wouldn't appear or exist, and it wouldn't have any reasonable basis of existence or any possibility of development. However, social stability isn't equal to social harmony, because the social stability presupposes the fact that the ruled obey the laws and the moral rules asserting the dominance of the ruler and is the outward manifestation of the stable dominance of the ruler. It is no real social harmony, because in terms of its overall social structure and social nature, it is still a society based on the antagonism of class interests.

This principle equally applies to the modern western developed capitalist society, in which the class at the dominant position practices policies that can ease social contradictions, carries out relatively good social security system and social welfare system, and has established a relatively perfect legal system, and exerts great impacts on the ideology and on the value guidance of the media, thus making the masses become the "One-dimensional Man" as Herbert Marcuse called. Masses have a high sense of identity about the bourgeois economic system and political system as well as a high degree of satisfaction about their living conditions, totally different from the workers that Frederick Engels described in *The Conditions of the Working Class in England* who were so angry, dissatisfied and slack in work and protested those in all kinds of means. Indeed, compared with the early capitalist society, the modern developed capitalist society is seeing relatively eased class contradiction and class antagonism, lacking both certain level of revolutionary trend and revolutionary enthusiasm. As I indicated above, the modern developed capitalist relations of production still have space for the rapid development of productive forces, but we cannot thereby hold the view that the social stability of the developed capitalist society appearing in the late half of the 20th century is a capitalist harmonious society. Since the basic social contradiction in the capitalist society has an antagonistic nature, those antagonistic classes or ranks can only get along with each other and keep peace temporarily, but the capitalist society can by no means become a harmonious society in which all classes share the common interests and cooperate with each other. In Preface to *A Contribution to the Critique of Political Economy* written in 1859, having examined the laws of the basic social contradictions of human society, Marx clearly pointed out, "The bourgeois mode of production is the last antagonistic form of the social process of production—antagonistic not in the sense of individual antagonism but of an antagonism that emanates from the individuals' social conditions of existence—but the productive forces developing within bourgeois society create also the material conditions for a solution of this antagonism. The prehistory of human society accordingly closes with this social formation."[1]

---

1 Karl Marx and Frederick Engels: Selected Works, 2nd Edition, Volume 2, p. 33, Beijing: People's Publishing House, 1995.

There are quite a lot of people in today's modern time having the sense of identity with the capitalist society based on their different views or values, but instead there is not the fact of harmonious social relations. The deviations of the value judgments and the illusory factual judgment of the nature of the capitalist society may continue to exist for a really long time, but the real fact that in all class societies including the capitalist society inevitably exist class struggles and interest antagonisms will not be overturned, or in a more fashionable word, be "deconstructed", because of men's different views of value or different feelings. Revolutions, civil wars, or even the large-scale suppressions of the rulers against the revolutionary people, in the long river of human history, are always short; most time in the history the state of daily life is relatively peaceful, but the contradictive, antagonistic nature among social members is always there and never fades away. As for the overall of the class society, the relatively peaceful state of daily life is actually a state of truce when the antagonistic parties are preparing for another struggle and the contradictions are being accumulated and intensified. A class society, based on private property, with dominance and exploitation as its basic class relation, can never become a truly harmonious society, whichever social formation it belongs to. We cannot assert when and how the western capitalist society will revolutionize, but we can say the so-called harmony in the capitalist society is actually the stability of social system; it is not a really social harmony. As far as I'm concerned, the description in *The Communist Manifesto* about class situations and class relations in class societies is still valid.

From the perspective of social development, the communist society is a harmonious society hypothesized by Marx and Engels, in which the conflicts between man and nature, man and man will have been sublated, the harmony between man and nature, man and man being realized, and the all-around development and the individualities of men are being set free. To realize this goal, socialist society is a particular and essential phase, and also based on the essence of socialist society, to construct a harmonious society goal is put forward. The harmonious society we want to construct is different from all the past societies, because its supreme goal is closely related with the communist society.

Social stability isn't equal to social harmony, but in a harmonious society social stability should be contained as the measurement of the degree of social harmony. The social stability of a harmonious society is different from that in an inharmonious society, because it isn't a social order that maintains the original inequality by virtue of external power but is the expression of the cohesion and composition of all forces inside the society. When talking about what socialism is, Deng Xiaoping clearly stated that, the essence of socialism is to "emancipate productive forces, develop productive forces, eliminate exploitation, eliminate polarization, and finally realize common prosperity"[2]. A society, based on highly developed productive forces, including that process of elimination of exploitation and polarization in the end, and common prosperity and sharing of produced results as goal, must be both harmonious and stable, if we look from the perspective that the possibility of constructing a harmonious society is just rooted deeply in the soil of socialist society different from all the other social formations. Without this kind of soil, no such fruit can be borne.

However, we cannot simply affirm now that our Chinese society has already been a harmonious society. If that had happened, we wouldn't have proposed the great historical mission of constructing a harmonious society. The realization of the essence of socialist society is a process, a process that keeps reforming, developing and maturing. In this process, some old contradictions having been solved, some new ones will spring up again, and there also exist the possibility and reality of intensifying contradictions due to mismanaging. We are now staying at the primary stage of socialism, the period of deepening social reforms, and thus we are also at a stage full of sharp and frequent contradictions. The reason that we proposed to construct a harmonious society lies in that the society we are living in isn't harmonious and has various inharmonious factors existing both in the relations between man and man and also between man and nature worthy of great and careful attention.

---

2   Selected Works of Deng Xiaoping, Volume 3, p. 373, Beijing: People's Publishing House, 1993.

Some scholars consider that the disharmony does not impede our society from being a harmonious society, because according to the law of the unity of opposites, contradiction should contain dual factors, both harmonious and inharmonious factors, which indeed replace the concrete analysis of practical contradictions with merely abstract talks.

Undoubtedly, harmony is not a state without any contradiction at all. But the contradictions we are faced with now are what we must spare no effort to solve to construct a socialist harmonious society. If we don't solve them one by one, then in theses contradictions will hide factors of insecurity and instability causing oppositions between social members, because some contradictions which are there are not what the essence of socialism should have or some contradictions which are there are not those beneficial for the social development, but are sarcomas attached on its organism, for example, the unfair social distribution, the polarization, the drain of state-owned property, the peasant problems caused by unreasonable land expropriation, all those malpractices and black holes existing in the reforms of education and medicine, and corruption, and so forth, are bottlenecks that estrange the social members and restrict further and deeper reforms. Of course, some other contradictions existing fall within the contradictions that are bound to occur due to the originally backward economy and culture, or due to the co-existence of multiple ownership forms and the diversified modes of distribution applied. Therefore, the situation we are faced with is interweaved with all kinds of contradictions, some of which are reasonable while some not, some of which are the necessary cost of reforms while some are the unexpected price paid for improper measures. Contradictions are not terrifying; the question is whether we pay due attention to them, whether we solve them, and how to solve them. The construction of a harmonious society is just proposed on the basis of admitting the contradictions and solving the contradictions. A socialist harmonious society can neither be a society without any contradiction nor a society that ends all contradictions. However, contradiction is anything but a still state of the unity of opposites; it is, on the basis of solving all current contradictions, a new contradiction will be appearing on a new harmonious, horizontal platform. Old contradictions solved and then new contradictions formed up, this kind of dependent progression is the process of social progress.

Faced with so many contradictions, we shouldn't thus deny the possibility of building a harmonious society. Our party could set up the goal of building a harmonious society because the contradictions we are facing now are different from those the non-socialist societies faced before. Except a few illegal acts, most of our social contradictions are contradictions among the people based on common fundamental interests. The nature and the type of the contradictions determine that we are likely to solve them according those principles good for the self-perfection of the socialist system. Therefore, in my mind, it is impossible to build any harmonious society without the guarantee of socialist system or without adhering to socialist principles; whereas, if we don't take the construction of a harmonious society as a goal or don't fully develop the advantages of socialist system, but let the existing contradictions keep being intensified, then the polarization and the antagonism between the rich and the poor will become more and more severe, the relation between man and nature will get worse and worse along with the development of modernization and industrialization, and the possibility of constructing the harmonious society will only become an abstract possibility. When the inharmonious side of contradiction overweighs the possibility that the two parties of contradiction can still stay within the same unity, the society is not likely to have a crisis; therefore, in essence, to stick to the socialist system and to construct a harmonious society are consistent with each other. If we ignored the practical basis of building a harmonious society, separated the construction of a harmonious society from socialism, but simply tossed about on the relation between contradiction and harmony, we would then turn the Marxist philosophy into empty talks.

3 WHY IS IT NECESSARY TO BUILD A HARMONIOUS SOCIETY?

Seen from the nature and the type of contradictions, socialism should be harmonious in essence, and could build a society in which all results both material and mental are shared by all social members. However, it should be doesn't mean it must be; it could be doesn't mean that it actually is so. Only through constructing a harmonious society can the essence of socialism be realized step by step, and can the advantages of socialist system be fully developed.

It is hard to understand a "socialism" that has always been on the verge of inner fights and has experienced perpetual class struggles and political movements, and in which most of the people live in poverty and misery, and lack normal democracy and lack rule by law, and this can never be the "socialism" in which the masses wholeheartedly support it, get satisfied with it and make every effort to protect it. This kind of socialism can be anything but not a solid/stable, everlasting and an energetic society with full of vitality. It has been manifested both by its negative and positive lessons throughout the dissolution of the Soviet Union and the fall of communism in the Eastern Europe, throughout the setbacks of international socialist movements and throughout our Chinese experience and lessons of constructing the socialist society that, to build a harmonious society is not a dispensable thing at all but is a great matter of life and death related to the prospect and fate of socialist society.

Before the state power is wrested, of course the proletariat and its political parties should launch class struggles including violent revolutions. And of all their activities, class struggles should be their primary task. However, having conquered the political power, the task of top priority needs to be shifted from taking over the regime and overthrowing the old ruler into the building of a new society. To take power is only the start of all socialist revolutions, it is the first step in the Long March. And the responsibilities shouldered by the destroyer of the old system are quite different from those shouldered by the constructor of the new system. As revolutionists, we could fix our eyes on the political power; while as socialist constructors, we should fix our eyes on the society. Since society is a unity, an organic unity including economy, politics and culture, and the relation between man and man and the relation between man and nature are inherent in this social structure, it is the essential requirements of the socialist society to build a society with its economy, politics and culture in coordination with each other, and which includes harmonious relations between man and man, man and nature. However, only under the contemporary international and national historical conditions we have and having gone through the pains and setbacks of constructing the socialist cause could the necessity of building a harmonious society be proposed. So to speak, the problem of constructing a harmonious society that we are faced with at present is actually a further development of Deng Xiaoping's questions about what socialism is and how to construct socialism.

Socialist society is a very long historical phase. After the proletariat has conquered the political power, there might be a time or times when class struggles are quite intense and fierce, which is an inevitable consequence of significant changes of class relations. Especially for Russia and China, the two big countries with relatively backward economy and culture and surrounded by developed capitalism, they had and have to face far sharper class struggles and heavier tasks of economic construction than developed countries. And we do have learnt a lot of lessons in how to deal with the relation between class relations and social harmony, between economic development and comprehensive social progress, which are all valuable theoretical resources for the construction of a harmonious society.

Seen from the history of the world's socialist practices, the Soviet Union has made significant mistakes in dealing with the two fundamental problems: Class contradiction and social harmony, secondly, economic development and social progress.

After the success of the October Revolution in 1917, the Soviet regime was faced with foreign armed interventions and domestic anti-revolutionary rebellions, it was threatened by sharp class struggles, so it was completely correct for the Bolsheviks to adopt harsh actions to protect the newly established Soviet regime. However, the problem is, after the death of Lenin when Stalin led the party and the nation, he handled the relation between social contradiction and social harmony in a metaphysically one-sided way during the period of economic construction, and led by this thinking method, he followed far "left" policy in dealing with internal social contradictions of the Soviet Union. On the one hand, he didn't admit there was any contradiction existing in the socialist society and claimed that the Soviet society was absolutely coherent both in politics and in morals; on the other hand, he also put forward a mistaken theory that the class struggles in the socialist society were becoming more and more severe. In his mind, socialist society should have no contradictions at all and all contradictions in the socialist society were class struggles and hostile struggles. In the article "The Economic Problems in the Soviet Socialism", Stalin began to admit that there were contradictions in the socialist society, but he had already been in his late ages and couldn't make up for the troubles his practical policies had resulted. The Soviet society had always been in an inharmonious state and had been faced with fierce class struggles, political movements as well as inner-party struggles both in political and cultural fields. Yes, before Stalin passed away, the Soviet society was stable, but it was only stable not a harmonious society, because this stability rested on Stalin's absolute authority and on the personality cult on him, maintained by the coercive power of the regime, as if a wooden cask tightly hooped by iron. The Soviet socialist society had never entered into a harmonious, benign development stage. When Stalin passed away, the constantly accumulated contradictions finally resulted in the dissolution of the socialist society. As for his latter successors, those including Mikhail Gorbachev and Boris Yeltsin not only failed to solve the contradictions, but further expanded and intensified them following the right line and also changed the nature and the type of the existing original contradictions. Now, these days Russian government has made the festival of October Revolution as the Day of National Reconciliation, to express their hope of social harmony, but as their socialist system was ended, the possibility of social harmony has also flown away.

In terms of economic development and social progress, the Soviet Union also left us many lessons worthy of learning. Under the planned economy, we ought to admit that the Soviet Union developed quite rapidly and even went beyond the capitalist countries to a certain extent, completely changing the backwardness prevalent in the epoch of tsar. Even the western critics acknowledge that Stalin led and brought the Russia using wooden ploughs into the atomic era. However, for its development, the Soviet Union paid an enormous price: the significant economic achievements of agricultural collectivization and industrialization couldn't counterbalance the excessive accumulation and overcome price scissors, thus making its economic development inconsistent, unbalanced, and unsustainable; the centralized planned system brought about a feeble economy with extreme imbalance between heavy industry and light industry, between industry and agriculture, between city and countryside, and between military industry and civil industry, difficult to sustain its development; the one-sided progress of heavy industry and military industry impeded the overall progress of social development. The Soviet socialism is truly a great experiment, which manifests the superiority of socialist system to an outstanding extent, but also shows that the socialist society can also lose the respect and support of the masses if without aiming social harmony. The tragedy of the Soviet socialism proves the necessity of building a socialist harmonious society.

China, as the Soviet Union, also gained the victory of the socialist revolution in a large country with backward economy and culture. Having taken power, China also experienced a storm of class struggles and political movements, but Mao Zedong, different from Stalin, admitted that there is contradiction inside a socialist society and it is essential to correctly deal with the contradictions in the socialist society. In his article "On correctly dealing with the contradictions among the people", he claimed we should distinguish two kinds of contradiction correctly and solve the contradictions among the people properly, so as to realize the internal solidarity of the socialist society through correctly dealing with contradictions. However, tragically, Mao also failed to correctly handle the relation between the two (struggle and unity) of contradiction of socialist society in practice, so the energetic and active political situation as he had longed for, in which democracy coexists with centralism, individual freedom with disciplines, wasn't established in the end. During a very long time from the establishment of the new China in 1949 to the end of the "Great Cultural Revolution" in 1976, class struggles were paid undue attention, and the society was in an abnormal unstable and inharmonious state, on the verge of breaking out, which severely influenced interpersonal relations including the relation of party and masses and the relation of cadres and masses, as well as the relations among the social members, even in family relations.

We also have drawn lessons concerning the economic development and social progress. One of the most painful lessons is that without a powerful and developed economy, we can never make our nation prosperous or our military force strong and efficient. A socialist society must develop its economy, and we did have made unprecedented achievements in the industrial field within a very short time. However, at that time, the Chinese people and the Chinese government were so much craving for rapid development, so they carried out quite a lot of measures, which, though reflecting their ambitious hope to build a wealthy and powerful nation, seriously violated the laws of economy and the laws of the coordinated development of economy and society, getting the result that was just the opposite to what they wished. The three years' disaster in 1960's had severely damaged the people's enthusiasm to build socialism and the development of other social causes.

We also need to consider the necessity of building a harmonious society from a global perspective. In the modern world, socialist society coexists with capitalist society. The antagonistic character of the basic contradictions in the developed capitalist society determines that it can never become a harmonious society, but these days the western capitalist society enjoys a relatively stable period through self-regulation, and its scientific development, per capita income, and practical living standards are higher than the existing socialist countries. In the past, theorists compared capitalism to a jade, and socialism to an eyas, to express their relation. However, the dissolution of the Soviet Union and the fall of communism in the Eastern Europe broke the wings of the tercel and greatly distorted the world's view about socialist society. Therefore, what kind of socialist society China, as a country sticking to the socialist road, will build, not only concerns our domestic affair, but also concerns the position of socialist theory and reality in the heart of the international public and especially of the progressive people of the world. From this perspective, the construction of the socialist harmonious society is quite necessary and is of great international significance, which will show the world a socialist country that has a harmonious, prosperous, powerful domestic society and that takes the pursuit of a harmonious world as its diplomatic policy. It will be the signal shell of the new victory of socialist theory and practice.

4 THE BASIC PRINCIPLES OF BUILDING A HARMONIOUS SOCIETY

In China, to build a harmonious society, to build the socialism with Chinese characteristics, and to stick to and deepen reform and opening up policy are in the same process. The construction of a harmonious society actually exists in the construction of the socialism with Chinese characteristics; and only by sticking to and deepening the reform and by advancing the opening up process can the harmonious society be built, while on the other side sticking to reform and deepening this reform must be aimed at building a harmonious society. If the so-called policy of reform and opening up didn't solve contradictions but instead constantly intensify the contradictions, then it wouldn't gain the support and respect of the masses, and would go inconsistent with the general purpose of building socialist harmonious society. Therefore, the reform and opening up must be beneficial for constructing a harmonious society, while the construction of a harmonious society must provide a stable social platform and promote the masses' psychological enduring capacity for following the policy of sticking to and deepening the reform and opening up. The key to combine these two is a correct line, which is the line of "One Centre and Two Basic Points"** put forward by Deng Xiaoping, and the line of Scientific Outlook on Development put forward by Hu Jintao which is a creative inheritance and development of the first.

The central position of economic construction can by no means be shaken. It can't work if a harmonious society has no highly developed economy or solid material basis. Up to now, socialism hasn't caught up with the level of production or that of scientific technology of the western developed capitalism. That is their advantage, our disadvantage. Lenin once said that the new productive forces were the guarantee for the new social system defeating the old one. His view is quite far-sighted. Poverty is no socialism, and it can never build harmonious socialism either.

**) "One Centre and Two Basic Points" approach was put forward by Deng Xiaoping. Center was economic development work or develop productive forces two points were insist on reform and opening grand policy and insist on Four Cardinal Principles in all the reform process as another grand policy.

There are two paragraphs written by Marx and Engels in *The German Ideology* that can help us correctly understand, from the perspective of social formation, the important role of economic development will play in building a harmonious society. They wrote that man's liberation didn't rest on self-consciousness, "it is only possible to achieve real liberation in the real world and by employing real means, slavery cannot be abolished without the steam-engine and the mule and spinning-jenny, serfdom cannot be abolished without improved agriculture, and that, in general, people cannot be liberated as long as they are unable to obtain food and drink, housing and clothing in adequate quality and quantity"[3].

When writing about communist revolutions in another place, they said the enormous growth and high development of productive forces are an absolutely necessary practical premise "because without that, want is merely made general, and with destitution the struggle for necessities and all the old filthy business would necessarily be reproduced"[4]. After over 160 years, when I review these words and combine them with the lessons and experience of the past international socialist movements, I couldn't help but marvel at the profound insight of the founders of Marxism.

As a creative new development of the socialist construction line with economic construction as the central task, the Scientific Outlook on Development policy has two major points: one is to develop, and the other is to be scientific.

If there is no development, then no scientific outlook on development is needed to be established. The law that development is of overriding importance should also be a fundamental principle of the outlook on development. When Stalin led the construction of the Soviet socialism, his conception of developing the Soviet economy by agricultural collectivization and industrialization was quite good and at that time, it did work out well and make great achievements amazing the whole capitalist world, but the Soviet economic development was also distorted and one-sided. On the other side Mao Zedong also laid stress on economic development, but he failed in the end when he tried to use unscientific methods to realize the "Great Leap

---

3   Karl Marx and Frederick Engels: Selected Works, 2nd Edition, Volume 1, p. 74.
4   ibid, p. 86.

Forward" in developing productive forces, such as steel production by rural communes, or highly close periods of grain planting, and so forth. It has been proved by experience that development can by no means be realized with good wishes only, but scientific approach is needed as well.

In the social field, the Scientific Outlook on Development policy is different from the unscientific, evolutionary outlook on development and social development is different form evolution as well. As a state, evolutional motion exists objectively, since the nature and the human society have always been in a non-stagnant state of motion. The evolution of the natural world is spontaneous, dominated by natural rules, but that of the social field contains the subjective selection and purposefulness of human acts. Which mode should be taken to develop economy, how to make this development beneficial for the balance and harmony of the whole social structure, and how to make human act for themselves, all these questions must be solved on the basis of objective laws. And this outlook on development based on objective laws is a scientific outlook on development.

Since the 1970s, in the western world, heated debates have been caused on questions about development. And some western scholars have proposed the problem of sustainable development, but they lacked the efficient guarantee of social systems because the problem of profits is far more important than that of environment for international capitalist companies, monopoly groups and private owners. This fact indicates that to solve the problem of development scientifically must be guaranteed by a reasonable social system. Furthermore, the word "scientific" in the Scientific Outlook on Development is concerned with all sciences including philosophy, social sciences, natural sciences, technical sciences, and etc, because it not only needs the guidance of scientific world outlook and methodology, but it also involves the theories and concrete calculations using economics and applied economics to bring about the appropriate relation between balance and harmony. It includes various researches in natural science and technical science on environment, population, the bearing capacity of nature, and renewable resources and non-renewable resources, and so forth. The implementation and practice of the Scientific Outlook on Development can be called as system engineering, which, at the same time, is the construction process of the socialist harmonious society.

When taking economic construction as our central task, we must stick to the two fundamental points as well, and first of all, stick to the Four Cardinal Principles**, which concerns the fundamental question that what kind of theoretical and political principles we should adopt to when striving to build a harmonious society.

Who will build it? Of course the leading role should be played by the China Communist Party at the dominant place only. And it is of decisive importance to adhering to the leading position of the CPC In the socialist China, to advertise multi-party rule can lead to mere

chaos rather than social harmony. The government must develop and perfect its governmental functions. Therefore, the construction of a harmonious society is above all, a test on the nature, the progressiveness and the governing capacity of the party and on the task performance capacity of the government. Without a communist party truly working for the public and ruling for the masses, without a honest and highly efficient government serving the people wholeheartedly, the blueprint of building a harmonious society will never work due to interruptions by corruption and inefficiency. On this point, the construction of a harmonious society is a serious test on the progressiveness and governing capacity of the CPC, especially on its leaders.

Towards which direction should the harmonious society be built? Undoubtedly, we must go along the socialist road. We have three versions of categories about socialist construction: to build the socialism with Chinese characteristics, to build a well-off society, and to build a harmonious society. In fact, these three expressions about socialist construction are mutually linked with each other and quite inseparable, each of which has its particular emphasis and aims at different theoretical and practical questions, advancing with the times.

**) Four Cardinal Principles were set by Deng Xiaoping in 1979, in the beginning period of reform and opening policy. They are, keeping to the socialist road, uphold the democratic dictatorship of the proletariat, uphold the leadership of the Communist Party, uphold Marxism-Leninism and Mao Zedong Thought.

The socialism with Chinese characteristics is a general expression in terms of the Chinese socialist construction road, which emphasizes that the Chinese socialist construction should neither be a reprint of the Soviet socialist road nor a mechanical application of Marx's and Engels' theories on socialism, but should have Chinese characteristics. China ought to walk on a socialist construction road of its own.

The well-off society is proposed as one milestone in the process of building socialism. We are now at the primary stage of socialism, and we are going to build a well-off society in an all-around way in a rather long time, which is the positioning of our socialist construction target that recovers the line of seeking truth from facts and is based on the reality and practices of China, but its emphasis is to take economic development level and per capita income as standards.

To build a harmonious society is raised on the basis of the socialist formation (society) and aims to warn against the contradictions we are facing and we must solve, which centres around adjusting the relation between man and man, between man and nature, and to construct the socialist society as a whole in an all-round way. However, the three are consistent in essence. The harmonious society is the harmonious society in the socialist society; without the fundamental system of socialism, there won't be any harmonious society at all. In this sense, the socialist society with Chinese characteristics, the well-off society, and the harmonious society are consistent in essence and have one thing in common, i.e. socialism. Of course, to build a harmonious society is also the duty of all social members of the society. Every part of the building process, from environmental protection to community/neighbourhood harmony, family harmony and interpersonal harmony, all cannot do without everyone's participation

The other fundamental point is to deepen the reform. We must stick to the reform and deepen the reform, because there won't be any way out if we go backward. Yes, in the past thirty years, the reform has made quite remarkable achievements, but to sum up the questions and contradictions appearing in it, should not be taken as an opposition to the reform. We ought to pay due attention when reflecting and summarizing our practical experiences in the reform.

It's true that we are now faced with so many contradictions, each of which has its own particular conditions. For example, the problem of unbalanced development, the problem of the urban-rural dual structure, the unsynchronized development between economy and society, and the ecological problem, and so forth, they are all old contradictions and problems which have existed even before the reform. Half a century ago, Mao Zedong listed ten contradictions at that time in his article—"On the Ten Major Relations". Corruption and the power exchange for-money type of misconduct are two global problems; but the new polarization and the unfair distribution in income including the power exchange for money type of misconduct, worsening corruption, some people making great fortunes overnight, moral bankruptcy, and upside-down turned views of values, and some other things that have been stamped out long time ago rise from the ashes again, they are all new problems for the socialist China in its social transition. For such a situation, there are many reasons with various aspects. We shouldn't overlook the changes of the social economic environment, because the market relations with money as the intermediary exert inducing effects on some symptoms. These are the negative effects of market economy, but theoretically we haven't done adequate researches, or thought of several legal and moral precautionary measures on the possibility that these negative effects may take place and we also lack high-level Marxist theoretical researches on what kind of influence the changes in the social economic environment may exert on thought. We haven't reasonably or fairly evaluated the role that the public ownership and the planned economy can play in the construction of Chinese socialism, and we are in need of theoretical evidences and efficient supervision mechanism ideas on how to maintain the subjective leadership position of the public ownership. All these questions also deserve to be answered both theoretically and practically through the practice of adhering to the reform and deepening the reform. Therefore, to adhere to the reform and to deepen the reform must be premised on sticking to the correct direction of reform and it must be guided by Deng Xiaoping's principle of "One Centre and Two Basic Points".

The people-oriented approach principle is the soul and core of the Scientific Outlook on Development, which also must stick to and deepen the reform and continue to enhance the soul of opening up. The policy of the reform and opening up itself is not the purpose, but is the inevitable course that China must experience to become prosperous and strong, and it is the successful line along which the socialism with Chinese characteristics develops and advances; it concerns the fundamental interests of all the people, thus how to reform and how to deepen the reform must represent the interests of the masses and should gain their support and acceptance. Only in this way can the principle of people-oriented approach could be really practiced in the reform and opening up course.

There is no doubt that to deepen the reform will face many important theoretical questions related to different subjects involved and thus it will need specialized studies. Limited by their positions, the masses generally may pay more attention to their personal interests, short-term interests, and direct interests, but that can't be taken as the evidence/pretext that the masses should be excluded from the reform. What the CPC has always advocated and applied is the mass line: principle "from the masses to the masses", concentrate all forces and apply that principle, and repeatedly test the correctness of Marxist policy-making methods. The ordinary masses of course don't have such a high theoretical level or cannot understand many different schools, but there is one thing of paramount importance that any reform must be closely related with both direct and indirect interests of all citizens. Who will be benefited? The majority or the minority? As for this question, it is the masses themselves who should directly benefit from the fruits of reform that have the most right to speak rather than some theorists. Their individual judgments may be limited, but the common feeling and experience of the masses do deserve great attention, because that is like a weather vane of social psychology and public opinions.

The experience learnt from the past three decades has proved that the masses of the Chinese people support the reform and are actually enjoying the fruits of reform to different extents. They don't hate the rich or oppose to that some of the people become wealthy first, gaining more money through their legal labour, but they hate the people who seek for personal gains in the name of reform, oppose to those greedy officials and unscrupulous merchants who make huge fortunes overnight, and despise all kinds of illegal acts. Our people are opposed to all these social parasites who amass their wealth by illegally and dishonestly taking advantage of the material resources, power resources and relational resources in their hands. This kind of opposition goes towards the same direction as the direction of the CPC, to combat corruption and build a clean government and rule the country by law. If the fruits of reform fall into the hands of a few people but the price is paid by all the people, this so-called reform will inevitably end in failure. In the final analysis, the fruits of the reform being shared by all citizens is the ultimate guarantee of the success of the reform. In this sense, during the process of deepening the reform, we must hold high the principle of people-oriented approach stipulated in the Scientific Outlook on Development, and only in this way can the socialist harmonious society be built.

APPENDIX V

CONTEMPORARINESS AND TEXTUAL INTERPRETATION IN MARXISM PHILOSOPHY*

Marxist philosophy should be realistic, and focus on the contemporary times and on the philosophical questions embodied in the questions of reality in the world and especially in China. There are all kinds of opinions in philosophy, debating with each other. Opinions can be subjective, diversified, and even insignificant, while questions are different. According to Marx, "questions are the time's mottoes; they are the supremely practical utterances proclaiming the state of its soul"[1]. Philosophy is called the essence of the time because it is the philosophic condensation of the questions of the time as well as the philosophic thinking to find solutions to the questions. The question about the contemporariness of Marxism basically is whether the Marxism philosophy can provide effective basic theories and thinking ways for grasping and answering the questions of our times.

---

1   Karl Marx and Frederick Engels: Collected Works, 1st Chinese Edition, Volume 40, p. 289-290.

*) The article was originally published in Social Sciences in China, 2007(5).

To equip the Marxist philosophy with contemporariness couldn't merely rest on the contemporary interpretation of the works of Marx and Engels. Undoubtedly, it is of great importance to do philological studies, textual researches, and collations from the classic works of Marxism. In the past, limited by the conditions and literatures, we fell behind the westerners; at present, people who are engaged in this field must make new contributions and breakthroughs in the field of Marxist research; they may discover some important statements that were ignored before, or they may correct some mistakes in the previous understanding, which has great academic value in correctly mastering the basic Marxist principles and correcting the previous wrong understandings or improper additions or supplements. However, only interpreting the classics could by no means be the only basis of the work to contemporarize the Marxist philosophy. The decisive standard of the truthfulness of the basic Marxist principles is the test of practice. Practice is like a tester and filter that can distinguish its basic principles from its individual theses of Marxist classics and thus distinguish the basic principles of Marxism from the mistaken understandings and improper additions to it.

If we just quoted some single sentence from one of the classic books but didn't test it in practice, we will throw ourselves into endless disputes, since all the cultural background, political background, research purpose, and application methods of the interpreter may influence his correctness of interpreting the text, let alone any interpretation limited within the context relation only, will be unreliable as well. Especially if we wouldn't pay due attention to the practices, the process of thoughts and all the works of Marx and Engels in their whole life but just interpret and evaluate each word of a certain book, or even a chapter, a section or a sentence of the book, in a scattered and fragmented way, it will be quite hard to see the forest through the trees. Furthermore, influenced by the idealism in the western hermeneutics, it will be easy for our scholars to distort Marxism with the method of textual interpretation, thus advocate the antagonism between Marx and Engels or even negate all the valuable literatures of Marxism produced after Marx.

All the texts of Marx and Engels were written at different times, under different backgrounds, aimed at different questions. Concerning the same question, the interpretations at different times may have many differences due to their different time and goals, so the interpretation relying on the context only and evaluating word by word always causes various ambiguities and leads to no permanent conclusion, which is a lesson we should have learned from the buried-and-forgotten fate of the hermeneutic ways of the ancient Chinese Confucians. Our literature research on Marxism must cooperate with the research on the basic principles, for only in this way can it help understand the basic principles not the other way around. Because ever since the foundation of Marxism by Marx and Engels, it is the basic principles of Marxism, not any certain sentence in a certain book, that have gone through all the storming and changeable tests of practice for over a century. No one has the right change any word or any sentence in the original texts, because these texts are historic and established; but a true Marxist has the right to enrich and develop the basic principles of Marxism in practice. In terms of the contemporariness of Marxism, we should take the test of practice as the standard rather than compare the classic texts word by word.

In the contemporary world, there are many different views about the one-dimensional and-multi-branched development of Marxism. It is impossible that only Lenin and Mao Zedong are the only representatives of orthodox school of Marxism while others are heresies; but on the other side it is also inappropriate to abstractly say that Marxism is "various or multiple" and thus any school can be attributed to Marxism as long as it claims itself Marxism; nobody has the right to excommunicate those claiming to be Marxists, otherwise, it will be to diminish our group and will be exclusionism. I couldn't make myself agree with this biased view. I believe there should be a specific standard to judge whether a school is a Marxist school or not. This standard is neither the quotation of classic texts nor an argumentation on who on earth learns and advocates the true essence of Marxism. In my opinion, this standard should be whether this school of thought accords with the nature of Marxism or not. Whichever claims that Marxism ought to be combined with the reality of each nation and takes the emancipation of the proletariat and the mankind as its supreme mission should be evaluated as Marxist and should belong to Marxism school. It is also normal even if they have divergent views, e.g. the choice of the mode and the road of revolution, and may have different opinions on what socialism is and how to construct socialism, because this kind of divergences are originated in the different practical environments they live in and in the different problems they are faced with. If this kind of divergence is not rooted in the practical needs of each nation but are only some different schools resulting from the different interpretations of Marxist books and if they are founded by some scholars who stay limited in their studies secluded from the outside world, deviate from and even abandon the emancipation cause of the proletariat and the mankind, which Marx and Engels have devoted their whole lives to, they can only be called the school of Marxology or the school of Marxism researchers, but not the school of Marxism, because their fundamental purpose and research goal have nothing to do with the historic mission and historic task of Marxism. What makes Marxism the Marxism rests in its historic mission which it shoulders. The eleventh point of Marx's theses on Feuerbach is not only the boundary line between Marxist philosophy and all the previous philosophies, but is also the touchstone to distinguish and test the contemporary schools of Marxism and those claiming to be schools of Marxism.

The basis of the contemporariness of Marxism philosophy couldn't rest on the common "threshold" called by the western modern philosophy or the postmodernism. It is unscientific to discuss how many common views and subjects Marxism has with the modern western philosophers and with the postmodernism, or discuss how well Marxism's critique of the malpractices in the western capitalist society fits with the reality as standard. I don't negate the critiques made by some western scholars at our times over the malpractices in the modern capitalism, especially the intense attacks made by postmodernism over the evils of the capitalist modernization. The fact is that they draw support from Marxism not Marxism draws support from the contemporary western philosophy or postmodernism, because to criticize capitalism and expose its inner contradiction has always been the historic mission of Marxism and something inherent in the basis of Marxism. Of course, it is advisable that the contemporary Marxists pay attention to the research results of the contemporary western philosophers and broaden their vision, but it can by no means be the reason to affirm that Marxism and the contemporary western philosophy stay at the same height, because they are two totally different kinds of critique with different theoretical heights and different social ideals. We could use their critique for reference but shouldn't unconditionally approve it.

The basic point of the contemporariness of Marxism lies in its basic principles and in the contemporary applicability of its world outlook and methodology. No matter when analyzing the contemporary capitalism, the socialism with Chinese characteristics, or when analyzing the problems due to the development of the modern science and technology, Marxist philosophy, as a world outlook and thinking method, is still the most effective tool ever. The essence of proceeding from questions is actually proceeding from the reality, for questions only exist in the reality. We are against the book worship; we don't proceed from books, and we don't proceed from questions and then match all the solutions of the questions to their corresponding books either. These two approaches, though different in forms, lead to the same destination. Quotation can't replace elucidations or demonstrations, even if it they are the quotations that come from Marxist texts; it can only increase the authority of demonstration rather than be demonstration itself.

Some people think that Marxism is a scientific theory that can be taken as the tool of theoretical analysis and cognition but can't be degraded as the tool of reason, otherwise it will degrade Marxism. This is false. Marx and Engels repeatedly emphasized that their theory is not a doctrine, not some texts that can be quoted everywhere but is a thinking method for further studies. Marxism will lose its value if it couldn't develop its function as a tool of cognition. No matter it is Marx and Engels, or Lenin and Mao Zedong, they all think highly of Marxism's function as a tool of cognition. Marxism obtains its contemporariness because its basic theories and thinking methods are still the most powerful and effective tools to understand the modern world not because we can find many quotations in them fitting our times.

In my mind, we can neither depend on the western philosophy or the postmodernism to observe the sophisticated reality of the modern world, nor use them to solve the contradictions in constructing the modern China, which equally applies for the Confucianism. They can supply us with abundant resources of ideas to enrich some judgments in Marxism but they have by no means transcended Marxism and can become the guiding principles for our society. We are still relying on the combination of the basic principles of Marxism and the reality of China, which is the only correct, socialist road to make the country powerful and the masses wealthy.

Needless to say that in the contemporary Chinese circle of philosophy, the debate between dialectic materialism and practical materialism is rather intense. Some scholars affirm that only the practical materialism is the most contemporary philosophy. As for myself, I never object to call Marxist philosophy as practical materialism, because this name is really beneficial to improve the comprehensive understanding of the function, position and effects of practice in Marxist philosophy. This debate in all these years is rewarding. However, I don't agree with that view which considers the relation between practical materialism and dialectic materialism the same as that between water and fire. If we take away materialism and dialectics from a practical thinking way, and say that all things which admits the objectivity of the world as well as the existence of the dialectic movement in the world is against the practical dialectics, isn't this practical thinking way, without the materialistic principle of seeking truth from the reality or ignores the dialectic principle of analyzing each case specifically and concretely is just an empty shell with no soul in it?

Some person wrote an article saying that to admit there is still a material world outside of practice is a view of the old materialism. In fact, this writer didn't understand that "there is no cognition outside of practice" and "there is no world outside of practice" are two totally different propositions. The former one is right, because man can only understand object in practice as Mao Zedong once said, "The question about how to understand the outside world cannot be solved outside of practice"[2]; while the second proposition is an ide-

---

2   The Philosophical Annotations By Mao Zedong, P22, Beijing: CC of CPC Literature Press, 1988.

alistic theory reversing the relation between the world and practice. "Existence is perception" and "human existence equals practice" are different paths leading to the same destination. According to this so-called practical materialist view, the superiority of the nature, the conversion between intrinsic nature and humanized nature, thing-in-itself and thing-for-us, are all wiped off. Can it be more ridiculous that the living world where man practices in is an unchangeable circle fixed by the practice of the subject? In fact, even the ancient Chinese philosopher, Chuang Tzu, had understood this truth. He said, a man may only need a little space to walk, but the reason making him continue is that: There is much space where he can keep going walking. (Works of Chuang Tzu Xu Wu Gui).

Every journey begins with a single step, but the journey shouldn't stop at the first step. If there is no world outside of practice, or the world without practice is of no meaning, then the practice of each epoch couldn't leave any "uncultivated virgin land" for the further development of the practice and knowledge of the later generations, which obviously doesn't conform to any history, to any fact or any existing knowledge.

Some people misunderstood the famous saying in Marx's *Economic and Philosophic Manuscripts of 1844*: "nature too, taken abstractly, for itself – nature fixed in isolation from man – is nothing for man."[3]

This is Marx's criticism on Hegel's idealistic conception of nature. Hegel, from the self-movement and alienation of absolute idea, deduced that that nature is not the real nature but the abstract nature isolated from man, which of course is "nothing". If the view that "there is no world outside of practice" could be called as "practical materialism", then I would rather choose bear the bad name of being "anti-practical materialism".

Also, there are some contemporary philosophers including some Chinese philosophers who keep condemning the dichotomy of subject and object of the western philosophy as if this view is of no contemporariness at all but is the "chief criminal" that causes the deterioration of the modern ecological environment. I call this

---

3   Karl Marx and Frederick Engels: Collected Works, 1st Chinese Edition, Volume 42, p. 178.

philosophical view as the absurdity of philosophy and the philosophy of absurdity. Please consider this question: if the world isn't
divided into subject or object but is a complete unity, will cognition
and practice possible? Can we correctly reflect objects and reform
objects? Any viewpoint that negates the dichotomy of subject and
object, opposes to divide subject and object or advocates to merge
the two together, could be nothing but idealism, which is self-centred
and only goes around its ego in circles. No wonder that Nietzsche
said, "We couldn't know things as what they are, because we cannot
think them at all." Why would Nietzsche say so? Because if subject
and object couldn't be divided, then cognition could only be the self-
reflection of man itself. He said, "We try to re-restrain the infinite
knowledge of philosophy and make it re-recognize the personification nature of all knowledge"[4].

If all knowledge including scientific knowledge is personalized
knowledge, science will be the reflection of man about his self-cog-
nition. It is even worse than witchcraft, because witchcraft still has
some object to pray for while science has nothing except itself. I want
to quote one sentence of Feuerbach that was once quoted by Lenin
too, "it is like to treat spermatorrhea and childbirth equally"[5]. And I
would like to add one sentence even more vulgar, "Masturbation is
not sex".

My dear readers, I really hope that you could refer to some words
said by Marx to criticize Max Stirner's idea of only admitting subject but not object, which are quite wonderful, "Philosophy and the
study of the actual world have the same relation to one another as
onanism and sexual love. Saint Sancho, in spite of his absence of
thought—which was noted by us patiently and by him emphatically—remains within the world of pure thoughts". Marx also said, "the
idealistic Dalai Lamas have this much in common with their real
counterpart: they would like to persuade themselves that the world
from which they derive their subsistence could not continue without
their holy excrement"[6].

---

4   Nietzsche, Philosophy and Truth, p. 189 and p. 186, Shanghai: Shanghai Academy
of Social Sciences, 1993.
5   Selected Works of Lenin, 2nd Edition, Volume 2, p. 103.
6   Karl Marx and Frederick, 1st Edition, Volume 3, p. 262 and p. 631.

Without the dichotomy of subject and object, without object, nothing can be generated from the ego. The dichotomy of subject and object and the "absolute dichotomy" of the two can never be the same. The dichotomy of subject and object refers that human is separated from the natural world and man became the subject; it is the most significant turn in the history of natural development, of human development and of social development, which makes man, envied by the God and all the other gods, the most beautiful flower in the nature, possess the wisdom and power to take the world as object. But the absolute antagonism and absolute dichotomy of subject and object is actually a wrong philosophic view.

I have always emphasized that we should distinguish the subject-object dichotomy in epistemology from the unity of subject and object in ontology. In epistemology, we should go for the dichotomy. There are divisions in cognition between cognitive subject and cognitive object, i.e. person who knows and object that is known, otherwise, there won't be practice and knowledge, which should be a very simple truth. It is a fact existing in human practices and their activities of objectifying knowledge at all time, but in fact which is just made so mysterious and sophisticated by some philosophers. But in ontology, we ought to treat the subject of cognition and the objection of cognition as two states in the same material world, inseparable, interactive, and interdependent, which is the question of matter/material unity in the world and in which also lie some reasonable factors of the "unity of nature and man" advocated by Chinese philosophy. Without the "one" (unity) in ontology, there won't be the "two" (dichotomy) in the epistemology either. If these two in epistemology was turned into a one in epistemology, it would be the idealism which is unable to distinguish subject and object; if the one in ontology was turned into a two in ontology, it would be a dualism in which subject and object absolutely oppose to each other; neither is correct.

As far as I think, in study to contemporarize Marxist philosophy, we should seek support from the Marxist philosophy itself and from the correctness of its basic principles. As long as we pay some careful attention to the contemporary western scholars and to some western Marxism scholars, we will find that though they have various kinds of opinions about Marxism, they all admit that Marx's thoughts are unparalleled and have great contemporary effects, because they know it clearly that Marx's ideas are theories produced to dissect and criticize capitalism and its malpractices. In an epoch that is still capitalist, in a world which is still bothered by different capitalist contradictions, only Marx's ideas can provide the source of theory to explain the modern development of the capitalist world. It is by no means fortuitous that Marx is reputed to be the greatest thinker in the western world of the past millennium.

I guess we can consider the socialism building with Chinese characteristics as contemporary, and all that is taking place in China is contemporary whether seen from the purpose and task of our socialist modernization or from the perspective of our century. With regard to the contemporariness of Marxist philosophy, we could consider that, putting the new-democratic revolution period aside, ever since the reform and opening up, from important thoughts of Deng Xiaoping to the "Three Represents" thoughts of Jiang Zemin, from the Scientific Outlook on Development to the building of a harmonious socialist society, which one of those innovative theories above isn't an innovative application of the basic principles of Marxist philosophy? Which important policy stated above couldn't prove the contemporary effectiveness of Marxist philosophy? In observing the modern world and in examining the socialist construction in China, Marxist philosophy is still the most effective theoretical and methodological tool for us; that is the contemporary one, also the biggest one, the examination of Marxist philosophy. If the world outlook and methodology of the basic theory being taken as the guiding principle by a nation with a population of over 1.3 billion are seen of no contemporary value, but instead some western social or philosophic trends which fail to indicate any direction for the mankind enjoy the most significant contemporary value and they still have the "final say" in measuring the contemporariness of Marxism, isn't it too ridiculous to understand?

In fact, philosophically and sociologically speaking, these postmodernist ideological trends, either of which emphasize contemporariness or criticize contemporariness, all have their sociological meanings in the west. Discarding the Marxist analysis of the social contradictions in the western world, we could even hardly understand why the question on contemporariness can be an important question at all. The contemporariness of a theory isn't a concept of time but a concept of value, an evaluation of the effectiveness of the theory itself.

To be honest, I feel very confused and disappointed about the current development of Marxist Philosophy in China, and this feeling gets much more intense especially when I read some articles. However, I believe the words that Mao Zedong said: "not all that is useful is truth, but all truth is useful"[7]. There is a stanza in Zhang Wenlong's poem (a poet in Qing dynasty), saying "the splendid music of xiao (a vertical bamboo flute) makes me the most pleasant when played by myself; a poem makes itself the best when expressing the poet's most sincere feelings and emotions (the original text: 天籁自鸣天趣足，好诗不过近人情 sounded as: tian lai zi ming tian qu zu, hao shi bu guo jin ren qing)", I admire this stanza which does have a point. A good poem must be understood, accepted by its readers, so is philosophy. Though some scholars hold different opinions on using the word "truth" in philosophy, I still insist that Marxist philosophy is a theory with truthfulness. Its principles are plain and concise but of great truthfulness. Because it has truthfulness, it necessarily has contemporariness. The contemporariness could never live without the modern world, since the modern world is still a world dominated by capitalism. Capitalism still exists in the world, and that's the objective basis of the contemporariness of Marxism.

---

7   The Philosophic Annotation Set of Mao Zedong, p. 149-150.

APPENDIX VI

ON THE WAY MARXIST PHILOSOPHY FOCUSES ON THE REALITY*

Marxist philosophy should neither be the mere "feast" of philosophers, nor be their personal whispers or monologues. The essence and function of Marxist philosophy together with its historical mission all demand Marxist philosophy to be realistic and to keep up with the times as well as to provide philosophic perspectives functioning as world outlook and methodology for grasping the questions in the modern world and in modern China. If the Marxist philosophy broke away with the reality, it would be like it exiled and marginalized itself.

Dialogue, it is a path that the contemporary philosophical field is exploring to get out of the dilemma of philosophy. However, dialogue, whether dialogue within philosophy or dialogue among the different subjects inside the scientific system of Marxism, can be of practical meaning only when it is beneficial for solving theoretical problems and practical problems.

---

*) The article was originally published in Social Sciences in China, 2008 (6).

1 PHILOSOPHY OUGHT TO DIALOGUE WITH THE REALITY THROUGH ECONOMIC THEORETICAL QUESTIONS

In the field of Marxist philosophy research, we researchers all advocate the "Oriental-Occidental Marxist" dialogue, which is rather essential for communicating different nations' philosophical thoughts, especially their modern philosophical development and fruits. Since Marxist philosophy should be an open system of thoughts, closedness and ossification will turn the Marxist philosophy in the contemporary China into an isolated, self-existing philosophy breaking away from the world cultures and from the national culture. This so-called Marxist philosophy is doomed to wither and die.

In fact, Marx and Engels kept conversing with their precursors of thought when establishing the Marxist philosophy. And we could easily recognize this point as long as we read Marx's letter to his father on November 10, 1837 when he was studying in the University of Bonn. He read lots of books on law and arts, and especially on philosophy, such as Johann Gottlieb Fichte, Immanuel Kant, and then Hegel, and said he "adopted the habit of making extracts from all the books I read"[1]. From Marx's *Notebooks on Epicurean Philosophy*, *Notes in Kreuznach*, *Notes in Paris*, and *Notes in London*, as well as *Notes on Anthropology* and *Notes on Historiography* in his late ages, we could tell that Marx had kept this habit for his whole life. In his notes, there are a large quantity of excerpts and annotations. The excerpts are thoughts and questions of the predecessors, while the annotations are answers Marx sought for. These reading notes are a way in which Marx made the thinking precursors talk with the thinkers at his own time.

If Marx and Engels, the two greatest Marxist thinkers, can do so, then the modern Chinese Marxist philosophers should pay more attention to philosophic dialogue. Nowadays, the situation in the Chinese philosophic field is that the western philosophic schools are quite prospering and diversified and are constantly introduced to China, like a new round of "the introduction of western learning to the east"; the traditional Chinese philosophy began to revive after

---

1 Karl Marx and Frederick Engels: Collected Works, 1st Chinese Edition, Volume 40, p. 14.

going through the terrible and cold current of the "Great Cultural Revolution", and especially, the Neo-Confucianism is likely to become a dominant discourse. The epoch when Marxist philosophy outshines all the others has gone with the wind, so it is in urgent need to expanding its philosophic vision, philosophic questions, and philosophic paradigms through the Oriental-Occidental Marxist dialogue.

However, the Oriental-Occidental Marxist dialogue is now faced with two difficult problems. One is that it is hard to form guiding thoughts and thinking ways agreed by all to practice the dialogue. Seemingly, the Chinese (Oriental) philosophy and the western (Occidental) philosophy both recognize the guidance of Marxist world outlook and methodology, but in fact, their divergence is difficult to be bridged as long as any concrete philosophic question is involved. The other question is that it is almost impossible to have the same consciousness of problems since the two sides have different focuses of attention and different interests, sometimes even in opposite directions. In the modern China, there is still a long way to go and heavy responsibilities to shoulder to establish a contemporary Chinese Marxist philosophy with Chinese style, Chinese spirit and Chinese characteristics, which is really guided by the basic theories and methods of Marxist philosophy and rooted in traditional Chinese philosophy, and which absorbs nourishment from the fruits of excellent western philosophers, and stands on the reality of the modern China. Furthermore, the pure Oriental-Occidental Marxist dialogue has its limitations as well, because it is still a dialogue among philosophers within the field of philosophy, and is the communication and collision between category and category, concept and concept, idea and idea. If it couldn't go beyond the purely philosophic sphere, then it would still wander around in the heaven of thoughts where the thoughts can be copied and extended, but can hardly create anything new based on practical questions.

The journal—*Social Sciences in China* and Shanghai University of Finance and Economics proposed to carry out the dialogue between philosophy and economics, which is a new way of thinking and a new way of dialogue. The dialogue between philosophy and economics is different from the purely philosophic dialogue. What economics faces is always the real life it lives in, or named as civil society. The theories of economics all serve for the living social economic operation and economic development it is directly faced with. In *The Poverty of Philosophy*, Marx said, "The classics, like Adam Smith and Ricardo, represent a bourgeoisie which, while still struggling with the relics of feudal society, works only to purge economic relations of feudal taints, to increase the productive forces and to give a new upsurge to industry and commerce."[2]. He also said, "Economists like Adam Smith and Ricardo, who are the historians of this epoch, have no other mission than that of showing how wealth is acquired in bourgeois production relations" These academic representatives produced by the bourgeoisie like Adam Smith and Ricardo are quite inseparable with the economic reality they were faced with.

Of course, economics also has its fundamental theories, categories, and specific ways of thinking. However, one of the important differences between philosophy and economics is that the categories, concepts and questions of the latter have characteristics of direct reality and are the direct abstractions of the realistic economic life, while the former one, philosophy, is indirect abstraction, or it can be seen as the re-abstract of the abstracts of all subjects. Economics is the closest to the economic base, while philosophy the farthest. Just as Marx said when he commented on Adam Smith and Ricardo, their mission is of "formulating these relations into categories, into laws, and of showing how superior these laws, these categories, are for the production of wealth to the laws and categories of feudal society"3 Philosophers can set themselves aloft in the sacred temple of philosophy, but economists must focus on the practical real life. If the dialogues among philosophers are those between thought and thought, then the dialogue between philosophers and economics is actually a dialogue between thoughts and the reality through economic theoretical questions.

Therefore, we ought to improve the Oriental-Occidental Marxist philosophic dialogue, and at the same time go beyond this kind of dialogue as well. And special attention should be paid to increasing the dialogues among all different subjects within the scientific system of Marxism.

2   Karl Marx and Frederick Engels: Collected Works, 1st Chinese Edition, Volume 4, p. 156.

2 MARXISM AND THE SUBJECTS BROUGHT FORWARD BY HISTORY: THE POLITICAL AND VALUE ORIENTATION OF PHILOSOPHY

Purely philosophic dialogues are not consistent with the nature of Marxist philosophy, because the Marxist philosophy is the most important constituent part of the scientific system of Marxism, and what determines its generation and development lies in its interaction with Marxist economics and scientific socialism on the basis of practice. In this sense, in the modern times, the dialogues between philosophy and economics inside Marxist subjects are more important and more urgent than the Oriental-Occidental Marxist dialogues in the purely philosophic field.

Marx could establish the Marxist philosophy because he didn't limit himself in the purely philosophic field; Marx could become a great philosopher not only because he inherited the essence of the German classic philosophy, but also because he extended himself from philosophy to economics and took an active part in the socialist labour movements and in the construction of socialist theories. The three sources and three constituent parts said by Lenin are by no means in a relation of one-to-one correspondence, but in a relation of interaction and mutual effects. The formation history of Marxism proves that the British classic economics and the three utopian socialist theories in the 19th century all play quite an important role as important idea resources for the establishment and mature of the Marxist philosophy. Without the theory of labour and labour value of the British classic economics, it would be very hard for alienation to rise into the theory of alienated labour, and then sublimate through the latter into the historical materialism that the mode of material production plays the decisive role in social life; without the idea resources of the utopian socialism in the 19th century, the Marxist philosophy would be degraded as an epistemology-type philosophy due to the lack of socialist value orientation.

Marxist philosophy is the unity of scientificalness and valueness. It is scientific, because it rests on the objectiveness of the world and takes practice as its basis and its laws as object. Believes that the regularity of world's historical development and the development of human society is apprehendable. But at the same time, it embodies valueness, thus does not restrict itself with some purely objective description of the laws of the world and laws of the human society.

It cares about the situation and the emancipation of the mankind, and emancipation and all-around development of individual man, intrinsically embodies appeals of socialism and humanism as its important elements. It is the least advisable to go for the epistemological inclination simply making the Marxist philosophy scientific and positivistic, because this kind of inclination will extremely weaken the attraction and cohesion of the Marxist philosophy. It is proper to say that the scientific and value-imbued Marxist philosophy has inherited all the excellent cultural heritage of the mankind, especially the best fruits of philosophy, economics and socialist theories of the 19th century.

In the scientific system of Marxism, the Marxist philosophy is not any part that is introduced from outside or that is attached and can be independent. In the 1840s, the subject brought forward by the history was how to turn socialism from imagination into science. To realize this mission, the first thing needed was a new world outlook completely different from the idealistic and abstract humanistic world outlook of various utopian socialism schools. No establishment of the new philosophy, no establishment of the scientific socialism. However, the Marxist scientific socialism is not philosophical communism; it is guided by philosophy, but it is no logical deduction of philosophic principles, so it is impossible to deduce the conclusions of scientific socialism by simply starting from the premise of philosophy. To transform socialism from imagination into science, then socialism must be built on the basis of reality. The so-called basis of reality is the practical bourgeois society itself, because socialism, whether as theory or practice, can be set up and produced only through the sublation and negation of capitalism. Therefore, to analyze the basis of reality of socialism, we must analyze the bourgeois civil society first, while the analysis of the civil society can seek help from no other place than political economy. In this sense, without economic theories, the historical materialism can never be formed and thus the integrated Marxism cannot be produced either.

The most famous, most concise, and most representative judgment made by Marx about the historical materialism appears in the Preface to *A Contribution to the Critique of Political Economy*, which is no accidental at all. Marx clearly claimed that his conclusions about the universal regularity of social development were drawn from his analysis of the civil society. He described his thinking process of how to establish historical materialism from his economic studies in a personal narrative way: "The study of this, which I began in Paris, I continued in Brussels, where I moved owing to an expulsion order issued by M. Guizot. The general conclusion at which I arrived and which, once reached, became the guiding principle of my studies can be summarized as follows."[3] Below this sentence is his classic description about the laws of historical materialism.

As for the regularity conclusions and value ideals of the scientific socialism, they are both conclusions deduced from the economic analysis of the bourgeois society. Marxist philosophy contains value judgment, but the scientific socialism isn't built on the basis of the moral evaluation on capitalism. Marx and Engels both had done a powerful moral incitement of the situation of the working class in the bourgeois society in which they were living, but their assertion of the historical necessity that socialism must take the place of capitalism is made on the basis of strict economic analyses rather than mere moral indignation, which is so both in their early days and late days. In the draft of the letter to Vera Ivanovna Zasulich in 1881, Marx still insisted on the economic analysis of the necessity that socialism must take the place of capitalism. He said, "Capitalist production, on the one hand, marvellously developed the productive forces of society, but on the other hand, it also shows an incompatibility with the social productive forces produced by itself. From now on, its history will be nothing but a history of confrontation, crisis, conflict and disaster. As a result, capitalist production will show every person (except those who are blinded by their own interests) its purely temporality."[4]

---

3   Karl Marx and Frederick Engels: Selected Works, 2nd Edition, Volume 2, p. 32.
4   Karl Marx and Frederick Engels: Collected Works, 1st Chinese Edition, Volume 19, p. 443.

History didn't exactly go along the road as Marx expected since the western capitalist world, having gone through civil confrontations, economic crises, world wars and other disasters, is still in a relatively stable stage and is going to enter into a developed stage through adjustment, but after the Second World War, in the western developed capitalist nations sprung out ideological trends of democratic socialism and of the third road, the metaphor signal implicated by which is quite clear: politicians and thinkers living in the developed capitalist society are still bothered and confused by all kinds of deficiencies in the capitalist society and they are seeking for new ways to improve capitalism. Of course, seen from the perspective of scientific socialism, capitalism can be improved but it can't exist permanently by virtue of improvement. The internal contradiction in the economic base of the capitalist society determines the necessity of its transition to a new higher social formation. Though the way and the time of this transition and where it will start cannot be predicted now, the capitalist society won't be ended by democratic socialism or the so-called third road. The historical dialectics of development of this social formation is irresistible.

Each constituent part of Marxism as a subject is relatively independent of each other, and they have inseparable inner connections, supporting and improving each other. Once they are separated, their essence of Marxism endowed with their integrity will be lost. As far as I'm concerned, some of the modern researches or dissertations on Marxist philosophy actually have lost the characteristics of Marxist philosophy, and are more like the transformation of western philosophy or traditional Chinese philosophy in the name of Marxist philosophy. As for myself, I don't oppose the Marxist philosophers to study western philosophy or traditional Chinese philosophy, but we ought to study them with Marxist philosophy rather than reconstruct the Marxist philosophy with them. These two routes are completely different, and so are their results.

The nature of Marxist philosophy requires it can never be purely academic. With regards to the political and value orientation, it must concern practical social problems, directly or indirectly related with the proletariat and with the historical mission of human emancipation. In the modern China, the Marxist philosophy must pay due attention to the philosophic questions in the economic construction of the socialism with Chinese characteristics; otherwise, it will be split up from the integrity of Marxism and turn into a philosophy that is nominally a Marxist philosophy but actually a speculative philosophy. In the same sense, if Marxist economics isn't guided by the Marxist world outlook or methodology and doesn't take the common ideal of socialism as purpose, it won't be a Marxist economics either but will turn into a "science to make fortunes" for the bourgeoisie as Engels talked about bourgeois economic theories in the Outline of *A Contribution to the Critique of Political Economy*; of course, the theory of scientific socialism, once without the guidance of Marxist philosophy or not based on the analysis of the economic reality of modern China, can but sink into the utopian socialism or some other socialism but can by no means be the scientific socialism of Marxism. The proper labour division of the internal subjects of Marxism shouldn't be taken as the reason to cut them apart.

The historical process in which the integrity of Marxism is formed is also a theoretical process in which all the theories help each other forward, argue with each other, and gradually merge into one, which actually is also the process of Marxism's establishment, gaining maturity, and development. One landmark in the formation process of Marxism is the publication of *Economic and Philosophic Manuscripts of 1844*, as the first book marking his transition to dissecting the capitalist civil society. The obvious features of the book are that it takes alienated labour and private property as centre, and combines theories of economics, philosophy and communism together through the analysis of capital, profit and wage in the capitalist society and through the analysis of the emergence and alienation of the private property system and of the sublation of alienation. This kind of combination was indeed at the primary level and immature, but it is the rudiment of the integrity of the Marxist system while its mature formation is the masterpiece—*Capital*. *Capital* is more than an economic work analyzing the capitalist social formation, and it is also logical, which is the outstanding model of applying Marxist historical materialism; and at the same time, it is the scientific demonstration of the socialist theory claiming the capitalist private property will inevitably be surpassed due to its inner contradictions.

When commenting on the value and meaning of the first volume of *Capital*, Engels said, "The press has already frequently mentioned Marx's intention to sum up the results of his many years' studies in a critique of the whole of political economy to date and thereby provide the scientific basis for socialist aspirations which neither Fourier nor Proudhon nor even Lassalle had been able to do"[5]. He also said, "Whatever one's attitude to socialism, one will at any rate have to acknowledge that in this work it is presented for the first time in a scientific manner"[6]. In this sense, the *Capital* is far more than a mere economic book, but is a Marxist classic integrating economics, Marxist philosophy and scientific socialism.

The contemporary theoretical system of the socialism with Chinese characteristics basically embodies the integrity of Marxism as well and includes therein the combination of philosophy, economics and scientific socialism principles with the reality of China. If any of the three parts were taken away, then the socialist theory with Chinese characteristics would be false. If we think over carefully Deng Xiaoping's theories of what socialism is and how to build socialism, and his definition of the essence of socialism which is to emancipate and develop productive forces, eliminate exploitation and polarization, and realize common wealth in the end, we could recognize that his theories are also unification of philosophy, economics and socialist social ideals. Without the philosophic thinking method of seeking truth from the reality and proceeding from the reality, without the new economic thoughts in various aspects, e.g. ownership and distribution, plan and market, fairness and efficiency, or without the social ideal of the scientific socialism about abolishing exploitation, establishing harmony between man and nature, harmony between man and man, and realizing common wealth, the socialist theory with Chinese characteristics can never come into being, and neither can the systematic idea of Scientific Outlook on Development.

---

5 Karl Marx and Frederick Engels: Collected Works, 1st Chinese Edition, Volume16, p. 242, Beijing: People's Publishing House, 1964.
6 Ibid., p. 411-412.

3 EXAMINE THE PROBLEMS OF MARKET ECONOMY FROM MULTIPLE PERSPECTIVES OF INTEGRATED MARXISM

It will be extremely harmful if philosophy and economics are split up from each other. The present Marxist philosophic study, to a certain extent, separates itself from social practice and lacks the theoretical basis of economics, as a result of which, it throws itself into such a predicament and always stays within the sphere of purely philosophic concepts, and at the same time breaks away from the theory and practice of scientific socialism. Some philosophers simply call the Marxist philosophy's serving socialist construction as "instrumentalism", or as "ideologicalization", and believe that the purer Marxism, the more academic it should be, which actually is castrating the critical and revolutionary nature of the Marxist philosophy. As long as we read some philosophic articles of this kind, we could then feel the estrangement and disgust brought by this emptiness, from its terminology to its writing style, for the readers.

To be honest, it is hardly possible to really understand the Marxist philosophy, especially the Marxist philosophy in the contemporary China, without any research basis of economics. The Marxist philosophy must be realistic, but it is the economic reality, the political and ideological structure built upon the basis of a definite mode of material production, that plays the fundamental and decisive role in the social life. If the Marxist philosophers didn't study economics at all, and didn't understand the economic structure of the modern Chinese society or the social stratifications based on economy/economics, they would be unable to understand the diversity of the modern Chinese social ideological trends or the nature of all the social phenomena. In my opinion, without the support of economic theories, the philosophical society would never go deep into the real society but would float on the surface of society forever, being nothing but empty talks.

I couldn't make myself believe that the philosophers who know nothing about economics can make any scientific and persuasive analysis of the basic social contradictions in the modern China and their movement laws, the contradictions among the Chinese people, the emancipation of the mankind, or the subjectivity of man. The most fundamental thing in human activities is the practice of production that produces material products to meet the needs of man's survival, which thus makes economic activities the most important and all the other activities will be practiced on the historical platform built by material production. If the philosophers don't recognize this point, and break away from the material production and all the social relations formed by it, they will never really understand man or man's nature however hard they emphasize that philosophy is the science of man and it should study man and man's nature. Without economics, the "man" of the philosophers will hang in the air forever.

What do our economic theories need the most nowadays? To me, they need the guidance of the basic theories and methodology of Marxist philosophy the most. Economics, of course, has its own particular categories and analytical methods, such as empirical, mathematical, statistical, model-based, and so forth, but the most fundamental guiding principles of Marxist economics should be dialectic materialism and historical materialism. I don't believe that an economist who doesn't admit the theory of social economic formation or the theory of the relations between productive forces and relations of production, economic base and superstructure, or opposes the theory and method of dialectic thinking, can be an excellent Marxist economist. Especially for those who are to found a socialist economic theory with Chinese characteristics, it will be like to fish in the air if they deviate from the guidance of Marxist philosophy and especially from that of historical materialism.

In fact, philosophy and economics should be inseparable. There is no economist who doesn't need a certain method of philosophic thinking. Economic thinking is no merely empirical thinking but needs to apply categories and concepts as well as a supporting point of philosophy. Adam Smith, the famous British classic economist had written *The Wealth of Nations* as well as *The Theory of Moral Sentiments*, but his philosophic theory had a contradiction with his economic theory. The man in *The Theory of Moral Sentiments* was a man with conscience and sympathy, while the man in *The Wealth of Nations* was a man caring about self-interest only. His invisible hand is based on the "Homo economicus Assumption". This kind of contradiction has caused dual damages: man's emotions lack the basis of economic interests, while the "Homo economicus" in economics lacks moral sympathy and self-discipline. The "invisible hand" uncovers the laws of market economy, but "Homo economicus" as the philosophic premise concerning man's nature excludes the possibility of founding any socialist market economy.

There is neither contradiction between philosophy and economics nor division between philosophic thinking method and economic theory in the system of Marxism. Therefore, for the Marxist economists, the largest danger comes from the contempt for Marxist philosophy and especially for historical materialism. If we can say, without historical materialism, Marx couldn't have exposed the operational laws of the capitalist economy and couldn't have written *Capital*; then without the dialectical materialism, Lenin couldn't have written *The Theory of Imperialism* since *The Theory of Imperialism* has the same connections of dialectical thinking method with his *Philosophical Notes*; Mao Zedong, without the theory of contradiction, couldn't have written *On The Ten Major Relationships*; and Deng Xiaoping couldn't have advocated a series of new economic policies or built the foundation for establishing the socialist political economy if he hadn't proceeded from the reality or sought truth from the reality or hadn't insisted on the philosophic thought that practice is the sole criterion for testing truth.

In the modern China, it is quite harmful both theoretically and practically if Marxist economics excludes Marxist philosophy but totally goes for the western economics. Only the Marxist philosophers can make correct philosophical analysis of the various economic phenomena existing in the Chinese socialist market economy.

The problem of market economy is not merely a problem of economics, so we shouldn't simply consider market economy as the allocation of resources and labour force but should see it as a philosophic problem and a problem of scientific socialism. It must be examined from multiple perspectives with Marxism as a scientific system.

From the early half of the 20th century, the early socialist nations, starting from Yugoslavia, then Poland and Hungary, and later Gorbachev and Boris Yeltsin of the Soviet Union, all have conducted market-oriented reforms which all turned out to be a failure and which also changed their original socialist colour. Why could China successfully realize its radical transition from planned economy to market economy and make its economy develop rapidly and enduringly? Why could the socialist system of China be constantly improved when realizing this transition? The basic question doesn't lie in whether we should conduct the reforms of market economy or not, but in what kind of guiding thought we should take when implementing the reforms of market economy and what kind of reforms related to market economy we should implement as well. When the reformers adopt neoliberal measures and integrate the reforms of market economy with the comprehensive implementation of privatization, they will definitely change the original socialist mode of production and thus lead to radical changes in social structure. However, the socialist theories with Chinese characteristics adhere to the principle of integrating the basic socialist system with the socialist reforms of market economy, insist on the basic socialist system, fully develop the fundamental functions of market economy in the allocation of resources, and mobilize the initiative of all ownerships forms to take part in market competitions, in order to facilitate the emancipation and development of productive forces, so as to realize the optimal effect of both rapidly developing the economy and as well realizing the self-perfection of socialism.

Some western scholars feel it difficult to understand why China, a nation with market economy, still adheres to the so-called "one-party dictatorship" of the China Communist Party in its superstructure and insists on the guiding position of Marxism in its ideology. According to their view, since China carries out market economy, then its political system should be a multi-party system and parliamentary system, and it should allow diversified guiding thoughts in the ideological field and practice liberty, democracy, and equality of capitalism, so as to accord with the principles of market economy. They expect that in China, either the reform will change the entire superstructure according to market economy principles, or the superstructure will be crashed by the positive strength of market economy due to its (superstructure's) constraints on the development of China's market economy, because they believe only this way conforms to historical materialism integrating economic base and superstructure. But that view really misinterprets the theory of historical materialism about economic base and superstructure. Deng Xiaoping once said, plan isn't equal to socialism, as capitalism also has plans; market isn't equal to capitalism, as socialism can have markets as well, which indicates that plan and market are economic operation ways rather than economic base.

According to the principles of historical materialism, economic base is the totality of all relations of production, with ownership as core. The bourgeois economic base is the totality of the relations of production with the core as capitalist private ownership; while as for the modern China in its primary stage of socialism, its economic base is the basic economic system with public ownership as the main body and with multiple ownerships developing together. The socialist superstructure in our nation does correspond to this kind of economic base. Naturally there are contradictions due to the disharmony between the two, (economic base and the superstructure) thus we must keep adjusting this kind of contradiction through reforms, but there is one thing we must keep in mind is that it is the basic socialist economic system with public ownership as main body, not the market economy which is the basis of our multi-party cooperation and political consultation system, our democratic system and our policy to adhere to the leading role of Marxism led by the CPC, in the superstructure spheres. Market economy isn't the economic base of the socialist China, but is an economic operation mode which is combined with our basic socialist economic system; it is important but not so critical for the superstructure. In fact, it is the socialist economic structure that directly exerts decisive effects on the above superstructure spheres. The operation ways, its effects and range of market economy are all conditioned and constrained by the basic socialist economic and our basic political system.

Of course, considering from the perspective of historical materialism, we cannot overlook the profound influences brought by the operational way of market economy to the social structure of the socialist society, that effect from economic base to superstructure. Market economy is quite beneficial to mobilize the enthusiasm of all social members to take part in economic activities and to boost up the development of productive forces, but it is very open to lead to the polarization of income and increase the gap between the poor and the rich. Furthermore, it is rather quite possible to invade into the political field and thus cause illegal power-for-money transactions, or into the ideological and moral field and thus result in a chaos of values and degradation of moral standards. In fact, how to fully develop the positive effects of market economy and at the same time to avoid enlarging and generalizing of its negative effects, is beyond a simple question that can be solved by a single subject of political economy. To solve this problem, we must put the political economics study on the market economy into the whole theoretical system of Marxism and into the system relating philosophy and scientific socialism theory, and then start our research.

To proceed the market economy reforms under the basic socialist system, we should condition and regulate market economy with the socialist system rather than change the entire socialist system with market economy, since among the two sides, one is the basic social economic system and political system, while the other is the way of conducting economic activities under this social system. What we pursue should be to observe the scientific socialism of Marxism and to practice socialist market economy other than to follow market socialism and change the basic socialist system with wholly marketized reforms.

When analyzing the features of market economy operations, we ought to hold economic views as well as philosophic views. Market relations materialize the relation between man and man, makes money the bond linking man and man, in terms of which, capitalist market economy and socialist market economy would have something in common. Historical materialism has fully recognized that money functions more than merely universal equivalent with the functions of exchange, circulation, measure of value, or storage, but also contains quite a lot of economic questions and philosophic questions. Philosophically, when the economic relation between man and man is intermediated by money, the worship of money and the perversion of values will be likely to be brought about. Marx had made many excellent analyses of money in his *Economic and Philosophic Manuscripts of 1844*. He said, "By possessing the property of buying everything, by possessing the property of appropriating all objects, money is thus the object of eminent possession. The universality of its property is the omnipotence of its being. It is therefore regarded as an omnipotent being. Money is the procurer between man's need and the object, between his life and his means of life. But that which mediates my life for me, also mediates the existence of other people for me. For me it is the other person."[7] "It is the visible divinity – the transformation of all human and natural properties into their contraries, the universal confounding and distorting of things: Impossibilities are soldered together by it." "It is the common whore, the common procurer of people and nations."[8] "The divine power of money – lies in its character as being men's estranged, alienating and self-disposing species-nature. Money is the alienated ability of mankind." Of course, these opinions of Marx contain the moral evaluation of money, which isn't in contrast to the positive effects of money in human society and in human civilization as Marx stated. Can socialist society abolish money? No! Abolishing money, abolishing commodities and abolishing markets can happen nowhere other than the Utopia. However, we must understand that even in the socialist society, the economic activities with money as intermediate could also exert negative effects on the various relations between man and man. Therefore, in the construction of socialist market economy, we must have a clear understanding about this point in philosophical theories, and thereby pay due attention to the moral construction within the ideological and cultural construction and oppose to money worship and extra-egoism.

Market economy is the economy of capital operation, so how to see the nature of capital is also an important philosophic question in the socialist market economy. Under the socialist conditions, the relations between man and man should be carried by objects. It is unwise if we avoid mentioning that there are different relations between man and man in different capital properties. In all kinds of capital of private property, the relation between capital owner and labourer is that between capital and wage labour, which violates historical materialism; while to abstract this relation between capital owner and labourer also violates historical materialism when examining bourgeois capital formations.

---

7   Karl Marx and Frederick Engels: Collected Works, 1st Chinese Edition, Volume 42, p. 150.
8   Ibid., p. 153.

Marx once said that the capital without labour would live longer than the labour without capital. It's true that in the capitalist society, capital has its own logic and its own laws, i.e. the pursuit of profits and the dominance over labour, including its grasp and control of political power in the political field and its holds on man's thoughts in the ideological field by possessing and controlling the media. Under the conditions of socialism, the circumstances of capital operation vary. The economic system and political system of socialism constrains the superior rights of capital over labour and protects the rights of labourers according to law, balancing the two sides properly. We must prevent capital from invading political power and making discourse hegemony by money and certainly watch out for this possibility, which is the requirement of basic socialist system itself. On this issue, philosophy can look farther than mere economics.

To perfect the socialist market economy is of paramount importance to further promote the reform process. However, to perfect market economy doesn't mean to marketize the whole social life, but means to make the operation mechanism of market economy more healthy and well-ordered and make the market economy favourable for building a socialist harmonious society and for building the socialism with Chinese characteristics. To perfect the socialist market economy involves perfecting governmental macro-control and bettering the basic economic structure of socialism and also involves correctly developing the economic and political functions of socialist states. The rescue activities conducted by the government in the Wenchuan Earthquake fully manifest that socialist states bear the economic and political functions for the society and that they won't and can't simply rest on market economy to allocate everything. Hundred thousand of soldiers and thousands of doctors hurrying off to the disaster area, the allocation and transfer of goods and materials, the selfless donations and support by the masses, all of these have given expression to the advantages of the socialist system and the macro-plan and macro-control functions of the state, which don't simply rely on the invisible hand. The failure of market is quite easy to happen not only in economic activities but also in the political activities concerning the interests of all people. When considering the functions of market within economics, we should neither abandon the basic principles of the scientific socialism nor break away from the theory on socialist state developed by historical materialism.

Some economists always avoid speaking up of the capitalist proper-ties of our private economy or exploitation, but rather call it civil economy or people-oriented economy, which to my mind is totally unnecessary. The capitalist sector of the economy of modern China was redeveloped by its leadership collective after over twenty years starting from 1956. Until 1956 CPC had practiced the public-private partnership in many industries for many years in which the party has led the Three Great Reconstructions, opposed to the capitalist private property, and practiced the public-private partnership with eagerness and zest, which was called as the great success of social-ism; at present, the capitalist private capital holds an important posi-tion in the whole national economy, which is now called as the great success of the socialism with Chinese characteristics. Times have changed, so the situations are different as well. If we didn't hold the view of Marxist historical materialism or if we adopted a dogmatic attitude towards the basic principles of Marxism, it would be impos-sible for us to understand such a change.

The rebirth and rapid development of capitalist economy in China is not merely an economic issue, but at the same time is a philo-sophical issue. It is rather difficult to understand the change without the laws of the mutual relations and interactions between productive forces and relations of production, interactions between economic base and superstructure. It is quite necessary to remember the social-ist reformation in 1956; if that transformation in 1956 hadn't been made, there wouldn't have been the strong state operated economy or the strong support of the relatively new born people's democratic regime supported by the basis of its powerful economic strength; no radical changes including those in the economic base and those related to superstructure would have happened, compared with the old China before people taking power, also due to the fact that it was the CPC that ruled the state and society. Otherwise, there wouldn't have been the economic and political basis upon which to conduct the reform and opening policy and develop multiple economic sec-tors later.

The problem is that after China practiced the socialist transformation of the capitalist sectors of the economy in 50'ies and formed a relatively strong state-owned economy, the state-owned economy had occupied the dominant position for a rather long time, and China, under the planned economy system, had one-sidedly strengthened the impacts of the superstructure on its economic base, which resulted in the disharmony between productive forces and relations of production, between economic base and superstructure, which had caused quite a lot of contradictions. So in 80'ies it was favourable for the emancipating and developing productive forces to reconstruct the capitalist economy after eliminating it in 1956, thus encourage the development of diverse sectors of economy, and take market economy as the means to allocate social resources and labour forces. In this sense, the nature of reform was to adjust the basic contradictions of socialist society and aimed the self perfection of socialist system. Only by standing on the height of historical materialism and focusing our study on the basic contradiction of socialist society can we really understand the position and function of capitalist economy in the new epoch. We don't have to change the name of capitalist private ownership, do need to avoid mentioning exploitation, or even modify the theory of labour value or the theory of surplus value, as long as we know that truth is concrete and there is no abstract truth. The capitalist private ownership, exploitation, and surplus value are not absolutely bad things under all conditions. When Engels was writing *The Condition of the Working Class in England*, capitalism was seeing quite a lot of troubles and contradictions in England and France; however, in Germany, it was welcomed as the newly rising sun.

Lenin criticized some members of the Communist Party when Russia was implementing the New Economic Policy, "Till today, 'we' still like to discuss like this, 'capitalism is evil, while socialism is happiness.' But this kind of discussion is incorrect, because it forgets the totality of all the existing social economic structures but only chooses two structures from them and looks at the two only"[9]. Lenin also stressed, "We must understand that it is a capitalism, which we can and we should allow its existence, which we can and we should

---

9   Selected Works of Lenin, 2nd Edition, Volume 4, p. 510.

bring into a certain range, because this capitalism is needed by the vast peasantry and private capital, while the latter of which can meet peasants' needs by doing business. Capitalist economy and capitalist circulation must run as usual, because that is what the people need and cannot live without."[10]

There is no need to be afraid of mentioning the capitalist nature of our private businesses if we could, in economic studies, adhere to the guidance of Marxist philosophy, understand historical material-ism, and know to adapt and change with time, location and condi-tion. We ought to know that according to the development stage of socialism and the development level of our society, the capitalist business existing within the basic socialist economic structure, is different from the private capitalism without the powerful public ownership as being the main body both in positional aspect and func-tional aspect. Remaining within the constraints of the basic socialist economic system, it can develop the productive forces of society, enhance state's comprehensive national strength, ease the pressure of employment, and increase supply; the surplus value can both increase the total social wealth and meet the eagerness of private capital for profits; private entrepreneurs can make their great con-tributions to the socialist construction with Chinese characteristics with their capital, managerial experience and technical innovation. It doesn't make much difference whether they are entrepreneurs or capitalists, whether it is surplus value or capital income; to debate on names is of little meaning for philosophy. Marxist philosophy is not philosophical semantics, and it demands to analyze any question by putting it into its corresponding time-and-space background.

We don't deny at all that there are social contradictions existing be-tween public ownership and private ownership, between capital and labour, between the rich and the poor, which are contradictions that must be solved to build a harmonious socialist society. The socialist superstructure, i.e. the state, surely should develop and enhance its regulatory function in the solving process. If these contradictions were mishandled, the economic sectors in the basic social economic system would lose their balance of structure and ideological trend of privatization would even become the mainstream, which would

---

10   Ibid., p. 671.

definitely threaten the socialist system. In addition, we will also fail to grasp the main points if we examine the problem of developing capitalist economy and the problem of developing multiple economic sectors co-existing together without considering them as the part of the whole social structure and consider them in the basic social contradiction movement at the primary stage of socialism of China. In this sense, historical materialism is most sharp-edged and essential weapon for our economists.

In fact, we not only should enhance the dialogue between philosophy and economics, but also should enhance the dialogue between the subjects of Marxist philosophy and the theoretical study on socialism theory. The socialism theory can't be scientific socialist theory if it breaks away from Marxist philosophy and economics. That was true when Marx and Engels set up the theory of scientific socialism and also true for contemporary China. Some scholars believe that the principal thing in socialism is the view of value, placing the so-called valuableness over the scientificity of the socialism theory and one-sidedly stressing the primacy of the values like liberty, equality, human rights, harmony, and justice and so forth. However, they forget the most fundamental principle of Marxist philosophy and economics: no social value is impending in the air but must rest on the social economic system and political system upon which it is created and where it exists. Engels once sharply criticized the view of bourgeois thinkers that concealed the nature of the capitalist economic system and political system and put value at the first place, "This, however, also removed the last justification for all the hypocritical phrases of the possessing classes to the effect that in the present social order right and justice, equality of rights and duties and a general harmony of interests prevail"[11].

This principle of historical materialism also applies to the theory of scientific socialism. We advocate the core values of socialism, encourage people-orientation, and promote liberty, equality, justice, and harmony, because our society is a socialist society, in which the economic base and the political system provides the economic and political basis to realize these values step by step. If our society weren't centred around economic construction, didn't have the

---

11   Karl Marx and Frederick Engels: Selected Works, 2nd Edition, Volume 3, p. 338.

highly developed productive forces or the people's democratic system led by the CPC, or in a word, if we didn't have the basic socialist economic system or political system, all our value goals would be like pie in the sky. The scientific socialism is different from the utopian socialism, which firmly established itself on the economic base since ever it was established and which believes that the mode of material production, in the final analysis, plays quite a decisive and significant role in the whole life of social formations. In the past Marx and Engels founded the theories of scientific socialism on the basis of historical materialism and the theory of surplus value; however, today, we are trying to put the theory of the socialism with Chinese characteristics into the theoretical framework of the New Kantian values again. How ridiculous it is!

What I want to highlight is the promotion of dialogue among all subjects within Marxism, such a dialogue that extremely needs to remove the division among the subjects within Marxism and which insist on and develop Marxism as a complete scientific system. However, I don't repel the dialogue between Marxism and non-Marxism. For example, in the aspect of economics, some Chinese scholars have made many achievements in their studies on the symbolic economics of Jean Baudrillard, a French postmodernist. Obviously, Baudrillard's critique of the capitalist consumer society is rather inspiring for us, but the starting point of his theory is hard to communicate with the historical materialism of Marxism. It is a universal law that material production is the basis of social existence and development. Any society, even a highly developed capitalist society, can't live if it stops production even just for a few weeks. A consumer society that is not based on the highly developed production doesn't exist at all. Therefore, Marx's analysis about production, distribution, exchange and consumption in his work "Introduction to *A Contribution to the Critique of Political Economy*" was totally correct to start from production. With the development of man's social production and the disappearance of the shortness of products, consumption will more and more transcend beyond the standard of human needs, and will become a luxury instead of a means to meet the living needs of human. Such a change is inevitable, but its basis is still the production.

Culture can be a new perspective to examine consumption, but it cannot replace the fundamental position of production in society. Consumption can have significance of symbol, since needs and the satisfaction of needs are the content of man's lifestyle while the life-style is the carrier of culture. Consumption is not only material but also has some kind of significance of symbol. In the feudal society, the pattern or the colour of clothes were all symbol of social status, for example, yellow symbolizes the imperial family. In the capital-ist epoch, this kind of constraints disappear along with the death of the feudal society, but the symbolic significance that clothes rep-resents as symbolizing nobleness, fashion, avant-garde or counter-secularism, or rebellion becomes even more strengthened. However, symbolic significance is cultural meaning, which can by no means change the nature of historical materialism.

In the same way, the alienation inclination in consumption has also shown up in the epoch of capitalism. Marx began to criticize the cap-italist consumption view in the "Human Requirements and Division of Labour under the Rule of Private Property and Under Socialism. Division of Labour in Bourgeois Society" in the "Third Manuscript" of *Economic and Philosophic Manuscripts of 1844*, and pointed out that in the capitalist production, "this appears partly in the fact that the extension of products and needs becomes a contriving and ever-calculating subservience to inhuman, sophisticated, unnatural and imaginary appetites. Private property does not know how to change crude need into human need. Its idealism is fantasy, caprice and whim; and no eunuch flatters his despot more basely or uses more despicable means to stimulate his dulled capacity for pleasure in or-der to sneak a favour for himself than does the industrial eunuch – the producer – in order to sneak for himself a few pieces of silver, in order to charm the golden birds out of the pockets of his dearly beloved neighbours in Christ"[12].

This alienation of consumption, manifested as that man becomes the slave of consumption goods, is rooted in the capitalist system of production itself. Thus, when pointing out the capitalist alienation of consumption, Marx at the same time also exposed the phenomenon

---

12   Karl Marx and Frederick Engels: Collected Works, 1st Chinese Edition, Volume 42, p. 132-133.

that capitalism was faced with insufficient consumption demand, i.e. "a bestial barbarization" of need. The modern capitalist society is not a society with universal high consumption. However the capitalist production develops, the total wealth increases, or the general living standards improves, the consumption standards of different classes or stratums will be still at different heights as long as there still exists capitalist private property, exploitation, and antagonism between the rich and the poor. With its mighty advertising publicity and by its invasion by commercial culture, capitalism truly can make high consumption as a cultural conception which is universally pursued in the capitalist society, but in reality it cannot achieve the universal high consumption which could include the whole society, which is an objective fact.

We can disagree with Baudrillard's view of replacing Marxist political economics with symbolic economics, but we can still learn something and get warned from his view, which advocates that contemporary capitalist consumption view has gradually assumed the dominant role in Western economy. We can get inspiration from his work about how to advocate and promote reasonable consumption, scientific consumption and civilized consumption and how to make the satisfaction of demands and consumption be beneficial for improving each men's personal qualities and all-around development of each member in our socialist society. At present, our major contradiction still lies in the insufficient consumption and the unbalances in the consumption levels. Therefore, our main task should be to develop production and meet the growing material and cultural demands of each man and also at the same time to prevent the generation and expansion of consumerism. We ought to consider the question raised by western scholars and try to find another answer. As for other dialogues with the western Marxism trends, we also should take this attitude.

All in all, philosophy is now in a "frozen" state, which does need to strengthen its dialogue with other subjects, and especially need to strengthen the dialogue within the scientific system of Marxism. Marxist philosophy cannot be too abstract or break away from the real life, especially from the economic life; on the contrary, economics cannot be too concrete or too microscopic, but must be guided by

Marxist philosophy, an should aim at advancing the self-perfection of socialist system, and really realize the functions of Marxist economics; while the theory of socialism must firmly stand on the basis of Marxist philosophy and Marxist economics, which should never go any closer towards the abstract theory of human nature or the "value" restricted views of idealism. If we could expand the dialogue between philosophy and economics into the dialogue among philosophy, economics and socialist theories, it will definitely contribute to comprehending the abundant content of our socialist theoretical system with Chinese characteristics from the perspective of the unity of philosophy, economics and socialism theories. And Marxist philosophy can also get itself out of the predicament of self-exile and self-marginalization through this strengthening of the philosophical dialogue.

ABOUT THE AUTHOR

Chen Xianda, born in 1930 in Jiangxi Province of China is honorary chairman of China Historical Materialism Association, member of Social Science Committee of Education Ministry of China. For long years he worked as researcher and tutor in the Department of Philosophy of Renmin University of China. In the last 30 years his more than 200 academic articles were published in the influential journals and newspapers. These articles involved issues on the basic principles of Marxism and the important problems of the history of Marxism, issues about culture and traditional Chinese culture.

His books include *Research on the Early Thoughts of Marx* co-authored with Jin Huiming. *History of Ideas of Marx and Engels,* monograph co-authored (1982); *Into the Depth of History*, monograph (1987); *A Course in the Basic Principles of Marxism* (1988); *Overview of Philosophy of Karl Marx and Frederick Engels*, in co-operation with his students (1989); In August 1990, he published *The Dismembered Marx*, focusing on the history of Marxism, carrying out a critical investigation on the contemporary Marxology. Chen Xianda's essays on philosophy: *Reverie and Ramble*; *Night Talking in the Garden of Peace*; *Philosophic Gnosis*; *A Return to Life*. In the 90'ies he spent nearly ten years on writing these four books which included more than one million characters. *Collected Works of Chen Xianda* (6 volumes) published by the China Renmin University Press, (2003); *The Philosophy of the Gap* published by Beijing Normal University Press. His books received many academic awards including the First Prize of China National Excellent Researches on Humanities and Social Science issued by Ministry of Education.

CANUT SERIES

Books in English

Defense for Marx
A New Interpretation of Marxist Philosophy
Yang Geng

A Marxist Reading of Young Baudrillard
Throughout His Ordered Masks
Zhang Yibing

A Deep Plough: Unscrambling Major Post-Marxist Texts
From Adorno to Žižek
Zhang Yibing

Problematic, Symptomatic Reading and Ideology
A Textological Interpretation of Althusser
Zhang Yibing

Lenin Revisited
A Post-textological Reading on Philosophical Notes
Zhang Yibing

The Subjective Dimension of Marxist Historical Dialectics
Zhang Yibing

Back to Marx.
The Change of Philosophical Discourse in the Context of Economics
Zhang Yibing

Into the Depths of History
Research on Marx's Historical Materialism
Chen Xianda

New Research into the New Edition of The German Ideology
Han Lixin

Marxist Theory of Economic Cycles and Crises
Liu Mingyuan

New Monistic Living Labor Theory of Value
The Normative and Positive Research of Labor Value
Cheng Enfu

A Review on Marxist and Left Debates

Post-marxism, Eco-marxism, Post-modernism, Market Socialism,
New Imperialism, Post-modern Feminism, Socialist Feminism,
Radical Democracy, Baudrillard's Political Economy, Future Socialism
Zeng Zhisheng

Marx's Practical Materialism
The Horizon of Post-Subjectivity Philosophy
Wang Nanshi, Xie Yongkang

Between Surging Ideas and Real Changes:
Contemporary Interpretation on Marx's Practice View
Ouyang Kang, Zhang Mingchang

History of Marxist Thought on Literature, Art, Aesthetics
Ideas of Major Critics and Political Thinkers
Zhou Houzhong

Books in German:

Verteidigung für Marx
Eine Neuinterpretation der Marxistischen Philosophie
Yang Geng

Ein Tiefer Pflug: Entschlüsselung der postmarxistischen Hauptwerke
von Adorno bis Žižek
Zhang Yibing

Zurück zu Lenin.
Eine post-textologische Lektüre der Philosophischen Notizen
Zhang Yibing

www.ingramcontent.com/pod-product-compliance
Lightning Source LLC
Chambersburg PA
CBHW031136020426
42333CB00013B/396